MAINE, VERMONT, & NEW HAMPSHIRE

11th Edition

Where to Stay and Eat for All Budgets

Must-See Sights and Local Secrets

Ratings You Can Trust

Excerpted from *Fodor's New England*

Fodor's Travel Publications   New York, Toronto, London, Sydney, Auckland

www.fodors.com

FODOR'S MAINE, VERMONT, & NEW HAMPSHIRE

Editor: Debbie Harmsen

Editorial Contributors: Christina Knight, Amanda Theunissen
Writers: Neva Allen, Stephen Allen, John Blodgett, Lelah Cole, Sherry Hanson, Mary Ruoff, Laura V. Scheel, George Semler, and Michael de Zayas

Editorial Production: Evangelos Vasilakis
Maps & Illustrations: David Lindroth, *cartographers*; Bob Blake, Rebecca Baer, *map editors;* William Wu, *information graphics*
Design: Fabrizio LaRocca, *creative director*; Guido Caroti, Siobhan O'Hare, *art directors*; Tina Malaney, Chie Ushio, Ann McBride, Jessica Walsh, *designers*; Melanie Marin, *senior picture editor;* Moon Sun Kim, *cover designer*
Cover Photo: (Barton, Vermont) Vladpans/eStock Photo
Production/Manufacturing: Matthew Struble

COPYRIGHT

Copyright © 2009 by Fodor's Travel, a division of Random House, Inc.

Fodor's is a registered trademark of Random House, Inc.

All rights reserved. Published in the United States by Fodor's Travel, a division of Random House, Inc., and simultaneously in Canada by Random House of Canada, Limited, Toronto. Distributed by Random House, Inc., New York.

No maps, illustrations, or other portions of this book may be reproduced in any form without written permission from the publisher.

11th Edition

ISBN 978-1-4000-0752-3

ISSN 1073-6581

SPECIAL SALES

This book is available at special discounts for bulk purchases for sales promotions or premiums. Special editions, including personalized covers, excerpts of existing books, and corporate imprints, can be created in large quantities for special needs. For more information, write to Special Markets/Premium Sales, 1745 Broadway, MD 6-2, New York, New York 10019, or e-mail specialmarkets@randomhouse.com.

AN IMPORTANT TIP & AN INVITATION

Although all prices, opening times, and other details in this book are based on information supplied to us at press time, changes occur all the time in the travel world, and Fodor's cannot accept responsibility for facts that become outdated or for inadvertent errors or omissions. So **always confirm information when it matters,** especially if you're making a detour to visit a specific place. Your experiences—positive and negative—matter to us. If we have missed or misstated something, **please write to us.** We follow up on all suggestions. Contact the Maine, Vermont, & New Hampshire editor at editors@fodors.com or c/o Fodor's at 1745 Broadway, New York, NY 10019.

PRINTED IN THE UNITED STATES OF AMERICA

10 9 8 7 6 5 4 3 2 1

Be a Fodor's Correspondent

Your opinion matters. It matters to us. It matters to your fellow Fodor's travelers, too. And we'd like to hear it. In fact, we need to hear it.

When you share your experiences and opinions, you become an active member of the Fodor's community. That means we'll not only use your feedback to make our books better, but we'll publish your names and comments whenever possible. Throughout our guides, look for "Word of Mouth," excerpts of your unvarnished feedback.

Here's how you can help improve Fodor's for all of us.

Tell us when we're right. We rely on local writers to give you an insider's perspective. But our writers and staff editors—who are the best in the business—depend on you. Your positive feedback is a vote to renew our recommendations for the next edition.

Tell us when we're wrong. We're proud that we update most of our guides every year. But we're not perfect. Things change. Hotels cut services. Museums change hours. Charming cafés lose charm. If our writer didn't quite capture the essence of a place, tell us how you'd do it differently. If any of our descriptions are inaccurate or inadequate, we'll incorporate your changes in the next edition and will correct factual errors at fodors.com immediately.

Tell us what to include. You probably have had fantastic travel experiences that aren't yet in Fodor's. Why not share them with a community of like-minded travelers? Maybe you chanced upon a beach or bistro or B&B that you don't want to keep to yourself. Tell us why we should include it. And share your discoveries and experiences with everyone directly at fodors.com. Your input may lead us to add a new listing or highlight a place we cover with a "Highly Recommended" star or with our highest rating, "Fodor's Choice."

Give us your opinion instantly at our feedback center at www.fodors.com/feedback. You may also e-mail editors@fodors.com with the subject line "Maine, Vermont, & New Hampshire Editor." Or send your nominations, comments, and complaints by mail to Maine, Vermont, & New Hampshire Editor, Fodor's, 1745 Broadway, New York, NY 10019.

You and travelers like you are the heart of the Fodor's community. Make our community richer by sharing your experiences. Be a Fodor's correspondent.

Happy traveling in Northern New England!

Tim Jarrell, Publisher

CONTENTS

MAPS

ABOUT THIS BOOK

Our Ratings

Sometimes you find terrific travel experiences and sometimes they just find you. But usually the burden is on you to select the right combination of experiences. That's where our ratings come in.

As travelers we've all discovered places whose worthiness is obvious. And sometimes a place is so wonderful that superlatives don't do it justice: you just have to see for yourself. These sights, properties, and experiences get our highest rating, **Fodor's Choice**, indicated by orange stars throughout this book.

Black stars highlight sights and properties we deem **Highly Recommended**, places that our writers, editors, and readers praise again and again for consistency and excellence.

By default, there's another category: any place we include in this book is by definition worth your time, unless we say otherwise. And we will.

Disagree with any of our choices? Care to nominate a place or suggest that we rate one more highly? Visit our feedback center at www.fodors.com/feedback.

Budget Well

Hotel and restaurant price categories from ¢ to $$$$ are defined in the opening pages of each chapter. For attractions, we always give standard adult admission fees; reductions are usually available for children, students, and senior citizens. Want to pay with plastic? **AE, D, DC, MC, V** following restaurant and hotel listings indicate if American Express, Discover, Diner's Club, MasterCard, and Visa are accepted.

Restaurants

Unless we state otherwise, restaurants are open for lunch and dinner daily. We mention dress only when there's a specific requirement and reservations only when they're essential or not accepted—it's always best to book ahead.

Hotels

Hotels have private bath, phone, TV, and air-conditioning, and operate on the European Plan (EP, without meals), unless we specify that they use the Continental Plan (CP, with continental breakfast), Breakfast Plan (BP, with full breakfast), Modified American Plan (MAP, with breakfast and dinner), or Full American Plan (FAP, with all means), or are all-inclusive (AI, with all meals and most activities). We always list facilities but not whether you'll be charged extra to use them.

Many Listings

★	Fodor's Choice
★	Highly recommended
⊠	Physical address
✛	Directions
⬤	Mailing address
☎	Telephone
⎙	Fax
⊕	On the Web
✍	E-mail
⛿	Admission fee
☉	Open/closed times
Ⓜ	Metro stations
▭	Credit cards

Hotels & Restaurants

⌂	Hotel
⇥	Number of rooms
♨	Facilities
❙❍❙	Meal plans
✕	Restaurant
✐	Reservations
↘	Smoking
	BYOB
✕⌂	Hotel with restaurant that warrants a visit

Outdoors

♣	Golf
⛺	Camping

Other

♧	Family-friendly
⇨	See also
⊠	Branch address
☞	Take note

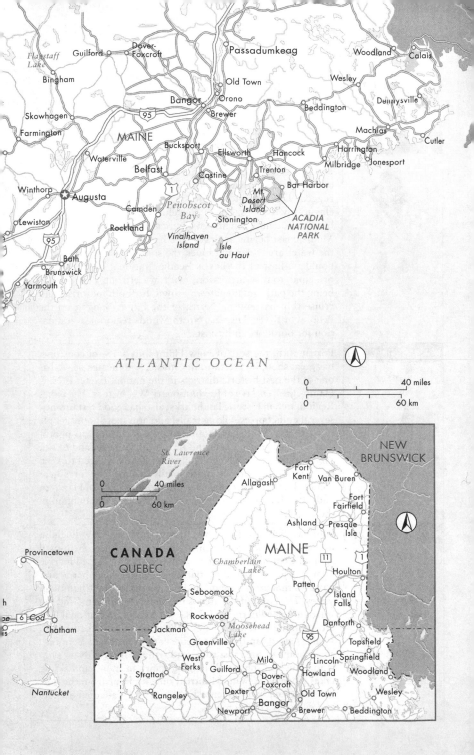

WHAT'S WHERE

MAINE 	Maine is by far the largest state in all of New England. At its extremes it measures 300 mi by 200 mi; all other New England states could fit within its perimeter. Maine's southernmost coastal towns are too overdeveloped to give you the rugged, Down East experience, but the Kennebunks will: classic townscapes, rocky shorelines punctuated by sandy beaches, quaint downtown districts. Purists hold that the Maine coast begins at Penobscot Bay, where the vistas over the water are wider and bluer, the shore a jumble of granite boulders. East of the bay is Acadia National Park, Maine's principal tourist attraction, with waterfront Bar Harbor being the park's main gateway town, for both motorists and cruise ship passengers. North of the bay is Bangor, on the Penobscot River. The vast North Woods region is a destination for outdoors enthusiasts.
NEW HAMPSHIRE	Portsmouth, the star of New Hampshire's 18-mi coastline, has great shopping, restaurants, music, and theater, as well as one of the best historic districts in the nation. Exeter is New Hampshire's enclave of Revolutionary War history. The Lakes Region, rich in historic landmarks, also has good restaurants, several golf courses, hiking trails, and antiques shops. People come to the White Mountains to hike and climb, to photograph the dramatic vistas and the vibrant foliage, and to ski. Western and central New Hampshire have managed to keep the waterslides and the outlet malls at bay. The lures here include Lake Sunapee, the charming college town of Hanover, and Mt. Monadnock, the second-most-climbed mountain in the world.
VERMONT 	Southern Vermont has farms, freshly starched New England towns, quiet back roads, bustling ski resorts, and strip-mall sprawl. Central Vermont's trademarks include famed marble quarries, just north of Rutland, and large dairy herds and pastures that create the quilted patchwork of the Champlain Valley. The heart of the area is the Green Mountains, and the surrounding wilderness of the Green Mountain National Forest. Both the state's largest city (Burlington) and the nation's smallest state capital (Montpelier) are in northern Vermont, as are some of the most rural and remote areas of New England. Much of the state's logging, dairy farming, and skiing takes place here. With Montréal only an hour from the border, the Canadian influence is strong, and Canadian accents and currency common.

NORTHERN NEW ENGLAND FOR KIDS

■ **Children's Museum of Maine, Portland, Maine.** How can kids not enjoy a museum with an exhibit called Attack of the Bloodsuckers? Located in the heart of Portland's Arts District, this interactive facility has been voted the nation's 14th best children's museum by Child Magazine. There's something scheduled most every day, and in the summer special camps are available. A first-floor exhibit called Our Town includes a lobster boat, car repair shop, and supermarket—all for hands-on learning.

■ **Southworth Planetarium, Portland, Maine.** This University of Southern Maine facility offers classes such as Night Sky Mythology and Introductory Astronomy. The 30-foot dome houses a star theater with lasers, digital sounds, and projector displaying more than 5,000 heavenly bodies.

■ **Montshire Museum of Science, Norwich, Vermont.** The kid-friendly museum uses more than 60 hands-on exhibits to explore nature and technology. Originally filled with resources from the closing of Dartmouth College's natural history museum, the Montshire Museum of Science sits amidst 110 acres of woodlands and nature trails. Permanent interactive exhibits abound, and cover topics such as air and weather, astronomy, and light and vision; there are even live animals on site.

■ **Shelburne Farms, Shelburne, Vermont.** This working dairy farm is also an educational and cultural resource center for children and adults alike. There are field trips, work and learn programs, and 4-H and summer camps. Day visitors can watch artisans make the farm's famous cheddar cheese from the milk of more than 100 purebred and registered Brown Swiss cows. A children's farmyard and walking trails round out the experience.

■ **Story Land, Glen, New Hampshire.** This fantasyland theme park has been entertaining young children and their parents since 1954. The $24 per person admission (ages 3 and older) covers all 21 rides, which include the Flying Fish, Swan Boats, Antique Cars, and the Huff Puff and Whistle Railroad. When summer gets too hot, kids can enjoy the Oceans of Fun Sprayground.

■ **Whale-watching, in Maine.** Few things speak of the great deep blue unknown like a whale, and any sighting of these magnificent creatures is dramatic and not soon forgotten. The whale-watching season varies by tour skipper, but generally is contained between the months of April and October. A few companies to sign on with for spotting these mighty creatures are Cap'n Fish's Boat Trips in Boothbay Harbor, which has both whale- and puffin-watching adventures; Bar Harbor Whale Watching Co., offering three-hour excursions via catamaran; Old Port Mariner Fleet, based in Portland and also offering fishing trips; and Island Cruises, which departs from Head Harbour Wharf in Wilson's Beach and allows passengers to spot whales while aboard a lobster boat.

QUINTESSENTIAL
MAINE, VERMONT, & NEW HAMPSHIRE

Artisans

Northern New England's independent artisans have built a thriving cottage industry. Some of the finest potters spin their wheels on the coast, and one-off, often whimsical jewelry is wrought in silver, pewter, and other metals. Modern furniture makers take classic simple New England designs, including those of the Shakers and Quakers, and refine them for buyers the world over who are willing to pay thousands for craftsmanship that has withstood the test of time. The varied landscapes throughout the three states have patiently sat for thousands of painters, whose canvases are sold in small shops and local museums. Visitors who come to Maine, Vermont, and New Hampshire to create their own art have plenty to paint or photograph. Photographers especially focus their lens on classic New England architecture, colorful lobster buoys, and the mighty windjammers.

The Coast

The coast of Maine and New Hampshire is both workplace and playground. Starting in the 17th century onward, boat-builders sprung up in one town after another to support the shipping and fishing trades. Today, the boatyards are far fewer than in historical times, but shipping and especially fishing remain important to the economy on the coast and beyond. But it's not all work and no play—some of the classic wooden sailboats now serve cruise-goers, and some fisherman have traded in their lobster boats for whale-watching vessels. Maine's Reid and Popham Beach state parks are a beachcomber's paradise, and the relatively chilly waters of the North Atlantic don't scare away swimmers come summertime.

If you want to get a sense of Northern New England culture, and indulge in some of its pleasures, start by familiarizing yourself with the rituals of daily life. Here are a few highlights of life in Maine, Vermont, and New Hampshire that you can sample with relative ease.

Fall Foliage

It's impossible to discuss Northern New England without mentioning that time of year when the region's deciduous trees explode in reds, yellows, oranges, and other rich hues. The season can be finicky, defined as much by the weather as it is by the species of trees—a single rainstorm can strip trees of their grandeur. But what happens in one region doesn't necessarily happen in another, and if you have the time you can follow the colors from one area to the next. Remember, you'll be competing with thousands of other like-minded leaf peepers, so be sure to book lodging early on the hotspots. Your preparedness will payoff the first time you drive down a winding country road aflame in the bright sun of a crisp Northern New England autumn day.

Food, Glorious Food

Maine will forever be famous for its delectable lobsters, and Vermont equally known for its maple treats. But Maine lobster and Vermont Grade A maple syrup are just samples to whet your appetite. Dining in Northern New England is a feast for the gastronomist to behold, and it runs the gamut from the simply prepared to the most artistic of presentations; from blueberry pie just like Grandma used to make to slow-cooked Long Island duck with kumquat, stuffed profiterole, glazed carrots, and long pepper. Beyond lobsters, also delicious are the area's shellfish: shrimp, clams (little redneck is a perennial favorite), scallops, crab, and mussels. Chefs who grew up here may leave to learn their trade, but often return and enrich the dining scene; the region is known for attracting newcomers as well.

IF YOU LIKE

Antiquing

Northern New England's rich history and heritage account for its share of antiques shops. A few regions and individual places worth exploring in Maine, Vermont, and New Hampshire for their antiques are listed below.

■ **The Down East Trail, Maine.** Antiquing doesn't get much more beautiful than this stretch of antiquing communities from Ellsworth to Stonington. Explore some of Maine's loveliest coves while browsing one antique shop after another along routes 172 and 175. Extend the trip with a stop at the shops on nearby Mt. Desert Island, where you can also visit Acadia National Park.

■ **U.S. 1, Maine.** Antique shops are clustered throughout the mid-coast and along U.S. 1 between Kittery and Scarborough.

■ **Burlwood Antique Center, New Hampshire.** Open daily from May through October and located near I-93 in Meredith, this center is home to 175 dealers. Specialties include furniture, china, books, and glass.

■ **Monadnock Region, New Hampshire.** Dealers abound here in barns and home stores strung along back roads—along Route 119, from Fitzwilliam to Hinsdale; Route 101, from Marlborough to Wilton; and in the towns of Hopkinton, Hollis, and Amherst.

■ **Newfane, Vermont.** In the Green Mountain State, antique shops and barns are scattered just about everywhere, but they're especially concentrated along the southern portions of U.S. 7 and Route 30.

■ **Williston Antique Center, Vermont.** Stop by this 3,800-square-foot facility on the way to or from the Burlington/Lake Champlain area. The setting is contemporary if simple, but it highlights the treasures inside. More than 45 dealers scour the state for old country tins, New England furniture, vintage quilts, and more.

The Beach

Long, wide beaches edge the Maine coast, and the short coastline of New Hampshire is nonetheless an attraction to beachgoers. Many are maintained by state and local governments and have lifeguards on duty; they may have picnic facilities, restrooms, changing facilities, and concession stands. Depending on the locale, you may need a parking sticker to use the lot. The waters are at their warmest in August, though they're cold even at the height of summer in much of Maine. Inland, small lake beaches abound.

■ **Reid State Park, Maine.** Located just east of Sheepscot Bay, right along the ocean, Reid State Park is a beach ambler's wonderland. The water is cold much of the year, and the waves roil during a storm (much to wet-suited surfers' delight), but it's a beautiful and quiet place to spend some solitary time looking for sand dollars or climbing amongst the rocks at low tide, exploring tidal pools.

■ **Old Orchard Beach, Maine.** Think Coney Island on a smaller scale. A ghost town in the off season, the main drag fills with cruising cars and amblers of all ages come summer. There's a white sand beach to be sure (lapped by cold North Atlantic waters), but many come to ride the Pirate Ship at

Palace Playland, drop quarters at the arcade, and browse the multitude of trinket-and-t-shirts shops. Grab a slice of pizza and French fries doused with white vinegar.

- **Hampton Beach State Park, New Hampshire.** New Hampshire's ocean shore is short compared to its neighbor to the north, so this state park along historic Route 1 takes full advantage of the space it has. In addition to swimming and fishing, there are campsites with full hookups for RVs and an amphitheater with band shell for fair-weather concerts.

Bicycling

Biking on a road through Northern New England's countryside is an idyllic way to spend a day. Every state in the region has its share of good choices for bicyclists, and many ski resorts allow mountain bikes in summer.

- **Acadia National Park, Maine.** At the heart of this popular park is the 45-mi network of historic carriage roads covered in crushed rock and shared only with equestrians and hikers. Sturdier cyclists can ride the road to the top of Cadillac mountain, but heavy traffic in the high season can make this a dangerous proposition.

- **Bear Brook State Park, New Hampshire.** The largest developed state park in New Hampshire at 10,000 acres, Bear Brook offers mountain biking trails to match the gumption of everyone in the family. The forty miles of dirt roads, double-track, and single-track trails also accommodate hikers and horseback riders, so be ready to slow your fat tires at short notice.

- **Killington Resort, Vermont.** Following the lead of many ski resorts in the Western United States, Killington allows fat-tire riders on many of its ski trails long after the snow has melted. Stunt riders can enjoy the jumps and bumps of the mountain bike park. Rent a bike on-site or bring your own.

Boating

Along many of Northern New England's larger lakes and along the ocean, sailboats, rowboats, canoes, and outboards are available for rent at local marinas. You may be required to prove your seaworthiness before renting a boat. Lessons are also frequently available.

- **Lake Winnipesaukee, New Hampshire.** By far New Hampshire's largest lake, Lake Winnipesaukee comprises 72 sq mi and has roughly 180 mi of shoreline. Boaters revel in having more than 240 islands to explore; some are private, while others, like 10-foot wide Becky's Garden, are rather small and might even disappear under the water when lake levels are high. The most common interpretation of the lake's name, given by American Indian tribes, is "Smile of the Great Spirit."

- **Allagash Wilderness Waterway.** Popular with canoeists since long before the Maine Legislature officially approved its designation in 1966, this scenic and remote waterway is 92 mi of lakes, ponds, rivers, and streams. It's part of the 740-mi Northern Forest Canoe Trail, which floats through New York, Vermont, Quebec, and New Hampshire as well as Maine.

- **Lake Champlain, Vermont.** Called by some the Sixth Great Lake, 435-sq mi Lake Champlain is bordered by Vermont's

Green Mountains to the east and the Adirondack's of New York to the west. Burlington, VT is the largest lakeside city, and a good bet for renting a boat—be it canoe, kayak, row boat, skiff, or motorboat. Attractions include numerous islands and deep blue water that's often brushed by pleasant breezes beneath sunny skies punctuated by clouds.

Dining

Seafood is king throughout Northern New England. Clams are a favorite, whether they're fried, steamed, or cooked in the famed New England chowder, made with milk or cream (unlike the tomato-based Manhattan version) and big, meaty quahogs. Some lobster classics include plain boiled lobster—a staple at "in the rough" picnic-bench-and-paperplate spots along the Maine Coast—and lobster rolls, a lobster meat and mayo (or just melted butter) preparation served in a hot dog bun. The leading fin fish is scrod—young cod or haddock—best sampled baked or broiled.

Inland specialties run to the plain and familiar dishes of old-fashioned Sunday-dinner America—pot roast, roast turkey, baked ham, hefty stacks of pancakes (with local maple syrup, of course), and apple pie. One regional favorite is Indian pudding, a long-boiled cornmeal-and-molasses concoction that's delicious with vanilla ice cream.

- **Zabby and Elf's Stone Soup, Burlington, Vermont.** This vegetarian/vegan spot is a good example of the "buy local" ethic of the progressive restaurants in Burlington and the Lake Champlain valley. Sandwiches cost under $10, and the soup of the day is hearty fare.

Juices are fresh, the coffee organic, and Saturday brunch includes quiche, lox, and eggs, yogurt and granola, and biscuits with herb gravy.

- **Black Trumpet Bistro, Portsmouth, New Hampshire.** Take a break from exploring Portsmouth's historic Old Port and spend some time in this bistro and wine bar that takes up two floors in a 200-year old brick building with exposed beams. The chef changes the menu every six weeks to ensure the freshest ingredients for inclusion in dishes that hint of Spanish, Turkish, and Mexican influence.

- **Gilbert's Chowderhouse/Becky's Diner, Portland, Maine.** Portland, Maine's waterfront Commercial Street is book ended by these two quintessential Maine diners. The former has one of the state's finest lobster rolls and homemade clam cakes; the latter opens for breakfast at 4 AM to feed the fisherman before they head out to sea. Order a slice of fresh pie.

Fishing

Anglers will find sport aplenty throughout the region—surf casting along the shore; deep-sea fishing in the Atlantic on party and charter boats; fishing for trout in streams; and angling for bass and landlocked salmon in freshwater lakes.

- **Rangeley Lakes Region, Maine and New Hampshire.** Located near the Maine-New Hampshire border, this collection of ponds, lakes, and rivers offer some of the finest fishing in New England. Brook trout and landlocked salmon are the big attractions. Big Kennebago Lake is the largest lake in the Northeast to allow only fly-fishing.

- **Lake Winnipesaukee, New Hampshire.** As fun to fish as it is to pronounce, the largest lake in New Hampshire is home to three species of trout, small and largemouth bass, bluegill, and more. Visitors 16 years old and older must purchase a one-, three-, or seven-day temporary fishing license.

- **Lake Champlain, Vermont.** Some Vermonters refer to this large lake as the state's West Coast. It's a major draw for anglers of all abilities and inclinations. Species include brook, lake, and rainbow trout, landlocked salmon, northern pike, walleye, and both large mouth and small mouth bass.

Golf

Northern New England has an ample supply of public and semiprivate courses, many of which are part of distinctive resorts or even ski areas.

- **The Gleneagles Golf Course At the Equinox, Vermont.** One of the most stately lodging resorts in all of New England, The Equinox opened in 1769 and has hosted the likes of Teddy Roosevelt and Mary Todd Lincoln. The golf course is par-71 and 6,423 yards, and is especially alluring in the fall when the deciduous trees that line the fairways explode in color. After golf, go to the 13,000-square-foot spa for some pampering. The resort is ringed by mountain splendor.

- **The Balsams Grand Resort, New Hampshire.** Golfing has attracted visitors from all over to this resort since 1897. Today, there are two courses, an 18-hole championship course and a 9-hole course. There are fine views of the White Mountains to the south.

- **Samoset Resort on the Ocean, Maine.** Few things match playing 18 holes on a championship course that's bordered by the North Atlantic Ocean. Located in Rockport, Maine along Penobscot Bay, this is a golf cart path only facility that's open from May through October. Book a room at the luxurious Samoset Resort Hotel to make it a complete golf vacation.

Hiking

The region's most famous trails are the 255-mi Long Trail, which runs north–south through the center of Vermont, and the Maine-to-Georgia Appalachian Trail, which runs through Maine and New Hampshire on both private and public land.

- **The Long Trail, Vermont.** Following the main ridge of the Green Mountains from one end of Vermont to the other, this is the nation's oldest long-distance trail. In fact, some say it was the inspiration for the Appalachian Trail. Hardy hikers make a go of its 270 mi length, but by no means should this scare away day hikers who can drop in and out at many places along the way.

- **Mt. Washington.** The cog railroad and the auto road to the summit are popular routes up New England's highest mountain, but for those with stamina and legs of steel it's one heckava hike. Actually, there are a handful of trails to the top, the most popular beginning at Pinkham Notch Visitor's Center. Be sure to dress in layers and have some warm clothing for the frequent winds toward the peak.

NORTHERN NEW ENGLAND'S TOP ATTRACTIONS

Acadia National Park

Maine's only national park is regularly one of the most visited in the United States. The scenic Loop Road leads all the way to the top of Cadillac Mountain, with 360-degree views of the surrounding coast. The road is typically closed in the winter months, but that doesn't stop snowshoers and cross-country skiers from getting deep into an experience of solitude and often frigid winds coming in off the North Atlantic. Built by John D. Rockefeller, Jr., the park's signature stone carriage roads are perfect for an afternoon stroll or relaxed bicycle ride.

Baxter State Park

Over the span of 32 years, from 1930 to 1962, former Maine governor Percival Baxter began buying and donating parcels of land, with the goal of creating a park in the wilds of Northern Maine. The result is Baxter State Park: more than 200,000 acres containing numerous lakes and streams, plus Mt. Katahdin, Maine's tallest peak and the northern terminus of the Appalachian Trail. Offering frequent sightings of moose, white-tailed deer, and black bear, the park provides a wilderness experience not found elsewhere in Northern New England.

Lake Champlain

Some call Lake Champlain the Sixth Great Lake. Bordered by New York to the west and Vermont to the east, the lake stretches 110 mi north to south and covers a total of 435 sq mi. The Adirondacks and Green Mountains provide mountainous vistas surrounding the valley. Burlington, Vermont, the largest city along the lake's shores, is progressive and friendly. A handful of marinas rent canoes, kayaks, and other boats.

Maine Coast

Counting all its nooks, crannies, and crags, the coast of Maine would stretch for thousands of miles if you could pull it straight. The Southern Coast is the most visited section, stretching north from Kittery to just outside Portland. Despite the cold North Atlantic waters, beachgoers enjoy miles of sandy or, more frequently, rocky beaches, which invite long walks and offer sweeping views of lighthouses, forested islands, and the wide-open sea.

Mt. Washington Observatory

Atop Northern New England's highest mountain, this New Hampshire research and educational institution has evolved from when meteorologists first took readings at the exposed summit in 1870. The observatory has a close relationship with the United States Weather Service. A world record to this day, a wind gust of 231 mph was recorded in April 1934—the highest wind speed to ever be recorded at a surface station. On one side, visitors can drive to the summit; on the other, a cog railway climbs to the top. Intrepid hikers can navigate a maze of trails.

Portland Head Light

Historic Portland Head Light, familiar to many from photographs and Edward Hopper's painting *Portland Head-Light (1927)*, was commissioned by George Washington and put into service in 1791. The towering white stone lighthouse stands over the keeper's house, a white home with a red roof. Besides a harbor view, its park has walking paths, picnic facilities, and wide grassy expanses perfect for flying a kite in the gusty ocean winds. The keeper's house is now the Museum at Portland Head Light. The lighthouse is in Fort Williams Park, about 2 mi from the town center of Cape Elizabeth.

NORTHERN NEW ENGLAND'S TOP EXPERIENCES

Hit the Slopes

Though the skiing in Northern New England is not as legendary as it is out West, and in fact can be downright unpleasant when packed powder turns into the scrape of crusty ice, the sport remains popular. Vermont has several ski areas, and its Killington is the largest resort in the Northeast, with 200 trails spanning seven mountains. Sunday River and Sugarloaf in Maine are perennial favorites with advanced intermediate and expert skiers. Beginners (and lift-ticket bargain hunters) can choose from a number of small but still fun hills in New Hampshire.

Rise and Shine at a B&B

Northern New England's distinct architecture, much of it originating in the 18th and 19th centuries, has resulted in beautiful buildings of all shapes and sizes, many of which have been restored as bed-and-breakfasts. These inns typify the cozy, down-home, and historic feel of the region, and as such are an ideal lodging choice, though prices are often more expensive than a hotel or motel.

Peep a Leaf

Tourist season in most of Northern New England is concentrated in the late spring and summer, but a resurgence happens in September and October when leaf peepers from all corners descend by the car-and bus-load upon deciduous woodlands to see the leaves turn red, yellow, orange, and all shades in between. Foliage season can be fragile—temperature, winds, latitude, and rain all influence when the leaves turn and how long they remain on the trees—but it makes the season even more precious. Don't discount the beauty of fallen leaves; watch them glisten in fall rains or float in the winds of approaching winter.

Watch a Whale

The deep, cold waters of the North Atlantic serve both as feeding ground and migration routes for a variety of whales, including the fin, humpback, the occasional blue, and the endangered right whales. Visit Maine's Southern Coast and Mid-Coast regions to hop aboard a whale-watching boat to motor 10 mi or more off the coast. Some boat captains go so far as to guarantee at least a single sighting.

Comb a Beach

Whether sandy or rocky, Maine and New Hampshire beaches (Vermont, of course, is landlocked) can be a veritable treasure trove of flotsam and jetsam—so long as you set your sights below, finding lost watches, jewelry, and the like. Anything from crab traps unmoored by heavy waves to colored glass worn smooth by the water can appear at your feet. Also common are shells of sea urchins, clams, and other bivalves that gulls have dropped from on high to crack open to eat the tender insides. During certain times of the year sand dollars of all sizes and colors are plentiful. You may even find one still whole.

Get the First Sight of First Light

Cadillac Mountain, in Maine's Acadia National Park, is the highest mountain on the entire length of the United States Eastern Seaboard. As such, the summit, which is reachable by car except when the Loop Road is closed in the winter, is an excellent vantage point, where you can, quite possibly, be the first person in the United States to witness the sunrise.

GREAT ITINERARIES

ESSENTIAL MAINE, NEW HAMPSHIRE, AND VERMONT

In a nation where distances can often be daunting, Northern New England packs its highlights into a remarkably compact area. Understanding Yankeedom might take a lifetime—but it's possible to get a good appreciation for the three-state region in a one week drive. The following itinerary assumes you're beginning your trip in Manchester, New Hampshire.

Day 1: Manchester & Concord

Manchester, New Hampshire's largest city, holds the Amoskeag Mills, a reminder of New England's industrial past. Smaller Concord is the state capital. Near the State House is the fine Museum of New Hampshire History, housing one of the locally built stagecoaches that carried Concord's name throughout the West. (⇨ *The Monadnocks & Merrimack Valley in Chapter 2.*)

Days 2 & 3: Green Mountains & Montpelier

Route 100 travels through the heart of the Green Mountains, whose rounded peaks assert a modest grandeur. Vermont's vest-pocket capital, Montpelier, has the gold-dome Vermont State House and the quirky Vermont Museum. (⇨ *Central Vermont & Northern Vermont in Chapter 3.*)

Days 4 & 5: White Mountains

U.S. 302 threads through New Hampshire's White Mountains, passing beneath brooding Mt. Washington and through Crawford Notch. In Bretton Woods, the Mt. Washington Cog Railway still chugs to the summit, and the Mount Washington Hotel recalls the glory days of White Mountain resorts. *If you have time, take an extra day here.* (⇨ *The White Mountains in Chapter 2.*)

Days 6 & 7: Portland

Maine's maritime capital shows off its restored waterfront at the Old Port. Nearby, two lighthouses on Cape Elizabeth, Two Lights and Portland Head, stand vigil. (⇨ *Portland & Environs in Chapter 1.*)

FALL FOLIAGE

In fall, Northern New England's dense forests explode into reds, oranges, yellows, and purples. This itinerary works its way south and west from west central Maine into northwestern Vermont. Nature's schedule varies from year to year; as a rule, it's best to begin this trip around the third week of September. Book accommodations well in advance.

Days 1 & 2: White Mountains & Lakes Region (Maine)

The Rangley Lakes region in west central Maine is a concentrated area of sparkling lakes and mountainous terrain, with peaks covered in flaming foliage. Some of Maine's taller mountains are here, and the lakes make for a nice foreground in photographs. Drive south toward the Rumford and Bethel regions and you run into even more mountains, including a couple of the state's premier ski areas and a section of White Mountain National Forest. (⇨ *Western Lakes & Mountains in Chapter 1*)

Days 3 & 4: White Mountains & Lakes Region (New Hampshire)

In New Hampshire, Interstate 93 narrows as it winds through craggy Franconia Notch. The sinuous Kancamagus Highway passes through the mountains to Conway. In Center Harbor, in the Lakes Region, you can ride the MS *Mount Washington* for views of the Lake Winnipesaukee shoreline, or ascend to Moultonborough's Castle in the Clouds for a falcon's-eye look at the colors. (⇨ *The White Mountains & Lakes Region in Chapter 2.*)

Day 5: Northeast Kingdom

After a side trip along Lake Willoughby, explore St. Johnsbury, where the St. Johnsbury Athenaeum and Fairbanks Museum reveal Victorian tastes in art and natural-history collecting. In Peacham, stock up for a picnic at the Peacham Store. (⇨ *Northern Vermont in Chapter 3.*)

Days 6 & 7: Northwestern Vermont

In Burlington, the elms will be turning color on the University of Vermont campus. A ferry ride across Lake Champlain affords great views of Vermont's Green Mountains and New York's Adirondacks. After visiting the resort town of Stowe, continue beneath the cliffs of Smugglers' Notch. The north country's palette unfolds in Newport, where the blue waters of Lake Memphremagog reflect the foliage. (⇨ *Northern Vermont in Chapter 3.*)

GREAT ITINERARIES

HIGHLIGHTS OF THE MAINE COAST

Much of the appeal of the Maine Coast lies in its geographical contrasts, from its long stretches of swimming and walking beaches, in the south to the cliff-edged, rugged rocky coasts in the north. And not unlike the physical differences of the coast, each town along the way reveals a slightly different character. This sampler tour will provide you with a good taste of what the Maine Coast offers; allow the individual chapters to invite you along other trails on the way.

Day 1: The Yorks

Start your trip in York Village with a leisurely stroll through the seven buildings of the Old York Historical Society, getting a glimpse of 18th-century life in this gentrified town. Spend time wandering amid the shops or walking the nature trails and beaches around York Harbor. There are several grand lodging options here, most with views of the harbor. If you prefer a livelier pace, continue on to York Beach, a haven for families with plenty of entertainment venues. Stop at Nubble Light for a seaside lunch or dinner.

Days 2 & 3: Ogunquit

For well over a century, Ogunquit has been a favorite vacation spot for those looking to combine the natural beauty of the ocean with a sophisticated environment. Take a morning walk along the Marginal Way to see the waves crashing on the rocks. In Perkins Cove, have lunch, stroll the shopping areas, or sign on with a lobster boat cruise to learn about Maine's most important fishery—the state's lobster industry supplies more than 90% of the world's lobster intake.

See the extraordinary collection at the Ogunquit Museum of American Art, take in a performance at one of the several theater venues, or just spend time on the beach.

Day 4: The Kennebunks

Head north to the Kennebunks, allowing at least two hours to wander through the shops and historic homes of Dock Square in Kennebunkport. This is an ideal place to rent a bike and amble around the backstreets, head out on Ocean Avenue to view the Bush estate, or ride to one of the several beaches to relax awhile.

Days 5 & 6: Portland

You can easily spend several days in Maine's largest city, exploring its historic neighborhoods, shopping and eating in the Old Port, or visiting one of several excellent museums. A brief side trip to Cape Elizabeth takes you to Portland Head Light, Maine's first lighthouse, which was commissioned by George Washington in 1790. The lighthouse is on the grounds of Fort Williams Park and is an excellent place to bring a picnic. Be sure to spend some time wandering the ample grounds. There are also excellent walking trails (and views) at nearby Two Lights State Park. If you want to take a boat tour while in Portland, get a ticket for Casco Bay Lines and see some of the islands that dot the bay.

Day 7: Bath to Camden

Head north from Portland to Bath, Maine's shipbuilding capital, and tour the Maine Maritime Museum or have lunch on the waterfront. Shop at boutiques and antiques shops, or view the plentitude of beautiful homes. Continue on U.S. 1 north, through the towns of Wiscasset and Damariscotta, where you

may find yourself pulling over frequently for outdoor flea markets or intriguing antiques shops.

Days 8 & 9: Camden

Camden is the picture-perfect image of a seaside tourist town: hundreds of boats bobbing in the harbor, immaculately kept antique homes, streets lined with boutiques and specialty stores, and restaurants serving lobster at every turn. The modest (by Maine standards, anyway) hills of nearby Mt. Battie offer good hiking and a great spot from which to picnic and view the surrounding area. Camden is one of the hubs for the beloved and historic windjammer fleet—there is no better way to see the area than from the deck of one of these graceful beauties. If you're an art lover, save some time for Rockland's Farnsworth Art Museum and the Wyeth Center.

Days 10 & 11: Mount Desert Island/ Acadia National Park

From Camden, continue north along U.S. 1, letting your interests dictate where you stop (or head south to explore the Blue Hill Peninsula, *see Chapter 5*). Once you arrive on Mount Desert Island, you can choose to stay in Bar Harbor, the busiest village in the area, or in the quieter Southwest Harbor area; either way, the splendor of the mountains and the sea surround you. If you have more time, several days can easily spent be exploring Acadia National Park, boating or kayaking in the surrounding waters, and simply enjoying the stunning panorama.

WHEN TO GO

Northern New England is a largely year-round destination, with winter popular with skiers, summer a draw for families and beach lovers, and fall a delight to those who love the bursts of autumnal color. Spring can also be a great time, with sugar shacks transforming maple sap into all sorts of tasty things and lilacs scenting the air. But, take note that you'll probably want to avoid rural areas during mud season (April) and black-fly season (mid-May to mid-June).

Memorial Day signals the migration to the beaches and the mountains; summer begins in earnest on July 4. Those who are driving to the Maine Coast in July or August should know that on Friday and Sunday weekenders clog Interstate 95 and U.S. 1.

Fall is the most colorful season, a time when many inns and hotels are booked months in advance by foliage-viewing visitors. Northern New England's dense hardwood forests explode in color as the green is stripped away from the leaves of maples, oaks, birches, beeches, and other deciduous species, revealing a rainbow of reds, oranges, yellows, purples, and other vivid hues. Generally, it's best to visit the northern reaches in late September and early October.

Climate

In winter, coastal Maine and New Hampshire is cold and damp; inland temperatures may be lower, but generally drier conditions make them easier to bear. Snowfall is heaviest in the interior mountains and can range up to several hundred inches per year in northern Maine, New Hampshire, and Vermont. Spring is often windy and rainy; in many years winter appears to segue almost immediately into

summer. Coastal areas can be quite humid in summer, while inland, particularly at higher elevations, there's a prevalence of cool summer nights. Autumn temperatures can be mild even into October, although northern portions of the region can be quite cold by Columbus Day. The charts below show the average daily maximum and minimum temperatures.

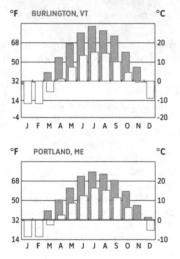

Maine

WORD OF MOUTH

"Getting up into Maine, the beach towns of York, Ogunquit, and Kennebunkport are wonderful. There are lighthouses, wide sandy beaches, and scenic rocky coastlines."

—zootsi

"Acadia National Park is one of Maine's jewels. You can drive around the Loop Road—about 20 miles or so—and stop at the various overlooks."

—massteacher

AS YOUR DRIVE ACROSS THE boarder into Maine, a sign plainly announces the state's philosophy: THE WAY LIFE SHOULD BE. Romantics luxuriate in the feeling of a down comforter on a yellow pine bed or in the sensation of the wind and salt spray on their faces while cruising in a historic windjammer. Families love the unspoiled beaches and safe inlets dotting the shoreline and the clear inland lakes. Hikers are revived by the exalting and exhausting climb to the top of Mt. Katahdin. Adventure seekers raft the Kennebec and Penobscot rivers or kayak along the coast, and skiers head for the snow-covered slopes of western and northern Maine.

There is an expansiveness to Maine, a sense of distance between places that hardly exists elsewhere in New England and, along with the sheer size and spread of the place, a variety of terrain. People speak of "coastal" Maine and "inland" Maine as though the state could be summed up under the twin emblems of lobsters and pine trees. Yet the topography and character in this state are a good deal more complicated.

Even the coast is several places in one. Rapidly gentrifying Portland may be Maine's largest metropolitan area, but its attitude is decidedly more big town than small city. South of Portland, Ogunquit, Kennebunkport, Old Orchard Beach, and other resort towns predominate along a reasonably smooth shoreline. North of Portland and Casco Bay, secondary roads turn south off U.S. 1 onto so many oddly chiseled peninsulas that it's possible to drive for days without retracing your route. Slow down to explore the museums, galleries, and shops in the larger towns and the antiques and curio shops and harborside lobster shacks in the smaller fishing villages on the peninsulas. Freeport is an entity unto itself, a place where numerous name-brand outlets and specialty stores have sprung up around the retail outpost of famous outfitter L. L. Bean. And no description of the coast would be complete without mention of popular Acadia National Park, with its majestic mountains that are often shrouded in mist.

Inland Maine likewise defies easy characterization. The terrain may be hilly or mountainous, heavily wooded or sprinkled with farms and villages. Much of the North Woods is virtually uninhabited. This is the land Henry David Thoreau wrote about in his evocative mid-19th-century portrait, *The Maine Woods*; in some ways it hasn't changed since the writer passed through.

If you come to Maine seeking an untouched fishing village with locals gathered around a potbellied stove in the general store, you'll likely come away disappointed; that innocent age has passed in all but the most remote spots like Way Down East or in the North Woods. Tourism has supplanted fishing, logging, and potato farming as Maine's number-one industry, and most areas are well equipped to receive the annual onslaught of visitors. But whether you are stepping outside a cabin for a walk in the woods or watching a boat rock at its anchor, you can sense the infinity of the natural world. Wilderness is always nearby, growing to the edges of the most urbanized spots.

MAINE TOP 5

■ **Freeport.** Main Street is like one giant mall—anchored by the L.L. Bean mother ship—except zoning laws ensure that the character and architecture of the street are maintained (witness, for example, the McDonald's located in a Victorian house, with a diminished logo and *without* a drive-thru).

■ **Portland Head Light.** The most familiar of Maine's 60-plus remaining lighthouses, it's accessible, photogenic, and historic. Watch tugboats head out to sea to escort large ships into Portland Harbor.

■ **Acadia National Park.** Maine has only one national park, and it's regularly one of the most visited in the United States. The scenic Loop Road leads all the way to the top of Cadillac Mountain, with 360-degree views of the surrounding coast. To head deeper into the park, walk along the carriage roads, built by John D. Rockefeller Jr.

■ **Seafood.** You should be sure to get some lobster while you're here, but you can also feast on clams, mussels, crabmeat, shrimp, scallops, halibut—the list goes on and on. You really can't go wrong, though—Maine seafood is about as fresh as it gets.

■ **Sailing.** No visit to the Maine Coast is complete without an ocean excursion, even if you don't leave the nearest bay. Take a ferry for an island tour, ride on a whale-watching boat, or sail aboard a grand old multimasted schooner from Maine's storied past.

EXPLORING MAINE

Maine is a large state that offers many different experiences. The York County Coast, in the southern portion of the state, is easily accessible and has long sand beaches, historic homes, and good restaurants. The coastal geography changes in Portland, the economic and cultural center of southern Maine. North of the city, long fingers of land jut into the sea, sheltering fishing villages. Penobscot Bay is famed for its rockbound coast, sailing, and numerous islands. Mount Desert Island lures crowds of people to Acadia National Park, which is filled with stunning natural beauty. Way Down East, beyond Acadia, the tempo changes; fast-food joints and trinket shops all but disappear, replaced by family-style restaurants and artisans' shops. Inland, the western lakes and mountains provide an entirely different experience. Summer camps, ski areas, and small villages populate this region. People head to Maine's North Woods to escape the crowds and to enjoy the great outdoors by hiking, rafting, camping, or canoeing.

ABOUT THE RESTAURANTS

Lobster and Maine are synonymous. As a general rule, the closer you are to a working harbor, the fresher your lobster will be. Aficionados eschew ordering lobster in restaurants, preferring to eat them "in the rough" at classic lobster pounds, where you select your dinner out of a pool and enjoy it at a waterside picnic table. Shrimp, scallops, clams, mussels, and crabs are also caught in the cold waters off Maine. Restaurants in Portland and in resort towns prepare shellfish in creative combinations with lobster, haddock, salmon, and swordfish.

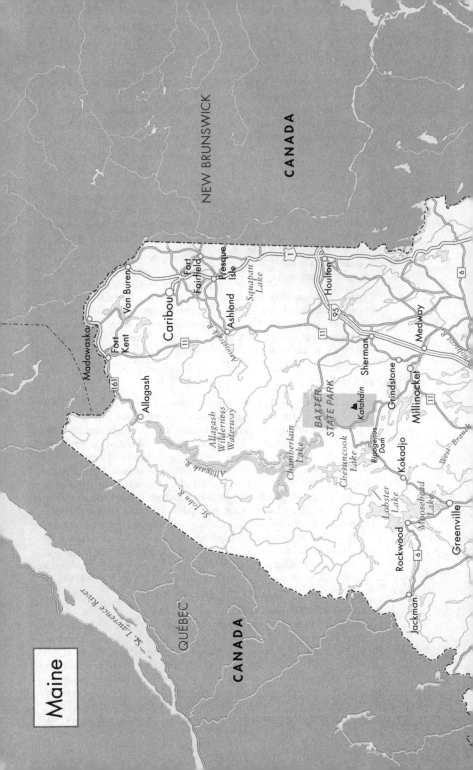

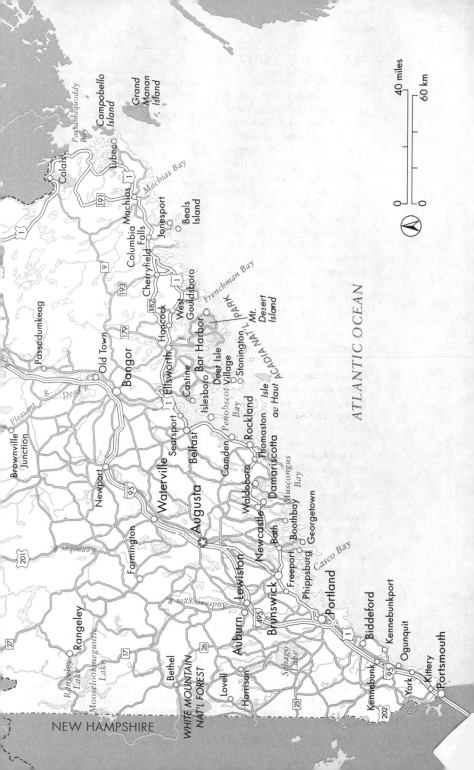

PLANNING YOUR TRIP

BUDGETING YOUR TRIP

You can spend days exploring just the coast of Maine, as these itineraries indicate, so plan ahead and decide whether you want to ski and dogsled in the western mountains, raft or canoe in the North Woods, or simply meander up the coast, stopping at museums and historic sites, shopping for local arts and crafts, and exploring coastal villages and lobster shacks. If you have only a few days, visit either Portland and Freeport or go farther north to Acadia National Park and Camden (and Rockport, if time). Whichever way you go, by all means try some lobster.

WHEN TO GO

In warm weather, the arteries along the coast and lakeside communities inland are clogged with out-of-state license plates, campgrounds are filled to capacity, and hotel rates are high. Even so, July to September is the choice time for a vacation in Maine. The weather is warmest in July and August, so throngs of people head to the beaches. September, when the days are still sunny, is far less crowded.

Fall foliage can be brilliant in Maine and is made even more so by its reflection in inland lakes or streams or off the ocean. Late September is peak season in the north country.

Elsewhere the prime viewing dates are in early or mid-October.

In winter, only a few places along the coast stay open for those who enjoy the solitude of the winter landscape. Maine's largest ski areas usually open in mid-November and provide good skiing often into April.

Springtime is mud season here, followed by spring flowers and the start of wildflowers in roadside meadows. Mid-May to mid-June is the main season for black flies, especially inland. It's best to schedule a trip after mid-June if possible, though this is prime canoeing time.

GETTING THERE & AROUND

Because Maine is large and rural, car transportation is essential, though buses operate in the larger cities. Interstate 95 is the Maine Turnpike, a toll road, from the New Hampshire border through Portland to Augusta. From there the interstate continues to Bangor and its terminus in Houlton at a Canadian border crossing. U.S. 1 winds through coastal regions, linking with peninsular routes. There are few public roads in Maine's North Woods, though private logging roads there are often open to the public (sometimes by permit only). ⇨ *See Maine Essentials at the end of this chapter for airport, train, and bus information.*

Blueberries are grown commercially in Maine, and local cooks use them generously in pancakes, muffins, jams, pies, and cobblers. Maine prohibits smoking in restaurants and bars.

ABOUT THE HOTELS

The beach communities in the south beckon with their weathered look. Stately digs can be found in the classic inns along the York County Coast. Bed-and-breakfasts and Victorian inns furnished with lace, chintz, and mahogany have joined the family-oriented motels of Ogunquit, Boothbay Harbor, Bar Harbor, and the Camden-Rockport region.

Although accommodations tend to be less luxurious away from the coast, Bethel, Carrabassett Valley, and Rangeley have sophisticated hotels and inns. Greenville has the largest selection of restaurants and accommodations in the North Woods region. Lakeside sporting camps, from the primitive to the upscale, are popular around Rangeley and the North Woods. Many have cozy cabins heated with woodstoves and serve three hearty meals a day. At some of Maine's larger hotels and inns with restaurants, rates may include breakfast and dinner during the peak seasons.

WHAT IT COSTS					
	¢	$	$$	$$$	$$$$
RESTAURANTS	under $8	$8–$12	$13–$20	$21–$28	over $28
HOTELS	under $80	$80–$120	$121–$170	$171–$220	over $200
CAMPING	under $10	$10–$17	$18–$35	$36–$49	over $50

Restaurant prices are per person, for a main course at dinner. Hotel prices are for a standard double room during peak season and not including tax or gratuities. Some inns add a 15% service charge.

WESTERN LAKES & MOUNTAINS

By Mary Ruoff   Less than 20 mi northwest of Portland and the coast, the sparsely populated lake and mountain areas of western Maine stretch north along the New Hampshire border to Quebec. In winter this is ski country; in summer the woods and waters draw vacationers.

The Sebago–Long Lake region bustles with activity in summer. Harrison and the Waterfords are quieter, Center Lovell is a dreamy escape, and Kezar Lake, tucked away in a fold of the White Mountains, has long been a hideaway of the wealthy. Bethel, in the valley of the Androscoggin River, is a classic New England town, its town common lined with historic homes. The more rural Rangeley Lake area brings long stretches of pine, beech, spruce, and sky—and stylish inns and B&Bs with access to golf, boating, fishing, and hiking. Snow sports, especially snowmobiling, are popular winter pastimes. Carrabassett Valley, just north of Kingfield, is home to Sugarloaf, a major ski resort with a challenging golf course.

SEBAGO LAKE

17 mi northwest of Portland.

Sebago Lake, which provides all the drinking water for Greater Portland, is Maine's best-known lake after Moosehead (⇨ *see The North Woods*). Many camps and year-round homes surround Sebago, which is popular with watersports enthusiasts.

WHAT TO SEE

Sabbathday Lake Shaker Museum. Established in the late 18th century, this is the last active Shaker community in the United States, with fewer than 10 members. Open for guided tours are four buildings with rooms of Shaker furniture, folk art, tools, farm implements, and crafts from the 18th to the early 20th century: the 1794 Meetinghouse, the 1839 Ministry's Shop, where the elders and eldresses lived until the early 1900s, the 1821 Sister's Shop, where household goods and candies were made for sale and still are on a smaller scale, and the 1816 Spinhouse, where changing exhibits are housed. A store sells herbs and goods handcrafted by the Shakers. ⊠707 Shaker Rd. (Hwy. 26, 20 mi north of Portland, 12 mi east of Naples, 8 mi west of Lewiston), New Gloucester ☎207/926–4597 ⊕www.shaker.lib.me.us ⊠Tour $6.50 ☉Late May–Columbus Day, Mon.–Sat. 10–4:30; first Sat. in Dec. for Christmas Fair.

SPORTS & THE OUTDOORS

Sebago Lake State Park. This 1,300-acre park on the north shore of the lake, provides swimming, picnicking, camping (250 sites), boating, and fishing (salmon and togue). ⊠11 Park Access Rd., Casco ☎207/693–6613 May–mid-Oct. only, 207/693–6231 ⊕www.maine.gov/doc/parks ⊠$4.50 mid-May–mid-Oct., $1.50 mid-Oct.–mid-May ☉Daily 9–sunset.

NAPLES

32 mi northwest of Portland.

Naples occupies an enviable location between Long and Sebago lakes. On clear days, the view down Long Lake takes in the Presidential Range of the White Mountains, highlighted by often-snowcapped Mt. Washington. The Causeway, which divides Long Lake from Brandy Pond, pulses with activity. Cruise and rental boats sail and motor on the lakes, open-air cafés overflow, and throngs of families parade along the sidewalk edging Long Lake. The town swells with seasonal residents and visitors in summer and all but shuts tight for winter.

☉ *Songo River Queen II,* a 92-foot stern-wheeler, takes passengers on hour-long cruises on Long Lake and longer voyages down the Songo River and through Songo Lock. ⊠U.S. 302, Naples Causeway ☎207/693–6861 ⊕www.songoriverqueen.net ⊠Long Lake cruise $8, Songo River ride $15 ☉July–Labor Day, 5 cruises daily.

WHERE TO STAY

$$$$ 🖬 **Migis Lodge.** The pine-paneled cottages scattered along the half mile
☉ of shorefront at this 125-acre resort have fieldstone fireplaces and are handsomely furnished with braided rugs and handmade quilts. A warm, woodsy feeling pervades the main lodge. The long front porch has views—marvelous at sunset—of Sebago Lake. All kinds of outdoor and indoor activities are included in the room rate, and canoes, kayaks, water-skiing and sailboats are available. Three fancy meals are served daily in the dining room. **Pros:** private island, waiters serve drinks at

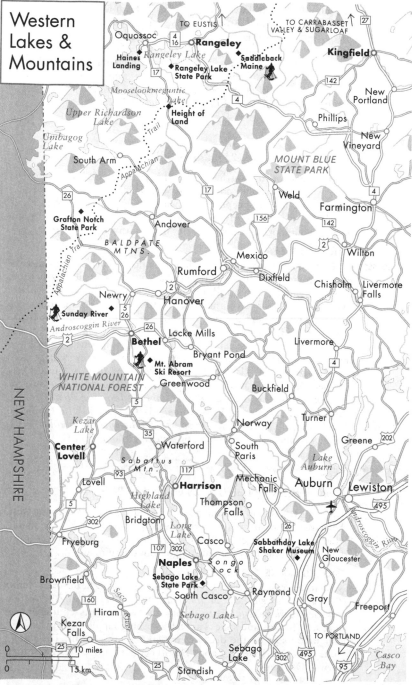

Western Lakes & Mountains

TO EUSTIS

TO CARRABASSET VALLEY & SUGARLOAF 27

Oquossoc 4 16 **Rangeley**

Kingfield

Haines Landing *Rangeley Lake* Saddleback Maine

17 Rangeley Lake State Park

142

New Portland

Mooselookmeguntic Lake 4

Upper Richardson Lake Height of Land

Phillips

Umbagog Lake

New Vineyard

Appalachian Trail

South Arm

MOUNT BLUE STATE PARK

4

26 17 Weld

Grafton Notch State Park Andover 156 142 Farmington

B A L D P A T E M T N S . Mexico Wilton 4

Rumford Dixfield Chisholm Livermore Falls

Newry 2 Hanover

Appalachian Trail

5 26 Sunday River

Androscoggin River 26 Locke Mills Livermore

2 **Bethel** Bryant Pond

WHITE MOUNTAIN NATIONAL FOREST Mt. Abram Ski Resort 4

5 Greenwood Buckfield

Kezar Lake 35 Norway Turner Greene 202

Center Lovell Waterford South Paris *Lake Auburn*

Sabattus Mtn. 117 Mechanic Falls **Auburn** **Lewiston**

Lovell 93 **Harrison** 26

5 *Highland Lake* Thompson Falls 495

302 Bridgton *Long Lake* Casco Sabbathday Lake Shaker Museum New Gloucester

Fryeburg 107 302 **Naples** *Songo Lock*

Sebago Lake State Park Gray Freeport

Brownfield 160 South Casco Raymond

Kezar Falls Hiram *Saco River* *Sebago Lake*

TO PORTLAND

Casco Bay

0 ____ 25 10 miles
0 ____ 15 km 25 Sebago Lake 302 495 95

Standish 25

NEW HAMPSHIRE

cocktail hour, fresh flowers from the gardens in lodgings. **Con:** week minimum in July and August (unless shorter openings occur). ⊠*30 Migis Lodge Rd., off U.S. 302, South Casco* ☎*207/655–4524* ⊕*www. migis.com* ↩*35 cottages, 6 rooms* ⚭*In-room: no a/c (some), refrigerator, Wi-Fi (some). In-hotel: restaurant, tennis courts, gym, spa, beachfront, water sports, bicycles, children's programs ages 0–12, public Internet, public Wi-Fi, airport shuttle (fee), no-smoking rooms* ⊟*No credit cards* ⊙*Closed mid-Oct.–mid-June* ℺*FAP.*

HARRISON

10 mi north of Naples, 25 mi south of Bethel.

Harrison anchors the northern end of Long Lake but is less commercial than Naples. The combination of woods, lakes, and views makes it a good choice for leaf-peepers. The nearby towns of North Waterford, South Waterford, and tiny Waterford, a National Historic District, are ideal for outdoors lovers who prefer to get away from the crowds.

WHERE TO STAY

$$–$$$$ ⬚**Bear Mountain Inn.** This rambling farmhouse inn has been meticu-
★ lously decorated in a woodsy theme. The luxurious Great Grizzly room has mesmerizing views and, like the other larger rooms, a fireplace, whirlpool bath for two, and wet bar. Cozy Sugar Bear Cottage is a romantic retreat, and the two-bedroom suites attract families. Breakfast is served in the dining room, which has a fieldstone fireplace and lake views. **Pros:** large lake-view deck with grill, benches and hammocks along riverside trail, "convenience area" with everything from beach bags to wine glasses to snacks. **Con:** one suite is considerably smaller. ⊠*Hwy. 35, Waterford, 04088* ☎*207/583–4404* ⊕*www.bear mtninn.com* ↩*9 rooms, 2 suites, 1 cabin* ⚭*In-room: no a/c (some), no phone, DVD (some), VCR (some), no TV (some), Wi-Fi. In-hotel: beachfront, no elevator, water sports, public Internet, public Wi-Fi, some pets allowed (cabin only), no-smoking rooms* ⊟*MC, V* ℺*BP.*

CENTER LOVELL

17 mi northwest of Harrison, 28 mi south of Bethel.

At Center Lovell you can glimpse the secluded Kezar Lake to the west, the retreat of wealthy and very private people. Sabattus Mountain, which rises behind Center Lovell, has a public hiking trail and stupendous views of the Presidential Range from the summit.

SPORTS & THE OUTDOORS

BOATING & Next to a town boat launch with a small beach, **Kezar Lake Marina**
FISHING (⊠*219 W. Lovell Rd., at the Narrows, Lovell* ☎*207/925–3000* ⊕*www.kezarlake.com*) rents boats and watersports equipment. A store sells T-shirts and snacks as well as fishing supplies and water skis. Dine indoors or on the decks at the lakeside restaurant, The Loon's Nest, open mid-June to Labor Day. The marina operates from mid-April to October.

WHERE TO STAY

$ □ **Center Lovell Inn.** The eclectic furnishings blend mid-19th and mid-20th centuries in a pleasing, homey style. In summer the best tables for dining at the on-site restaurant ($$–$$$$) are on the wraparound porch, which has sunset views over Kezar Lake and the White Mountains. Entrées may include pan-seared Muscovy duck, fillet of bison, or fresh swordfish. Breakfast is by reservation only (no lunch). Rooms are upstairs and in the adjacent Harmon House. **Pros:** suite has apartment feel. **Con:** no common TV. ⊠*1107 Main St. (Hwy. 5), 04016* ☎*207/925–1575 or 800/777–2698* ⊕*www.centerlovellinn.com* ⇨*8 rooms, 6 with bath; 1 suite* �&*In-room: no a/c, no phone, no TV (some). In-hotel: restaurant, no elevator, no-smoking rooms* ▭*D, MC, V* ⊙*Closed Nov.–late Dec. and Apr.–mid-May.*

$$$$ □ **Quisisana.** This delightful cottage resort on Kezar Lake makes music a main focus. The staff—students and graduates of the country's finer music schools—perform everything from Broadway tunes to concert-piano pieces throughout your stay. Most of the white clapboard cottages have screened porches, pine-paneled living areas, fireplaces, and simple wicker and country furnishings. **Pros:** Tuesday cocktail party, dinner-hour children's program. **Con:** one-week minimum in peak season (unless shorter openings occur). ⊠*42 Quisisana Dr., off Pleasant Point Rd., 04016* ☎*207/925–3500* ⊕*www.quisisanaresort.com* ⇨*11 rooms in 2 lodges, 32 cottages* �&*In-room: no a/c, no phone, no TV. In-hotel: restaurant, bar, tennis courts, beachfront, water sports, no elevator, public Internet, public Wi-Fi, airport shuttle, no-smoking rooms* ▭*No credit cards* ⊙*Closed Sept.–mid-June* ⧉*FAP.*

BETHEL

28 mi north of Lovell, 66 mi north of Portland.

Bethel is pure New England, a town with white clapboard houses and white-steeple churches and a mountain vista at the end of every street. In winter, this is ski country: Sunday River ski area in Newry is only a few miles north.

WHAT TO SEE

Regional History Center. A stroll in Bethel should begin at this history center at the Bethel Historical Society. The center's campus comprises two buildings, the 1821 O'Neil Robinson House and the 1813 Dr. Moses Mason House; both are listed on the National Register of Historic Places. The Robinson House has exhibits pertaining to the region's history; the Moses Mason House has nine period rooms and a front hall and stairway wall decorated with murals by folk artist Rufus Porter. Pick up materials for a walking tour of Bethel Hill Village. ⊠*10–14 Broad St.* ☎*207/824–2908 or 800/824–2910* ⊕*www.bethelhistorical. org* ⧉*$3* ⊙*O'Neil Robinson House: Tues.–Fri. 10–noon and 1–4; July–Aug. also Sat.–Sun. 1–4; Dr. Moses Mason House: July–Labor Day, Tues.–Sun. 1–4, and by appointment year-round.*

SPORTS & THE OUTDOORS

Grafton Notch State Park. At this park 14 mi north of Bethel, you can take an easy nature walk to Mother Walker Falls or Moose Cave and see the spectacular Screw Auger Falls, or you can hike to the summit of Old Speck Mountain, the state's third-highest peak. If you have the stamina and the equipment, you can pick up the Appalachian Trail here, hike over Saddleback Mountain, and continue on to Mt. Katahdin. The **Maine Appalachian Trail Club** (✉ *Box 283, Augusta 04330* ⊕ *www.matc. org*) publishes a map and trail guide. ✉ *Hwy. 26* ☎ *207/824–2912 mid-May–mid-Oct., 207/624–6080* ✉ *Mid-May–mid-Oct. $2, mid-Oct.–mid-May $1.50* ☉ *Daily 9–sunset.*

White Mountain National Forest. This forest straddles New Hampshire and Maine, with the highest peaks on the New Hampshire side. The Maine section, however, has magnificent rugged terrain, camping and picnic areas, and hiking from hour-long nature loops to a day hike up Speckled Mountain. Highway 113 through the forest is closed in the winter. ✉ *Evans Notch Visitor Center, 18 Mayville Rd. (U.S. 2)* ☎ *207/824–2134* ⊕ *www.fs.fed.us/r9/white* ✉ *Day pass $3, week pass $5* ☉ *Forest daily, 24 hours. Center Fri. and Sat. 8–4:30.*

CANOEING **Bethel Outdoor Adventure and Campground** (✉ *121 Mayville Rd.* ☎ *207/824–4224 or 800/533–3607* ⊕ *www.betheloutdooradventure. com*) rents canoes, kayaks, and bikes, guides fishing, kayak, and canoe trips, and operates a hostel and riverside campground.

DOGSLEDDING **Mahoosuc Guide Service** (✉ *1513 Bear River Rd., Newry* ☎ *207/824–2073* ⊕ *www.mahoosuc.com*) leads day and multiday dogsledding expeditions on the Maine–New Hampshire border, as well as canoeing trips. Its **Mahoosic Mountain Lodge** (⊕ *www.mahoosucmountainlodge. com*) has dorm and bed-and-breakfast lodging.

HORSEBACK RIDING **Sparrowhawk Mountain Ranch** (✉ *120 Fleming Rd.* ☎ *207/836–2528* ⊕ *www.sparrowhawkmountainranch.com*) leads one-hour to daylong trail rides and also has an indoor arena. Parties of up to 10 can rent the guest house for overnight stays.

SKI AREAS **Bethel Inn Nordic Ski and Snowshoe Center** (✉ *Village Common* ☎ *207/824–6276* ⊕ *www.bethelinn.com*) has 25 mi of cross-country trails, 5 mi of packed snowshoe trails, and provides ski and snowshoe rentals as well as lessons. It is located at the Bethel Inn Resort, which has a hotel and townhouse rentals. **Carter's Cross-Country Ski Center** (✉ *786 Intervale Rd.* ☎ *207/824–3880 or 207/539–4848* ⊕ *www. cartersxcski.com*) has 33 mi of trails for all levels of skiers; lessons and snowshoe, ski, and sled (to pull children) rentals are provided. It also rents lodging rooms and ski-in cabins.

What was once a sleepy little ski area with minimal facilities has evolved into a sprawling resort that attracts skiers from as far away as Europe. Spread throughout the valley at **Sunday River** (✉ *15 S. Ridge Rd., Turn on Sunday River Rd. from U.S. 2, Newry* ☎ *207/824–3000 main number, 207/824–5200 snow conditions, 800/543–2754 reservations* ⊕ *www.sundayriver.com*) are three base areas, two condominium hotels, trailside condominiums, town houses, and a ski dorm. Sunday River is home to the Maine Handicapped Skiing program, which provides lessons and services for skiers with disabilities. There's plenty else to do, including cross-country skiing, ice-skating, tubing, hiking, and mountain biking. Family-friendly **Mt. Abram Ski Resort** (🏠 *Box 240, Greenwood 04255*) 📞*207/875–5000* 🌐*www. skimtabram.com*), south of Bethel, has night skiing.

SNOW- **Sun Valley Sports** (✉ *129 Sunday River Rd.* 📞*207/824–7533 or*
MOBILING *877/851–7533* 🌐*www.sunvalleysports.com*) gives guided snowmobile tours (rentals provided). It also operates fly-fishing trips, canoe and kayak rentals, guided ATV tours, and moose and wildlife safaris.

WHERE TO STAY

$–$$ 🏨**Victoria Inn.** It's hard to miss this turreted inn, with its teal-, mauve-, and beige-painted exterior and attached carriage house topped with a cupola. Inside, Victorian details include ceiling rosettes, stained-glass windows, elaborate fireplace mantels, and gleaming oak trim. Guest rooms vary in size (suites sleep three to eight); most are furnished with reproductions of antiques. The restaurant ($$–$$$$) is open most days for dinner, lunch, and (with 24-hour notice) afternoon tea. Choose from entrées like rack of lamb with basil and mint pesto, and duck with pomegranate sauce. **Pros:** lots of breakfast choices, homemade cookies in your room. **Con:** lofts in suites lack decor. ✉*32 Main St.* 📞*207/824–8060 or 888/774–1235* 🌐*www.thevictoria-inn.com* 🛏*10 rooms, 4 suites* ⚙*In-room: Wi-Fi (some). In-hotel: restaurant, no elevator, Wi-Fi, no-smoking rooms* ▤*AE, D, MC, V* 🍽*BP.*

EN
ROUTE
The routes north from Bethel to the Rangeley district are all scenic, particularly in autumn when the maples are aflame with color. In the town of Newry, make a short detour to the **Artist's Bridge** (turn off Highway 26 onto Sunday River Road and drive about 4 mi), the most painted and photographed of Maine's eight covered bridges. Highway 26 continues north to the gorges and waterfalls of **Grafton Notch State Park.** Past the park, Highway 26 continues to Errol, New Hampshire, where Highway 16 will return you east around the north shore of Mooselookmeguntic Lake, through Oquossoc, and into Rangeley.

RANGELEY

67 mi north of Bethel.

Rangeley, on the north side of Rangeley Lake on Highways 4 and 16, has long lured anglers and winter-sports enthusiasts to its more than 40 lakes and ponds and 450 square mi of woodlands. Equally popular in summer or winter, Rangeley has a rough, wilderness feel to it. Lodgings are in the woods, around the lake, and along the golf course.

SPORTS & THE OUTDOORS

Rangeley Lake State Park. On the south shore of Rangeley Lake, this park has superb lakeside scenery, swimming, picnic tables, a boat ramp, showers, and 50 campsites. ✉*S. Shore Dr., off Hwy. 17 or Hwy. 4* 📞*207/864–3858 May 15–Oct. 1 only, 207/624–6080* 🌐*www.state. me.us/doc/parks* 💲*$3* 🕐*May 15–Oct. 1.*

<table>
<tr><td>BOATING &
FISHING</td><td>Rangeley and Mooselookmeguntic lakes are good for canoeing, sailing, and motorboating. Fishing for brook trout and salmon is at its best in May, June, and September; the Rangeley area is especially popular with fly-fishers.</td></tr>
</table>

SKI AREAS **Rangeley Lakes Trail Center** (⊠ *524 Saddleback Mountain Rd.* ☎*207/864–4309* ⊕*www.xcskirangeley.com*) rents cross-country skis and snowshoes and has about 30 mi of groomed trails surrounding Saddleback Mountain.

A family atmosphere prevails at **Saddleback Maine** (⊠*976 Saddleback Mountain Rd., follow signs from Hwy. 4* ☎*207/864–5671 or 866/918–2225, 207/864–5441 or 877/864–5441 reservations* ⊕*www.saddlebackmaine.com*), where the quiet, lack of crowds, and spectacularly wide valley views draw return visitors. The 60 trails, accessed by five lifts, are about evenly divided between novice, intermediate, and advanced. On-site is also a day-care center, ski school, rental and retail shop, and trailside condominium lodging. Hiking (the Appalachian Trail crosses Saddleback's summit ridge), mountain biking, canoeing, fly-fishing, and birding are big draws in warm weather.

WHERE TO EAT & STAY

$$–$$$ ✗**Gingerbread House Restaurant.** A big fieldstone fireplace, well-spaced
AMERICAN tables, and an antique marble soda fountain, all with views of the woods beyond, make for comfortable surroundings at this gingerbread-trim establishment, which is open for breakfast, lunch, and dinner. Soups, salads, and sandwiches at lunch give way to entrées such as Maine crab cakes and barbequed ribs with blueberry chipotle sauce and maple syrup. ⊠ *55 Carry Rd. (Hwy. 4), Oquossoc* ☎*207/864–3602* ▤*AE, D, MC, V* ⊗*Closed Nov. and Apr.; and Mon. and Tues., Dec.–Mar. No lunch or dinner Sun., Dec.–Mar. and May–mid-June.*

$–$$ ⊞**Country Club Inn.** Built in 1920 as the country club for the adjacent
⟳ Mingo Springs Golf Course, this secluded hilltop retreat has sweeping lake and mountain views. Fieldstone fireplaces anchor both ends of the lodge-like common room. Rooms downstairs in the main building and in the adjacent 1950s motel are cheerfully, if minimally, decorated. Inside the glassed-in dining room ($$–$$$$)—open to nonguests by reservation only—you can dine on such entrées as veal Gruyère and roast duck Montmorency. **Pros:** loads of lawn and board games, lots of photos of Rangeley's long-gone resorts. **Con:** smallish rooms in main building. ⊠*56 Country Club Rd.* ☎*207/864–3831* ⊕*www.countryclubinnrangeley.com* ⟿*19 rooms* ⟁*In-room: no a/c (some), no TV, refrigerators (some). In-hotel: restaurant, bar, pool, no elevator, public Internet, some pets allowed, no-smoking rooms* ▤*AE, MC, V* ⊗*Closed Nov. and Apr.* ❍*BP, MAP.*

¢–$ ⊞**Rangeley Inn and Motor Lodge.** From Main Street you see only the large three-story blue inn, built in the early 1900s for wealthy urbanites on vacation. Behind it is a motel wing with decks on most rooms and views of Haley Pond, a lawn, and a garden. Some of the inn's sizable rooms have iron-and-brass beds. Some baths are marble, some have claw-foot tubs, others have whirlpool tubs. **Pros:** historic hotel last of its kind the region. **Con:** elegant dining room closed at this writing. ⊠*2443 Main*

1

St., 04970 ☎207/864–3341 or 800/666–3687 ⊕www.rangeleyinn. com ⟶35 inn rooms, 15 motel rooms (including 1 suite) ♿In-room: no a/c (some), kitchen (some). In-hotel: restaurant, some pets allowed (fee) ☰AE, D, MC, V ⊘Closed Apr.–May and Nov.–Dec.

KINGFIELD

33 mi east of Rangeley, 15 mi west of Phillips.

In the shadows of Mt. Abram and Sugarloaf Mountain, Kingfield has everything a "real" New England town should have: a general store, historic inns, and white clapboard churches. Sugarloaf has golf and tennis in summer.

SPORTS & THE OUTDOORS

SKI AREAS Abundant natural snow, a huge mountain, and the only above-tree-
★ line lift-service skiing in the East have made **Sugarloaf** (⊠*5092 Access Rd., Carrabassett Valley* ☎*207/237–2000, 207/237–6808 snow conditions, 800/843–5623 reservations* ⊕*www.sugarloaf.com)* one of Maine's best-known ski areas. Two slope-side hotels and hundreds of slope-side condominiums provide ski in, ski-out access, and the base village has restaurants and shops. The Outdoor Center has more than 60 mi of cross-country ski trails as well as snowshoeing, snow tubing, and ice-skating activities. There's also plenty for the kids, from day care to special events. Once you are here, a car is unnecessary—a shuttle connects all mountain operations. Summer is much quieter than winter, but you can bike, fish, and hike, plus golf at the superb 18-hole, Robert Trent Jones Jr.–designed golf course.

THE NORTH WOODS

By Mary Ruoff Maine's North Woods, the vast area in the north-central section of the state, is best experienced by canoe or raft, on a hiking, snowshoe or snowmobile trip, or on a fishing trip. Some great theaters for these activities are Moosehead Lake, Baxter State Park, and the Allagash Wilderness Waterway—as well as the summer resort town of Greenville. Maine's largest lake, Moosehead supplies more in the way of rustic camps, guides, and outfitters than any other northern locale. Its 420 mi of shorefront, three-quarters of which is owned by paper manufacturers, is virtually uninhabited.

GREENVILLE

160 mi northeast of Portland, 71 mi northwest of Bangor.

Greenville, the largest town on Moosehead Lake, is an outdoors lover's paradise. Boating, fishing, and hiking are popular in summer, while snowmobiling, skiing, and ice fishing reign in winter. The town also has the greatest selection of shops, restaurants, and inns in the region—note that some of these, however, are closed mid-October to mid-June.

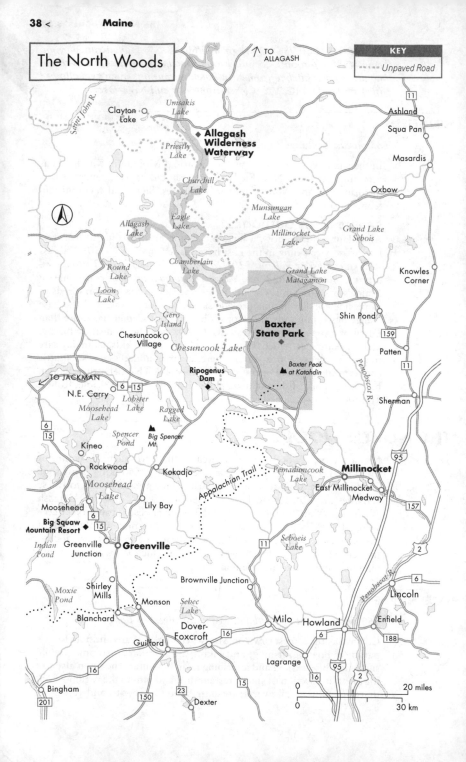

The North Woods

KEY

Unpaved Road

TO ALLAGASH

Saint John R.

Clayton Lake

Umsakis Lake

Ashland

Squa Pan

Allagash Wilderness Waterway

Priestly Lake

Masardis

Churchill Lake

Oxbow

Munsungan Lake

Grand Lake Sebois

Eagle Lake

Allagash Lake

Millinocket Lake

Knowles Corner

Round Lake

Chamberlain Lake

Grand Lake Matagamon

Loon Lake

Baxter State Park

Shin Pond

159

Patten

Gero Island

Chesuncook Village

Chesuncook Lake

Baxter Peak at Katahdin

11

TO JACKMAN

Ripogenus Dam

6 15

N.E. Carry

Lobster Lake

Ragged Lake

Penobscot R.

Sherman

Moosehead Lake

6 15

Spencer Pond

Big Spencer Mt.

95

Kineo

Rockwood

Kokadjo

Pemadumcook Lake

Millinocket

Moosehead Lake

Appalachian Trail

East Millinocket

Medway

Moosehead

Lily Bay

157

Big Squaw Mountain Resort

6 15

Indian Pond

Greenville Junction

Greenville

11

Seboeis Lake

2

Moxie Pond

Shirley Mills

Brownville Junction

Penobscot R.

Lincoln

6

Blanchard

Monson

Sebec Lake

Milo

Howland

Enfield

188

Guilford

Dover-Foxcroft

16

6

95

16

Lagrange

2

16

Bingham

150

23

Dexter

15

0   20 miles

0   30 km

201

WHAT TO SEE

Moosehead Historical Society. The historical society leads guided tours of the Eveleth-Crafts-Sheridan House, a late-19th-century Victorian mansion filled with period antiques, most original to the home. Special exhibits and displays change annually. A small lumberman's museum and a fine exhibit of American Indian artifacts dating from 9,000 BC to the 1700s are in the Carriage House. ⊠ *444 Pritham Ave.* ☎ *207/695–2909* ⊕ *www.mooseheadhistory.org* 🖾 *$4* ⊙ *Eveleth-Crafts-Sheridan House mid-June–Sept., Wed.–Fri. 1–4. Carriage House Tues.–Fri. 9–4 or by appointment.*

OFF THE BEATEN PATH

Mt. Kineo. Once a thriving summer resort for the wealthy, the Mount Kineo Hotel (the original was built in 1830, its last successor torn down in the 1940s) was accessed primarily by steamship. Today Kineo makes a pleasant day trip. You can take the Kineo Shuttle, which departs from the State Dock in **Rockwood,** or rent a motorboat in Rockwood and make the journey across the lake in about 15 minutes. It's an easy hike to Kineo's summit for awesome views down the lake. A map is available at the Moosehead Lake Region Chamber of Commerce.

SPORTS & THE OUTDOORS

Lily Bay State Park. Eight miles northeast of Greenville on Moosehead Lake, this park has a good swimming beach, two boat-launching ramps, and two campgrounds with 91 sites. ⊠ *13 Myrle's Way, off Lily Bay Rd.* ☎ *207/695–2700 May 15–Oct. 15 only, 207/941–4014* ⊕ *www.state.me.us/doc/parks* 🖾 *$3* ⊙ *May 15–Oct. 15, daily 9–sunset.*

BIKING Mountain biking is popular in the Greenville area, but bikes are not allowed on some logging roads. Expect to pay about $20 per day for a rental bicycle. **Northwoods Outfitters** (⊠ *5 Lily Bay Rd., Greenville* ☎ *207/695–3288* ⊕ *www.maineoutfitter.com*) rents mountain bikes, kids bikes, and more.

FISHING Togue (lake trout), landlocked salmon, small mouth bass, and brook trout lure thousands of anglers to the region from ice-out in mid-May until September; the hardiest return in winter to ice fish.

RAFTING The Kennebec and Dead rivers and the west branch of the Penobscot River provide thrilling white-water rafting (guides are strongly recommended). These rivers are dam-controlled, so trips run rain or shine daily from mid-April to mid-October (day and multiday trips are conducted). Many rafting outfitters operate resort facilities in their base towns. **Raft Maine** (☎ *800/723–8633* ⊕ *www.raftmaine.com*) has lodging and rafting packages and information about outfitters.

SKIING **Big Squaw Mountain Resort.** This remote but pretty resort overlooking Moosehead Lake is open weekends, holidays, and Maine school-vacation weeks. The chairlift to the black diamond trails has been shut down since a 2004 accident, and the hotel is closed, but with downright cheap prices, families still come here to ski. There are plans to expand the resort and fully reopen. ⊠ *Hwys. 6/15* ☎ *207/695–1000 or 800/754–6246* ⊕ *www.bigsquawmountain.com.*

TOURS **Katahdin.** The Moosehead Marine Museum runs three- and five-hour
★   trips on Moosehead Lake (eight-hour foliage cruise in late fall) aboard
the *Katahdin,* a 115-foot 1914 steamship (now diesel). Also called *The
Kate,* the ship carried passengers to Mt. Kineo until 1933 and then
was used in the logging industry until 1975. The trips range in price
from $30 to $35. The boat and the shore-side museum have displays
about the steamships that transported people and cargo on the lake
more than 100 years ago. ⊠*12 Lily Bay Rd.* ☞*(board on shoreline by
museum)* ☎*207/695–2716* ⊕*www.katahdincruises.com* ⊘*Memorial
Day weekend–Columbus Day.*

▌OFF THE
BEATEN
PATH
Gulf Hagas. From the site of the old Katahdin Iron Works, a hiking
trail leads over fairly rugged terrain to Gulf Hagas, a National Natural Landmark with natural chasms, cliffs, a 5.2-mi gorge, waterfalls,
pools, exotic flora, and rock formations. Access is on land managed by
North Maine Woods (☎*207/435–6213* ⊕*www.northmainewoods.org*)
for public use. From Greenville, take Pleasant Street east (road becomes
gravel) about 19 mi, follow signs to gulf. From Millinocket, take Hwy.
11 south about 32 mi to the Katahdin Iron Works Checkpoint, continue 7 mi on dirt road, follow signs.

WHERE TO STAY

$$$$ 🏨**Blair Hill Inn.** Beautiful gardens and a hilltop location with marvelous
★   views over the lake distinguish this 1891 estate. So do fine antiques,
plush bedding, and elegant baths, some with oversized or footed tubs.
Guest rooms are spacious; all have sitting areas and four have fireplaces. A restaurant (reservations required) serves a prix-fixe five-
course dinner ($$$$) from mid-June to mid-October on Friday and
Saturday nights. Arrive early to enjoy cocktails on the wraparound
porch. The inn hosts a music series in July and August. **Pros:** third-floor
deck the length of the inn; 15 acres with stone paths, wooded picnic
area, and trout pond, flowers from gardens in rooms. **Con:** steep drive-
way. ⊠*351 Lily Bay Rd. 04441* ☎*207/695–0224* ⊕*www.blairhill.
com* ♥*7 rooms, 1 suite* ⚒*In-room: no a/c (some), no phone. In-hotel:
restaurant, no elevator, public Internet, no-smoking rooms* ▤*D, MC,
V* ⊘*Closed Apr. and Nov.* ⏃*BP.*

$$$$ 🏨**Little Lyford Pond Camps.** When you want to get away from everything—including electricity, plumbing, and phones—head to this
remote, rustic wilderness retreat, part of the Appalachian Mountain
Club lodging network. Gulf Hagas is a 2-mi hike away, moose abun-
dantly populate the area, and the fly-fishing, snowshoeing, and backcountry skiing are excellent. Cabins boast woodstoves and gas and
kerosene lanterns. The home-cooked fare is served family style in the
main lodge. **Pros:** family adventure camps in summer, cedar sauna
in winter. **Con:** winter access is by cross-country ski or snowmobile
transport (for a fee). ⊠*About 10 mi east of Greenville, access via logging roads* ☎*603/466–2727* ⊕*www.outdoors.org/lodging* ♥*7 cabins, 12-bed bunkhouse* ⚒*In-room: no a/c, no phone, no TV. In-hotel:
restaurant, water sports, no-smoking rooms* ▤*AE, MC, V* ⊘*Closed
Apr.–mid-May and Nov.–late Dec.* ⏃*FAP.*

NORTH WOODS OUTFITTERS

BOATING

Allagash Canoe Trips (⊠ *8 Bigelow, Carrabassett Valley* ☎ *207/237-3077* ⊕ *www.allagash-canoetrips.com*) operates guided trips on the Allagash Waterway, plus the Moose, Penobscot, and St. John rivers. **Beaver Cove Marina** (☎ *207/695-3526* ⊕ *www.beavercovemarina.com*) rents boats. **Katahdin Outfitters** (⊠ *Less than ¼ mi outside Millinocket on Baxter State Park Rd.* ☎ *207/723-5700 or 800/862-2663* ⊕ *www.katahdinoutfitters.com*) outfits canoeing and kayaking expeditions. **North Woods Ways** (⊠ *2293 Elliottsville Rd., Willimantic* ☎ *207/997-3723* ⊕ *www.northwoodsways.com*) leads overnight canoe and snowshoe trips (gear is hauled on toboggans).

If requested, most canoe-rental operations will also arrange transportation, help plan your route, and provide a guide. Transportation to wilderness lakes can be handled through various regional flying services (⇨ *By Air* in *Maine Essentials*).

MULTI-SPORT

Moose Country Safaris (☎ *207/876-4907* ⊕ *www. moosecountrysafaris.com*) leads moose safaris and canoe, kayak, Jeep, snowshoe, and hiking trips. **New England Outdoor Center** (☎ *207/723-5438 or 800/766-7238* ⊕ *www.neoc.com*) rents snowmobiles and canoes and offers guided snowmobile, whitewater rafting, fishing, canoe, hiking, and moose-watching trips. It also has campgrounds and rents cabins. **Northwoods Outfitters** (⊠ *5 Lilly Bay Rd* ☎ *207/695-3288* ⊕ *www. maineoutfitter.com*) outfits for moose watching, biking, skiing, snowmobiling, snowboarding, canoeing, kayaking, and fishing; leads trips for many of these activities; and rents canoes, kayaks, bikes, snowmobiles, snowshoes and more. Shop, get trail advice, and kick back in the Internet café at its downtown outfitters store.

RAFTING

Raft Maine (☎ *800/723-8633* ⊕ *www.raftmaine.com*) is an association of white-water outfitters licensed to lead trips down the Kennebec and Dead rivers and the west branch of the Penobscot River. Rafting season begins in mid-April and continues through mid-October.

SCENIC DRIVE

For a scenic backwoods trip, travel the Golden Road from the Greenville area east toward Baxter State Park and Millinocket. The road is named for the amount of money it took the Great Northern Paper Company to build it. From downtown Greenville, take Lily Bay Road north to Kokadjo and follow the dirt Sias Hill/Greenville Road to its end, then turn right on the Golden Road (it soon becomes paved). Note: keep to the right, as logging trucks have the right of way. Turn left on Rip Dam Road to drive across **Ripogenus Dam**, at the head of Ripogenus Lake (east of Chesuncook Lake) and granite-walled **Ripogenus Gorge**. It is about 20 mi northeast of Kokadjo, and 16 mi southeast of Chesuncook Village by floatplane.

The turnaround north of the dam has the best gorge views. The Penobscot River drops more than 70 feet per mile through the gorge, giving white-water rafters a hold-on-for-your-life ride. The best spot to watch the rafters is from the overlook at the rock-choked Crib Works Rapid (a Class V rapid). To get there, continue on the Golden Road and turn left on Telos Road. The parking area is just after the single-lane bridge (don't loiter on bridge).

Returning to the Golden Road, take photos of Mt. Katahdin from the footbridge alongside one-lane Abol Bridge (park well off the road)—this view is famed. Turn left at North Woods Trading Post to connect with Highway 157; turn left again for Baxter State Park or right for Millinocket.

MILLINOCKET

67 mi north of Bangor, 88 mi northwest of Greenville via Hwys. 6 and 11.

Millinocket, a paper-mill town with a population of 5,000, is a gateway to Baxter State Park and Maine's North Woods. Although it has a smattering of motels and restaurants, Millinocket is the place to stock up on supplies, fill your gas tank, or grab a hot meal or shower before heading into the wilderness. Numerous rafting and canoeing outfitters and guides are based here.

SPORTS & THE OUTDOORS

★ **Allagash Wilderness Waterway.** A spectacular 92-mi corridor of lakes and rivers, the waterway cuts across 170,000 acres of wilderness, beginning at the northwest corner of Baxter State Park and running north to the town of Allagash, 10 mi from the Canadian border. From mid-May to October, this is prime canoeing (and camping) country, but it should not be undertaken lightly. On the lakes, strong winds can halt your progress for days; on the river, conditions vary greatly with the depth and volume of water, and although the Allagash rapids are ranked Class I and Class II (very easy and easy, respectively), the river is not a piece of cake. The complete 92-mi course requires seven to 10 days. The best bet for a novice is to go with a guide; a good outfitter will help plan your route and provide your craft and transportation. ⊠ *Maine Bureau of Parks and Lands, 106 Hogan Rd., Bangor* ☎ *207/941–4014* ⊕ *www.maine.gov/doc/parks.*

Fodor's Choice **Baxter State Park.** A gift from Governor Percival Baxter, this is the jewel
★ in the crown of northern Maine, a 209,501-acre wilderness area that surrounds **Mt. Katahdin,** Maine's highest mountain (5,267 feet at Baxter Peak) and the terminus of the Appalachian Trail. Katahdin draws thousands of hikers every year for the daylong climb to the summit and the stunning views of woods, mountains, and lakes. Three trailheads lead to its peak; some routes include the hair-raising Knife Edge Ridge. The crowds climbing Katahdin can be formidable on clear summer days, so if you crave solitude, tackle one of the 45 other mountains in the park, 17 of which exceed an elevation of 3,000 feet and all of which are accessible from an extensive network of trails. South Turner can be climbed in a morning (if you're fit), and its summit has a great view of Katahdin across the valley. On the way you'll pass Sandy Stream

Pond, where moose are often seen at dusk. The Owl, the Brothers, and Doubletop Mountain are good day hikes.

Day-use parking areas fill quickly in season at Baxter; it's best to arrive early, between 5 and 6 AM (limited parking held until 8 AM for Maine residents by reservation). No pets, domestic animals, oversize vehicles, radios, all-terrain vehicles, motorboats, or motorcycles are allowed in the park, and there are no pay phones, gas stations, stores, running water, or electricity. The camping is primitive, and sites typically fill up well ahead for peak season. The visitor center is at the southern entrance outside Millinocket. You can also get information about Baxter in town at park headquarters. ✉ *64 Balsam Dr., Millinocket* ✛ *Togue Pond Gate (southern entrance): Hwy. 157, 18 mi northwest of Millinocket; Matagamon Gate (northern entrance): Grand Lake Rd., 26 mi northwest of Patten via Hwy. 159 and Grand Lake Rd.* ☎ *207/723–5140* ⊕ *www.baxterstateparkauthority.com* 💰 *$13 per vehicle (free to Maine residents)* ☉ *Daily, sunrise to sunset.*

WHERE TO STAY

CAMPING
$$–$$$

⚠ **Baxter State Park Authority.** Camping spaces at the park's 10 primitive campgrounds (no electricity or running water) must be reserved by mail or in person (check or cash) within four months of your trip, or by phone (MC or V only) two weeks prior. Phones reservations are much harder to come by for July, August, and fall weekends, but cancellations do open up spots. There are also primitive backcountry sites. **Pro:** cabins at Daicey Pond and Kidney Pond campgrounds. **Con:** winter access is by ski or snowshoe. ✉ *64 Balsam Dr., Millinocket* ✛ *Togue Pond Gate (southern entrance): Hwy. 157, 18 mi northwest of Millinocket; Matagamon Gate (northern entrance): Grand Lake Rd., 26 mi northwest of Patten via Hwy. 159 and Grand Lake Rd.* ☎ *207/723–5140* ⊕ *www.baxterstateparkauthority.com* ⚠ *22 cabins, 4 bunkhouses, 57 lean-tos, 75 tent sites, 13 group tent sites* ♿ *Pit toilets, fire grates, fire rings, picnic tables, ranger stations, swimming (pond, lake, stream)* ▤ *MC, V* ☉ *Closed mid-Oct.–Nov. and Apr.–mid-May.*

THE SOUTHERN COAST

By Laura V.
Scheel

Maine's southernmost coastal towns—Kittery, the Yorks, Ogunquit, the Kennebunks, and the Old Orchard Beach area—reveal a few of the stunning faces of the state's coast, from the miles and miles of inviting sandy beaches to the beautifully kept historic towns and carnival-like attractions. There is something for every taste, whether you seek solitude in a kayak or prefer being caught up in the infectious spirit of fellow vacationers. The Southern Coast is best explored on a leisurely holiday of two days—more if you require a fix of solid beach time.

North of Kittery, long stretches of hard-packed white-sand beach are closely crowded by nearly unbroken ranks of beach cottages, motels, and oceanfront restaurants. The summer colonies of York Beach and Wells brim with crowds and ticky-tacky shorefront overdevelopment, but nearby, quiet wildlife refuges and land reserves promise an easy escape. York evokes yesteryear sentiment with its acclaimed historic

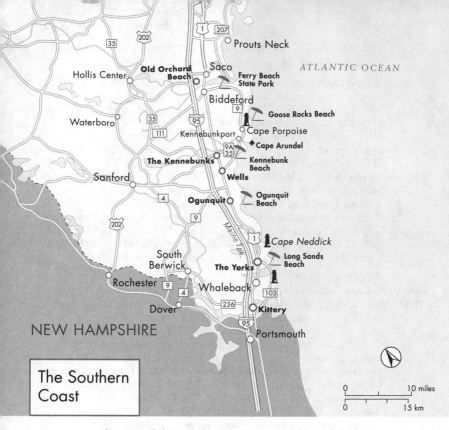

The Southern Coast

district, while upscale Ogunquit tantalizes stylish and sporty visitors with its array of shops and a cliff-side walk.

The Kennebunks—and especially Kennebunkport—provide the complete Maine Coast experience: classic townscapes where white clapboard houses rise from manicured lawns and gardens; rocky shorelines punctuated by sandy beaches; quaint downtown districts packed with gift shops, ice-cream stands, and visitors; harbors with lobster boats bobbing alongside yachts; rustic, picnic-tabled restaurants specializing in lobster and fried seafood (aka lobster pounds in Maine lingo); and well-appointed dining rooms. As you continue north, the scents of french fries, pizza, and cotton candy hover in the air above Maine's version of Coney Island, Old Orchard Beach.

KITTERY

55 mi north of Boston; 5 mi north of Portsmouth, New Hampshire.

One of the earliest settlements in the state of Maine, Kittery suffered its share of British, French, and American Indian attacks throughout the 17th and 18th centuries, yet rose to prominence as a vital shipbuilding center. The tradition continues; despite its New Hampshire name, the Portsmouth Naval Shipyard is part of Maine and has been one of the leading researchers and builders of U.S. submarines since its inception in 1800. The shipyard has the distinction of being the oldest naval shipyard continuously operated by the U.S. government and is a major source of local employment. It's not open to the public.

Kittery has come to more recent light as a major shopping destination thanks to its complex of factory outlets. Flanked on either side of U.S. 1 are more than 120 stores, which attract hordes of shoppers year-round. For something a little less commercial, head east on Route 103 to the hidden Kittery most people miss: the lands around **Kittery Point.** Here you can find hiking and biking trails and, best of all, great views of the water.

SHOPPING

Kittery has more than 120 outlet stores. Along a several-mile stretch of U.S. 1 you can find just about anything, from hardware to underwear. Among the stores are Crate & Barrel, Eddie Bauer, Jones New York, Esprit, Waterford/Wedgwood, Lenox, Ralph Lauren, and J. Crew.

WHERE TO EAT

$$–$$$
SEAFOOD
✕ **Warren's Lobster House.** A local institution, this waterfront restaurant specializes in seafood and has a huge salad bar. The pine-sided dining room leaves the impression that little has changed since Warren's opened in 1940. Dine outside overlooking the water when the weather is nice. ⊠ *U.S. 1 and Water St.* ☎ *207/439–1630* ▭ *AE, MC, V.*

$–$$$
★
SEAFOOD
✕ **Chauncey Creek Lobster Pound.** From the road you can barely see this restaurant's red roof hovering below the trees, but chances are you can see the cars parked at this popular spot amid the high banks of the tidal river. The menu has lots of fresh lobster items and a raw bar with locally harvested offerings like clams and oysters. Bring your own beer or wine if you desire alcohol. In season, it's open daily for lunch and dinner. ⊠ *Chauncey Creek Rd., Kittery Point* ☎ *207/439–1030* ▭ *MC, V* ⊗ *Closed Nov.–Apr.*

THE YORKS

Beginning about 6 mi north of Kittery on Highway 103 or U.S. 1A.

The Yorks—York Village, York Harbor, York Beach, and Cape Neddick—are typical of small-town coastal communities in New England and are smaller than most. Many of their nooks and crannies can be explored in a few hours. The beaches are the big attraction here.

Not unlike siblings in most families, the towns within this region reveal vastly different personalities. York Village and York Harbor, 3 mi farther north, abound with old money, picturesque mansions, impeccably manicured lawns, and gardens and shops that cater to a more staid and wealthy clientele. Continue 6 mi north along U.S. 1A to York Beach and soon all the pretense falls away like autumn leaves in a storm—it's family vacation time (and party time), with scores of T-shirt shops, ice-cream and fried-seafood joints, arcades and bowling, and motor court–style motels. Left from earlier days are a number of trailer and RV parks spread across the road from the beach—in prime real estate that must have developers and moneyed old-timers in pure agony. About 4 mi north of York Beach, Cape Neddick blends back into more peaceful and gentle terrain.

WHAT TO SEE

Mount Agamenticus Park. Maintained by the York Parks and Recreation Department, this humble summit of 692 feet above sea level is said to be the highest peak along the Atlantic seaboard. That may not seem like much, but if you choose to hike to the top, you will be rewarded with incredible views that span all the way to the White Mountains in New Hampshire. If you don't want to hoof it (though it's not very steep), there is parking at the top. The Nature Conservancy has chosen the site as very significant owing to the variety of unusual natural flora and fauna. To get here, take Mountain Road just off U.S. 1 in Cape Neddick (just after Flo's Steamed Hot Dogs) and follow the signs. The area is open daily, with no charge. It's a popular place for equestrians and cyclists as well as families and hikers. *York Parks and Recreation Department, 200 U.S. Rte. 1 S, York 03909* ☎*207/363–1040.*

Nubble Light. Head out a couple of miles on the peninsula to see one of the most photographed lighthouses on the globe. Set out on a hill of rocks, the lighthouse is still in use. Direct access is prohibited, but an informational center shares the 1879 light's history. Find parking at Sohier Park, at the end of Nubble Road, as well as restrooms and plenty of benches. ✉*End of Nubble Rd., York Beach, off U.S. 1A.*

SHOPPING

Home furnishings with an antique feel are the specialty of **Jeremiah Campbell & Company** (✉*1537 U.S. 1, Cape Neddick* ☎*207/363–8499*). Everything here is handcrafted, from rugs, decoys, furniture, and lighting to glassware. The shop is closed Wednesday. Quilt and fabric lovers will delight in a visit to **Knight's Quilt Shop** (✉*1901 U.S. 1, Cape Neddick* ☎*207/361–2500*), where quilts and everything needed to make them—including instructional classes—can be found.

NIGHTLIFE & THE ARTS

Inn on the Blues (✉*7 Ocean Ave., York Beach* ☎*207/351–3221*) is a hopping blues club that attracts national bands.

WHERE TO EAT

¢ ✗**Flo's Steamed Hot Dogs.** Yes, it seems crazy to highlight a hot dog
★ stand, but this is no ordinary place. Who would guess that a hot dog
AMERICAN could make it into *Saveur* and *Gourmet* magazines? But there is something grand about this shabby, red-shingle shack that has been dealing dogs since 1959. The line is out the door most days but the operation is so efficient that the wait is not long at all. Flo has passed but her granddaughter keeps the business going, selling countless thousands of hot dogs each year. Be sure to ask for the special sauce—consisting of, among other things, hot sauce and mayo (you can take a bottle of the sauce home, and you'll want to). ✉*1359 U.S. 1, Cape Neddick* ☎*No phone* ▤*No credit cards* ⊘*Closed Wed.*

$$$ ✗**Foster's Downeast Clambake.** Save your appetite for this one. Special-
SEAFOOD izing in the traditional Maine clambake—a feast consisting of rich clam

1

chowder, a pile of mussels and steamers, Maine lobster, corn on the cob, roasted potatoes and onions, bread, butter, and Maine blueberry crumb cake (phew!)—this massive complex provides entertainment as well as belly-busting meals. You can also opt to have clambake fixings shipped to your home or have a special event catered. ⌂5 *Axholme Rd., York Village* ☎*207/363–3255 or 800/552–0242* ▭*AE, MC, V.*

¢–$ ✗**The Goldenrod.** If you wanted to—and you are on vacation—you
AMERICAN   could eat nothing but the famous taffy here, made just about the same way today as it was back in 1896. The famous Goldenrod Kisses, made to the tune of 65 tons per year, are a great attraction and people line the windows to watch the process. Aside from the famous taffy, this eating place is family oriented, very reasonably priced, and a great place to get ice cream from the old-fashioned soda fountain. Breakfast is served all day while the simple lunch menu doubles as dinner; choose from sandwiches and burgers. There is even penny candy for sale for, yes, a penny apiece. ⌂*Railroad Ave., York Beach* ☎*207/363–2621* ▭*AE, MC, V* ☉*Closed Columbus Day–late May.*

WHERE TO STAY

$$$–$$$$ 🏨**Chapman Cottage.** Set proudly atop a grassy lawn is this impeccably
Fodor'sChoice   restored inn, named for the woman who had it built as her summer
★   cottage in 1899. The luxuriant bedspreads, fresh flowers, antiques, and beautiful rugs only hint at the indulgence found here. Innkeepers Donna and Paul Archibald spoil their guests with sumptuous breakfasts, afternoon hors d'oeuvres, port, sherry, and homemade chocolate truffles, all prepared by Paul, a professionally trained chef. Most rooms have fireplaces and whirlpool tubs; all are spacious, bright, and airy. It's a five-minute walk to either York Village or the harbor, but you may never wish to leave. What used to be an off-season hobby is now a year-round, ambitious little restaurant that serves dinner Wednesday– Sunday ($$–$$$), as well as offers a tasty tapas menu; a great accompaniment to the wine/martini bar. **Pros:** beautifully restored historic lodging, luxury appointments, and attention to detail. **Con:** no water views, most rooms located on upper floors (and no elevator). ⌂*370 York St., York Harbor* ☎*207/363–2059 or 877/363–2059* ⊕*www. chapmancottagebandb.com* ⇥*6 rooms* ⌂*In-room: no phone, Wi-Fi. In-hotel: restaurant, bar, no elevator, no kids under 12, no-smoking rooms* ▭*AE, D, MC, V* ⦿*BP.*

$$–$$$$ 🏨**York Harbor Inn.** A mid-17th-century fishing cabin with dark timbers
★   and a fieldstone fireplace forms the heart of this inn, while several wings and outbuildings have been added over the years, making for quite a complex with a great variety of styles and appointments. The rooms are furnished with antiques and country pieces; many have decks overlooking the water, and some have whirlpool tubs or fireplaces. The nicest rooms are in two adjacent buildings, Harbor Cliffs and Harbor Hill. The dining room ($$$–$$$$; no lunch off-season) has great ocean views. For dinner, start with Maine crab cakes and then try the lobster-stuffed chicken breast, or the scallops Dijon. Ask about various packages and Internet specials. **Pros:** many rooms have harbor views, close to beaches and scenic walking trails, some luxury appointments. **Cons:** rooms vary greatly in style and appeal, many rooms accessed via

stairways (no elevator). ⊠*Rte. 1A, York Harbor 03911* ☎*207/363–5119 or 800/343–3869* ⊕*www.yorkharborinn.com* ⮩*54 rooms, 2 suites* ♿*In-room: Wi-Fi. In-hotel: restaurants, bar, no elevator, executive floor, no-smoking rooms* ☰*AE, DC, MC, V* ⧇*CP.*

OGUNQUIT

10 mi north of the Yorks via Rte. 1A and 1 or Shore Rd.

A resort-village in the 1880s, stylish Ogunquit gained fame as an artists' colony. Today it has become a mini Provincetown, with a gay population that swells in summer. Many inns and small clubs cater to a primarily gay and lesbian clientele. For a scenic drive, take Shore Road through downtown toward the 100-foot Bald Head Cliff; you'll be treated to views up and down the coast. On a stormy day the surf can be quite wild here.

The **Ogunquit Trolley** is one of the best things that happened to this area. Parking in the village is troublesome and expensive, beach parking is costly and often limited, and so it's often just easier to leave your car parked at the hotel. The trolley begins operation in May and stays in service until Columbus Day. The fare is $1.50 (at each boarding) and kids under 10 ride free with an adult. Stops are numerous along the route that begins at Perkins Cove and follows Shore Road through town, down to Ogunquit Beach, and out along U.S. 1 up to Wells (where a connecting Wells trolley takes over for northern travel). Maps are available wherever you find brochures and at the chamber of commerce Welcome Center on U.S. 1, just as you enter Ogunquit from the south. ⌂*Box 2368, Ogunquit 03907* ☎*207/646–1411.*

WHAT TO SEE

★ **Perkins Cove.** A neck of land connected to the mainland by Oarweed Road and a pedestrian drawbridge, Perkins Cove has a jumble of sea-beaten fish houses. These have largely been transformed by the tide of tourism to shops and restaurants. When you've had your fill of browsing and jostling the crowds, stroll out along the **Marginal Way,** a mile-long footpath between Ogunquit and Perkins Cove that hugs the shore of a rocky promontory known as Israel's Head. Benches along the route give walkers an opportunity to stop and appreciate the open sea vistas, flowering bushes, and million-dollar homes.

NIGHTLIFE & THE ARTS

Much of the nightlife in Ogunquit revolves around the precincts of Ogunquit Square and Perkins Cove, where people stroll, often enjoying an after-dinner ice-cream cone or espresso. Ogunquit is popular with gay and lesbian visitors, and its club scene reflects this.

One of America's oldest summer theaters, the **Ogunquit Playhouse** (⊠*U.S. 1* ☎*207/646–5511* ⊕*www.ogunquitplayhouse.org*) mounts plays and musicals with well-known actors of stage and screen from late June to Labor Day.

1

WHERE TO EAT & STAY

¢–$

★

AMERICAN

✕**Amore Breakfast.** One could hardly find a more-satisfying, full-bodied breakfast than at this smart and busy joint between Ogunquit and Perkins Cove. Amid a lighthearted mix of enamel-topped tables and retro advertising design touches, breakfast is a sophisticated affair. You won't find tired standards here—the only pancakes are German potato—rather, you'll have a hard time choosing among the options. The Oscar Madison omelet combines crabmeat with asparagus and Swiss, topped with a dill hollandaise. For a real decadent start, opt for the Banana Foster: pecan-coated, cream cheese–stuffed French toast with a side of sautéed bananas in rum syrup. The offers of a half-, three-quarter-, or full order give an indication of this item's richness. If you're especially lucky, you'll catch the sometimes special of corned beef hash—this version is made from hearty pieces of the briny beef rather than the often-seen, through-the-blender kind of hash. To ease the wait for a morning table, a self-serve coffee bar is available. ✉*178 Shore Rd.* ☎*207/646–6661* ▤*D, MC, V* ☉*Closed Christmas–Mar., and Wed. and Thurs. in spring and fall. No lunch.*

$$$$

Fodor's Choice

★

ECLECTIC

✕**Arrows.** Elegant simplicity is the hallmark of this restaurant in an 18th-century farmhouse, 2 mi up a back road. Grilled salmon and radicchio with marinated fennel and baked polenta, and Chinese-style duck glazed with molasses are typical entrées on the daily-changing menu—much of what appears is dependent on what is ready for harvest in the restaurant's abundant 1-acre garden. The Maine crabmeat mousse and lobster risotto appetizers, and desserts such as strawberry shortcake with Chantilly cream, are also beautifully executed. The accolades are continual: *Gourmet* magazine rated this small-town restaurant 14th of the 50 best restaurants in the country. ✉*41 Berwick Rd.* ☎*207/361–1100* ♨*Reservations essential* ▤*MC, V* ☉*Closed Mon. and mid-Dec.–mid-Apr. No lunch.*

$$$–$$$$

Fodor's Choice

★

🏠**Black Boar Inn.** The original part of this inn dates to 1674, an era that is reflected in the beauty of the wide-pine floors and the fireplaces in every room. A sense of absolute luxury pervades here. The interior is exquisite, with bead board, richly colored rugs and comforters, William Morris–like wallpaper, tiled bathrooms, and many antiques. Although the manager wasn't sure where the "wild boar" name originated, evidence of the beast abounds in art and sculpture throughout. Wine and hors d'ouevres are served on weekend afternoons and can be enjoyed on the front terrace, overlooking the massive gardens and the world of Main Street beyond. Cottages are rented by the week and are notable for their exposed wood, vaulted ceilings, and full kitchens. **Pros:** gracious, historic lodging; most rooms have fireplaces; quiet retreat in the center of town. **Cons:** most rooms accessed via steep stairs; due to home's age, rooms are on the smaller (though uncrowded) side. ✉*277 Main St.* ☎*207/646–2112* ⊕*www.blackboarinn.com* ➷*6 rooms, 3 cottages* ⚘*In-room: no phone, Wi-Fi. In-hotel: no elevator, no-smoking rooms* ▤*MC, V* ☉*Closed Nov.–late May* ⏚*BP.*

WELLS

5 mi north of Ogunquit on U.S. 1.

Lacking any kind of noticeable village center, Wells could be easily overlooked as nothing more than a commercial stretch on U.S. 1 between Ogunquit and the Kennebunks. But look more closely—this is a place where people come to enjoy some of the best beaches on the coast. Part of Ogunquit until 1980, this family-oriented beach community has 7 mi of densely populated shoreline, along with nature preserves where you can explore salt marshes and tidal pools, and see birds and waterfowl.

Leave your car at your hotel and take the **Wells Trolley** to the beach or to the shops on U.S. 1. The seasonal trolley makes pickups at the Wells Transportation Center when the *Downeaster* (the Amtrak train with service from Boston to Portland) pulls in. If you want to continue south toward Ogunquit, the two town trolleys meet at the Wells Chamber of Commerce on U.S. 1; get a route map here. Fare is $2. ☎207/646–2451 ⊕*www.wellschamber.org*.

NEED A BREAK?

How would you like a doughnut...a really superior one that the same family has been making since 1955? The doughnuts from **Congdon's** (✉*U.S. 1* ☎*207/646–4219*) easily rival (many say there is no contest) some of those other famous places we won't mention here. Choose from about 30 different varieties, though the plain really gives you an idea of just how good these doughnuts are. There's a drive-through window so you don't have to get out of the car; or you can take a seat inside and have breakfast or lunch.

SPORTS & THE OUTDOORS

Rachel Carson National Wildlife Refuge. Spot migrating birds and waterfowl of many varieties in a white-pine forest that borders the mile-long loop nature trail through a salt marsh and along the Little River. ✉*Hwy. 9* ☎*207/646–9226*

BEACHES With its thousands of acres of marsh and preserved land, Wells is a great place to spend a lot of time outdoors. Nearly 7 mi of sand stretch along the boundaries of Wells, making beach going a prime occupation. Tidal pools sheltered by rocks are filled with all manner of creatures awaiting discovery. Parking is available for a fee (take the trolley!) at **Crescent Beach,** along Webhannet Drive; **Wells Beach** (at the end of Mile Road off U.S. 1) has public restrooms and two parking areas. There is another lot at the far end of Wells Beach, at the end of Atlantic Avenue. Across the jetty from Wells Harbor is **Drakes Island Beach** (end of Drakes Island Road off U.S. 1), which also has parking and public restrooms. Lifeguards are on hand at all the beaches.

WHERE TO EAT & STAY

$-$$
SEAFOOD

✗**Billy's Chowder House.** Locals head to this simple restaurant in a salt marsh for the generous lobster rolls, haddock sandwiches, and chowders. Big windows in the bright dining rooms overlook the marsh. ✉*216 Mile Rd.* ☎*207/646–7558* ▭*AE, D, MC, V* ⊙*Closed mid-Dec.–mid-Jan.*

$–$$
AMERICAN
✕**Maine Diner.** It's the real thing here—one look at the nostalgic (and authentic 1953) exterior and you start craving good diner food. You'll get a little more here…how many greasy spoons make an award-winning lobster pie? That's the house favorite, as well as a heavenly seafood chowder. There's plenty of fried seafood in addition to the usual diner fare, and breakfast is served all day, just as it should be. Be sure to check out the adjacent gift shop, Remember the Maine. ⊠*2265 U.S. 1* ☎*207/646–4441* ▤*D, MC, V* ⊘*Closed 1 wk in Jan.*

$$–$$$$
Fodor'sChoice
★
🖼 **Haven by the Sea.** Once the summer mission of St. Martha's Church in Kennebunkport, this stunning, exquisite inn has retained many of the original details from its former life as a seaside church. The cathedral ceilings and stained-glass windows remain, all gathering and spreading the grand surrounding light. The guest rooms are spacious, some with serene marsh views. Four common areas, including one with a fireplace, are perfect spots for afternoon refreshments. The inn is one block from the beach. **Pros:** unusual structure with elegant appointments, nightly happy hour, walk to beach. **Cons:** some rooms upstairs, not an in-town location. ⊠*59 Church St.* ☎*207/646–4194* ⊕*www. havenbythesea.com* ➳*6 rooms, 2 suites, 1 apartment* ⚬*In-room: Wi-Fi. In-hotel: no elevator, no kids under 12, no-smoking rooms* ▤*AE, MC, V* ⏀*BP.*

THE KENNEBUNKS

6 mi north of Wells via U.S. 1; 23 mi south of Portland via Maine Tpke.

The Kennebunks encompass Kennebunk, Kennebunk Beach, Goose Rocks Beach, Kennebunkport, Cape Porpoise, and Arundel. This cluster of seaside and inland villages provides a little bit of everything—salt marshes, sand beaches, jumbled fishing shacks, and architectural gems.

Handsome white clapboard homes with shutters give Kennebunk, an early-19th-century shipbuilding center, a quintessential New England look. The many boutiques and galleries surrounding Dock Square draw visitors to Kennebunkport. People flock to Kennebunkport mostly in summer, but some come in early December when the Christmas Prelude is celebrated on two weekends. Santa arrives by fishing boat, and the Christmas trees are lighted as carolers stroll the sidewalks.

In Kennebunkport, get a good overview of the sights with an **Intown Trolley** tour. The narrated 45-minute jaunts leave every hour starting at 10 AM at the designated stop on Ocean Avenue, around the corner of Dock Square. The fare is valid for the day so you can hop on and off at your leisure. ⊠*Ocean Ave., Kennebunkport* ☎*207/967–3686* ⊕*www.intowntrolley.com* ✉*$13 all-day fare* ⊘*Late May–mid-Oct., daily 10–5.*

WHAT TO SEE

★
☾
Seashore Trolley Museum. This museum displays streetcars built from 1872 to 1972 and includes trolleys from major metropolitan areas and world capitals—Boston to Budapest, New York to Nagasaki, San

Francisco to Sydney—all beautifully restored. Best of all, you can take a trolley ride for nearly 4 mi over the tracks of the former Atlantic Shoreline trolley line, with a stop along the way at the museum restoration shop, where trolleys are transformed from junk into gems. Both guided and self-guided tours are available. ✉*195 Log Cabin Rd., Kennebunkport* ☎*207/967–2800* ⊕*www.trolleymuseum.org* 🎟*$8.50* ⊙*Early May–mid-Oct., daily 10–4:30; reduced hrs in spring and fall, call ahead.*

SPORTS & THE OUTDOORS

Kennebunk Beach has three parts: Gooch's Beach, Mother's Beach, and Kennebunk Beach. Beach Road, with its cottages and old Victorian boardinghouses, runs right behind them. Gooch's and Kennebunk attract teenagers; Mother's Beach, which has a small playground and tidal puddles for splashing, is popular with families.

BOATING & FISHING
Find and catch fish with **Cast Away Fishing Charters** (✉*Box 245, Kennebunkport 04046* ☎*207/284–1740* ⊕*www.castawayfishingcharters. com*). **First Chance** (✉*4-A Western Ave., Kennebunk* ☎*207/967–5507 or 800/767–2628*) leads whale-watching cruises and guarantees sightings in season. Daily scenic lobster cruises are also offered aboard *Kylie's Chance.* For half- or full-day fishing trips as well as discovery trips for kids, book some time with **Lady J Sportfishing Charters** (✉*Arundel Wharf, Ocean Ave.* ☎*207/985–7304* ⊕*www.ladyjcharters.com*).

SHOPPING

The **Gallery on Chase Hill** (✉*10 Chase Hill Rd., Kennebunk* ☎*207/967– 0049*) presents original artwork by Maine and New England artists. **Mast Cove Galleries** (✉*Mast Cove La., Kennebunkport* ☎*207/967– 3453*) sells graphics, paintings, and sculpture by 105 artists. **Tom's of Maine Natural Living Store** (✉*52 Main St., Kennebunk* ☎*207/985–6331*) sells all-natural personal-care products.

WHERE TO EAT

$$–$$$$
ITALIAN
✗**Grissini.** This popular trattoria draws high praise for its northern Italian cuisine. Dine by the stone hearth on inclement days or on the patio when the weather's fine. You can mix and match appetizers, pizzas, salads, pastas, and entrées from the menu to suit your hunger and budget. ✉*27 Western Ave., Kennebunk* ☎*207/967–2211* ▭*AE, MC, V.*

$$$$
★
AMERICAN
✗**White Barn Inn.** Formally attired waiters, meticulous service, and exquisite food have earned this restaurant accolades as one of the best in New England. Regional New England fare is served in a rustic but elegant dining room. The three-course, prix-fixe menu ($90), which changes weekly, might include steamed Maine lobster nestled on fresh fettuccine with carrots, ginger, and snow peas. ✉*37 Beach Ave., Kennebunk* ☎*207/967–2321* ⟡*Reservations essential Jacket required* ▭*AE, MC, V* ⊙*Closed 3 wks in Jan. No lunch.*

WHERE TO STAY

$$$$
Fodor'sChoice
★
🛏**Captain Lord Mansion.** Of all the mansions in Kennebunkport's historic district that have been converted to inns, the 1812 Captain Lord Mansion is the most stately and sumptuously appointed. Distinctive architecture, including a suspended elliptical staircase, gas fireplaces in

all rooms, and near-museum-quality accoutrements, make for a formal but not stuffy setting. Six rooms have whirlpool tubs. The extravagant suite has two fireplaces, a double whirlpool, a hydro-massage body spa, a TV/DVD and stereo system, and a king-size canopy bed. Day-spa services are available for added luxury. **Pros:** elegant and luxurious historic lodging, in-town location, beautiful landscaped grounds and gardens. **Cons:** not for those on a tight budget, not a beachfront location. ⊠ *Pleasant and Green Sts., Box 800, Kennebunkport 04046* ☎ *207/967–3141* ⊕ *www.captainlord.com* ⊃ *15 rooms, 1 suite* ₺ *In-room: no TV, Wi-Fi. In-hotel: bicycles, no elevator, public Internet, no kids under 12, no-smoking rooms* ▤ *D, MC, V* ⦿ *BP.*

$$$–$$$$
Fodor'sChoice
★
⊡ **The Colony.** You can't miss this place—it's grand, white, and incredibly large, set majestically atop a rise overlooking the ocean. The hotel was built in 1914 (after its predecessor caught fire in 1898), and much of the splendid glamour of this earlier era remains. Many of the rooms in the main hotel (there are two other outbuildings) have breezy ocean views from private or semiprivate balconies. All are outfitted with antiques and hardwood floors; the bright white bed linens nicely offset the colors of the Waverly wallpaper. The restaurant ($$–$$$$) features New England fare, with plenty of seafood, steaks, and other favorites. **Pros:** lodging in the tradition of grand old hotels, many ocean views, plenty of activities and entertainment for all ages. **Cons:** not for those looking for more intimate or peaceful lodging, rooms with ocean views come at steep prices. ⊠ *Ocean Ave.* ☎ *207/967–3331 or 800/552–2363* ⊕ *www.thecolonyhotel.com/maine* ⊃ *124 rooms* ₺ *In-room: no a/c (some), no TV (some), Wi-Fi. In-hotel: restaurant, room service, bar, pool, beachfront, bicycles, no-smoking rooms, some pets allowed* ▤ *AE, MC, V* ⊗ *Closed Nov.–mid-May* ⦿ *BP.*

$$$$
☺
⊡ **The Seaside.** This handsome seaside property has been in the hands of the Severance family since 1667. The modern hotel units, all with sliding-glass doors that open onto private decks or patios (half with ocean views), are appropriate for families; so are the cottages with one to four bedrooms. You can't get much closer to Kennebunk Beach. **Pros:** ideal beachfront location, lawn games available, great ocean views from upper-floor rooms. **Cons:** rooms are hotel standard and a little outdated (but fairly sized), not an in-town location. ⊠ *80 Beach Ave., Kennebunk* ☎ *207/967–4461 or 866/300–6750* ⊕ *www.kennebunkbeachmaine.com* ⊃ *22 rooms, 11 cottages* ₺ *In-room: refrigerator, Wi-Fi. In-hotel: beachfront, no elevator, laundry service, public Internet, no-smoking rooms* ▤ *AE, MC, V* ⊗ *Cottages closed Nov.–May* ⦿ *CP.*

$$$$
★
⊡ **White Barn Inn.** For a romantic overnight stay, you need look no further than the exclusive White Barn Inn, known for its attentive, pampering service. No detail has been overlooked in the meticulously appointed rooms, from plush bedding and reading lamps to robes and slippers. Rooms are in the main inn and adjacent buildings. Some have fireplaces, hot tubs, and luxurious baths with steam showers. The inn is within walking distance (10–15 minutes) of Dock Square and the beach. **Pros:** elegant, luxurious lodging; full-service; in a historic building. **Cons:** no water views or beachfront, overly steep lodging prices,

CLOSE UP

All About Lobsters

Judging from the current price of a lobster dinner, it's hard to believe that lobsters were once so plentiful that servants in rich households would have contracts stating they could be served lobster "no more than two times a week."

The going price for lobsters in the 1840s was three cents per lobster—not per pound, per lobster. Today, Maine is nearly synonymous with lobsters, the fishery being one of Maine's primary industries. Well over 60 million pounds of lobster are landed a year in the state, making Maine, by far, the biggest supplier in the nation.

Because of the size restrictions, most of the lobsters you find in restaurants weigh 1¼ to 1½ pounds. However, lobsters can actually grow much larger and live to a ripe old age. The largest lobster ever caught off the coast of Maine weighed in at nearly 45 pounds and was more than 50 years old!

For an authentic, Maine-style lobster dinner, you must go to a lobster pound, and they're not hard to find. Generally, these places are rustic and simple—they look more like fish-packing plants than restaurants. Hundreds of freshly caught lobsters of varying sizes are kept in pens, waiting for customers. Service is simple in the extreme. You usually sit at a wooden picnic table, and eat off a thick paper plate. A classic "Downeast" feast includes lobster—boiled or steamed—with clam chowder, steamers, potato, and corn on the cob—and, of course, a large bib tied around your neck.

—Stephen Allen

not in town. ✉ *37 Beach Ave., Kennebunk* ☎ *207/967–2321* ⊕ *www. whitebarninn.com* ⚲ *16 rooms, 9 suites* △ *In-room: VCR, DVD, Wi-Fi. In-hotel: restaurant, bar, pool, spa, bicycles, no elevator, concierge, laundry service, public Internet, no kids under 12, no-smoking rooms* ▤ *AE, MC, V* ⦿ *CP.*

OLD ORCHARD BEACH AREA

15 mi north of Kennebunkport, 18 mi south of Portland.

Back in the late 19th century, Old Orchard Beach was a classic, upscale, place-to-be-seen resort area. The railroad brought wealthy families who were looking for entertainment and the benefits of the fresh sea air. Although a good bit of this aristocratic hue has dulled in more-modern times—admittedly, the place is more than a little pleasantly tacky these days—Old Orchard Beach remains a good place for those looking for entertainment and thrills by the sea.

The center of the action is a 7-mi strip of sand beach and its accompanying amusement park, which resembles a small Coney Island. Despite the summertime crowds and fried-food odors, the atmosphere can be captivating. During the 1940s and '50s, in the heyday of the Big Band era, the pier had a dance hall where stars of the time performed. Fire claimed the end of the pier—at one time it jutted out nearly 1,800 feet into the sea—but booths with games and candy concessions still line both sides. In summer the town sponsors fireworks (on Thursday night). Places to stay run the gamut from cheap motels to cottage colonies to full-service seasonal hotels. You won't find free parking in town, but there are ample lots. Amtrak has a seasonal stop here.

WHAT TO SEE

Ocean Park. A world away from the beach scene, Ocean Park lies on the southwestern edge of town. Locals and visitors like to keep the separation distinct, touting their area as a more peaceful and wholesome family-style village. This vacation community was founded in 1881 by Free Will Baptist leaders as an interdenominational retreat with both religious and educational purposes, following the example of Chautauqua, New York. Today the community still hosts an impressive variety of cultural happenings, including movies, concerts, recreation, workshops, and religious services. Most are presented in the Temple, which is on the National Register of Historic Places. Although the religious nature of the place is apparent in its worship schedule and some of its cultural offerings, visitors need not be a member of any denomination; all are welcome. There's even a public shuffleboard area for those not interested in the neon carnival attractions several miles up the road. Get an old-fashioned raspberry-lime rickey at the Ocean Park Soda Fountain (near the library, at Furber Park); it's also a good place for breakfast or a light lunch. ⊠ *Southwestern edge of town* ☎ *207/934–9068 Ocean Park Association* ⊕ *www.oceanpark.org. .*

SPORTS & THE OUTDOORS

Not far from Old Orchard Beach is the Maine Audubon–run **Scarborough Marsh Nature Center,** where you can rent a canoe and explore on your own, or sign up with a guided trip. The salt marsh is Maine's largest and is an excellent place for bird-watching and peaceful paddling amid its winding ways. The Nature Center has a discovery room for kids, programs for all ages ranging from basket making to astronomy, birding and canoe tours, and a good gift shop. ⊠ *Pine Point Rd. (Rte. 9), Scarborough* ☎ *207/883–5100* ⊕ *www.maineaudubon.org* ✉ Free, guided tours begin at $5 ⊙ *Memorial Day–Sept. daily, 9:30–4*

WHERE TO EAT

$-$$ ✗ **DennyMike's.** In Old Orchard Beach, you can't help but notice the
AMERICAN heavenly smells of briskets and ribs wafting down the street from this bold and authentic barbecue joint. If you've had your fill of lobster and fried seafood, bring your appetite here. Owner DennyMike is no Texan, but that's where he learned the secret of his craft. Portions are very generous; dinner feasts come with a choice of two sides—absolutely get the beans. There's also a good selection of giant burgers, specialty barbecue sandwiches, and hand-cut fries that rival any sold on the pier. It just might be the best barbecue in New England. Takeout and delivery are available. ⊠ *27 W. Grand Ave., Old Orchard Beach* ☎ *207/934–2207* ▤ *MC, V* ⊙ *Closed mid-Oct.–mid-May.*

$$-$$$ ✗ **The Landmark.** This restaurant almost feels as if it doesn't belong
★ here, at least not in this modern transformation of Old Orchard Beach.
ECLECTIC Tables are set either on the glassed-in porch or within high, tin-ceiling rooms. Candles and a collection of giant fringed art-nouveau lamps

provide a warm, gentle light. The menu has a good selection of seafood and meats, many treated with either Asian or Mediterranean flavors; the mahimahi might be seared and served with a coconut cream sauce. It's the kind of menu that encourages you to try new things and you definitely won't be disappointed. The tiramisu is divine. Reservations are recommended. ⊠ *25 E. Grand Ave., Old Orchard Beach* ☎ *207/934–0156* ⊟ *AE, D, MC, V* ⊘ *Closed early Jan.–late Mar.*

PORTLAND & ENVIRONS

By John
Blodgett

Maine's largest city is considered small by national standards—its population is just 64,000—but its character, spirit, and appeal make it feel much larger. In fact, it is a cultural and economic center for a metro area of 230,000 residents—one-quarter of Maine's entire population. Portland and its environs are well worth a day or two of exploration.

North of Portland, Freeport was made famous by its L.L. Bean store, whose success led to the opening of scores of other outlets. Meanwhile, the Boothbays attract hordes of vacationing families and flotillas of pleasure craft.

PORTLAND

Several distinct neighborhoods reveal the many faces of a city that embraces its history as well as its art, music, and multicultural scenes.

The most visited section, the restored **Old Port** features a real working waterfront where emblematic lobster boats share ports with modern cruise ships, ferries, and vintage sailing yachts, and renovated redbrick warehouses. Nightlife thrives here, with numerous clubs, taverns, and bars pouring out the sounds of live music and lively patrons. Exceptional restaurants, shops, and galleries, many featuring locally produced goods, abound here as well.

Downtown Portland has emerged from a years-long on-again, off-again funk, during which much retail commerce was lost to shopping malls in the outlying suburbs. Its burgeoning Arts District—which starts at the top of Exchange Street (near the upper end of the Old Port) and extends up past the Portland Museum of Art. Much of Portland's economic heart is here, including several large banking firms. The district's central artery, revitalized Congress Street, is peppered with shops, restaurants, numerous performing arts venues, and excellent museums.

Just beyond the Arts District is the **Western Promenade**, an area of extensive architectural wealth. Predominantly residential, the neighborhood is filled with stunning examples of both the city's historical and economic prominence and its emphasis on preserving this past. A handful of historic homes are open to tours.

Portland is wonderfully walkable; an able-bodied explorer can easily take in the Old Port, the Downtown/Arts District, and the Western Promenade. In fact, in much of the city it's best to park your car and explore on foot. You can park at the city garage on Fore Street (between Exchange and Union streets) or opposite the U.S. Customs House at the corner of Fore and Pearl streets. A helpful hint: Look for the PARK & SHOP sign on garages and parking lots and get one hour of free parking for each stamp collected at participating shops.

Greater Portland's Metro runs seven bus routes in Portland, South Portland, and Westbrook. The fare is $1.25; exact change is required. Buses run from 5:30 AM to 11:45 PM. The **Portland Explorer** (☎207/774–9891 or 207/774–0351 ⊕www.transportme.org) has express shuttle service to the Old Port from the Portland Jetport, the **Portland Transportation Center** (☎207/828–1151), and other downtown locations. The shuttle runs hourly, seven days a week, from noon to 7 PM. Fare is $2. For service around Portland, there's the Metro and shuttle bus service.

If you want a taxi, your best bet is to call ahead (try **ABC Taxi,** ☎207/772–8685; **Elite Cab,** ☎207/871–7667; or **South Portland Taxi,** ☎207/767–5200). However, the small size is an advantage in getting around, for many destinations in downtown are in close proximity. There is even a water taxi (**Portland Express Water Taxi,** ☎207/415–8493) to get to and from the islands of Casco Bay. Meter rates are $1.40 for the first 1/9 mi, 25¢ for each additional 1/9 mi throughout Portland.

Numbers in the margin correspond to numbers on the Portland map.

WHAT TO SEE

② **Children's Museum of Maine.** Touching is okay at Portland's relatively small but fun Children's Museum, where kids can pretend they are lobster fishermen, shopkeepers, or computer experts. The majority of the museum's exhibits, many of which have a Maine theme, are best for children 10 and younger. Camera Obscura, an exhibit about optics, provides fascinating panoramic views of the city. The museum's newest addition, L. L. Bear's Discovery Woods, takes imagination to the great outdoors, with explorations below the sea, up a tree, on top of Maine's tallest mountain, and within a flowing stream. ⊠142 Free St. ☎207/828–1234 ⊕www.childrensmuseumofme.org ☑Museum (including Camera Obscura) $6, Camera Obscura (without museum) $3 ☉Memorial Day–Labor Day, Mon.–Sat. 10–5, Sun. noon–5; day after Labor Day–day before Memorial Day, Tues.–Sat. 10–5, Sun. noon–5.

① **The Old Port.** A major international port and a working harbor since the early 17th century, the Old Port bridges the gap between the city's historical commercial activities and those of today. It is home to fishing boats docked alongside whale-watching charters, luxury yachts, cruise ships, and oil tankers from throughout the globe. Busy Commercial Street parallels the water and is lined with brick buildings and warehouses that were built following the Great Fire of 1866, and were intended to last for ages. In the 19th century, candle makers and sail stitchers plied their trades here; today, specialty shops, art galleries, and restaurants have taken up residence. While in Old Port, visit the **Harbor Fish Market** (⊠9 Custom House Wharf ☎207/775–0251 or 800/370–1790 ⊕www.harborfish.com). A Portland favorite for more than 30 years, this freshest of the fresh seafood markets now ships lobsters and other Maine seafood delectables anywhere in the country from its waterfront location on a working wharf. A bright-red facade opens into a bustling space with bubbling lobster pens, clams, and other shellfish on ice, and employees as skilled with a fillet knife as a sushi chef. For a lively and sensory-filled (you may want to hold your nose) glimpse into the Old Port's active fish business, take a free tour of the **Portland Fish Exchange** (⊠*6 Portland Fish Pier, Old Port* ☎*207/773–0017* ⊕*www.pfex.org*). Watch as the fishing boats unload their daily haul, the catch gets weighed in, and prices are settled through an auction process. It's a great behind-the-scenes view of this dynamic market. Auctions take place Sunday at 11 AM and Monday through Thursday at noon.

❸ ★ **Portland Museum of Art.** Maine's largest public art institution has a number of strong collections, including fine seascapes and landscapes by Winslow Homer, John Marin, Andrew Wyeth, Edward Hopper, Marsden Hartley, and other painters. Homer's *Pulling the Dory* and *Weatherbeaten*, two quintessential Maine Coast images, are here; the museum owns and displays more than 20 other works by Homer. The Joan Whitney Payson Collection of impressionist and postimpressionist art includes works by Monet, Picasso, and Renoir. Harry N. Cobb, an associate of I. M. Pei, designed the strikingly modern Charles Shipman Payson building. The nearby and entirely renovated McLellan House contains additional galleries housing the museum's 19th-century collection and decorative art as well as interactive educational stations. ⊠*7 Congress Sq.* ☎*207/775–6148* ⊕*www.portlandmuseum.org* ⊞*$10, free Fri. 5–9* ☉*Memorial Day–Columbus Day, Mon.–Thurs. and weekends 10–5, Fri. 10–9; day after Columbus Day–day before Memorial Day, Tues.–Thurs. and weekends 10–5, Fri. 10–9.*

❹ ★ **Victoria Mansion.** This Italianate-style mansion was built between 1858 and 1860 and is widely regarded as the most sumptuously ornamented dwelling of its period remaining in the country. Architect Henry Austin designed the house for hotelier Ruggles Morse and his wife, Olive. The interior design—everything from the plasterwork to the furniture (much of it original)—is the only surviving commission of New York designer Gustave Herter. Inside the elegant brownstone exterior of this National Historic Landmark are colorful frescoed walls and ceilings, ornate marble mantelpieces, gilded gas chandeliers, a magnificent 6-foot by 25-foot stained-glass ceiling window, and a freestanding mahogany staircase; guided tours, running about 45 minutes, cover all the details. The mansion reopens during the Christmas season, richly ornamented and decorated to reveal the opulence and elegance of the Victorian era. ⊠*109 Danforth St.* ☎*207/772–4841* ⊕*www.victoria mansion.org* ⊞*$10* ☉*May–Oct., Mon.–Sat. 10–4, Sun. 1–5; Christmas tours Nov. 24–Dec. 31.*

❺ **Wadsworth Longfellow House.** The boyhood home of the poet—which was the first brick house in Portland—is particularly interesting because most of the furnishings are original to the house. The late-Colonial-style structure, built in 1785, sits back from the street and has a small

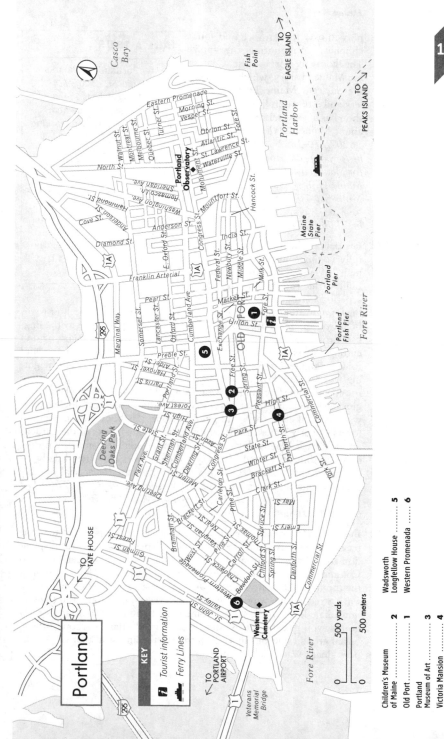

portico over its entrance and four chimneys surmounting the roof. The house is part of the Center for Maine History, which includes the adjacent Maine History Gallery and a research library; the gift shop has a good selection of books about Maine. ⊠ *489 Congress St.* ☎ *207/774–1822* ⊕ *www.maine-history.org* ☜ *House $7, Center for Maine History $4* ⊙ *House and Maine History Gallery May–Oct., Mon.–Sat. 10–5, Sun. noon–5 (last tour at 4); Nov. and Dec., call for hrs. Library Tues.–Sat. 10–3.*

OFF THE BEATEN PATH

Tate House. This magnificent house fully conjures up the style—even high style—of Colonial Maine. Built astride rose granite steps and a period herb garden overlooking the Stroudwater River on the outskirts of Portland, the 1755 house was built by Captain George Tate. Tate had been commissioned by the English Crown to organize "the King's Broad Arrow"—the marking and cutting down of gigantic forest trees, which were transported overland to water and sent to England to be fashioned as masts for English fighting frigates. The house has several period rooms, including a sitting room with some fine English Restoration chairs. With its clapboard still gloriously unpainted, its impressive Palladian doorway, dogleg stairway, unusual clerestory, and gambrel roof, this house will delight all lovers of Early American decorative arts. Guided tours of the gardens are held each Wednesday from mid-June to mid-September, with tea and refreshments served afterward. House tours are offered daily in-season except Monday. Call or visit the Web site for special holiday programs during December. ⊠ *1270 Westbrook St.* ☎ *207/774–6177* ⊕ *www.tatehouse.org* ☜ *$5* ⊙ *Mid-June–Mid-Oct., Tues.–Sat. 10–4, Sun. 1–4 (1st Sun. each month only).*

❻ The Western Promenade. On the National Register of Historic Places, the neighborhood reveals an extraordinary display of architectural splendor, from High Victorian Gothic to lush Italianate, Queen Anne to Colonial Revival. A leisurely walk through the area should begin at the top of the Downtown/Arts District. From the Old Port, take Danforth Street all the way up to Vaughn Street; take a right and then an immediate left onto Western Promenade. In addition to seeing stately homes, you pass by the Western Cemetery, Portland's second official burial ground laid out in 1829 (inside is the ancestral plot of famous poet Henry Wadsworth Longfellow).

TAKE A TOUR

Greater Portland Landmarks (⊠ *165 State St.* ☎ *207/774–5561* ☜ *$7*) conducts 1½-hour walking tours of the city from July through September. **Working Waterfront** (☎ *207/415-0765* ⊠ *Meet at Union Wharf Market on Commercial St.* ☜ *$10*) walking tours are led by local Angela Clark, who shares a good deal of uncommon history about the docks and alleys of the Old Port. The hour-long tours run weekdays at 11 AM and 2 PM; Saturday at 9 AM and 11 AM. The cost is $10 per person.

NIGHTLIFE & THE ARTS

NIGHTLIFE Portland has a nicely varied nightlife, with a great emphasis on local, live music and pubs serving award-winning local microbrews. Big, raucous dance clubs are few, but darkened taverns and lively bars (smoke-free by law) pulse with the sounds of rock, blues, alternative, and folk tunes. Several hip wine bars have cropped up, serving appetizers along with a full array of specialty wines and whimsical cocktails. It's a fairly youthful scene in Portland, in some spots even rowdy and rough-around-the-edges, but there are plenty of places where you don't have to shout over the din to be heard.

Brian Boru (⊠ *57 Center St.* ☎ *207/780–1506*) is an Irish pub with occasional entertainment, ranging from Celtic to reggae, and an outside deck. For nightly themed brew specials, plenty of Guinness, and live entertainment, head to **Bull Feeney's** (⊠ *375 Fore St.* ☎ *207/773–7210*), a lively two-story Irish pub and restaurant. **Gritty McDuff's** (⊠ *396 Fore St.* ☎ *207/772–2739*) brews fine ales and serves British pub fare and seafood dishes.

THE ARTS Art galleries and studios have spread throughout the city; many are concentrated along the Congress Street downtown corridor; others are hidden amid the boutiques and restaurants of the Old Port and the East End. A great way to get acquainted with the city's artists is to participate in the **First Friday Art Walk** (⊕ *www.firstfridayartwalk.com*), a self-guided, free tour of galleries, museums, and alternative art venues happening, you guessed it, on the first Friday of each month, from May to December. **Portland Stage Company** (⊠ *25-A Forest Ave.* ☎ *207/774–0465*) mounts productions year-round on its two stages.

SPORTS & THE OUTDOORS

Portland has quite a bit of green space in its several parks; in the heat of summer these places make for cool retreats with refreshing fountains and plenty of shade. Local sports teams are the Portland Sea Dogs (baseball) and the Portland Pirates (hockey).

BOAT TRIPS **Casco Bay Lines** (⊠ *Maine State Pier, 56 Commercial St.* ☎ *207/774–7871* ⊕ *www.cascobaylines.com*) provides narrated cruises and transportation to Casco Bay Islands.

SHOPPING

Trendy Exchange Street is great for arts and crafts browsing, while Commercial Street caters to the souvenir hound—gift shops are eager to sell Maine moose, nautical items, and lobster emblems emblazoned on everything from T-shirts to shot glasses.

Several art galleries bring many alternatives to the ubiquitous New England seaside painting. Modern art, photography, sculpture, pottery, and artful woodwork now fill the shelves of many shops, revealing the sophisticated and avant-garde faces of the city's art scene.

ART & **Abacus** (⊠ *44 Exchange St.* ☎ *800/206–2166* ⊕ *www.abacusgallery.*
ANTIQUES *com*), an appealing crafts gallery, has unusual gift items in glass, wood, and textiles, plus fine modern jewelry. **F.O. Bailey Antiquarians** (⊠ *35 Depot Rd., Falmouth* ☎ *207/781–8001* ⊕ *www.fobailey.com*),

carries antique and reproduction furniture and jewelry, paintings, rugs, and china. The **Institute for Contemporary Art** (✉*522 Congress St.* ☎*207/775–3052*), at the Maine College of Art, showcases contemporary artwork from around the world.

BOOKS   **Longfellow Books** (✉*1 Monument Way* ☎*207/772–4045*) is a grand success story of the independent bookstore triumphing over the massive presence of the large chains. Longfellow's is known for its good service and very thoughtful literary selection. Author readings are scheduled regularly.

CLOTHING   Family-owned **Casco Bay Wool Works** (✉*10 Moulton St.* ☎*207/879–9665 or 888/222–9665* ⊕*www.cascobaywoolworks.com*) sells beautiful, handcrafted wool capes, shawls, blankets, and scarves.

WHERE TO EAT

$$$–$$$$ ✕**Fore Street.** Two of Maine's best chefs, Sam Hayward and Dana
Fodor'sChoice   Street, opened this restaurant in a renovated, airy warehouse on the
★   edge of the Old Port (heating-oil delivery trucks once were parked
AMERICAN   here—honest). The menu changes daily to reflect the freshest local ingredients available. Every copper-top table in the two-level main dining room has a view of the enormous brick oven and hearth and the open kitchen, where sous-chefs seem to dance as they create entrées such as three cuts of Maine island lamb, Atlantic monkfish fillet, and breast of Moulad duckling. Desserts include artisanal cheeses. ✉*288 Fore St.* ☎*207/775–2717* ▤*AE, MC, V* ☯*No lunch.*

$$ ✕**Gilbert's Chowder House.** This is the real deal, as quintessential as
★   Maine dining can be. Clam rakes, nautical charts, and a giant plastic
SEAFOOD   marlin hang from the walls of this unpretentious waterfront diner. The flavors are from the depths of the North Atlantic, prepared and presented simply: fish, clam, and corn chowders; fried shrimp, haddock, clam strips, and extraordinary clam cakes. A chalkboard of daily specials is a must-read, and often features steamed mussels, oysters, and peel-and-eat shrimp. But don't miss out on the lobster roll—a toasted hot dog roll bursting with claw and tail meat unadulterated by mayo or other ingredients. It sits on a leaf of lettuce, but who needs more? It's classic Maine, fuss-free and presented on a paper plate. ✉*92 Commercial St.* ☎*207/871–5636* ▤*AE, MC, V.*

$$$$ ✕**Hugo's.** Chef-owner Rob Evans has turned Hugo's into one of the
★   city's best restaurants. The warmly lighted dining room is small and
ECLECTIC   open, yet you can hold a conversation without raising your voice. The four-course prix-fixe menu changes weekly, but a pub menu is available to mix and match downsized items for $10 to $20 a dish. These could include herb-crusted Maine wolffish, Maine diver scallops with beef tartare, and risotto steeped deep red by beets. Few other restaurants in downtown are so devoted to preparing and serving the freshest local organic foods. ✉*88 Middle St.* ☎*207/774–8538* ▤*AE, MC, V* ☯*Closed Sun. and Mon. No lunch.*

$$–$$$ ✕**Ri-Ra.** Whether you're in the mood for a pint of beer and corned beef
IRISH   and cabbage, or a crock of mussels and whole roasted rainbow trout, Ri-Ra delivers. Settle into a comfy couch in the downstairs pub or take a table in the upstairs dining room, where walls of windows overlook

the busy ferry terminal. After dinner every Thursday, Friday, and Saturday, the lower level gets loud with live local bands playing until closing time. ✉️*72 Commercial St.* ☎️*207/761–4446* 🟰*AE, MC, V.*

$$–$$$
SEAFOOD
✗**Street and Co.** Fish and seafood are the specialties in this Old Port basement establishment. You enter through the bustling kitchen and dine amid dried herbs and shelves of staples, at one of the copper-top tables (so your waiter can place a skillet of sizzling seafood directly in front of you). The daily specials are usually a good bet, and pasta dishes are popular (garlic and olive oil lovers rejoice; they're loaded with both). Listen to your server—chances are your plate is very hot indeed. ✉️*33 Wharf St.* ☎️*207/775–0887* 🟰*AE, MC, V* 🕙*No lunch.*

$$–$$$
AMERICAN
✗**Walter's Cafe.** Capturing the 19th-century spirit of the Old Port, with its brick walls and wood floors, this casual, busy place in the heart of the Old Port's shopping area manages a good balance of local seafood and meats with Asian and more eclectic flavors. Begin with lobster bisque or deep-fried lemongrass shrimp sticks; then move on to a shrimp and andouille bake. ✉️*15 Exchange St.* ☎️*207/871–9258* 🟰*AE, MC, V* 🕙*No lunch Sun.*

WHERE TO STAY

$$–$$$
🏨**Inn on Carleton.** After a day of exploring Portland's museums and shops, you can find a quiet retreat at this elegant brick town house on the city's Western Promenade. Built in 1869, it is furnished throughout with period antiques as well as artwork by contemporary Maine artists. A trompe l'oeil painting by Maine artist Charles Schumacher, known for the technique, greets you at the entryway, and more fine examples of his work in this style are either on display or in the process of being uncovered and restored. **Pros:** European-style elegance, English garden, Western Promenade location. **Con:** it's a long walk to the Old Port. ✉️*46 Carleton St.* ☎️*207/775–1910 or 800/639–1779* 🌐*www.innoncarleton.com* 🛏*6 rooms* 🔑*In-room: no phone, no TV. In-hotel: no elevator, public Wi-Fi, no kids under 9, no-smoking rooms* 🟰*D, MC, V* 🍴*BP.*

$$$–$$$$
Fodor'sChoice
★
🏨**Pomegranate Inn.** The classic architecture of this handsome inn in the architecturally rich Western Promenade area gives no hint of the surprises within. Vivid hand-painted walls, floors, and woodwork combine with contemporary artwork, and the result is both stimulating and comforting. Rooms are individually decorated, and five have fireplaces. Room 8, in the carriage house, has a private garden terrace. **Pros:** near Western Promenade. **Con:** not within reasonable walking distance of Old Port and waterfront. ✉️*49 Neal St.* ☎️*207/772–1006 or 800/356–0408* 🌐*www.pomegranateinn.com* 🛏*8 rooms* 🔑*In-room: Wi-Fi. In-hotel: no elevator, no kids under 16, no-smoking rooms* 🟰*AE, D, DC, MC, V* 🍴*BP.*

$$$$
🏨**Portland Harbor Hotel.** Making luxury its primary focus, the Harbor Hotel has become a favorite with business travelers seeking meetings on a more-intimate scale, and vacationing guests who want high-quality service and amenities. In season, eat on the enclosed peaceful garden patio. **Pros:** luxurious amenities, amid the action of the Old Port and waterfront. **Con:** not for the quaint of heart. ✉️*468 Fore St.* ☎️*207/775–9090 or 888/798–9090* 🌐*www.portlandharborhotel.com*

⇨85 rooms, 12 suites ⛄In-room: Wi-Fi. In-hotel: restaurant, laundry service, concierge, public Internet, no-smoking rooms ▤AE, D, DC, MC, V.

$$$$ ⬚**Portland Regency Hotel and Spa.** One of the few major hotels in the center of the Old Port, the brick Regency building was Portland's armory in the late 19th century. Most rooms have four-poster beds, tall standing mirrors, floral curtains, and love seats. The spa features a licensed massage therapist, pedicures and manicures, and even its own healthy cuisine, such as yogurt, salads, and sandwiches. **Pros:** convenient to shops, restaurants, and museums; has all the extras you'd want. **Con:** more luxurious than charming. ⬚20 Milk St. ☎207/774–4200 or 800/727–3436 ⊕www.theregency.com ⇨87 rooms, 8 suites ⛄In-room: refrigerator, Ethernet, Wi-Fi. In-hotel: restaurant, gym, spa, laundry service, public Wi-Fi, no-smoking rooms ▤AE, D, DC, MC, V.

ISLANDS OF CASCO BAY

The islands of Casco Bay are also known as the Calendar Islands because an early explorer mistakenly thought there was one for each day of the year (in reality there are only 140). Some islands are uninhabited; others support year-round communities as well as stores and restaurants. Nearest to Portland (and in fact considered a suburb of it), **Peaks Island** is the most developed of the Calendar Islands. A trip here allows you to commune with the wind and sea, explore an old fort, and ramble along the alternately rocky and sandy shore without having to venture too far away. A bit farther out, 17-acre **Eagle Island** contains the 1904 home of Admiral Robert E. Peary, the American explorer of the North Pole. It also has a rocky beach and myriad trails.

GETTING The brightly painted ferries of **Casco Bay Lines** (☎207/774–7871
THERE ⊕www.cascobaylines.com) are the islands' lifeline. A ride on the bay is a great way to experience the dramatic shape of the Maine Coast while offering a glimpse of some of its hundreds of islands.

CAPE ELIZABETH TO PROUTS NECK

WHAT TO SEE

Fodor'sChoice **Portland Head Light.** Familiar to many from photographs and Edward
★ Hopper's painting *Portland Head-Light (1927)*, this historic lighthouse was commissioned by George Washington in 1790. The towering white stone lighthouse stands over the keeper's house, a white home with a blazing red roof. Besides a harbor view, its park has walking paths and picnic facilities. The keeper's house is now the Museum at Portland Head Light. The lighthouse is in Fort Williams Park, about 2 mi from the town center. *Museum* ⬚1000 Shore Rd., Cape Elizabeth ☎207/799–2661 ⊕www.portlandheadlight.com ⬚$2 ⊙Memorial Day–mid-Oct., daily 10–4; Apr., May, Nov., and Dec., weekends 10–4.

★ **Two Lights State Park.** On just over 40 acres of Maine's quintessential rocky shoreline, this park is named for the two lighthouses atop the hill

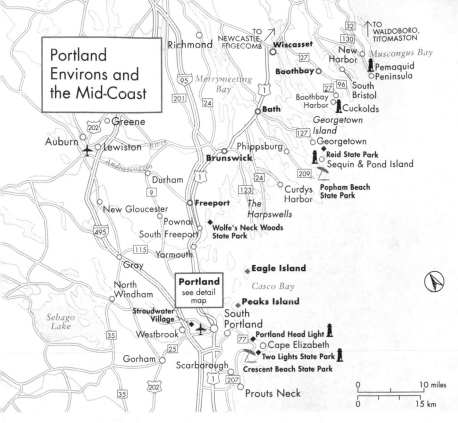

Portland
Environs and
the Mid-Coast

(one is now privately owned, the other still in use since 1828. The park has ample beach access, picnic facilities, and great views of the activities of Portland Harbor. ⊠ *Rte. 77, Cape Elizabeth* ☎ *207/799–5871* ⊠ *$1.50* ⊙ *Daily 9 AM–sunset.*

WHERE TO EAT

$$–$$$
SEAFOOD

✕ **Joe's Boathouse.** The two small dining rooms of this establishment are simple, clean, and finished in sea-foam green, with large windows looking out to a marina. The ocean motif extends to a lobster boat on a mantle and a bar that houses an aquarium. Dinner specials include tuna steak and lemon tarragon sea scallops; for lunch try the Red Riot, a sandwich featuring spicy sausage, capicola, and red peppers. In summer diners can enjoy the flavors and the scenery from the vantage of a patio. Altogether, it is low-key, casual, and a hit with the locals. ⊠ *1 Spring Point Dr.* ☎ *207/741–2780* ⊟ *AE, MC, V.*

¢–$$
SEAFOOD

✕ **Lobster Shack.** You can't beat the location—right on the water, below the lighthouse pair that gives Two Lights State Park its name—and the food's not bad either. Just as the name implies, fresh lobster is the watchword here, and you can choose your meal right from the tank. Other menu must-haves include chowder, fried clams, and fish-and-chips. It's been a classic spot since the 1920s. Eat inside or out. ⊠ *225 Two Lights Rd.* ☎ *207/799–1677* ⊟ *MC, V* ⊙ *Closed Nov.–late Mar.*

WHERE TO STAY

$$$$ 🏨 **Black Point Inn.** Toward the tip of the peninsula that juts into the ocean at Prouts Neck stands this stylish, tastefully updated historic resort with spectacular views up and down the coast. The extensive grounds contain beaches, trails, and sports facilities—including use of the tennis courts and golf course at the nearby country club. Finer touches abound, such as nightly turndown service and in-room terry robes. The Cliff Walk, a pebbled path that wanders past Winslow Homer's former studio, runs along the Atlantic headlands that Homer often painted. The inn is 12 mi south of Portland and about 10 mi north of Old Orchard Beach. **Pros:** stunning water views, set amid scenery that inspired Winslow Homer. **Con:** driving required to get to area attractions. ⊠ *510 Black Point Rd., Scarborough* ☎ *207/883–2500* ⊕ *www. blackpointinn.com* ⇆ *25 rooms* ⟐ *In-room: DVD (some), Wi-Fi. In-hotel: restaurant, bar, pools, bicycles* ⊟ *AE, D, MC, V* �aMAP.*

$$$–$$$$ 🏨 **Inn by the Sea.** Every unit in this all-suites inn includes a kitchen and a view of the Atlantic. It's a short walk down a private boardwalk to sandy Crescent Beach, a popular family spot. Dogs are welcomed with a room-service pet menu, evening turndown treats, and oversize beach towels. The Audubon dining room ($$$–$$$$), open to non-guests, serves fine seafood and regional dishes. The shingle-style design, typical of turn-of-the-20th-century New England shorefront cottages and hotels, includes a varied roofline punctuated by turretlike features and gables, balconies, a covered porch supported by columns, an open deck, and large windows. **Pros:** on Crescent Beach and a short drive to Two Lights, Portland Head, and Portland. **Con:** a bit large to be considered charming. ⊠ *40 Bowery Beach Rd., Cape Elizabeth (7 mi south of Portland)* ☎ *207/799–3134 or 800/888–4287* ⊕ *www.innby thesea.com* ⇆ *43 suites* ⟐ *In-room: kitchen, refrigerator, VCR, dial-up. In-hotel: restaurant, bar, tennis court, pool, laundry service, public Internet, some pets allowed* ⊟ *AE, D, MC, V.*

FREEPORT

17 mi northeast of Portland.

Many who come to the area do so simply to shop—L. L. Bean is the store that put Freeport on the map, and plenty of outlets and some specialty stores have settled here. But those who flock straight to L. L. Bean and see nothing else of Freeport are missing out on some real New England beauty. Beyond the shops are charming back streets lined with historic buildings and old clapboard houses, a pretty little harbor on the south side of the Harraseeket River, and bucolic nature preserves with miles of walking trails.

SPORTS & THE OUTDOORS

It shouldn't come as a surprise that one of the world's largest outdoor clothing and supply outfitters also provides its customers with instructional adventures to go with their products. L. L. Bean's year-round **Outdoor Discovery Schools** (☎ *888/552–3261* ⊕ *www.llbean.com/ods*) include half- and one-day classes, as well as longer trips that teach canoeing, shooting, photography, kayaking, fly-fishing, cross-country skiing, and other sports. Classes are for all skill levels; it's best to sign up several months in advance. Check their schedule for special activities held regularly during the summer months.

SHOPPING

The *Freeport Visitors Guide* (☎207/865–1212, 800/865–1994 *for a copy*) lists the more than 100 shops and factory outlet stores that can be found on Main Street, Bow Street, and elsewhere, including such big-name designers as Coach, Brooks Brothers, Polo Ralph Lauren, and Cole-Haan. Don't overlook the specialty stores and crafts galleries. **Thos. Moser Cabinetmakers** (✉*149 Main St.* ☎*207/865–4519*) sells high-quality handmade furniture with clean, classic lines.

Fodor'sChoice Founded in 1912 as a mail-order merchandiser of products for hunters,
★ guides, and anglers, **L. L. Bean** (✉*95 Main St. [U.S. 1]* ☎*800/341–4341*) attracts 3.5 million shoppers a year to its giant store (open 24 hours a day) in the heart of Freeport's shopping district. You can still find the original hunting boots, along with cotton, wool, and silk sweaters; camping and ski equipment; comforters; and hundreds of other items for the home, car, boat, and campsite. The **L.L. Bean Factory Store** (✉*Depot St.* ☎*800/341–4341*) has seconds and discontinued merchandise at discount prices. **L.L. Bean Kids** (✉*8 Nathan Nye St.* ☎*800/341–4341*) specializes in children's merchandise and has a climbing wall and other activities that appeal to kids.

NIGHTLIFE & THE ARTS

Once a week in July and August, sit outside under the stars for the **L. L. Bean Summer Concert Series** (✉*Morse St.* ☎*800/559–0747 Ext. 37222* ⊕*www.llbean.com*). The free concerts start at 7:30 PM in downtown Freeport at L. L. Bean's Discovery Park. The entertainment ranges from folk, jazz, and country to rock and includes some pretty big names. Bring a blanket and refreshments. Look for special Sunday concert events in late fall and in the winter holiday season. Previous summer acts have included Livingston Taylor, zydeco and bluegrass musicians, and the Don Campbell Band.

WHERE TO EAT & STAY

$$–$$$$ ✕**Broad Arrow Tavern.** On the main floor of the Harraseeket Inn, this
Fodor'sChoice dark-paneled tavern with mounted moose heads, decoys, snowshoes,
★ and other outdoor sporty decor is known for both its casual nature and
AMERICAN its sumptuous menu. The chefs use only organically grown food, with a nearly exclusive emphasis on Maine products, to create treats such as steaks and seafood wood-grilled in a large brick hearth. About the only non-Maine ingredient is the farm-raised South Dakota buffalo, though the burger it makes is a real favorite. For lunch, choose from the ample menu or graze on the well-stocked buffet. Lunch and dinner are served daily from 11 AM. ✉*162 Main St.* ☎*207/865–9377* ⌫*Reservations not accepted* ▭*AE, D, DC, MC, V.*

$–$$ ✕**Harraseeket Lunch & Lobster Co.** Seafood baskets and lobster dinners
SEAFOOD are the focus at this bare-bones place beside the town landing in South Freeport. Order at the counter and find a seat inside or out, depending

on the weather. ✉*On pier, end of Main St.* ☎*207/865–4888* ⚓*Reservations not accepted* ⊟*No credit cards* ⊘*Closed mid-Oct.–Apr.*

$$$$
Fodor'sChoice
★

⊡ **Harraseeket Inn.** Despite modern appointments such as elevators and whirlpool baths in some rooms, this 1850 Greek Revival home provides a pleasantly old-fashioned, country-inn experience just a few minutes' walk from L.L. Bean. Guest rooms have print fabrics and reproductions of Federal quarter-canopy beds. Ask for a second-floor, garden-facing room. The formal Maine Dining Room ($$$–$$$$) specializes in contemporary American regional (and organic) cuisine such as pan-roasted lobster and all-natural filet mignon. **Pros:** excellent on-site dining, walk to shopping district, afternoon tea. **Con:** building updates over the years have diminished some authenticity. ✉*162 Main St.* ☎*207/865–9377 or 800/342–6423* ⊕*www.harraseeketinn. com* ↩*84 rooms* ⚷*In-room: refrigerator (some), dial-up. In-hotel: 2 restaurants, pool, no-smoking rooms* ⊟*AE, D, DC, MC, V* ⦿*BP.*

THE MID-COAST REGION

By Sherry
Hanson

Lighthouses dot the headlands of Maine's Mid-Coast region, where thousands of miles of coastline wait to be explored. Defined by chiseled peninsulas stretching south from U.S. 1, this area has everything from the sandy beaches and sandbars of Popham Beach to the jutting cliffs of Monhegan Island. If you are intent on hooking a trophy-size fish or catching a glimpse of a whale, there are plenty of cruises available. If you want to explore deserted beaches and secluded coves, kayaks are your best bet.

The charming towns, too, each have their array of attractions. Brunswick has rows of historic wood and clapboard homes, while Bath is known for its maritime heritage. Wiscasset Harbor has docks where you can stroll and waterfront seafood restaurants where you can enjoy the catch of the day—Damariscotta, too, is worth a stop for its seafood restaurants. Boothbay has lots of little stores that are perfect for window shopping, while Thomaston and environs offer scenic drives through fishing villages surrounded by water on all sides.

BRUNSWICK & THE HARPSWELLS

10 mi north of Freeport, 30 mi northeast of Portland.

Lovely brick-and-clapboard buildings are the highlight of Brunswick's Federal Street Historic District, which includes Federal Street and Park Row and the stately campus of Bowdoin College. From the intersection of Pleasant and Maine streets, in the center of town, you can walk in any direction and discover an impressive array of restaurants. Plus, from pushcart vendors on the shady town green, known as the Mall, you can sample finger foods such as hamburgers, clam rolls, and that old Maine favorite, steamed hot dogs.

From Brunswick, Routes 123 and 24 take you to the peninsulas and islands known collectively as the Harpswells. Small coves along

Harpswell Neck shelter lobster boats, and summer cottages are tucked away amid birch and spruce trees. On your way down to Land's End at the end of Route 24, stop at Mackerel Cove to see a real fishing harbor; there are a few parking spaces where you can stop and picnic and look for beach glass, or put in your kayaks.

NEED A
BREAK? The scent of freshly baked scones and breads may draw you into the **Wild Oats Bakery** (⊠ *149 Maine St., Brunswick* ☎ *207/725–6287* ▭*D, MC, V*), inside the Tontine Mall downtown. There are also hot soups and chowders or made-to-order sandwiches and salads.

SPORTS & THE OUTDOORS

The coast near Brunswick is full of hidden nooks and crannies waiting to be explored. By kayak you can seek out secluded beaches and tucked-away coves along the shore, and watch gulls and cormorants diving for fish. **H2Outfitters** (⊠ *Rte. 24, Orr's Island* ☎ *207/833–5257 or 800/205–2925* ⊕ *www.h2outfitters.com*) provides top-notch kayaking instruction and gear for people of all skill levels.

WHERE TO EAT

$$–$$$
Fodor's Choice
★
SEAFOOD

✕ **Cook's Lobster House.** Inhale the salt breeze as you cross the world's only cribstone bridge (designed so that water flows freely through gaps between the granite blocks) on your way south on Route 24 from Cook's Corner in Brunswick to this famous seafood restaurant 15 mi away, which began as a lobster shack on Bailey Island. Try the lobster casserole, or the delectable haddock sandwich. Several specialties come in smaller portions. Lobster dishes are in the $$$$ price range. Whether you choose inside or deck seating, you can watch the activity on the water: men checking lobster pots on the water and kayakers fanning across the bay. ⊠ *68 Garrison Cove Rd., Bailey Island* ☎ *207/833–2818* ⪦ *Reservations not accepted* ▭*D, MC, V* ☉ *Closed New Year's Day–mid-Feb.*

BATH

11 mi northeast of Brunswick, 38 mi northeast of Portland.

Bath has been a shipbuilding center since 1607. The venerable Bath Iron Works completed its first passenger ship in 1890 and is still building ships today, turning out frigates for the U.S. Navy. Along Front and Centre streets, in the heart of Bath's historic district are some charming 19th-century Victorian homes. Among them are the 1820 Federal-style Pryor House, at 360 Front Street; the 1810 Greek Revival–style mansion at 969 Washington Street, covered with gleaming white clapboards; and the Victorian gem at 1009 Washington Street, painted a distinctive shade of raspberry. All three operate as inns. ■TIP➔It's a good idea to avoid U.S. 1 on weekdays from 3:15 to 4:30 pm, when a major shift change at the factory takes place.

WHAT TO SEE

Fodor's Choice
★ **Reid State Park.** This park on Georgetown Island has 1½ mi of sand split between two beaches. From the top of rocky Griffith Head, you can spot the lighthouses on Seguin Island, the Cuckolds, and Hendricks Head. In summer, parking lots fill by 11 AM on weekends and holidays. If swimming, be aware of the possibility of an undertow. During a storm, this is a great place to observe the ferocity of the waves crashing onto the shore. ⊠ *Rte. 127* ☎ *207/371–2303*

OFF THE BEATEN PATH

Popham Beach State Park (⊠ *Rte. 209, Phippsburg* ☎ *207/389–1335*) has bathhouses and picnic tables. There are no restaurants at this end of the beach, so pack a picnic or get takeout from Spinney's Restaurant near the Civil War–era Fort Popham or Percy's Store behind Spinney's, at 6 Sea Street, phone number 207/389–2010. At low tide you can walk miles of tidal flats and also out to a nearby island, where you can explore tide pools or fish off the ledges. Drive past the entrance to the park and on the right you can see a vista often described as "Million Dollar View." The confluence of the Kennebec and Morse rivers creates an ever-shifting pattern of sandbars.

WHERE TO EAT

$–$$
BARBECUE
✕ **Beale Street Barbecue.** Ribs are the thing at this barbecue joint. For hearty eaters, ask for one of the platters piled high with pulled pork, pulled chicken, or shredded beef. If you can't decide, there's always the massive barbecue sampler. Jalapeño popovers and chili served with corn bread are terrific appetizers. Enjoy a beer at the bar while waiting for your table. ⊠ *215 Water St.* ☎ *207/442–9514* ▭ *MC, V.*

$$
AMERICAN
✕ **Mae's Café & Bakery.** Some of the region's tastiest pies, pastries, and cakes are baked in this restaurant, a local favorite since 1977. Rotating selections of works by local artists hang in the two turn-of-the-20th-century houses joined together. Dine inside or on the front deck, where you can gaze down at the "City of Ships." The satisfying contemporary cuisine includes savory omelets and seafood quiche as well as seafood specials and traditional chicken, beef, and pasta dishes. Meals also can be packed to go. ⊠ *160 Centre St.* ☎ *207/442–8577* ▭ *D, MC, V.*

$$$–$$$$
Fodor's Choice
★
AMERICAN
✕ **Robinhood Free Meetinghouse.** Though owned by acclaimed chef and owner Michael Gagné—whose 72-layer cream-cheese biscuits are shipped all over the country—this 1855 Greek Revival–style meetinghouse serves meals that are primarily made by chef de cuisine Troy Mains. The menu changes daily but always has a variety of seafood, vegetables, and dairy products purchased locally. You might begin with the lobster and crab cakes, then move on to grilled fillet of beef stuffed with crab or the confit of duck. Finish up with the signature Obsession in Three Chocolates. The wine list offers an array of choices to accompany Mains's creations. The service is excellent. The dining room evokes its meetinghouse past with cream-color walls, pine floorboards, and cherry Shaker-style chairs. Crisp linens add an elegant touch. ⊠ *210 Robinhood Rd., Georgetown* ☎ *207/371–2188* ▭ *AE, D, MC, V* ⊘ *No lunch.*

WHERE TO STAY

$$$–$$$$

☺

Fodor's Choice

★

Sebasco Harbor Resort. This destination family resort, spread across 575 acres at the foot of the Phippsburg Peninsula, has an exceptional range of accommodations and services, to which it continues to add. Comfortable guest rooms in the clapboard-covered main building have antique furnishings and new bathrooms, while rooms in a building designed to resemble a lighthouse have wicker furniture, paintings by local artists, and rooftop access. The Fairwinds, a luxury waterfront spa, was added in 2007; prices for room-and-treatment packages hover around $400. Also added in 2007 was the Harbor Village Suites, set into exquisitely landscaped grounds and featuring 18 spacious and air-conditioned rooms. These units rent for around the same rate, though sometimes a bit lower. The resort's Pilot House restaurant ($$–$$$) is known for its innovative take on classic dishes. Entrées include haddock stuffed with a trio of scallops, shrimp, and vegetables. **Pros:** ocean location, excellent food and service. **Con:** pricey. ⊠ *Rte. 217* ⊡ *Box 75, Sebasco Estates 04565* ☎ *207/389–1161 or 800/225–3819* ⊕ *www. sebasco.com* ⇆ *115 rooms, 23 cottages* ☺ *In-room: no a/c (some), Wi-Fi (some). In-hotel: 3 restaurants, bar, golf course, tennis courts, pool, gym, bicycles, public Wi-Fi, airport shuttle, no-smoking rooms* ⊟ *AE, D, MC, V* ☺ *Closed Nov.–mid-May* ⊙ *MAP.*

WISCASSET

10 mi north of Bath, 46 mi northeast of Portland.

Settled in 1663, Wiscasset sits on the banks of the Sheepscot River. It bills itself "Maine's Prettiest Village," and it's easy to see why: it has graceful churches, old cemeteries, and elegant sea captains' homes (many converted into antiques shops or galleries). U.S. 1 becomes Main Street, and traffic often slows to a crawl. If you park in town, you can walk to most galleries, shops, restaurants, and other attractions. ■ TIP→ Try to arrive early in the morning to find a parking space—you'll likely have success if you try to park on Water Street rather than Main.

SHOPPING

Not to be missed is **Edgecomb Potters** (⊠ *727 Boothbay Rd., Edgecomb* ☎ *207/882–9493* ⊕ *www.edgecombpotters.com*), which specializes in pricey exquisitely glazed porcelain. Open year-round, the shop has one of the best selections in the area and also carries jewelry. **Sheepscot River Pottery** (⊠ *34 U.S. 1, Edgecomb* ☎ *207/882–9410* ⊕ *www.sheepscot. com*) boasts beautifully glazed kitchen tiles as well as kitchenware and home accessories. A second store is located in Damariscotta.

OFF THE BEATEN PATH

When Portlanders want a break from city life, many come north to the **Boothbay region,** which is made up of Boothbay proper, East Boothbay, and Boothbay Harbor. This part of the shoreline is a craggy stretch of inlets where pleasure craft anchor alongside trawlers and lobster boats. Commercial Street, Wharf Street, Townsend Avenue, and the By-Way are lined with shops and ice-cream parlors. You can browse for hours in the trinket shops, crafts galleries, clothing stores, and boutiques around the harbor, or take a walk through the 248-acre **Coastal Maine Botanical Garden** (⊠ *Barters Island Rd.* ☎ *207/633–4333*).

Excursion boats leave from the piers off Commercial Street; some allow you to see the two lighthouses standing at attention near Boothbay Harbor: **Burnt Island Light** and **Cuckolds Light**. Boats to Monhegan Island are also available. Drive out to Ocean Point in East Boothbay for some incredible scenery, or rent a kayak and explore from a lower perspective. You can also catch a ride on a lobster boat and help haul the traps. Boothbay is 13 mi southeast of Wiscasset via U.S. 1 to ME-27.

NEWCASTLE

18 mi north of Boothbay Harbor via Rte. 27 and U.S. 1.

Between the Sheepscot and the Damariscotta rivers, the town of Newcastle was settled in the early 1600s. The earliest inhabitants planted apple trees, but the town later became an industrial center, home to several shipyards and a couple of mills. The oldest Catholic church in New England, St. Patrick's, is here, and the church still rings its original Paul Revere bell to call parishioners to worship.

WHERE TO EAT & STAY

$$$–$$$$
SEAFOOD
✕⌂ **Newcastle Inn.** A riverside location and an excellent dining room make this country inn a classic. All the guest rooms are filled with antiques and decorated with sumptuous fabrics; some rooms have fireplaces and whirlpool baths. On pleasant mornings, breakfast is served on the back deck overlooking the river. The dining room ($$$$), which is open to the public by reservation, serves six-course meals and is open Tuesday through Saturday in season. The emphasis is on local seafood. **Pros:** innkeepers' reception evenings with cocktails and hors d'oeuvres. **Con:** away from town. ⊠ *60 River Rd.* ☎ *207/563–5685 or 800/832–8669* ⊕ *www.newcastleinn.com* ⇆ *14 rooms, 3 suites* ⌂ *In-room: no phone, no TV (some). In-hotel: restaurant, bar, no elevator, no kids under 12, no-smoking rooms* ⊟ *AE, MC, V* ⦿ *BP.*

▌OFF THE BEATEN PATH
Six miles east of Newcastle, the Damariscotta region comprises several communities along the rocky coast. The town of **Damariscotta**, which sits on the water, is filled with attractive shops and several good restaurants. **Bremen**, which encompasses more than a dozen islands and countless rocky outcrops, offers numerous sporting activities. **Nobleboro** was settled in the 1720s by Colonel David Dunbar, sent by the British to build the fort at Pemaquid. Neighboring **Waldoboro** is situated on the Medomak River and was settled largely by Germans in the early 1770s. You can still visit the old German Meeting House, built in 1772. The peninsula stretches south to include Bristol, Round Pond, South Bristol, New Harbor, and Pemaquid.

PEMAQUID POINT

17 mi south of Damariscotta via U.S. 1 to Rte. 129 to Rte. 130.

Route 130 brings you to Pemaquid Point, home of the famous lighthouse and its attendant fog bell and tiny museum. New Harbor is about 4 mi away, and Round Pond is 6 mi beyond that. To reach those towns, take a left onto Route 32 where it intersects Route 130 just before Pemaquid Point.

WHAT TO SEE

☾ ★ **Pemaquid Point Light.** Route 130 terminates at this lighthouse that looks as though it sprouted from the ragged, tilted chunk of granite that it commands. The former lighthouse keeper's cottage is now the Fishermen's Museum, which displays historic photographs, scale models, and artifacts that explore commercial fishing in Maine. Also here is the original fog bell and bell house built in 1897 for the two original Shipman engines. Pemaquid Art Gallery, on-site, mounts exhibitions by area artists in July and August, and admission to the gallery, once you have paid your fee to be on the lighthouse property, is free. Restrooms, picnic tables, and barbecue grills are all available on this site. Next door to this property is the Sea Gull Shop, with a dining room, gift shop, and ice-cream parlor. ⊠*Rte. 130 (Bristol Rd.), Pemaquid* ☎*207/677–2494* ⌨*$2* ☉*Memorial Day–Columbus Day, Mon.–Sat. 10–5, Sun. 11–5.*

STATE BEVERAGE

It's difficult to get very far in Maine without running into Moxie—the nation's oldest soft drink, invented by Dr. Augustin Thompson of Union, Maine, in 1884. You'll recognize it by its bright orange label. It comes in bottles and cans and is sold in just about every supermarket and convenience store in Maine. A word of warning, however; you gotta get past that first taste!

SPORTS & THE OUTDOORS

CRUISES   You can take a cruise to Monhegan with **Hardy Boat Cruises** (⊠*Shaw's Wharf, New Harbor* ☎*207/677–6026*). On the sightseeing cruises you can spot seals and puffins.

SHOPPING

The **Granite Hall Store** (⊠*9 Back Shore Rd., Round Pond* ☎*207/529–5864*) has penny candy, wicker baskets, and cards on the first floor and antiques and books on the second. Order ice-cream cones through a window on the side. It's open May to mid-October.

WHERE TO STAY

$$ ⬚**Unique Yankee Bed & Breakfast.** Spectacular views of the Gulf of
Fodor'sChoice   Maine, John's Bay, and Monhegan Island and the sound of crashing
★   surf greet you at this hilltop B&B. The facility is at Christmas Cove, named when explorer Captain John Smith anchored here one Christmas Eve in the early 1600s. Since that time the cove has been a snug harbor for watercraft of all kinds. If you are looking for an oasis away from the crowds, you will enjoy the 11 gorgeous perennial gardens and the fact that this 2.3-acre property is surrounded by a 2-acre greenbelt. The owners' artwork from all over the world adorns the walls.

Extensive libraries of books, videos, and DVDs wind around the staircases going up to the cupola towers, and you will even find a couple of pieces of exercise equipment tucked in a corner on the way. The hosts offer afternoon snacks and a selection of wines every evening. If you are looking for the experience of a lifetime, take that glass of wine up two or three floors to the tower, inside or on the outdoor decks. You can see all the way to Monhegan Island. Each of the guest rooms has a four-season electric fireplace, microwave, coffee pot, and two-person jetted bath (plus separate shower). The inn accepts kids and pets—in fact, pets have their own outdoor courtyard. **Pros:** amenities, view, grounds, hosts. **Con:** dogs on premises. ⊠ *53 Coveside Rd., South Bristol* ☎ *207/644–1502 or 866/644–1502* ⊕ *www.uniqueyankeeofmaine. com* ↩*4 rooms* ♿ *In-room: refrigerator, DVD, Wi-Fi. In-hotel: no elevator, some pets allowed, no-smoking rooms* ☱ *MC, V* ⏀*BP.*

WALDOBORO

10 mi northeast of Damariscotta.

Veer off U.S. 1 onto Main Street or down Route 220 or 32, and you can discover a seafaring town with a proud shipbuilding past. Waldoboro's Main Street is lined with houses representing numerous architectural styles: Cape Cod, Queen Anne, Stick, Greek Revival, and Italianate.

WHAT TO SEE

Old German Church. One of the oldest churches in Maine, the Old German Church was built in 1772. It originally sat on the eastern side of the Medomak River, then was moved across the ice to its present site in 1794. Inside you can find box pews and a 9-foot-tall chalice pulpit. ⊠ *Rte. 32* ☎ *No phone* ☉ *July and Aug., daily 1–3.*

Olson House. Between 1893 and 1968, Andrew Wyeth painted his famous Christina pictures in the Olson House. Reproductions of many of these enigmatic portraits are hung throughout this historic house, now part of the Farnsworth Museum. ⊠ *384 Hathorn Point Rd., Cushing* ☎ *207/354–0102* ⊕ *www.farnsworthmuseum.org* ⊠*$4* ☉ *Memorial Day–Columbus Day, daily 11–4.*

SHOPPING

The **Waldoboro 5 & 10** (⊠ *17 Friendship St.* ☎ *207/832–4624*) is the oldest continually operated five-and-ten in the country. It offers deli-type sandwiches, soups, and ice cream, plus it sells a nice selection of toys. There's also a penny-candy counter popular with kids.

PENOBSCOT BAY

By Stephen and Neva Allen

Few could deny that Penobscot Bay is one of Maine's most dramatically beautiful regions. Its 1,000-mi-long coastline is made up of rocky granite boulders, wild and often undeveloped shore, a sprinkling of colorful towns, and views of the sea and shore that are a photographer's dream. It is home to hundreds of islands.

Initially, shipbuilding was the primary moneymaker here. In the 1800s, during the days of the great tall ships, or Down Easters as they were often called, more wooden ships were built along Penobscot Bay than in any other place in America. This golden age of billowing sails and wooden sailing ships did not last long, however. It came to an end with the development of the steam engine. Ships propelled by steam-fed pistons were faster, safer, more reliable, and could hold more cargo. By 1900, sailing ships were no longer a viable commercial venture in Maine. However, as you will see when traveling the coast, the tall ships have not disappeared—they have simply been revived as recreational boats, known as windjammers.

■ **TIP→** If you're driving at night, be wary of moose crossing the road.

THOMASTON

10 mi northeast of Waldoboro, 72 mi northeast of Portland.

Dotted with antiques and specialty shops, the seaside town of Thomaston is a delightful town known for the clapboard houses lining its streets. A National Historic District encompasses parts of High, Main, and Knox streets.

WHERE TO EAT

$$–$$$ ╳ **Thomaston Café & Bakery.** A changing selection of works by local artAMERICAN ists adorns the walls of this small café, and you are next door to an independent bookstore. You might actually run into a writer or an artist or two here, since this is a popular meeting place for locals. Entrées, prepared with locally grown ingredients, include seared fresh tuna on soba noodles, lobster ravioli with lobster sauce, and filet mignon with béarnaise sauce. Soups and sandwiches are delicious. ⊠*154 Main St.* ☎*207/354–8589* ▤*MC, V* ☉*No dinner Sun.–Thurs.*

TENANTS HARBOR

13 mi south of Thomaston.

On a rocky part of the coast, Tenants Harbor is a quintessential coastal town—its harbor is dominated by lobster boats, its shores are slippery, and its downtown streets are lined with clapboard houses, a church, and a general store. It's a favorite with artists, and galleries and studios welcome browsers.

WHERE TO STAY

$$–$$$ ▦ **Craignair Inn.** From Route 1 just east of Thomaston, take Route 131
Fodor'sChoice south 6 mi, then turn left on Route 73 for a mile, right at Clark Island
★ Road 1½ mi, all the way to the end of the road to find this lodging dating from 1928. Sitting on four acres right on the water, it was originally built to house granite workers from nearby quarries. The annex was the chapel where the stonecutters and their families worshipped. Rooms are comfortably furnished with antique furniture, and the beds are piled high with colorful quilts. Most rooms have views of the water, and the semi-suite rents for $200 a night. A recent addition here is an

Lighting the Way

Ever wonder what makes Maine's more than five dozen lighthouses so bright? It has to do with the lens; you need the right kind of lens to magnify the light. Resembling giant beehives, the original Fresnel lenses used in these lighthouses were made of prisms that redirected light from a lamp into a concentrated beam.

The first Fresnel lens was made in France in 1822 by French physicist Augustine Fresnel. Most lenses that were placed in lighthouses along the coasts of Europe and North America were handmade and shipped unassembled from France. The largest of these lenses, called a first-order lens, could be as much as 12 feet tall. Rings of glass prisms arranged above and below the center drum were intended to bend the light beam. Later designs incorporated a bull's eye into the center of the lens, which acted like a magnifying glass to make the beam even more powerful.

You can see some of the smaller original lenses in museums in Maine, but you can also see a first-order lens in the Mid-Coast area in the lighthouse on Seguin Island, 10 mi from shore, accessible by boat from the Maine Maritime Museum. The Seguin Light is the only first-order lens in Maine, and one of only two remaining lenses still in use north of Virginia. The lens shines with 282 prisms.

The Seguin Island Light was commissioned by George Washington in 1795, and is one of the oldest lighthouses in the United States. Most of the original lenses used in lighthouses in this part of the country were mounted on mercury bases that were designed to rotate; these lenses were later replaced because of the danger of mercury poisoning. The lens at Seguin is a fixed light, meaning that it does not rotate. It used no mercury, so it could be kept in place. Ships can see this beacon 20 mi out to sea. Today the lens reflects the light of a 1,000-watt bulb. Before electricity, incandescent oil vapor was used.

Early Fresnel lenses were fairly standard in size and shape, but that posed problems as more and more lighthouses were built along the coasts. The captain of a ship could not tell one light from another in the dark and stormy night, so he didn't know what headland or ledge he was approaching. The lenses eventually were designed to have different "personalities" that made them easily identifiable. Many lights became known for their distinctive flash patterns. Seguin Island Light is a fixed white light, whereas the Pemaquid Point Light is a white light that flashes every 6 seconds. Monhegan Island Light, visible from Port Clyde, has a white light that flashes for 2.8 seconds every 30 seconds. In Phippsburg, Pond Island Light shines a white beam with 6-second intervals of white and dark.

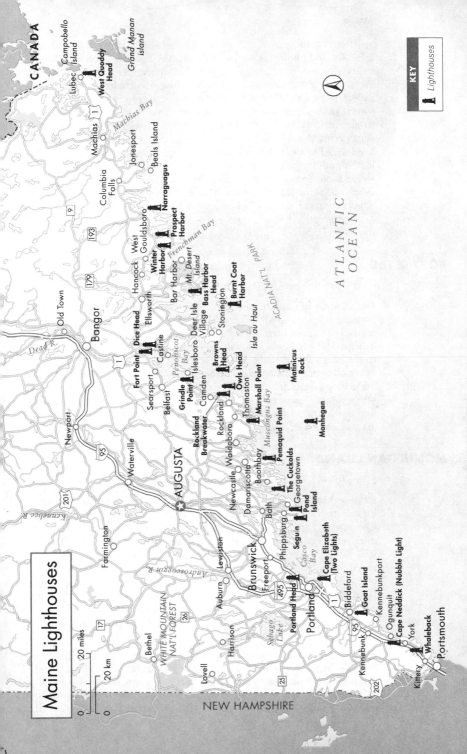

Maine Lighthouses

NEW HAMPSHIRE

CANADA

ATLANTIC OCEAN

KEY

Lighthouses

0   20 miles

0   20 km

Lovell
Bethel
WHITE MOUNTAIN NAT'L FOREST
Harrison
Sebago Lake
Farmington
Lewiston
Auburn
Brunswick
Freeport
Portland
Casco Bay
Cape Elizabeth (Two Lights)
Portland Head
Biddeford
Goat Island
Kennebunkport
Kennebunk
Ogunquit
Cape Neddick (Nubble Light)
York
Whaleback
Portsmouth
Kittery

Newport
Waterville
AUGUSTA
Phippsburg
Bath
Georgetown
Pond Island
Seguin
The Cuckolds
Boothbay
Newcastle
Damariscotta
Waldoboro
Pemaquid Point
Monhegan
Marshall Point
Thomaston
Rockland
Rockland Breakwater
Owls Head
Camden
Belfast
Grindle Point
Islesboro
Searsport
Browns Head
Matinicus Rock
Muscongus Bay

Bangor
Old Town
Dead R.
Fort Point
Castine
Penobscot Bay
Stonington
Isle au Haut
Deer Isle
Village
Bass Harbor Head
Burnt Coat Harbor
ACADIA NAT'L PARK
Mt. Desert Island
Bar Harbor
Frenchman Bay
Ellsworth
Dice Head
Hancock
West Gouldsboro
Winter Harbor
Prospect Harbor
Narraguagus
Columbia Falls
Jonesport
Beals Island
Machias
Machias Bay
Lubec
West Quoddy Head
Campobello Island
Grand Manan Island

Dead R.
Kennebec R.
Androscoggin R.

apartment with kitchen, gas fireplace, washer and dryer, ceiling fans, cable TV and phone, as well as a private deck, water access, and two kayaks for use by apartment guests. The apartment rents for $200 a night. Chef extraordinaire Chris Seiler, most recently from the Samoset Resort, wins awards for his creative cuisine served in the inn's dining room ($$$). You might want to start with the Caribbean jerk grilled shrimp brochettes, or steamed great eastern mussels, and move on to pecan-crusted salmon, bacon-wrapped tenderloin, or baked stuffed haddock. The dessert menu might feature pastry chef Meg Joseph's lemon pudding cake, key lime square, or a mini crème brûleé. **Pros:** stellar food, some air-conditioned rooms. **Con:** pets allowed in some rooms. ⊠*5 3rd St., Spruce Head* ☎*207/594–7644 or 800/320–9997* ⊕*www.craignair.com* ⬅*21 rooms, 13 with bath* ⚲*In-room: no a/ c. In-hotel: public Wi-Fi, no elevator, some pets allowed, no-smoking rooms* ▭*D, MC, V* ⦶*BP.*

PORT CLYDE

2 mi south of Tenants Harbor via Rte. 131.

Port Clyde, a fishing village at the end of the St. George Peninsula, is the jumping-off point to Monhegan Island. Shipbuilding was the first commercial enterprise here, and later the catching and canning of seafood. You can still buy Port Clyde sardines. Port Clyde's boat landing is home to the *Laura B,* the mail boat that serves nearby Monhegan Island. It's operated by the **Monhegan Boat Line** (☎*207/372–8848*). Several artists make their homes in Port Clyde, so check to see if their studios are open while you are visiting. From here you also can visit Owls Head Light and the Marshall Point Lighthouse, the latter of which has inspired artists like Jamie Wyeth.

MONHEGAN ISLAND

East of Pemaquid Peninsula, 10 mi south of Port Clyde.

Remote Monhegan Island, with its high cliffs fronting the sea, was known to Basque, Portuguese, and Breton fishermen well before Columbus discovered America. About a century ago, Monhegan was discovered again by some of America's finest painters, including Rockwell Kent, Robert Henri, A. J. Hammond, and Edward Hopper, who sailed out to paint its open meadows, savage cliffs, wild ocean views, and fishermen's shacks. Tourists followed, and today three excursion boats dock here *(at the end of this chapter).* The village bustles with activity in summer, when many artists open their studios. You can escape the crowds on the island's 17 mi of hiking trails, which lead to the lighthouse and to the cliffs.

Enjoy the silence and serenity of Cathedral Woods on your way to or from the high cliffs at White Head, Black Head, and Burnt Head. Bring drinking water or plan to purchase same, as there is no potable drinking water except in restaurants, inns, and private cottages. You might consider bringing a picnic if you're visiting during the day, or eat at one of the island's restaurants, though they are busy at lunch. If you are planning on hiking, bring sunblock and insect repellant, as well as a hat, and a jacket for the boat trip, which will be an hour or longer, depending on where your boat originates. Plan to pack out whatever trash you generate while you are out and about, as there are few trash receptacles in public places. All trash on Monhegan Island has to be taken off the island by boat. Use the toilet on your boat before you come ashore; the only public toilets on the island are located behind the old Monhegan House, and these are privately maintained and the owners appreciate a small donation. All that being said, if you love the rocky cliffs, this is your place. And if you happen to be an artist you might never leave. Studios and galleries are all over the island and all schedule certain days to be open. Several shops are available for browsers. Bring your camera!

ROCKLAND

4 mi northeast of Thomaston, 14 mi northeast of Tenants Harbor.

The name "Rockland" defines this area's history. If you set fishing aside, rock cutting—specifically granite and limestone—was once the area's principal occupation. In fact, numerous government buildings across the United States were built using granite blocks from Rockland and other nearby quarries. Just outside the town of Rockland, a large cement factory on U.S. 1 serves as a reminder of this rocky past.

Though once merely a place to pass through on the way to tonier ports like Camden, Rockland now attracts attention on its own, thanks to this trio of attractions: the renowned Farnsworth Museum, the increasingly popular summer Lobster Festival, and the lively North Atlantic Blues Festival. Its Main Street Historic District, with its Italianate, Mansard, Greek Revival, and Colonial Revival buildings, is on the National Register of Historic Places. Specialty shops and galleries line the main street, and at least one of the restaurants, Primo, has become nationally famous. The town has a growing popularity as a summer destination, but it is still a large fishing port and the commercial hub of this coastal area. You can find plenty of working boats moored alongside the yachts.

Rockland Harbor is the berth of more windjammer ships than any other port in the United States. The best place in Rockland to view these beautiful vessels as they sail in and out of the harbor is the mile-long granite breakwater, which bisects the outer portion of Rockland Harbor. To get there, go north on U.S. 1, turn right on Waldo Avenue, and right again on Samoset Road; go to the end of this short road.

WHAT TO SEE

Fodor's Choice ★ **Farnsworth Art Museum.** This is one of the most important small museums in the country. The **Wyeth Center** is devoted to Maine-related works of the famous Wyeth family: N. C. Wyeth, an accomplished illustrator whose works were featured in many turn-of-the-20th-century books; his son Andrew, one of America's best-known painters; and Andrew's

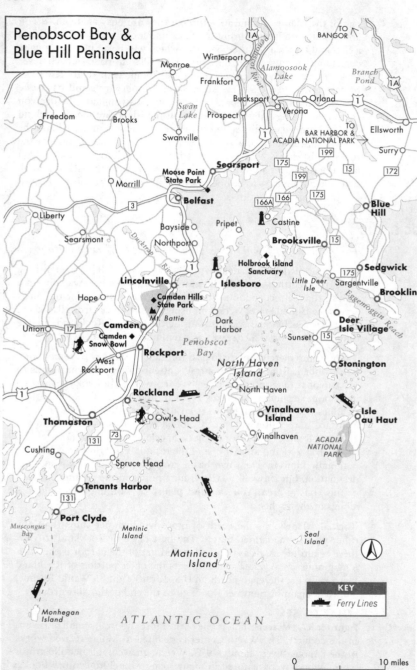

Penobscot Bay & Blue Hill Peninsula

TO BANGOR

Winterport

Penobscot River

Alamoosook Lake

Branch Pond

1A

Monroe

Frankfort

Bucksport   Orland   1

Swan Lake   Prospect   Verona

TO BAR HARBOR & ACADIA NATIONAL PARK

Ellsworth

Freedom   Brooks   Swanville   199   Surry

172

Searsport   175   15

Moose Point State Park   199   175

Morrill   Belfast   166A   166   175   Blue Hill

Liberty   Bayside   Pripet   Castine   Brooksville   15

Searsmont   Northport   Sedgwick

Hope   Lincolnville   Holbrook Island Sanctuary   Little Deer Isle   175   Sargentville   Brooklin

Camden Hills State Park   Islesboro   Eggemoggin Reach

Union   17   Mt. Battie   Dark Harbor   Deer Isle Village

Camden   Sunset   15

Camden Snow Bowl   Penobscot Bay   Stonington

West Rockport   Rockport   North Haven Island

Rockland   North Haven

Thomaston   Owl's Head   Vinalhaven Island   Isle au Haut

Cushing   131   73   Vinalhaven   ACADIA NATIONAL PARK

Spruce Head

Tenants Harbor

131   Seal Island

Port Clyde   Metinic Island

Muscongus Bay   Matinicus Island

Monhegan Island   ATLANTIC OCEAN

KEY

Ferry Lines

0 ——— 10 miles
0 ——— 15 km

son James, also an accomplished painter who lives nearby on an island. Some works from the personal collection of Andrew and Betsy Wyeth include *The Patriot, Adrift, Maiden Hair, Dr. Syn, The Clearing,* and *Watch Cap.* Also on display are works by Fitz Hugh Lane, George Bellows, Frank W. Benson, Edward Hopper (his paintings of old Rockland are a highlight), Louise Nevelson, and Fairfield Porter. Works by living Maine artists are shown in the **Jamien Morehouse Wing.** The **Farnsworth Homestead,** a handsome circa-1852 Greek Revival dwelling that is part of the museum, retains its original lavish Victorian furnishings. There is a museum store next to the Morehouse Wing (⇨ *Shopping*). In Cushing, a tiny town a few miles south of Thomaston, on the St. George River, the museum also operates the **Olsen House** (⊠*Hathorn Point Rd., Cushing*), which is depicted in Andrew Wyeth's famous painting *Christina's World.* ⊠*16 Museum St., Rockland* ☎*207/596–6457* ⊕*www.farnsworthmuseum.org* 🎫*Museum and Olsen House $10, Olsen House alone $4* ⊙*Daily 10–5.*

🔄 **Maine Lighthouse Museum.** The museum displays the largest collection of
★ the famed Fresnel lighthouse lenses to be found anywhere in the world. It also displays a collection of lighthouse artifacts and Coast Guard memorabilia. Sharing the same building is the Penobscot Bay Regional Chamber of Commerce, where tourists and visitors can pick up maps and area information. ⊠*1 Park Dr.* ☎*207/594–3301* ⊕*www.maine lighthousemuseum.com* 🎫*$5* ⊙*Weekdays 9–5, weekends 10–4.*

SHOPPING

ART GALLERIES The **Caldbeck Gallery** (⊠*12 Elm St.* ☎*207/594–5935* ⊕*www.caldbeck. com*) displays contemporary Maine works. The **Gallery at 357 Main** (⊠*357 Main St.* ☎*207/596–0084*) specializes in marine paintings.

BOOKS & TOYS The motto at **Planet Inc.** (⊠*318 Main St.* ☎*207/596–5976*), Maine's largest toy store, is "You're never too old to play." Planet Inc. also has a store in Camden. **Rock City Books & Coffee** (⊠*328 Main St.* ☎*207/594– 4123*) is a wonderful place for book lovers. There's a huge selection, the staff is friendly, and you can enjoy coffee and a homemade pastry while browsing.

NIGHTLIFE & THE ARTS

FESTIVALS Rockland's annual **Maine Lobster Festival** (☎*207/596–0376 or 800/562–*
🔄 *2529* ⊕*www.mainelobsterfestival.com*), in early August, is more than
★ 60 years old and has become the biggest local event of the year. People come from all over the country to sample lobster in every possible form: steamed, fried, chowder, lobster rolls—you name it. During the few days of the festival, tons of lobsters (about 10 tons, to be exact) are steamed in the world's largest lobster cooker—you have to see it to believe it. In addition, there's shrimp in its many forms, steamed clams, and Maine mussels. The festival, held in Harbor Park, includes a parade, entertainment, craft and marine exhibits, food booths— and, of course, the crowning of the Maine Sea Goddess. More than a dozen well-known artists gather for the **North Atlantic Blues Festival** (☎*207/593–1189* ⊕*www.northatlanticbluesfestival.com*), a two-night affair each July. The show officially takes place at Harbor Park,

but it also includes a Blues Club Crawl through downtown Rockland, which gives this staid old Maine town the atmosphere of New Orleans. Admission is $25.

WHERE TO EAT

$$ ✕**Amalfi.** A well-chosen and affordable wine list and excellent service
★ have made this storefront bistro a hit with locals and visitors alike.
MEDITERRANEAN Chef-owner David Cooke serves delicious Mediterranean cuisine, influenced by the culinary traditions of France, Spain, Italy, Greece, and Morocco. The menu changes seasonally but may include the house paella with chorizo or the duck risotto. The seafood is always fresh. ⊠*421 Main St.* ☎*207/596–0012* ▤*AE, MC, V* ⊗*Closed Mon. No lunch.*

$$$–$$$$ ✕**Primo.** Owner-chef Melissa Kelley and her world-class gourmet res-
Fodor'sChoice taurant in a restored Victorian home has won many awards and been
★ written about favorably in several high-quality publications, *Vanity*
CONTINENTAL *Fair, Town and Country,* and *Food and Wine* among them. The cuisine combines fresh Maine ingredients with Mediterranean influences. The menu, which changes daily, may include wood-roasted black sea bass, local crab-stuffed turbot, or diver-harvested-scallop and basil ravioli. The co-owner is pastry chef Price Kushner, who offers a number of unusual and delectable desserts. One of the best is his Cannoli Sicili-ana, featuring crushed pistachios and amarena cherries. ⊠*2 S. Main St., Rockland* ☎*207/596–0770* ⊕*www.primorestaurant.com* ▤*AE, D, DC, MC, V* ⊗*Closed mid-Jan.–mid-Apr.*

$–$$ ✕**Rockland Cafe.** It may not look like much from the outside, but the
Fodor'sChoice Rockland Café is probably the most popular eating establishment in
★ town, especially among locals. It's famous for the size of its breakfasts
SEAFOOD and is also open for lunch and dinner. The restaurant is a real bargain if you go for the all-you-can-eat seafood special. At dinner, the seafood combo of shrimps, scallops, clams, and fish is excellent, or there's the classic liver and onions. ⊠*441 S. Main St., Rockland* ☎*207/596–7556* ⊕*www.rocklandcafe.com* ▤*AE, DC, MC, V.*

WHERE TO STAY

$$$–$$$$ ▥**Berry Manor Inn.** Originally the residence of prominent Rockland
★ merchant Charles H. Berry, this 1898 inn is in a historic residential neighborhood. The large guest rooms are elegantly furnished with antiques and reproduction pieces. All rooms have fireplaces; TVs are available upon request, and some rooms have whirlpools. A guest pantry is stocked with sweets. **Pros:** in a nice, quiet neighborhood, within walking distance of downtown and the harbor. **Con:** not handi-cap accessible. ⊠*81 Talbot Ave.* ☎*207/596–7696 or 800/774–5692* ⊕*www.berrymanorinn.com* ☜*12 rooms* ⚘*In-room: no TV, Wi-Fi. In-hotel: public Wi-Fi, no-smoking rooms* ▤*AE, MC, V* ▥◯*BP.*

$$–$$$ ▥**Limerock Inn.** This inn is in the center of town, so you can easily walk
★ to the Farnsworth Museum or any of the other downtown attractions and restaurants. The house is built in the Queen Anne–Victorian style, and among the meticulously decorated rooms is one called Island Cottage, which features a whirlpool tub and doors that open onto

a private deck overlooking a garden. The Grand Manan room has a fireplace, a whirlpool tub, and a four-poster king-size bed. Room TVs are available upon request. **Pro:** free Wi-Fi. **Con:** no dinner options within walking distance. ✉96 Limerock St. ☎207/594–2257 or 800/546–3762 ⊕www.limerockinn.com ➡8 rooms ♿In-room: no phone, no TV, Wi-Fi. In-hotel: no-smoking rooms ▤AE, DC, MC, V ⊙BP.

VINALHAVEN

★ *East of Rockland via Maine State Ferry on U.S. 1.*

The largest inhabited island in Maine, Vinalhaven has 1,200 residents. It's nearly 8 mi long by 5 mi wide and is mostly wooded. At one time the granite industry was booming here, but the quarries are now mostly used for swimming and fishing. Many islanders work in the lobster-harvesting business. They even have a special season when they can gather lobsters while those on the mainland cannot (to compensate them for living on an island).

Most of Penobscot Bay's islands have infrequent ferry service, or are totally uninhabited. Vinalhaven, however, is relatively accessible—*relatively* being the key word here. There are six ferry trips per day to and from Vinalhaven in summer. The Maine State Ferry Terminal is right in the center of Rockland, on U.S. 1, across from the Navigator Motor Inn. The ferry runs throughout the year (except on major holidays), but the times change somewhat from the end of October through December, so it's best to call first. Ferry service to North Haven and to Mantinicus, a small island 23 mi from Rockland, is also available.

■TIP➜ These old ferries are very minimal in their amenities. You won't find a restaurant, snack bar, lounge, or even a vending machine.

The village of Vinalhaven is small and easy to explore. There is a designated walking path on the north side of Main Street that runs from the ferry terminal to the center of town. Within a 1-mi radius of the ferry dock you will find two town parks and a nature conservancy area. There is only one road on the island, so it's pretty easy to find your way around. Biking the island can be fun, though there are no designated bike paths and the road can be a little rough outside the village. There is no public transportation on the island.

CATCH THE FERRY

Be aware of the ferry schedule. If you miss the last ferry back, or if there simply is not enough room for your car on the last ferry, you will have to spend the night on the island, and chances are you'll be sleeping in your car since there is not a lot in the way of accommodations on Vinalhaven. ■TIP➜ A good way not to get caught overnight on the island is not to take your vehicle—merely board as a walk-on passenger. The fare is about a third of what it is if you take your vehicle, and Vinalhaven can be easily explored on foot.

THE PRETTIEST WALK IN THE WORLD

A few years ago, *Yankee*, the quintessential magazine of New England, did a cover story on what it called "the prettiest walk in the world." The two-lane paved road, which winds up and down, with occasional views of the ocean, connects Rockport to Camden. To judge the merits of this approximately 2-mi journey for yourself, you can travel by foot or by car. Begin at the intersection of U.S. 1 and Pascal Road. Take a right off U.S. 1 toward Rockport harbor, then cross the bridge and go up the hill. On your left is Russell Avenue. Take that all the way to Camden. Lining the way are some of the most beautiful homes in Maine, surrounded by an abundance of flora and fauna. Keep an eye out for a farm with Belted Galloway cows, as well as views of the sparkling ocean—for those who may not know, these rare white cows get their name from the foot-wide black "belt" around their middles. The walk or drive is beautiful at any time of the year, but in fall it's breathtaking. Like the rest of New England, the coast of Maine gets a large number of fall foliage "leaf peepers," and the reds and golds of the chestnut, birch, and elm trees along this winding route are especially beautiful.

WHERE TO EAT

$$-$$$
SEAFOOD
✕**Harbor Gawker.** Decorated with old wooden lobster traps and fishing gear, this mariner-theme restaurant has been in business for 30 years. The fare, seafood of course, is abundant and tasty. Try a lobster dinner or the ever-popular lobster roll. ✉*Main St.* ☎*207/863–9365* ▤*MC, V* ☉*Closed Sun. and mid-Nov.–mid-Apr.*

ROCKPORT

4 mi north of Rockland on U.S. 1.

Heading north on U.S. 1, you come to Rockport before you reach the tourist mecca of Camden. The most interesting part of Rockport—the harbor—is not right on U.S. 1, so many people drive by without realizing it's here. You can get there by following the first ROCKPORT sign you see off U.S. 1 at Pascal Road. The cutting and burning of limestone was once a major industry in this area. The stone was cut in nearby quarries and then burned in hot kilns. The resulting lime powder was used to create mortar. Some of the massive kilns are still here.

WHERE TO EAT & STAY

$$$-$$$$
Fodor'sChoice
★
FRENCH
✕**Marcel's.** If you're a serious gourmet and only have time to sample one dining experience in the Rockport-Rockland-Camden area, this lavish restaurant in the big Samoset Resort ought to be the one. Marcel's offers a fine array of Continental cuisine. Enjoy table-side preparation of a classic rack of lamb, châteaubriand, or Steak Diane while admiring the bay view. The menu includes a variety of Maine seafood and a fine wine list. The Sunday brunch buffet, with some of the finest seafood along the coast, is famous and draws a crowd. ✉*220 Warrenton St., off U.S. 1* ☎*207/594–2511* ⚖*Reservations essential Jacket required* ▤*AE, D, DC, MC, V* ☉*No lunch.*

1

$$–$$$$ ⓣ **SAMOSET RESORT. THIS 230-ACRE,** all-encompassing, ocean-side
Fodor'sChoice resort on the Rockland-Rockport town line offers luxurious rooms and
★ suites, all with a private balcony or patio, and an ocean or garden view.
The spacious rooms are decorated in deep green and burgundy tones.
The resort has three dining options: the Breakwater Cafe, the Clubhouse
Grille, and the flagship restaurant, Marcel's (⇨ Where to Eat). For a
less-formal affair, try the Breakwater Cafe, featuring basic New Eng-
land fare, such as homemade chowder and lobster rolls; there's outdoor
seating when the weather is nice. The Clubhouse Grille, catering to the
golf crowd, serves casual food, which you can enjoy inside or on the
porch. *Golf Digest* called the resort's 18-hole championship golf course
the "Top Ranked Resort Course in New England," and the "Seventh
Most Beautiful Course in America." **Pro:** this is a resort property that
seems to meet every need. **Con:** not within walking distance of Rockland
or Camden shops. ⊠ *220 Warrenton St.* ☎ *207/594–2511 or 800/341–
1650* ⊕ *www.samoset.com* ⇆ *156 rooms, 22 suites* ♿ *In-room: dial-up,
Wi-Fi. In-hotel: 3 restaurants, bar, golf course, tennis courts, pools, gym,
children's programs (ages 3–12), laundry service, concierge, public Inter-
net, airport shuttle, no-smoking rooms* ▤ *AE, D, DC, MC, V* ⍩ *CP.*

CAMDEN

2 mi north of Rockport, 5 mi south of Lincolnville.

★ More than any other town along Penobscot Bay, Camden is the per-
fect picture-postcard of a Maine coastal village. It is one of the most
popular destinations on the Maine Coast, so June through September
the town is crowded with visitors—but don't let that scare you away;
Camden is worth it. Just come prepared for busy traffic on the town's
Main Street (U.S. 1), and make lodging reservations well in advance.
You'll also want to make restaurant reservations whenever possible.

"The Jewel of the Maine Coast" is the publicity slogan for Camden-
Rockport-Lincolnville, and it is an apt description. Camden is famous
not only for its geography but also for its large fleet of windjammers—
relics and replicas from the age of sailing—with their romantic histo-
ries and great billowing sails. At just about any hour during the warm
months, you're likely to see at least one windjammer tied up in the
harbor. The excursions, whether for an afternoon or a week, are best
from June through September.

The town's compact size makes it perfect for exploring on foot: shops,
restaurants, and galleries line Main Street (U.S. 1), as well as side streets
and alleys around the harbor. Especially worth inclusion on your walk-
ing tour is Camden's residential area. It is quite charming and filled
with many fascinating old period houses from the time when Federal,
Greek Revival, and Victorian architecture were the rage among the
wealthy. Many of them now are B&Bs. The chamber of commerce, at
the Public Landing, can provide you with a walking map.

★ One of the biggest and most colorful events of the year in Cam-
den is **Windjammer Weekend** (☎ *207/374–2993 or 800/807–9463*

CLOSE UP

Windjammer Excursion

Nothing defines the Maine coastal experience more than a sailing trip on a windjammer. Windjammers were built throughout the East Coast in the 19th and early 20th centuries. Designed to carry cargo primarily, these iron- or steel-hulled beauties have a rich past—the *Nathaniel Bowditch* served in World War II, for example, while others plied the waters in the lumbering and oystering trades. They vary in size, but could be as small as 40 feet and hold six passengers (plus a couple of crew members), or more than 130 feet and hold 40 passengers and 10 crew members. During a windjammer excursion, not only do passengers have the opportunity to ride on a historical vessel, but in most cases they are able to participate in the navigation, be it hoisting a sail or playing captain at the wheel.

The majority of windjammers are berthed in Rockland, Rockport, or Camden. You can get information on the fleets by contacting one of two windjammer organizations: The Maine Windjammer Association (☎800/807-9463 ⊕www.sail-

mainecoast.com) or Maine Windjammer Cruises (☎207/236-2938 or 888/692-7245 ⊕www.mainewindjammercruises.com). Cruises can be anywhere from one day or one overnight to up to eight days. The price, ranging from nearly $200 to $900, depending on length of trip, includes all meals. Trips leave from Camden, Rockland, and Rockport.

Here is a selection of some of the best windjammer cruises in the area.

Camden-Rockport *Angelique,* Yankee Packet Co., 207/236-8873. *Appledore,* which can take you out for just a day sail, 207/236-8353. *Mary Day,* Coastal Cruises, 207/236-2750. *Olad,* Downeast Windjammer Packet Co., 207/236-2323. *Yacht Heron,* 207/236-8605 or 800/599-8605.

Rockland *American Eagle* and *Schooner Heritage,* North End Shipyard, 207/594-8007. *Nathanial Bowditch,* 207/273-4062. *Summertime,* 800/562-8290. *Victory Chimes,* 207/265-5651. *Wendameen,* 207/594-1751.

⊕*www.windjammerweekend.com*), which usually takes place at the beginning of September and includes the single largest gathering of windjammer ships in the world, plus lots of good eats.

SPORTS & THE OUTDOORS

☾
★ Although their height may not be much more than 1,000 feet, the hills in **Camden Hills State Park** (✉*U.S. 1 just north of Camden* ☎*207/236-3109*) are lovely landmarks for miles along the low, rolling reaches of the Maine Coast. The 5,500-acre park contains 25 mi of hiking trails, including the easy nature trail up Mt. Battie. Hike or drive to the top for a magnificent view over Camden and island-studded Penobscot Bay. There also is a campground here.

SAILING For the voyage of a lifetime, you and your family should think seriously
☾ about a **windjammer trip**—which can be as little as a couple of hours or
★ as much as a week. The following day-sailer windjammers leave from Camden Harbor; most are of the schooner type: **Lazy Jack** (☎*207/230-0602* ⊕*www.schoonerlazyjack.com*); **Olad** (☎*207/236-2323*

www.maineschooners.com); **Shantih II** (☎207/236–8605 or 800/599–8605 *www.woodenboatco.com*); and **Windjammer Surprise** (☎207/236–4687 *www.camdenmainesailing.com*). Prices range from $395 to $875, with all meals included—and often that means a lobster bake on a deserted island beach.

SKIING

☺

★

The Maine Coast isn't known for skiing, but the **Camden Snow Bowl** (✉*Hosmer Pond Rd.* ☎207/236–3438, 207/236–4418 *snow phone* *www.camdensnowbowl.com*) has a 950-foot-vertical mountain with 11 trails accessed by one double chair and two T-bars. The complex also includes a small lodge with a cafeteria, and ski and toboggan rentals. Activities include skiing, night skiing, snowboarding, tubing, tobogganing, and ice-skating—plus magnificent views over Penobscot Bay. The North American Tobogganing Championships, a tongue-in-cheek event open to anyone, is held annually in early February. At **Camden Hills State Park** (✉*U.S. 1 just north of downtown Camden* ☎207/236–0849), there are 10 mi of cross-country skiing trails.

SHOPPING

Camden has some of the best shopping in the region. The downtown area is a shopper's paradise with lots of interesting places to spend money. Most of the shops and galleries are along Camden's main drag, U.S. 1, so you can easily complete a shopping tour on foot. Start at the Camden Harbor, turn right on Bay View, and walk to Main/High Street. ■TIP→ **U.S. 1 has three different names within the town limits—it starts as Elm Street, changes to Main Street, then becomes High Street. So don't let the addresses listed below throw you off.**

Bayview Gallery (✉*33 Bay View St.* ☎207/236–4534 *www.bayview-gallery.com*) specializes in original art, prints, and posters, most with Maine themes. **Maine Gold** (✉*12 Bay View St.* ☎702/236–2717) sells authentic Maine maple syrup. **Planet Toys** (✉*10 Main St.* ☎207/236–4410) has unusual gifts—including books, toys, and clothing—from Maine and other parts of the world.

NIGHTLIFE

Offering live music, dancing, pub food, and local brews, **Gilbert's Public House** (✉*12 Bay View St., underneath Peter Ott's pub* ☎207/236–4320) is the favorite drinking place of the windjammer crowd.

WHERE TO EAT

$–$$

★

SEAFOOD

✕**Cappy's Chowder House.** Cappy's has been around for so long (more than two decades) it's become somewhat of a Camden institution. As you would expect from the name, Cappy's "chowdah" is the thing to order here—it's been written up in the *New York Times* and in *Bon Appétit* magazine—but there are plenty of other seafood specials on the menu, too. Don't be afraid to bring the kids—this place has many bargain meals. ✉*1 Main St.* ☎207/236–2254 ⌨*Reservations not accepted* ▭*MC, V.*

$$–$$$

FRENCH

✕**Natalie's.** Fine dining with a French-American menu is the name of the game here. There's also a prix-fixe meal and a Grand Lobster dish. The lounge is a perfect place for a cocktail in front of the big fireplace. ✉*83 Bay View St.* ☎207/236–7008 ▭*AE, DC, MC, V.*

WHERE TO STAY

$$–$$$$ ⊞**Hartstone Inn.** This downtown 1835 mansard-roofed Victorian
★   home has been turned into an elegant and sophisticated retreat and
a fine culinary destination. No detail has been overlooked, from soft
robes, down comforters, and chocolate truffles in the guest rooms to
china, crystal, and silver in the elegantly decorated dining room. The
inn hosts seasonal food festivals. **Pro:** on-site restaurant is excellent.
Con: not handicapped accessible. ✉*41 Elm St. (U.S. 1)* ☎*207/236–
4259 or 800/788–4823* ⊕*www.hartstoneinn.com* ⬅*6 rooms, 6
suites* ⬙*In-room: dial-up. In-hotel: restaurant, no-smoking rooms*
⊟*MC, V* ⳩*BP.*

$$$$ ⊞**Inn at Sunrise Point.** Guests are offered a spectacular setting in this
★   luxury inn. (The Irish manager prides himself on having the highest
rates of any Camden inn.) The main house and cottages are right on the
ocean, resulting in beautiful ocean views from nearly all rooms. Ame-
nities such as plush robes and oversize tubs and showers are standard;
some rooms include romantic wood-burning fireplaces and Jacuzzis.
One of the cottages is accessible for people with disabilities. All rooms
have flat-screen TVs with DVD players. **Pros:** spectacular views, a
delightful Irish manager. **Cons:** pricey, no restaurants nearby. ✉*U.S.
1* ☎*207/236–7716* ⊕*www.sunrisepoint.com* ⬅*3 rooms, 4 cottages,
2 suites* ⬙*In-room: no a/c, Wi-Fi. In-hotel: no elevator, no-smoking
rooms* ⊟*MC, V* ⳩*BP.*

$$$–$$$$ ⊞**Lord Camden Inn.** The Lord Camden Inn is an excellent location if
★   you want to be in the very center of town near the harbor. The exterior
of the building is red brick with bright blue-and-white awnings. The
colorful interior is furnished with restored antiques and paintings by
local artists. Despite being downtown, the inn offers plenty of ocean
views from the upstairs rooms, and some of the rooms have lovely
old-fashioned, four-poster beds. There's no on-site restaurant but you
can find plenty of dining options within walking distance. Two of the
rooms are handicapped accessible, including the bathrooms. All of the
rooms are no-smoking, but the hotel is pet-friendly. An elevator goes
to the upper floors. **Pro:** the most centrally located accommodation in
Camden. **Con:** U.S. 1 traffic may keep you awake in the front rooms.
✉*24 Main St. (U.S. 1)* ☎*207/236–4325 or 800/336–4325* ⊕*www.
lordcamdeninn.com* ⬅*37 rooms* ⬙*In-room: refrigerator (some), dial-
up. In-hotel: no-smoking rooms* ⊟*AE, MC, V* ⳩*BP.*

$$$–$$$$ ⊞**Norumbega.** The Norumbega is probably the most unusual-looking
Fodor's Choice   B&B you'll ever see. When you see this ivy-coated, gray stone castle,
★   from the outside you may think, *"Wow, Count Dracula would feel
right at home here."* But inside it's cheerier, and elegant, with many
of the antique-filled rooms offering fireplaces and private balconies
overlooking the bay. The inn was built in 1886 by local businessman
and inventor (of duplex telegraphy) Joseph Stearns. Before erecting
his home, he spent a year visiting the castles of Europe and adapting
the best ideas he found. He named the castle after the original 17th-
century name for what is now Maine, "Norumbega." The home was
converted into a B&B in 1984 and has been named by the *Maine Times*
as the most-photographed piece of real estate in the state. There are

no ground-floor guest rooms, and no elevator. Pets are not allowed. **Pro:** you will never again stay in a place this dramatic looking. **Con:** while this is an unusually beautiful property, guests with mobility problems or who have difficulty climbing stairs will not find it comfortable. ⊠ *63 High St. (U.S. 1), just a little north of downtown Camden* ☎ *207/236–4646 or 877/363–4646* ⊕ *www.norumbegainn.com* ⮐ *13 rooms* ⌂ *In-room: no a/c, dial-up, Wi-Fi. In-hotel: no elevator, no-smoking rooms* ⊟ *AE, DC, MC, V* ⃝ *BP.*

$$–$$$ 🏨 **Whitehall Inn.** One of Camden's best-known inns, the Whitehall is an
★ 1834 white clapboard sea captain's home just north of town. The Millay Room, off the lobby, preserves memorabilia of the poet Edna St. Vincent Millay, who grew up in the area and read her poetry here. The inn is a delightful blend of the old and the new. The telephones are antiques, but the electronics are brand new. The rooms, remodeled in 2007, have dark-wood bedsteads, white bedspreads, and claw-foot tubs. The dining room serves traditional and creative American cuisine as well as many seafood specialties, and the popular prix-fixe dinner is $36 a person. One room is handicapped accessible. **Pro:** Edna St. Vincent Millay—wow! **Con:** no air-conditioning, but usually it's fine without it. ⊠ *52 High St.* ☎ *207/236–3391 or 800/789–6565* ⊕ *www.whitehall-inn.com* ⮐ *50 rooms, 45 with bath* ⌂ *In-room: no a/c, no phone (some), Wi-Fi. In-hotel: restaurant, tennis court, public Internet, no-smoking rooms* ⊟ *AE, MC, V* ⊗ *Closed mid-Oct.–mid-May* ⃝ *BP.*

LINCOLNVILLE

6 mi north of Camden via U.S. 1.

Looking at a map, you may notice there are two parts to Lincolnville: Lincolnville Beach on U.S. 1 and the town of Lincolnville Center a little inland on Route 73. The area of most interest—where you can find the restaurants and the ferry to Islesboro—is Lincolnville Beach. This is a tiny area; you could be through it in less than a minute. Still, it has a history going back to the Revolution, and you can see a few small cannons on the beach that were intended to repel the British in the War of 1812 (they were never used). Lincolnville is close to Camden, so it's a great place to stay if rooms in Camden are full—or if you just want someplace a little quieter.

WHERE TO EAT & STAY

$–$$ ✕ **Lobster Pound Restaurant.** If you're looking for an authentic place to
Fodor's Choice have your Maine lobster dinner, this is it. This simple restaurant looks
★ more like a cannery than a restaurant, with rustic wooden picnic tables
SEAFOOD and hundreds of live lobsters swimming in tanks—you can pick out (if you want) your own lobster. It'll be served to you with clam chowder and corn. Forget about ordering a predinner cocktail or wine with dinner; have an ice tea instead. On U.S. 1, right on the edge of the sea, the Lobster Pound provides beautiful views from both its indoor and outdoor seating. On the menu here you will see the classic "Shore Dinner," which consists of lobster stew or fish chowder, steamed or fried clams, 1½-pound lobster, potato, and dessert. Lobster and seafood are,

LOBSTER TRIVIA

How old is this lobster on my plate? It is probably around seven years old. It takes them that long to reach a size where you would want to eat them (about 1½ pounds).

What's that yucky-looking green stuff on its belly? That's the lobster's liver. It won't kill you; some people like it, most don't.

Why do lobsters start out being green and then turn red when they're cooked? Like fall leaves, the red was there all the time as background. The other colors disappear when the lobster is cooked.

Do lobsters feel pain when they are cooked? There is some controversy about this. According to the state's Lobster Institute, the lobsters feel no pain because they don't have complex brains like you and I do but rather a cortex of ganglia that reacts to stimuli, sort of like an involuntary muscle reaction. A recent Norwegian study also concluded that lobsters' nervous systems don't register pain. People for the Ethical Treatment of Animals (PETA) and some scientists disagree.

For more on lobsters, check out the book *The Secret Life of Lobsters: How Fishermen and Scientists Are Unraveling the Mysteries of Our Favorite Crustacean* by Trevor Corson.

of course, the reason to come here, though turkey and steak are also available. This restaurant has seating for nearly 300, so even if it's a busy time, you won't have to wait long. There's also a 70-seat picnic area if you want to take your food to go. ⊠*2521 Atlantic Hwy. (U.S. 1)* ☎*207/789–5550* ⊟*AE, DC, MC, V* ⊗*Closed Nov.–Apr.*

$$$$
Fodor'sChoice
★

🖪 **Inn at Ocean's Edge.** This beautiful white inn on 22 acres has one of the loveliest settings in the area, with heavy forest on one side and the ocean on the other. The inn looks as if it has been here for decades, but the original building was only built in 1999, with the upper building following in 2001. The rooms are styled simply but with old-fashioned New England elegance: a lot of quilts and throws and Colonial-style furniture. Every room has a king-size bed, an ocean view, a fireplace, and a whirlpool for two. One room is handicapped accessible; and there is an elevator for the upper floors. The elevator is small and unobtrusive, not affecting the basic look of the hotel. The inn also includes a fine restaurant, the Edge, with oceanfront dining. **Pro:** it would be tough to find an accommodation in a more beautiful setting than this. **Cons:** abundant shopping and dining options not within walking distance, lodging is pricey. ⊠*20 Stone Coast Rd. (U.S. 1), Lincolnville* ⌂ ☎*207/236–0945* ⊕*www.innatoceansedge.com* ⌨*29 rooms, 3 suites* △*In-room: VCR, DVD, dial-up, Wi-Fi. In-hotel: bar, gym, pool, restaurant, no-smoking rooms* ⊟*AE, DC, MC, V* ⫶⊙⫶*BP.*

ISLESBORO

★ *3 mi east of Lincolnville via Islesboro Ferry (terminal on U.S. 1).*

If you would like to visit one of Maine's area islands but don't have much time, Islesboro is the best choice. The island is only a 20-minute ferry ride off the mainland. You can take your car with you. The drive from one end of the island to the other (on the island's only road) is lovely. It takes you through Warren State Park, a nice place to stop for a picnic and the only public camping area on the island. There are two stores on the island where you can buy supplies for your picnic: the Island Market is a short distance from the ferry terminal on the main road; and Durkee's General Store is 5 mi farther north at 863 Main Road. Next to the island's ferry terminal are the Sailor's Memorial Museum and the Grindle Point Lighthouse, both worth a brief look.

The permanent year-round population of Islesboro is about 625, but it swells to around 3,000 in summer. Most of the people who live on the island full time earn their living in one way or another from the sea. Some of them work at the three boatyards on the island, others are fishermen, and still others run small businesses. Seasonal residents may include some familiar faces: John Travolta and his wife, Kelly Preston, have a home here, as does Kirstie Alley.

The **Islesboro Ferry,** operated by the Maine State Ferry Service, departs from Lincolnville Harbor, a few hundred feet from the Lobster Pound Restaurant. Try to head out on one of the early ferries so you have enough time to drive around and get back. If you miss the last ferry, you'll have to stay on the island overnight. The ferry runs back and forth nine times a day from April through October and seven times a day from November through March. There are fewer runs on Sunday. The round-trip cost for a vehicle and one passenger is $22.25, slightly more with additional passengers, less if you leave the vehicle behind. Call for schedules. ☎207/789–5611.

BELFAST

10 mi north of Lincolnville.

The farther you get up the coast and away from Camden, the less touristy the area becomes and the more you see of the real Maine. Traffic jams and crowded restaurants give way to a more-relaxed and casual atmosphere, and locals start to treat you like a potential neighbor.

A number of Maine coastal towns, such as Wiscasset and Damariscotta, like to think of themselves as the prettiest little town in Maine, but Belfast may be the true winner of this title. It has a full variety of charms: a beautiful waterfront; an old and interesting main street climbing up from the harbor; a delightful array of B&Bs, restaurants, and shops; and a friendly population. The downtown even has old-fashioned street lamps, which set the streets aglow at night. If you like looking at old houses, many of which go all the way back to the Revolution, just drive up and down some of the side streets. In 2007, Belfast was called "one of the top 10 culturally cool towns in the country" by *USA Today*. The biggest employer in town is Bank of America.

WHAT TO SEE

In the mid-1800s, Belfast was home to a number of wealthy business magnates. Their mansions still stand along High Street, offering some excellent examples of Greek Revival and Federal architecture. **The Belfast Chamber of Commerce Visitor Center** (⊠ *17 Main St., at harbor* ☎ *207/338–5900*) can provide you with a free walking tour brochure that describes the various historic homes and buildings, as well as the old business section in the harbor area.

■**TIP**➔ As you walk around Belfast, you will see a number of cream-color signs labeled THE MUSEUM IN THE STREETS. Be sure to read them. They will tell you in easy-to-access fashion everything that you'd want to know about the history of Belfast. They are written in both English and French, for the benefit of Maine's neighbors to the north.

SHOPPING

Colburn Shoe Store (⊠ *79 Main St.* ☎ *207/338–1934 or 877/338–1934*) is worth a visit simply because it's the oldest shoe store in America. At one time, the making of shoes was a major industry in Belfast. The **Shamrock, Thistle & Rose** (⊠ *39 Main St.* ☎ *207/338–1864* ⊕ *www.shamrockthistlerose.com*) sells clothing, jewelry, art, and music from Ireland, Scotland, and England.

■ **NEED A BREAK?** If you're looking for a quick and easy place to have lunch, **Alexia's** (☎ *207/338-9676*), at the main corner of Main and High streets, serves the best pizza in town, plus sandwiches and Italian food.

NIGHTLIFE & THE ARTS

NIGHTLIFE

★ **Rollie's Bar & Grill** (⊠ *37 Main St.* ☎ *207/338-4502* ⊟ *MC, V*) looks like it's been here 100 years, but actually it's been here only since 1972. The tavern is right in the heart of Main Street, and at first glance it might look like a bikers bar. It is that—and a lot more. If you recognize the interior, it's because it was used as a setting in the Stephen King film *Thinner*. The vintage bar is from an 1800s sailing ship. Rollie's is the most popular watering spot in town with the locals, and it just may serve the best cheeseburger in the state of Maine.

WHERE TO EAT & STAY

$-$$

★

CONTINENTAL

✕ **Darby's Restaurant and Pub.** Darby's, a charming old-fashioned restaurant and bar, is probably the most popular restaurant in town with the locals. The building, with pressed-tin ceilings, was constructed in 1865 and has been a bar or a restaurant ever since. The antique bar is an original and has been there since 1865. The first Darby is long gone, but his name remains. Artwork on the walls is by local artists and may be purchased. A lot of the regular items on the menu, such as the pad thai and the seafood à la grecque, are quite unusual for a small-town restaurant. It also has hearty homemade soups and sandwiches, as well as dishes with an international flavor. ⊠ *155 High St.* ☎ *207/338-2339* ⊟ *AE, DC, MC, V.*

$$

Fodor's Choice

★

SEAFOOD

✕ **Young's Lobster Pound.** The place looks more like a corrugated steel fish cannery than a restaurant, but this is one of the places to have an authentic Maine lobster dinner. Young's sits right on the edge of the water, across the river from Belfast Harbor (cross Veterans Bridge to get here and turn right on Mitchell Avenue). When you first walk in, you'll see tanks and tanks and tanks of live lobsters of varying size. The traditional meal here is the Shore Dinner: fish or clam chowder; steamed clams or mussels; a 1½-pound boiled lobster; corn on the cob; and rolls and butter. Order your dinner at the counter then find a table inside or on the deck. ■ TIP→ **If you are enjoying your lobster at one of the outside tables, don't leave the table with no one to man it. Seagulls are notorious thieves—and they LOVE lobster.** ⊠ *2 Fairview St.* ☏ *207/338–1160* ▭ *AE, DC, MC, V* ☾ *Closed Labor Day–Easter.*

$-$$
Fodor'sChoice
★

🖭 **Penobscot Bay Inn.** Formerly the Belfast Bay Meadows Inn, this lovely accommodation is on five meadowed acres overlooking Penobscot Bay and is owned and managed by Kristina and Valentinas Kurapka. The rooms are bright and airy and decorated in pastel shades, with old-fashioned New England quilts on the beds. Some of the rooms even have their own fireplaces. The inn's Continental gourmet restaurant ($$–$$$$) is one of the best in the area. **Pro:** you don't have to go out for dinner. **Con:** if you want to explore Belfast's colorful downtown, you will have to drive. ⊠ *192 Northport Ave.* ☏ *207/338–5715 or 800/335–2370* ⊕ *www.penobscotbayinn.com* ➾ *19 rooms* ⌂ *In-hotel: restaurant, no elevator, no-smoking rooms* ▭ *AE, DC, MC, V* ⏣ *BP.*

SEARSPORT

6 mi northeast of Belfast.

Searsport is well known as the antique and flea market capital of Maine, and with good reason: the Antique Mall alone, on U.S. 1 just north of town, contains the offerings of 70 dealers, and flea markets during the visitor season line both sides of U.S. 1. But antiques are not the town's only point of interest; Searsport also has a rich history of shipbuilding and seafaring. In the early to mid-1800s, there were 10 shipbuilding facilities in Searsport and the town was home to more than 200 sailing ship captains.

WHAT TO SEE

Fodor'sChoice
★
�

Penobscot Marine Museum. This museum is dedicated to the history of Penobscot Bay and the maritime history of Maine. The exhibits, artifacts, souvenirs, and paintings are displayed in a unique setting of seven historic buildings, including two sea captains' houses, and five other buildings in an original seaside village. The various exhibits provide fascinating documentation of the region's seafaring way of life. The museum's outstanding collection of marine art includes the largest gathering in the country of works by Thomas and James Buttersworth. Also of note are photos of local sea captains; a collection of China-trade merchandise; artifacts of life at sea (including lots of scrimshaw); navigational instruments; tools from the area's history of logging, granite cutting, fishing, and ice cutting; treasures collected by seafarers from around the globe; and models of famous ships. The museum also has a rotating exhibit every year on a different theme. Two recent themes have been "Pirates!" and "Lobstahs!" Next to the museum, you can find the Penobscot Marine Museum Store, where you can buy anything nautical. ⊠ *5 E. Main St. (US. 1)* ☏ *207/548–2529*

⊕*www.penobscotmarinemuseum.org* ⌨*$8* ◷*Memorial Day–mid-Oct., Mon.–Sat. 10–5, Sun. noon–5.*

The 2,120-foot-long **Penobscot Narrows Bridge** ✉*711 Ft. Knox Rd., at U.S. 104416)*, about 9 mi north of Searsport, has been declared an engineering marvel. It is certainly beautiful to look at or to drive over (no toll). Spanning the Penobscot River at Bucksport, the bridge replaced the old Waldo-Hancock bridge, built in 1931. The best part of it is the three-story observation tower at the top of the western pilon. This was the first bridge observation tower built in America and, at 420 feet above the river, it's the highest bridge observation tower in the world. An elevator shoots you to the top. The cost is $5. Don't miss it—the view, which encompasses the river, the bay, and the sea beyond, is breathtaking.

SHOPPING

ANTIQUES In Searsport, shopping usually implies antiques or flea markets. Both stretch along both sides of U.S. 1 a mile or so north of downtown. **All Small Antiques** (✉*357 W. Main St.* ☎*207/338–1613*) has just what the name implies. In the very heart of town, **Captain Tinkham's Emporium** (✉*34 E. Main St.* ☎*207/548–6465*) offers antiques, collectibles, old books, magazines, records, paintings, and prints. The biggest collection of antiques is in the **Searsport Antique Mall** (✉*149 E. Main St. [U.S. 1]* ☎*207/548–2640*), which has more than 70 dealers.

BANGOR

133 mi northeast of Portland, 20 mi northwest of Bucksport, 46 mi west of Bar Harbor.

The second-largest city in the state (Portland being the first), Bangor is about 20 mi from the coast and is the unofficial capital of northern Maine. Back in the 19th century its most important product and export in the "Queen City" was lumber from the state's vast North Woods. Bangor's location on the Penobscot River helped make it the world's largest lumber port. A 31-foot-tall statue of legendary lumberman Paul Bunyan stands in front of the Bangor Auditorium.

Lumber is no longer at the heart of its economy, but Bangor has thrived in other ways. Because of its airport, Bangor has become a gateway to Mount Desert Island, Bar Harbor, and Acadia National Park. The city is also home to author Stephen King, who lives in an old Victorian house on West Broadway notable for its bat-winged iron gate.

Bangor has a very good bus system the **BAT Community Connector** (☎*207/992–4670* ⊕*www.bgrme.org*), which goes in a number of directions and as far away as Hampden to the south.

WHAT TO SEE

☾ **Maine Discovery Museum.** The the largest children's museum north of Boston, the Maine Discovery Museum has three floors with more than 60 interactive exhibits. Kids can explore Maine's ecosystem in Nature Trails, travel to foreign countries in Passport to the World, and walk through Maine's literary classics in Booktown. ⊠ *74 Main St.* ☎ *207/262–7200* ⊕ *www.mainediscoverymuseum.org* ⊠ *$5.50* ⊙ *Tues.–Thurs. and Sat. 9:30–5, Fri. 9:30–8, Sun. 11–5.*

NIGHTLIFE & THE ARTS

The **Penobscot Theatre Company** (⊠ *131 Main St.* ☎ *207/942–3333*) stages live classic and contemporary plays from October to May. From mid-July to mid-August, the company hosts the **Maine Shakespeare Festival** on the riverfront. Admission to the festival is $17.

WHERE TO STAY

$–$$
Fodor'sChoice
★

⊞ **Lucerne Inn.** This is one of the most famous and respected inns in New England. Nestled in the mountains, the Lucerne overlooks beautiful Phillips Lake. The inn was established in 1814, and in keeping with that history, every room is furnished with antiques. The rooms all have a view of the lake, gas-burning fireplaces, and a whirlpool tub; some have wet bars, refrigerators, and balconies as well. There's a golf course directly across the street. The inn's restaurant ($$–$$$$) is nearly as famous as the inn and draws many of the local people for its lavish Sunday brunch buffet. The traditional dinner among guests is the boiled Maine lobster. The inn is about 15 mi from Bangor. Several rooms are available for smokers; two rooms are handicapped accessible. **Pros:** some of the rooms have lovely views of Phillips Lake (you can request one), and the Sunday brunch is famous—but be sure to make a reservation for it. **Con:** the inn, while famous, has been around for awhile, and some of the rooms are a little on the shabby side. ⊠ *2517 Main St. (Rte. 1A), Dedham* ☎ *207/843–5123 or 800/325–5123* ⊕ *www.lucerneinn. com* ⇄ *31 rooms, 4 suites* ⚴ *In-room: Wi-Fi. In-hotel: restaurant, bar, pool, no-smoking rooms* ⊟ *AE, DC, MC, V* ⏍ *CP.*

BLUE HILL PENINSULA & ENVIRONS

By Lelah Cole
Updated
by George
Semler

If you want to see unspoiled Down East Maine land- and seascapes, explore art galleries, savor exquisite meals, or simply enjoy life at a relaxed and unhurried pace, you should be quite content on the Blue Hill Peninsula. The area is not at all like its coastal neighbors, as very little of it has been developed. There aren't any must-see attractions, so you are left to investigate the area on your own terms, seeking out the villages, hikes, artists, restaurants, or views that interest you most. Blue Hill and Castine are the area's primary business hubs.

The peninsula, approximately 16 mi wide and 20 mi long, juts out into Penobscot Bay. Not far from the mainland are the islands of Deer Isle, Little Deer Isle, and the picturesque fishing town of Stonington. It lacks the mountains, lakes, ponds, and vast network of trails of neighboring Mount Desert Island. Instead, a twisting labyrinth of roads rolls over fields and around coves, linking the towns of Blue Hill, Brooksville, Sedgwick, and Brooklin. This is a place to meander for views of open fields reaching to the water's edge or, around the next bend, a tree-shaded farmhouse with an old stone wall marking the property line.

Painters, photographers, sculptors, and other artists are drawn to the area. You can find more than 20 galleries on Deer Isle and Stonington, and at least half as many on the mainland. And with its small inns, charming bed-and-breakfasts, and outstanding restaurants scattered across the area, the Blue Hill Peninsula may just persuade you to leave the rest of the coastline to the tourists.

CASTINE

30 mi southeast of Searsport.

A summer destination for more than 100 years, Castine is a well-preserved seaside village rich in history. Although a few different American Indian tribes inhabited the area before the 1600s, French explorer Samuel de Champlain was the first European to record its location on a map. The French established a trading post here in 1613, naming the area Pentagoet. A year later, Captain John Smith claimed the area for the British. The French regained control of the peninsula with the 1667 Breda Treaty, and Jean Vincent d'Abbadie de St. Castin obtained a land grant in the Pentagoet area, which would later have his name. Castine's strategic position on Penobscot Bay and its importance as a trading post meant there were many battles for control until 1815. The Dutch claimed the area in 1674 and 1676, and England made it a stronghold during the Revolutionary War. In the 19th century, Castine was an important port for trading ships and fishing vessels. The Civil War and the advent of train travel brought its prominence as a port to an end, but by the late 1800s, some of the nation's wealthier citizens discovered Castine as a pleasant summer retreat.

WHAT TO SEE

Federal- and Greek Revival–style architecture, spectacular views of Penobscot Bay, and a peaceful setting make Castine an ideal spot to spend a day or two. Well worth exploring are its lively harbor front, two small museums, and the ruins of a British fort. For a nice stroll, park your car at the landing and walk up Main Street toward the white Trinitarian Federated Church. Among the white clapboard buildings ringing the town common are the Ives House (once the summer home of poet Robert Lowell), the Abbott School, and the Unitarian Church, capped by a whimsical belfry.

SPORTS & THE OUTDOORS

At Dennett's Wharf, **Castine Kayak Adventures** (⊠ *15 Sea St.* ☎ *207/326–9045*) operates tours with a registered Maine guide. Walk through the restaurant to the deck, where you can sign up for a half day of kayaking along the shore, or a full day of kayaking by shipwrecks, reversing falls, and islands in Penobscot Bay. The steam launch **Laurie Ellen** (⊠ *Dennett's Wharf* ☎ *207/326–9045 or 207/266–2841*) is the only wood-fired, steam-powered passenger steam launch in the country. Climb aboard for a trip around Castine Harbor and up the Bagaduce River.

WHERE TO EAT

$–$$$
AMERICAN ✕**Dennett's Wharf.** Originally built as a sail rigging loft in the early 1800s, this longtime favorite is a good place for fresh seafood. The waterfront restaurant also serves burgers, sandwiches, and other light fare. There are several microbrews on tap, including the tasty Dennett's Wharf Rat Ale. Eat in the dining room or outside on the deck. ⊠*15 Sea St.* ☎*207/326–9045* ▭*MC, V* ⊙*Closed Columbus Day–May.*

BLUE HILL

19 mi east of Castine.

Snuggled between 943-foot Blue Hill mountain and Blue Hill bay, the village of Blue Hill is perched dramatically over the harbor. Originally known for its granite quarries, copper mines, and shipbuilding, today the town charms with its pottery, and a plethora of galleries, shops, and studios line its streets. Blue Hill is also a good spot for shopping, as there are numerous bookstores and antiques shops. The Blue Hill Fair (⊕*www.bluehillfair.com*), held Labor Day weekend, is a tradition in these parts, with agricultural exhibits, food, rides, and entertainment.

SHOPPING

ART GALLERIES
★ **Blue Hill Bay Gallery** (⊠*11 Tenny Hill* ☎*207/374–5773* ⊕*www.blue hillbaygallery.com* ⊙*Daily, Memorial Day–Labor Day; weekends mid-May–Memorial Day and Labor Day–mid-Oct.*) sells oil and watercolor paintings of the local landscape. Bird carvings and other items are also available. **Leighton Gallery** (⊠*24 Parker Point Rd.* ☎*207/374–5001* ⊕*www.leightongallery.com*) shows oil paintings, lithographs, watercolors, and other contemporary art. Many pieces are abstract. Outside, granite, bronze, and wood sculptures are displayed in a gardenlike setting under apple trees and white pines.

POTTERY **Rackliffe Pottery** (⊠*126 Ellsworth Rd., Blue Hill* ☎*207/374–2297*) sells colorful pottery made with lead-free glazes. You can choose among water pitchers, tea-and-coffee sets, and sets of canisters. **Rowantrees Pottery** (⊠*9 Union St.* ☎*207/374–5535*) has an extensive selection of dinnerware, tea sets, vases, and decorative items. The shop makes many of the same pieces it did 60 years ago, so if you break a favorite item, you can find a replacement.

WINE In what was once a barn out behind one of Blue Hill's earliest houses, the **Blue Hill Wine Shop** (⊠*138 Main St.* ⊕*Halfway between intersection of Rtes. 172 and 176 and Rte. 15 in center of town* ☎*207/374–2161*) carries more than 1,000 carefully selected wines. Wine tastings are held on the last Saturday of every month.

WHERE TO EAT & STAY

$$–$$$
Fodor'sChoice
★
CONTINENTAL ✕**Arborvine.** Glowing (albeit ersatz) fireplaces, period antiques, exposed beams, and hardwood floors covered with Oriental rugs create an elegant and comforting atmosphere in each of the four candlelit dining rooms in this renovated Cape Cod–style house. You might begin with a salad of mixed greens, sliced beets, and pears with blue cheese crumbled on top. For your entrée, choose from among dishes such as medal-

lions of beef and goat cheese with shoelace potatoes, or pork tenderloin with sweet cherries in a port-wine reduction. The specials and fresh fish dishes are superb, as are the crab cakes. Be sure to save room for a dessert, such as lemon mousse or wonderfully creamy cheesecake. A take-out lunch menu is available at the adjacent Moveable Feasts deli, where the Vinery serves drinks and tapas in the evening. ⊠ *33 Tenney Hill* ☎ *207/374–2119* ⊟ *AE, DC, MC, V* ⊗ *Closed Mon. and Tues. Sept.–June. No lunch.*

$$$–$$$$ 📺 **Blue Hill Inn.** This rambling inn dating from 1830 is a comfortable
★   place to relax after climbing Blue Hill mountain or exploring nearby shops and galleries. Original pumpkin pine and painted floors set the tone for the mix of Empire and early-Victorian pieces that fill the two parlors and guest rooms, several of which have working fireplaces. One of the nicest rooms is No. 8, which has exposures on three sides and views of the flower gardens and apple trees. Two rooms have antique claw-foot tubs perfect for soaking. The spacious Cape House Suite (available after the rest of the inn has closed for the season) has a bed as well as two pullout sofas, a full kitchen, and a private deck. The inn has a bar offering an ample selection of wines and whiskies. Here you can enjoy appetizers before you head out to dinner or try specialty coffees and liqueurs when you return. **Pro:** the bedroom fireplaces and the antique floorboards make you want to stay here forever. **Cons:** rooms are on the small side, and the walls are thin. ⊠ *40 Union St.,* ☎ *207/374–2844 or 800/826–7415* ⊕ *www.bluehillinn.com* 🛏 *11 rooms, 1 suite* ♿ *In-room: no phone, no TV. In-hotel: bar, no elevator, public Internet, no-smoking rooms* ⊟ *AE, MC, V* 🍴 *BP.*

EN ROUTE   Offering kayakers surfable currents when the tide is running full force, **Blue Hill falls** is a reversing falls on Route 175 between Blue Hill and Brooklin. Water flowing in and out of the salt pond from Blue Hill bay roars in and out under the Stevens Bridge. See it by foot or by kayak (use extreme caution, especially with children, on the bridge itself as the hydraulic roar drowns out the sound of oncoming motorists). ⊠ *Rte. 175 south of Blue Hill.*

SEDGWICK, BROOKLIN & BROOKSVILLE

Winding through the hills, the roads leading to the villages of Sedgwick, Brooklin, and Brooksville take you past rambling farmhouses, beautiful ocean coves, and blueberry fields with the occasional mass of granite. It's a perfect leisurely drive, ideal for a Sunday afternoon.

Incorporated in 1798, **Sedgwick** runs along much of Eggemoggin Reach, the body of water that separates the mainland from Deer Isle, Little Deer Island, and Stonington. The village of **Brooklin,** originally part of Sedgwick, established itself as an independent town in 1849. Today, it is home to the world-famous Wooden Boat School, a 64-acre oceanfront campus offering courses in woodworking, boatbuilding, and seamanship. The town of **Brooksville,** incorporated in 1817, is almost completely surrounded by water, with Eggemoggin Reach, Walker Pond, and the Bagaduce River marking its boundaries.

WHAT TO SEE

Blue Poppy Garden. Gardens filled with brightly colored poppies, as well as lovely perennials, are the attraction here. A nature trail winds through the woods past native plants identified by small signs. There's a dining room that serves lunch and afternoon tea in July and August. At the gift shop you can purchase blue poppy plants and seeds. ⊠*1000 Reach Rd., Sedgwick* ☎*207/359–8392* ⊕*www.bluepoppygarden.com* ☎*Free* ☉*Mid-May–mid-Oct.*

SHOPPING

The **Gallery at Caterpillar Hill** (⊠*328 Caterpillar Hill Rd.* ☎*207/359–4600*) is a spectacular refuge for looking at landscape paintings and other artifacts competing, sometimes successfully, with the Penobscot Bay panorama out the window. On Rte. 15 just north of Caterpillar Hill, **Old Cove Antiques** (⊠*106 Caterpillar Hill Rd.* ☎*207/359–8585*) specializes in antique furniture, quilts, wood carvings and more.

WHERE TO EAT & STAY

$$
Fodor's Choice
★
AMERICAN
✕**Buck's.** Popular among cruisers mooring in Buck's Harbor, this fine dining gem is behind **Buck's Harbor Market,** itself a key food destination for its wines, cheeses, olive oils, and sandwiches. Jonathan Chase, formerly of the Pilgrim's Inn in Deer Isle Village, has put together a superlative and constantly changing market-based menu strong in local ingredients, starring fresh fish, scallops, duck, and lamb. The seared duck breast with cranberries, beer, and maple barbecue sauce is a favorite, as are the sautéed sea scallops. The restaurant has a reasonably priced, carefully selected wine list and a deck for outdoor dining in summer. ⊠*6 Cornfield Hill Rd., at Rte. 176, South Brooksville* ☎*207/326–8683* ▤*MC, V* ☉*Closed Sun.–Tues. Sept.–June.*

$–$$
★
▥**Brooklin Inn.** A comfortable yet elegant atmosphere distinguishes this B&B in downtown Brooklin. There are plenty of homey touches like hardwood floors and an upstairs deck. The sunny rooms have attractive bureaus and beds piled with cozy quilts. The restaurant ($$–$$$$) specializes in fresh fish and locally raised beef, poultry, and lamb. It also has fine soups, salads, and desserts worth saving room for. In summer you can dine on the enclosed porch. An Irish pub downstairs showcases local musicians most Saturday nights. **Pro:** bedroom fireplaces and the antique floorboards make you want to stay here forever. **Cons:** rooms are small, walls are paper thin. ⊠*Rte. 175, Brooklin* ☎*207/359–2777* ⊕*www.brooklininn.com* ▧*5 rooms, 3 with bath* ⅋*In-room: no a/c, no phone, no TV. In-hotel: restaurant, no elevator, no-smoking rooms* ▤*AE, D, DC, MC, V* ⍜*BP.*

DEER ISLE VILLAGE

16 mi south of Blue Hill.

Around Deer Isle Village, thick woods give way to tidal coves. Stacks of lobster traps populate the backyards of shingled houses, and dirt roads lead to secluded summer cottages. This region is prized by artists, and studios and galleries are plentiful.

WHAT TO SEE

Haystack Mountain School of Crafts. People of all skill levels can sign up for two- and three-week-long courses in crafts such as blacksmithing, basketry, printmaking, and weaving. Artisans from around the world present evening lectures throughout summer (*see Blue Heron Gallery in Shopping to learn about buying their work*). You can take a free tour of the facility at 1 PM on Wednesday, June through September. In autumn, shorter courses are available to New England residents. The school is 6 mi from Deer Isle Village, off Route 15. ⊠*89 Haystack School Dr., Deer Isle* ☎*207/348–2306* ⊕*www.haystack-mtn.org.*

SPORTS & THE OUTDOORS

While enjoying miles of woodland and shore trails at the **Edgar M. Tennis Preserve** (⊠*Tennis Rd. off Sunshine Rd., Deer Isle* ☎*No phone* ☞ *Free* ☉*Daily dawn–dusk*), you can look for hawks, eagles, and ospreys, and wander among old apple trees and fields of wildflowers. A mixture of hard- and soft-wood trees, including birch, oak, maple, and white pine, make an excellent habitat for songbirds at **Shore Acres Preserve** (⊠ *Greenlaw District Rd. off Sunshine Rd., Deer Isle* ☎*No phone* ☞*Free* ☉*Daily dawn–dusk*) on the eastern edge of Deer Isle. On a 1½-mi walking trail you can see native plants like juniper, blueberry, and cranberry, as well as mushrooms, mosses, and ferns. You might even spot a fox, red squirrel, or hawk.

SHOPPING

Purchase a handmade quilt from **Dockside Quilt Gallery** (⊠*33 Church St.* ☎*207/348–2849 or 207/348–2531* ⊕*www.docksidequiltgallery. com*). If you don't see anything you like, you can commission a custom-designed quilt. **Nervous Nellie's Jams and Jellies** (⊠*598 Sunshine Rd.* ☎*207/348–6182 or 800/777–6825* ⊕*www.nervousnellies.com*) sells jams and jellies, operates the Mountain View café, and has a sculpture garden with work by Peter Beerits.

WHERE TO STAY

$$–$$$ ▦ **Pilgrim's Inn.** A four-story gambrel-roof house, this inn dates from
  ★   about 1793. Wing chairs and Oriental rugs fill the library; a downstairs taproom has a huge brick fireplace and pine furniture. Individually furnished guest rooms—each filled with quilts, some with exposed beams and supports, others with canopy frames overhead—overlook a mill pond and harbor. Three cottages—Rugosa Rose, Ginny's One, and Ginny's Two—are perfect for families. The dining room ($$$–$$$$) is rustic yet elegant with exposed beams, hardwood floors, and French oil lamps. Try an appetizer of ouzo-flamed gulf shrimp with black olives and feta or a warm salad of spinach, smoked mussels, goat cheese, and pine nuts. For the main course, you can try traditional boiled Maine lobster, or go for something entirely different like sautéed venison with shiitake mushrooms. Be sure to save room for desserts like the mocha mousse. **Pros:** memorable architecture and early-American interior, an oasis of fine cuisine. **Cons:** creaky floors, squeaky bedsprings, and only adequate bathrooms. ⊠*20 Main St.* ☎*207/348–6615 or 888/778–7505* ⊕*www.pilgrimsinn.com* ⇆*12 rooms, 3 cottages* ﹠*In-room: no a/c, no phone, no TV. In-hotel: restaurant, bicycles, no elevator,*

some pets allowed, no-smoking rooms $\equiv$*AE, D, MC, V* $\odot$*Closed mid-Oct.–mid-May* $\lceil\odot\rceil$*BP.*

STONINGTON

7 mi south of Deer Isle.

Stonington is rather isolated, which has helped retain its small-town flavor. The boutiques and galleries lining Main Street cater mostly to out-of-towners, but the town remains a fishing community at heart. The principal activity is at the waterfront, where boats arrive overflowing with the day's catch. The sloped island that rises to the south is Isle au Haut, which contains a remote section of Acadia National Park; it's accessible by mail boat from Stonington.

WHAT TO SEE

Deer Isle Granite Museum. This tiny museum documents Stonington's quarrying tradition. The centerpiece is an 8- by 15-foot working model of quarrying operations on Crotch Island and the town of Stonington at the turn of the last century. $\boxtimes$*51 Main St.* $\textcircled{2}$*207/367–6331* $\boxtimes$*Free* $\odot$*Memorial Day–Labor Day, Mon.–Sat. 10–5, Sun. 1–5.*

Settlement Quarry. Once a busy mine employing hundreds of men, Settlement Quarry closed in the 1980s. Visit the grounds for the panoramic views and easy walking trails. $\boxtimes$*Off Oceanville Rd.* $\boxtimes$*Free* $\odot$*Daily.*

OFF THE
BEATEN
PATH

Off-Shore Islands. Many of the uninhabited islands near Deer Isle and Stonington are open for public use. One of the most popular is Green Island, which has an old quarry that is perfect for swimming. Some are for day-use only, while others allow overnight camping. All of these islands operate on a "leave no trace" basis, meaning that you must stay on marked trails and carry out what you carry in. For more information, contact **Island Heritage Trust** ($\boxtimes$*3 Main St.,* $\textcircled{D}$*Box 42, Deer Isle 04627* $\textcircled{2}$*207/348–2455*) or the **Maine Island Trail Association** ($\boxtimes$*328 Main St., Box C, Rockland 04841* $\textcircled{2}$*207/596–6456* $\oplus$*www.mita.org*)

SPORTS & THE OUTDOORS

Old Quarry Ocean Adventures ($\boxtimes$*130 Settlement Rd.* $\textcircled{2}$*207/367–8977* $\oplus$*www.oldquarry.com*) rents bicycles, canoes, and kayaks, and offers guided tours of the bay. Captain Bill Baker's three-hour boat tours take you past Stonington Harbor on the way to the outer islands. You can see Crotch Island, which has the area's only active stone quarry, and Green Island, where you can take a dip in a water-filled quarry. Tours cover the region's natural history, the history of Stonington, and the history of the granite industry. Sunset cruises are also available.

SHOPPING

Art and antiques are for sale at the **Clown** ($\boxtimes$*6 Thurlow's Hill* $\textcircled{2}$*207/367–6348*), as are specialty foods and wine. Facing the harbor, **Dockside Books & Gifts** ($\boxtimes$*62 W. Main St.* $\textcircled{2}$*207/367–2652*) stocks an eclectic selection of books.

WHERE TO EAT & STAY

$–$$ ✕**Lily's.** Homemade baked goods,
★ delicious sandwiches, and fresh
AMERICAN salads are on the menu at this
friendly café. Try the Italian turkey sandwich, which has slices
of oven-roasted turkey and Jack
cheese on homemade sourdough
bread. The dining room's glass-
top tables reveal the seashells
and various treasures inside. A

WORD OF MOUTH

Stonington is a real lobster village and very, very remote. The
scenery is gorgeous and [Janu-
ary] is the most quiet time of the
year...some fish year-round, but
the fleet will have thinned out.
–bassharborbaby

produce stand behind the restaurant sells some of the same organic
foods used by the chefs here. ✉*Corner of Rte. 15 and Airport Rd.*
☎*207/367–5936* ▤*MC, V.*

CAMPING ⛺**Old Quarry Campground.** This oceanfront campground offers both
$$–$$$ open and wooded campsites with raised platforms for tents, table,
chairs, and fire rings. Carts are available to tote your gear to your site.
Another property, Sunshine Campground, is on Deer Isle. **Pro:** campsites on the water with spectacular views. **Con:** somewhat uproarious
in the height of summer when fully booked. ✉*130 Settlement Rd.,
off Oceanville Rd.* ☎*207/367–8977* ⊕*www.oldquarry.com* ⛺*10 tent
sites* ⚲*Flush toilets, drinking water, guest laundry, showers, public
telephone, general store, swimming* ▤*MC, V* ☉*Closed Nov.–Apr.*

ISLE AU HAUT

14 mi south of Stonington.

Isle au Haut thrusts its steeply ridged back out of the sea south of
Stonington. French explorer Samuel D. Champlain discovered Isle au
Haut—or "High Island"—in 1604, but heaps of shells suggest that
native populations lived on or visited the island prior to his arrival.
The island is accessible only by mail boat, but the 45-minute journey
is well worth the effort. As you pass between the tiny islands of Merchants Row, you might see terns, guillemots, and harbor seals. The
ferry makes two trips a day between Stonington and the Town Landing
from Monday to Saturday, and adds a Sunday trip from mid-May to
mid-September. From mid-June to mid-September, the ferry also stops
at Duck Harbor, located within Acadia National Park. The ferry will
not unload bicycles, kayaks, or canoes at Duck Harbor, however.

Except for a grocery store and a natural-foods store, Isle au Haut does
not have any opportunities for shopping. The island is ideal for day-
trippers intent on exploring its miles of trails, or those seeking a night
or two of low-key accommodations and delicious homemade meals.

SPORTS & THE OUTDOORS

There's no place to rent bicycles on Isle au Haut. If you want to bike
around the island, head to **Old Quarry Ocean Adventures** (✉*130 Settlement Rd., Stonington* ☎*207/367–8977* ⊕*www.oldquarry.com*). The
mainland company can transport you and your bikes to Isle au Haut.

WHERE TO STAY

$$$$ 🏠 **Inn at Isle au Haut.** This sea captain's home from 1897 retains its architectural charm. On the eastern side of the island, the seaside inn has views of sheep roaming around distant York Island and Cadillac Mountain. Comfortable wicker furniture is scattered around the porch, where appetizers are served when the weather is good. Downstairs, the dining room has original oil lamps and a model of the sea captain's boat (which sank just offshore). Breakfast includes granola and a hot dish like a spinach, tomato, and cheese frittata. Dinner is an elaborate five-course meal usually incorporating local seafood. One night a week the inn has a lobster bake on the shore. The first-floor Captain's Quarters, the only room with a private bath, has an ocean view, as do two of the three upstairs rooms. All have colorful quilts and frilly canopies. **Pros:** nonpareil views and first-class dining. **Cons:** shared baths, thin walls. ⊠ *78 Atlantic Ave.,* ☎ *207/335–5141* ⊕ *www.innatisleauhaut. com* 🛏 *4 rooms, 1 with bath* ⚐ *In-room: no a/c, no phone, no TV. In-hotel: bicycles, no elevator, no-smoking rooms* ⊟ *No credit cards* ⏱ *Closed Oct.–May* ⍾ *FAP.*

MOUNT DESERT ISLAND & ACADIA NATIONAL PARK

By Stephen and Neva Allen

With some of the most dramatic and varied scenery on the Maine Coast, and home to Maine's one and only national park, Mount Desert (pronounced "Mount Dessert" by locals) Island, it's no wonder this is Maine's most popular tourist destination, attracting more than 2 million visitors a year. Much of the approximately 12-mi-long by 9-mi-wide island belongs to Acadia National Park. The rocky coastline rises starkly from the ocean, appreciable along the scenic drives. Trails for hikers of all skill levels lead to the rounded tops of the mountains, providing views of Frenchman and Blue Hill bays, and beyond. Ponds and lakes beckon you to swim, fish, or boat. Ferries and charter boats provide a different perspective on the island and a chance to explore the outer islands, all of which are a part of Maine but not a part of Mount Desert. A network of old carriage roads lets you explore Acadia's wooded interior, filled with birds and other wildlife.

Mount Desert Island has four different townships, each with its own personality. The town of Bar Harbor is on the northeastern corner of the island, and includes Bar Harbor and the little villages of Hulls Cove, Salisbury Cove, and Town Hill. The town of Mount Desert comprises the southeastern corner of the island and parts of the western edge, and includes Mount Desert and the little villages of Somesville, Hall Quarry, Beech Hill, Pretty Marsh, Northeast Harbor, Seal Harbor, and Otter Creek. As its name suggests, the town of Southwest Harbor is on the southwestern corner of the island, although the town of Tremont is at the southernmost tip of the west side. This area includes the villages of Southwest Harbor, Manset, Bass Harbor, Bernard, and Seal Cove. The island's major tourist destination is Bar Harbor, which has plenty of accommodations, restaurants, and shops. Less congested are the smaller communities of Northeast Harbor, Southwest Harbor, and Bass Harbor. Mount Desert Island is a place with three personalities: the hustling, bustling tourist mecca of Bar Harbor, the "quiet side" of the island composed of the little villages, and the vast natural expanse that is Acadia National Park.

Acadia's Park Loop Road provides an excellent overview of the island, but to get a feel for the island's natural beauty, you must leave your car behind. Instead, seek as many opportunities as you can for hiking, biking, and boating. And while Bar Harbor is the best-known town on Mount Desert Island, there's plenty to see and do around the entire island. Take a scenic drive along Sargent Drive for spectacular views of Somes Sound—the only fjord on the East Coast. Visit the villages of Northeast Harbor, Somesville, and Southwest Harbor, each with its own unique character. The west side of the island—also known as the "back side" or the "quiet side"—has its own restaurants and accommodations. To get a unique perspective of the island, take a cruise. Away from the crowds and traffic, you'll have plenty of time to discover some of the island's less-obvious charms.

> ### FUN THINGS TO DO ON MOUNT DESERT ISLAND
>
> ■ Take the circle drive through Acadia National Park.
>
> ■ Hike—or drive—to the 1,532-foot top of Cadillac Mountain for a spectacular view.
>
> ■ Climb down the rocks to the edge of the ocean to shoot the most photographed lighthouse in Maine, Bass Harbor Head Light.
>
> ■ Hop a ride on The CAT (high-speed catamaran) from Bar Harbor to Nova Scotia, Canada.

In Mount Desert Island, the free **Island Explorer (Downeast Transportation)** (☎ 207/667–5796 ⊕ *www.exploreacadia.com*) shuttle service circles the island from the end of May to September, with limited service continuing through mid-October. Buses, which are equipped with racks for bicycles, service the major campgrounds, Acadia National Park, and Trenton's Hancock County–Bar Harbor Airport. They also run from Bar Harbor to Ellsworth.

BAR HARBOR

160 mi northeast of Portland, 22 mi southeast of Ellsworth.

★ A resort town since the 19th century, Bar Harbor is the artistic, culinary, and social center of Mount Desert Island. It also serves visitors to Acadia National Park with inns, motels, and restaurants. The island's unique topography was shaped by the glaciers of the most recent Ice Age. Around the turn of the last century—before the days of air-conditioning—the island was known as the summer haven of the very rich because of its cool breezes; lavish mansions were built throughout the island. Many of them were destroyed in a great fire that devastated the island in 1947, but many of those that survived have been converted into businesses. Shops are clustered along Main, Mount Desert, and Cottage streets. Take a stroll down West Street, a National Historic District, where you can see some fine old houses.

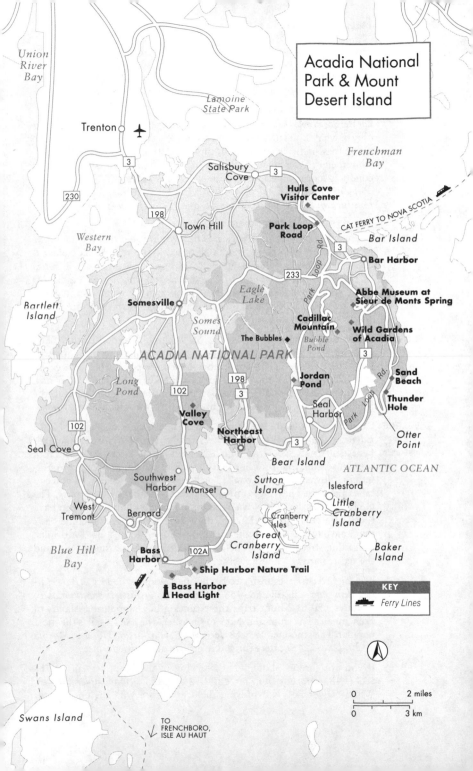

Acadia National Park & Mount Desert Island

Union River Bay

Lamoine State Park

Trenton

Frenchman Bay

230

Salisbury Cove

3

Hulls Cove Visitor Center

3

Park Loop Road

CAT FERRY TO NOVA SCOTIA

Bar Island

198

Town Hill

Bar Harbor

Western Bay

233

Somesville

Eagle Lake

Abbe Museum at Sieur de Monts Spring

Bartlett Island

Somes Sound

Cadillac Mountain

Wild Gardens of Acadia

The Bubbles

Bubble Pond

ACADIA NATIONAL PARK

3

Long Pond

102

198

Jordan Pond

Sand Beach

3

Thunder Hole

Seal Harbor

102

Valley Cove

3

Otter Point

Seal Cove

Northeast Harbor

3

Bear Island

ATLANTIC OCEAN

Sutton Island

Islesford

Southwest Harbor

Manset

Little Cranberry Island

West Tremont

Bernard

Cranberry Isles

Great Cranberry Island

Baker Island

Blue Hill Bay

Bass Harbor

102A

Ship Harbor Nature Trail

Bass Harbor Head Light

0   2 miles

0   3 km

Swans Island

TO FRENCHBORO, ISLE AU HAUT

The island and its surrounding Gulf of Maine are home to a great variety of wildlife: whales, seals, eagles, falcons, ospreys, puffins (probably the most unusual-looking birds in the world), and denizens of the forest, such as moose, deer, foxes, coyotes, and black bears.

WHAT TO SEE

☾ **Bar Harbor Whale Museum.** Learn about the history of whaling, the anatomy of whales, and how biologists are working to gain more information about these massive creatures at this interesting museum. All proceeds from the gift shop benefit Allied Whale, a nonprofit organization that conducts marine mammal research. ⊠*52 West St.* ☎*207/288–0288* ⊕*www.barharborwhalemuseum.org* ⊠*Free* ⊗*June, daily 10 am–8 pm; July and Aug., daily 9–9; Sept. and Oct., 10 am–8 pm.*

SPORTS & THE OUTDOORS

AIR TOURS   There are few places in America as beautiful to see from the air as the
★   Mount Desert Island and Acadia National Park areas. **Scenic Biplane & Glider Rides Over Bar Harbor** (⊠*968 Bar Harbor Rd. [Rt. 3], Trenton* ☎*207/667–7627* ⊕*www.acadiaairtours.com*) is a part of Acadia Air Tours and provides exactly what the name suggests: biplane and glider rides over Bar Harbor and Acadia National Park. It also offers helicopter tours.

BICYCLING   **Acadia Bike Rentals** (⊠*48 Cottage St.* ☎*207/288–9605 or 800/526–8615*) rents mountain bikes good for negotiating the trails in Acadia National Park. The **Bar Harbor Bicycle Shop** (⊠*141 Cottage St.* ☎*207/288–3886 or 800/824–2453*) rents bikes by the half- or full day. **Caution:** Riding a bike around Bar Harbor is fun, but be careful; the town is full of gawking tourists, and many of the streets are narrow.

BOATING   Surely, the best boat excursions…must be the rides on **The CAT** (⊠*12*
☾   *Eden St.* ☎*888/249–7245* ⊕*www.catferry.com*), North America's
Fodor's Choice   fastest international ferry. This is a high-speed (55 mph) catamaran
★   that, in season, jets from Bar Harbor across the Gulf of Maine to Yarmouth, Nova Scotia, and back. You can do it all in one day, or you can take one of the one- or two-night package trips that include tours. The CAT can whisk you to Nova Scotia in a mere 2¾ hours. You can have lunch at a waterside restaurant, do a little shopping, and come back the same day. On board, you will find a café for food, a bar for drinks, and a duty-free gift shop. The morning departure is around 7:45, and the returns are at 1 and 8:30 PM.

☾   The big 151-foot four-masted schooner **Margaret Todd** (⊠*Bar Har-*
★   *bor Inn Pier* ☎*207/288–4585* ⊕*www.downeastwindjammer.com*) operates 1½- to 2-hour trips three times a day among the islands of Frenchman's Bay from mid-May to October. The sunset sail is the most popular. The schooner **Rachel B. Jackson** (⊠*Harborside Hotel & Marina* ☎*207/288–2216*) offers three-day cruises and sunset cruises.

☾   If you are curious about what's lurking in the deep, set sail on **The Seal** (⊠*Bar Harbor Inn Pier* ☎*207/288–3483* ⊕*www.divered.com*). While "Diver Ed" is exploring the sea bottom with his underwater video camera, you can see what he finds by watching an LCD screen on the boat; also get an up-close look at the creatures he brings back.

WHALE-
WATCHING
There are two truly unique experiences you can have at Bar Harbor, and both of them are ideal for family outings. One is a trip on the fast CAT boat to Nova Scotia. The other, also at sea, is whale-watching.

☾ **Bar Harbor Whale Watch Co.** (⊠*1 West St.* ☎*207/288–2386 or 800/*
★ *WHALES–4 (800/942–5374)* ⊕*www.whalesrus.com*) merged with the Acadian Whale Watcher to make one big company with four boats, one of them a 138-foot jet-propelled catamaran with spacious decks. In season, the outfit also offers a lobster-fishing and seal-watching cruise, a nature cruise, and a puffin-watching cruise. How likely are you to actually see a whale? Very. In fact, the company can practically guarantee it—they apparently have some sort of arrangement with the whales.

SHOPPING

★ Bar Harbor is a shoppers paradise, but not necessarily for bargains. Tourism shoppers not only come from the land, they also come from the sea, since some cruise ships, including very large ones like the *Queen Elizabeth,* have made this a destination. (Imagine how delighted the store owners are to see her arrive, with thousands of passengers!)

ARTWORK
Fodor'sChoice
★
Paint your own pottery or piece together a mosaic at **All Fired Up** (⊠*101 Cottage St.* ☎*207/288–3130* ⊕*www.acadiaallfiredup.com*). The gallery also sells glass sculptures, pendants, paintings, and pottery. The **Alone Moose Fine Crafts** (⊠*78 West St.* ☎*207/288–4229*) is the oldest made-in-Maine gallery on the island. It offers bronze wildlife sculpture, jewelry, pottery, and watercolors. The **Eclipse Gallery** (⊠*12 Mount Desert St.* ☎*207/288–9048*) carries handblown glass, ceramics, and wood furniture. **Island Artisans** (⊠*99 Main St.* ☎*207/288–4214*) sells basketry, pottery, fiber work, and jewelry created by more than 100 of Maine's artisans. The gallery is a co-op owned and operated by the artists. **Native Arts Gallery** (⊠*99 Main St.* ☎*207/288–4474* ⊕*www. nativeartsgallery.com*) sells American Indian silver and gold jewelry.

SPORTING
GOODS
One of the best sporting-goods stores in the state, **Cadillac Mountain Sports** (⊠*28 Cottage St.* ☎*207/288–4532* ⊕*www.cadillacmountainsports.com*), has developed a following of locals and visitors alike. You can find top-quality climbing, hiking, and camping equipment. In winter you can rent cross-country skis, ice skates, and snowshoes. **Michael H. Graves Antiques** (⊠*10 Albert Meadow* ☎*207/288–3830*) specializes in maps and books focusing on Mount Desert Island.

TREATS
Ben and Bill's Chocolate Emporium (⊠*66 Main St.* ☎*207/288–3281*) is a chocolate lover's nirvana. It also has more than 20 flavors of ice cream, including the popular KGB (Kahlua, Grand Marnier, and Bailey's).

NIGHTLIFE & THE ARTS

★ The **Bar Harbor Music Festival** (⊠*59 Cottage St.* ☎*207/288–5744*) hosts jazz, classical, and pop concerts by young professionals from July to early August at the Criterion Theater. It has recently started including one opera every season and has done *La Bohème* and *La Traviata.*

WHERE TO EAT

$$–$$$
SEAFOOD

✕**Quarterdeck.** If you would like to dine while enjoying a view of the colorful harbor, head here. The majority of menu items are seafood—a good choice is the baked stuffed lobster. If you like your seafood uncooked, take a look at the raw bar, which overflows with oysters. ✉*1 Main St.* ☎*207/288–1161* ▤*AE, DC, MC, V.*

$$$–$$$$
Fodor'sChoice
★
CONTINENTAL

✕**Reading Room at the Bar Harbor Inn & Spa.** This elegant waterfront restaurant serves mostly Continental fare. Look for Maine specialties such as lobster pie and Indian pudding. There's live music nightly. When the weather is nice, what could be more romantic than dining out under the stars at the inn's Terrace Grille with the ships of beautiful Bar Harbor right at your feet? The natural thing to order here would be the Maine lobster bake with all the fixings. For something different, you might try the lobster stew, which is served in a bread bowl. The restaurant is also famous for its Sunday brunch, 11:30–2:30. ✉*Newport Dr.* ☎*207/288–3351 or 800/248–3351* ⌁*Reservations essential* ▤*AE, DC, MC, V* ✆*Closed late Nov.–late Mar.*

ACADIA LEAF PEEPING

The fall foliage in Maine can be spectacular. Because of the moisture, the fall foliage comes later along the coast than it does in the interior of the state. In the interior, it's usually the last week of September, whereas along the coast, it's usually around the middle of October. The best way to catch the colors along the coast is travel on the Acadia National Park Loop Road. In fall 2007, the National Park Service placed Acadia National Park on its fall foliage list of "The 10 Best Places in the U.S. to Take Photographs." For up-to-date information, go online to www.mainefoliage.com.

WHERE TO STAY

$$$–$$$$
Fodor'sChoice
★

🏨**Bar Harbor Inn & Spa.** Originally established in the late 1800s as a men's social club, this waterfront inn has rooms spread out over three buildings on well-landscaped grounds. Most rooms have gas fireplaces and balconies with great views. Rooms in the Oceanfront Lodge have private decks overlooking the ocean. Many rooms in the main inn have balconies overlooking the harbor. Should you need more room, there are also some two-level suites. A relatively new addition to the inn is a luxury spa, which offers everything from massages and mud wraps to aroma therapy and facials. The inn is a short walk from town, so you're close to all the sights, and a terrific restaurant, the Reading Room, is on-site *(⇨ Where to Eat)*. **Pros:** this is one of those resort hotels that truly seems to meet every need, plus it's right at the harbor. **Con:** not as close to Acadia National Park as some other Bar Harbor properties, though still just a short drive. ✉*Newport Dr.* ☎*207/288–3351 or 800/248–3351* ⊕*www.barharborinn.com* ↝*138 rooms, 15 suites* ⌖*In-room: safe, refrigerator, DVD. In-hotel: 2 restaurants, pool, gym, no-smoking rooms* ▤*AE, DC, MC, V* ✆*Closed late Nov.–late Mar.* ⍟*CP.*

$$–$$$$

🏨**Bluenose Inn–Bar Harbor Hotel.** This resort is perched on the top of a hill overlooking Frenchman Bay. Most of the guest rooms have excellent views, and all of them have gas fireplaces. After touring Acadia

National Park, you can relax in the hotel's hot tub or steam room, or swim a few laps in the indoor or outdoor pool. Fine dining is provided at the Rose Garden restaurant ($$$$), which features seafood and beef entrées on the three-course prix-fixe and five-course tasting menus. To start, try the strudel filled with asparagus or the Maine lobster bisque. For the main entrée, order North Atlantic salmon, Maine lobster, rack of lamb, or the pan-seared venison steak. Finally, choose from desserts such as a warm apple tart, vanilla-bean crème brûlée, or flourless chocolate cake. **Pros:** spectacular views of the bay and outer islands, wonderful on-site dining. **Con:** a bit of a hike to town (you'll probably want to drive). ⊠*90 Eden St.04609* ☎*207/288–3348 or 800/445–4077* ⊕*www.bluenoseinn.com* ⊲*97 rooms, 1 suite* ⚬*In-room: safe, refrigerator, DVD. In-hotel: 2 restaurants, bar, pools, gym, public Internet. In-room: Wi-Fi, no-smoking rooms* ▭*AE, D, DC, MC, V* ☉*Closed Nov.–late Apr.*

ACADIA NATIONAL PARK

4 mi northwest of Bar Harbor.

Fodor's Choice
★

With more than 30,000 acres of protected forests, beaches, mountains, and rocky coastline, Acadia National Park is the second-most-visited national park in America (the first is the Great Smoky Mountains National Park). According to the national park service, more than 2.2 million people visit Acadia each year. The park holds some of the most spectacular scenery on the eastern seaboard: a rugged coastline of surf-pounded granite, and an interior graced by sculpted mountains, quiet ponds, and lush deciduous forests. Cadillac Mountain (named after an American Indian, not the car), the highest point of land on the Eastern Coast, dominates the park. Although it's rugged, Acadia National Park also has graceful stone bridges, horse-drawn carriages, and the elegant Jordan Pond House restaurant.

The 27-mi Park Loop Road provides an excellent introduction, but to truly appreciate the park, you must get off the main road and experience it by walking, biking, sea kayaking, or taking a carriage ride. If you get off the beaten path, you can find places you can have practically to yourself. Mount Desert Island was once the site of summer homes for the very rich (still is for some), and, because of this, Acadia is the only national park in America that was largely created by the donations of private land. A small part of the park is on the Isle au Haut, which is out in the ocean and more than 10 mi away.

PARK ESSENTIALS

Admission Fee. A user fee is required if you are anywhere in the park. The fee is $20 per vehicle for a seven-consecutive-day pass. Or use your National Park America the Beautiful Pass, which allows entrance to any national park in the United States. See www.nps.gov for details.

Admission Hours. The park is open 24 hours a day, year-round, though the roads often are closed in winter because of snow. Operating hours are 8 AM–4:30 PM April 15–October and until 6 PM in July and August.

Camping. There are more than 500 campsites in the park. Ask for a guide at the Hulls Cove Visitor Center. Blackwoods Campground has 16 wheelchair-accessible sites. There are no hook-ups, though some sites can fit RVs.

Pets. Pets are allowed at all park locations, but they must be on leashes no longer than six feet.

Visitor Information. ⓓ*Acadia National Park, Box 177, Bar Harbor 04609* ☎*207/288–3338* ⊕*www.nps.gov/acad.*

WHAT TO SEE

HISTORIC SITES & MUSEUMS

★ **Bass Harbor Head Light.** Originally built in 1858, this lighthouse is one of the most photographed in Maine. The light, now automated, marks the entrance to Blue Hill Bay. The grounds and residence are Coast Guard property, but two trails around the facility provide excellent views. ■**TIP→ The best place to take a picture of this small but beautiful lighthouse is from the rocks below—but watch your step, they can be slippery.** ⊠*Rte. 102, halfway between Tremont and Manset Bass Harbor* 🖃*Free* ⊙*Daily 9–sunset.*

SCENIC DRIVES & STOPS

★ **Cadillac Mountain.** At 1,532 feet, this is the first place in America to see the sun's rays at break of day. It is the highest mountain on the eastern seaboard north of Brazil. Dozens of visitors make the trek to see the sunrise or, for those less inclined to get up so early, sunset. From the smooth summit you have an awesome 360-degree view of the jagged coastline that runs around the island. Decades ago a train took visitors to a hotel at the summit. Today a small gift shop and some rest rooms are the only structures at the top. The road up the mountain is generally closed from the end of October through March because of snow.

Ⓒ **Park Loop Road.** This 27-mi road provides a perfect introduction to the
★ park. You can do it in an hour, but allow at least half a day or more for the drive so that you can explore the many sites along the way. Traveling south on Park Loop Road toward Sand Beach, you'll reach a small ticket booth, where, if you haven't already, you will need to pay the park's good-for-seven-consecutive-days $20 entrance fee (the fee is not charged from November through April). Traffic is one-way from the Route 233 entrance to the Stanley Brook Road entrance south of the Jordan Pond House. The section known as Ocean Drive is open year-round.

VISITOR CENTER

Ⓒ At the Hulls Cove entrance to Acadia National Park, northwest of Bar Harbor on Route 3, the **Hulls Cove Visitor Center,** operated by the National Park Service, is a great spot to get your bearings. A large relief map of Mount Desert Island

---

BOOK A CARRIAGE RIDE

If you would like to take a horse-drawn carriage ride down one of these roads, from mid-June to mid-October, you can do so by making a reservation with Wildwood Stables (☎207/276–3622). Two of their carriages can accommodate two wheelchairs each.

gives you the lay of the land, and you can watch a free 15-minute video about everything the park has to offer. Pick up guidebooks, maps of hiking trails and carriage roads, schedules for naturalist-led tours, and recordings for drive-it-yourself tours. Don't forget the *Acadia Beaver Log*, the park's free newspaper detailing guided hikes and other ranger-led events. Junior-ranger programs for kids, nature hikes, photography walks, tide-pool explorations,

> **CAUTION**
>
> A couple of people a year fall off one of the park's trails or cliffs and are swept out to sea. There is a lot of loose, rocky gravel along the shoreline, and sea rocks can often be slippery—so watch your step. Don't bring a sudden end to your visit by trying to get that "impossible" photo op.

and evening talks are all popular. The visitor center is off Route 3 at Park Loop Road. ⊠ *Park Loop Rd., Hulls Cove* ☎ *207/288–3338* ⊕ *www. nps.gov/acad* ⊙ *Mid-June–Aug., daily 8–6; mid-Apr.–mid-June, Sept., and Oct., daily 8–4:30.*

The **Acadia National Park Headquarters** is on Route 233 in the park not far from the north end of Eagle Lake. It serves as the park's visitor center during the off-season.

SPORTS & THE OUTDOORS

The best way to see Acadia National Park is to get out of your vehicle and explore by foot, bicycle, or boat. There are more than 40 mi of carriage roads that are perfect for walking and biking in the warmer months, and cross-country skiing and snowshoeing in winter. There are more than 115 mi for hiking, numerous ponds and lakes for canoeing or kayaking, two beaches for swimming, and steep cliffs for rock climbing.

HIKING Acadia National Park maintains more than 120 mi of hiking paths, from easy strolls around lakes and ponds to rigorous treks with climbs up rock faces and scrambles along cliffs. Although most hiking trails are on the east side of the island, the west side also has some scenic trails. For those wishing for a long climb, try the trails leading up Cadillac Mountain or Dorr Mountain. Another option is to climb Parkman, Sargeant, and Penobscot mountains. Most of the hiking is done from mid-May to mid-October. Snow falls early in Maine, so from late October to the end of March, cross-country skiing and snowshoeing replace hiking.

■ TIP➔ **The Hulls Cove Visitor Center and area bookstores have trail guides and maps and will help you match a trail with your interests and abilities. You can park at one end of any trail and use the free shuttle bus to get back to your starting point.**

★ **Ocean Patch Trail.** This 3.6-mi, easily accessible trail runs parallel to the Loop Road from Sand Beach to Otter Point. It has some of the best scenery in Maine: the cliffs and boulders of pink granite at the ocean's edge, the twisted branches of the dwarf jack pines, and ocean views that stretch to the horizon. ⊠ *Sand Beach or Otter Point parking area.*

★ The **Acadia Mountain Trail** is the king of the trails. The 2½-mi round-trip climb up Acadia Mountain is steep and strenuous—but the payoff is grand: views of Somes Sound and Southwest Harbor. If you want a guided trip, look into the ranger-led hikes for this trail. ⊠ *Acadia Mountain parking area, on Rte. 102.*

SKIING When the snow falls on Mount Desert Island, the more than 40 mi of carriage roads used for biking and hiking during the rest of the year are transformed into a cross-country skiing paradise. With so few visitors on the island at this time of year, you can ski or snow-shoe for miles without seeing anyone else. Be sure to bring a carriage road map with you. Snowshoe tracks are usually to the right of or between the ski trails.

> **THE EARLY BIRD GETS THE SUN**
>
> During your visit to Mount Desert, pick a day when you are willing to get up very early, around 4:30 or 5 AM. Drive with a friend to the top of Cadillac Mountain in Acadia National Park. Stand on the highest rock you can find there and wait for the sun to come up. When it does, have your friend take a photo of you looking at it from behind. Then you can label the photo something like: "The first person in America to see the sun come up on June 1, 2008."

SWIMMING The park has two beaches that are perfect for swimming, Sand Beach and Echo Lake Beach. Sand Beach, along Park Loop Road, has changing rooms, restrooms, and a lifeguard on duty from Memorial Day to Labor Day. The water temperature here rarely reaches above 55°F. Echo Lake Beach, on the western side of the island just north of Southwest Harbor, has much warmer water. There are changing rooms, restrooms, and a lifeguard on duty throughout summer.

WHERE TO STAY

Acadia National Park does not have its own hotel, and there are no cabins or lodges. But 500 campgrounds within the park for RVers and tenters are available. There are also five primitive sites on the part of the park on the Isle au Haut, out to sea 10 mi away. Visitors with RVs do need to be warned, however, that facilities at both of the Acadia National Park campgrounds are deliberately kept minimal. There are no hookups. So if you are used to and like a lot of facilities, you may wish to opt for campgrounds outside the park. Both campgrounds within the park are wooded, and both are within a 10-minute walk of the ocean, but neither is located right on the ocean.

CAMPING **Blackwoods Campground.** One of only two campgrounds located $$ inside inland Acadia National Park, Blackwoods is open throughout the year (though restrictions apply for winter camping; call ahead for details). Reservations are handled by the National Recreation Reservation Service ☎ 877/444–6777, not by the park. Reservations for high season (May–October) can be made up to six months in advance. During the off-season, a limited number of campsites are available for primitive camping, and a camping permit must be obtained from the park headquarters. Rates drop by 50% for the shoulder season

(April and November). **Pros:** shuttle bus. **Cons:** no hookups or utilities. ⊠*Rte. 3, 5 mi south of Bar Harbor, Otter Creek* ☎*207/288–3274 or 800/365–2267* ⚑*35 RV sites; 198 tent sites* ⚐ *Flush toilets, running water, showers, fire pits, picnic tables* ▭*DC, MC, V.*

$-$$ ⚑**Seawall Campground.** On the "quiet side" of the island, this campground does not accept reservations, but offers space on a first-come, first-served basis, starting at 8 AM. Seawall is open from late May to late September. Walk-in tent sites are $14 per night, while drive-in sites for tents and RVs are $20. **Pros:** quiet. **Cons:** no hookups or utilities. ⊠*Rte. 102A, 4 mi south of Southwest Harbor, Manset* ☎*207/244–3600* ⚑*42 RV sites; 163 tent sites* ⚐ *Flush toilets, showers, picnic tables, fire pits* ▭*MC, V* ⊗*Closed late Sept.–late May.*

NORTHEAST HARBOR

12 mi south of Bar Harbor via Rtes. 3 and 198 or Rtes. 233 and 198.

The summer community for some of the nation's wealthiest families, Northeast Harbor is a quiet place to stay. The village has one of the best harbors on the coast, and fills with yachts and powerboats during peak season. It's a great place to sign up for a cruise around Somes Sound or to the Cranberry Islands. Other than that, there isn't much to hold your attention for long. There's a handful of restaurants, boutiques, and art galleries on the downtown streets.

SOMESVILLE

7 mi northwest of Northeast Harbor via Rtes. 198 and 102.

Most visitors pass through Somesville on their way to Southwest Harbor, but this well-preserved village, the oldest on the island, is more than a stop along the way. Originally settled by Abraham Somes in 1763, this was once a bustling commercial center with shingle, lumber, and wool mills; a tannery; a varnish factory; and a dye shop. Today, Route 102, which passes through the center of town, takes you past a row of white clapboard houses with black shutters and well-manicured lawns. Designated a historic district in 1975, Somesville has one of the most-photographed spots on the island: a small house with a footbridge that crosses an old mill pond. Get out your camera. In spring, summer, or fall, this scene will remind you of a Thomas Kinkade painting. Maybe even in winter, too.

WHERE TO STAY

CAMPING   ⚑**Mount Desert Campground.** Near the village of Somesville, this camp-
$$–$$$ ground has one of the best locations imaginable. It lies at the head of Somes Sound, the only fjord on the East Coast. The campground prefers tents, so vehicles longer than 20 feet are not allowed. Many sites are along the waterfront, and all are tucked into the woods for a sense of privacy. Restrooms and showers are placed sensibly throughout the campground and are kept meticulously clean. Canoes and kayaks are available for rent, and there's a dock with access to the ocean. The Gathering Place has baked goods in the morning, and ice cream

and coffee in the evening. **Pro:** a lovely location for sightseeing. **Con:** fills up quickly during peak season. ✉ *516 Sound Dr., Mount Desert* ☎ *207/244–3710* 🌐 *www.mountdesertcampground.com* ⛺ *150 sites* ♿ *Flush toilets, drinking water, showers, fire pits, food service, swimming (ocean)* 💳 *MC, V* ⏲ *Closed mid-Sept.–mid-June.*

BASS HARBOR

4 mi south of Southwest Harbor via Rte. 102 or Rte. 102A

Bass Harbor is a tiny lobstering village with a relaxed atmosphere and a few accommodations and restaurants. If you're looking to get away from the crowds, consider using this hardworking community as your base. Although Bass Harbor does not draw as many tourists as other villages, the Bass Harbor Head Light in Acadia National Park is one of the region's most popular attractions and is undoubtedly the most-photographed lighthouse in Maine. (The best picture is taken from the rocks below, but be careful: they can be slippery.) From Bass Harbor you can hike on the Ship Harbor Nature Trail or take a ferry to Frenchboro.

WHERE TO EAT

¢–$$ SEAFOOD ✕ **Thurston's Lobster Pound.** On the peninsula across from Bass Harbor, Thurston's is easy to spot because of its bright yellow awning. You can buy fresh lobsters to go or sit at outdoor tables. Order everything from a grilled cheese sandwich to a boiled lobster served with clams or mussels. ✉ *1 Thurston Rd., at Steamboat Wharf, Bernard* ☎ *207/244–7600* 💳 *MC, V* ⏲ *Closed Columbus Day–Memorial Day.*

WAY DOWN EAST

By Mary Ruoff

Way Down East covers roughly a fourth of the state's coast, at least as the crow flies. The raw, mostly undeveloped coast in this remote region is more accessible than it is farther south. Pleasure craft don't crowd out lobster boats and draggers in small harbor towns the way they do in other coastal towns. Even in summer here you're likely to have rocky beaches and shady hiking trails to yourself. The slower pace is as calming as a sea breeze.

The region's offerings include national wildlife refuges, state parks, historic sites and preserves, and increasingly, conservancy-owned public land. Cutler's Bold Coast, with its dramatic granite headlands, is protected from development. Waters near Eastport have some of the world's highest tides. Lakes perfect for canoeing and kayaking are sprinkled inland. Rivers snake through marshland as they near the many bays. Boulders are strewn on blueberry barrens. Rare plants thrive in coastal bogs and heaths. Dark-purple-and-pink lupines line the roads in late June.

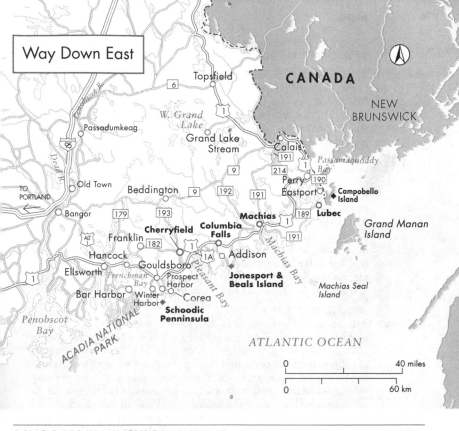

Way Down East

SCHOODIC PENINSULA

16 mi southeast of Hancock via U.S. 1 and Rte. 186, 25 mi east of Ellsworth.

The landscape of Schoodic Peninsula makes it easy to understand why the overflow from Bar Harbor's wealthy summer population settled in Winter Harbor. The craggy coastline, the towering evergreens, and views over Frenchman Bay are breathtaking year-round. A drive through the well-to-do summer community of Grindstone Neck shows what Bar Harbor might have been like before so many mansions there were destroyed in the Great Fire of 1947. Artists and artisans have opened galleries in and around Winter Harbor. Anchored at the foot of the peninsula, Winter Harbor was once part of Gouldsboro, which wraps around it.

WHAT TO SEE

Within Gouldsboro on the Schoodic Peninsula are several small coastal villages. You drive through **Wonsqueak** and **Birch Harbor** after leaving the Schoodic section of Acadia National Park. Near Birch Harbor you can find **Prospect Harbor,** a small fishing village nearly untouched by tourism. There's also **Corea,** where there's little to do besides watch the fishermen at work, wander along stone beaches, or gaze out to sea—and that's what makes it so special.

Fodor'sChoice
★
The only section of **Acadia National Park** that sits on the mainland is at the southern side of the Schoodic Peninsula. A few miles east of Winter Harbor, the park has a scenic 6-mi one-way loop that edges along the coast and yields views of Grindstone Neck, Winter Harbor, and Winter Harbor Lighthouse. At the tip of the point, huge slabs of pink granite lie jumbled along the shore, thrashed unmercifully by the crashing surf (stay away from water's edge), and jack pines cling to life amid the rocks. Fraser Point at the beginning of the loop is an ideal place for a picnic. Work off lunch with a hike up Schoodic Head for the panoramic views up and down the coast. A free bus called the Island Explorer (☎ *207/288–4573 [late June–Columbus Day] or 207/667–5796* ⊕ *www.exploreacadia.com*) takes passengers from Prospect Harbor, Birch Harbor, and Winter Harbor and drops them off anywhere in the park. In Winter Harbor you can get off at the ferry to Bar Harbor. The $10 park admission fee is generally not charged when you're just visiting Schoodic. ⊠ *Rte. 186, Winter Harbor* ☎ *207/288–3338* ⊕ *www.nps.gov/acad* ☜ *$10* ☉ *Year-round, 24/7.*

NIGHTLIFE & THE ARTS

FESTIVALS
Afternoon and evening musical, poetry, puppet, magic and theater performances, and speakers are part of the **Schoodic Arts Festival** (☎ *207/963–2569* ⊕ *www.schoodicarts.org*), which takes place at venues throughout the peninsula during the first two weeks of August. Schoodic Steel, a community steel pan band, drums up a lot of excitement at its evening performance on the last weekend of the festival. An art show is held on the second Saturday, and you can take workshops in everything from dance to writing. Lobster boats from up and down the Maine Coast race in the **Winter Harbor Lobster Festival** (☎ *207/963–7658* ⊕ *www.acadia-schoodic.org*) on the second Saturday of August. The free event also includes a parade, an arts-and-crafts fair, an art show, a pancake breakfast, and a lobster dinner that draws hundreds.

SPORTS & THE OUTDOORS

KAYAKING
Registered Master Maine Guides lead all-day, half-day, and overnight sea kayaking and hiking trips to the region's less visited islands and trails for **Ardea EcoExpeditions** (⊠ *242 S. Gouldsboro Rd., Gouldsboro [Rte. 186]* ☎ *207/460–9731* ⊕ *www.ardea-ecoexpeditions.com*). Learning is part of the fun on these ecotourism adventures. The company also offers sunrise birding and sunset kayaking tours, expeditions that lend a hand to ecological research and conservation projects, and cross-country skiing and snowshoeing trips.

GOLFING
You can see the ocean from every green at the 9-hole **Grindstone Neck Golf Course** (⊠ *106 Grindstone Ave., Winter Harbor* ☎ *207/963–7760* ⊕ *www.grindstonegolf.com*), one of Maine's oldest courses. Greens fees are $20 to $45.

SHOPPING

ANTIQUES & MORE

Hand-cast bronze doorbells and wind bells are among the items sold at **U.S. Bells** (⊠*56 W. Bay Rd. (Rte. 186), Prospect Harbor* ☎*207/963–7184* ⊕*www.usbells.com*). You can also buy finely crafted quilts, wood-fired pottery, and wood and bronze outdoor furniture, all made by family members of the foundry owner. Tours of the foundry are given frequently. The shop is open June through December and by appointment. Children appear in many of the watercolor, pastel, and Asian ink paintings of Down East landscapes by Wendilee Heath O'Brien, the friendly artist-owner of **whopaints** (⊠*316 Main St., Winter Harbor* ☎*207/963–2076* ⊕*www.whopaints.com*); the artist's studio-gallery is beside her home. You're welcome to listen in if she's teaching a class. Open year-round. Step back in time at **Winter Harbor 5 & 10** (⊠*349 Main St., Winter Harbor* ☎*207/963–7927* ⊕*www.winterharbor5and10.com*), a tried-and-true dime store with a big selection of local T-shirts and sweatshirts. Open year-round.

ART GALLERIES

Handcrafts by area artisans, including jewelry and wool items, and the owner's colorful hooked rugs with animal and nature themes are sold in an old school at **Chapter Two** (⊠*611 Corea Rd. [Rte. 195], Corea* ☎*207/963–7269*) You can enjoy a cup of tea, and you might catch a hooking group or class in action. Art of the Schoodic Peninsula is sold in the house-turned-gallery next door, and the garage is stocked with used books. Glass wildlife sculptures, flowers, goblets, and beads are for sale at **Gypsy Moose Glass Co.** (⊠*20 Williamsbrook Rd., off Rte. 186, Gouldsboro* ☎*207/963–2674* ⊕*www.gypsymoose.com*), whose owner gives glassblowing demonstrations. It's open March to December.

FOOD & WINE

The wines sold at **Bartlett Maine Estate Winery** (⊠*175 Chicken Mill Rd., off U.S. 1, Gouldsboro* ☎*207/546–2408* ⊕*www.bartlettwinery.com*) are produced from locally grown apples, pears, blueberries, and other fruit. Ask the vintners what foods to pair them with while sampling different wines in the tasting room. It's open late May through mid-October and by appointment. Along with mostly organic local produce, **Winter Harbor Farmers' Market** (⊠*10 Main St. [Rte. 186], Winter Harbor* ☎*207/963–2984*) sells goat cheese, beef and chicken, hand-spun yarn, knitted items, and maple syrup, chutney, and preserves. The market operates on Tuesday mornings from late June to early September.

WHERE TO EAT

$$$–$$$$
SEAFOOD

✕**Bunker's Wharf.** On a narrow harbor that is home to an 18-boat lobster fleet and opens onto the ocean, this restaurant sits near Acadia National Park. Enjoy the views from the stone patio or from the large windows in the blond-wood dining room. Some seats in the bar face the water. The setting—quintessential Maine—isn't all that keeps locals coming back. Lobster (served with roasted corn-bread pudding) is bought off boats in the harbor. The restaurant is also known for generous portions and scrumptious fare, from fried clams on a baguette at lunch to baked haddock with focaccia-bread stuffing at dinner. ⊠*260 E. Schoodic Dr., Birch Harbor* ☎*207/963–2244* ▭*MC, V* ☺*Closed some days Sept.–June; call for hours.*

$-$$ ✕ **J.M. Gerrish Provisions.** The store that opened here in the early 1900s
CAFE   was where locals and visitors alike went for ice cream. The name
remains and part of the old marble counter, but this is now a deli and
café where folks bustle in for fudge and coffee and linger at tables inside
and on the porch. A simple menu has soups, salads, and savory sandwiches such as turkey and Jarlsberg cheese topped with peach salsa.
The deli case offers salads and dishes such as scallops with roasted
tomatoes. Baked goods crowd the counter, a building out back that's
to open in 2008 will sell wine and beer, and, yes, you can still buy an
ice cream. ⊠*352 Main St., Winter Harbor* ☎*207/963–2727* ▤*MC,
V* ⊘*Closed mid-Oct.–mid-May.*

WHERE TO STAY

$-$$ ▦ **Bluff House Inn.** Combining the service of a hotel with the ambi-
☾   ence of a cozy lodge, this modern two-story inn on a secluded hillside
★   has expansive views of Frenchman Bay. You can see the bay's granite
shores from the inn's partially screened wraparound porches. There's a
picnic area with grill (a lobster pot is available for those who want to
boil their own dinner). A stone fireplace warms one of the knotty-pine
lounge areas. The individually decorated guest rooms have furnishings
from around the state. **Pros:** close to things but secluded, apartment
has two bedrooms. **Con:** hill to water a bit steep. ⊠*57 Bluff House
Rd., off Rte. 186, Gouldsboro* ☎*207/963–7805* ⊕*www.bluffinn.com*
↯*8 rooms, 1 apartment* ☾*In-room: no a/c, no TV (some), kitchen
(some), DVD (some). In-hotel: no elevator, no-smoking rooms* ▤*AE,
MC, V* ⦿*CP.*

$$-$$$ ▦ **Oceanside Meadows Inn.** This place is a must for nature lovers. Trail
☾   maps guide you through a 200-acre preserve dotted with woods,
Fodor's Choice   streams, salt marshes, and ponds. Inspired by the moose, eagles, and
★   other wildlife that thrive here, the innkeepers created the Oceanside
Meadows Innstitute for the Arts & Sciences, which holds lectures,
musical performances, art exhibits, and other events in the restored
barn. Furnished with antiques, country pieces, and family treasures,
and scented with flowers from the gardens, the inn has sunny, inviting
living rooms with fireplaces and a separate guest kitchen. Guest rooms
are spread between two white clapboard buildings fronting a private
beach shaded by granite ledges. Breakfast is an extravagant multicourse
affair that includes chilled fruit soup. **Pros:** one of the region's few sand
beaches, many spacious rooms, handicapped-accessible room with
water view. **Con:** need to cross road to beach. ⊠*202 Corea Rd. (Rte.
195), Prospect Harbor* ☎*207/963–5557* ⊕*www.oceaninn.com* ↯*12
rooms, 3 suites* ☾*In-room: no a/c, no TV, Wi-Fi. In-hotel: beachfront,
no elevator, public Internet, public Wi-Fi, no-smoking rooms, some
pets allowed* ▤*AE, D, DC, MC, V* ⊘*Closed Nov.–Apr.* ⦿*BP.*

**EN
ROUTE**   Visitors are welcome at **Petit Manan National Wildlife Refuge,** a 2,166-
acre sanctuary of fields, forests, and rocky shorefront near Millbridge
(35 mi east of Ellsworth). The wildlife viewing and bird-watching are
renowned. In August the park is a popular spot for picking wild blueberries. You can explore the refuge on two walking trails; the shore trail
looks out on sand-color Petit Manan Lighthouse, Maine's second-tall-

1

est light. ⊠*Pigeon Hill Rd.* ☎*207/546–2124* ⊕*www.fws.gov/north east/mainecoastal* ⊠*Free* ☉*Daily, sunrise–sunset.*

CHERRYFIELD

6 mi north of Milbridge via U.S. 1.

In the 1800s, the Narraguagus River was lined with lumber mills, and Cherryfield was a lumbering center. Now this stretch is a lovely waterway (with native salmon) overlooked by a gazebo in a small town park. The industry's legacy remains in the surprising number of ornate Victorian homes, unusual for a small New England village. The town has 52 buildings on the National Historic Register in such styles as Colonial Revival, Greek Revival, Italianate, and Queen Anne. The historic district runs along U.S. 1 and the handful of side streets.

Cherryfield is also known as the "Blueberry Capital of the World." Maine's two largest blueberry plants sit side by side on Route 193. To see the area's wild blueberry barrens, head north past the factories and take a right onto Ridge Road.

OFF THE BEATEN PATH In nearby Millbridge the largest annual event is the **Milbridge Days Celebration** (☎*207/546–2422* ⊕*www.milbridgedays.com*), held each year on the last weekend of July. There's a blueberry-pancake breakfast, clam-and-lobster bake, parade, crafts show, and most famously, a codfish relay race. There's only one screen at **Milbridge Theatre** (⊠*26 Main St.* ☎*207/546–2038*), but it's a large one and the price is right—$4.50. The owner of the only movie theater between Ellsworth and Calais is likely to greet you in the little lobby—he hasn't missed a show since opening the place in 1978. If you're lucky, you'll catch one of the player-piano performances. The theater is open daily Memorial Day through early January and weekends in April and May.

COLUMBIA FALLS

11 mi northeast of Cherryfield via U.S. 1.

Founded in the late 18th century, Columbia Falls is a pretty village along the Pleasant River. True to its name, a waterfall tumbles into the river in the center of town. Once a prosperous shipbuilding center, Columbia Falls still has a number of stately homes dating from that era. U.S. 1 used to pass through the center of town, but now it passes to the west. It's worth driving through even if you don't have time to stop.

WHAT TO SEE

★ **Ruggles House.** Judge Thomas Ruggles, a wealthy lumber dealer, store owner, postmaster, and justice of the Court of Sessions, built this home about 1820. The house's distinctive Federal architecture, flying staircase, Palladian window, and intricate woodwork were crafted over three years by Massachusetts wood-carver Alvah Peterson. ⊠*146 Main St.* ☎*207/483–4637* ⊕*www.ruggleshouse.org* ⊠*$5* ☉*June– mid-Oct., Mon.–Sat. 9:30–4:30, Sun. 11–4:30.*

Wild for Blueberries

There's no need to inquire about the cheesecake topping if you dine out in August when the wild blueberry crop comes in. Anything but blueberries would be unthinkable.

Way Down East, wild blueberries have long been a favorite food—and a key ingredient In cultural and economic life. Maine produces about a third of the commercial harvest, which totals about 70 million pounds annually, with Canada supplying virtually all the rest. Washington County yields 65% of Maine's total crop, which is why the state's largest blueberry processors are here: Cherryfield Foods' predecessor and Jasper Wyman & Son were founded shortly after the Civil War.

Wild blueberries, which bear fruit every other year, thrive in the region's cold climate and sandy, acidic soil. Undulating blueberry barrens stretch for miles in Deblois and Cherryfield—"the Blueberry Capital of the World"—and are scattered throughout Washington County. Look for tufts among low-lying plants along the roadways. In spring, fields shimmer as the small-leaf plants turn myriad shades of mauve, honey orange, and lemon yellow. White flowers appear in June. Fall transforms the barrens into a sea of red.

Amid Cherryfield's barrens, a plaque on a boulder lauds the late J. Burleigh Crane for helping advance an industry that's not as wild as it used to be. Honeybees have been brought in to supplement native pollinators. Fields are irrigated. Barrens are burned and mowed to rid plants of disease and insects, reducing the need for pesticides. Most fields are owned by the large blueberry processors.

About 80% of Maine's crop is now harvested with machinery. That requires moving boulders, so the rest continues to be harvested by hand with blueberry rakes, which resemble large forks and pull the berries off their stems. Years ago, year-round residents did the work. Today migrant workers make up two-thirds of this seasonal labor force.

Blueberries get their dark color from anthocyanins, believed to provide their antioxidant power. Wild blueberries have more of these antiaging, anticancer compounds than their cultivated cousins. Smaller and more flavorful than cultivated blueberries, wild ones are mostly used in packaged foods. Less than 1% of the state's crop—about 500,000 pints—is consumed fresh, mostly in Maine. Look for fresh berries (sometimes starting in late July and lasting until early September) at roadside stands, farmers' markets, and supermarkets.

Wild Blueberry Land in Columbia Falls sells everything blueberry, from muffins and ice cream to socks and books. Find farm stores, stands, and markets statewide, many selling blueberries and blueberry jams and syrups, at www.getrealgetmaine.com, a Maine Department of Agriculture site that promotes Maine foods.

—Mary Ruoff

1

SHOPPING

Next door to historic Ruggles House, **Columbia Falls Pottery** (⊠*150 Main St.* ☎*207/483–4075* ⊕*www.columbiafallspottery.com*) carries owner April Adams's hand-thrown earthernware pottery. Her work is decorated with local flora (blueberry, columbine, and bunchberry are popular), ships, and lighthouses. It's open June through October and by appointment.

WHERE TO STAY

¢–$

♻

★

Pleasant Bay Bed & Breakfast. This Cape Cod–style inn takes advantage of its riverfront location. Stroll the nature paths on the 110-acre property, which winds around a peninsula and out to Pleasant Bay—you can even take one of the inn's llamas along for company. A screened porch and deck overlook the Pleasant River, and the suite has a private deck. The country-style rooms, all with water views, are decorated with antiques, as are the roomy common areas. A library with a fireplace is tucked away from the family room. **Pros:** fireplace at one of three waterfront picnic areas, river mooring, extra bed or pullout couch in most quarters. **Con:** just a Continental breakfast for late risers. ⊠*386 West Side Rd., Box 222, Addison* ☎*207/483–4490* ➬*3 rooms, 1 with bath; 1 suite* ♿*In-room: no a/c, no phone (some), kitchen (some), TV (some), Wi-Fi. In-hotel: no elevator, public Wi-Fi, no-smoking rooms* ▭*MC, V* ❍*BP.*

JONESPORT & BEALS ISLAND

12 mi northeast of Columbia Falls via U.S. 1 and Rte. 187, 20 mi southwest of Machias.

The birding is superb around Jonesport and Beals Island, a pair of fishing communities joined by a bridge over the harbor. A handful of stately homes is tucked away on Jonesport's Sawyer Square, where Sawyer Memorial Congregational Church's exquisite stained-glass windows are illuminated at night. But the towns are less geared to travelers than those on the Schoodic Peninsula. Lobster traps are still piled in the yards, and lobster-boat races near Moosabec Reach are the highlight of the community's annual Independence Day celebration.

SPORTS & THE OUTDOORS

In business since 1940, **Norton of Jonesport** (☎*207/497–5933* ⊕*www. machiassealisland.com*) takes passengers on day trips to Machias Seal Island, where thousands of puffins nest. Arctic terns, razorbill auks, common murres, and many other seabirds also nest on the rocky island. Trips, which cost $100 per person, are offered from late May through August.

WHERE TO EAT

$–$$$

SEAFOOD

✕**Tall Barney's.** Salty accents add plenty of flavor at this down-home restaurant, which serves breakfast, lunch, and dinner (some nights). Reserved for fishermen, the "liar's table" near the entrance is about as legendary as the namesake. The breakfast menu tells of Tall Barney, a brawny fisherman who left truly tall tales in his wake. Your server may

PEEP AT PUFFINS

Set sail from Jonesport on a cruise to Machias Seal Island, the state's largest puffin colony. Many people come Way Down East just to visit this treeless, rocky isle 10 mi off the coast, a summer home puffins share with scores of other seabirds, including razorbills, common terns, arctic terns, common murres, black guillemots, and common eiders. With clownish ways and a "stuffed toy" look—white breasts beneath jet-black coats, goggle-like eyes, and blue bands on red-orange beaks—

thousands of puffins steal the show. Canada and the United States dispute ownership of the migratory bird sanctuary, but tour operators cooperate with the Canadian Wildlife Service to control access. Weather can prevent boat landings, as there is no pier, but if you go ashore, you can walk on boardwalks and grassy paths to closetlike blinds where four people can stand comfortably as puffins court, clatter, and nuzzle. Bring layers: temperatures in July and August can drop to 50°F.

be among his multitudinous descendants. The menu includes five types of seafood stew, grilled as well as fried seafood, and oversize desserts such as molasses cookies, a local favorite. ⊠ 52 Main St. ☎ 207/497–2403 ═ MC, V ⊘ Closed Feb. Closed Sun.–Tues. late Oct.–Jan. and Mar. and Apr. No dinner Sun.–Tues. May–mid-Oct.

MACHIAS

20 mi northeast of Jonesport.

The Machias area—Machiasport, East Machias, and Machias, the Washington County seat—lays claim to being the site of the first naval battle of the Revolutionary War, which took place in what is now Machiasport. Despite being outnumbered and outarmed, a small group of Machias men under the leadership of Jeremiah O'Brien captured the armed British schooner *Margaretta*. That battle, fought on June 12, 1775, is now known as the "Lexington of the Sea." The Margaretta Days Festival on the second weekend in June commemorates the event with a Colonial dinner, period reenactors, and a parade. The town's other claim to fame is wild blueberries. On the third weekend in August, the annual Machias Wild Blueberry Festival is a community celebration complete with parade, crafts fair, concerts, and plenty of blueberry dishes.

WHAT TO SEE

★ The **Burnham Tavern Museum**, housed in a building dating from 1770, details the colorful history of Job Burnham and other early residents of the area. It was in this tavern that the men of Machias laid the plans that culminated in the capture of the *Margaretta* in 1775. Period furnishings show what life was like in Colonial times. ⊠ 98 Main St. (Rte. 192 section) ☎ 207/255–6930 ⊕ www.burnhamtavern.com ⊠ $5 ⊘ Early June–Fri. before Labor Day, weekdays 9–5, or by appointment.

WHERE TO EAT & STAY

$ ✕🏠**Riverside Inn & Restaurant.** A bright yellow exterior invites a stop at
★ this delightful inn perched on the banks of the Machias River. Inside
AMERICAN you can find hammered-tin ceilings and lots of hand-carved wood.
The spacious guest rooms have antique furnishings and colorful quilts.
The upstairs suite in the coach house has a private balcony overlook-
ing the river. The restaurant ($$$–$$$$) has maintained its excellent
reputation. The chef brings a special flair to traditional dishes such
as pork served with a pistachio crust. His signature dish is salmon
stuffed with crabmeat and shrimp. In summer the menu includes an
updated take on the chef salad. Try pairing it with standout appetizers
like hake cakes and red tuna wontons. Ask for a table in the intimate
sunroom. **Pros:** suites a good value, garden overlooks river, walk to
riverside park. **Con:** small grounds. ⊠*608 Main St. (U.S. 1)* 📭*Box
373, East Machias 04630* 📞*207/255–4134 or 888/255–4344* ⊕*www.
riversideinn-maine.com* 🛏*2 rooms, 2 suites* ⚒*In-room: no a/c (some),
no phone, kitchen (some), refrigerator (some). In-hotel: no elevator,
restaurant, no-smoking rooms* 🗖*AE, MC, V* ⊗*Closed Jan.–early Feb.
Restaurant closed Mon.–Wed. mid-Feb.–May and Nov. and Dec. No
lunch* 🍴*BP.*

LUBEC

28 mi northeast of Machias via U.S. 1 and Rte. 189.

Lubec is the first town in the United States to see the sunrise. A popular
destination for outdoor enthusiasts, there are plenty of opportunities
for hiking and biking, and the birding is renowned. It's a good base
for day trips to New Brunswick's Campobello Island, reached by a
bridge—the only one to the island—from downtown Lubec. The vil-
lage is perched at the end of a narrow strip of land, so you often can
see water in three directions.

FUN TOUR

On educational tours by **Tours of Lubec and Cobscook** (⊠*24 Water St.*
📞*207/733–2997 or 888/347–9302* ⊕*www.toursoflubecandcobscook.
com*) you can visit historic locales and lighthouses, walk the shoreline to
learn about the area's high tides and tide pools, tour a ninth-generation farm
on Cobscook Bay, explore a bog, and visit artist galleries.

SPORTS & THE OUTDOORS

★ The easternmost point of land in the United States, **Quoddy Head State
Park,** is marked by candy-striped West Quoddy Head Light. In 1806
President Thomas Jefferson signed an order authorizing construction of
a lighthouse on this site. You can't climb the tower, but the former light
keeper's house has a museum with a video showing the interior. The
museum also has displays on Lubec's maritime past and the region's
marine life. A gallery displays lighthouse art by locals. A mystical 2-mi
path along the cliffs here, one of four trails, yields magnificent views of
Canada's cliff-clad Grand Manan island. Whales can often be sighted
offshore. The 540-acre park has a picnic area. ⊠*S. Lubec Rd., off Rte.
189* 📞*207/733–0911 or 207/941–4014* ⊕*www.state.me.us/doc/parks*
🎟*$2* ⊗*May 15–Oct. 15, 9–sunset.*

WHERE TO EAT & STAY

$–$$$
SEAFOOD

✕ **Uncle Kippy's Restaurant.** There isn't much of a view from the picture windows, but locals don't mind—they come here for the satisfying seafood. There's one large dining room with a bar beside the main entrance. The menu includes seafood dinners and combo platters, and the fresh-dough pizza is popular. A take-out window and ice-cream bar are open spring through fall. ✉ *170 Main St.* ☎ *207/733–2400* ▭ *MC, V* ⊘ *Generally closed Mon. Sept. and Oct.; Mon. and Tues. Apr.–June, Nov., and Dec.; and Mon.–Wed. Jan.–Mar.*

$–$$
★

▦ **Peacock House.** Five generations of the Peacock family lived in this white clapboard house before it was converted into an inn. With a large foyer, library, and living room, the 1860 sea captain's home has plenty of places where you can relax. Minglers are drawn to the sunroom, which opens to the deck and has a handsome bar with glasses for your wine or spirits. The best of the rooms has a separate sitting area and a wet bar and gas fireplace. **Pros:** piano in library, lovely garden off deck, handicapped accessible suite. **Con:** only one off-street parking space. ✉ *27 Summer St.* ☎ *207/733–2403 or 888/305–0036* ⊕ *www.peacockhouse.com* ⌕ *5 rooms, 2 suites* ⚬ *In-room: no a/c, no phone, refrigerator (some), VCR (some), no TV (some), Wi-Fi. In-hotel: no elevator, public Wi-Fi, no-smoking rooms* ▭ *MC, V* ⊘ *Closed Nov.–Apr.* ⧉ *BP.*

▌ OFF THE
BEATEN
PATH

A popular excursion from Lubec, New Brunswick's Campobello Island has two fishing villages, Welshpool and Wilson's Beach; it's also home to the **Roosevelt Campobello International Park,** a joint project of the American and the Canadian governments. The only bridge to Campobello Island is from Lubec, but in summer a car ferry shuttles passengers from Campobello Island to Deer Island, where you can continue on to the Canadian mainland. U.S. citizens need a passport or other federal government–approved ID when traveling to Canada.

Stop at the information center (open mid-May to mid-October) after passing customs for an update on tides—specifically, when you will be able to walk to **East Quoddy Head Lighthouse** (✉ *East end of Rte. 774, Wilson's Beach*). On a tiny island off the eastern end of Campobello, this distinctive lighthouse is marked with a large red cross and is accessible only at and around low tide, but it's worth a look no matter the sea level. You may spot whales in the island-dotted waters off the small park on the rock-clad headland across from the light.

Spot whales and other creatures from a 20-passenger lobster boat operated by **Island Cruises** (✉ *1 Head Harbour Wharf Rd., Wilson's Beach* ☎ *506/752–1107 or 888/249–4400*). It operates daily from July to September. Cruises cost $48 and depart from Head Harbour Wharf.

SPORTS & OUTDOORS IN MAINE

1

BIRDING

The **Maine Audubon Society** (✉ *20 Gilsland Farm Rd., Falmouth* ☎ *207/781–6180* ⊕ *www.maine audubon.org*) provides information on birding in Maine and hosts field trips for novice to expert birders.

CAMPING

Reservations for state park campsites (excluding Baxter State Park) can be made through the **Bureau of Parks and Lands** (✉ *State House Station 22, Augusta* ☎ *207/287–3821, 800/332–1501 in Maine* ⊕ *www. maine.gov/doc/parks*), which also can tell you if you need a camping permit and where to obtain one. The **Maine Campground Owners Association** (✉ *10 Falcon Rd., Lewiston* ☎ *207/782–5874* ⊕ *www. campmaine.com*) publishes a helpful annual directory of its members.

FISHING

For information about fishing and licenses, contact the **Maine Department of Inland Fisheries and Wildlife** (✉ *284 State St., Augusta* ☎ *207/287–8000* ⊕ *www. mefishwildlife.com*). Guides are available through most wilderness camps, sporting goods stores, and canoe outfitters. For assistance in finding a fishing guide, contact the **Maine Professional Guides Association** (✉ *Box 336, Augusta 04332* ☎ *No phone* ⊕ *www.maine guides.org*), which maintains and mails out listings of its members and their specialties.

HORSEBACK RIDING

Owned by registered Maine guides Judy Cross-Strehlke and Bob Strehlke, **Northern Maine Riding Adventures** (✉ *186 Garland Line Rd., Dover-Foxcroft* ☎ *207/564–3451*

⊕ *www.mainetrailrides.com*) conducts one-day and two-day trips through parts of Piscataquis County. Or take day rides during a weeklong stay at a wilderness cabin.

KAYAKING & RAFTING

Maine Professional Guides Association (✉ *Box 336, Augusta 04332* ☎ *No phone* ⊕ *www.maineguides. org*) represents kayaking guides. **Raft Maine** (✉ *Box 78, West Forks 04985* ☎ *800/723–8633* ⊕ *www. raftmaine.com*) provides information on white-water rafting on the Kennebec, Penobscot, and Dead rivers.

SKIING

Weather patterns that create snow cover for Maine ski areas may come from the Atlantic or from Canada, and Maine may have snow when other New England states do not—and vice versa. Sunday River in Carrabassett Valley and Sugarloaf outside Bethel in Newry are the state's largest ski areas. It's worth the effort to get to Sugarloaf, which provides the only above-tree-line lift-service skiing in New England.

For information on alpine and cross-country skiing, contact **Ski Maine** (✉ *Box 7566, Portland 04112* ☎ *207/773–7669, 888/624–6345 snow conditions* ⊕ *www. skimaine.com*).

SNOWMOBILING

The **Maine Snowmobile Association** (✉ *Box 80, Augusta 04332* ☎ *207/622–6983* ⊕ *www.mesnow. com*) distributes an excellent statewide trail map of about 3,500 mi of trails.

MAINE ESSENTIALS

Research prices, get travel advice, and book your trip at fodors.com.

TRANSPORTATION

BY AIR

Two primary airports serve Maine: Portland International and Bangor International. Logan International in Boston (about 65 mi from Maine's southern end) is also an option. Additionally, Manchester Boston Regional Airport, in New Hampshire, is only some 45 mi from the beginning of the Maine Coast and a number of discount airlines fly there. Trenton's Hancock County–Bar Harbor Airport offers the closest airport to the Mount Desert Island region, including Acadia National Park; however, only one commuter airline, Colgan Air (operated by US Airways Express), services the airport. Most people going to Mount Desert Island, as well as the Blue Hill peninsula and Penobscot Bay, prefer Bangor International Airport, an hour's drive from the island, though there can be frequent cancellations at this small airport.

Regional flying services, operating from regional and municipal airports, provide access to remote lakes and wilderness areas as well as to Penobscot Bay islands. For visiting the North Woods, Katahdin Air Service offers charter flights by seaplane from points throughout Maine to smaller towns and remote lake and forest areas. It can help you find a guide and also does scenic flights over the Katahdin area. Currier's Flying Service offers sightseeing flights over the Moosehead Lake region. In the mountains and lakes region, Lake Region Air provides access to remote areas, scenic flights, and charter-fishing trips.

Airport Information Bangor International (BGR) (⊠ *287 Godfrey Blvd., Bangor* ☎ *207/992–4600 or 207/947–0384* ⊕ *www.flybangor.com*). **Hancock County–Bar Harbor Airport** (⊠ *E Rte. 3, Trenton* ☎ *207/667–7329* ⊕ *www.bhbairport.com*). **Logan International (BOS)** (⊠ *1 Harborside Dr., East Boston, MA* ☎ *800/235–6426* ⊕ *www.massport.com/logan*). **Manchester Boston Regional Airport (MHT)** (⊠ *1 Airport Rd., Manchester, NH* ☎ *603/624–6539* ⊕ *www.flymanchester.com*). **Portland International Jetport (PWM)** (⊠ *1001 Westbrook St., off Rte. 9, Portland* ☎ *207/774–7301* ⊕ *www.portlandjetport.org*).

Regional Flying Services Currier's Flying Service (⊠ *Greenville Junction* ☎ *207/695–2778* ⊕ *www.curriersflyingservice.com*). **Katahdin Air Service** (⊠ *Millinocket* ☎ *207/723–8378* ⊕ *www.katahdinair.com*). **Lake Region Air** (⊠ *Rangeley* ☎ *207/864–5307*).

BY BUS

Concord Coach Lines (☎ *207/945–4000 or 800/639–3317* ⊕ *www.concordcoach lines.com*) operates a luxury bus service (including snacks, drinks, and an "in-flight" movie) that travels the length of the coast from Orono (not far from Bangor) to Logan International Airport in Boston, stopping in every major town along the way. **Greyhound** (☎ *800/552–8737 or 800/642–3133* ⊕ *www.greyhound.com*) services towns throughout Maine and northern New England.

1

BY CAR

A car is helpful when visiting the Maine Coast, and is essential to tour Maine's western lakes and mountains and to negotiate the vast North Woods region—though it may not be useful to someone spending a vacation entirely at a wilderness camp. Interstate 95 is the fastest route to and through the state from coastal New Hampshire and points south; it turns inland at Portland and goes on to Bangor and the Canadian border. U.S. 1, more leisurely and scenic, is the principal coastal highway from New Hampshire to Canada.

Interstate 95 also provides the quickest access to the North Woods, linking with Highway 15, the road to Greenville, in Bangor, and with Highway 11 near Millinocket. U.S. 201 is the major route to Jackman and to Quebec. Highway 15 connects Jackman to Greenville and Bangor. The Golden Road is a private logging company–operated road that links the Greenville area and Millinocket. Be sure to have a full tank of gas before heading onto the many private roads in the region.

Travelers visiting the Mid-Coast region in summer and early fall may encounter fog, especially on the peninsulas and points of land. It's best to leave headlights on. Fog may stay around all day, or it may burn off by late morning. Winter driving in Maine can be challenging when snow and ice coat the roads. "Black ice" is a special hazard along the coast, as the road may appear clear but is actually covered by a nearly invisible coating of ice. Four-wheel-drive vehicles are recommended for driving in winter. Always carry warm clothing and blankets, as well as food and drinking water in case of an emergency.

Public roads in the North Woods are scarce, but lumber companies maintain private roads that are often open to the public (sometimes by permit only). When driving on a logging road, always give lumber-company trucks the right of way. Be aware that loggers must drive in the middle of the road and often can't move over or slow down for cars.

BY TRAIN

Amtrak (☎ 800/872–7245 ⊕ *www.amtrak.com*) connects Portland with Boston. The train makes five runs to and from Boston each day and makes eight stops along the way, with stops in Wells and Saco and a seasonal stop in Old Orchard Beach.

CONTACTS & RESOURCES

VISITOR INFORMATION

State Tourism Contacts Maine Tourism Association (⊠ *327 Water St., Hallowell* ☎ *207/623–0363 or 800/767–8709* ⊕ *www.mainetourism.com*).

Local Tourism Contacts Bar Harbor Chamber of Commerce (⊠ *93 Cottage St. ⌂ Box 158, Bar Harbor 04609* ☎ *207/288–3393, 207/288–5103, or 800/288–5103* ⊕ *www.barharborinfo.com*). **Camden-Rockport-Lincolnville Chamber of Commerce** (⊠ *2 Public Landing, Camden 04843* ☎ *207/236–4404 or 800/223–5459* ⊕ *www.visitcamden.com*). **Boothbay Harbor Region Chamber of Commerce** (⌂ *Box 356, 04538* ☎ *207/633–2353* ⊕ *www.boothbayharbor.com*). **Convention**

and Visitors Bureau of Greater Portland (☎ *207/772–5800* ⊕ *www.visitportland. com*). **Deer Isle–Stonington Chamber of Commerce** (⊠ *Rte. 15, Deer Isle04627* ☎ *207/348–6124* ⊕ *www.deerisle.com*). **Searsport Chamber of Commerce** (⊠ *1 Union St., Searsport 04974* ☎ *207/548–0173* ⊕ *www.searsportme.com*).

Regional Tourism Contacts Blue Hill Peninsula Chamber of Commerce (⊠ *28 Water St., Blue Hill* ☎ *207/374–3242* ⊕ *www.bluehillpeninsula.org*). **Mount Desert Chamber of Commerce** (⊠ *Sea St., Northeast Harbor 04662* ☎ *207/276–5040* ⊕ *www.mountdesertchamber.org*). **Penobscot Regional Chamber of Commerce** (⊠ *1 Park Dr., Rockland* ☎ *207/596–0376 or 800/562–2529* ⊕ *www. therealmaine.com*).

Vermont

WORD OF MOUTH

"Vermont is probably the most bucolic and relaxing state in the Northeast. Towns like Woodstock, Chester, Stowe and Waitsfield make good choices. The Round Barn Inn in Waitsfield is very idyllic, as is Marshland Farm in Quechee...."

—zootsi

By Michael
de Zayas

VERMONT IS AN ENTIRE STATE of hidden treasures. Sprawl has no place here. The pristine countryside is dotted with farms and tiny towns with church steeples, village greens, and clapboard colonial-era houses. Highways are devoid of billboards by law, and on some roads, cows still stop traffic twice a day, en route to and from the pasture. In spring, sap boils in sugarhouses, some built generations ago, and up the road, a chef trained at the New England Culinary Institute in Montpelier might use the maple syrup to glaze a pork tenderloin.

It's the landscape, for the most part, that attracts people to Vermont. The rolling hills belie the rugged terrain underneath the green canopy of forest growth. In summer, clear lakes and streams provide ample opportunities for swimming, boating, and fishing; the hills attract hikers and mountain bikers. The more than 14,000 mi of roads, many of them only intermittently traveled by cars, are great for road biking. In fall, the leaves have their last hurrah, painting the mountainsides a stunning array of yellow, gold, red, and orange. In winter, Vermont's ski resorts are the prime enticement. Here you'll find the best ski resorts in the eastern U.S., centered along the spine of the Green Mountains north to south. The traditional heart of skiing is the town of Stowe.

Vermont may, in many ways, seem locked in time, but technological sophistication appears where you least expect it: wireless Internet access in a 19th-century farmhouse-turned-inn and cell phone coverage from the state's highest peaks. Luckily, these 21st-century perks have been able to infiltrate without many visual cues. Like an old farmhouse under renovation, Vermont's historic exterior is still the main attraction.

EXPLORING VERMONT

Vermont can be divided into three regions. The southern part of the state, flanked by Bennington on the west and Brattleboro on the east, played an important role in Vermont's Revolutionary War–era drive to independence (yes, there was once a Republic of Vermont) and its eventual statehood. The central part is characterized by rugged mountains and the gently rolling dairy lands near Lake Champlain. Northern Vermont is home to the state's capital, Montpelier, and its largest city, Burlington, as well as its most rural area, the Northeast Kingdom.

ABOUT THE RESTAURANTS

Home to the New England Culinary Institute, Vermont tends to keep the chefs who train here. The result: cuisine in Vermont is often exceptional. Seasonal menus use local fresh herbs and vegetables, along with native game. Look for imaginative approaches to native New England foods such as maple syrup (Vermont is the largest U.S. producer), dairy products (especially cheese), native fruits and berries, "new Vermont" products such as salsa and salad dressings, and venison, quail, pheasant, and other game.

VERMONT TOP 5

■ **Small-town charm.** Vermont rolls out a seemingly never-ending supply of tiny, picturesque towns made of steeples, general stores, village squares, red barns, and B&Bs.

■ **Skiing.** The East's best skiing takes place in uncrowded, modern facilities, with great views and lots and lots of fresh snow.

■ **Fall foliage.** Perhaps the most vivid colors in North America wave from the trees in September and October, when the whole state is ablaze.

■ **Gorgeous landscapes.** A sparsely populated, heavily forested state, this is an ideal place to find peace and quiet amid the mountains and valleys.

■ **Tasty and healthy eats.** The state's great soil and focus on local farming and ingredients yields great cheeses, dairies, orchards, local food resources, and restaurants.

Many of the state's restaurants belong to the Vermont Fresh Network (⊕www.vermontfresh.net), a partnership that encourages chefs to create menus from local produce. A participating chef might have picked the mesclun greens on your salad plate that morning, or the butternut squash in your soup might have been harvested by the restaurant's neighboring farmer. The food is delicious and the chefs are helping to keep Vermont's farmers in business. Your chances of finding a table for dinner vary with the season: lengthy waits are common at peak times (a reservation is always advisable); the slow months are April and November. Some of the best dining is found at country inns.

ABOUT THE HOTELS

Vermont's only large chain hotels are in Burlington and in Rutland. Elsewhere you'll find just quaint inns, bed-and-breakfasts, and small motels. The many lovely and sometimes quite luxurious inns and B&Bs provide what many people consider the quintessential Vermont lodging experience. Most areas have traditional base ski condos; at these you'll sacrifice charm for ski and stay deals and proximity to the lifts. Rates are highest during foliage season, from late September to mid-October, and lowest in late spring (April is typically the heart of "mud season") and November, although many properties close during these times. Winter, of course, is high season at Vermont's ski resorts.

WHAT IT COSTS					
	¢	$	$$	$$$	$$$$
RESTAURANTS	under $10	$10–$16	$17–$24	$25–$35	over $35
HOTELS	under $100	$100–$149	$150–$199	$200–$250	over $250

Prices are per person, for a main course at dinner. Prices are for a standard double room during peak season and not including tax or gratuities. Some inns add a 15%–18% service charge.

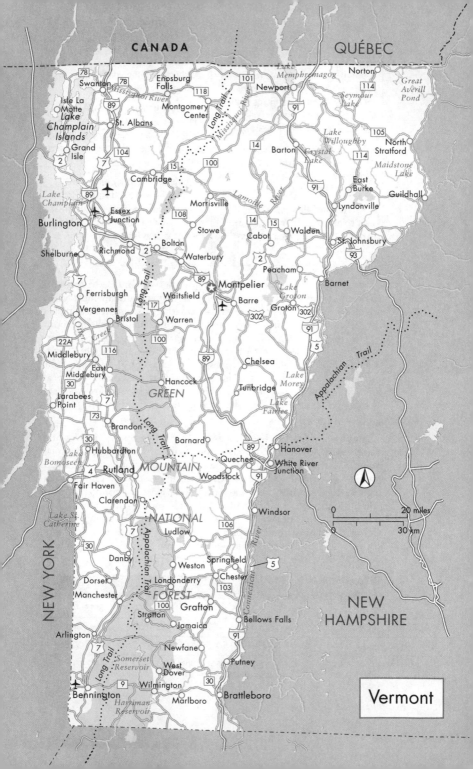

2

PLANNING YOUR TRIP

BUDGETING YOUR TIME

There are many ways to take advantage of Vermont's beauty—skiing or hiking its mountains, biking or driving its back roads, fishing or sailing its waters, shopping for local products, visiting its museums and sights, or simply finding the perfect inn and never leaving the front porch.

Distances are relatively short, yet the mountains and many back roads will slow a traveler's pace. You can see a representative north–south section of Vermont in a few days; if you have up to a week you can hit the highlights. Note that many inns have two-night minimum stays on weekends and holidays.

WHEN TO GO

In summer, the state is lush and green, while in winter, the hills and towns are blanketed with snow and skiers travel from around the East Coast to challenge Vermont's peaks. Fall is one of the most amazing times to come. If you have never seen a kaleidoscope of autumn colors, a trip to Vermont is worth braving the slow-moving traffic and paying the extra money for fall lodging. The only time things really slow down is during "mud" season—otherwise known as late fall and spring. Even innkeepers have told guests to come another time.

GETTING THERE & AROUND

Vermont is bifurcated by a mountainous north–south middle; on either side are two main highways: scenic Route 7 on the western side, and I-91 on the east (I-91 begins in New Haven, and runs through Hartford, central Massachussets, and along the Connecticut River in Vermont to the Canadian border). Flights from Boston connect to Rutland; otherwise the only major airport is Burlington.

SOUTHERN VERMONT

Cross into the Green Mountain State from Massachusetts on Interstate 91, and you might feel as if you've entered a new country. There isn't a town in sight. What you see are forested hills punctuated by rolling pastures. When you reach Brattleboro, no fast-food joints or strip malls line the exits to signal your arrival at southeastern Vermont's gateway city. En route to downtown, you pass by Victorian-era homes on tree-lined streets. From Brattleboro, you can cross over the spine of the Green Mountains toward Bennington and Manchester.

The state's southwest corner is the southern terminus of the Green Mountain National Forest, dotted with lakes, threaded with trails and old forest roads, and home to four big ski resorts: Bromley, Stratton, Mt. Snow, and Haystack Mountain.

The towns are listed in counterclockwise order in this chapter, beginning in the east in Brattleboro, then traveling west along Route 9 toward Bennington, then north to Manchester and Weston and south along scenic Routes 100 and 30 back to Townshend and Newfane.

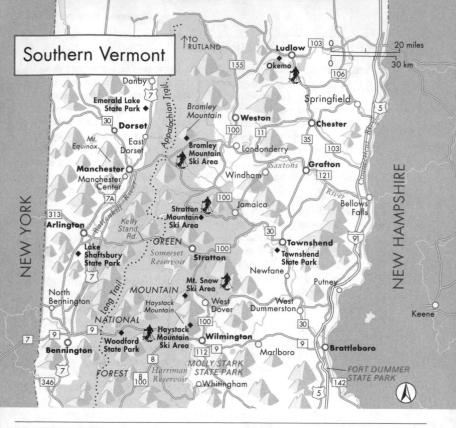

BRATTLEBORO

60 mi south of White River Junction.

Brattleboro has drawn political activists and earnest counterculturists since the 1960s. Today, the city of 12,000 is still politically and culturally active, making it Vermont's hippest city outside of Burlington.

WHAT TO SEE

Brattleboro Museum and Art Center. Downtown is the hub of Brattleboro's art scene, with this museum in historic Union Station at the forefront. It presents changing exhibits created by locally, nationally, and internationally renowned artists. ✉ *10 Vernon St.* ☎ *802/257–0124* ⊕ *www.brattleboromuseum.org* 🎟 *$4, free 1st Fri. each month 5–8:30* ☉ *Wed.–Mon. 11–5, 1st Fri. each month 11–8:30.*

SPORTS & THE OUTDOORS

CANOEING **Vermont Canoe Touring Center** (✉ *451 Putney Rd.* ☎ *802/257–5008*) conducts guided and self-guided tours, rents canoes and kayaks, and provides a shuttle service.

2

SHOPPING

ARTWORK   **Gallery in the Woods** (⊠*143 Main St.* ☎*802/257–4777* ⊕*www.galleryinthewoods.com*) sells art, jewelry, and glassware from around the world. To get a sense of the vibrant works being produced by young local artists, head to the back of Brattleboro's **Turn it Up** record shop to find **Through the Music** (⊠*2 Elliot St.* ☎*802/779–3188*), an otherwise easy-to-miss gallery. The excellent contemporary art spans genres from painting to pottery. **Vermont Artisan Designs** (⊠*106 Main St.* ☎*802/257–7044* ⊕*www.vtartisans.com*) displays ceramics, glass, wood, clothing, jewelry, and furniture from over 300 artists. **Vermont Center for Photography** (⊠*49 Flat St.* ☎*802/251–6051*) exhibits works from Vermont, New Hampshire, and Massachusetts photographers.

BOOKS   **Brattleboro Books** (⊠*106 Main St.* ☎*802/257–7044*) boasts over 75,000 used books and is a great source for local goings-on.

OFF THE BEATEN PATH

Putney. Nine miles upriver, this small town, with a population of just over 2,000, is the country cousin of bustling Brattleboro and is a haven for writers, artists, and craftspeople. There are dozens of pottery studios to visit and a few orchards. The town also has a great general store. Watch wool being spun into yarn at the **Green Mountain Spinnery** (⊠*7 Brickyard La., off I–91 Exit 4* ☎*802/387–4528 or 800/321–9665* ⊕*www.spinnery.com*). The factory shop sells yarn, knitting accessories, and patterns. Tours are conducted at 1:30 on the first and third Tuesday of the month. **Harlow's Sugar House** (⊠*563 Bellows Falls Rd., Putney* ☎*802/387–5852* ⊕*www.vermontsugar.com*), 2 mi north of Putney, has a working cider mill and sugarhouse, as well as seasonal apple and berry picking. You can buy cider, maple syrup, and other items in the gift shop.

NIGHTLIFE & THE ARTS

NIGHTLIFE   **Mole's Eye Cafe** (⊠*4 High St.* ☎*802/257–0771*) hosts an open-mike night every Thursday, and live bands Friday and Saturday. **Tinderbox** (⊠*17 Elliot St., 3rd floor* ☎*no phone*) hosts indie rock shows. **Lathis Theater** (⊠*50 Main St.* ☎*802/254–6300*) hosts art exhibits when movies aren't playing.

ARTS   Brattleboro has a gallery walk on the first Friday of each month from 5:30 to 8:30 PM.

NEED A BREAK?

The authentic gathering spot in town for coffee and conversation is **Mocha Joe's** (⊠*82 Main St.* ☎*802/257–7794*), which takes great care in sourcing beans from places like Kenya, Ethiopia, and Guatemala. This is ground zero for Brattleboro's contemporary bohemian spirit.

WHERE TO EAT

¢–$ ✕ **Brattleboro Food Co-op.** Pick up a pre-made sandwich or order a plate

AMERICAN   of curry chicken at the deli counter, then eat it in a small sitting area in this busy market. The focus is on the natural and organic, with everything from tofu sandwiches to beef satay. The delicatessen is connected to a natural-food market, and serves breakfast. ⊠*2 Main St.* ☎*802/257–0236* ▭*MC, V.*

$$–$$$
ITALIAN

✕**Max's.** Pasta creations at this trendy place include artichoke-mascarpone ravioli or Tuscan-style cauliflower with linguine. Complementing this *nuovo* Italian menu are eclectic entrées such as mahimahi in parchment, and lavender tea–smoked salmon. Sunday brunch is both traditional and adventurous, with everything from eggs to curry rice kedgeree. ✉*889 Putney Rd.* ☎*802/254–7747* ▬*MC, V* ⊗*No dinner Mon. Closed Tues.*

$$–$$$
★
STEAKHOUSE

✕**Peter Havens.** In a town better known for tofu than toniness, this chic little bistro knows just what to do with a filet mignon: serve it with Roquefort walnut butter. One room is painted a warm red, another in sage; both are punctuated by copies of Botero paintings creating a look that is one of the most sophisticated in the state. Try the house-cured gravlax made with lemon vodka or the fresh seasonal seafood, which even includes a spring fling with soft-shell crabs. The wine list is superb. ✉*32 Elliot St.* ☎*802/257–3333* ▬*AE, MC, V* ⊗*Closed Sun. and Mon. No lunch.*

$$$$
Fodor'sChoice
★
ECLECTIC

✕**T.J. Buckley's.** It's easy to miss this tiny restaurant, but those who know about it consider it one of the most romantic little restaurants in southern Vermont. Open the doors to the sleek black 1920s diner, and you'll enter what amounts to an intimate—a very intimate—theater. There are 18 seats for the show. The stage is an open kitchen, the kitchen flames a few feet away. And working under the whisper of vocal jazz and candlelight is the star of the show: Michael Fuller, the dashing owner and sole chef who has been at the helm for 25 years. The three tactful waitresses are delightful supporting players. The contemporary menu is conveyed verbally each day and is based on locally available ingredients. It's pre-theater dinner and theater all in one, a romantic triumph. ✉*132 Elliot St.* ☎*802/257–4922* ⊲*Reservations essential* ▬*No credit cards* ⊗*No lunch. Closed Mon. and Tues.*

¢–$
SOUTHERN

✕**Top of the Hill Grill.** Hickory-smoked ribs, beef brisket, apple-smoked turkey, and pulled pork are a few of the favorites at this barbecue just outside town. Larger parties can opt for "family-style" dinners. Homemade pecan pie is the dessert of choice. You can sit indoors in the informal dining room with big windows, but the best seats are outdoors at picnic tables overlooking the West River. ✉*632 Putney Rd.* ☎*802/258–9178* ▬*No credit cards* ⊗*Closed Nov.–mid-Apr.*

WHERE TO STAY

$$

▦**Forty Putney Road.** Tim and Amy Brady, the young and engaging couple who took over the property in 2007, have breathed new life into this French-style manse, restoring some of its more interesting original features, like nickel plated bathroom fixtures, and adding new ones like flat screen TVs. They've also made sure that it's full of thoughtful and comforting details, like a mini-fridge stocked with complimentary soda, water, granola bars, and chips. Other treats include a hot tub, a billiard table, and the neighboring Retreat Meadows, a bird sanctuary at the junction of the West and Connecticut rivers that offers good hiking trails. There's no restaurant, but a decent pub menu and wine are offered. Stay here if you want a good B&B within walking distance of downtown. **Pros:** caring hosts; clean, remodeled rooms. **Cons:** short walk into town. ✉*192 Putney Rd.* ☎*802/254–6268 or 800/941–2413*

⊕*www.fortyputneyroad.com* ⤶*5 rooms, 1 suite* &*In-room: DVD, Wi-Fi. In-hotel: room service, bar, no elevator, laundry service, public Internet, public Wi-Fi, no kids under 12, no-smoking rooms* ≡*AE, D, MC, V* |○|*BP.*

$$–$$$
Fodor'sChoice
★

Hickory Ridge House. If you're looking for a relaxing country getaway in southeast Vermont, this historic, redbrick, 1808 Federal-style mansion, a former sheep farm set on a wide meadow, is a sure bet. The house has a sturdy comfort that distinguishes it from daintier inns. Owners Gillian and Dennis,

> **BILLBOARDS NO MORE**
>
> Did you know that there are no billboards in Vermont? The state banned them in 1967 (similar laws exist in Maine, Alaska and Hawaii). The last one came down in 1975. The motive, of course, was so that when you look out your window, you see trees and other scenic sights, not advertisements. (It may, however, make playing the Alphabet Game with your child a bit difficult.)

along with their dog Jack, bring an English touch to it all. Most rooms have Rumford fireplaces and canopy beds; they all have fine linens. A separate two-bedroom cottage has a full kitchen. Thousands of acres of nature preserve surround the property's eight acres of meadow, making it great for hiking and cross-country skiing. **Pros:** peaceful, scenic property; terrific house; quintessential B&B experience. **Cons:** can be expensive. ⊠*53 Hickory Ridge Rd., 11 mi north of Brattleboro, Putney* ☎*802/387–5709 or 800/380–9218* ⊕*www.hickoryridgehouse. com* ⤶*6 rooms, 1 cottage* &*In-room: DVD, VCR (some), Wi-Fi. In-hotel: no elevator, public Internet, public Wi-Fi, some pets allowed, no-smoking rooms* ≡*MC, V* |○|*BP.*

¢–$$

Latchis Hotel. To stay in the heart of town at a low rate, you can do no better than the Latchis. The three-story art deco landmark is run by a non-profit group dedicated to preserving and restoring the 1938 building. Rooms are not lavish, but they are clean and functional, and have original sinks and tiling in the bathrooms. Most overlook Main Street, with New Hampshire's mountains in the background. The lobby has original and notably colorful terrazzo floors. Downstairs you can catch a movie under the impressive zodiac ceiling of the Latchis Theater or eat at the Flat St. Brew Pub. **Pros:** heart-of-town location; inexpensive. **Cons:** clean but dull furnishings. ⊠*50 Main St.* ☎*802/254–6300 or 800/798–6301* ⊕*www.latchis.com* ⤶*30 rooms, 3 suites* &*In-room: refrigerator, Wi-Fi. In-hotel: public Wi-Fi, no smoking rooms* ≡*AE, MC, V* |○|*CP.*

EN ROUTE

Tiny Marlboro, 10 mi west of Brattleboro, draws musicians from around the world each summer to the Marlboro College campus for the **Marlboro Music Festival** (⊠*Marlboro Music Center, Marlboro College* ☎*802/254–2394, 215/569–4690 Sept.–June* ⊕*www.marlboro-music.org*). Founded by Rudolf Serkin, who was joined for many years by Pablo Casals, the festival presents weekend chamber music concerts from mid-July to mid-August.

WILMINGTON

18 mi west of Brattleboro.

The village of Wilmington, with its classic Main Street lined with 18th- and 19th-century buildings, anchors the Mt. Snow Valley. Most of the valley's lodging and dining establishments, however, line Route 100, which travels 5 mi north to West Dover and Mt. Snow, where skiers flock on winter weekends. The area abounds with cultural activity year-round, from concerts to art exhibits.

WHAT TO SEE

Adams Farm. At this working farm you can collect fresh eggs from the chicken coop, feed a rabbit, milk a goat, ride a tractor or a pony, and jump in the hay—and run through the corn maze in summer and take sleigh rides in winter. The indoor livestock barn is open Wednesday through Sunday, November to mid-June; an outdoor version is open daily the rest of the year. The farm store sells more than 200 handmade quilts and sweaters. Open all year Wednesday–Sunday 10–5. ⊠*15 Higley Hill Rd., 3 mi north of Wilmington, off Rte. 100* ☎*802/464–3762* ⊕*www.adamsfamilyfarm.com.*

Southern Vermont Natural History Museum. This museum, 5 mi east of Wilmington on Route 9, houses one of New England's largest collections of mounted birds, including three extinct birds and a complete collection of mammals native to the Northeast. The museum also has live hawk and owl exhibits. ⊠*Rte. 9* ☎*802/464–0048* ⛚*$3* ☉*Memorial Day–late Oct., daily 10–5; late Oct.–Memorial Day, most weekends 10–4, call ahead.*

SPORTS & THE OUTDOORS

BOATING **Green Mountain Flagship Company** (⊠*Rte. 9, 2 mi west of Wilmington* ☎*802/464–2975* ⊕*www.greenmountainflagship.com*) runs *Mt. Mills,* a 55-passenger cruise boat on Lake Whitingham. The 90-minute cruise takes you by New England's largest nudist beach. You can also rent canoes, kayaks, and sailboats from May to late October.

FISHING Eight-mile-long **Lake Whitingham (Harriman Reservoir)** is the largest body of water completely within the state's boundaries. It has good fishing and 28 mi of undeveloped shoreline. Boat-launch areas are at Wards Cove, Whitingham, Mountain Mills, and the Ox Bow.

HIKING **Molly Stark State Park** (⊠*Rte. 9 east of Wilmington* ☎*802/464–5460*) has a hiking trail that leads to a vista from a fire tower on Mt. Olga.

SKI AREA The closest major ski area to all of the Northeast's big cities, **Mount Snow Resort** (⊠*400 Mountain Rd., Mount Snow* ☎*802/464–3333, 802/464–2151 snow conditions, 800/245–7669 lodging* ⊕*www. mountsnow.com*), is also one of the state's premier family resorts and has a full roster of year-round activities. The almost 800-acre facility encompasses a hotel, 10 condo developments, an 18-hole golf course, a health club and spa, 45 mi of mountain-biking trails, and an extensive network of hiking trails.

Mount Snow prides itself on its 101 fan guns, which has given it the earliest open time of any ski area in the state. More than half of the 107 trails down its 1,700-foot vertical summit are intermediate, wide, and sunny. There are four major downhill areas. The main mountain is where you'll find most of the beginner slopes, especially toward the bottom. The North Face is where you'll find the majority of expert terrain. Corinthia used to be a separate ski mountain, but is now connected with a mix of trail levels. The south face, Sunbrook, has wide, sunny trails. The trails are served by 19 lifts, including 3 high-speed quads. Snowmaking covers 85% of the terrain. There are 98 acres of glades. The ski school's instruction program is designed to help skiers of all ages and abilities. Mount Snow also has five terrain parks of different skill levels, and a 400-foot halfpipe with 18-foot walls. Skiing programs start with the Cub Camp, designed for kids age 3. Snow Camp teaches kids 4 to 6, and Mountain Camp and Mountain Riders is for kids 7 to 14.

Two cross-country ski centers near Mount Snow provide more than 68 mi of varied terrain. **Timber Creek** (⊠*Rte. 100, north of Mount Snow* ☎*802/464–0999* ⊕*www.timbercreekxc.com*) is appealingly small with 9 mi of groomed loops. The groomed trails at the **White House of Wilmington** (⊠*178 Rte. 9* ☎*802/464 2135* ⊕*www.whitehouseinn. com*) cover 30 mi. Both areas have Nordic equipment and snowshoes for rent.

SNOWMOBILE **High Country Tours** (⊠*Rte. 100, West Dover* ☎*802/464–2108*) runs
TOURS one-hour, two-hour, and ½-day snowmobile tours from two locations: one near Mount Snow, the other west of Wilmington in Searsburg.

SHOPPING
Downtown Wilmington is lined with unique shops and galleries. **Quaigh Design Centre** (⊠*11 W. Main St. [Rte. 9]* ☎*802/464–2780*) sells artwork from Britain and New England—including works by Vermont woodcut artists Sabra Field and Mary Azarian—and Scottish woolens and tartans. **Young and Constantin Gallery** (⊠*10 S. Main St.* ☎*802/464–2515*) sells handblown glassware, ceramics, and art from local and nationally known artisans.

THE ARTS
ARTS A year-round roster of music, theater, film, and fine art is presented at the **Memorial Hall Center for the Arts** (⊠*14 W. Main St.* ☎*802/464–8411*). In addition to steak and Mexican specialties, the standard fare on weekends at **Poncho's Wreck** (⊠*S. Main St.* ☎*802/464–9320*) is acoustic jazz or mellow rock.

WHERE TO EAT
¢–$ ✕**Dot's Restaurant.** Look for the classic red neon sign (one of only a
DINER handful still permitted in Vermont) at the main corner of Wilmington: Dot's is a local landmark. A photo inside depicts the interior in the early 1940s—except for the soda fountain, all else is identical, from the long counter with swivel chairs to the fireplace in the back. This friendly place is packed with locals and skiers; the menu ranges from chicken cordon bleu to homemade rost beef. Berry berry pancakes

are de rigeur for breakfast, and a bowl of turkey chili for lunch. A second location is in a strip mall in West Dover. ⊠ *3 West Main St.* ☎ *802/464–7284* ☐ *MC, V.*

$$$-$$$$
Fodor's Choice
★
CONTINENTAL

✕ **Inn at Sawmill Farm.** No other restaurant in Vermont aims as high with its haute Continental food, wine, and service as the restaurant at Sawmill. Order a beer and the bottle is served chilled in a small ice bucket, as if it were champagne. This reverent service, and deference to potables, comes from the top: chef and owner Brill Williams passionately cares for his 17,000-bottle cellar, the biggest restaurant collection in the state. It's also Vermont's only Wine Spectator Grand Award winner. The aim is haute Continental. Try the potato-crusted fish of the day served in beurre blanc sauce, or grilled loin of venison. Gourmands of Mount Snow, this is your place, if only because nobody is trying harder. ⊠ *7 Crosstown Rd., at Rte. 100, West Dover* ☎ *802/464–8131 or 800/493–1133* ⊕ *www.theinnatsawmillfarm.com* ☐ *AE, D, MC, V* ⊘ *Closed Easter–late May.*

WHERE TO STAY

$$-$$$
▥ **Deerhill Inn.** The exterior of this inn leaves something to be desired, but the interior makes up for it. The common living room features a large stone fireplace and works by local artists hang on the walls. Guest rooms are cozy and adorned with English floral linens; balcony rooms are more spacious. The wonderful dining room headed by chef and owner Michael Allen is one of the best in town. **Pros:** great restaurant, nicely renovated rooms. **Cons:** building exterior is unimpressive. ⊠ *Valley View Rd., West Dover* ⌂ *Box 136, West Dover 05356* ☎ *802/464–3100 or 800/993–3379* ⊕ *www.deerhill.com* ⇲ *12 rooms, 2 suites* ⊘ *Closed weekdays in Apr. and Nov.* ⌖ *In-room: no a/c, no phone, DVD (some), no TV (some), Wi-Fi. In-hotel: restaurant, bar, pool, no elevator, public Internet, public Wi-Fi, no kids under 12, no-smoking rooms* ☐ *AE, MC, V* ⍓ *BP, MAP.*

$$$$
▥ **Grand Summit Hotel.** The 200-room base lodge at Mount Snow will be an easy choice for skiers who don't care about anything but getting on the slopes as quickly as possible. Ski-in ski-out ease is the main sell and package deals can make the lodging cheap. The lobby has the look of a traditional ski lodge, with a big center fireplace, but the overall feel is that of an efficient, new hotel. Rooms are clean and fairly basic. A big outdoor heated pool sits beside two hot tubs at the base of the slopes. In summer guests enjoy the property golf and tennis courts. **Pros:** easy ski access; clean, modern property. **Cons:** somewhat bland decor in rooms. ⊠ *Mount Snow Rd., West Dover 05356* ☎ *800/451–4211* ⊕ *www.mountsnow.com/grandsummit.html* ⇲ *104 rooms, 96 suites* ⌖ *In room: kitchen (some), refrigerator (some), DVD (some), VCR (some), Wi-Fi. In-hotel: 2 restaurants, bar, golf course, tennis courts, pool, gym, spa, children's programs (ages 4–14), laundry service, public Internet, public Wi-Fi, no-smoking rooms* ☐ *AE, D, MC, V.*

$$$$
▥ **Inn at Sawmill Farm.** Full of character and charm, this inn in a converted barn has common rooms elegantly accented with English chintzes, antiques, and Oriental rugs. Each of the guest rooms—in the main inn or in cottages scattered on the property's 22 acres—is individually decorated, and many have sitting areas and fireplaces. Dinner

in the formal dining room, as well as a full breakfast, is included in the price of a stay. **Pros:** spacious grounds, attentive service. **Cons:** overload of floral prints in some rooms. ✉7 Crosstown Rd., at Rte 100, West Dover ☎802/464–8131 or 800/493–1133 ⊕www.theinnatsaw millfarm.com ↩21 rooms ☒In-room: no phone, no TV. In-hotel: restaurant, tennis court, pool, no kids under 8, no-smoking rooms ☐AE, D, MC, V ⊗Closed Easter–late May ⦿BP, MAP.

$$ ⚑ **White House of Wilmington.** It's hard to miss this 1915 Federal-style ☪ mansion standing imposingly atop a high hill off Route 9 east of Wilmington. Indeed if the President took up residence in Vermont, he (or she) would surely feel at home here. Grand balconies and the main balustraded terrace overlook the hill. If you have kids, you can trust they'll create memories tubing down the hill in winter (tubes are provided). The grand staircase leads to rooms with antique bathrooms and brass wall sconces; some rooms have fireplaces and lofts. There is a cross-country ski touring and snowshoeing center on-site along with 7 mi of groomed trails. The restaurant has an extensive wine list and undeniably romantic dining in the Mahogany Room, which has its original fireplace and wood paneling. And for anyone who thinks they've seen it all: take a dunk in the small indoor pool, which is formed from an old coal bin and surrounded by hand-painted murals of Roman bath scenes. **Pros:** great for kids and families; intriguing, big, old-fashioned property; intimate dining. **Cons:** removed from town activity. ✉178 Rte. 9, Wilmington, ☎802/464–2135 or 800/541–2135 ⊕www. whitehouseinn.com ↩24 rooms, 1 cottage ☒In-room: no a/c (some), no phone, no TV, Wi-Fi (some). In-hotel: restaurant, bar, pools, no elevator, laundry service, public Internet, public Wi-Fi, no-smoking rooms ☐AE, D, MC, V ⦿BP.

BENNINGTON

21 mi west of Wilmington.

Bennington is the commercial focus of Vermont's southwest corner. It's really three towns in one: Downtown Bennington, Old Bennington, and North Bennington. Downtown Bennington, where U.S. 7 and U.S. 9 intersect, has retained much of the industrial character it developed in the 19th century, when paper mills, gristmills, and potteries formed the city's economic base.

West of downtown, Old Bennington is a National Register Historic District centered along the axis of Monument Avenue and well endowed with stately Colonial and Victorian mansions. Here, at the Catamount Tavern (now a private home just north of Church Street), Ethan Allen organized the Green Mountain Boys, who helped capture Fort Ticonderoga in 1775.

WHAT TO SEE

Fodor'sChoice ★ **Old First Church.** In the graveyard of this church, the tombstone of the poet Robert Frost proclaims, "I had a lover's quarrel with the world." ✉Church St. and Monument Ave.

♻ **Bennington Battle Monument.** This 306-foot stone obelisk (with an elevator to the top) commemorates General Stark's victory over the British, who attempted to capture Bennington's stockpile of supplies. Inside the monument you can learn all about the battle, which took place near Walloomsac Heights in New York State on August 16, 1777, and helped bring about the surrender of the British commander "Gentleman Johnny" Burgoyne two months later. The summit provides commanding views of the Massachusetts Berkshires, the New York Adirondacks, and the Vermont Green Mountains. ⊠*15 Monument Cir., Old Bennington* ☎*802/447–0550* ⊠*$2* ⊙*Mid-Apr.–Oct., daily 9–5.*

Bennington Museum. The rich collections at this museum include military artifacts, early tools, dolls, toys, and the Bennington Flag, one of the oldest Stars and Stripes in existence. One room is devoted to early Bennington pottery, and two rooms cover the history of American glass (fine Tiffany specimens are on display). The museum displays the world's largest public collection of the work of Grandma Moses (1860–1961), the popular self-taught folk artist who lived and painted in the area. ⊠*75 Main St. (Rte. 9)* ☎*802/447–1571* ⊕*www.bennington museum.com* ⊠*$8* ⊙*Thurs.–Tues. 10–5.*

North Bennington. Just north of Old Bennington is this village, home to Bennington ·College, lovely mansions, Lake Paran, three covered bridges, and a wonderful old train depot. Contemporary stone sculpture and white-frame neo-Colonial dorms surrounded by acres of cornfields punctuate the green meadows of **Bennington College**'s placid campus (⊠*Rte. 67A off U.S. 7 (look for stone entrance gate)* ☎*802/442–5401*). The architecturally significant **Park-McCullough House** (⊠*Corner of Park and West Sts.* ☎*802/442–5441* ⊕*www. parkmccullough.org* ⊠*$8* ⊙*Mid-May–mid-Oct., daily 10–4; last tour at 3)* is a 35-room classic French Empire–style mansion, built in 1865 and furnished with period pieces. Several restored flower gardens grace the landscaped grounds, and a stable houses a collection of antique carriages. Call for details on the summer concert series.

Robert Frost Stone House Museum. A few miles north along Route 7A is the town of Shaftsbury. It was here that Robert Frost came in 1920 "to plant a new Garden of Eden with a thousand apple trees of some unforbidden variety." The museum tells the story of the nine years (1920–29) Frost spent living in the house with his wife and four children. (Frost spent the 1930s in a house up the road in Shaftsbury, now owned by a Hollywood movie producer.) It was here that he penned "Stopping by Woods on a Snowy Evening" and published two books of poems. Seven of the Frost family's original 80 acres can be wandered. Among the apple boughs you just might strike inspiration of your own. ⊠*75 Main St. (Rte. 9)* ☎*802/447–1571* ⊕*www.frostfriends.org* ⊠*$5* ⊙*May–Christmas daily 10–5.*

SPORTS & THE OUTDOORS
Lake Shaftsbury State Park (⊠*Rte. 7A, 10½ mi north of Bennington* ☎*802/375–9978*) has a swimming beach, nature trails, boat and canoe rentals, and a snack bar. **Woodford State Park** (⊠*Rte. 9, 10 mi east of*

2

Bennington ☎*802/447–7169)* has an activities center on Adams Reservoir, playground, boat and canoe rentals, and nature trails.

SHOPPING

BAKED GOODS The **Apple Barn and Country Bake Shop** (✉*U.S. 7 S* ☎*802/447–7780)* sells home-baked goodies, fresh cider, Vermont cheeses, and maple syrup and has a cornfield maze. The shop is open from September to mid-October.

BOOKS **Now & Then Books** (✉*439 Main St.* ☎*802/442–5566* ⊕*www. nowandthenbooksvt.com),* is a great used bookstore located in an upstairs shop. **The Bennington Bookshop** (✉*467 Main St.* ☎*802/442– 5050),* sells new books and gifts and has free Wi-Fi.

THE ARTS

The **Bennington Center for the Arts** (✉*Rte. 9 at Gypsy La.* ☎*802/442– 7158)* hosts cultural events, including exhibitions by local and national artists. The on-site **Oldcastle Theatre Co.** (☎*802/447–0564)* hosts fine regional theater from May through October. The **Basement Music Series** (✉*29 Sage St.North Bennington* ☎*802/442–5549),* run by the nonprofit Vermont Arts Exchange, is a funky basement cabaret venue in an old factory buiding. It hosts the best contemporary music performances in town.

WHERE TO EAT

¢ ✕**Blue Benn Diner.** Breakfast is served all day in this authentic diner,
AMERICAN where the eats include turkey hash and breakfast burritos with scrambled eggs, sausage, and chilies, plus pancakes of all imaginable varieties. The menu lists many vegetarian selections. Lines may be long, especially on weekends: locals and tourists alike can't stay away. ✉*314 North St.* ☎*802/442–5140* ⊜*Reservations not accepted* ⊟*No credit cards* ⊗*No dinner Sat.–Tues.*

$$–$$$ ✕**Four Chimneys Inn.** It's a treat just to walk up the long path to this
CONTINENTAL classic Old Bennington mansion, the most refined setting around. The dining room is a discrete, quiet room lit by candlelight and a gas fireplace. Thom Simonetti creates a sophisticated seasonal menu. If you're lucky you might find a wonderful hand-crafted agnolotti pasta with angus beef—braised in port with a shallot confit and cherry ragout and topped with a local blue cheese. The poached salmon comes in a lemon-dill beurre blanc sauce. Desserts are hit or miss. ✉*21 West Rd. (Rte. 9), Old Bennington* ☎*802/447–3500* ⊕*www.fourchimneys.com* ⊜*Reservations essential* ⊟*AE, D, MC, V* ⊗*No lunch. Nov.–Aug. closed Mon. and Tues.; Sept.–Oct. closed Mon.*

$–$$ ✕**Pangaea Lounge.** Don't let the dusty old storefront fool you, Benning-
★ ton's in-the-know crowd comes here before anywhere else for afford-
ECLECTIC able comfort food and an excellent bar. Directly next door is Pangaea, the fancier twin restaurant, where the menu is somewhat overpriced. We prefer the Lounge, which is handsome and irresistible, with its scuffed-up floor, intimate proportions, and fine approach to simple food and service. At the helm at the corner bar is Jason, an impressive mixologist. The eclectic pub fare includes such dishes as pot roast chimichangas, Cobb salad with Danish blue cheese, salmon burgers,

and seared pork loin with a potato croquette. On weekends in warmer months, follow the crowd out the back stairs to the deck. ⊠*3 Prospect St., 3 mi north of Bennington, North Bennington* ☎*802/442–7171* ⊟*AE, MC, V* ⊘*No lunch.*

WHERE TO STAY

¢–$ ★ ⊞ **Eddington House.** You can thank Patti Eddington for maintaining this three-bedroom house, probably the best value in all of Vermont. You get a spotless and updated room in a house you can't help but feel is all your own. Patti lives in an attached barn, giving you all the privacy you need. Homemade desserts and wine are always out on the counter. The house is in the heart of North Bennington, across the street from a market and two restaurants. The most expensive room, the Village Suite, is $109, a fantastic value. Another at $89 has a four-poster bed with a lovely old tub, separate shower, and great light. Ask about the excellent dinner package. **Pros:** spotlessly clean home and rooms; privacy and gentle service. **Cons:** slightly off usual tourist track. ⊠*21 Main St., North Bennington,* ☎*802/442–1551* ⊕*www.eddingtonhouseinn.com* ↩*3 rooms* ⌂*In room: no phone, no TV (some), Wi-Fi. In-hotel: no elevator, public Wi-Fi, some pets allowed, no children under 12, no-smoking rooms* ⊟*AE, MC, V* ⦿*BP.*

$$–$$$
Fodor's Choice
★
⊞ **Four Chimneys Inn.** This is the quintessential Old Bennington mansion, and one of the best inns in Vermont. The three-story 1915 neo-Georgian looks out over a substantial lawn and a wonderful old stone wall. On the second floor, rooms 1, 3, and 11 have great bay windows and fireplaces. One has a chandelier hung over a hot tub, reproduction antique washstands, and a flat screen TV cleverly concealed by a painting. All rooms are light and bright. This property has long been an inn but only recently did it spring back to life in high style, under the careful attention of new owner and innkeeper Lynn Green. Luster was returned to the original hardwood floors in 2008. Two cottages in back (a two-story brick former ice house, and a former carriage house) overlook a pond. **Pros:** stately mansion that's extremely well kept; formal dining; very clean, spacious, renovated rooms. **Cons:** common room/bar closes early. ⊠*21 West Rd. (Rte. 9), Old Bennington,* ☎*802/447–3500* ⊕*www.fourchimneys.com* ↩*9 rooms, 2 suites* ⌂*In-room: DVD, Ethernet, Wi-Fi. In-hotel: restaurant, bar, bicycles, no elevator, laundry service, public Wi-Fi, no kids under 5, no-smoking rooms* ⊟*AE, D, MC, V* ⦿*BP.*

ARLINGTON

15 mi north of Bennington.

Smaller than Bennington and more down to earth than upper-crust Manchester to the north, Arlington exudes a certain Rockwellian folksiness. And it should. Illustrator Norman Rockwell lived here from 1939 to 1953, and many of the models for his portraits of small-town life were his neighbors.

2

WHAT TO SEE

Norman Rockwell Exhibition. Although no original paintings are displayed at this gallery, the rooms are crammed with reproductions of the illustrator's works, arranged in every way conceivable: chronologically, by subject matter, and juxtaposed with photos of the models, several of whom work here. ⊠ *Main St. (Rte. 7A)* ☎ *802/375–6423* 💲 *$3* 🕙 *May–Oct., daily 9–5; Nov.–Apr., Fri.–Mon. 9–5.*

OFF THE BEATEN PATH

The endearing town of **East Arlington** (⊠ *1 mi east of Arlington on East Arlington Rd.*) sits on the shore of Roaring Brook just east of Arlington. An 18th-century gristmill is now home to a fine antiques shop, one of a few in town, and other fun shops, including a fudge and teddy bear store (⇨ Shopping).

A covered bridge leads to the quaint town green of **West Arlington** ⊠ *West of Arlington on Rte. 313 West*), where Norman Rockwell once lived. River Road follows along the south side of the Battenkill River, a scenic drive. If you continue west along Route 313, you'll come to the Wayside General Store, a real charmer where you can pick up sandwiches and chat with locals. The store is frequently mentioned (anonymously) in the Vermont columns written by Christopher Kimball, editor of *Cooks Illustrated*.

SPORTS & THE OUTDOORS

★ **BattenKill Canoe** (⊠ *6328 Rte. 7A, Sunderland* ☎ *802/362–2800 or 800/421–5268* ⊕ *www.battenkill.com*) rents canoes for trips along the Battenkill River, which runs directly behind the shop. If you're hooked, they also run bigger white-water trips as well as inn-to-inn tours.

SHOPPING

ANTIQUES   More than 70 dealers display their wares at **East Arlington Antiques Center** (⊠ *East Arlington Rd., East Arlington* ☎ *802/375–6144*), which is in a converted 1930s movie theater.

Fodor'sChoice   **Gristmill Antiques** (⊠ *316 Old Mill Rd.,East Arlington* ☎ *802/375–
★   2500*) is a beautiful two-floor shop in a historic mill that looks out over Roaring Brook.

GIFTS   **The Bearatorium** (⊠ *Old Mill Rd., East Arlington* ☎ *802/375–6037*) has 🐻 a chocolate museum where you can learn all about chocolate. It does wine and chocolate pairings, sells fudge and other candies, and has a large collection of teddy bears for sale. In the winter, it's closed on Tuesdays and Wednesdays.

NIGHTLIFE & THE ARTS

The **Friday Night Fireside Music Series** in the cozy tavern at the West Mountain Inn (⊠ *River Rd., West Arlington* ☎ *802/375–6516*) features great live music acts every other Friday evening from November through May. There's a $10 cover.

WHERE TO STAY

$$–$$$ 🏨 **Arlington Inn.** Greek-revival columns at this 1848 home lend it an imposing presence in the middle of town, but the atmosphere is friendly and old-fashioned. Rooms are dainty and Victorian, dressed heavily in florals, and are spread among the main inn, parsonage, and carriage house. Landscaping includes a garden, gazebo, pond, and waterfall. The inn runs one of the most repsected restaurants in town, and its bar is one of the most colonial in the state. **Pros:** heart-of-town location, friendly atmosphere. **Cons:** rooms are dated. ⊠*Rte. 7A* ☎*802/375-6532 or 800/443-9442* ⊕*www.arlingtoninn.com* ➥*13 rooms, 5 suites* ⚘*In-room: Wi-Fi. In-hotel: restaurant, bar, no elevator, public Wi-Fi, no-smoking rooms* ⊟*AE, D, MC, V* ¶⊙¶*BP, MAP.*

$$$–$$$$ 🏠**West Mountain Inn.** This 1810 farmhouse sits on 150 acres on the
☾ side of a mountain, offering plenty of hiking trails and easy access
Fodor'sChoice to the Battenkill River where you can canoe or go tubing. In winter
★ you can sled down a former ski slope, or borrow the inn's snow shoes or cross-country skis. It's a beautiful place made more so by blithe innkeeper Amie Emmons, who lines the front yard in summer with Adirondack chairs that overlook the mountains. Families will love the alpacas, and there's a kids room painted with Disney characters and filled with games and videos. (Amie's young son Owen and Siriu, the inn's golden retriever, are the resident play pals.) Since the house is a patchwork of additions and gables, rooms have eccentric configurations. Though they are not luxurious or flawless, they are comfortable and have great views and interesting sitting areas. The onsite restaurant is well-respected; dishes have a strong focus on organic and locally grown vegetables and meats. **Pros:** mountainside location, great for families, lots of outdoor activities. **Cons:** slightly outdated bedding and carpets. ⊠*River Rd., Arlington* ☎*802/375-6516* ⊕*www.west mountaininn.com* ➥*16 rooms, 6 suites* ⚘*In-room: no phone, no TV. In-hotel: restaurant, bar, water sports, bicycles, no elevator, laundry service, no- smoking rooms* ⊟*AE, D, MC, V* ¶⊙¶*BP, MAP.*

MANCHESTER

★ *9 mi northeast of Arlington.*

Well-to-do Manchester has been a popular summer retreat since the mid-19th century when city dwellers traveled north to take in the cool clean air at the foot of 3,816-foot Mt. Equinox. Manchester Village's tree-shaded marble sidewalks and stately old homes—Main Street here could hardly be more picture perfect—reflect the luxurious resort life-style of more than a century ago. A mile north on 7A, Manchester Center is the commercial twin to colonial Manchester Village. This is where you'll find the town's famed upscale factory outlets doing business in attractive faux-colonial shops. If you're coming here from Arlington, take scenic Route 7A.

WHAT TO SEE

Manchester Village is home to the world headqurters of Orvis, the outdoors goods brand that began here in the 19th century. Its complex includes a fly-fishing school with lessons in its casting ponds and the Battenkill River (⇨Sports & the Outdoors).

American Museum of Fly Fishing. This museum houses the world's largest collection of angling art and angling-related objects. Displays include more than 1,500 rods, 800 reels, 30,000 flies, and the tackle of famous people like Winslow Homer, Bing Crosby, and Jimmy Carter. ⊠*4070 Main St. (Rte. 7A)* ☎*802/362–3300* ⊕*www.amff.com* ⊠*$5* ⊙*Daily 10–4.*

Fodor'sChoice
★ **Hildene.** The "Lincoln Family Home" is a twofold treat, providing historical insight into the life of the Lincolns while escorting you into the lavish Manchester life of the 1900s. Abraham had only one son who survived to adulthood, Robert Todd Lincoln, who served as secretary of war and head of the Pullman Company. Robert bought the beautifully preserved 412-acre estate and built a 24-room mansion where he and his descendants lived from 1903–75. The entire grounds are open for exploration—you can hike, picnic, and ski; use the astronomical observatory; loll across beautiful gardens; and walk through the sturdy Georgian-revival house, which holds the family's original furniture, books, and possessions. One of three surviving stovepipe hats owned by Abraham Lincoln and Robert's Harvard yearbook are among the treasures you'll find. When the 1,000-pipe aeolian organ is played, the music reverberates as though from the mansion's very bones. The highlight, though, may be the elaborate formal gardens: in June a thousand peonies bloom. When snow conditions permit, you can cross-country ski and snowshoe on the property. Robert's carriage house now houses the attractive gift shop and visitor center that showcases his daughter's 1928 vintage Franklin. ⊠*Rte. 7A* ☎*802/362–1788* ⊕*www.hildene. org* ⊠*Tour $12.50, grounds pass $5* ⊙*Daily 9:30–4:30.*

Southern Vermont Arts Center. Rotating exhibits and a permanent collection of more than 700 pieces of 19th- and 20th-century American art are showcased at this 12,500-square-foot museum. The arts center's original building, a graceful Georgian mansion set on 407 acres, is the frequent site of concerts, performances, and film screenings. In summer and fall, a pleasant restaurant with magnificent views serves lunch. ⊠*West Rd.* ☎*802/362–1405* ⊕*www.svac.org* ⊠*$8* ⊙*Tues.–Sat. 10–5, Sun. noon–5.*

SPORTS & THE OUTDOORS

FISHING **Battenkill Anglers** (⊠*6204 Main St., Manchester* ☎*802/379–1444*) teaches the art and science of fly-fishing in both private and group lessons. **Orvis Co.** (⊠*Rte. 7A, Manchester Center* ☎*800/235–9763*) hosts a nationally known fly-fishing school on the Battenkill, the state's most famous trout stream, with 2- and 2½-day courses offered weekly between June and October.

HIKING One of the most popular segments of Vermont's **Long Trail** starts from a parking lot on Route 11/30 and goes to the top of Bromley Mountain. The 6-mi round-trip trek takes about four hours. The **Mountain Goat** (⊠*4886 Main St.* ☎*802/362–5159*) sells hiking and backpacking equipment and rents snowshoes and cross-country and telemark skis.

SHOPPING

ART &   In Manchester Village, **Frog Hollow at Equinox** (✉3566 Main St. [Rte.
ANTIQUES   7A] ☎802/362–3321) is a nonprofit collective that sells such contem-
★   porary works as jewelry, glassware, and home furnishings from a huge
range of Vermont artisans.

Long Ago and Far Away (✉Green Mountain Village Shops, 4963 Main
St. ☎802/362–3435 ⊕www.longagoandfaraway.com) specializes in
fine indigenous artwork, including Canadian Inuit stone sculpture. The
large **Tilting at Windmills Gallery** (✉24 Highland Ave. ☎802/362–3022
⊕www.tilting.com) displays and sells the paintings and sculpture of
nationally known artists.

BOOKS   **Northshire Bookstore** (✉4869 Main St. ☎802/362–2200 or 800/437–
Fodor'sChoice   3700) is the heart of Manchester Center, and no wonder—it's a huge
★   independently owned bookseller with a massive children's section and
is considered one of the finest bookstores in the country. Connected to
the bookstore is the Spiral Press Café, where you can sit for a grilled
pesto-chicken sandwich on focaccia bread or a latte and scone.

CLOTHING   The two-story, lodge-like **Orvis Flagship Store** (✉4200 Rte. 7A
★   ☎802/362–3750) has a trout pond as well as the company's latest
clothing and accessories.

Fodor'sChoice   Spread out across Manchester Center, **Manchester Designer Outlets**
★   (✉U.S. 7 and Rte. 11/30 ☎802/362–3736 or 800/955–7467 ⊕www.
manchesterdesigneroutlets.com) is the most upscale collection of stores
in northern New England—and every store is a discount outlet! Adding
to the allure, town ordinances decree the look of the shops be in tune in
with the surrounding historic homes, making these the most attractive
and decidedly colonial-looking outlets you'll ever see. In 2008, three
new outlets opened: Michael Kors, Betsey Johnson, and Ann Taylor.
These add to such esteemed lines as Tumi, Escada, Armani, Coach,
Polo Ralph Lauren, Brooks Brothers, and Theory. There's also a few
less expensive brands like Gap and Banana Republic.

NIGHTLIFE & THE ARTS

Near Bromley Mountain, **Johnny Seesaw's** (✉3574 Rte. 11 ☎802/824–
5533) is a classic rustic ski lodge, with live music on weekends and an
excellent "comfort food" menu. It's closed April through Memorial
Day. The **Marsh Tavern** (✉3567 Main St. [Rte. 7A] ☎802/362–4700) at
the Equinox resort hosts folk music and jazz from Thursday to Sunday
in summer and on weekends in winter. The **Perfect Wife** (✉2594 Depot
St. [Rte. 11/30] ☎802/362–2817) hosts live music on Friday.

WHERE TO EAT

$$$ ✕**Bistro Henry.** The active presence of chef and owner Henry Bronson
FRENCH   accounts for the continual popularity of this friendly place that's about
$5 per dish cheaper than the other good restaurants in town. The menu
works off a bistro foundation, with a peppery steak au poivre and a
medium rare duck breast served with a crispy leg, and mixes things up
with eclectic dishes like seared tuna with wasabi and soy; crab cakes
in a Cajun rémoulade; and a delicious scallop dish with Thai coconut

2

curry and purple sticky rice. The wine list is extensive. Dina Bronson's desserts are memorable—indulge in the "gooey chocolate cake," a great molten treat paired with a homemade malt ice cream. ⊠ *1942 Rte. 11/30, 3 mi east of Manchester Center* ☎ *802/362–4982* ⊟ *AE, D, DC, MC, V* ⊘ *Closed Mon. No lunch.*

$$$-$$$$
CONTINENTAL
✕ **Chantecleer.** There is something wonderful about eating by candlelight in an old barn. Chantecleer's dining rooms (in winter ask to sit by the great fieldstone fireplace) are wonderfully romantic, even with a collection of roosters atop the wooden beams. The menu leans toward the Continental with starters like a fine escargot glazed with Pernod in a hazlenut and parsely butter. Crowd pleasers include Colorado rack of lamb, and whole Dover sole filleted table-side. A recipe from the chef's Swiss hometown makes a winning dessert: Basel Rathaus Torte, a delicious hazlenut layer cake. ⊠ *Rte. 7A, 3½ mi north of Manchester, East Dorset* ☎ *802/362–1616* ⟁ *Reservations essential* ⊟ *AE, DC, MC, V* ⊘ *Closed Mon. and Tues. No lunch.*

$
PIZZA
✕ **Depot 62 Cafe.** The best pizzas in town are topped with terrific fresh ingredients and served in the middle of a high-end antiques showroom, making it a local's secret worth knowing about. The wood-fired yields masterful results—like the arugula pizza, a beehive of fresh greens atop a thin crust base. This a great place for lunch or an inexpensive but satisfying dinner. Sit on your own or at the long communal table. ⊠ *515 Depot St.* ☎ *802/366–8181* ⊟ *MC, V.*

$$$-$$$$
FRENCH
✕ **Mistral's.** This classic French restaurant is tucked in a grotto off Route 11/30 on the climb to Bromley Mountain. The two dining rooms are perched over the Bromley Brook, and at night, lights magically illuminate a small waterfall. Ask for a window table. Specialties include chateaubriand béarnaise and rack of lamb with rosemary for two. Chef Dana Markey's crispy sweetbreads with porcini mushrooms are a favorite. ⊠ *10 Toll Gate Rd.* ☎ *802/362–1779* ⊟ *AE, DC, MC, V* ⊘ *Closed Wed. No lunch.*

$-$$
ECLECTIC
✕ **Perfect Wife.** Owner-chef Amy Chamberlain, the self-proclaimed aspiring flawless spouse, creates freestyle cuisine like turkey schnitzel and grilled venison with a caramelized shallot and dried cranberry demi-glace. The upstairs tavern serves burgers and potpies, plus Vermont microbrews on tap. ⊠ *2594 Depot St. (Rte. 11/30), 2½ mi east of Manchester Center* ☎ *802/362–2817* ⊟ *AE, D, MC, V* ⊘ *Closed Sun. No lunch.*

WHERE TO STAY

$$$$
Fodor'sChoice
★
▦ **The Equinox.** Though this multi-building property is the geographic center and historic heart of Manchester Village, and though it has been *the* fancy hotel in town—in the state—since the 18th century, the Equinox had lost its luster in the past decade. That all changed in 2008, however, thanks to a complete renovation that's elevated the property, finally, to the lofty tier befitting its white columns. Rooms now have huge flat-screen TVs, leather chairs, contemporary carpets, and two-tone cream wallpaper, new plush-top mattresses, and marble bathrooms with granite sinks and Molton Brown toiletries. If you crave colonial, the Equinox bought the pink 1811 House across the street, which had been an independent B&B and is one of New England's most heart-grabbing

properties. If you've got big bucks, ask for a room in the Charles Orvis Inn, which has a billiard room, hot tubs, and private porches. The spa is the best in southern Vermont, you can take falconry lessons, the resort's golf course is across the street, and there's a new wine bar in addition to the good restaurant. **Pros:** heart-of-town location, full-service hotel, great golf and spa. **Cons:** big-hotel feeling, overrun by New Yorkers on weekends. ⊠3567 Main St. (Rte. 7A) 🕾802/362–4700 or 888/367–7625 ⊕www.equinoxresort.com ⇜154 rooms, 29 suites ⌂In-room: kitchen (some), refrigerator (some), Wi-Fi. In-hotel: 2 restaurants, bar, golf course, tennis courts, pool, spa, laundry service, concierge, public Wi-Fi, no-smoking rooms ☰AE, D, DC, MC, V.

$$$–$$$$ **Wilburton Inn.** A few miles south of Manchester and overlooking the Battenkill Valley from a hilltop all its own, this turn-of-the-20th-century complex is centered around a Tudor mansion with 11 bedrooms and suites, and richly paneled common rooms containing part of the owners' vast art collection. Besides the main inn, five guest buildings are spread over the grounds, dotted with more owner-created sculpture. Rooms at the Wilburton vary greatly in condition, so choose carefully. The dining room is an elegant affair, with a menu to match the wood-paneled interiors and the bucolic surroundings. Entrées might include poached Maine lobster with gnocchi or a roasted antelope chop with bordelaise sauce. One note: weddings take place here most summer weekends. **Pros:** beautiful setting with easy access to Manchester; fine dining. **Cons:** rooms in main inn, especially, need updating. ⊠River Rd. 🕾802/362–2500 or 800/648–4944 ⊕www.wilburton.com ⇜30 rooms, 4 suites ⌂In-hotel: restaurant, tennis courts, pool, no-smoking rooms ☰AE, MC, V ⍾BP.

DORSET

★ *7 mi north of Manchester.*

Lying at the foot of many mountains and blessed with a village green surrounded by white clapboard homes and inns, Dorset has a solid claim on the title of Vermont's most picture-perfect town. It also has two of the state's best and oldest general stores (⇨Shopping). The town has just 2,000 residents.

The country's first commercial marble quarry was opened here in 1785. Dozens followed suit. They provided the marble for the main research branch of the New York City Public Library and many Fifth Avenue mansions, among other notable landmarks, as well as the sidewalks that border the streets here and in Manchester. A remarkable private home made entirely of marble can be seen on Dorset West Road, a beautiful residential road just west of the town green. The marble Dorset Church on the green features two Tiffany stained-glass windows.

WHAT TO SEE

Fodor's Choice **Dorset Quarry.** On hot summer days the sight of dozens of families jump-
★   ing, swimming, and basking in the sun around this massive swimming hole makes it one of the most wholesome and picturesque recreational spots in all America. Mined in 1785, this is the oldest marble quarry in

the United States. The popular area visible from Route 30 is actually just the lower quarry. Footpaths lead to the quiet upper quarry. ⊠*Rte. 30, 1 mi south of Dorset green* ☎*No phone* ☎*Free.*

☾ **Merck Forest and Farmland Center.** This 3,100-acre farm and forest is a
★ nonprofit educational center with 30 mi of nature trails for hiking, cross-country skiing, snowshoeing, and horseback riding. You can visit the farm, which grows organic fruits and vegetables (and purchase them at the farm stand), and check out the pasture-raised horses, cows, sheep, pigs, and chickens. There are also remote cabins and tent sites. ⊠*3270 Rte. 315, Rupert* ☎*802/394–7836* ⊕*www.merckforest.org* ☎*Free* ☉*Daily, dawn–dusk.*

SPORTS & THE OUTDOORS

Emerald Lake State Park (⊠*U.S. 7, East Dorset* ☎*802/362–1655*) has a small beach, marked nature trail, an on-site naturalist, boat rentals, and a snack bar.

SHOPPING

The **H.N. Williams General Store** (⊠*2732 Rte. 30* ☎*802/824–3184* ⊕*www.hnwilliams.com*) is quite possibly the most authentic and comprehensive general store in the state. It was started in 1840 by William Williams and has been run by the same family for six generations. This is one of those unique places where you can buy maple syrup and a rifle, and catch up on posted town announcements. A farmer's market (⊕*www.dorsetfarmersmarket.com*) is held outside on Sundays in summer. The **Dorset Union Store** (⊠*Dorset Green* ☎*802/867–4400* ⊕*www. dorsetunionstore.com*) first opened in 1816 as a village co-op. Today this privately owned general store makes good prepared dinners, has a big wine selection, rents DVDs, and sells food and gifts.

THE ARTS

Dorset is home to a prestigious summer theater troupe that presents the annual Dorset Theater Festival. Plays are held in a wonderful converted pre-Revolutionary barn, the **Dorset Playhouse** (⊠*104 Cheney Rd., off town green* ☎*802/867–2223 or 802/867–5777*). The playhouse also hosts a community group in winter.

WHERE TO EAT

$–$$ ✕**Dorset Inn.** The inn that houses this restaurant has been continuously
AMERICAN operating since 1796, and even today you can count on three meals a day, every day of the year. The comfortable tavern, which serves the same menu as the more formal dining room, is popular with locals, and Patrick, the amiable veteran bartender, will make you feel at home. The menu features ingredients from local farms. Popular choices include fried yam fritters served in maple syrup, and a lightly breaded chicken breast saltimbocca, stuffed with prosciutto and mozzarella. ⊠*Dorset Green at Rte. 30, Dorset* ☎*802/867–5500* ⊕*www.dorsetinn.com* ☰*AE, MC, V.*

$$$ ✕**West View Farm.** Chef-owner Raymond Chen was the lead line cook at
★ New York City's The Mercer Kitchen under Jean-Georges Vongerichten
ECLECTIC before opening this local-ingredient-friendly restaurant. Like Dorset's other eateries, you'll find traditional floral wallpaper and soft classical

music; but that's where the similarities end. Chen's dishes are skillful and practiced, starting with an amuse-bouche like brandade (salt cod) over pesto. French influences are evident in the sautéed mushrooms and mascarpone ravioli in white truffle oil. Asian notes are evident, too, as in the lemongrass ginger soup with shiitake mushrooms that's ladled over grilled shrimp. A tavern serves enticing, inexpensive small dishes. ✉*2928 Rte. 30, Dorset* ☎*802/867–5715 or 800/769–4903* ⊕*www. westviewfarm.com* ☐*AE, MC, V* ⊘*Closed Tues. and Wed.*

WHERE TO STAY

$$–$$$ 🏠**Squire House.** This 10-acre estate sits on a wonderfully quiet road. The house has an excellent mix of modern comforts and antique fixtures. And there's enough space and quiet, with three big common rooms (and only three guest rooms), that it can feel like home. The house was built in 1918 and was designed with 9-foot ceilings and great light throughout. Rooms are newly carpeted, and clean freaks will breathe easy here. Owners Gay and Roger Squire are rightly proud of their breakfasts served in a richly paneled dining room. Roger is a flute player and enjoys the company of other musicians, who get a 10% discount. **Pros:** big estate feels your own, spotless. **Cons:** bathrooms less exciting than rooms, no credit cards. ✉*3395 Dorset West Rd.* ☎*802/867–0281* ⊕*www.squirehouse.com* ⬚*2 rooms, 1 suite* ♨*In-room: no phone, refrigerator (some), DVD (some), no TV (some), Wi-Fi. In-hotel: no elevator, laundry service, public Wi-Fi, no kids under 14, no-smoking rooms* ☐*No credit cards* ⦿|*BP.*

$–$$ 🏠**Inn at West View Farm.** While these aren't the best rooms in town, they're not bad and they offer an inexpensive way to stay in an old farmhouse with comfortable common rooms—along with easy access to perhaps the best dining room in southwestern Vermont (⇨West View Farm *under* Where to Eat). The white clapboard farmhouse is part of a former 1870 dairy farm. A deck in back looks out at the smaller farm buildings that dot the 5-acre yard. Rooms display imperfections, like an occasional stain or crack, and the carpeting could use an update, but they are very clean, and the furniture and wallpaper satisfy the colonial farmhouse urge. **Pros:** great restaurant. **Cons:** rooms aren't perfectly maintained. ✉*2928 Rte. 30* ☎*802/867–5715* ⊕*www.innatwestviewfarm.com* ⬚*9 rooms, 1 suite* ♨*In-room: Wi-Fi. In-hotel: restaurant, bar, no elevator, laundry service, public Wi-Fi, no kids under 10, no-smoking rooms* ☐*AE, MC, V* ⦿|*BP.*

STRATTON

26 mi southeast of Dorset.

Stratton is really Stratton Mountain Resort—a mountaintop ski resort with a self-contained "town center" of shops, restaurants, and lodgings clustered at the base of the slopes. When the snow melts, golf, tennis, and a host of other summer activities are big attractions, but the ski village remains quiet. For those arriving from the north along Route 30, Bondville is the town at the base of the mountain. At the juncture of Rtes. 30 and 100 is the tiny Vermont village of Jamaica, with its own cluster of inns and restaurants on the east side of the mountain.

SPORTS & THE OUTDOORS

SKI AREA ★ About 30 minutes from Manchester, sophisticated, exclusive **Stratton Mountain** (⊠ *5 Village Rd., Bondville. Turn off Rte 30 and go 4 mi up access road* ☎ *802/297–2200, 802/297–4211 snow conditions, 800/787–2886 lodging* ⊕ *www.stratton.com*) draws affluent families and young professionals from the New York–southern Connecticut corridor. An entire village, with a covered parking structure for 700 cars, is at the base of the mountain. Activities are afoot year-round. Stratton has 15 outdoor tennis courts, 27 holes of golf, a climbing wall, horseback riding, hiking accessed by a gondola to the summit, and instructional programs in tennis and golf. The sports center, open year-round, has two indoor tennis courts, three racquetball courts, a 25-meter indoor swimming pool, a hot tub, a steam room, a fitness facility with Nautilus equipment, and a restaurant. Adjacent to the base lodge are a condo-hotel, restaurants, and about 25 shops lining a pedestrian mall.

In terms of downhill skiing, Stratton prides itself on its immaculate grooming, making it excellent for cruising. The lower part of the mountain is beginner to low-intermediate, served by several chairlifts. The upper mountain is served by several high-speed quads and a 12-passenger gondola. Down the face are the expert trails, and on either side are intermediate cruising runs with a smattering of wide beginner slopes. The third sector, the Sun Bowl, is off to one side with two high-speed, six-passenger lifts and two expert trails, a full base lodge, and plenty of intermediate terrain. Snowmaking covers 95% of the slopes. Every March, Stratton hosts the U.S. Open Snowboarding championships; its snowboard park has a 380-foot half-pipe. A Ski Learning Park provides its own Park Packages for novice skiers. In all, Stratton has 15 lifts that service 92 trails and 90 acres of glades. There is a ski school for children ages 4–12. The resort also has more than 18 mi of cross-country skiing and the Sun Bowl Nordic center.

NIGHTLIFE & THE ARTS

Popular **Mulligan's** (⊠ *Mountain Rd.* ☎ *802/297–9293*) hosts bands or DJs in the late afternoon and on weekends in winter. Year-round, the **Red Fox Inn** (⊠ *Winhall Hollow Rd., Bondville* ☎ *802/297–2488*) is probably the best nightlife spot in southern Vermont. It hosts Irish music Wednesday night; an open mike Thursday night; and rock and roll at other times.

WHERE TO EAT

$$$–$$$$ AMERICAN ✗ **Red Fox Inn.** This two-level converted barn has the best nightlife in southern Vermont, and a fun dining room to boot. The restaurant has been here for 30 years, but you'd believe 100. The upper level is the dining room—the big A-frame has wagon wheels and a carriage suspended from the ceiling. Settle in near the huge fireplace for rack of lamb, free-range chicken, or penne à la vodka. Downstairs is the tavern where there's Irish music, half-price Guinness, and fish-and-chips

on Wednesday. Other nights there might be live music, karaoke, or video bowling. The bar operates daily year-round. ⊠ *Winhall Hollow Rd., Bondville* ☎802/297–2488 ⊟*AE, MC, V* ⊘*No lunch. Closed Mon.–Wed. June–Oct.*

$$$$
CONTEMPORARY
Fodor's Choice
★

✕**Three Mountain Inn.** If you're in the Stratton area and can splurge on an expensive meal, don't miss dinner at this charming inn. The prix fixe meal include amuse bouche, starter, salad, entrée, and dessert for $55. (It also includes the best restaurant bread in Vermont, a homemade herb focaccia). A starter might be baked Malpec oysters with a chorizo and fennel jam; entrées include grilled swordfish with toasted couscous, with a mint cucumber sauce. Fireplaces in each dining room and common areas have terrific original wall and ceiling beams. A romantic winner. ⊠*3732 Rte. 30/100, Jamaica* ☎802/874–4140 ⊟*AE, D, MC, V* ⊘*No dinner Mon., Tues.*

WHERE TO STAY

$$

🏨**Long Trail House.** Directly across the street from Stratton's ski village, this fairly new condo complex is one of the best choices close to the slopes. Units have fully equipped kitchens with ovens and dishwashers. The studios are an excellent value; they come with Murphy beds that fold into the living room area for additional sleepers. **Pros:** across from skiing, good rates available, outdoor heated pool. **Cons:** individualistic rooms, two-night stay required on weekends. ⊠*Middle Ridge Rd.* ☎802/297–2200 or 800/787–2886 ⊕*www.stratton.com* ⟋*100 units* ⌂*In-room: safe (some), kitchen, refrigerator, DVD (some), VCR (some). In-hotel: pool, laundry facilities, no-smoking rooms* ⊟*AE, D, DC, MC, V.*

$$–$$$

🏨**Red Fox Inn.** Stay here for great mid-week rates (50% off Sunday through Thursday) and relaxed, no-frills accommodations off the noisy mountain. Tom and Cindy Logan's "white house," an early 1800s farmhouse, is set in an open meadow 4 mi from Stratton and 8 mi from Bromley. The feeling here is warm and cozy, with original wood floors and simple furnishings. Downstairs rooms have bay windows; upstairs rooms are smaller. **Pros:** great nightlife and food next door, real local hosts, secluded. **Cons:** a drive to ski, weekends overpriced. ⊠*Winhall Hollow Rd., Bondville* ☎802/297–2488 ⊕*www.redfox-inn.com* ⟋*8 rooms, 1 suite* ⌂*In-room: no a/c, no phone, no TV, Wi-Fi. In-hotel: restaurant, bar, no elevator, public Wi-Fi, no-smoking rooms* ⊟*AE, MC, V.*

$$$–$$$$
Fodor's Choice
★

🏨**Three Mountain Inn.** A 1780s tavern, this romantic inn in downtown Jamaica (10 mi northeast of Stratton) feels authentically Colonial, from the wide paneling to the low ceilings. It's one of the coziest inns in Vermont. Rooms are appointed with a blend of historic and modern furnishings, including featherbeds. Most rooms have fireplaces and mountain views, and three have private decks. Owners Ed and Jennifer Dorta-Duque attend to your stay, and oversee truly romantic dinners. **Pros:** charming, authentic, romantic, small town B&B; well-kept and clean rooms; great dinners. **Cons:** can be expensive. ⊠*3732 Rte. 30/100* ☎802/874–4140 ⊕*www.threemountaininn.com* ⟋*14 rooms, 1 suite* ⌂*In-room: DVD (some), no TV (some), Wi-Fi. In-hotel: restaurant, bar, pool, bicycles, no elevator, laundry service, public Internet,* *public Wi-Fi, some pets allowed, no kids under 12, no-smoking rooms* ⊟*AE, D, MC, V* �"⊘"*BP.*

WESTON

2

17 mi north of Stratton.

Best known for the Vermont Country Store, Weston was one of the first Vermont towns to discover its own intrinsic loveliness—and marketability. With its summer theater, pretty town green with a Victorian bandstand, and an assortment of shops, the little village really lives up to its vaunted image.

SHOPPING

For paintings, prints, and sculptures by Vermont artists and craftspeople, go to the **Todd Gallery** (⊠*614 Main St.* ☎*802/824–5606* ⊕*www. toddgallery.com*). It's open Thursday–Monday, 10–5.

★ The **Vermont Country Store** (⊠*Rte. 100* ☎*802/824–3184* ⊕*www. vermontcountrystore.com*) sets aside one room of its old-fashioned emporium for Vermont Common Crackers and bins of fudge and other candy. The retail store and its mail-order catalog carry nearly forgotten items such as Lilac Vegetol aftershave and horehound drops, and practical items such as sturdy outdoor clothing and even typewriters. Nostalgia-evoking implements dangle from the store's walls and ceiling. (There's another store on Route 103 in Rockingham.)

THE ARTS

The members of the **Weston Playhouse** (⊠*703 Main St., Village Green, off Rte. 100* ☎*802/824–5288* ⊕*www.westonplayhouse.org*), the oldest professional theater in Vermont, produce Broadway plays, musicals, and other works. Their season runs from late June to early September. Throughout the summer, the **Kinhaven Music School** (⊠*354 Lawrence Hill Rd.* ☎*802/824–4332*) stages free student concerts on Friday at 4 and Sunday at 2:30. Faculty concerts are Saturday at 8 PM.

WHERE TO STAY

¢–$ 🏠**Colonial House Inn & Motel.** You'll find warmth and charm at this family-friendly complex just 2 mi south of the village. Relax on comfortable furniture in the large living room or enjoy the sun in the solarium. Homey, country furnishings adorn the inn rooms and the motel units. Breakfast includes fresh goodies from the family-owned bakery; a family-style dinner is served Thursday–Saturday nights. **Pros:** inexpensive. **Cons:** located outside of town. ⊠*287 Rte. 100* ☎*802/824–6286 or 800/639–5033* ⊕*www.cohoinn.com* ➫*9 motel units, 6 inn rooms without bath* ♿*In-room: no a/c, no TV (some). In-hotel: restaurant, no-smoking rooms* ⊟*D, MC, V* "⊘"*BP, MAP.*

$$–$$$ 🏠**Inn at Weston.** Highlighting the country elegance of this 1848 inn, a short walk from the Vermont Country Store and Weston Playhouse, is innkeeper Bob Aldrich's collection of 500 orchid species—rare and beautiful specimens surround the dining table in the gazebo and others enrich the indoors. Rooms in the inn, carriage house, and Coleman House (across the street) are comfortably appointed, and some

have fireplaces. The restaurant ($$$; closed Monday) serves contemporary regional cuisine amid candlelight. Vermont cheddar cheese and Granny Smith–apple omelets are popular choices for breakfast. **Pros:** great rooms; terrific town location. **Cons:** top end rooms are expensive. ⊠*Rte. 100* ☎*802/824–6789* ⊕*www.innweston.com* ⟲*13 rooms* ⌂*In-room: no TV (some). In-hotel: restaurant, bar, no kids under 12, no-smoking rooms* ▤*AE, DC, MC, V* ⍟*BP.*

LUDLOW

9 mi northeast of Weston.

Ludlow was once a nondescript factory town that just happened to have a small ski area—Okemo. Today, that ski area is one of Vermont's largest and most popular resorts, and downtown Ludlow is a collection of restored buildings with shops and restaurants.

SPORTS & THE OUTDOORS

HORSEBACK RIDING **Cavendish Trail Horse Rides** (⊠*20 Mile Stream Rd., Proctorsville* ☎*802/226–7821*) operates horse-drawn sleigh rides in snowy weather, wagon rides at other times, and guided trail rides from mid-May to mid-October.

SKI AREA Family-owned since 1982 and still run by Tim and Diane Mueller, **Okemo Mountain Resort** (⊠*77 Okemo Ridge Rd.* ☎*802/228–4041, 802/228–5222 snow conditions, 800/786–5366 lodging* ⊕*www. okemo.com*) has evolved into a major year-round resort, now with two base areas. Known for its wide, well-groomed trails, it's a favorite among intermediates. The Jackson Gore expansion, a new base village north of Ludlow off Route 103, has an inn, restaurants, a child-care center, and shops. The resort offers numerous ski and snowboarding packages. There's also ice skating at the Ice House, a covered, open-air ice skating rink open 10–9 daily in the winter. The Spring House next to the entrance of Jackson Gore Inn has a great kids pool with slides, a racquetball court, fitness center, and sauna. The yoga and Pilates studio has classes a few times a week. A day pass is $12.

At 2,200 feet, Okemo has the highest vertical drop of any resort in southern Vermont. The beginner trails extend above both base areas, with more challenging terrain higher on the mountains. Intermediate trails are the theme here, but experts will find steep trails and glades at Jackson Gore and on the South Face. Of the 113 trails, 42% have an intermediate rating, 33% are rated novice, and 25% are rated for experts. They are served by an efficient system of 18 lifts, including nine quads, three triple chairlifts, and six surface lifts; 95% are covered by snowmaking. Okemo has four terrain parks for skiers and snowboarders, including one for beginners; two 400-foot-long Superpipes, and a mini half-pipe.

For cross-country skiing, the **Okemo Valley Nordic Center** (⊠*Fox La.* ☎*802/228–1396*) has 16 mi of groomed cross-country trails and 6 mi of dedicated snowshoe trails, and rents equipment.

If you're looking for non-snow-related activities, you can play basketball and tennis at the Ice House next to Jackson Gore Inn, or perfect your swing at the 18-hole, par-70, 6,400-yard, Heathland-style course at the Okemo Valley Golf Club. Seven target greens, four putting greens, a golf academy, an indoor putting green, swing stations, and a simulator provide plenty of ways to improve your game year-round. The newer, off-site 9-hole **Tater Hill Golf Course** (⊠ *6802 Popple Dungeon Rd., Windham, 22 mi south of Ludlow* ☎ *802/875–2517*) has a pro shop, putting green, and a driving range.

WHERE TO EAT

$-$$

ITALIAN

✕ **Cappuccino's.** This local's place in town serves mostly Italian fare. Pasta dishes include Pasta Pink, which is loaded with crabmeat and shrimp in a sherry cream tomato sauce, and Pasta Balsamic, with chicken and tomatoes. ⊠ *41 Depot St.* ☎ *802/228–7566* ▤ *MC, V* ⊗ *No lunch. Closed Mon.*

$$-$$$

AMERICAN

✕ **Coleman Brook Tavern.** Slopeside at the Jackson Gore Inn, Colebrook is the fanciest and most expensive of Okemo's 19 places to eat, but it's not formal—you'll find ski-boot-wearing diners crowding the tables at lunch. Big wing chairs and large banquettes line window bays. If possible, ask to sit in the Wine Room, a separate seating section where tables are surrounded by the noteworthy collection of wines. Start with a pound of steamed clams steamed in butter, garlic, white wine, and fresh herbs. Then move on to the sesame seed-crusted ahi tuna served over green-tea soba noodles in a ginger-miso broth. If you're with kids, they'll love the s'mores dessert, cooked with a tabletop "campfire." ⊠ *Jackson Gore, Okemo* ☎ *802/228–1435* ▤ *AE, D, DC, MC, V.*

¢-$

☺

PIZZA

✕ **Goodman's American Pie.** This pizzeria has the best wood-fired oven pizza in town, maybe even in the state. It also has character to spare— sit in chairs that are old ski lifts, and order from a counter that's an old purple VW bus. Though it's on Main Street, it's set back and kind of hidden—you may consider it your Ludlow secret. Locals and Okemo regulars already in the know stop by to design their own pizza from 25 ingredients; there is also a section of six specials. The Rip Curl has mozzarella, Asiago, ricotta, chicken, fresh garlic, and fresh tomatoes. Slices are available. Arcade games are in the back. ⊠ *106 Main St.* ☎ *802/228–4271* ▤ *No credit cards* ⊗ *Closed Wed.*

$-$$

ECLECTIC

✕ **Harry's.** The local favorite when you want to eat a little out of town, this casual roadside restaurant 5 mi northwest of Ludlow is an oasis of eclectic food. The menu ranges from such traditional contemporary entrées as pork tenderloin to Mexican dishes. The large and tasty burrito, made with fresh cilantro and black beans, is one of the best bargains around. Chef-owner Trip Pearce also owns the equally popular Little Harry's in Rutland. ⊠ *Rte. 103, Mount Holly* ☎ *802/259–2996* ▤ *AE, MC, V* ⊗ *Closed Mon. and Tues. No lunch.*

$$$

Fodor's Choice

★

ECLECTIC

✕ **Inn at Weathersfield.** Just 15 mi east of Ludlow is this culinary gem, one of Vermont's best restaurants, located in a rural 1792 inn. A chalkboard in the foyer lists the area farms that grow the food you'll eat here, and it's no gimmick: chef Jason Tostrup (a former sous chef at David Keller's Bouchon in Napa, and a veteran of New York's Vong, Daniel, and Jean George) is passionate about local ingredients. Get converted to "farm-to-table" via a daily five-course "VerTerra" prix-fixe menu ($65) that might feature stuffed local quail in a cider-soy glaze or local "humanely-rasied" veal served two ways—veal breast braised over heirloom polenta and sautéed liver over mashed potatoes, topped with a single onion ring—each is masterful. Service is excellent and the wine list is large and reasonably priced. ☒*1342 Rte. 106, Perkinsville* ☎*802/263–9217* ▤*AE, D, MC, V* ☙*No lunch. Closed Mon. and Tues. and Apr. and beginning of Nov.*

WHERE TO STAY

$$–$$$ ▦ **Inn at Water's Edge.** Want to ski but resent the busy Ludlow and Okemo scene? You'll find a happy middle ground at this inn 10 mi north of town. Former Long Islanders Bruce and Tina Verdrager converted their old ski house and barns into this comfortably refined haven. The centerpiece of the relaxed common areas is a huge 1850 English bar, with comfortable banquettes, a big double sided fireplace, and a billiards table. Rooms are standard Victorian B&B affairs, clean and nice, but uninspiring compared to the grounds and setting. While most guests come for skiing, golf and spa packages are also available, and in summer the inn's dock has two canoes and a small sailboat on charming Echo Lake. **Pros:** bucolic setting on a lakefront; interesting, big house. **Cons:** ordinary rooms. ☒*45 Kingdom Rd.* ☎*802/228–8134 or 888/706–9736* ⊕*www.innatwatersedge.com* ➲*9 rooms, 2 suites* ⌂*In-room: no phone, no TV, Wi-Fi. In-hotel: restaurant, room service, bar, water sports, laundry service, public Internet, public Wi-Fi, no kids under 12, no-smoking rooms* ▤*AE, MC, V* ☉I*BP, MAP.*

$$$$ ▦ **Jackson Gore Inn.** This slope-side base lodge is the place to stay if
Ⓒ your aim is convenience to Okemo's slopes. The resort includes three restaurants and a martini bar ($12 a pop, but they're served in generous portions), plus an arcade. You can use the Spring House health center, which includes a fitness center, a raquetball court, hot tubs, a sauna, and great kid pools with slides. Right next to the original Jackson Gore structure are the newest annexes, Adams House (which opened in 2007) and Bixby House (2008), which feature whirlpool tubs and slightly more contemporary furnishings. Most units have full kitchen facilities. Besides Jackson Gore, Okemo offers 145 other condo units all across the mountain. **Pros:** ski-in, ski-out at base of mountain; good for families. **Cons:** chaotic and noisy on weekends. ☒*Okemo Ridge Rd. off Rte. 103* ☎*802/228–1400 or 800/786–5366* ⊕*www.okemo. com* ➲*263 rooms* ⌂*In-room: kitchen (some), refrigeraor, DVD, VCR, Wi-Fi. In-hotel: 3 restaurants, bar, golf courses, tennis courts, pools, gym, spa, children's programs (ages 2–12), laundry facilities, concierge, public Internet, public Wi-Fi, some pets allowed, no-smoking rooms* ▤*AE, MC, V.*

CHESTER

13 mi southeast of Ludlow.

At the junction of Routes 11 and 103, Chester is the town that time forgot. Gingerbread Victorians line the town green, the pharmacy on

Main Street has been in continuous operation since the 1860s, and the hardware store across from the train station opened in 1858.

TRAIN RIDE

From the Chester Depot, dating from 1852, you can board the historic **Green Mountain Flyer** (⊠ *Rte. 103* ☎ *802/463–3069 or 800/707–3530* ⊕ *www. rails-vt.com* ✉ *$14* ☉ *Late June–mid-Sept., Tues.–Sun.; mid-Sept.–late-Oct., daily. Call for schedule*) for a two-hour round-trip journey to Bellows Falls. The route passes covered bridges and goes through the Brockway Mills gorge. Fall foliage trips are spectacular.

SHOPPING

More than 125 dealers sell antiques and country crafts at **Stone House Antique and Craft Center** (⊠ *Rte. 103 S* ☎ *802/875–4477*).

WHERE TO EAT & STAY

$–$$

AMERICAN

✗ **Raspberries and Thyme.** Breakfast specials, homemade soups, a large selection of salads, homemade desserts, and a menu listing more than 40 sandwiches make this one of the area's most popular spots for casual dining. ⊠ *On the green* ☎ *802/875–4486* ▤ *AE, D, MC, V* ☉ *No dinner Tues.*

$–$$

▥ **Chester House Inn.** All of the rooms in this handsomely restored 1780 historic inn on the green have private baths. Five have gas fireplaces, and three have hot tubs or steam showers. Breakfast is served in the elegant Keeping Room, which has a fireplace. **Pros:** quaint and friendly B&B. **Cons:** not luxurious. ⊠ *266 Main St.* ☎ *802/875–2205 or 888/875–2205* ⊕ *www.chesterhouseinn.com* ⇖*7 rooms* ⌂ *In-room: no TV. In-hotel: bar, no-smoking rooms* ▤ *DC, MC, V* ☉*BP.*

GRAFTON

★ *8 mi south of Chester.*

Out-of-the-way Grafton is as much a historical museum as a town. During its heyday, citizens grazed some 10,000 sheep and spun their wool into sturdy yarn for locally woven fabric. When the market for wool declined, so did Grafton. Then in 1963, the Windham Foundation—Vermont's second-largest private foundation—commenced the town's rehabilitation. Not only was the Old Tavern preserved, but many other commercial and residential structures in the village center were as well. The **Historical Society** (⊠ *Main St. [Rte. 121]* ☎ *802/843–1010* ✉ *$3* ☉ *Memorial Day–Columbus Day, weekends and holidays 10–noon and 2–4*) documents the town's renewal.

SHOPPING

Gallery North Star (⊠ *151 Townshend Rd.* ☎ *802/843–2465*) exhibits the oils, watercolors, lithographs, and sculptures of Vermont-based artists. Sample the best of Vermont cheddar at the **Grafton Village Cheese Company** (⊠ *533 Townshend Rd.* ☎ *802/843–2221*).

WHERE TO STAY

$$$–$$$$ 🖼 **Old Tavern at Grafton.** Two-story white-column porches wrap around
★   this commanding 1801 inn, one of Vermont's greatest lodging assets.
While the rooms don't show the marks of a designer's touch (and they
could use it, without forgoing a link to the past), languid pleasures are
to be had lingering with a book by the fire in the library, on the porches,
and the authentically Colonial common rooms. In the main building
are 11 guest rooms; the rest are dispersed among six other close-by
buildings. Two dining rooms ($$$), one with formal Georgian furni-
ture, the other with rustic paneling and low beams, serve American
fare. The bar at the Phelps Barn is available only to guests, and offers
much character. The inn runs the nearby Grafton Ponds Cross-Country
Ski Center. **Pros:** classic Vermont inn and tavern; professionally run;
appealing common areas. **Cons:** rooms are attractive but not stellar.
✉*Rte. 121* ☎*802/843–2231 or 800/843–1801* ⊕*www.old-tavern.
com* ⚟*39 rooms, 7 suites* ⚐*In-room: no a/c (some), no TV, Wi-Fi.
In-hotel: 2 restaurants, bar, tennis court, bicycles, public Internet, pub-
lic Wi-Fi, no-smoking rooms* ▤*AE, MC, V* ⊘*Closed Apr.* ❍|*BP.*

TOWNSHEND

9 mi south of Grafton.

One of a string of pretty villages along the banks of the West River,
Townshend embodies the Vermont ideal of a lovely town green pre-
sided over by a gracefully proportioned church spire. The spire belongs
to the 1790 Congregational Meeting House, one of the state's oldest
houses of worship. Just north on Route 30 is the Scott Bridge (closed
to traffic), the state's longest single-span covered bridge.

**OFF THE
BEATEN
PATH**

With a village green surrounded by pristine white buildings, **Newfane**,
6 mi southeast of Townshend, is sometimes described as the quintessential New England small town. The 1839 First Congregational Church
and the Windham County Court House, with 17 green-shuttered windows and a rounded cupola, are often open. The building with the
four-pointed spire is Union Hall, built in 1832.

SPORTS & THE OUTDOORS

At **Townshend State Park** (✉*Rte. 30 N* ☎*802/365–7500*) you'll find a
sandy beach on the West River and a trail that parallels the river for 2½
mi, topping out on Bald Mountain Dam. Up the dam, the trail follows
switchbacks literally carved into the stone apron.

SHOPPING

The **Big Black Bear Shop** (✉*Rte. 30* ☎*802/365-4160 or 888/758–2327*
⊕*www.bigblackbear.com*) at Mary Meyer Stuffed Toys Factory, the
state's oldest stuffed toy company, offers discounts of up to 70% on
stuffed animals of all sizes. The **Newfane Country Store** (✉*Rte. 30,
Newfane* ☎*802/365-7916* ⊕*www.newfanecountrystore.com*) carries
many quilts (which can also be custom ordered), homemade fudge, and
other Vermont foods, gifts, and crafts.

WHERE TO EAT

¢ ✕**Townshend Dam Diner.** Folks come from miles around to enjoy tradi-
AMERICAN tional fare such as Mom's meat loaf, chili, and roast beef croquettes,
as well as Townshend-raised bison burgers, and creative daily specials.
Breakfast, served all day every day, includes such tasty treats as raspberry chocolate-chip walnut pancakes and homemade French toast.
You can sit at any of the collection of 1930s enamel-top tables or at the
big swivel-chairs at the big U-shaped counter. The diner is a few miles
northwest of the village on Route 30. ✉*5929 Rte. 30 West Townshend*
☎*802/874–4107* ▭*No credit cards* ⊙*Closed Tues.*

$$$ ✕**Windham Hill Inn.** This remote inn is a fine choice for a romantic din-
CONTINENTAL ner. Chef Michael Pelton heads up the Frog Pond dining room (don't
worry, no frog legs on the menu). Start with a spiced Vermont quail,
served with hand-rolled pappardelle and a wild mushroom ragout.
Entrees include a Moroccan-spiced rack of lamb. There's a notably
large wine list. A four-course prix fixe is $50. ✉*311 Lawrence Dr.,
West Townshend* ☎*802/874–4080* ⌖*Reservations essential* ▭*AE,
D, MC, V.*

WHERE TO STAY

¢–$ ⊡**Boardman House.** This handsome Greek-revival home on the town
green combines modern comfort with the relaxed charm of a 19th-
century farmhouse. It also happens to be one of the cheapest stays in
Vermont. The uncluttered guest rooms are furnished with Shaker-style
furniture, colorful duvets, and paintings. Both the breakfast room and
front hall have trompe l'oeil floors. **Pros:** cheap, perfect town green
location. **Cons:** no phone and cell-phone reception is bad. ✉*On the
green* ☎*802/365–4086* ⇆*4 rooms, 1 suite* ⌂*In-room: no phone, no
TV, Wi-Fi. In-hotel: no elevator, public Wi-Fi, no kids under 5, no-
smoking rooms* ▭*No credit cards* ⲓⵙⵏ*BP.*

$$–$$$ ⊡**Four Columns Inn.** Rooms and suites in this white-columned, 1834
★ Greek-revival mansion were designed for luxurious romantic getaways.
The inn is right in the heart of town on the lovely Newfane green,
giving you the quintessential Vermont village experience. Some of the
suites have cathedral ceilings; all have gas fireplaces and double whirl-
pool baths, and one has a 12-head spa shower. The elegant restaurant
($$$–$$$$; closed Tuesday) serves new American cuisine. Come here
for a serene getaway, as tiny Newfane is adorable, but quiet. **Pros:** great
rooms, heart-of-town location. **Cons:** little area entertainment. ✉*On
the green, 6 mi southeast of Townshend, Newfane* ⌖*Box 278, 05345*
☎*802/365–7713 or 800/787–6633* ⊕*www.fourcolumnsinn.com* ⇆*6
rooms, 9 suites* ⌂*In-room: no TV (some), Wi-Fi. In-hotel: restaurant,
bar, pool, no elevator, laundry service, public Internet, public Wi-Fi,
some pets allowed, no-smoking rooms* ▭*AE, DC, MC, V* ⲓⵙⵏ*BP.*

$$–$$$ ⊡**Windham Hill Inn.** Since there's not too much to do nearby, you might
★ find yourself sitting by a fire or swimming in the outdoor pool at this
calm, quiet retreat. And that's a good thing. The 165 hillside acres
have magnificent views of the West River valley and are perfect for
real relaxing. Period antiques, Oriental carpets, and locally made fur-
niture are hallmarks of the 1825 brick farmhouse. The white barn
annex has a great rough-hewn parlor that leads to the rooms, most of

which have fireplaces. The Marion Goodfollow room has a staircase up to a cozy private cupola with 360-degree views. **Pros:** quiet getaway, good food, lovely setting. **Cons:** little by way of entertainment. ✉ *311 Lawrence Dr., West Townshend* ☎ *802/874–4080 or 800/944–4080* 🌐 *www.windhamhill.com* *21 rooms* *In-hotel: restaurant, bar, tennis court, pool, no elevator, laundry service, public Internet, no kids under 12, no-smoking rooms* *AE, D, MC, V* *BP.*

CENTRAL VERMONT

Central Vermont's economy once centered on marble quarrying and mills. But today, as in much of the rest of the state, tourism drives the economic engine. The center of the dynamo is Killington, the East's largest downhill resort. However, central Vermont has more to discover than high-speed chairlifts and slope-side condos. The old mills of Quechee and Middlebury are now home to restaurants and shops, giving wonderful views of the waterfalls that once powered the mill turbines. Woodstock has upscale shops and America's newest national historic park. Away from these settlements, the protected (except for occasional logging) lands of the Green Mountain National Forest are laced with hiking trails.

Our coverage of towns begins with Norwich, on U.S. 5 near Interstate 91 at the state's eastern edge; winds westward toward U.S. 7; then continues north to Middlebury before heading over the spine of the Green Mountains to Waitsfield.

NORWICH

6 mi north of White River Junction.

On the shores of the Connecticut River, Norwich boasts beautifully maintained 18th- and 19th-century homes set about a handsome green.

WHAT TO SEE

Fodor's Choice ★ **Montshire Museum of Science.** Numerous hands-on exhibits here explore nature and technology. Kids can make giant bubbles, watch fish and turtles swim in giant aquariums, explore wind, and wander a maze of outdoor trails by the river. An ideal destination for a rainy day, this is one of the finest museums in New England. ✉ *1 Montshire Rd.* ☎ *802/649–2200* 🌐 *www.montshire.org* *$9* *Daily 10–5.*

SHOPPING

★ Are you a baker? **King Arthur Flour Baker's Store** (✉ *135 Rte. 5 S* ☎ *802/649–3881 or 800/827–6836*) is a must-see for those who love bread. The shelves are stocked with all the ingredients and tools in the company's *Baker's Catalogue,* including flours, mixes, and local jams and syrups. The bakery has a viewing area where you can watch products being made.

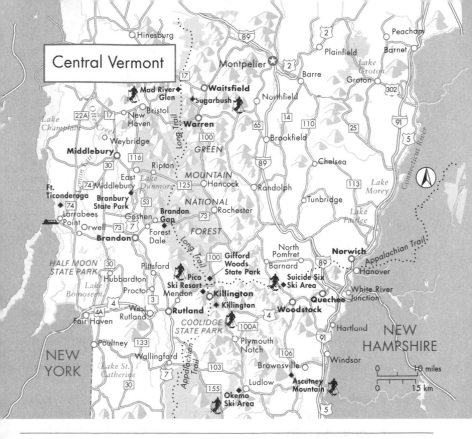

Central Vermont

QUECHEE

11 mi southwest of Norwich, 6 mi west of White River Junction.

A historic mill town, Quechee sits just upriver from its namesake gorge, an impressive 165-foot-deep canyon cut by the Ottauquechee River. Most people view the gorge from U.S. 4. To escape the crowds, hike along the gorge or scramble down one of several trails to the river.

WHAT TO SEE

Simon Pearce. The main attraction in the village is this glassblowing factory, which an Irish glassmaker by the same name set up in 1981 in a restored woolen mill by a waterfall. Water power still drives the factory's furnace. Visitors may take a free self-guided tour of the factory floor and see the glassblowers at work. The store in the mill sells contemporary glass and ceramic tableware and home furnishings, such as glass lamps and clocks. Seconds and discontinued items are reduced 25%. A fine restaurant here uses the Simon Pearce glassware and is justly popular. ⊠ *The Mill, 1760 Main St.* ☎ *802/295–2711* ⊕ *www. simonpearce.com* ⊙ *Store daily 9–9; glassblowing Tues.–Sat. 9–9, Sun. and Mon. 9–5.*

☺ **Vermont Institute of Natural Science (VINS) Nature Center.** Next to Quechee Gorge, this science center has 17 raptor exhibits, including bald eagles, peregrine falcons, and a variety of owls. All the caged birds have been found injured and are unable to survive in the wild. Predators of the Sky, a 30-minute-long live bird program, starts daily at 11, 1, and 3:30. ⊠*Rte. 4* ☎*802/359–5000* ⊕*www.vinsweb.org* ☜*$8* ☽*May–Oct., daily 10–5; Nov.–Apr., daily 10–4.*

SPORTS & THE OUTDOORS

FISHING   The **Vermont Fly Fishing School/Wilderness Trails** (⊠*1119 Main St.* ☎*802/295–7620*) leads workshops, rents fishing gear and mountain bikes, and arranges canoe and kayak trips. In winter, the company conducts cross-country and snowshoe treks.

POLO   **Quechee Polo Club** (⊠*Dewey's Mill Rd., ½ mi north of U.S. 4* ☎*802/295–7152*) draws hundreds of spectators on summer Saturdays to its matches near the Quechee Gorge. Admission is $8 per carload.

SHOPPING

ANTIQUES &   The 40 dealers at the **Hartland Antiques Center** (⊠*U.S. 4* ☎*802/457–*
CRAFTS   *4745*) stock furniture, paper items, china, glass, and collectibles. More than 350 dealers sell their wares at the **Quechee Gorge Village** (⊠*573 Woodstock Rd., off U.S. 4* ☎*802/295–1550 or 800/438–5565* ⊕*www.quecheegorge.com*), an antiques and crafts mall in an immense reconstructed barn that also houses a country store and a classic diner. A merry-go-round and a small-scale working railroad operate when weather permits.

CLOTHING &   **Scotland by the Yard** (⊠*U.S. 4* ☎*802/295–5351 or 800/295–5351*) sells
MORE   all things Scottish, from kilts to Harris tweed jackets and tartan ties.

WINE   **Ottauquechee Valley Winery** (⊠*5967 Woodstock Rd. [U.S. 4]* ☎*802/295–9463*), in a historic 1870s barn complex, has a tasting room and sells fruit wines, such as apple and blueberry.

WHERE TO EAT & STAY

$$–$$$ ✗ **Simon Pearce.** Candlelight, sparkling glassware from the studio down-
Fodor'sChoice   stairs, exposed brick, and large windows overlooking the falls of the
★   roaring Ottauquechee River create an ideal setting for contemporary
AMERICAN   American cuisine. The food is widely considered to be worthy of a pilgrimage. Sesame-seared tuna with noodle cakes and wasabi as well as roast duck with mango chutney sauce are house specialties; the wine cellar holds several hundred vintages. The lunch menu might include a roasted duck quesadilla or Mediterranean lamb burger. ⊠*The Mill, 1760 Main St.* ☎*802/295–1470* ▭*AE, D, DC, MC, V* ⋈*Reservations not accepted.*

$$–$$$ ▣ **Parker House.** This beautiful house on the National Historic Register was once home to the mill owner who ran the textile mill next door (which is now Simon Pearce). Rooms are bright and clean with queen and king beds. Walter and Joseph are the names of the two cute rooms that face the river in back. Downstairs is an attractive bar area and a good French restaurant with a nightly changing menu. **Pros:** in-town; riverfront location; spacious, cute rooms. **Cons:** no yard. ⊠*1792 Main St.*

2

☎802/295–6077 ⊕*www.theparkerhouseinn.com* ↩*7 rooms, 1 suite*
⇃*In-room: no TV, Wi-Fi. In-hotel: restaurant, room service, bar, no
elevator, laundry service, public Internet, public Wi-Fi, some pets
allowed, no-smoking rooms* ⊟*AE, MC, V* ⦿|*BP.*

$–$$ 🔲 **Quechee Inn at Marshland Farm.** Each room in this handsomely
restored 1793 country home has Queen Anne–style furnishings and
period antiques. From the old barn, the inn runs bike and canoe rentals, a fly-fishing school, and kayak and canoe trips. Eleven miles of
cross-country and hiking trails are on property. Guests also have privi-
leges at the Quechee Club, a private golf, tennis, and ski club. The
dining room's ($$–$$$) creative entrées include shellfish bouillabaisse
and rack of lamb with green peppercorn pesto. **Pros:** historic, spacious property. **Cons:** bathrooms are clean but out-of-date. ⊠*Main
St.,* ☎*802/295–3133 or 800/235–3133* ⊕*www.quecheeinn.com* ↩*22
rooms, 3 suites* ⇃*In-room: Wi-Fi. In-hotel: restaurant, bar, water
sports, bicycles, no elevator, public Wi-Fi, no-smoking rooms* ⊟*AE,
D, DC, MC, V* ⦿|*BP.*

WOODSTOCK

★ *4 mi west of Quechee.*

Woodstock is a Currier & Ives print come to life. Well-maintained Federal-style houses surround the tree-lined village green, which is not far
from a covered bridge. The town owes much of its pristine appearance
to the Rockefeller family's interest in historic preservation and land
conservation, and to town native George Perkins Marsh, a congress-
man, diplomat, and conservationist who wrote the pioneering book
Man and Nature in 1864 about man's use and abuse of the land. Only
busy U.S. 4 detracts from the town's quaintness.

WHAT TO SEE

☝ **Billings Farm and Museum.** Founded by Frederick Billings in 1871 as a
model dairy farm, this is one of the oldest dairy farms in the country
and sits on the property that was the childhood home of George Perkins Marsh. Concerned about the loss of New England's forests to
overgrazing, Billings planted thousands of trees and put into practice
Marsh's conservationist farming ideas. Exhibits in the reconstructed
Queen Anne farmhouse, school, general store, workshop, and former
Marsh homestead demonstrate the lives and skills of early Vermont settlers. ⊠*Rte. 12, ½ mi north of Woodstock* ☎*802/457–2355* ⊕*www.
billingsfarm.org* 🎫*$9.50* ⊗*May–late Oct., daily 10–5; call for winter
holiday and weekend schedules.*

Marsh-Billings-Rockefeller National Historical Park. This 500-acre park is
Vermont's only national park and the nation's first to focus on natural
resource conservation and stewardship. The park encompasses the forest lands planned by Frederick Billings according to Marsh's principles,
as well as Frederick Billings's mansion, gardens, and carriage roads.
The entire property was the gift of Laurance S. Rockefeller, who lived
here with his late wife, Mary, Billings's granddaughter. The residential
complex is accessible by guided tour only, but you can explore the

extensive network of carriage roads and trails on your own. ⊠ *Rte. 12* ☎ *802/457–3368* ☞ *Tour $6* ⊗ *May–Oct., mansion and garden tours 10–5; grounds daily dawn–dusk.*

OFF THE
BEATEN
PATH

Plymouth Notch Historic District. U.S. president Calvin Coolidge was born and buried in Plymouth Notch, a town that shares his character: low-key and quiet. The perfectly preserved 19th-century buildings resemble nothing so much as a Vermont town frozen in time. In addition to the homestead—where "Silent Cal" was sworn in as president at 2:47 AM on August 3, 1923, after the sudden death of President Harding—there is a visitor center, a general store once run by Coolidge's father (a room above it was once used as the summer White House), a cheese factory, two large barns displaying agricultural equipment, and a one-room schoolhouse. Coolidge's grave is in the cemetery across Route 100A. ⊠ *Rte. 100A, 6 mi south of U.S. 4, 1 mi east of Rte. 100* ☎ *802/672–3773* ⊕ *www.historicvermont.org/coolidge* ⊗ *Late May–mid-Oct., daily 9:30–5.*

SPORTS & THE OUTDOORS

BIKING **Biscuit Hill Bike and Outdoor Shop** (⊠ *490 Woodstock Rd.* ☎ *802/457–3377*) rents, sells, and services bikes and also distributes a free touring map of local rides.

GOLF Robert Trent Jones Sr. designed the 18-hole, par-70 course at **Woodstock Country Club** (⊠ *14 The Green* ☎ *802/457–1100*), which is run by the Woodstock Inn. Green fees are $67 weekdays, $85 weekends; cart rentals are $18.

HORSEBACK **Kedron Valley Stables** (⊠ *Rte. 106, South Woodstock* ☎ *802/457–1480*
RIDING *or 800/225–6301*) conducts one-hour guided trail rides and horse-drawn sleigh and wagon rides.

SHOPPING

ARTWORK In downtown Woodstock, **Stephen Huneck Studio** (⊠ *49 Central St.* ☎ *802/457–3206*) invites canines and humans to visit the artist's gallery, filled with whimsical animal carvings, prints, and furniture.

CLOTHING **Who Is Sylvia?** (⊠ *26 Central St.* ☎ *802/457–1110*), in the old firehouse,
★ sells vintage clothing and antique linens, lace, and jewelry.

FOOD The **Woodstock Farmer's Market** (⊠ *468 Woodstock Rd., U.S. 4* ☎ *802/457–3658*) is a year-round buffet of local produce, fresh fish, and excellent sandwiches and pastries. The maple-walnut scones go fast every morning except Monday, when the market is closed. Near Taftsville, **Sugarbush Farm Inc.** (⊠ *591 Sugarbush Farm Rd.* ☎ *802/457–1757 or 800/281–1757*) demonstrates how maple sugar is made. The farm also makes excellent cheeses. In winter and spring, the road can be messy, so call ahead for road conditions. East of town, the **Taftsville Country Store** (⊠ *U.S. 4, Taftsville* ☎ *802/457–1135 or 800/854–0013*) sells a wide selection of Vermont cheeses, moderately priced wines, and Vermont specialty foods.

2

WHERE TO EAT

$-$$ ✕ **Barnard Inn.** The dining room in this 1796 brick farmhouse breathes
★ 18th century, but the food is decidedly 21st century. Former San Fran-
ECLECTIC cisco restaurant chef-owners Will Dodson and Ruth Schimmelpfennig
create inventive four-course prix-fixe menus with delicacies such as
beef carpaccio and pan-seared escolar in lemon-and-caper herb butter. In the back is a local favorite, Max's Tavern, which serves upscale
pub fare such as beef with Gorgonzola mashed potatoes and panfried
trout with almond *beurre noisette* (browned butter). ⊠*5518 Rte. 12,
8 mi north of Woodstock, Barnard* ☎*802/234–9961* ⊟*AE, MC, V*
⊗*Closed Sun. and Mon. No lunch* ⚅*Reservations essential.*

$-$$ ✕ **Keeper's Café.** Creative, moderately priced fare draws customers from
CAFE all over the region to this café. Chef Eli Morse's menus include such
light fare as pancetta salad and fresh corn soup as well as such elaborate entrées as herb garlic roast chicken with a sherry caper sauce.
Blackboard specials change daily. Housed inside a former general
store, the small dining room feels relaxed, with locals table-hopping
to chat with friends. ⊠*Rte. 106, 12 mi south of Woodstock, Reading*
☎*802/484–9090* ⊟*AE, MC, V* ⊗*Closed Sun. and Mon. No lunch.*

$$ ✕ **Pane e Saluto.** One of the most exciting little restaurants in Vermont
Fodor'sChoice is run by the young couple Deirdre Heekin and Caleb Barker. Hip con-
★ temporary decor, an intimately small space, and Deirdre's discretely
ITALIAN passionate front-of-house direction all come together to complement
the chef's slow-food-inspired passion for flavorful, local and farm-
raised dishes. Try *ragu d'agnello e maiale,* spaghetti with an abruzzese
ragu from roasted pork and lamb, followed by *cotechino e lenticche,*
a garlic sausage with lentils. You might expect such a gem in Berkeley
or Brooklyn—here this *osteria* seems to pump life into the blood of old
Woodstock. Ask about the culinary tours the team leads each year in
Italy. ⊠*61 Central Woodstock, upstairs* ☎*802/457–4882* ⊟*AE, MC,
V* ⊗*No lunch. Closed Tues. and Wed. and Apr. and Nov.*

$-$$ ✕ **Prince & the Pauper.** Modern French and American fare with a Ver-
★ mont accent is the focus of this candlelit Colonial restaurant off the
FRENCH Woodstock green. The grilled duck breast might have an Asian five-
spice sauce; lamb and pork sausage in puff pastry comes with a honey-
mustard sauce. A three-course prix-fixe menu is available for $46; a
less-expensive bistro menu is available in the lounge. ⊠*24 Elm St.*
☎*802/457–1818* ⊟*AE, D, MC, V* ⊗*No lunch.*

WHERE TO STAY

$$-$$$ ⌂ **Fan House.** Do you have an elusive dream, one that hankers for an
★ authentic home in the heart of a very small, quaint Vermont town?
Take the one-minute walk from the perfect general store in Barnard to
this 1840 white colonial: and here it is. The three rooms put together
by Sara Widness—who happens to be an expert on luxury travel—are
cozy, comfortable, and avoid romantic clichés. The rooms are simply
adorned with tapestries, antique rugs, claw-foot tubs, comfy sofas, and
old bed frames guarding soft linens and a mountain of pillows. The
living room hearth, the old wood stove in the kitchen, and the library
nook create a real sense of home. **Pros:** center of old town, homey
comforts, good library. **Cons:** upstairs rooms can be cool in winter.

✉ *Rte. 12 N* ✉ *Box 294, 05031* ☎ *802/234–6704* ⊕ *www.thefan house.com* ▦ *3 rooms* ⚒ *In room: no TV, no phone. In-hotel: no elevator, public Internet, no kids under 12, no-smoking rooms* ▭ *No credit cards* ⊘ *Closed Apr.* ⱺ *BP.*

$$–$$$ ⚏ **Kedron Valley Inn.** Two 19th-century buildings and a 1968 log lodge make up this inn on 15 acres. Many of the rooms have a fireplace or a Franklin stove, and some have private decks or terraces. The motel units in the log lodge boast country antiques and reproductions. A big spring-fed pond has a white sand beach with toys for kids. In the restaurant ($$–$$$$), the chef creates French masterpieces such as fillet of Norwegian salmon stuffed with herb seafood mousse in puff pastry. **Pros:** good food, quiet setting, beach. **Cons:** 5 mi south of Woodstock. ✉ *Rte. 106* ☎ *802/457–1473 or 800/836–1193* ⊕ *www.kedronvalley inn.com* ▦ *21 rooms, 6 suites* ⚒ *In-room: no a/c (some), no phone. In-hotel: restaurant, bar, no elevator, public Internet, some pets allowed, no-smoking rooms* ▭ *AE, MC, V* ⊘ *Closed Apr.* ⱺ *BP.*

$$$ ⚏ **Maple Leaf Inn.** Nancy and Mike Boyle operate this traditional B&B set back far from the main road on 16 wooded acres near the center of little Barnard. The house was built in 1994 and has modern features like radiant floor heat. Victorian appointments make it feel like its been here quite a while—while still maintaining a spotless order. The light and airy rooms have king-size beds and big whirlpool or soaking tubs. Most rooms have wood-burning fireplaces and sitting areas. The inn includes a pillow library, where you can "check out" pillows of varying firmness. **Pros:** clean, quaint rooms; great front porch. **Cons:** a 10-minute drive from Woodstock, doesn't feel rustic. ✉ *Rte. 12, 8 mi north of Woodstock, Barnard* ☎ *802/234–5342 or 800/516–2753* ⊕ *www. mapleleafinn.com* ▦ *7 rooms* ⚒ *In-room: VCR, Wi-Fi. In-hotel: bicycles, no elevator, public Internet, public Wi-Fi, no kids under 14, no-smoking rooms* ▭ *AE, D, MC, V* ⱺ *BP.*

$$ ⚏ **Shire Riverview Motel.** Some rooms in this immaculate motel have decks—and almost all have views—overlooking the Ottauquechee River. Rooms are simple, a step above usual motel fare, with four-poster beds and wing chairs; two rooms have hot tubs and the suite has a full kitchen. Complimentary coffee is served each morning; in summer take it on the riverfront veranda. The real key here is walking distance to the green and all shops. **Pros:** inexpensive access to the heart of Woodstock, views. **Cons:** dull rooms. ✉ *46 Pleasant St.* ☎ *802/457–2211* ⊕ *www.shiremotel.com* ▦ *42 rooms, 1 suite* ⚒ *In-room: kitchen (some), refrigerator, no-smoking rooms* ▭ *AE, D, MC, V.*

$$$$ ⚏ **Twin Farms.** Let's just get out with it: Twin Farms is the best lodg-
Fodor's Choice   ing choice in Vermont. (Some even say it's the best small property in
★   America.) And if you can afford it—stays begin at well over $1,000 a night—you'll want to experience it. Three rooms are in the beautiful main building, which was once home to writer Sinclair Lewis. The rest are individual cottages, secluded among 300 acres. Each incredible room and cottage is furnished with a blend of high art (Jasper Johns, Milton Avery, Cy Twombly), gorgeous folk art, and furniture that goes beyond comfortable sophistication. The food may be the best in Vermont. The service—suave, relaxed—definitely is. Prices include

2

all meals, alcohol and activities—there's a good spa, a pub within a big game room, and a private ski hill. **Pros:** impeccable service; stunning rooms; sensational meals. **Cons:** astronomical prices. ✉ *Royalton Turnpike, Barnard* ☎ *802/234-9999* ⊕ *www.twinfarms.com* ⟟ *3 rooms, 10 cottages* ⬙ *In room: DVD, Wi-Fi. In-hotel: restaurant, room service, bars, tennis courts, pool(s), gym, spa, water sports, bicycles, no elevator, laundry service, public Internet, public Wi-Fi, no kids under 12, no-smoking rooms* ☰ *AE, D, DC, MC, V* ☺ *Closed Apr.* ⓄⅠAI.

$$$
Fodor'sChoice
★

🛉 **Woodstock Inn and Resort.** If this is your first time in Woodstock and you want to feel like you're in the middle of it all, stay here. Set back far from the main road but still on the town's gorgeous green, the Inn is the town's beating heart. You'll feel that right away when looking at the main fireplace, set immediately through the front doors, which burns impressive three-foot-long logs. Rooms are contemporary and luxurious, with huge flat screen TVs, sleek furniture and great bathrooms done in clean-looking subway tiles. The resort also owns and gives you access to Suicide Six ski mountain and the Woodstock Golf Club. **Pros:** exciting, big property; contemporary furnishings; professionally run **Cons:** can lack intimacy. ✉ *14 The Green, U.S. 4* ☎ *802/457-1100 or 800/448-7900* ⊕ *www.woodstockinn.com* ⟟ *135 rooms, 7 suites* ⬙ *In-room: safe, refrigerator, Ethernet (some), Wi-Fi (some). In-hotel: 2 restaurants, room service, bar, golf course, tennis courts, pools, gym, bicycles, laundry service, concierge, public Internet, no-smoking rooms* ☰ *AE, D, MC, V.*

KILLINGTON

15 mi east of Rutland.

With only a gas station, post office, motel, and a few shops at the intersection of Routes 4 and 100, it's difficult to tell that the East's largest ski resort is nearby. The village of Killington is characterized by unfortunate strip development along the access road to the ski resort. But the 360-degree views atop Killington Peak, accessible by the resort's gondola, make it worth the drive.

SPORTS & THE OUTDOORS

BIKING **True Wheels Bike Shop** (✉ *Killington Rd.* ☎ *802/422-3234*) sells and rents bicycles and has information on local mountain and bicycle routes.

FISHING Kent Pond in **Gifford Woods State Park** (✉ *Rte. 100, ½ mi north of U.S. 4* ☎ *802/775-5354*) is a terrific fishing spot.

GOLF At its namesake resort, **Killington Golf Course** (✉ *4763 Killington Rd.* ☎ *802/422-6700*) has a challenging 18-hole course. Green fees are $52 midweek and $57 weekends; carts run for $17.

SKI AREA
★
"Megamountain," "Beast of the East," and plain "huge" are apt descriptions of **Killington** (✉ *4763 Killington Rd.* ☎ *802/422-6200, 802/422-3261 snow conditions, 800/621-6867 lodging* ⊕ *www.killington.com*). The American Skiing Company operates Killington and its neighbor, **Pico,** and over the past several years has improved

lifts and snowmaking capabilities. Thanks to its extensive snowmaking system, the resort typically opens in October and the lifts often run into May. Killington's après-ski activities are plentiful and have been rated the best in the East by national ski magazines. With a single call to Killington's hotline or a visit to its Web site, skiers can plan an entire vacation: choose accommodations, book air or railroad transportation, and arrange for rental equipment and ski lessons. Killington ticket holders can also ski at Pico: a shuttle connects the two areas.

The Killington–Pico complex has a host of activities, including an alpine slide, a golf course, two waterslides, a skateboard park, and a swimming pool. The resort rents mountain bikes and advises hikers. The K-1 Express Gondola takes you up the mountain, Vermont's second-highest summit.

In terms of downhill skiing, it would probably take several weeks to test all 200 trails on the seven mountains of the Killington complex, even though all except Pico interconnect. About 70% of the 1,182 acres of skiing terrain can be covered with machine-made snow. Transporting skiers to the peaks of this complex are 32 lifts, including 2 gondolas, 12 quads (including 6 high-speed express quads), 6 triples, and a Magic Carpet. The K-1 Express Gondola goes to the area's highest elevation, 4,241-foot Killington Peak. The Skyeship Gondola starts on U.S. 4, far below Killington's main base lodge, and savvy skiers park here to avoid the more crowded access road. After picking up more passengers at a mid-station, the Skyeship tops out on Skye Peak. Although Killington has a vertical drop of 3,050 feet, only gentle trails—Juggernaut and Great Eastern—go from top to bottom. The skiing includes everything from Outer Limits, one of the East's steepest and most challenging mogul trails, to 6½-mi Great Eastern. In the Fusion Zones, underbrush and low branches have been cleared away to provide tree skiing. Killington's Superpipe is one of the best rated in the East. Instruction programs are available for youngsters ages 3–8; those from 6 to 12 can join an all-day program.

Mountain Top Inn and Resort (⊠ *195 Mountaintop Rd., Chittenden* ☎ *802/483–6089 or 800/445–2100* ⊕ *www.mountaintopinn.com*) has 50 mi of hilly trails groomed for nordic skiing, 37 mi of which can be used for skate skiing. You can also enjoy snowshoeing, dogsledding, ice skating, and snowmobile and sleigh rides. In the summer there's horseback riding, fishing, hiking, biking, and water sports.

NIGHTLIFE & THE ARTS
On weekends, listen to live music and sip draft Guinness at the **Inn at Long Trail** (⊠ *U.S. 4* ☎ *802/775–7181*). The **Nightspot Outback** (⊠ *Killington Rd.* ☎ *802/422–9885*) serves all-you-can-eat pizza on Monday nights in winter, and $2 Long Trail pints on Sunday. It's open year-round. During ski season, the **Pickle Barrel Night Club** (⊠ *Killington Rd.* ☎ *802/422–3035*) has a band every happy hour on Friday and Saturday. After 8, the crowd moves downstairs for dancing, sometimes to big-name bands. Twentysomethings prefer to dance at the **Wobbly Barn** (⊠ *Killington Rd.* ☎ *802/422–3392*), open only during ski season.

WHERE TO EAT & STAY

$$$$ ✕**Hemingway's.** With a national reputation, Hemingway's is as good
★ as dining gets. Among the house specialties are the cream of garlic
CONTINENTAL soup and a seasonal kaleidoscope of dishes created by chef-owner
Ted Fondulas. Native baby pheasant with local chanterelles or seared
scallops with truffles and caramelized onions are just two entrées that
might appear on the menu. Diners can opt for the prix-fixe, three- to
six-course menu or the wine-tasting menu. Request seating in either
the formal vaulted dining room, the intimate wine cellar, or the garden room. ⊠*4988 U.S. 4* ☎*802/422–3886* ⌂*Reservations essential*
✉*AE, D, DC, MC, V* ☉*Closed Mon. and Tues., early Nov., and mid-
Apr.–mid-May. No lunch.*

$$ ⊡**Birch Ridge Inn.** A slate-covered carriageway leads uphill to one of
Killington's newest inns, a former executive retreat in two renovated A-
frames. Rooms range in style from Colonial and Shaker to Mission, and
all have a sitting area with a TV hidden behind artwork (in one room,
a dollhouse rotates up to reveal the TV). Six rooms have gas fireplaces,
and four have whirlpool baths. In the intimate slate-floored dining
room ($$–$$$$; closed Monday and Tuesday), choose either a four-
course prix-fixe dinner or order à la carte. **Pros:** quirky. **Cons:** oddly
furnished, slightly older rooms. ⊠*37 Butler Rd.* ☎*802/422–4293 or
800/435–8566* ⊕*www.birchridge.com* ⇗*10 rooms* ⌂*In-room: no a/c
(some), Wi-Fi. In hotel: restaurant, bar, no elevator, public Wi-Fi, no
kids under 12, no-smoking rooms* ✉*AE, D, MC, V* ☉*Closed May*
❡⊙*BP, MAP.*

$$$$ ⊡**Woods Resort & Spa.** These clustered upscale two- and three-bedroom town houses stand in wooded lots along a winding road leading
to the spa. Most units have master baths with saunas and two-person whirlpool tubs. Vaulted ceilings in the living rooms give an open,
airy feel. The resort has a private shuttle to the ski area. **Pros:** contemporary facility; clean, spacious rooms; lots of room choices. **Cons:**
lacks traditional Vermont feeling. ⊠*53 Woods La.* ☎*802/422–3139
or 800/642–1147* ⊕*www.woodsresortandspa.com* ⇗*107 units* ⌂*In-
room: no a/c, kitchen, VCR, Wi-Fi. In-hotel: tennis courts, pool, gym,
spa, no elevator, laundry facilities, some pets allowed, no-smoking
rooms* ✉*AE, MC, V.*

RUTLAND

15 mi southwest of Killington, 32 mi south of Middlebury.

On and around U.S. 7 in Rutland are strips of shopping centers and
a seemingly endless row of traffic lights. Two blocks west, however,
stand the mansions of the marble magnates. Preservation work has
uncovered white and verde marble facades; the stonework harkens
back to the days when marble ruled what was once Vermont's second-largest city.

WHAT TO SEE

Paramount Theatre. The highlight of downtown is this 700-seat, turn-of-the-20th-century gilded playhouse. ⊠*30 Center St.* ☎*802/775–0570* ⊕*www.paramountvt.org.*

Chaffee Art Center. The former mansion of the local Paramount Theatre's founder, this arts center exhibits the work of more than 200 Vermont artists. ⊠*16 S. Main St.* ☎*802/775–0356* ⊕*www.chaffeeartcenter.org* ☞*Free* ☼*Tues.–Sat. 10–5, Sun. noon–4.*

Vermont Marble Exhibit. North of Rutland, this monument to marble highlights one of the main industries in this region, and illustrates marble's many industrial and artistic applications. The hall of presidents has a carved bust of each U.S. president, and in the marble chapel is a replica of Leonardo da Vinci's *Last Supper.* Elsewhere you can watch a sculptor-in-residence shape the stone into finished works of art, compare marbles from around the world, and also check out the Vermont Marble Company's original "stone library." Factory seconds and foreign and domestic marble items are for sale. A short walk away is the original marble quarry in Proctor. Marble from here became part of the U.S. Supreme Court building and the New York Public Library. ⊠*52 Main St., 4 mi north of Rutland, off Rte. 3, Proctor* ☎*802/459–2300 or 800/427–1396* ⊕*www.vermont-marble.com* ☞*$7* ☼*Mid-May–Oct., daily 9–5:30.*

Wilson Castle. This 32-room mansion built in 1875 comes complete with 84 stained-glass windows (one inset with 32 Australian opals), hand-painted Italian frescos, and 13 fireplaces. It's magnificently furnished with European and Asian objets d'art. ⊠*W. Proctor Rd., Proctor* ☎*802/773–3284* ⊕*www.wilsoncastle.com* ☞*$8.50* ☼*Late May–mid-Oct., daily 9–5:30.*

SPORTS & THE OUTDOORS

BOATING Rent pontoon boats, speedboats, waterskiing boats, Wave Runners, and water toys at **Lake Bomoseen Marina** (⊠*145 Creek Rd., off Rte. 4A, 1½ mi west of Castleton* ☎*802/265–4611*).

HIKING **Deer's Leap** (⊠*Starts at the Inn at Long Trail on Rte. 4 west of Rutland*) is a 3-mi round-trip hike to a great view overlooking Sherburne Gap and Pico Peak. **Mountain Travelers** (⊠*147 Rte. 4 E* ☎*802/775–0814*) sells hiking maps and guidebooks, and gives advice on local hikes.

NIGHTLIFE & THE ARTS

Crossroads Arts Council (⊠*39 E. Center St.* ☎*802/775–5413*) presents films, music, opera, dance, jazz, and theater year-round at venues throughout the region.

WHERE TO EAT & STAY

¢–$ ✕**Little Harry's.** Locals have packed this restaurant ever since chef-owners
ECLECTIC Trip (Harry) Pearce and Jack Mangan brought Vermont cheddar-cheese ravioli and lamb lo mein to downtown Rutland in 1997. The 17 tabletops are adorned with laminated photos of the regulars. For big appetites on small budgets, the Pad Thai and burrito are huge meals for under $8. ⊠*121 West St.* ☎*802/747–4848* ▭*MC, V* ☼*No lunch.*

2

$$ ⌂**Inn at Rutland.** If you love B&Bs and are tired of Rutland's chain motels this stately 1889 Victorian mansion on Main Street is a welcome sight. Large plate-glass windows illuminate the entryway, library, and sitting room. A large table dominates the dining room, which has hand-tooled leather wainscoting. Upstairs, the rooms have antiques; two rooms have private porches and whirlpool tubs. **Pros:** solid, non-motel choice. **Cons:** unexciting rooms. ⌂*70 N. Main St.* ☎*802/773–0575 or 800/808–0575* ⊕*www.innatrutland.com* ⟲*8 rooms* ⌂*In-room: Wi-Fi. In-hotel: restaurant, no elevator, public Internet, public Wi-Fi, no-smoking rooms* ▭*AE, D, MC, V.*

BRANDON

15 mi northwest of Rutland.

Thanks to an active artists' guild, Brandon is making a name for itself. In 2003 the Brandon Artists Guild, led by American folk artist Warren Kimble, auctioned 40 life-size fiberglass pigs painted by local artists. The "Really Really Pig Show" raised money for the guild (as well as other organizations) and brought fame to this once overlooked community. Since then themes have been birdhouses, rocking chairs, artist palettes, cats and dogs, and in 2008, "Thinking Outside the Box." The works are spread throughout town.

WHAT TO SEE

New England Maple Museum and Gift Shop. Maple syrup is Vermont's signature product and this museum south of Brandon explains the history and process of turning maple sap into syrup with murals, exhibits, and a slide show. ⌂*U.S. 7, Pittsford, 9 mi south of Brandon* ☎*802/483–9414* ⌂*Museum $2.50* ⊙*Late May–Oct., daily 8:30–5:30; Nov., Dec., and mid-Mar.–late May, daily 10–4.*

SPORTS & THE OUTDOORS

The **Moosalamoo Association** (☎*800/448–0707*) manages, protects, and provides stewardship for more than 20,000 acres of the Green Mountain National Forest, just northeast of Brandon. More than 60 mi of trails take hikers, mountain bikers, and cross-country skiers through some of Vermont's most gorgeous mountain terrain. Attractions include Branbury State Park, on the shores of Lake Dunmore; secluded Silver Lake; and sections of both the Long Trail and Catamount Trail (the latter is a Massachusetts-to-Quebec ski trail).

GOLF **Neshobe Golf Club** (⌂*Rte. 73 east of Brandon* ☎*802/247–3611*) has 18 holes of par-72 golf on a bent-grass course totaling nearly 6,500 yards. The Green Mountain views are terrific.

HIKING For great views from a vertigo-inducing cliff, hike up the Long Trail to **Mt. Horrid.** The steep, hour-long hike starts at the top of Brandon Gap (about 8 mi east of Brandon on Route 73). A large turnout on Route 53 marks a moderate trail to the **Falls of Lana.** West of Brandon, four trails—two short ones of less than 1 mi each and two longer ones—lead to the old abandoned Revolutionary War fortifications at **Mt. Independence.** To reach them, take the first left turn off Route 73 west of Orwell and go right at the fork. The road will turn to gravel and once again will fork; take a sharp left-hand turn toward a small marina. The parking lot is on the left at the top of the hill.

WHERE TO EAT & STAY

$–$$
CAFE

✕**Café Provence.** One story above the main street, this large, high-ceilinged café with hints of Provence (flowered seat cushions and dried-flower window valences) specializes in eclectic farm-fresh dishes. Goat-cheese cake with mesclun greens, braised veal cheeks and caramelized endive, and a portobello pizza from the restaurant's hearth oven are just a few of the choices. Breakfast offerings include buttery pastries, eggs Benedict, and breakfast pizza. Umbrellas shade outdoor seating. ✉*11 Center St.* ☎*802/247–9997* ▭*MC, V.*

$$–$$$
★

▦**Blueberry Hill Inn.** In the Green Mountain National Forest, 5½ mi off a mountain pass on a dirt road, you'll find this secluded inn with its lush gardens and a pond with a wood-fired sauna on its bank. Many rooms have views of the mountains; all are furnished with antiques and quilts. The restaurant prepares a four-course prix-fixe ($$$$) menu nightly, with dishes such as venison fillet with cherry sauce. This is a very popular place for weddings–the grounds are gorgeous and there's lots to do if you're into nature: biking, hiking, and a cross-country ski center with 43 mi of trails. **Pros:** peaceful setting witin the national forest; terrific property with lots to do; great food. **Cons:** forest setting not right for those who want to be near town. ✉*1307 Goshen–Ripton Rd., Goshen* ☎*802/247–6735 or 800/448–0707* ⊕*www.blueberryhill inn.com* ↪*12 rooms* ♿*In-room: no a/c, no phone, no TV, Wi-Fi. In-hotel: restaurant, bicycles, no elevator, public Internet, public Wi-Fi, some pets allowed, no-smoking rooms* ▭*AE, MC, V* ❙◎❙*MAP.*

$$–$$$

▦**Brandon Inn.** Built in 1786, this large hotel exudes an aura of elegance from centuries past. The foyer has marble flooring, and this theme continues throughout the three-story inn. The Victorian-furnished common rooms and multipillared dining room, used only for special groups, are expansive (and underutilized). In the main lobby, the state's oldest elevator (circa 1901) leads to two upper floors with comfortable and spacious guest rooms. **Pros:** in-town location. **Cons:** unexciting rooms. ✉*20 Park St.* ☎*800/639–8685* ⊕*www.historicbrandoninn. com* ↪*39 rooms* ♿*In-room: no TV. In-hotel: restaurant, pool, no-smoking rooms* ▭*AE, D, MC, V* ❙◎❙*BP.*

$$–$$$

▦**Lilac Inn.** This Greek-revival mansion's spacious common areas are filled with lovely antiques. The rooms, all furnished with claw-foot tubs and handheld European showerheads, are charming, and the grand suite has a pewter canopy bed, whirlpool bath for two, and fireplace. Overlooking the gardens, the elegant dining room ($$) serves unique creations such as fig-mango pork short ribs. **Pros:** big manor house, walking distance to town. **Cons:** busy in summer with weddings. ✉*53 Park St. (Rte. 73)* ☎*802/247–5463 or 800/221–0720* ⊕*www.lilacinn. com* ↪*9 rooms* ♿*In-room: no a/c. In-hotel: restaurant, public Internet, public Wi-Fi, no kids under 12, some pets allowed, no-smoking rooms* ▭*AE, MC, V* ❙◎❙*BP.*

MIDDLEBURY

★ *17 mi north of Brandon, 34 mi south of Burlington.*

In the late 1800s Middlebury was the largest Vermont community west of the Green Mountains, an industrial center of river-powered wool and grain mills. This is Robert Frost country: Vermont's late poet laureate spent 23 summers at a farm east of Middlebury. Still a cultural and economic hub amid the Champlain Valley's serene pastoral patchwork, the town and countryside invite a day of exploration.

WHAT TO SEE

Middlebury College. Founded in 1800, Middlebury College was conceived as a more godly alternative to the worldly University of Vermont. The college has no religious affiliation today, however. Set in the middle of town, the early-19th-century stone buildings contrast provocatively with the postmodern architecture of the Center for the Arts and the sports center. Music, theater, and dance performances take place throughout the year at the **Wright Memorial Theatre** and **Center for the Arts** *(802/443–5000).*

Vermont Folklife Center. Located in the Masonic Hall, exhibits include photography, antiques, folk paintings, manuscripts, and other artifacts and contemporary works that examine facets of Vermont life. ⊠*3 Court St. 802/388–4964 Donations accepted Gallery May–Dec., Tues.–Sat. 11–4.*

Vermont State Craft Center/Frog Hollow. More than a crafts store, this arts center mounts changing exhibitions and displays exquisite works in wood, glass, metal, clay, and fiber by more than 250 Vermont artisans. The center, which overlooks Otter Creek, sponsors classes taught by some of those artists. Burlington and Manchester also have centers. ⊠*1 Mill St. 802/388–3177 www.froghollow.org Call for hrs.*

UVM Morgan Horse Farm. The Morgan horse—Vermont's official state animal—has an even temper, stamina, and slightly truncated legs in proportion to its body. The University of Vermont's Morgan Horse Farm, about 2½ mi west of Middlebury, is a breeding and training center where in summer you can tour the stables and paddocks. ⊠*74 Battell Dr., off Morgan Horse Farm Rd. (follow signs off Rte. 23), Weybridge 802/388–2011 $4 May–Oct., daily 9–4.*

Robert Frost Interpretive Trail. About 10 mi east of town on Route 125 (1 mi west of Middlebury College's Bread Loaf campus), this easy ¾-mi trail winds through quiet woodland. Plaques along the way bear quotations from Frost's poems. A picnic area is across the road from the trailhead.

OFF THE BEATEN PATH

Fort Ticonderoga Ferry. Established in 1759, the Fort Ti cable ferry crosses Lake Champlain between Shoreham and Fort Ticonderoga, New York, at one of the oldest ferry crossings in North America. The trip takes seven minutes. ⊠*4675 Rte. 74 W, 18 mi southwest of Middlebury, 9 mi south of Brandon, Shoreham 802/897–7999 Cars, pickups,* *and vans with driver and passenger $8; bicycles $2; pedestrians $1* ⊙ *May–last Sun. of Oct., daily 8–5:45.*

SHOPPING

ARTWORK **Historic Marble Works** (✉*Maple St.* ☎*802/388–3701*), a renovated marble manufacturing facility, is a collection of unique shops set amid quarrying equipment and factory buildings. One of them, **Danforth Pewter** (☎*802/388–0098*), sells handcrafted pewter vases, lamps, and tableware.

WHERE TO EAT & STAY

¢–$ ✕**American Flatbread.** On weekends this is the most happening spot
★ in town, and no wonder: the pizza is extraordinary and the attitude
PIZZA is pure Vermont. Wood-fired clay domes create masterful crusts from organically grown wheats. Besides the innovative, delicious pizzas, try an organic mesclun salad tossed in a house raspberry-ginger vinaigrette. During the week, when the restaurant is closed, the space is used to manufacture pizzas for gourmet stores across the country—but if you pop in at any time you can buy whatever is in the oven for a flat $10. (And whatever is in the oven is sure to be delicious.) ✉*137 Maple St., at the Marble Works* ☎*802/388–3300* ⬧*Reservations not accepted* ⊟*MC, V* ⊙*Closed Sun.–Thurs. No lunch.*

$$–$$$ ✕**Mary's at Baldwin Creek.** People drive from the far reaches of Vermont
Fodor's Choice to eat at this restaurant in Bristol, 13 mi northeast of Middlebury. Chef-
★ owner Douglas Mack founded the Vermont Fresh Network; member-
ECLECTIC ship in this group, which facilitates farm-fresh ingredients, is now a hallmark of the state's best restaurants. The innovative fare includes a superb garlic soup and entrées with whimsical names like Swimming with Noodles (shrimp, shiitake mushrooms, roasted tomato, and asparagus sautéed in garlic white wine and served over fettuccine), and What's Eating Gilbert Crepe (sesame-and-ginger-marinated tofu in a crepe). A café menu is also available. ✉*1869 Rte. 116, Bristol* ☎*802/453–2432* ⊟*MC, V* ⊙*Closed Mon. and Tues. No lunch.*

$$–$$$ ✕**Storm Café.** Locals rave about the eclectic ever-changing menu at this
ECLECTIC small restaurant in the old Frog Hollow Mill overlooking the Otter Creek Falls. Chef-owner John Goettelmann's creations include stormy Thai stew, Jamaican jerk-seasoned pork tenderloin, and melt-in-your-mouth desserts like an apricot soufflé. Outdoor seating by the river is available in nice weather. ✉*3 Mill St.* ☎*802/388–1063* ⊟*MC, V* ⊙*No lunch Sun.*

$–$$ ⌂**Swift House Inn.** The 1824 Georgian home of a 19th-century governor showcases white-panel wainscoting, mahogany furnishings, and marble fireplaces. The stellar rooms—most with Oriental rugs and nine with fireplaces—have period reproductions such as canopy beds, curtains with swags, and claw-foot tubs. Some bathrooms have double whirl-pool tubs. Rooms in the attractive Gatehouse suffer from street noise but are charming and a solid value. The seven-room carriage house has more expensive rooms with wood fireplaces and king-size beds. **Pros:** attractive, spacious, well-kept rooms; professionally run. **Cons:** near, but not quite in the heart of town. ✉*25 Stewart La.* ☎*802/388–9925* ⊕*www.swifthouseinn.com* ⊶*20 rooms* ⌃*In-room: DVD (some),*

VCR (some), Wi-Fi. In-hotel: restaurant, room service, bar, laundry service, public Wi-Fi, some pets allowed, no-smoking rooms ⊟*AE, D, DC, MC, V* ⊺◎⏐*BP.*

WAITSFIELD & WARREN

32 mi northeast (Waitsfield) and 25 mi east (Warren) of Middlebury.

Skiers discovered the high peaks overlooking the pastoral Mad River valley in the 1940s. Now the valley and its two towns, Waitsfield and Warren, attract the hip, the adventurous, and the low-key. Warren is tiny and adorable, with a general store that attracts tour buses. The gently carved ridges cradling the valley and the swell of pastures and fields lining the river seem to keep notions of ski-resort sprawl at bay. With a map from the Sugarbush Chamber of Commerce you can investigate back roads off Route 100 that have exhilarating valley views.

SPORTS & THE OUTDOORS

OUTFITTER **Clearwater Sports** (⊠*4147 Main St. [Rte. 100]* ☎*802/496–2708*) rents canoes, kayaks, and camping equipment and leads guided river trips and white-water instruction in the warm months; in winter, the store leads snowshoe and backcountry ski tours and rents telemark equipment, snowshoes, and one person Mad River Rocket sleds.

GOLF Great views and challenging play are the trademarks of the Robert Trent Jones–designed 18-hole mountain course at **Sugarbush Resort** (⊠*Golf Course Rd.* ☎*802/583–6725*). The green fees run from $48 to $58; a cart (sometimes mandatory) costs $18 per person.

SLEIGH RIDES **Mountain Valley Farm** (⊠*1719 Common Rd.* ☎*802/496–9255*) offers in horse-drawn carriage and sleigh rides. Reservations are required.

SKI AREAS **Blueberry Lake Cross-Country Ski Area** (⊠*Plunkton Rd., Warren* ☎*802/496–6687*) has 18 mi of trails through thickly wooded glades.

The hundreds of shareholders who own **Mad River Glen** (⊠*Rte. 17* ☎*802/496–3551, 802/496–2001 snow conditions, 800/850–6742 cooperative office* ⊕*www.madriverglen.com*) are dedicated, knowledgeable skiers devoted to keeping skiing what it used to be—a pristine alpine experience. Mad River's unkempt aura attracts rugged individualists looking for less-polished terrain: the area was developed in the late 1940s and has changed relatively little since then. It remains one of only three resorts in the country that ban snowboarding.

Mad River is steep, with natural slopes that follow the mountain's fall lines. The terrain changes constantly on the 45 interconnected trails, of which 30% are beginner, 30% are intermediate, and 40% are expert. Intermediate and novice terrain is regularly groomed. Five lifts—including the world's last surviving single chairlift—service the mountain's 2,037-foot vertical drop. Most of Mad River's trails are covered only by natural snow. The kids ski school runs classes for little ones ages 4 to 12.

Known as the "Mecca of Free-Heel Skiing," Mad River Glen sponsors telemark programs throughout the season. Every March, the North America Telemark Organization (NATO) Festival attracts up to 1,400. Snowshoeing is also an option. There is a $5 fee to use the snowshoe trails, and rentals are available.

Sugarbush (⊠*Sugarbush Access Rd., accessible from Rtes. 100 or 17* ⌂*Box 350, Warren 05674* ☏*802/583–6300, 802/583–7669 snow conditions, 800/537–8427 lodging* ⊕*www.sugarbush.com*) has remade itself as a true skier's mountain, with steep, natural snow glades and fall-line drops. Not as rough around the edges as Mad River Glen, Sugarbush also has well-groomed intermediate and beginner terrain. A computer-controlled system for snowmaking has increased coverage to nearly 70%. At the base of the mountain are condominiums, restaurants, shops, bars, and a sports center.

Sugarbush is two distinct, connected mountain complexes connected by the Slide Brook Express quad. Lincoln Peak, with a vertical of 2,400 feet, is known for formidable steeps, especially on Castlerock. Mount Ellen has more beginner runs near the bottom, with steep fall-line pitches on the upper half of the 2,650 vertical feet. There are 115 trails in all: 23% beginner, 48% intermediate, 29% expert. The resort has 18 lifts: seven quads (including four high-speed versions), three triples, four doubles, and four surface lifts. There's half- and full-day instruction available for children ages 4–12, ski/day care for 3-year-olds, and supervised ski and ride programs for teens. Sugarbear Forest, a terrain garden, has fun bumps and jumps.

SHOPPING

All Things Bright and Beautiful (⊠*Bridge St.* ☏*802/496–3997*) is a 12-room Victorian house jammed to the rafters with stuffed animals of all shapes, sizes, and colors as well as folk art, prints, and collectibles. One of the rooms is a coffee and ice-cream shop. **Cabin Fever Quilts** (⊠*4276 Main St. No. 1 [Rte. 100]* ☏*802/496–2287*), inside a converted old church, sells fine handmade quilts.

NIGHTLIFE & THE ARTS

NIGHTLIFE **Chez Henri** (⊠*Lincoln Peak base area, Sugarbush Village, Warren* ☏*802/583–2600*) is the place to go après-ski. Live bands play most weekends at **Purple Moon Pub** (⊠*Rte. 100* ☏*802/496–3422*).

★ In the basement of the Pitcher Inn, **Tracks** (⊠*275 Main St. Warren* ☏*802/493–6350*) is a public bar run by the Relais & Châteaux property. It has billiards, darts, and a really fun game like shuffle board played on a long table with sawdust. There's a full tavern menu and a giant moose head.

ARTS The **Green Mountain Cultural Center** (⊠*Inn at the Round Barn Farm, 1661 E. Warren Rd.* ☏*802/496–7722*) hosts concerts, art exhibits, and educational workshops. The **Valley Players** (⊠*Rte. 100, Waitsfield* ☏*802/496–9612*) present musicals, dramas, follies, and more.

WHERE TO EAT

$$–$$$
AMERICAN

✕ **1824 House.** Much like the Common Man up the hill closer to Sugarbush, this reconverted barn is floor-to-ceiling wood. The 1870 post-and-beam construction is hung with chandeliers and is an enticing setting for a fancy meal cooked up by owner John Lumbra. A specialty is the French onion soup made with Tarentaise, an excellent cheese made only in Vermont. Entrées might include lobster pancakes, filet mignon stuffed with blue cheese and wrapped in bacon, and a lemon sabayon–pine-nut tart. ⊠ *2150 Main St., Waitsfield* ☎ *802/496–7555 or 800/426–3986* ▤ *AE, MC, V* ⊘ *No lunch. Dec.–Feb. closed Mon. and Tues.; June–Aug. closed Tues. and Wed.*

¢–$
Fodor'sChoice
★
PIZZA

✕ **American Flatbread.** Is this the best pizza experience in the world? It just may be. In summer, dining takes place outside around fire pits in the beautiful valley, a setting and meal not to be forgotten. The secret is in the love, of course, but some clues to the magic are in the organically grown flour and vegetables and the wood-fired clay ovens. The "new Vermont sausage" is Waitsfield pork in a maple-fennel sausage baked with sundried tomatoes, caramelized onions, cheese, and herbs; it's a dream, as are the more traditional pizzas. This is the original American Flatbread location, and the retail bakery is open Monday–Thursday 7:30 AM–8 PM; if you're here during that time anything in the oven is yours for $10. As a restaurant, it's open only Friday and Saturday evenings. Plan your trip around it. ⊠ *46 Lareau Rd., off Rte. 100, Waitsfield* ☎ *802/496–8856* ⌖ *Reservations not accepted* ▤ *MC, V* ⊘ *Closed Sun.*

$$$–$$$$
ECLECTIC

✕ **Common Man.** A local institution since 1972, this restaurant is in a big 1800s barn with hand-hewn rafters and crystal chandeliers hanging from the beams. That's the Common Man for you: fancy and après-ski at once. Bottles of Moët & Chandon signed by the customers who ordered them sit atop the beams. The eclectic New American cuisine highlights locally grown produce and meats. The menu might include an appetizer of sautéed sweetbreads and apples, a salad of organic field greens, and entrées ranging from fish stew in tomato and saffron broth to grilled venison or sautéed and confited rabbit. Dinner is served by candlelight. Couples sit by the big fireplace. ⊠ *3209 German Flats Rd., Warren* ☎ *802/583–2800* ▤ *AE, DC, MC, V* ⊘ *Closed Mon. mid-Apr.–mid-Dec. No lunch.*

¢–$
CAFE

✕ **The Green Cup.** You can count on products and ingredients from the community at this local favorite. Chef-owner Jason Galiano is famed for his egg specialties, making this the best place around for breakfast (served every day except Wednesday); or just to hang out with a cup of coffee (there's free Wi-Fi). Jason's sister Sarina works front of house and preps orders. Egg specials, soups, and pastries are all made form scratch. Dinner is served Sunday and Monday nights, filling a void in the area. Dinner plates are designed to be shared. ⊠ *40 Bridge St., Waitsfield* ☎ *802/496–4963* ▤ *MC, V* ⊘ *No dinner Tues.–Sat.*

WHERE TO STAY

$$

▥ **1824 House.** Not to be confused with Manchester's 1811 House, this 10-gable farmhouse north of Waitsfield is a traditional Vermont farmhouse converted into an elegant inn with cozy rooms and featherbeds. There are just two room types: queen rooms are simple and cute; king rooms have larger sitting areas. Innkeepers Trae Greene and John Lumbra (the chef) take their dining seriously. The renovated rustic barn is home to good, and expensive, prix-fixe dinners. **Pros:** clean, cheery rooms in a historic inn. **Cons:** on Route 100, slightly outside of town. ⊠*2150 Main St. (Rte. 100), Waitsfield* ☎*802/496–7555 or 800/426–3986* ⊕*www.1824house.com* ⊲*8 rooms* ⌂*In-room: no a/c, no TV, Wi-Fi. In-hotel: restaurant, bar, no elevator, public Internet, public Wi-Fi, some pets allowed, no kids under 7, no-smoking rooms* ⊟*AE, MC, V* ⦿*BP, MAP.*

$$ ▦**Inn at the Round Barn Farm.** A Shaker-style round barn (one of only
★ five in Vermont) is the physical hallmark of this B&B, but what you'll remember when you leave is how comfortable a stay here is. In winter, you toss your shoes under a bench when you come in and put on a pair of slippers from a big basket. There's magic in that gesture, breaking down barriers between guests and giving you permission to really kick back. You'll feel like a kid in the downstairs rec room with its TV, games, and billiard table. The guest rooms, inside the 1806 farmhouse, have eyelet-trimmed sheets, elaborate four-poster beds, rich-color wallpapers, and brass wall lamps for easy bedtime reading. Many have fireplaces and whirlpool tubs. Cooper, the inn dog, is your guide—literally—as you snowshow or hike the miles of trails on this beautiful property filled with gardens and sculpture. Plan a winter trip around one of the moonlit snowshoe walks, which terminate with hot chocolate in an old cabin. **Pros:** great trails, gardens, and rooms; nice breakfast. **Cons:** no restaurant. ⊠*1661 E. Warren Rd., Waitsfield* ☎*802/496–2276* ⊕*www.theroundbarn.com* ⊲*11 rooms, 1 suite* ⌂*In-room: no TV, Wi-Fi. In-hotel: pool, no elevator, public Internet, public Wi-Fi, no kids under 15, no-smoking rooms* ⊟*AE, D, MC, V* ⦿*BP.*

$$$$ ▦**Pitcher Inn.** Across from the justly famous Warren General Store is
Fodor'sChoice the elegant Pitcher Inn, Vermont's only Relais & Châteaux property.
★ Ari Sadri, the hands-on manager, exudes an easygoing sophistication that makes staying here a delight. Each comfortable room has its own unusual and elaborate motif—which you'll either love or hate. The Mountain Room, for instance, is designed as a replica of a fire tower in the Green Mountains, with murals on some walls and others covered in stone and glass to resemble a mountain cliff. All the bathrooms, however, are uniformly wonderful, with rain showerheads and Anchini linens and superb toiletries. **Pros:** exceptional service, great bathrooms, fun pub, great location. **Cons:** many rooms can be considered kitschy or downright silly. ⊠*275 Main St., Warren* ☎*802/496–6350 or 888/867–4824* ⊕*www.pitcherinn.com* ⊲*9 rooms, 2 suites* ⌂*In-room: refrigerator (some), VCR, Wi-Fi. In-hotel: restaurant, bar, spa, water sports, bicycles, public Internet, public Wi-Fi, no-smoking rooms* ⊟*AE, MC, V* ⦿*BP.*

NORTHERN VERMONT

Vermont's northernmost region reveals the state's greatest contrasts. To the west, Burlington and its suburbs have grown so rapidly that rural wags now say that Burlington's greatest advantage is that it's "close to Vermont." The north country also harbors Vermont's tiny capital, Montpelier, and its highest mountain, Mt. Mansfield, site of the famous Stowe ski resort. To the northeast of Montpelier is a sparsely populated and heavily wooded territory that former Senator George Aiken dubbed the "Northeast Kingdom." It's the domain of loggers, farmers, and avid outdoors enthusiasts.

Our coverage of towns begins in the state capital, Montpelier; moves west toward Stowe and Burlington; then goes north through the Lake Champlain Islands, east along the boundary with Canada toward Jay Peak, and south into the heart of the Northeast Kingdom.

MONTPELIER

38 mi southeast of Burlington, 115 mi north of Brattleboro.

With only about 8,000 residents, Montpelier is the country's smallest capital city. The well-preserved downtown bustles with state and city workers walking to meetings or down the street for coffee or lunch.

WHAT TO SEE

Vermont State House. With a gleaming gold dome and columns of Barre granite 6 feet in diameter, the state house is home to the oldest legislative chambers in their original condition in the United States. The goddess of agriculture tops the gilded dome. Interior paintings and exhibits make much of Vermont's sterling Civil War record. ⊠ *115 State St.* ☎ *802/828–2228* ⊞ *Donations accepted* ⊙ *Weekdays 8–4; tours July–mid-Oct., weekdays every ½ hr 10–3:30 (last tour at 3:30), Sat. 11–3 (last tour at 2:30).*

Vermont Museum. Next door to the capitol, in the Pavilion building, this museum preserves all things Vermont, from a catamount to Ethan Allen's shoe buckles. ⊠ *109 State St.* ☎ *802/828–2291* ⊕ *www.state. vt.us/vhs* ⊞ *$5* ⊙ *May–Oct., Tues.–Sat. 10–4, Sun. noon–4.*

OFF THE BEATEN PATH

Rock of Ages Granite Quarry. The attractions here range from the awe-inspiring (the quarry resembles the Grand Canyon in miniature) to the mildly ghoulish (you can consult a directory of tombstone dealers throughout the country) to the whimsical (an outdoor granite bowling alley). You might recognize the sheer walls of the quarry from *Batman and Robin*, the film starring George Clooney and Arnold Schwarzenegger. At the crafts center, skilled artisans sculpt monuments; at the quarries themselves, 25-ton blocks of stone are cut from sheer 475-foot walls by workers who clearly earn their pay. ⊠ *Exit 6 off I–89, follow Rte. 63, 7 mi southeast of Montpelier, Barre* ☎ *802/476–3119* ⊞ *Tour of active quarry $4, craftsman center and self-guided tour free* ⊙ *Visitor center May–Oct., Mon.–Sat. 8:30–5, Sun. 10–5; narrated tour on Sat. (call for times).*

CLOSE UP

Slopes Less Traveled

Since America's first ski tow opened in a farmer's pasture near Woodstock in January 1934, skiers have flocked to Vermont in winter. The Green Mountains are dotted with 18 ski resorts, from Mt. Snow in the south to Jay Peak near the Canadian border. They range in size from Killington, in central Vermont, with its 200 trails and 31 lifts, to the Bear Creek Mountain Club, also in central Vermont, with only 15 trails and one chairlift. On weekends and holidays, the bigger resorts—Mt. Snow, Stratton, and Okemo in southern Vermont; Killington, Sugarbush, and Mad River Glen in the central part of the state; and Stowe, Smugglers' Notch, and Jay Peak in the north—attract most of the skiers and snowboarders. To escape the crowds, try these smaller ski resorts.

SOUTHERN VERMONT

Near Stratton, **Bromley** (⊠ Rte. 11, Peru ☎ 802/824–5522 or 800/865–4786 ⊕ www.bromley.com) is a favorite with families. The 43 trails are evenly divided between beginner, intermediate, and expert. The resort runs a child care center, for kids ages 6 weeks to 4 years, and hosts children's programs, for ages 3–12. An added bonus: the trails face south, making for glorious spring skiing and warm winter days.

CENTRAL VERMONT

Once only a faint blip on skiers' radar, **Ascutney** (⊠ Rte. 44, Brownsville ☎ 802/484–7711 or 800/243–0011 ⊕ www.ascutney.com) has remade itself into a bona-fide destination. The 56 trails on an 1,800-foot vertical drop are served by six lifts, including a high-speed quad chairlift accessing double-diamond terrain near the summit. Day care is available for children

ages 6 weeks to 6 years, with learn-to-ski programs for toddlers and up. On Saturday from 5–8 PM, children ages 4–12 can join Cheddar's Happy Hour and movie night. When weekend hordes hit Killington, the locals head to **Pico** (⊠ Rte. 4, Killington ☎ 802/422–6200 or 866/667–7426 ⊕ www.picomountain.com). One of Killington's "seven peaks," Pico is physically separated from its parent resort. The 50 trails range from elevator-shaft steeps to challenging intermediate trails near the summit, with easier terrain near the bottom of the mountain's 2,000-foot vertical. The learning slope is separated from the upper mountain, so hotshots won't bomb through it. The lower express quad can get crowded, but the upper one rarely has a line.

NORTHERN VERMONT

About an hour's drive from Montpelier is **Burke Mountain** (⊠ Mountain Rd., East Burke ☎ 802/626–3322 ⊕ www.skiburke.com). Racers stick to the Training Slope, served by its own poma lift. The other 44 trails and glades are a quiet playground. Near Burlington, **Bolton Valley Resort** (⊠ 4302 Bolton Valley Access Rd., Bolton ☎ 802/434–3444 or 877/926–5866 ⊕ www.boltonvalley. com) is a family favorite. In addition to 61 downhill ski trails (over half rated for intermediates), Bolton has night skiing Wednesday–Saturday, 62 mi of cross-country and snowshoe trails, and a sports center.

For skiing information, contact **Ski Vermont/Vermont Ski Areas Association** (⊠ 26 State St., Montpelier ☎ 802/223–2439 ⊕ www. skivermont.com).

Northern Vermont

Lake Champlain Islands

QUÉBEC

CANADA

QUÉBEC

NEW YORK

NEW HAMPSHIRE

Great Averill Pond

Seymour Lake

Lake Memphremagog

Maidstone Lake

Connecticut River

Missisquoi

Lake Champlain

Crystal Lake

Willoughby Lake

Winooski R.

Lamoille

Black

Long Trail

Long Trail

Painfield Lake

Norton
Island Pond
Guildhall
Burke Mountain
East Burke
Lyndonville
Westmore
Lake Willoughby
Barton
Glover
Craftsbury
The Craftsburys
Greensboro
Morrisville
Hardwick
Walden
Cabot
Peacham
St. Johnsbury
Lower Waterford
Barnet
Groton
Northfield
Montpelier
Rock of Ages Granite Quarry
Waterbury
Ben & Jerry's Ice Cream Factory
Stowe
Stowe Mountain Resort
Smugglers' Notch Resort
Johnson
Cambridge
Jeffersonville
Bolton
Bolton Valley
LITTLE RIVER STATE PARK
Richmond
Huntington
Hinesburg
Shelburne
Burlington
Winooski
South Burlington
Essex Junction
Colchester
St. Albans
Kill Kare State Park
Burton Island State Park
Swanton
Alburg Center
Isle La Motte
North Hero State Park
Grand Isle State Park
Grand Isle
South Hero
Sand Bar State Park
East Berkshire
Eelosburg Falls
Montgomery/ Jay
Montgomery Center
Jay
Jay Peak
Newport
Waitsfield
Ferrisburg
Vergennes
Bristol
Basin Harbor
Barre
Waterbury

102
105
114
105
101
242
118
100
91
5A
5A
5
14
16
15
14
2
302
91
63
14
89
100
108
130
15
104
36
78
89
7
2
89
116
22A
7
5A
122
91

0 ———— 15 miles

0 ———— 25 km

Cabot Creamery. The major cheese producer in the state, midway between Barre and St. Johnsbury, has a visitor center with an audiovisual presentation about the dairy and cheese industry. You can taste samples, purchase cheese and other Vermont products, and tour the plant. ⊠*2870 Main St. (Rte. 215), 3 mi north of U.S. 2, Cabot* ☎*800/837–4261* ▨*$2* ☉*June–Oct., daily 9–5; Nov., Dec., and Feb.–May, Mon.–Sat. 9–4; Jan., Mon.–Sat. 10–4; call ahead to check cheese-making days.*

SHOPPING

Unique shops attract locals and tourists alike to Montpelier. For hip children's clothing made-in-Vermont, head to **Zutano** (⊠*79 Main St.* ☎*802/223–2229*).

WHERE TO EAT

$–$$$
Fodor's Choice
★
ECLECTIC
✕**Ariel's.** Well off the beaten path, this small restaurant overlooking a lake is worth the drive down a dirt road. Chef Lee Duberman prepares eclectic treats such as scallop, lobster, and shrimp ravioli in a ginger shiitake broth. Her husband and sommelier Ricard Fink recommends selections from the wine cellar. The full menu is offered Friday and Saturday; a pub menu ($–$$) is served Wednesday, Thursday, and Sunday. ⊠*29 Stone Hill Rd., 8 mi south of Montpelier, Brookfield* ☎*802/276–3939* ▤*DC, MC, V* ☉*Closed Nov. and Apr.; Mon. and Tues. May–Oct.; Mon.–Thurs. Dec.–Mar.*

$$
★
AMERICAN
✕**Chef's Table.** Nearly everyone working here is a student at the New England Culinary Institute. Although this is a training ground, the quality and inventiveness are anything but beginner's luck. The menu changes daily. Dining is more formal than at the sister operation downstairs, the Main Street Bar and Grill (open daily for lunch and dinner). A 15% gratuity is added to the bill. ⊠*118 Main St.* ☎*802/229–9202, 802/223–3188 grill* ▤*AE, D, DC, MC, V* ☉*Closed Sun. and Mon. No lunch.*

$–$$
SOUTHERN
✕**River Run Restaurant.** Mississippi-raised chef Jimmy Kennedy has brought outstanding Southern fare to northern Vermont. Fried catfish, hush puppies, collard greens, and whiskey cake are just a few of the surprises awaiting diners at this rustic, hip eatery. Try the buttermilk biscuits at breakfast. There is a full bar. ⊠*Main St., 10 mi east of Montpelier, Plainfield* ☎*802/454–1246* ▤*No credit cards* ☉*Closed Mon.*

¢–$
ITALIAN
✕**Sarducci's.** Legislative lunches have been a lot more leisurely since Sarducci's came along to fill the trattoria void in Vermont's capital. These bright, cheerful rooms alongside the Winooski River are a great spot for pizza fresh from wood-fired ovens, wonderfully textured homemade Italian breads, and imaginative pasta dishes such as pasta *pugliese,* which marries penne with basil, black olives, roasted eggplant, portobello mushrooms, and sun-dried tomatoes. ⊠*3 Main St.* ☎*802/223–0229* ▤*AE, MC, V* ☉*No lunch Sun.*

WHERE TO STAY

$–$$ ⚐**Inn at Montpelier.** This inn consists of side-by-side homes built in the early 1800s. The architectural detailing, antique four-poster beds, Windsor chairs, and classical guitar on the stereo attract the leisure trade as well as those heading to the capital on business. The formal sitting room has a wide wraparound Colonial-revival porch, perfect for reading a book or watching the townsfolk stroll by. The rooms are small and can be chilly on cool summer days. **Pros:** beautiful home, relaxed setting. **Cons:** small rooms ⊠*147 Main St.* ☎*802/223–2727* ⊕*www.innatmontpelier.com* ⥲*19 rooms* ⌂*In-room: Wi-Fi. In-hotel: bar, laundry service, no elevator, no-smoking rooms* ☰*AE, D, DC, MC, V* ⦿*CP.*

EN ROUTE   On your way to Stowe from Interstate 89, be sure to stop at **Ben & Jerry's Ice Cream Factory,** the Valhalla for ice-cream lovers. Ben and Jerry began selling ice cream from a renovated gas station in Burlington in the 1970s. The tour only skims the surface of the behind-the-scenes goings-on at the plant—a flaw forgiven when the free samples are dished out. ⊠*Rte. 100, 1 mi north of I–89, Waterbury* ☎*802/846-1500* ⊕*www.benjerry.com* ⬛*Tour $3* ⊙*Late Oct.–June, daily 10–6; July–mid-Aug., daily 9–9; mid-Aug.–late Oct., daily 9–7. Tours run every half hour.*

STOWE

Fodor'sChoice
★   *22 mi northwest of Montpelier, 36 mi east of Burlington.*

Long before skiing came to Stowe in the 1930s, the rolling hills and valleys beneath Vermont's highest peak, the 4,395-foot Mt. Mansfield, attracted summer tourists looking for a reprieve from city heat. Most stayed at one of two inns in the village of Stowe. When skiing made the town a winter destination, the arriving skiers outnumbered the hotel beds, so locals took them in. This spirit of hospitality continues, and many of these homes are now lovely country inns. The village itself is tiny, just a few blocks of shops and restaurants clustered around a picture-perfect white church with a lofty steeple, but it serves as the anchor for Mountain Road, which leads north past restaurants, lodges, and shops on its way to Stowe's fabled slopes.

WHAT TO SEE

Mt. Mansfield. With its elongated summit ridge resembling the profile of a recumbent man's face, Mt. Mansfield has long attracted the adventurous. The mountain is ribboned with hiking and ski trails.

Gondola. Mt. Mansfield's "Chin" area is accessible by the eight-seat gondola. At the gondola's summit station is the **Cliff House Restaurant** (☎*802/253–3558 Ext. 237*), where lunch is served daily 11–3. ⊠*Mountain Rd., 8 mi off Rte. 100* ☎*802/253–3000* ⬛*Gondola $14* ⊙*Mid-June–mid-Oct., daily 10–5; early Dec.–late Apr., daily 8–4.*

Trapp Family Lodge. Built by the von Trapp family, of *Sound of Music* fame, this Tyrolean lodge and its surrounding pastureland are the site

Spa Vacations

Vermont's destination spas have come a long way since the days its *au natural* mineral springs attracted affluent 19th-century city dwellers looking to escape the heat, but the overall principle remains the same. The state remains a natural place to restore mind and body.

Stowe has two destination spas. The largest spa in New England, **Spa at Stoweflake** (✉ *1746 Mountain Rd. [Rte. 108], Stowe* ☎ *802/760–1083 or 800/253–2232* ⊕ *www.stoweflake. com*) features a massaging hydrotherapeutic waterfall, a Hungarian mineral pool, 30 treatment rooms, a hair and nail salon, and 120 services, such as the Bingham Falls Renewal, named after a local waterfall. This treatment begins with a seasonal body scrub (e.g., immune builder in winter) that's rinsed in a Vichy shower, followed by an aromatherapy oil massage. The spacious men's and women's sanctuaries and locker rooms have saunas, steamrooms, and Jacuzzis.

Opened in early 2005, the **Spa at Topnotch** (✉ *4000 Mountain Rd. [Rte. 108], Stowe* ☎ *802/253–8585* ⊕ *www.topnotchresort.com*) provides an aura of calm, with its birch wood doors and accents, hardwood floors, natural light, chrome fixtures, and cool colors. Signature services include a Vermont wildflower or woodspice treatment, which includes a warm herb wrap, exfoliation, and massage. Locker areas are spacious, with saunas, steam rooms, and Jacuzzis. The spa also has a full-service salon.

Next door to the swank Pitcher Inn, the **Alta Day Spa** (✉ *247 Main St., Warren* ☎ *802/496–2582* ⊕ *www. altadayspa.com*) is an Aveda concept spa offering massage, masques,

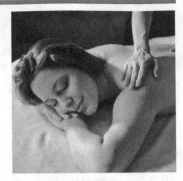

Slopeside spas like Stoweflake's can soothe muscles weary from skiing.

wraps, and facials in four light, airy treatment rooms in a renovated 19th-century house. A two-night spa package through the inn might include daily manicures and hydrating pedicures, facials, and massages, plus lodging and breakfast.

At Killington, the **Woods Resort and Spa** (✉ *53 Woods La., Killington* ☎ *802/422–3139* ⊕ *www.woods resortandspa.com*) is a European spa within an upscale condo complex. At the resort's clubhouse, the spa has a 75-foot indoor pool, a sauna, steamroom, and weight room. Spa services include massages, hot stone therapies, facials, salt scrubs, maple-sugar polishes, and mud treatments.

Okemo's ski area has a very similar spa facility to Killington's at the **Jackson Gore Resort** (✉ *Okemo Ridge Rd., off Rte. 103, Ludlow* ☎ *802/228–1400* ⊕ *www.okemo.com*), with a slopeside outdoor heated pool, hot tubs, a sauna, steam rooms, a fitness center, and massages like Swedish, deep tissue, and hot stone.

2

of a popular outdoor music series in summer and an extensive cross-country ski-trail network in winter. A tea house serves food and drinks. ⊠*Luce Hill Rd.* ☎*802/253–8511 or 800/826–7000.*

Vermont Ski Museum. The state's skiing history is documented here with myriad exhibits. ☎*802/253–9911.*

SPORTS & THE OUTDOORS

CANOEING & KAYAKING
Umiak Outdoor Outfitters (⊠*849 S. Main St. [Rte. 100], just south of Stowe Village* ☎*802/253–2317*) rents canoes and kayaks for day trips and leads overnight excursions. The store also operates a rental outpost at Lake Elmore State Park in Elmore, on the Winooski River off Route 2 in Waterbury, at North Beach in Burlington, and on the Lamoille River in Jeffersonville.

FISHING
The **Fly Rod Shop** (⊠*Rte. 100, 1½ mi south of Stowe* ☎*802/253–7346 or 800/535–9763*) provides a guiding service; gives fly-tying, casting, and rod-building classes in winter; rents fly tackle; and sells equipment, including classic and collectible firearms.

GOLF
Stowe Country Club (⊠*Mountain Rd.* ☎*802/253–4893*) has a scenic 18-hole, par-72 course; a driving range; and a putting green. Green fees are $45–$75; cart rental is $18.

HIKING
Ascending **Mt. Mansfield** makes for a scenic day hike. Trails lead from Route 108 (Mountain Road) to the summit ridge, where they meet the north-to-south Long Trail. Views from the summit take in New Hampshire's White Mountains, New York's Adirondacks across Lake Champlain, and southern Quebec. The Green Mountain Club publishes a trail guide.

ICE-SKATING
Jackson Arena (⊠*Park St.* ☎*802/253–6148*) is a public ice-skating rink, with skate rentals available.

SKI AREA
★
To be precise, the name of the village is Stowe and the name of the mountain is Mt. Mansfield, but to generations of skiers, the area, the complex, and the region are just plain Stowe. **Stowe Mountain Resort** (⊠*5781 Mountain Rd.* ☎*802/253–3000, 802/253–3600 snow conditions, 800/253–4754 lodging* ⊕*www.stowe.com*) is a classic that dates from the 1930s. Even today, the area's mystique attracts as many serious skiers as social skiers. Improved snowmaking, new lifts, and free shuttle buses that gather skiers from lodges, inns, and motels along Mountain Road have added convenience to the Stowe experience. Yet the traditions remain: the Winter Carnival in January, the Sugar Slalom in April, ski weeks all winter. Three base lodges provide the essentials, including two on-mountain restaurants. In 2004 the resort broke ground on its 10-year expansion plan at the Spruce Peak base area. Plans are to include new base lodges and lifts, a hotel, retail shops, and a golf course.

The resort provides hiking, in-line skating, an alpine slide, gondola rides, and an 18-hole golf course. It also has 22 mi of groomed cross-country trails and 24 mi of backcountry trails. Four interconnecting cross-country ski areas have more than 90 mi of groomed trails within the town of Stowe.

Mt. Mansfield, with an elevation of 4,395 feet and a vertical drop of 2,360 feet, is one of the giants among eastern ski mountains. The mountain's symmetrical shape allows skiers of all abilities long, satisfying runs from the summit. The famous Front Four (National, Liftline, Starr, and Goat) are the intimidating centerpieces for tough, expert runs, yet there is plenty of mellow intermediate skiing, with 59% of the runs rated at that level. One long beginner trail, the Toll Road Trail, is 3½ mi. Mansfield's satellite sector is a network of intermediate trails and one expert trail off a basin served by a gondola. Spruce Peak, separate from the main mountain, is a teaching hill and a pleasant experience for intermediates and beginners. In addition to the high-speed, eight-passenger gondola, Stowe has 11 lifts, including two quads, two triples, and five double chairlifts, plus one handle tow, to service its 48 trails. Night-skiing trails are accessed by the gondola. The resort has 73% snowmaking coverage. Snowboard facilities include a half-pipe and two terrain parks—one for beginners, at Spruce Peak, and one for experts, on the Mt. Mansfield side. Children's programs are headquartered at Spruce Peak., with ski-school programs for ages 4 to 12.

SHOPPING

In Stowe, Mountain Road is lined with shops from town up toward the ski area. North of Stowe, shops line Route 100 from Interstate 89. Watch apples pressed into cider at the **Cold Hollow Cider Mill** (⊠ *Rte. 100, 3 mi north of I–89* ☎ *802/244–8771 or 800/327–7537*), a very popular tourist attraction. The on-site store sells cider, baked goods, Vermont produce, and specialty foods. On Route 100 south toward Waterbury, between the cider mill and Ben & Jerry's, you can visit the **Cabot Cheese Annex Store** (⊠ *Rte. 100, 2½ mi north of I–89* ☎ *802/244–6334*). South of Waterbury, don't miss the freshly baked, maple-glazed sticky buns at the **Red Hen Baking Company** (⊠ *Rte. 100* ☎ *802/244–0966*).

NIGHTLIFE & THE ARTS

NIGHTLIFE The **Matterhorn Night Club** (⊠ *4969 Mountain Rd.* ☎ *802/253–8198*) hosts live music and dancing Thursday–Saturday nights and has a separate martini bar. The **Rusty Nail** (⊠ *1190 Mountain Rd.* ☎ *802/253– 6245*) rocks to live music on weekends.

THE ARTS **Stowe Performing Arts** (☎ *802/253–7792*) sponsors a series of classical and jazz concerts in July in the Trapp Family Lodge meadow. **Stowe Theater Guild** (⊠ *Town Hall Theater, Main St.* ☎ *802/253–3961 summer only*) performs musicals in summer and performs plays in September.

WHERE TO EAT

$$–$$$ ✕ **Mes Amis.** At this small bistro, locals queue up for house specialties
FRENCH such as fresh oysters, lobster bisque, braised lamb shanks, roast duck (secret recipe), and bananas Foster. You can dine in the candlelit dining room or outside on the patio, especially appealing on a warm summer's night. ⊠ *311 Mountain Rd.* ☎ *802/253–8669* ▭ *AE, D, MC, V* ⊙ *Closed Mon.*

$$–$$$ ✕ **Michael's on the Hill.** Swiss-born chef Michael Kloeti trained in Europe
CONTINENTAL and New York before opening this dining establishment in a 19th-century farmhouse outside Stowe. In addition to a la carte options,

Milchael's four-course prix-fixe menus ($60) highlight European cuisine such as roasted rabbit with mirepoix or ravioli with braised autumn vegetables. There's live piano music weekends. ✉4182 Stowe-Waterbury Rd. (Rte. 100), 6 mi south of Stowe, Waterbury Center ☎802/244–7476 ☐AE, DC, MC, V ☉Closed Tues. No lunch.

$–$$ ✕**Red Basil.** Stowe's new "in" dinner spot enhances its traditional Thai
THAI entrées with fresh cilantro, Kaffir lime leaves, lemongrass, and ginger. The Panang curry (sauteed meat in spicy Panang curry paste, coconut milk, bell peppers, and fresh basil leaves) is smooth, just a bit hot, and delicious; you can also order from the sushi bar. The martini bar has 18 varieties of James Bond's favorite libation. ✉294 Mountain Rd. ☎802/253–4478 ☐AE, MC, V ☉No lunch weekends.

WHERE TO STAY

$$–$$$ ⊞**Green Mountain Inn.** Welcoming guests since 1833, this classic red-brick inn is across from the landmark Community Church and gives you access to the buzz of downtown. Rooms in the main building and annex still feel like a country inn, with Early American furnishings. Newer buildings have luxury rooms and suites. The Whip Bar & Grill ($$–$$$) puts an interesting twist on comfort food, as in cheddar-cheese-and-apple-stuffed chicken; and the outdoor heated pool is open year-round. **Pros:** fun location, lively tavern. **Cons:** farther from skiing than other area hotels. ✉18 Main St. ☎802/253–7301 or 800/253–7302 ⊕www.greenmountaininn.com ⇨105 rooms ⚲In-room: kitchen (some), refrigerator (some), DVD (some), Wi-Fi. In-hotel: restaurant, bar, pool, gym, laundry service, public Internet, public Wi-Fi, no-smoking rooms ☐AE, D, MC, V.

$$$$ ⊞**Stone Hill Inn.** This is a contemporary B&B—built in 1998—where classical music plays in the halls. Each soundproof guest room has a king-size bed. Squeaky-clean bathrooms have two-sink vanities and two-person whirlpools in front of two-sided fireplaces. (Can you tell it's for couples?) A pantry is stocked with complimentary snacks and drinks. Common areas include a sitting room and a game room, and the 10 acres of grounds are beautifully landscaped with gardens and waterfalls. The inn is high up Mountain Road not far from the ski resort. **Pros:** clean and new, very comfortable. **Cons:** very expensive, a bit stiff. ✉89 Houston Farm Rd. ☎802/253–6282 ⊕www.stonehillinn.com ⇨9 rooms ⚲In-room: no phone, safe, DVD, VCR, Wi-Fi. In-hotel: no elevator, laundry facilities, public Internet, public Wi-Fi, no kids under 18, no-smoking rooms ☐AE, D, DC, MC, V ⊺⊙┃BP.

$ ⊞**Stowe Motel & Snowdrift.** This family-owned motel sits on 16 acres across the river from the Stowe recreation path. Accommodations range from one-room studios with small kitchenettes to modern two-bedroom fireplace suites. Late-model mountain bikes, kids' bikes, tricycles, bike trailers, and helmets are available to guests. A game room has Ping-Pong and a pool table. The motel is owned by Peter

Ruschp, whose father Sepp founded the Mt. Mansfield ski school in 1936. **Pros:** cheap, complimentary bikes and games. **Cons:** basic, motel-style accommodations. ⊠*2043 Mountain Rd. (Rte. 108)* ☎*802/253–7629 or 800/829–7629* ⊕*www.stowemotel.com* ⇆*52 rooms, 4 suites* ⌂*In-room: kitchen (some), refrigerator. In-hotel: tennis court, pools, bicycles, no elevator, public Internet, public Wi-Fi, some pets allowed, no-smoking rooms* ⊟*AE, D, MC, V* ⍰*CP.*

$$$ 🏨**Stoweflake Mountain Resort and Spa.** Stoweflake has a lot in common with Topnotch; these two properties have the best and biggest spas in the state, and a contemporary, serious approach to rooms and service. Stoweflake probably has a slightly better spa, perhaps due to the fun of the Bingham hydrotherapy waterfall, a nice 12-foot rock formation cascading into a hot tub. Accommodations range from standard hotel rooms to luxurious suites with fireplaces, refrigerators, double sinks, and whirlpool tubs. One- to three-bedroom town houses sit on the resort's perimeter. The spa overlooks an herb and flower labyrinth and is connected to the fitness center via a faux covered bridge. Stoweflake also hosts Stowe's annual Hot Air Balloon Festival. **Pros:** great spa, excellent service. **Cons:** urban-style resort. ⊠*1746 Mountain Rd.* ☎*802/253–7355* ⊕*www.stoweflake.com* ⇆*94 rooms, 30 town houses* ⌂*In-room: kitchen (some), refrigerator, DVD, VCR, Ethernet (some), Wi-Fi (some). In-hotel: 2 restaurants, room service, bar, golf course, tennis courts, pools, gym, spa, bicycles, laundry service, concierge, public Internet, public Wi-Fi, no-smoking rooms* ⊟*AE, D, DC, MC, V.*

$$$$ 🏨**Topnotch at Stowe Resort and Spa.** One of the state's poshest resorts occupies 120 acres overlooking Mt. Mansfield. Floor-to-ceiling windows, a freestanding metal fireplace, and heavy stone walls distinguish the lobby. Topnotch is almost a twin to its main competitor, Stoweflakem but it tops it in country-chic, spacious rooms with plush beds, Anichini linens, and other accents like painted barn-board walls. Norma's restaurant ($$–$$$) serves contemporary Continental cuisine in a romantic setting surrounded by torches. Service throughout the resort is impeccable. The tennis center has marvelous indoor and outdoor courts (easily the best facilities in Vermont) and a world-class instructional staff. **Pros:** near the mountain; world-class tennis center; good dining; top spa. **Cons:** the urban look and feel may not be for everyone. ⊠*4000 Mountain Rd.* ☎*802/253–8585 or 800/451–8686* ⊕*www.topnotch-resort.com* ⇆*71 rooms, 9 suites, 14 town houses* ⌂*In-room: safe, Wi-Fi. In-hotel: 2 restaurants, bar, tennis courts, pools, spa, public Internet, public Wi-Fi, no-smoking rooms* ⊟*AE, D, DC, MC, V* ⍰*BP, FAP, MAP.*

THE CRAFTSBURYS

27 mi northeast of Stowe.

The three villages of the Craftsburys—Craftsbury Common, Craftsbury, and East Craftsbury—are among Vermont's finest and oldest towns. Handsome white houses and barns, the requisite common, and terrific views make them well worth the drive. Craftsbury General Store in Craftsbury Village is a great place to stock up on picnic supplies and local information. The rolling farmland hints at the way Vermont used to be: the area's sheer distance from civilization and its rugged weather have kept most of the state's development farther south.

WHERE TO STAY

$$ ☷ **Craftsbury Outdoor Center.** If you think simplicity is bliss and love the outdoors, give this place a try. In winter it's a mecca for cross-country skiing (50 mi of groomed trails). In summer there's a giant lake for swimming and boating (sculling and running camps are held here). Two two-story simple lodges have rooms with communal TV/library areas. Many share baths. The simplest rooms have two twin beds and a wooden peg to hang a towel. Meals are served buffet-style. Cabin D is a paradisiacal setup, a simple three-bedroom cabin right on the edge of the lake. **Pros:** outdoor heaven, activities galore. **Cons:** many rooms have a shared bath, many are sparely furnished. ✉ *535 Lost Nation Rd., Craftsbury Common* ☎ *802/586–7767 or 800/729–7751* ⊕ *www.craftsbury.com* ⇆ *49 rooms, 10 with bath; 4 cabins; 2 suites* ♨ *In-room: no a/c, no phone, kitchen (some), refrigerator (some) no TV, Wi-Fi (some). In-hotel: restaurant, tennis court, gym, water sports, bicycles, no elevator, laundry facilities, public Internet, public Wi-Fi, some pets allowed, no-smoking rooms* ⊟ *MC, V* ⦿ *MAP.*

$$ ☷ **Inn on the Common.** All guest rooms at these three renovated Federal-style homes are appointed with antiques and hand-stitched quilts and have sitting areas. Some rooms have fireplaces or woodstoves. The Trellis Restaurant ($$–$$$), which serves excellent "innovative country" cuisine, has indoor and outdoor seating overlooking the gardens. **Pros:** beautiful setting, simple rooms. **Cons:** breakfast ends at 9 AM. ✉ *1162 N. Craftsbury Rd., Craftsbury Common* ☎ *802/586–9619 or 800/521–2233* ⊕ *www.innonthecommon.com* ⇆ *14 rooms, 2 suites* ♨ *In-room: no a/c, no TV. In-hotel: restaurant, no-smoking rooms* ⊟ *AE, D, DC, MC, V* ⦿ *BP, MAP.*

GREENSBORO

10 mi southeast of Craftsbury Common.

Tucked along the southern shore of Caspian Lake, Greensboro has been a summer resort for literati, academics, and old-money types for more than a century. Yet it exudes an unpretentious, genteel character where most of the people running about on errands seem to know each other. A town beach is right off the main street.

SHOPPING

The **Miller's Thumb** (✉ *Main St.* ☎ *802/533–2960 or 800/680–7886*) sells Italian pottery, Vermont furniture, crafts and antiques, and April Cornell clothing and linens. **Willey's Store** (✉ *Main St.* ☎ *802/533–2621*) is a classic general store of the "if-we-don't-have-it-you-don't-need-it" kind.

WHERE TO STAY

$$$$ ☷Highland Lodge. Tranquillity reigns at this 1860 house overlooking a pristine lake. The lodge's 120 acres of rambling woods and pastures are laced with hiking and skiing trails (ski rentals available). Comfortable guest rooms have Early American–style furnishings; most have views of the lake. The one- to three-bedroom cottages are more private (four with gas stoves stay open in winter). The lodge has canoes, kayaks, Sunfish, and paddleboats. There's also a game room with foosball, Ping-Pong, puzzles, and books. In winter there's a complete cross-country touring center; 31 mi of groomed trails connect to the Craftsbuty Outdoor Center. The traditional dinner menu might include such entrées as roast leg of lamb. **Pros:** across from lake, lots of activities, private beach. **Cons:** remote, expensive. ⊠*1608 Craftsbury Rd.* ☎*802/533–2647* ⊕*www.highlandlodge.com* ⇆*8 rooms, 11 cottages* ⌂*In-room: no a/c, no phone, kitchen, refrigerator, Wi-Fi (some). In-hotel: restaurant, tennis court, water sports, bicycles, no elevator, laundry service, public Internet, public Wi-Fi, no-smoking rooms* ▭*D, MC, V* ☉*Closed mid-Mar.–late May and mid-Oct.–mid-Dec.* ⏻*BP, MAP.*

JEFFERSONVILLE

36 mi west of Greensboro, 18 mi north of Stowe.

Jeffersonville is just over Smugglers' Notch from Stowe but miles away in feel and attitude. In summer, you can drive over the notch road as it curves precipitously around boulders that have fallen from the cliffs above, then pass open meadows and old farmhouses and sugar shacks on the way down to town. Below the notch, Smugglers' Notch Ski Resort is the hub of much activity year-round. Downtown Jeffersonville, once home to an artist colony, is quiet but has excellent dining and sophisticated art galleries.

WHAT TO SEE

Boyden Valley Winery. West of town, this winery conducts tours and tastings and showcases an excellent selection of Vermont specialty products and local handicrafts, including fine furniture. The winery is closed Monday, June–December, and Monday–Thursday, January–May. ⊠*Junction of Rtes. 15 and 104, Cambridge* ☎*802/644–8151.*

SPORTS & THE OUTDOORS

KAYAKING **Green River Canoe & Kayak** (☎*802/644–8336 or 802/644–8714*), at the junction of routes 15 and 108 behind Jana's Restaurant, rents canoes and kayaks on the Lamoille River and leads guided canoe trips to Boyden Valley Winery.

LLAMA RIDES **Applecheek Farm** (⊠*567 McFarlane Rd., Hyde Park* ☎*802/888–4482*) runs daytime and evening (by lantern) hay and sleigh rides, llama treks, and farm tours. **Northern Vermont Llamas** (⊠*766 Lapland Rd., Waterville* ☎*802/644–2257*) conducts half- and full-day treks from May through October along the cross-country ski trails of Smugglers' Notch. The llamas carry everything, including snacks and lunches. Advance reservations are essential.

SKI AREA ☼★ **Smugglers' Notch Resort** (✉ *Rte. 108* ☎ *802/644–8851 or 800/451–8752* ⊕ *www.smuggs.com*) consistently wins accolades for its family programs. Its children's ski school is one of the best in the country—possibly *the* best. But skiers of all levels come here (Smugglers' was the first ski area in the East to designate a triple-black-diamond run—the Black Hole). All the essentials are available in the village at the base of the Morse Mountain lifts, including lodgings, restaurants, and several shops. Smugglers' has a full roster of summertime programs, including pools, complete with waterfalls and waterslides; the Giant Rapid River Ride (the longest water ride in the state); lawn games; mountain biking and hiking programs; and craft workshops for adults.

The self-contained village has outdoor ice-skating and sleigh rides. The numerous snowshoeing programs include family walks and backcountry trips. SmuggsCentral has an indoor pool, hot tub, Funzone playground with slides and miniature golf, and a teen center, open from 5 PM until midnight. In terms of nordic skiing, the area has 18 mi of groomed and tracked trails and 12 mi of snowshoe trails.

For downhill skiing, Smugglers' has three mountains. The highest, Madonna, with a vertical drop of 2,610 feet, is in the center and connects with a trail network to Sterling (1,500 feet vertical). The third mountain, Morse (1,150 feet vertical), is adjacent to Smugglers' "village" of shops, restaurants, and condos; it's connected to the other peaks by trails and a shuttle bus. The wild, craggy landscape lends a pristine wilderness feel to the skiing experience on the two higher mountains. The tops of each of the mountains have expert terrain—a couple of double-black diamonds (and the only triple-black diamond trail in the east) make Madonna memorable. Intermediate trails fill the lower sections. Morse has many beginner and advanced beginner trails. Smugglers' 70 trails are served by eight lifts, including six chairs and two surface lifts. Top-to-bottom snowmaking on all three mountains allows for 62% coverage. There are four progression terrain parks, including one for early beginners. Night skiing and snowboarding classes are given at the new Learning and Fun Park.

Ski camps for kids ages 3–17 provide excellent instruction, plus movies, games, and other activities. Wednesday, Thursday, and Saturday are kids' nights at Treasures, with dinner and supervised activities for children ages 3–11.

SHOPPING

ANTIQUES The **Green Apple Antique Center** (✉ *60 Main St.* ☎ *802/644–2989*) has a good bakery in the back of the store. **Smugglers' Notch Antique Center** (✉ *906 Rte. 108* ☎ *802/644–8321*) sells antiques and collectibles of 60 dealers in a rambling barn.

CLOTHING Fodor'sChoice ★ **Johnson Woolen Mills** (✉ *Main St., 9 mi east of Jeffersonville, Johnson* ☎ *802/635–2271*) is an authentic factory store with deals on woolen blankets, yard goods, and the famous Johnson outerwear.

CRAFTS **Vermont Rug Makers** (✉ *Rte. 100C, 10 mi east of Jeffersonville, East Johnson* ☎ *802/635–2434*) weaves imaginative rugs and tapestries from fabrics, wools, and exotic materials. Its International Gallery displays rugs and tapestries from around the world.

WHERE TO EAT & STAY

$-$$
AMERICAN

✕ **158 Main.** As soon as this restaurant opened in January 2004, locals were lining up at the door. Its menu selections range from sesame-seared yellowfin tuna with jasmine rice and wasabi to the locals' favorite breakfast: eggs, homemade toast, and home fries for $2.58. Portions are big, prices are not. Sunday brunch is served 8 AM–2 PM. ⊠*158 Main St.* ☎*802/644–8100* ⌲*Reservations not accepted* ⊟*AE, DC, MC, V* ⊘*Closed Mon. No dinner Sun.*

$$$$
♻
Fodor's Choice
★

🎲 **Smugglers' Notch Resort.** From watercolor workshops to giant water parks to weeklong camps for kids, this family resort has a plethora of activities. In winter, the main activity is skiing, but children's programs abound. Lodging is in clustered condominium complexes, with the condos set away from the resort center. Rates are packages for three, five, and seven nights and can include use of all resort amenities and lift tickets and ski lessons in season. **Pros:** great place for families and to learn to ski. **Cons:** with so many kids around, it's not right for couples. ⊠*4232 Rte. 108 S05464* ☎*802/644–8851 or 800/451–8752* ⊕*www.smuggs.com* ⋟*550 condominiums* ⌂*In-room: no a/c (some). In-hotel: 4 restaurants, bar, tennis courts, pools, children's programs (ages 3–17), no-smoking rooms* ⊟*AE, DC, MC, V.*

BURLINGTON

Fodor's Choice
★

31 mi southwest of Jeffersonville, 76 mi south of Montreal, 349 mi north of New York City, 223 mi northwest of Boston.

As you drive along Main Street toward downtown Burlington, it's easy to see why the city is so often called one of America's most livable small cities. Downtown is filled with hip restaurants and nightclubs, art galleries, and the Church Street Marketplace—a bustling pedestrian mall with trendy shops, craft vendors, street performers, and sidewalk cafés. Just beyond, Lake Champlain shimmers beneath the towering Adirondacks on the New York shore. On the shores of the lake, Burlington's revitalized waterfront teems with outdoors enthusiasts who stroll along its recreation path and ply the waters in sailboats and motor craft in summer.

WHAT TO SEE

♻ ★ **ECHO Leahy Center for Lake Champlain.** Part of the waterfront's revitalization, this aquarium and science center gives kids a chance to check out 100 hands-on, interactive wind and water exhibits and a sunken shipwreck. ⊠*1 College St.* ☎*802/864–1848* ⊕*www.echovermont.org* ⌐*$9* ⊘*Daily 10–5, Thurs. until 8.*

Ethan Allen Homestead. One of the earliest residents of the Intervale was Ethan Allen, Vermont's Revolutionary-era guerrilla fighter, who remains a captivating figure. Exhibits at the on-site visitor center answer questions about his flamboyant life. The house holds such frontier hallmarks as rough saw-cut boards and an open hearth for cooking. A re-created Colonial kitchen garden resembles the one the Allens would have had. After the tour and multimedia presentation, you can stretch your legs on scenic trails along the Winooski River. ⊠*North Ave., off Rte. 127, north of Burlington* ☎*802/865–4556* ⊕*www.ethanallen-homestead.org* ⊠*$5* ☉*May–Oct., Mon.–Sat. 10–4, Sun. 1–4.*

University of Vermont. Crowning the hilltop above Burlington is the campus of the University of Vermont, known simply as UVM for the abbreviation of its Latin name, Universitas Viridis Montis—the University of the Green Mountains. With more than 10,000 students, UVM is the state's principal institution of higher learning. The most architecturally interesting buildings face the green, which has a statue of UVM founder Ira Allen, Ethan's brother. ☎*802/656–3131.*

SPORTS & THE OUTDOORS

BEACHES The **North Beaches** (⊠*North Beach Park off North Ave.* ☎*802/864–0123* ⊠*Leddy Beach, Leddy Park Rd. off North Ave.*) are on the northern edge of Burlington. Leddy Beach is a good spot for sailboarding.

BIKING Burlington's 10-mi Cycle the City loop runs along the waterfront, connecting several city parks and beaches. It also passes the Community Boathouse and runs within several blocks of downtown restaurants and shops. **North Star Cyclery** (⊠*100 Main St.* ☎*802/863–3832*) rents bicycles and provides maps of bicycle routes. **Ski Rack** (⊠*85 Main St.* ☎*802/658–3313 or 800/882–4530*) rents and services bikes and provides maps.

BOATING **Burlington Community Boathouse** (⊠*Foot of College St., Burlington Harbor* ☎*802/865–3377*) rents 19-foot sailboats. **Shoreline Cruise's** *Spirit of Ethan Allen III.* This 500-passenger, three-level cruise vessel has narrated cruises and dinner and sunset sailings with awesome views of the Adirondacks and Green Mountains. ⊠*Burlington Boat House, College and Battery Sts.* ☎*802/862–8300* ⊕*www.soea.com* ⊠*$12* ☉*Cruises late May–mid-Oct., daily 10–9.*

Waterfront Boat Rentals (⊠*Foot of Maple St. on Perkins Pier, Burlington Harbor* ☎*802/864–4858*) rents kayaks, canoes, rowboats, skiffs, and Boston whalers. Affordable sailing lessons are available.

OFF THE BEATEN PATH
Green Mountain Audubon Nature Center. This is a wonderful place to discover Vermont's outdoor wonders. The center's 300 acres of diverse habitats are a sanctuary for all things wild, and the 5 mi of trails provide an opportunity to explore the workings of differing natural communities. Events include dusk walks, wildflower and birding rambles, nature workshops, and educational activities for children and adults. The center is 18 mi southeast of Burlington. ⊠*255 Sherman Hollow Rd., Huntington* ☎*802/434–3068* ⊠*Donations accepted* ☉*Grounds daily dawn–dusk, center Mon.–Sat. 8–4.*

SHOPPING

CRAFTS In addition to its popular pottery, **Bennington Potters North** (⊠*127 College St.* ☎*802/863–2221 or 800/205–8033*) stocks interesting gifts, glassware, furniture, and other housewares. **Vermont State Craft Center/Frog Hollow** (⊠*85 Church St.* ☎*802/863–6458*) is a nonprofit collective that sells contemporary and traditional crafts by more than 200 Vermont artisans.

MARKETS **Church Street Marketplace** (⊠*Main St. to Pearl St.* ☎*802/863–1648*), a pedestrian thoroughfare, is lined with boutiques, cafés, and street vendors. Look for bargains at the rapidly growing **Essex Outlet Fair** (⊠*Junction of Rtes. 15 and 289, Essex* ☎*802/878–2851*), with such outlets as BCBG, Brooks Brothers, Polo Ralph Lauren, and Levi's, among others.

NIGHTLIFE & THE ARTS

NIGHTLIFE The music at **Club Metronome** (⊠*188 Main St.* ☎*802/865–4563*) ranges from cutting-edge sounds to funk, blues, and reggae. National and local musicians come to **Higher Ground** (⊠*1214 Williston Rd., South Burlington* ☎*802/265–0777*). The band Phish got its start at **Nectar's** (⊠*188 Main St.* ☎*802/658–4771*). This place is always jumping to the sounds of local bands and never charges a cover. **Ri Ra** (⊠*123 Church St.* ☎*802/860–9401*) hosts live entertainment with an Irish flair. **Vermont Pub and Brewery** (⊠*144 College St.* ☎*802/865–0500*) makes its own beer and fruit seltzers and is arguably the most popular spot in town. Folk musicians play here regularly.

THE ARTS The **Fire House Art Gallery** (⊠*135 Church St.* ☎*802/865–7165*) exhibits works by local artists. **Flynn Theatre for the Performing Arts** (⊠*153 Main St.* ☎*802/652–4500 information, 802/863–5966 tickets* ⊕*www.flynncenter.org*), a grandiose old structure, is the cultural heart of Burlington; it schedules the Vermont Symphony Orchestra, theater, dance, big-name musicians, and lectures. **St. Michael's Playhouse** (⊠*St. Michael's College, Rte. 15, Colchester* ☎*802/654–2281 box office, 802/654–2617 administrative office*) stages performances in the McCarthy Arts Center. The **Vermont Symphony Orchestra** (☎*802/864–5741*) performs throughout the state year-round and at the Flynn from October through May.

WHERE TO EAT

¢–$ ✗**American Flatbread–Burlington Hearth.** It might be worth going to college in Burlington just to be able to gather with friends at this wildly popular and delicious, organic pizza place. On weekends, it's standing room only (seating is first-come, first-served) as kids bustle for house-made brews. The wood-fired clay dome oven combines with all organic ingredients to create masterful results, like the Punctuated Equilibrium, which has kalamata olives, roasted red peppers, local goat's cheese, fresh rosemary, red onions, mozzarella, and garlic. Here's to the college life! ⊠*115 St. Paul St.* ☎*802/861–2999* ⊟*MC, V.*

Fodor'sChoice
★
PIZZA

$$$–$$$$ ✗**Butler's Restaurant.** This formal restaurant is run by instructors and second-year students at the New England Culinary Institute, one of America's best. It's a joy to sample the menu and even the wine selection pulses with enthusiam and vigor. Dishes can be hit or miss, but the high notes can be among the highest in the state. Service is taken very seriously. Adjacent to Butler's is The Tavern, run by the same kitchen, which has a grilled flatbread pizza of the day and a bounty of local draft beers. Expect only local ingredients at both restaurants.

Fodor'sChoice
★
AMERICAN

2

⊠*70 Essex Way, Essex Junction* ☎*802/878–1100* ▤*AE, D, DC, MC, V* ⊘*No dinner Sun. in winter.*

$–$$ ✕**Cannon's.** Don't let the shopping center location deter you. This fam-
ITALIAN ily-style Italian restaurant has more than just spaghetti on the menu.
Pasta selections are diverse and include such items as fettuccine with
sautéed chicken strips and snow peas, and noodle-less eggplant lasagna. Entrées range from traditional Italian (shrimp scampi) to American (sirloin steak). ⊠*1127 North Ave.* ☎*802/652–5151* ▤*DC, MC,
V* ⊘*No lunch Sat.*

$–$$ ✕**Ri Ra.** Brought to Burlington from Ireland in pieces and reassembled
IRISH on-site, this Irish pub serves classic fare such as bangers-and-mash
and fish-and-chips, along with burgers and fish. ⊠*123 Church St.*
☎*802/860–9401* ▤*AE, MC, V.*

$–$$ ✕**A Single Pebble.** The creative, authentic Asian selections served in
CHINESE the first floor of this residential rowhouse include traditional clay-pot
dishes as well as wok specialties, such as sesame catfish and kung pao
chicken. The dry-fried green beans (sautéed with flecks of pork, black
beans, preserved vegetables, and garlic) are a house specialty. All dishes
can be made without meat. ⊠*133-135 Bank St.* ☎*802/865–5200*
⌂*Reservations essential* ▤*AE, D, MC, V* ⊘*No lunch weekends.*

$–$$ ✕**Trattoria Delia.** Didn't manage to rent that villa in Umbria this year?
★ The next best thing, if your travels bring you to Burlington, is this
ITALIAN superb Italian country eatery just around the corner from City Hall
Park. Game and fresh produce are the stars, as in wild boar braised in
red wine, tomatoes, rosemary, and sage served on soft polenta. Wood-
grilled items are a specialty. ⊠*152 St. Paul St.* ☎*802/864–5253* ▤*AE,
D, DC, MC, V* ⊘*No lunch.*

WHERE TO STAY

¢ ⌂**G.G.T. Tibet Inn.** This motel probably has the cheapest rates in all of
Vermont—$49 for two people in winter, and $59 to $69 in summer. But
that's not the main attraction. The lure here is the friendly face and evident care of the motel's Tibetan owner, whose name is Kalsang G.G.T.
(Yes, G.G.T. really is his real last name.) Bhuddist prayer flags flap
from the exterior. All rooms have a microwave and a refrigerator, and
basic motel furnishings with a big TV. Kalsang's smile at check-in will
bring you back. **Pros:** great price, locally owned. **Cons:** no high-speed
Internet. ⊠*1860 Shelburne Rd., South Burlington* ☎*802/863–7110*
⊕*www.ggttibetinn.com* ⇰*21 rooms* ⌂*In-room: dial-up. In-hotel:
pool, no elevator, no-smoking rooms* ▤*AE, D, MC, V.*

$$ ⌂**Inn at Essex.** "Vermont's Culinary Resort" is a hotel and conference
center about 10 mi from downtown Burlington, with two good res-
taurants run by the New England Culinary Institute. The best part
of a stay here is access to cooking classes offered each day in profes-
sional test kitchens on site. Very comfortable Susan Sargent–designed
rooms are adorned with her vibrant colors in everything from the wall
paint to the pillow covers; 30 rooms have fireplaces. A 19,000-square-
foot spa is slated to open in fall 2008, along with an Orvis-endorsed
fly-fishing pond. **Pros:** daily cooking classes, colorful rooms, free air-
port shuttle. **Cons:** odd location in suburb of Burlington. ⊠*70 Essex
Way, off Rte. 289, Essex Junction* ☎*802/878–1100 or 800/727–4295*

⊕*www.vtculinaryresort.com* ⇦*60 rooms, 60 suites* ☼*In-room: Wi-Fi. In-hotel: 2 restaurants, bar, golf course, tennis courts, pool, no-smoking rooms* ⊟*AE, D, MC, V.*

$ ▦**Willard Street Inn.** High in the historic hill section of Burlington, this
★   ivy-covered grand house with an exterior marble staircase and English gardens incorporates elements of Queen Anne and Colonial–Georgian-revival styles. The stately foyer, paneled in cherry, leads to a more formal sitting room with velvet drapes. The solarium is bright and sunny with marble floors, many plants, and big velvet couches for contemplating views of Lake Champlain. All the rooms have down comforters and phones; some have lake views and canopied beds. Orange French toast is among the breakfast favorites. **Pros:** lovely old mansion loaded with character and details; friendly attention; common room snacks. **Cons:** walk to downtown. ⊠*349 S. Willard St.* ☎*802/651–8710 or 800/577–8712* ⊕*www.willardstreetinn.com* ⇦*14 rooms* ☼*In-room: Wi-Fi. In-hotel: no elevator, public Internet, public Wi-Fi, no kids under 12, no-smoking rooms* ⊟*AE, D, MC, V* ⦿❘*BP.*

SHELBURNE

5 mi south of Burlington.

A few miles south of Burlington, the Champlain Valley gives way to fertile farmland, affording stunning views of the rugged Adirondacks across the lake. In the middle of this farmland is the village of Shelburne, chartered in the mid-18th century and now largely a bedroom community for Burlington.

WHAT TO SEE

↻   **Shelburne Farms.** Founded in the 1880s as a private estate, this 1,400-
FodorsChoice   acre farm is an educational and cultural resource center with, among
★   other things, a working dairy farm, a Children's Farmyard, and a spot for watching the farm's famous cheddar cheese being made. Frederick Law Olmsted, co-creator of New York's Central Park, designed the magnificent grounds overlooking Lake Champlain. For an additional charge of $3, you can tour the 1891 breeding barn. ⊠*West of U.S. 7 at Harbor and Bay Rds.* ☎*802/985–8686* ⊕*www.shelburnefarms.org* ▱*Day pass $6, tour an additional $5* ⊙ *Visitor center and shop daily 10–5; tours mid-May–mid-Oct. (last tour at 3:30); walking trails daily 10–4, weather permitting.*

FodorsChoice   **Shelburne Museum.** You can trace much of New England's history simply
★   by wandering through the 45 acres and 37 buildings of this museum. The outstanding 80,000-object collection of Americana consists of 18th- and 19th-century period homes and furniture, fine and folk art, farm tools, more than 200 carriages and sleighs, Audubon prints, an old-fashioned jail, and even a private railroad car from the days of steam. The museum also has an assortment of duck decoys, an old stone cottage, a display of early toys, and the *Ticonderoga*, a side-wheel steamship, grounded amid lawn and trees. ⊠*U.S. 7* ☎*802/985–3346* ⊕*www.shelburnemuseum.org* ▱*$18* ⊙*May–Oct., daily 10–5.*

Vermont Teddy Bear Company. On the 25-minute tour of this fun-filled factory you'll hear more puns than you ever thought possible and learn how a few homemade bears, sold from a cart on Church Street, have turned into a multimillion-dollar business. A children's play tent is set up outdoors in summer, and you can wander the beautiful 57-acre property. ✉*6655 Shelburne Rd.* ☎*802/985–3001* 🎟*Tour $2* ⊙*Tours Mon.–Sat. 9:30–5, Sun. 10:30–4; store daily 9–6.*

SHOPPING

When you enter the **Shelburne Country Store** (✉*Village Green off U.S. 7* ☎*802/985–3657*) you'll step back in time. Walk past the pot-bellied stove and take in the aroma emanating from the fudge neatly piled behind huge antique glass cases. The store specializes in candles, weather vanes, glassware, and local foods.

WHERE TO EAT & STAY

$$–$$$
★
FRENCH

✕**Café Shelburne.** This popular restaurant serves creative French bistro cuisine. Specialties include sweetbreads with a port wine and mushroom sauce in puff pastry, and homemade fettuccine with Vermont goat cheese. Desserts such as the sweet chocolate layered terrine and maple-syrup mousse with orange terrine are fabulous. ✉*U.S. 7* ☎*802/985–3939* ▤*AE, MC, V* ⊙*Closed Sun. and Mon. No lunch.*

$$–$$$
Fodor'sChoice
★

▨**Inn at Shelburne Farms.** This turn-of-the-20th-century Tudor-style inn, once the home of William Seward and Lila Vanderbilt Webb, overlooks Lake Champlain, the distant Adirondacks, and the sea of pastures that make up this 1,400-acre working farm. Each room is different, from the wallpaper to the period antiques. The dining room ($$–$$$) defines elegance, and Sunday brunch (not served in May) is one of the area's best. Breakfast is served Monday–Saturday. **Pros:** unbeatable setting within the Shelburne Farms property. **Cons:** some may miss not having a TV in the room. ✉*Harbor Rd.* ☎*802/985–8498* ⊕*www.shelburne farms.org* 🛏*24 rooms, 17 with bath; 2 cottages* ⚘*In-room: no a/c, no TV. In-hotel: restaurant, tennis court, no-smoking rooms* ▤*D, DC, MC, V* ⊙*Closed mid-Oct.–mid-May.*

VERGENNES

12 mi south of Shelburne.

Vermont's oldest city, founded in 1788, is also the third oldest in New England. The downtown area is a compact district of Victorian homes and public buildings. Main Street slopes down to Otter Creek Falls, where cannonballs were made during the War of 1812. The statue of Thomas MacDonough on the green immortalizes the victor of the Battle of Plattsburgh in 1814.

OFF THE
BEATEN
PATH

Lake Champlain Maritime Museum. This museum documents centuries of activity on the historically significant lake. Climb aboard a replica of Benedict Arnold's Revolutionary War gunboat moored in the lake, learn about shipwrecks, and watch craftsmen work at traditional boatbuilding and blacksmithing. Among the exhibits are a nautical archaeology center, a conservation laboratory, and a restaurant. ✉*Basin Harbor*

Rd., 7 mi west of Vergennes, Basin Harbor ☎*802/475–2022* ✉*$9* ⊘*May–mid-Oct., daily 10–5.*

SHOPPING

Dakin Farm (✉*Rte. 7, 5 mi north of Vergennes* ☎*800/993–2546*) sells cob-smoked ham, aged cheddar cheese, and other specialty foods.

WHERE TO EAT & STAY

$–$$ ✕**Starry Night Café.** This chic restaurant is one of the hottest spots
ECLECTIC around and it's increased in size to meet growing demand. Appetizers include house specials such as honey-chili glazed shrimp and gazpacho. Among the French-meets-Asian entrées are lobster-stuffed sole, pan-seared scallops, and grilled New York steak. ✉*5371 Rte. 7, 5 mi north of Vergennes, Ferrisburg* ☎*802/877–6316* ⊕*www.starrynight-cafe.com* ▭*MC, V* ⊘*Closed Mon. and Tues. No lunch.*

$$$$ ⊞**Basin Harbor Club.** On 700 acres overlooking Lake Champlain, this
Fodor'sChoice ultimate family resort provides luxurious accommodations and a full
★ roster of amenities, including an 18-hole golf course, boating (with a 40-foot tour boat), a 3,200-foot grass airstrip, and daylong children's programs. Some rooms in the guesthouses have fireplaces, decks, or porches. The cottages are charming and have one to three bedrooms. The restaurant menu ($–$$$) is classic American, the wine list excellent. Jackets and ties are required in common areas after 6 PM from late-June through Labor Day. **Pros:** gorgeous lakeside property; activities galore. **Cons:** open only half the year. ✉*48 Basin Harbor Rd.* ☎*802/475–2311 or 800/622–4000* ⊕*www.basinharbor.com* ➪*36 rooms, 2 suites in 3 guesthouses, 77 cottages* ⌂*In-room: no a/c, no TV. In-hotel: 3 restaurants, golf course, tennis courts, pool, gym, bicycles, children's programs (ages 3–15), some pets allowed, no-smoking rooms* ▭*MC, V* ⊘*Closed mid-Oct.–mid-May* ⦿*BP.*

LAKE CHAMPLAIN ISLANDS

43 mi north of Vergennes, 20 mi northwest of Shelburne, 15 mi northwest of Burlington.

Lake Champlain, which stretches more than 100 mi southward from the Canadian border, forms the northern part of the boundary between New York and Vermont. Within it is an elongated archipelago composed of several islands—Isle La Motte, North Hero, Grand Isle, South Hero—and the Alburg Peninsula. With a temperate climate, the islands hold several apple orchards and are a center of water recreation in summer and ice fishing in winter. A scenic drive through the islands on U.S. 2 begins at Interstate 89 and travels north to Alburg Center; Route 78 takes you back to the mainland.

WHAT TO SEE

Herrmann's Royal Lipizzan Stallions. These beautiful stallions, cousins of the noble white horses bred in Austria since the 16th century, perform intricate dressage maneuvers for delighted spectators for a brief period each summer on North Hero. These acrobatic horses are descendants of animals rescued from the turmoil of World War II by General George

Patton and members of the Herrmann family. ⊠*U.S. 2, North Hero* ☎*802/372–5683* ✑*Barn visits free between performances, shows $17* ☽*Early July–late Aug., Thurs. and Fri. at 6 PM, weekends at 2:30 PM.*

Snow Farm Vineyard and Winery. Take a self-guided tour, sip some samples in the tasting room, and listen to music at the free concerts on the lawn Thursday evenings, mid-June through Labor Day. ⊠*190 W. Shore Rd., South Hero* ☎*802/372–9463* ✑*Free* ☽*May–Dec., daily 10–5; tours May–Oct. at 11 and 2.*

St. Anne's Shrine. This shrine marks the site where French soldiers and Jesuits put ashore in 1665 and built a fort, creating Vermont's first European settlement. The state's first Roman Catholic Mass was celebrated here on July 26, 1666. ⊠*W. Shore Rd., Isle La Motte* ☎*802/928–3362* ✑*Free* ☽*Mid-May–mid-Oct., daily 9–4.*

SPORTS & THE OUTDOORS

On the mainland east of the Alburg Peninsula, **Missisquoi National Wildlife Refuge** (⊠*Tabor Rd., 36 mi north of Burlington, Swanton* ☎*802/868–4781*) consists of 6,642 acres of federally protected wetlands, meadows, and woods. It's a beautiful area for bird-watching, canoeing, or walking nature trails. **Sand Bar State Park** (⊠*U.S. 2, South Hero* ☎*802/893–2825* ✑*$3.50* ☽*Mid-May–Labor Day, daily dawn–dusk*) has one of Vermont's best swimming beaches.

BOATING **Apple Island Resort** (⊠*U.S. 2, South Hero* ☎*802/372–5398*) rents sailboats, rowboats, canoes, kayaks, and motorboats. **Hero's Welcome** (⊠*U.S. 2, North Hero* ☎*802/372–4161 or 800/372–4376*) rents bikes, canoes, kayaks, and paddleboats.

WHERE TO STAY

$–$$ **North Hero House Inn and Restaurant.** This inn has four buildings right on Lake Champlain, including the 1891 Colonial-revival main house with nine guest rooms, the restaurant, a pub room, library, and sitting room. Many rooms have water views, and each possesses country furnishings and antiques. The beach is a popular spot for lake swimming in summer, and there are boat rentals nearby. The Homestead, Southwind, and Cove House have adjoining rooms that are good for families. Dinner ($$–$$$) is served in the informal glass greenhouse or Colonial-style dining room. **Pros:** relaxed vacation complex; superb lakefront setting. **Cons:** open just May to November. ⊠*U.S. 2, North Hero* ☎*802/372–4732 or 888/525–3644* ⊕*www.northherohouse. com* ⇌*26 rooms* ♿*In-room: no a/c (some). In-hotel: restaurant, bar, no-smoking rooms* ⊟*AE, MC, V* ⦿*CP* ☽*Closed Dec.—Apr.*

$ **Ruthcliffe Lodge.** Good food and splendid scenery make this off-the-beaten-path motel directly on Lake Champlain a great value. If you're looking for a cheap, DIY summer place to take in the scenery, canoe the lake, or bicycle, this will do quite nicely. The lodge is on Isle La Motte—a rarely-visited island. Rooms are very clean and simple: bed, dresser, night table, and stenciled wall border. Owner-chef Mark Infante specializes in Italian pasta, fish, and meat dishes; there's al fresco seating that overlooks a lawn leading to the lakeshore. A full breakfast is included as well. **Pros:** inexpensive; serene setting;

laid-back. **Cons:** rooms simple, not luxurious. ⊠*1002 Quarry Rd.,
Isle La Motte* ☎*802/928–3200* ⊕*www.ruthcliffe.com* ⊶*7 rooms*
♨*In-hotel: restaurant, bicycles, boating, no-smoking rooms* ⊟*MC, V*
†◎†*BP* ⊘*Closed Columbus Day–mid-May.*

MONTGOMERY/JAY

32 mi east of St. Albans, 51 mi northeast of Burlington.

Montgomery is a small village near the Canadian border and Jay Peak ski
resort. Amid the surrounding countryside are seven covered bridges.

Trout River Store (⊠*Main St., Montgomery Center* ☎*802/326–3058*),
an old-time country store with an antique soda fountain, is a great
place to stock up on picnic supplies, eat a hearty bowl of soup and an
overstuffed sandwich, and check out local crafts.

**OFF THE
BEATEN
PATH**

Lake Memphremagog. Vermont's second-largest lake, Lake Memphremagog extends from Newport 33 mi north into Canada. Prouty Beach
in Newport has camping facilities, tennis courts, and paddleboat and
canoe rentals. Watch the sun set from the deck of the **East Side Restaurant**
(⊠*Lake St., Newport* ☎*802/334–2340*), which serves excellent burgers and prime rib. ⊠*Veterans Ave.* ☎*802/334–7951.*

SPORTS & THE OUTDOORS

SKI AREA **Hazen's Notch Cross Country Ski Center and B&B** (⊠*Rte. 58* ☎*802/326–
4799*), delightfully remote at any time of the year, has 40 mi of marked
and groomed trails and rents equipment and snowshoes.

★ Sticking up out of the flat farmland, **Jay Peak** (⊠*Rte. 242, Jay*
☎*802/988–2611, 800/451–4449 outside VT* ⊕*www.jaypeakresort.
com*) averages 355 inches of snow a year—more than any other Vermont ski area. Its proximity to Quebec attracts Montrealers and dis-
courages eastern seaboarders; hence, the prices are moderate and the
lift lines shorter than at other resorts. The area is renowned for its glade
skiing and powder.

Off season, Jay Peak runs tram rides to the summit from mid-June
through Labor Day, and mid-September through Columbus Day ($10).
In the winter, snowshoes can be rented, and guided walks are led by a
naturalist. Telemark rentals and instruction are available.

In terms of its downhill-skiing options, Jay Peak has two interconnected mountains, the highest reaching nearly 4,000 feet with a vertical
drop of 2,153 feet. The smaller mountain has straight-fall-line, expert
terrain that eases mid-mountain into an intermediate pitch. The main
peak is served by Vermont's only tramway and transports skiers to
meandering but challenging intermediate trails. Beginners should stick
near the bottom on trails off the Metro lift. Weekdays at 9:30 AM and
1:30 PM, mountain ambassadors conduct a free tour. The area's 76
trails, including 21 glades and two chutes, are served by eight lifts,
including the tram and the longest detachable quad in the East. The
area also has two quads, a triple, and a double chairlift; one T-bar;

and a moving carpet. Jay has 80% snowmaking coverage. The area also has four terrain parks, each rated for different abilities. There are ski-school programs for children ages 3–18.

WHERE TO STAY

$$$$ ⌂**Hotel Jay & Jay Peak Condominiums.** Centrally located in the ski resort's base area, the hotel and its simply furnished rooms are a favorite for families. Kids 13 and under stay and eat free, and during non-holiday times, they can ski free, too. Farther afield (but still mostly slope-side) are studio to five-bedroom condominiums and town houses, with fireplaces, modern kitchens, and washer/dryers. Complimentary child care is provided to hotel and condo guests 9 AM–4 PM for kids ages two to seven. **Pros:** great for skiers and summer mountain adventurers. **Cons:** not an intimate, traditional Vermont stay. ⊠*Rte. 242* ☎*802/988–2611, 800/451–4449 outside VT* ⊕*www.jaypeakresort. com* ⊷*48 rooms, 94 condominiums* ☼*In-room: no a/c. In-hotel: restaurant, bar, tennis courts, pool, no-smoking rooms* ⊟*AE, D, DC, MC, V* ⊺©*MAP.*

$ ⌂**Inn on Trout River.** Guest rooms at this 100-year-old riverside inn sport a country-cottage style, and all have down quilts and flannel sheets in winter. Lemoine's Restaurant ($–$$) specializes in American and continental fare. Try the raviolini stuffed with Vermont cheddar cheese and walnuts topped with pesto, and the medallions of pork tenderloin in a maple syrup demi-glace sauce. Hobo's Café, also at the inn, serves simpler fare. **Pros:** traditional B&B. **Cons:** rooms heavy on the florals. ⊠*Main St., Montgomery Center* ☎*802/326–4391 or 800/338–7049* ⊕*www.troutinn.com* ⊷*9 rooms, 1 suite* ☼*In-room: no a/c, no TV. In-hotel: restaurant, bar, no-smoking rooms* ⊟*AE, DC, MC, V* ⊺©*BP, MAP.*

EN ROUTE   Routes 14, 5, 58, and 100 make a scenic drive around the **Northeast Kingdom,** named for the remoteness and stalwart independence that have helped preserve its rural nature. You can extend the loop and head east on Route 105 to the city of Newport on Lake Memphremagog. You will encounter some of the most unspoiled areas in all Vermont on the drive south from Newport on either U.S. 5 or Interstate 91 (Interstate 91 is faster, but U.S. 5 is prettier).

LAKE WILLOUGHBY

30 mi southeast of Montgomery (summer route; 50 mi by winter route), 28 mi north of St. Johnsbury.

The cliffs of Mt. Pisgah and Mt. Hor drop to the edge of Lake Willoughby on opposite shores, giving this beautiful, deep, glacially carved lake a striking resemblance to a Norwegian fjord. The trails to the top of Mt. Pisgah reward hikers with glorious views.

WHAT TO SEE

☾ **Bread and Puppet Museum.** This ramshackle barn houses a surrealistic ★ collection of props used by the world-renowned Bread and Puppet Theater. The troupe has been performing social and political commentary with the towering (they're supported by people on stilts), eerily expressive puppets for about 30 years. They perform at the museum every Sunday June–August at 3 PM. ⊠*753 Heights Rd. (Rte. 122), 1 mi east of Rte. 16, Glover* ☎*802/525–3031* ✆*Donations accepted* ☉*June–Oct., daily 10–6.*

EAST BURKE

17 mi south of Lake Willoughby.

Once a sleepy village, East Burke is now the Northeast Kingdom's outdoor-activity hub. The Kingdom Trails attract thousands of mountain bikers in summer and fall. In winter, many trails are groomed for cross-country skiing. Contact the **Kingdom Trails Association** (✆*Box 204, East Burke 05832* ☎*802/626–0737* ⊕*www.kingdomtrails.org*) for details and maps.

SPORTS & THE OUTDOORS

East Burke Sports (⊠*Rte. 114, East Burke* ☎*802/626–3215*) rents mountain bikes, kayaks, and skis, and provides guides for cycling, hiking, paddling, skiing, and snowshoeing. **Village Sport Shop** (⊠*511 Broad St., Lyndonville* ☎*802/626–8448*) rents bikes, canoes, kayaks, paddleboats, rollerblades, skis, and snowshoes.

⇨ "Slopes Less Traveled" box on page 396 for information on Burke Mountain ski area.

WHERE TO EAT & STAY

$–$$ ✕**River Garden Café.** You can eat lunch, dinner, or brunch outdoors on
AMERICAN the enclosed porch, on the patio amid perennial gardens, or inside this bright and cheerful café. The excellent fare includes lamb tenderloin, warm artichoke dip, bruschetta, pastas, and fresh fish, and the popular salad dressing is bottled for sale. ⊠*Rte. 114, East Burke* ☎*802/626–3514* ⊟*AE, D, MC, V* ☉*Closed Mon. and Tues. Nov.–Apr.*

$$ ⊡**Wildflower Inn.** The hilltop views are breathtaking at this rambling,
♻ family-oriented complex of old farm buildings on 570 acres. Guest rooms in the restored Federal-style main house and three other buildings are furnished with reproductions and contemporary furnishings. In summer, supervised day and evening programs engage the kids, allowing parents to explore the many nature trails on their own. You can play with farm animals at the petting barn, go biking, and play tennis and volleyball. In winter sleigh rides, snowshoeing, and cross country skiing are popular. Junipers ($–$$; closed Sunday) serves comfort food such as meat loaf and lemon herb chicken, and offers a kids' menu. **Pros:** mega kid-friendly nature resort; best of the Northeast Kingdom's expansiveness; relaxed. **Cons:** most rooms are simply furnished. ⊠*2059 Darling Hill Rd., 5 mi west of East Burke, Lyndonville* ☎*802/626–8310 or 800/627–8310* ⊕*www.wildflowerinn.com* ⇌*10 rooms, 13 suites, 1 cottage* ⅄*In-room: no a/c (some), kitchen (some), no TV. In-hotel: restaurant, tennis court, pool, children's programs (infant–age 17), no-smoking rooms* ⊟*MC, V* ☉*Closed Apr. and Nov.* ⅃⊙|BP.*

ST. JOHNSBURY

16 mi south of East Burke, 39 mi northeast of Montpelier.

St. Johnsbury, the southern gateway to the Northeast Kingdom, was chartered in 1786. But its identity was established after 1830, when Thaddeus Fairbanks invented the platform scale, a device that revolutionized weighing methods. The Fairbanks family's philanthropic efforts gave the city a strong cultural and architectural imprint.

WHAT TO SEE

Maple Grove Museum and Factory. East of downtown, this is the world's oldest and largest maple candy factory. On a tour, watch how maple candy is made, then sample some in the gift shop. ⊠*1052 Portland St. (Rte. 2)* ☎*802/748–5141* ⊕*www.maplegrove.com* ☜*Tour $1* ☉*May–Dec., weekdays 8–2.*

Fodor'sChoice **St. Johnsbury Athenaeum.** With its dark rich paneling, polished Victo-
★ rian woodwork, and ornate circular staircases, this building is both the town library and one of the oldest art galleries in the country, housing over 100 original works mainly of the Hudson River School. Albert Bierstadt's enormous *Domes of Yosemite* dominates the gallery. ⊠*1171 Main St.* ☎*802/748–8291* ⊕*www.stjathenaeum.org* ☜*Free* ☉*Mon. and Wed. 10–8; Tues., Thurs., and Fri. 10 5:30; Sat. 9:30–4.*

OFF THE BEATEN PATH **Peacham.** Tiny Peacham, 10 mi southwest of St. Johnsbury, is on almost every tour group's list of "must-sees." With views extending to the White Mountains of New Hampshire and a white-steeple church, Peacham is perhaps the most photographed town in New England. *Ethan Frome,* starring Liam Neeson, was filmed here. One of the town's gathering spots, the **Peacham Store** (⊠*Main St.* ☎*802/592–3310*), sells gourmet soups and stews. Next door, the **Peacham Corner Guild** sells local handcrafts.

WHERE TO STAY

$$$ **Rabbit Hill Inn.** Few inns in New England have the word-of-mouth
★ buzz that Rabbit Hill seems to earn from satisfied guests. Most of the spacious, elegant rooms have fireplaces, two-person whirlpool tubs, and views of the Connecticut River and New Hampshire's White Mountains. The grounds have 10 acres of walking trails. The intimate candlelit dining room serves a three- or five-course prix-fixe dinner ($$$$) featuring contemporary new American and regional dishes such as grilled venison loin with cranberry-juniper orange glaze. Afternoon tea in the parlor, horseshoes, garden strolls: this inn is great for small pleasures. **Pros:** attractive, spacious rooms; lovely grounds; good food. **Cons:** might be too quiet a setting for some. ⊠*Rte. 18, 11 mi south of St. Johnsbury, Lower Waterford,* ☎*802/748–5168 or 800/762–8669* ⊕*www.rabbithillinn.com* ⇖*19 rooms* ⚏*In-room: no TV. In-hotel: restaurant, bar, no kids under 14, no-smoking rooms* ▭*AE, D, MC, V* ☉*Closed 1st 3 wks in Apr., 1st 2 wks in Nov.* ⏍*BP, MAP.*

VERMONT ESSENTIALS

Research prices, get travel advice, and book your trip at fodors.com.

TRANSPORTATION

BY AIR

Continental, Delta, JetBlue, United, and US Airways fly into **Burlington International Airport (BTV)** (✉ *1200 Airport Dr., 4 mi east of Burlington off U.S. 2* ☎ *802/863–1889* ⊕ *www.burlingtonintlairport.com*). **Rutland State Airport (RUT)** (✉ *1004 Airport Rd., North Clarendon* ☎ *802/773–3348*) has daily service to and from Boston on US Airways Express. West of Bennington and convenient to southern Vermont, **Albany International Airport (ALB)** (✉ *737 Albany Shaker Rd., Albany* ☎ *518/242–2200* ⊕ *www.albanyairport.com*) in New York State is served by 10 major U.S. carriers.

BY BIKE

Vermont is a popular destination for cyclists, who find villages and towns—with their inns, B&Bs, and restaurants—spaced closely enough for comfortable traveling. **Vermont Bicycle Touring** (✉ *Monkton Rd., Bristol* ☎ *802/453–4811 or 800/245–3868*) leads numerous tours in the state.

BY BOAT

Lake Champlain Ferries (☎ *802/864–9804* ⊕ *www.lakechamplainferries.com*) operates three ferry crossing routes between the lake's Vermont and New York shores: Grand Isle–Plattsburgh, NY; Burlington–Port Kent, NY; and Charlotte–Essex, NY. Two of the routes are in operation year-round, through thick lake ice in winter; the Burlington–Port Kent route functions from late May to mid-October. This is a convenient means of getting to and from New York State, as well as a pleasant way to spend an afternoon.

BY BUS

Vermont Transit (☎ *800/552–8737* ⊕ *www.greyhound.com*), operated by Greyhound, connects Bennington, Brattleboro, Burlington, Manchester, Montpelier, Rutland, Waterbury, and many other Vermont cities and towns with Albany, Boston, Springfield, Newport, New York, Montreal, and cities in New Hampshire. Local service in Burlington and surrounding communities is provided by **Chittenden Country Transportation Authority** (☎ *802/864–0211*).

BY CAR

Interstate 91, which stretches from Connecticut and Massachusetts in the south to Quebec in the north, serves most points along Vermont's eastern border (as does U.S. 5). Interstate 89, from New Hampshire to the east and Quebec to the north, crosses central Vermont from White River Junction to Burlington. North of Interstate 89, Routes 104 and 15 provide a major east–west transverse. From Barton, near Lake Willoughby, U.S. 5 and Route 122 south are beautiful drives. Strip-mall drudge bogs down the section of U.S. 5 around Lyndonville.

Southwestern Vermont can be reached by U.S. 7 from Massachusetts and U.S. 4 from New York. U.S. 7 and Route 30 are the north–south highways in the west (the more scenic drive is Route 7A). Interstate 89 links White River Junction with Montpelier to the north. U.S. 4,

2

the major east–west route, stretches from White River Junction in the east to Fair Haven in the west. Traffic can be slow through Woodstock. Route 100 is the scenic route. It splits the region in half along the eastern edge of the Green Mountains. In the south the principal east–west highway is twisty Route 9, the Molly Stark Trail, from Brattleboro to Bennington.

The official speed limit in Vermont is 50 mph, unless otherwise posted; on the interstates it's 65 mph. Right turns are permitted on a red light unless otherwise indicated. You can get a state map, which has mileage charts and enlarged maps of major downtown areas, free from the Vermont Department of Tourism and Marketing.

The *Vermont Atlas and Gazetteer,* sold in many bookstores, shows nearly every road in the state and is great for driving on the back roads.

For current road conditions, call 800/429–7623.

BY TRAIN

Amtrak (☎ *800/872-7245* ⊕ *www.amtrak.com*) has daytime service linking Washington, D.C., with Brattleboro, Bellows Falls, White River Junction, Montpelier, Waterbury, Essex Junction, and St. Albans via its Vermonter line. Amtrak's Adirondack, which runs from New York City to Montreal, serves Albany, Ft. Edward (near Glens Falls), Ft. Ticonderoga, and Plattsburgh, allowing relatively convenient access to western Vermont. The Ethan Allen Express (also Amtrak) connects New York City with Fair Haven and Rutland.

CONTACTS & RESOURCES

VISITOR INFORMATION

State Contacts Vermont Department of Tourism and Marketing (⊠ *6 Baldwin St., Drawer 33, Montpelier* ☎ *802/828–3676 or 800/837–6668* ⊕ *www.vermont vacation.com*). The **Foliage and Snow Hot Line** (☎ *802/828–3239*) has tips on peak foliage viewing locations and times, up-to-date snow conditions, and events in Vermont.

Regional Contacts Forest Supervisor, Green Mountain National Forest (⊠ *231 N. Main St., Rutland* ☎ *802/747–6700*). **Lake Champlain Regional Chamber of Commerce** (⊠ *60 Main St., Suite 100, Burlington* ☎ *802/863–3489 or 877/686– 5253* ⊕ *www.vermont.org*). **Northeast Kingdom Chamber of Commerce** (⊠ *51 Depot Sq., Suite 3, St. Johnsbury* ☎ *802/748–3678 or 800/639–6379* ⊕ *www. nekchamber.com*). **Northeast Kingdom Travel and Tourism Association** (⊓ *Box 465, Barton 05822* ☎ *802/525–4386 or 800/884–8001* ⊕ *www.travelthekingdom. com*). **Vermont North Country Chamber of Commerce** (⊠ *246 The Causeway, Newport* ☎ *802/334–7782 or 800/635–4643* ⊕ *www.vtnorthcountry.org*).

Local Contacts Addison County Chamber of Commerce (⊠ *2 Court St., Middlebury* ☎ *802/388–7951 or 800/733–8376* ⊕ *www.midvermont.com*). **Bennington Area Chamber of Commerce** (⊠ *Veterans Memorial Dr., Bennington* ☎ *802/447– 3311 or 800/229–0252* ⊕ *www.bennington.com*). **Brattleboro Area Chamber of Commerce** (⊠ *180 Main St., Brattleboro* ☎ *802/254–4565 or 877/254–4565* ⊕ *www.brattleborochamber.org*). **Chamber of Commerce, Manchester and the**

SPORTS & OUTDOORS IN VERMONT

BIKING

Vermont, especially the often deserted roads of the Northeast Kingdom, is great bicycle-touring country. Many companies lead weekend tours and weeklong trips throughout the state. If you'd like to go it on your own, most chambers of commerce have brochures highlighting good cycling routes in their area.

P.O.M.G. Bike Tours of Vermont (✍️ *Richmond Box 1080, 05477* ☎️ *802/434–2270 or 888/635–2453* 🌐 *www.pomgbike.com*) leads weekend and five-day bike tours.

CAMPING

Call Vermont's **Department of Forests, Parks, and Recreation** (☎️ *888/409–7579* 🌐 *www.vtfpr.org*) for the *Vermont Campground Guide*, listing public and private campgrounds in the state.

FISHING

Central Vermont is the heart of the state's warm-water lake and pond fishing area. Harriman and Somerset reservoirs have both warm- and cold-water species; Harriman has a greater variety. Rainbow trout pulled out of Lake Dunmore have set state records; Lakes Bomoseen and St. Catherine are good for rainbows and largemouth bass. In the east, Lakes Fairlee and Morey hold bass, perch, and chain pickerel, while the lower part of the Connecticut River bursts with smallmouth bass, walleye, and perch; shad are returning via the fish ladders at Vernon and Bellows Falls.

In northern Vermont, rainbow and brown trout inhabit the Missisquoi, Lamoille, Winooski, and Willoughby rivers. Lakes Seymour, Willoughby, and Memphremagog and Great Averill Pond in the Northeast Kingdom

are good for salmon and lake trout. The Dog River near Montpelier has one of the best wild populations of brown trout in the state, and landlocked Atlantic salmon are returning to the Clyde River following removal of a controversial dam.

Lake Champlain, stocked annually with salmon and lake trout, has become the state's ice-fishing capital; walleye, bass, pike, and channel catfish are also taken. Ice fishing is also popular on Lake Memphremagog. For information about fishing, including licenses, contact the **Vermont Fish and Wildlife Department** (☎️ *802/241–3700* 🌐 *www. vtfishandwildlife.com*).

HIKING

Vermont is an ideal state for hiking—80 percent of the state is forest, and trails are everywhere. The Appalachian Trail runs the length of the state. In fact, it was the first portion of the trail to be completed, and in Vermont it is called the Long Trail.

The **Green Mountain Club** (✉️ *4711 Waterbury-Stowe Rd. (Rte. 100), Waterbury Center* ☎️ *802/244–7037* 🌐 *www.greenmountainclub. org*) publishes hiking maps and guides. The club also manages the Long Trail, the north–south trail that traverses the entire state.

SPORT TOURS

Country Inns Along the Trail (✍️ *Box 59, Montgomery 05470* ☎️ *802/326–2072 or 800/838–3301* 🌐 *www.inntoinn.com*) arranges self-guided hiking, skiing, and biking trips from inn to inn in Vermont.

VERMONT SKI AREAS

This list is composed of ski areas in Vermont with at least 150 skiable acres.

Ski Area	Vertical Drop (in feet)	Skiable Acres	# of Lifts	Terrain Type*	Boarding Options
Ascutney Mountain	1,800	150	6	30% B 40% I 30% A	Terrain Park
Bolton Valley	1,704	165	6	27% B 47% I 26% A	Terrain Park and Half-pipe
Bromley	1,334	177	10	35% B 34% I 31% A	Terrain Park
Burke Mountain	2,011	250	4	25% B 45% I 30% A	Terrain Park
Jay Peak	2,153	385	8	20% B 40% I 40% A	Terrain Park
Killington	3,050	1,001	26	29% B 29% I 42% A	Terrain Park, Half-pipe
Mount Snow	1,700	590	19	14% B 73% I 13% A	Terrain Park, Half-pipe
Okemo	2,200	624	19	32% B 36% I 32% A	Terrain Park, Half-pipe
Pico Mountain	1,967	214	6	20% B 48% I 32% A	No Terrain Park
Smugglers' Notch	2,610	310	8	19% B 56% I 25% A	Terrain Park, Half-pipe
Stowe	2,360	485	13	16% B 59% I 25% A	Terrain Park, Half-pipe
Stratton	2,003	600	16	42% B 31% I 27% A	Terrain Park, Half-pipe
Sugarbush	2,600	508	16	20% B 45% I 35% A	Terrain Park, Half-pipe

* B = Beginner, I = Intermediate, A = Advanced

Mountains (✉ *5046 Main St., Manchester* ☎ *802/362–2100 or 800/362–4144* ⊕ *www.manchestervermont.net*). **Lake Champlain Islands Chamber of Commerce** (✉ *3537 Rte. 2, Suite 100, North Hero* ☎ *802/372–8400 or 800/262–5226* ⊕ *www.champlainislands.com*). **Mt. Snow Valley Chamber of Commerce** (✉ *W. Main St.* ⌂ *Box 3, Wilmington 05363* ☎ *802/464–8092 or 877/887–6884* ⊕ *www.visitvermont.com*). **Quechee Chamber of Commerce** (✉ *1789 Quechee St.* ⌂ *Box 106, Quechee 05059* ☎ *802/295–7900 or 800/295–5451* ⊕ *www.quechee.com*). **Stowe Area Association** (✉ *Main St., Box 1320, Stowe* ☎ *802/253–7321 or 877/467–8693* ⊕ *www.gostowe.com*). **Sugarbush Chamber of Commerce** (✉ *Rte. 100* ⌂ *Box 173, Waitsfield 05673* ☎ *802/496–3409 or 800/828–4748* ⊕ *www.madrivervalley.com*). **Woodstock Area Chamber of Commerce** (✉ *18 Central St.* ⌂ *Box 486, Woodstock 05091* ☎ *802/457–3555 or 888/496–6378* ⊕ *www.woodstockvt.com*).

New Hampshire

WORD OF MOUTH

"If you are looking for sights, the cog railway trip up Mt. Washington is fun, and the Mt. Washington Hotel in Crawford Notch is lovely. It's one of the few remaining grand old hotels. A gorgeous drive from there would be taking Rt. 302 through North Conway to Rt. 112 (Kancamagus Highway) to Lincoln, then back up Rt. 3 to Bretton Woods...Lots to see along the way. It's slow going, but worth the time."

—colbeck

By Michael de
Zayas

CRUSTY, AUTONOMOUS NEW HAMPSHIRE IS often defined more by what it is not than by what it is. It lacks Vermont's folksy charm, and its coast isn't nearly as grand as that of Maine. However, it has a strong political history: it was the first colony to declare independence from Great Britain, the first to adopt a state constitution, and the first to require that constitution be referred to the people for approval.

From the start, New Hampshire residents took their hard-won freedoms seriously. Twenty years after the Revolutionary War's Battle of Bennington, New Hampshire native General John Stark, who led the troops to that crucial victory, wrote a letter to be read at the reunion he was too ill to attend. In it, he reminded his men, "Live free or die; death is not the worst of evils." The first half of that sentiment is now the Granite State's motto.

New Hampshire's independent spirit, mountain peaks, clear air, and sparkling lakes have attracted trailblazers and artists for centuries. Ralph Waldo Emerson, Henry David Thoreau, Nathaniel Hawthorne, and Louisa May Alcott all visited and wrote about the state, sparking a strong literary tradition that continues today. Filmmaker Ken Burns, writer J. D. Salinger, and poet Donald Hall all make their homes here.

The state's diverse terrain makes it popular with everyone from avid adventurers to young families looking for easy access to nature. You can hike, climb, ski, snowboard, snowshoe, and fish as well as explore on snowmobiles, sailboats, and mountain bikes. Natives have no objection to others enjoying the state's beauty as long as they leave some money behind. New Hampshire has long resisted both sales and income taxes, so tourism brings in much-needed revenue.

With a few of its cities consistently rated among the most livable in the nation, New Hampshire has seen considerable growth over the past decade or two. Longtime residents worry that the state will soon take on two personalities: one of rapidly growing cities to the southeast and the other of quiet villages to the west and north. Although the influx of newcomers has brought change, the independent nature of the people and the state's natural beauty remain constant.

EXPLORING NEW HAMPSHIRE

Generally speaking, New Hampshire has four geographic areas: the coast, the central Lakes Region, the White Mountains in the north, and Merrimack Valley and the southwest. The main attractions of southern New Hampshire's coast are historical Portsmouth and bustling Hampton Beach; several somewhat quieter communities such as Durham and Exeter are a bit farther inland. The Lakes Region has good hiking trails, antiques shops, and, of course, water sports. For winter activities, there's no match for the mighty White Mountains, where you can experience the state's best hiking and skiing. The southwest is hemmed in to the east by the central Merrimack Valley, which has a string of fast-growing communities along Interstate 93 and U.S. 3 but for the most part retains its quiet, small-town life.

PLANNING YOUR TRIP

BUDGETING YOUR TIME

Some people come to New Hampshire to hike or ski the mountains, fish and sail the lakes, or cycle along the back roads. Others prefer to drive through scenic towns, visiting museums and shops. Although New Hampshire is a small state, roads curve around lakes and mountains, making distances longer than they appear. You can get a taste of the coast, lake, and mountain areas in three to five days; eight days gives you time to make a more comprehensive loop.

WHEN TO GO

Summer and fall are the best times to visit most New Hampshire. Winter is a great time to visit the White Mountains, but most other tourist sites in the state, including the Portsmouth museums and the Lake attractions, are closed. In summer, people flock to seaside beaches, mountain trails, and lake boat ramps. In the cities, festivals showcase music, theater, and crafts.

Fall brings leaf-peepers, especially to the White Mountains and along the Kancamagus Highway (Route 112). Skiers take to the slopes in winter, when Christmas lights and carnivals brighten the long, dark nights. Spring's unpredictable weather—along with April's mud and late May's black flies—tends to deter visitors. Still, the season has its joys, not the least of which is the appearance of the state flower, the purple lilac, from mid-May to early June.

GETTING THERE & AROUND

New Hampshire is an easy drive north from Boston, and serves as a good base for exploring northern New England. Its major destinations are easily located off major highways, so getting around by car is a great way to go in the state.

Though Boston's Logan Airport is nearby, it's easy to reach the state by air directly as well. Manchester Airport is the state's largest airport and has nonstop service to more than 20 cities.

ABOUT THE RESTAURANTS

New Hampshire prides itself on seafood—not just lobster but also salmon pie, steamed mussels, fried clams, and seared tuna. Across the state you'll find country taverns with upscale continental and American menus, many of them embracing regional ingredients. A dearth of agriculture in the state means that you won't find an emphasis on local ingredients like you might in Vermont, and the level of culinary sophistication is lacking. Alongside a growing number of contemporary eateries are such state traditions as greasy-spoon diners, pizzerias, and pubs that serve hearty comfort fare. Reservations are almost never required, and dress is casual in nearly every eatery.

ABOUT THE HOTELS

In the mid-19th century, wealthy Bostonians retreated to imposing New Hampshire country homes in summer months. Grand hotels were built across the state, especially in the White Mountains, when the area was competing with Saratoga Springs, Newport, and Bar Harbor to draw the nation's elite vacationers. Today a handful survive, with their large cooking staffs and tradition of top-notch service. Many of the vacation

NEW HAMPSHIRE TOP 5

■ **The White Mountains:** Great for hiking and skiing, these rugged, dramatic peaks and notches are unforgettable.

■ **Lake Winnipesaukee:** Water parks, arcades, boat cruises, and classic summer camps make for a family fun extravaganza.

■ **Fall Foliage:** Head to the Kancamagus Highway in the fall for one of America's best drives.

■ **Portsmouth:** Less than an hour from the state capital, this great American city has coastline allure, cute and colorful colonial architecture, and a real small-city energy.

■ **Pristine Towns:** Jaffrey Center, Walpole, Tamworth, Center Sandwich, and Jackson are among the most charming tiny villages in New England.

3

houses have been converted into inns. The smallest have only a couple of rooms and are typically done in period style. The largest contain 30 or more rooms and have in-room fireplaces and even hot tubs. Amenities increase each year at some of these inns, which, along with bed-and-breakfasts, dominate New Hampshire's lodging scene. You'll also find a great many well-kept, often family-owned motor lodges—particularly in the White Mountains and Lakes regions. In the ski areas expect the usual ski condos and lodges. In the Merrimack River valley, as well as along major highways, chain hotels and motels prevail.

WHAT IT COSTS					
	¢	$	$$	$$$	$$$$
RESTAURANTS	under $10	$10–$16	$17–$24	$25–$35	over $35
HOTELS	under $100	$100–$149	$150–$199	$200–$250	over $250

Prices are per person, for a main course at dinner. Prices are for a standard double room during peak season and not including tax or gratuities. Some inns add a 15%–18% service charge.

THE COAST

New Hampshire's 18-mi stretch of coastline packs in a wealth of scenery and diversions. The honky-tonk of Hampton Beach gets plenty of attention, good and bad, but first-timers are often surprised by the significant chunk of shoreline that remains pristine—especially through the town of Rye. This section begins in the regional hub, Portsmouth; cuts down the coast to the beaches; branches inland to the quintessential prep-school town of Exeter; and then runs back up north through Dover, Durham (home of the University of New Hampshire), and Rochester. From here it's a short drive to the Lakes Region.

New Hampshire Coast

TO ROCHESTER
Dover
MAINE
95
9
202
108
16
Piscataqua River
4
202
Durham
4
TO
CONCORD
125
108
4
16
Newmarket
Great
Bay
Portsmouth
New Castle
Greenland
Odiorne Point
State Park
TO
MANCHESTER
85
33
1
Rye
Wallis Sands
State Beach
101
Stratham
95
Winnicut
Jenness
State Beach
Exeter
Exeter R.
88
Rye Beach
Isles of
Shoals
North Hampton
111
108
Hampton
1A
Country
Pond
108
107
Hampton Falls
Hampton
Beach
Seabrook
Hampton Beach
State Park
ATLANTIC
OCEAN
95
1
MASSACHUSETTS

0   10 miles
0   15 km

PORTSMOUTH

★ *47 mi southeast of Concord; 50 mi southwest of Portland, Maine; 56 mi north of Boston.*

Settled in 1623 as Strawbery Banke, Portsmouth became a prosperous port before the Revolutionary War, and like similarly wealthy Newport, Rhode Island, it harbored many Tory sympathizers throughout the campaign. Filled with grand residential architecture spanning the 18th through early 20th century, this city of 23,000 has numerous house museums, including the collection of 40-plus buildings that make up the Strawbery Banke Museum. With hip eateries, quirky shops, swank cocktail bars, respected theaters, and jumping live-music venues, this sheltered harbor city is a hot destination. Downtown, especially around elegant Market Square, buzzes with conviviality.

WHAT TO SEE

John Paul Jones House. The yellow, hip-roof home was a boarding-house when the Revolutionary War hero lived here while supervising shipbuilding for the Continental Navy. The 1758 structure, now the headquarters of the Portsmouth Historical Society, contains furniture, costumes, glass, guns, portraits, and documents from the late

SIGHTSEEING TRAILS & TROLLEYS

TRAILS

One of the best ways to learn about town history is on the guided tour along the **Portsmouth Harbour Trail** (✉ *Downtown through the South End and along State and Congress Sts.* ☎ *603/427–2020 for guided tour* ⊕ *www.seacoastnh. com/harbourtrail* ✉ *$8 for guided tour* ⊙ *Highlights tour Thurs.–Sat., Mon. 10:30 AM, Sun. 1:30 PM. Twilight tour Thurs.–Sat. and Mon. 5:30 PM).* You can purchase a tour map ($2.50) at the information kiosk in Market Square, at the chamber of commerce, and at several house museums. Guided walks are conducted late spring to early fall.

Sites important to African-American history in Portsmouth are along the self-guided walk on the **Portsmouth Black Heritage Trail** (✉ *Downtown, starting at Prescott Park wharf* ☎ *603/431–2768* ⊕ *www.seacoast nh.com/blackhistory*). Included are the **New Hampshire Gazette Printing Office,** where skilled slave Primus Fowle operated the paper's printing press for some 50 years beginning in 1756, and the city's 1866 **Election Hall,** outside of which the city's black citizens held annual celebrations of the Emancipation Proclamation.

TROLLEYS

On the **Seacoast Trolley** (✉ *Departs from Market Sq. or from 14 locations en route* ☎ *603/431–6975* ⊕ *www.locallink.com/seacoasttrolley* ✉ *$5)* guides conduct narrated tours of Portsmouth, Rye, and New Castle, with views of the New Hampshire coastline and area beaches. The 17-mi round-trip, which you can hop on and off at several stops, runs from mid-June through Labor Day

Portsmouth is also served by the **Downtown Loop Coastal Trolley** (✉ *Departs from Market Sq. every half hour* ☎ *603/743–5777* ⊕ *www.coastbus.org/downtown. html* ✉ *50¢).* Running from late June to early September, the tours are narrated 90-minute round-trips through downtown and around the waterfront. You can hop on and off at numerous stops.

18th century. ✉ *43 Middle St.* ☎ *603/436–8420* ✉ *$5* ⊙ *June–Oct., daily 10–5.*

Moffatt-Ladd House. The period interior of this 1763 home tells the story of Portsmouth's merchant class through portraits, letters, and fine furnishings. The Colonial-revival garden includes a horse chestnut tree planted by General William Whipple when he returned home after signing the Declaration of Independence in 1776. ✉ *154 Market St.* ☎ *603/436–8221* ✉ *$6, garden and house tour $1* ⊙ *Mid-June–mid-Oct., Mon.–Sat. 11–5, Sun. 1–5.*

NEED A BREAK?

Drop by **Annabelle's Natural Ice Cream** (✉ *49 Ceres St.* ☎ *603/436–3400*) for a dish of Ghirardelli chocolate chip or Almond Joy ice cream. Breaking New Grounds (✉ *14 Market Sq.* ☎ *603/436–9555*) is a big hangout in town and serves coffee, pastries, and gelato.

Port of Portsmouth Maritime Museum. The USS *Albacore,* built here in 1953, is docked at this museum in Albacore Park. You can board the prototype submarine, which was a floating laboratory assigned to test an innovative hull design, dive brakes, and sonar systems for the Navy. The nearby Memorial Garden and its reflecting pool are dedicated to those who have lost their lives in submarine service. ⊠ *600 Market St.* ☎ *603/436–3680* ⊑ *$5* ⊙ *Daily 9:30–5.*

Redhook Ale Brewery. Tours here end with a beer tasting. If you don't have time to tour, stop in the Cataqua Public House to sample the fresh ales and have a bite to eat (open daily for lunch and dinner). The building is visible from the Spaulding Turnpike. ⊠ *Pease International Tradeport, 35 Corporate Dr.* ☎ *603/430–8600* ⊕ *www.redhook.com* ⊑ *$1* ⊙ *Tours weekdays at 2, weekends at 2 and 4; additional tours at noon, 1, and 3 summer weekends.*

FodorsChoice
★
Strawbery Banke Museum. The first English settlers named the area around today's Portsmouth for the wild strawberries abundant along the shores of the Piscataqua River. The name survives in this 10-acre neighborhood, continuously occupied for more than 300 years and now doing duty as an outdoor history museum, one of the largest in New England. The compound has 46 buildings dating from 1695 to 1820—some restored and furnished to a particular period, some used for exhibits, and some viewed from the outside only—as well as restored or re-created period gardens. Half the interior of the Drisco House, built in 1795, depicts its use as a dry-goods store in Colonial times, whereas the living room and kitchen are decorated as they were in the 1950s, showing how buildings were adapted over time. The Shapiro House has been restored to reflect the life of the Russian Jewish immigrant family who lived in the home in the early 1900s. Perhaps the most opulent house, done in decadent Victorian style, is the 1860 Goodwin Mansion, former home of Governor Ichabod Goodwin. ⊠ *Marcy St.* ☎ *603/433–1100* ⊕ *www.strawberybanke.org* ⊑ *$15* ⊙ *May–Oct., daily 10–5; Feb.–Apr., Nov., and Dec., Wed.–Sat. 10–2.*

Wentworth-Coolidge Mansion Historic Site. A National Historic Landmark now part of Little Harbor State Park, this home site was originally the residence of Benning Wentworth, New Hampshire's first royal governor (1753–70). Notable among its period furnishings is the carved pine mantelpiece in the council chamber. Wentworth's imported lilac trees bloom each May. The visitor center stages lectures and exhibits and contains a gallery with changing exhibits. ⊠ *375 Little Harbor Rd., near South Street Cemetery* ☎ *603/436–6607* ⊑ *$3* ⊙ *Grounds daily; mansion mid-May–Aug., Wed.–Sat. 10–3, Sun. 1–5; Sept.–mid-May, by appointment.*

OFF THE
BEATEN
PATH
Though it consists of a single square mile of land, the small island of **New Castle,** 3 mi southeast from downtown via Route 1B, was once known as Great Island. The narrow roads and coastal lanes are lined with prerevolutionary houses making for a beautiful drive or stroll. **Wentworth-by-the-Sea,** the last of the state's great seaside resorts, towers over the southern end of New Castle on Route 1B. It was the site of the signing of the Russo-Japanese Treaty in 1905, when Russian and Japanese delegates stayed at the resort and signed an agreement ending

the Russo-Japanese War. President Theodore Roosevelt won a Nobel Peace Prize for bringing this about. The property was vacant for 20 years before reopened as a luxury resort in 2003. Also on New Castle Island, **Ft. Constitution** (✉ *Wentworth St. off Rte. 1B, at the Coast Guard Station* ☎ *603/436–1552* ⊕ *www.nhstateparks.com/fortconstitution. html* ✉ *Free* ⊙ *Daily 9–4*) was built in 1631 and then rebuilt in 1666 as Ft. William and Mary, a British stronghold overlooking Portsmouth Harbor. The fort earned fame in 1774, when patriots raided it in one of revolutionary America's first overtly defiant acts against King George III. The rebels later used the captured munitions against the British at the Battle of Bunker Hill. Panels explain its history. Park at the dock and walk into the Coast Guard installation to the fort.

OFF THE BEATEN PATH

Isles of Shoals. Many of these nine small, rocky islands (eight at high tide) retain the earthy names—Hog and Smuttynose, to cite but two—given them by transient 17th-century fishermen. A history of piracy, murder, and ghosts surrounds the archipelago, long populated by an independent lot who, according to one writer, hadn't the sense to winter on the mainland. Not all the islands lie within the state's border: after an ownership dispute, five went to Maine and four to New Hampshire.

Celia Thaxter, a native islander, romanticized these islands with her poetry in *Among the Isles of Shoals* (1873) and celebrated her garden in *An Island Garden* (1894; now reissued with the original color illustrations by Childe Hassam). In the late 19th century, **Appledore Island** became an offshore retreat for Thaxter's coterie of writers, musicians, and artists. The island is now used by the Marine Laboratory of Cornell University. **Star Island** contains a nondenominational conference center and is open to those on guided tours.

From late May to late October you can cruise of the Isles of Shoals or take a ferry to Star Island with **Isles of Shoals Steamship Company** (✉ *315 Market St.* ☎ *800/441–4620 or 603/431–5500* ⊕ *www.isles ofshoals.com*).

SPORTS & THE OUTDOORS

Great Bay Estuarine Research Reserve. Just inland from Portsmouth is one of southeastern New Hampshire's most precious assets. Amid its 4,471 acres of tidal waters, mudflats, and about 48 mi of inland shoreline, you can spot blue herons, ospreys, and snowy egrets, particularly during spring and fall migrations. Winter eagles also live here. The best public access is via the **Sandy Point Discovery Center** (✉ *89 Depot Rd., off Rte. 33, Stratham* ☎ *603/778–0015* ⊕ *www.greatbay. org* ⊙ *May–Sept., Wed.–Sun. 10–4; Oct., weekends 10–4*). The facility has year-round interpretive programs, indoor and outdoor exhibits, a library and bookshop, and a 1,700-foot boardwalk as well as other trails through mudflats and upland forest. The center, about 15 mi southeast of Durham and 6 mi west of Exit 3 from Interstate 95 in Portsmouth, also distributes maps and information. ⓘ *Information: New Hampshire Fish & Game Dept., 225 Main St., Durham 03824* ☎ *603/868–1095* ✉ *Free* ⊙ *Daily dawn–dusk.*

Prescott Park. Picnicking is popular at this waterfront park. A large formal garden with fountains is perfect for whiling away an afternoon. The park also contains Point of Graves, Portsmouth's oldest burial ground, and two 17th-century warehouses. ⊠*Between Strawbery Banke Museum and the Piscataqua River.*

Water Country. New Hampshire's largest water park has a river tube ride, large wave pool, white-water rapids, and 12 large waterslides. ⊠*Rte. 1, 3 mi south of downtown Portsmouth* ☎*603/427–1112* ☞*$29* ⊙*Mid-June–Labor Day, daily 10–6; until 7:30 in July and early Aug.*

BOAT TOURS **Granite State Whale Watch** (⊠*Rye Harbor State Marina, Rte. 1A, Rye* ☎*603/964–5545 or 800/964–5545* ⊕*www.whales-rye.com*) conducts naturalist-led whale-watching tours aboard the 150-passenger MV *Granite State* out of Rye Harbor State Marina from May to early October, and narrated Isles of Shoals cruises in July and August.

From May to October, **Portsmouth Harbor Cruises** (⊠*Ceres Street Dock* ☎*603/436–8084 or 800/776–0915* ⊕*www.portsmouthharbor.com*) operates tours of Portsmouth Harbor, foliage trips on the Cocheco River, and sunset cruises aboard the MV *Heritage.*

The **Isles of Shoals Steamship Co.** (⊠*Barker Wharf, 315 Market St.* ☎*603/431–5500 or 800/441–4620* ⊕*www.islesofshoals.com*) runs a three-hour Isles of Shoals, lighthouses, and Portsmouth Harbor cruise out of Portsmouth aboard the *Thomas Laighton,* a replica of a Victorian steamship, from April through December (twice daily in summer). Lunch and light snacks are available on board or you can bring your own. There are also fall foliage cruises, narrated sunset cruises visiting five local lighthouses, and special holiday cruises.

One of the questions visitors to Portsmouth ask most frequently is whether they can tour the familiar red tugboats plying the waters of Piscataqua River and Portsmouth Harbor. Unfortunately, the answer is no, but you can get a firsthand look at Portsmouth's working waterfront aboard the **Tug Alley Too** (⊠*2 Ceres St.* ☎*603/430–9556* ⊕*www. tugboatalley.com*), a six-passenger replica. The 90-minute tours pass lighthouses, the Portsmouth Naval Shipyard, and Wentworth Marina. Tours are conducted daily from July through September, Monday through Saturday.

Explore the waters, sites, and sea life of the Piscataqua River Basin and the New Hampshire coastline on a guided kayak tour with **Portsmouth Kayak Adventure** (⊠*185 Wentworth Rd.* ☎*603/559–1000*). Beginners are welcome (instruction is included). Tours are run daily from June through mid-October, at 10 and 2. Sunset tours take off at 6. They also run a kids camp. If you'd rather pedal than drive, stop by **Portsmouth Rent & Ride** (⊠*37 Hanover St.* ☎*603/433–6777*) for equipment, maps, and suggested bike routes to Portsmouth sites, area beaches, and attractions. Guided two-hour tours of the seacoast area are also offered.

SHOPPING

Market Square, in the center of town, has gift and clothing boutiques, book and card shops, and exquisite crafts stores. **Nahcotta** (⊠*110 Congress St.* ☎ *603/433–1705*) is a wonderful contemporary art gallery, and has a well-chosen selection of contemporary housewares, artist-crafted jewelry, and glassware. **Byrne & Carlson** (⊠*121 State St.* ☎*888/559–9778*) produces handmade chocolates in the finest European tradition. **N. W. Barrett** (⊠*53 Market St.* ☎*603/431–4262*) specializes in leather, jewelry, pottery, and other arts and crafts. It also sells furniture, including affordable steam-bent oak pieces and one-of-a-kind lamps and rocking chairs.

NIGHTLIFE & THE ARTS

MUSIC Fans of the local music scene should discover **The Red Door** (⊠*401 State St.* ☎*603/431–5202* ⊕*www.reddoorportsmouth.com*), which has a bar and different music series and DJs nightly. Indie music fans shouldn't miss Monday nights at 8 for the acclaimed live acts curated by the Hush Hush Sweet Harlot series. The **Portsmouth Gas Light Co.** (⊠*64 Market St.* ☎*603/430–9122*), a brick-oven pizzeria and restaurant, hosts local rock bands in its lounge, courtyard, and slick upstairs space. People come from as far away as Boston and Portland to hang out at the **Press Room** (⊠*77 Daniel St.* ☎*603/431–5186*), which showcases folk, jazz, blues, and bluegrass performers.

BARS The town's newest bar and its only martini bar is at little **Two Ceres Street** (⊠*2 Ceres St.* ☎*603/431–5967*). If vodka is your thing you'll do no better than the book-lined English oak bar **The Library** (⊠*401 State St.* ☎*603/431–5202*), which has more than 100 brands.

THE ARTS Five galleries participate in the Art 'Round Town Reception, a gallery walk that takes place the second Friday of each month. Check out ⊕*www.artroundtown.org* for more information. Beloved for its acoustics, the 1878 **Music Hall** (⊠*28 Chestnut St.* ☎*603/436–2400, 603/436–9900 film line* ⊕*www.themusichall.org*) brings the best touring events to the seacoast—from classical and pop concerts to dance and theater. The hall also hosts art-house film series. The **Prescott Park Arts Festival** (⊠*105 Marcy St.* ☎*603/436–2848* ⊕*www.prescottpark. org*) presents theater, dance, and musical events outdoors from June through August.

WHERE TO EAT

$$ ✕**Blue Mermaid Island Grill.** This is a fun, colorful place for great fish,
ECLECTIC sandwiches and quesadillas, as well as house-cut sweet-potato chips. Specialties include plantain-encrusted grouper topped with grilled mango vinaigrette and served with black-eyed pea–sweet potato hash; and wood-grilled flat-iron steak with a cilantro-hoisin glaze, cucumber-citrus relish, and noodles. In summer you can eat on a deck that overlooks the adorable Colonial homes of the Hill neighborhood. Entertainers perform (outdoors in summer) on Wednesday through Saturday. ⊠*409 The Hill* ☎*603/427–2583* ▤*AE, D, DC, MC, V.*

$–$$ ✕**Chiangmai Thai.** Portsmouth's first authentic Thai restaurant remains
THAI one of its favorites among locals and visitors. The dining room is small,

but the menu lists an extensive array of creative Thai dishes. Duck is a specialty (try it roasted, then lightly fried in egg batter; topped with ginger, scallions, and a spicy red-chili sauce; and served over crispy noodles and roasted pine nuts). Or you can create your own dish with an assortment of sauces and curries. ⊠ *128 Penhallow St.* ☎ *603/433– 1289* ⊟ *AE, D, MC, V* ☺ *Closed Mon. and Feb.*

↺ ¢–$
★
AMERICAN

✕ **Friendly Toast.** The biggest and best breakfast in town (as well as lunch and dinner) is served at this funky, wildly colorful diner-style restaurant loaded with bric-a-brac. Almond Joy cakes (buttermilk pancakes, chocolate chips, coconut, and almonds), orange French toast, and hefty omelets (lots of combinations) are favorites. The homemade breads and muffins are a hit, too. A late-night crowd gathers in the wee hours after the bars close, since the restaurant is open 24 hours on weekends. ⊠ *121 Congress St.* ☎ *603/430–2154* ⊟ *AE, D, MC, V.*

$$
SEAFOOD

✕ **Jumpin' Jay's.** A wildly popular spot downtown, this offbeat, dim-lighted eatery presents a changing menu of world-beat seafood, and nary a red-meat platter is served. Try the steamed Prince Edward Island mussels with a spicy lemongrass and saffron sauce, Jonah crab–and-vegetable lasagna, or the Chilean sea bass with a ginger-orange marinade. Singles often gather at the central bar for dinner and schmoozing. ⊠ *150 Congress St.* ☎ *603/766–3474* ⊟ *MC, V* ☺ *No lunch.*

$$–$$$
★
STEAKHOUSE

✕ **The Library.** Have an insatiable appetite for words? Don't miss having a cocktail or a fine meal this steak house in a former luxury hotel where there are bookcases on every wall, and the check arrives between the pages of a vintage best-seller. The 12-foot hand-painted dining room ceiling was constructed by the Pullman Car Woodworkers in 1889. There is hand-carved Spanish mahogany paneling, and original lighting fixtures inlaid with semiprecious stones. Although the kitchen churns out such light dishes as pan-roasted salmon with basmati rice, the mainstays are thick-cut steaks and chops. Order a vodka in the English-style pub—there are more than 100 to choose from. Also, Sunday brunch is a big to-do. ⊠ *401 State St.* ☎ *603/431–5202* ⊟ *AE, D, DC, MC, V.*

$
SOUTHERN

✕ **Muddy River Smokehouse.** A wall of red barn shingles, fake trees, and a ceiling painted with stars evoke an outdoor summer barbecue joint at this fun BBQ place. Roll up your sleeves and dig into corn bread and molasses baked beans as well as blackened catfish or a burger. Devotees swear by the Pig City platter of grilled ribs, smoked sweet sausage, and pulled pork. There's a big bar, and downstairs, live music on weekends. ⊠ *21 Congress St.* ☎ *603/430–9582* ⊟ *AE, MC, V.*

$$–$$$
★
SEAFOOD

✕ **Pesce Blue.** Sleek, modern, and hip, this restaurant specializes in fresh seafood blended with simple Italian flavors. You pass a wall of flickering votives before entering the main dining room, which has an industrial feel: cinder-block walls, black industrial grid ceiling, wood and chrome accents, and mosaic blue tiles. The menu changes daily but may include grilled Greek sardines, fried anchovies, grilled jumbo prawns with sweet garlic custard, and a selection of local catches. There's patio dining in summer. ⊠ *103 Congress St.* ☎ *603/430–7766* ⊕ *www.pesce blue.com* ⊟ *AE, D, MC, V* ☺ *No lunch Sat.*

$–$$ ✕**Poco's.** Sure, Poco's boisterous downstairs bar and spacious outside
★ deck have earned it a reputation as a local hangout, but the upstairs
LATIN dining room turns out exceptional Southwest and pan-Latin cuisine—
AMERICAN and at great prices. Avocado-wrapped fried oysters with chipotle tar-
tar sauce, fried calamari, and lobster quesadilla are among the better
choices. Most tables have great views of the Piscataqua River. ⊠*37
Bow St.* ☎*603/431–5967* ▭*AE, D, MC, V.*

WHERE TO STAY

$$$ ⊞**Governor's House.** Of Portsmouth's inns and small hotels, the Gover-
Fodor'sChoice nor stands apart. Small, plush, and quiet, this four-room inn, a couple
★ blocks from the historic downtown area, is the perfect place for dis-
cerning couples. It was the home of Charles Dale, formerly the gov-
ernor of New Hampshire, from 1930 to 1964. Frette linens, down
comforters, in-room Bose CD stereos with 300 CDs to choose from,
high-speed wireless, a guest computer, in-room massages, complimen-
tary wine, a private tennis court, as well as DVDs that include col-
lection featuring the last 55 Academy Award winners are among the
extras at this 1917 Georgian Colonial house turned bed-and-breakfast.
Innkeeper Bob Chaffee is a discerning host. Ask him to tell the his-
tory of the hand-painted bathroom tiles. **Pros:** great rooms and home,
free bicycle rental, great location. **Cons:** king beds, most showers are
small. ⊠*32 Miller Ave.* ☎*603/427–5140 or 866/427–5140* ⊕*www.
governors-house.com* ☞*4 rooms* ⏃*In-room: DVD, refrigerator, Wi-
Fi. In-hotel: tennis court, bicycles, no elevator, laundry service, public
Internet, public Wi-Fi, no kids under 15, no-smoking rooms* ▭*D,
MC, V* ⦿*CP.*

$ ⊞**Martin Hill Inn.** Once you see it from the street you may fall in love
with this adorable yellow 1815 house surrounded by gardens. It's a
10- to 15-minute walk from the historic district and the waterfront.
The quiet rooms are furnished with antiques and decorated in formal
Colonial or country-Victorian styles. The Greenhouse Suite has a solar-
ium. You'll get to know your fellow travelers at a communal breakfast
served at 8:30 each morning at a common table. **Pros:** very clean, real
antiques, communal breakfast. **Cons:** not inside historic district, no
common spaces, early breakfast. ⊠*404 Islington St.* ☎*603/436–2287*
⊕*www.martinhillinn.com* ☞*4 rooms, 3 suites* ⏃*In-room: no phone,
no TV, Wi-Fi. In-hotel: no elevator, public Wi-Fi, no kids under 14,
no-smoking rooms* ▭*MC, V* ⦿*BP.*

$$$ ⊞**Wentworth by the Sea.** What's not to love about this white colos-
Fodor'sChoice sus overlooking the sea on New Castle island? The closest thing New
★ Hampshire has to a Ritz-Carlton, Wentworth by the Sea has luxurious rooms that are lushly carpeted, come with gas fireplaces, and have
modern and opulent amenities. There's has a good spa and an attractive
indoor heated pool. The coastline and island location are superb. The
luxury property was built in 1874 as a summer resort for East Coast
socialites, wealthy patrons, and former presidents. It reopened in spring
2003 after literally being rebuilt. All of the bright airy rooms have
ocean and harbor views—the huge sunny suites occupy a new building
right on the water, facing the marina. **Pros:** great spa and restaurants,
sense of history, oceanfront perch. **Cons:** not in downtown Portsmouth.

✉ *588 Wentworth Rd. New Castle* ☎ *603/422–7322 or 866/240–6313*
⊕ *www.wentworth.com* ⟲ *127 rooms, 34 suites* ⌂ *In-room: DVD,*
Wi-Fi. In-hotel: 3 restaurants, room service, bar, golf course, tennis
courts, pools, gym, spa, concierge, laundry service, no-smoking rooms
☰ *AE, D, DC, MC, V.*

RYE

8 mi south of Portsmouth.

On Route 1A as it winds south through Rye, you'll pass a group of late-
19th- and early-20th-century mansions known as **Millionaires' Row.**
Because of the way the road curves, the drive south along this route
is especially breathtaking. In 1623 the first Europeans established a
settlement at Odiorne Point in what is now the largely undeveloped
and picturesque town of Rye, making it the birthplace of New Hampshire. Today the area's main draws are a lovely state park, oceanfront
beaches, and the views from Route 1A. Strict town laws have prohib-
ited commercial development in Rye, creating a dramatic contrast with
its frenetic neighbor Hampton Beach.

SPORTS & THE OUTDOORS

☾ **Odiorne Point State Park.** This site encompasses more than 330 acres of
★ protected land, on the site where David Thompson established the first
permanent European site in what is now New Hampshire. Stroll several nature trails with interpretive panels describing the park's military
history or simply enjoy the vistas of the nearby Isles of Shoals. The
rocky shore's tidal pools shelter crabs, periwinkles, and sea anemo-
nes. Throughout the year, the **Seacoast Science Center** conducts guided
walks and interpretive programs and has exhibits on the area's natural
history. Displays trace the social history of Odiorne Point back to the
Ice Age, and the tidal-pool touch tank and 1,000-gallon Gulf of Maine
deepwater aquarium are popular with kids. Day camp is offered for
grades K–8 throughout summer and during school vacations. Popular music concerts are held here on Thursday evenings in summer.
✉ *570 Ocean Blvd. (Rte. 1A), north of Wallis Sands, Rye State Beach*
☎ *603/436–8043 science center, 603/436–1552 park* ⊕ *www.seacentr.*
org ⛶ *$3* ⊙ *Science center daily 10–5 (closed Sun. Nov.–Mar.), park*
daily 8 AM*–dusk.*

☾ **Rye Airfield.** If you've got active kids with you, consider spending the
day at this extreme-sports park with an indoor in-line-skate and skateboard arena and two BMX tracks. ✉ *U.S. 1* ☎ *603/964–2800.*

BEACHES Good for swimming and sunning, **Jenness State Beach** (✉ *Route 1A*
☎ *603/436–1552*) is a favorite with locals. The facilities include a
bathhouse, lifeguards, and metered parking. **Wallis Sands State Beach**
(✉ *Route 1A* ☎ *603/436–9404* ⛶ *$10*) is a swimmers' beach with
bright white sands and a bathhouse. There's plenty of parking.

FISHING For a full- or half-day deep-sea angling charter, try **Atlantic Fishing**
and Whale Watch Fleet (✉ *Rye Harbor* ☎ *603/964–5220 or 800/*
942–5364).

WHERE TO EAT & STAY

$$–$$$ ✗**The Carriage House.** Walk across scenic Ocean Boulevard from Jenness
★ Beach to this elegant cottage eatery that serves innovative dishes with
AMERICAN a continental flair. Standouts include crab cakes served with a spicy
jalepeño sauce, a penne *alla vodka* teeming with fresh seafood, creative
Madras curries, and a delectable steak au poivre. Upstairs is a rough-
hewn-wood-paneled tavern serving lighter fare. Savor a hot fudge–ice
cream croissant or an indulgent tiramisu for dessert while enjoying the
ocean views. ✉*2263 Ocean Blvd.* ☎*603/964–8251* ▤*AE, MC, V*
☺*No lunch.*

$$ ▥**Rock Ledge Manor.** You can avoid the crowds of Hampton but still
enjoy the beach at this three-room B&B. Built out on a point, this
mid-19th-century gambrel-roof house with a wraparound porch once
anchored a resort colony. Rooms are quite small, with little bathrooms;
they do have partial water views. The real joy is sitting out on the porch
overlooking the ocean. Owners Karen and Noel Rix serve breakfast
in the sunny dining room. **Pros:** great views, quiet, very clean. **Cons:**
small rooms and baths, continental breakfast only. ✉*1413 Ocean
Blvd.* ☎*603/431–1413* ⊕*www.rockledgemanor.com* ⇌*3 rooms*
⌂*In-room: no phone, Wi-Fi. In-hotel: no elevator, public Wi-Fi, no
kids under 11, no-smoking rooms* ▤*AE, MC, V* ▯❙*CP.*

HAMPTON BEACH

⟳ *8 mi south of Rye.*

Hampton Beach, from Route 27 to where Route 1A crosses the cause-
way, is an authentic seaside amusement center—the domain of fried-
dough stands, loud music, arcade games, palm readers, parasailing, and
bronzed bodies. An estimated 150,000 people visit the town and its
free public beach on the Fourth of July, and it draws plenty of people
until late September, when things close up. The 3-mi boardwalk, where
kids can play games and see how saltwater taffy is made, looks like a
leftover from the 1940s; in fact, the whole community remains remark-
ably free of modern franchises. Free outdoor concerts are held on many
a summer evening, and once a week there's a fireworks display. Tal-
ent shows and karaoke performances take place in the Seashell Stage,
right on the beach. Each August, locals hold a children's festival, and
they celebrate the end of the season with a huge seafood feast on the
weekend after Labor Day.

SPORTS & THE OUTDOORS

BEACHES **Hampton Beach State Park** (✉*Rte. 1A* ☎*603/926–3784*) is a quiet stretch
of sand on the southwestern edge of town at the mouth of the Hampton
River. It has picnic tables, a store (seasonal), parking ($8 on summer
weekends, $5 weekdays in summer, free Nov.–Apr.), and a bathhouse.

FISHING Several companies conduct whale-watching excursions as well as half-
& WHALE- day, full-day, and nighttime cruises. Most leave from the Hampton
WATCHING State Pier on Route 1A. **Al Gauron Deep Sea Fishing** (☎*603/926–2469*)
maintains a fleet of three boats for whale-watching cruises and fishing
charters. **Eastman Fishing Fleet** (✉*Seabrook* ☎*603/474–3461*) offers

whale-watching and fishing cruises, with evening and morning charters. **Smith & Gilmore Deep Sea** (☎603/926–3503 *or 877/272–4005*) conducts deep-sea fishing expeditions and whale-watching trips.

NIGHTLIFE

Despite its name, the **Hampton Beach Casino Ballroom** (✉169 *Ocean Blvd.* ☎603/929–4100) isn't a gambling establishment but rather a late-19th-century, 2,000-seat performance venue that has hosted everyone from Janis Joplin to Jerry Seinfeld, George Carlin, and B. B. King. Performances are scheduled weekly from April through October.

WHERE TO EAT & STAY

$$–$$$ ✕**Ron's Landing at Rocky Bend.** Amid the motels lining Ocean Boule-
AMERICAN   vard is this casually elegant restaurant. Pan-seared ahi over mixed greens with a Thai peanut dressing makes a tempting starter. For an entrée, try the oven-roasted salmon with a hoisin (soybeans, garlic, and chili peppers) glaze, a Frangelico cream sauce, slivered almonds, and sliced apple or the baked haddock stuffed with scallops and lobster and served with lemon-dill butter. From many tables you can enjoy a sweeping Atlantic view. Brunch is served on Sunday. ✉379 *Ocean Blvd.* ☎603/929–2122 ▤*AE, D, DC, MC, V* ☉*No lunch.*

$ ▥**Ashworth by the Sea.** You'll be surprised how contemporary this center-of-the-action, across-from-the-beach hotel is, especially after you see its classic old neon sign outside. From the cheery modern lobby to rooms with new carpeting and furniture, this Hampton Beach classic hotel is clean and up-to-the-minute. Most rooms have decks, but request a beachside room for an ocean view; otherwise you'll look out onto the pool or street. The Sand Bar, on the roof deck between the hotel's two buildings, is a great place to watch the town's fireworks each Wednesday, and have food and drinks. **Pros:** center-of-town location and across from beach, open all year. **Cons:** breakfast not included, very busy. ✉295 *Ocean Blvd.* ☎603/926–6762 *or 800/345–6736* ⊕*www.ashworthhotel.com* ↔*105 rooms* △*In-room: Wi-Fi. In-hotel: 3 restaurants, room service, pool, laundry service, public Wi-Fi, no-smoking rooms* ▤*AE, D, DC, MC, V.*

EN ROUTE   At the 400-acre **Applecrest Farm Orchards** you can pick your own apples and berries or buy fresh fruit pies and cookies. Fall brings cider pressing, hay rides, pumpkins, and music on weekends. In winter a cross-country ski trail traverses the orchard. Author John Irving worked here as a teenager, his experiences inspiring the book *The Cider House Rules.* ✉133 *Rte. 88, Hampton Falls* ☎603/926–3721 ⊕*www.applecrest.com* ☉*Daily 9–5.*

EXETER

★   *9 mi northwest of Hampton, 52 mi north of Boston, 47 mi southeast of Concord.*

In the center of Exeter, contemporary shops mix well the esteemed Phillips Exeter Academy, which opened in 1783.

During the Revolutionary War, Exeter was the state capital, and it was here amid intense patriotic fervor that the first state constitution and the first Declaration of Independence from Great Britain were put to paper. These days Exeter shares more in appearance and personality with Boston's blue-blooded satellite communities than the rest of New Hampshire—indeed, plenty of locals commute to Beantown. There are a handful of cheerful cafés and coffeehouses in the center of town, making it a nice spot for a snack break.

WHAT TO SEE

American Independence Museum. Adjacent to Phillips Exeter Academy in the Ladd-Gilman House, this museum celebrates the birth of the nation. The story unfolds during the course of a guided tour focusing on the Gilman family, who lived in the house during the Revolutionary era. See drafts of the U.S. Constitution and the first Purple Heart as well as letters and documents written by George Washington and the household furnishings of John Taylor Gilman, one of New Hampshire's early governors. In July the museum hosts the American Independence Festival. ⊠*1 Governor's La.* ☎*603/772–2622* ⊕*www.independence museum.org* ⊠*$5* ☉*Mid-May–Oct., Wed.–Sat. 10–4 (last tour at 3).*

Phillips Exeter Academy. Above all else, the town is energized by the faculty and 1,000 high school students of the Phillips Exeter Academy. The grounds of the Academy's 129 buildings, open to the public, resemble an elite Ivy League university campus. In fact, with over 619 acres, it's bigger than most Ivy schools. The Louis Kahn–designed library contains the largest seconday school book collection in the world. ⊠*20 Main St.* ☎*603/772–4311.*

SHOPPING

A Picture's Worth a Thousand Words (⊠*65 Water St.* ☎*603/778–1991*) stocks antique and contemporary prints, old maps, town histories, and rare books. Prestigious **Exeter Fine Crafts** (⊠*61 Water St.* ☎*603/778–8282*) shows an impressive selection of juried pottery, paintings, jewelry, textiles, glassware, and other fine creations by some of northern New England's top artists.

WHERE TO EAT

¢ **Fodor'sChoice** ★ AMERICAN

✕ **Loaf and Ladle.** There are three components to this extraordinary place: quality, price, and location. The name refers to homemade bread—there are over 30 kinds—and soup—there are over 100 varieties. A bowl of soup, which is a full meal, is $5. It's hard to spend more than that here. Choose a chunk of bread to go with your soup, and take your meal to one of the two decks that hover over the Exeter River, or one of the cafeteria-style tables, and enjoy. It's simplicity. It's a masterpiece. ⊠*9 Water St.* ☎*603/778–8955* ⊘*Reservations not accepted* ☐*AE, D, DC, MC, V.*

$$–$$$ AMERICAN

✕ **Tavern at River's Edge.** A convivial downtown gathering spot on the Exeter River, this downstairs tavern pulls in parents of prep-school kids, University of New Hampshire (UNH) students, and suburban yuppies. It may be informal, but the kitchen turns out surprisingly sophisticated chow. You might start with sautéed ragout of portobello and shiitake mushrooms, sun-dried tomatoes, roasted shallots, garlic, and Asiago cheese. Move on to New Zealand rack of lamb with rosemary-port demi-glace and minted risotto. In the bar, lighter fare is served daily 3–10. ⊠*163 Water St.* ☎*603/772–7393* ⊟*AE, D, DC, MC, V* ⊗*No lunch.*

WHERE TO STAY

$$ 🖭**The Exeter Inn.** This elegant brick Georgian-style inn on the Phillips
★ Exeter Academy campus has been the choice of visiting parents since it opened in the 1930s. After a complete overhaul, completed in the spring of 2008, the place looks better than ever. Rooms have a clubby Ralph Lauren design, with striped wallpapers, 10-inch pillowtop mattresses, and flat-screen TVs. There's a good lounge and restaurant serving three meals a day. **Pros:** contemporary, well-designed, clean rooms; near Academy. **Cons:** not close to town shops. ⊠*90 Front St.* ☎*603/772–5901 or 800/782–8444* ⊕*www.theexeterinn.com* ☞*41 rooms, 5 suites* ⚘*In-room: Wi-Fi. In-hotel: restaurant, room service, bar, gym, laundry service, public Wi-Fi, no-smoking rooms* ⊟*AE, D, DC, MC, V.*

$$ 🖭**Inn by the Bandstand.** If you're visiting someone at the academy and
★ want to stay in a B&B, you're bound to love this place smack dab in the heart of town. Rooms are individually furnished—in the extreme. One might be floral Victorian. Another might be the Lakeheath Lodge, which takes a rustic outdoorsy approach, with exposed ceiling beams and antlers over the brick fireplace and pine strung over the headboard. Pillows are piled in profusion atop the Ralph Lauren sheets. Character and comfort continue in all rooms, with crystal decanters of sherry. It's one of the best B&Bs in the state. Note that breakfast is served at one set time: 8:30. **Pros:** perfect location in town, richly furnished rooms. **Cons:** early breakfast. ⊠*4 Front St.* ☎*603/772–6352 or 877/239–3837* ⊕*www.innbythebandstand.com* ☞*7 rooms, 2 suites* ⚘*In-room: refrigerator, Wi-Fi. In-hotel: room service, no elevator, public Wi-Fi, no-smoking rooms* ⊟*AE, D, MC, V* ⭐*BP.*

DURHAM

12 mi north of Exeter, 11 mi northwest of Portsmouth.

Settled in 1635 and the home of General John Sullivan, a Revolutionary War hero and three-time New Hampshire governor, Durham was where Sullivan and his band of rebel patriots stored the gunpowder they captured from Ft. William and Mary in New Castle. Easy access to Great Bay via the Oyster River made Durham a maritime hub in the 19th century. Among the lures today are the water, farms that welcome visitors, and the University of New Hampshire (UNH), which occupies much of the town's center.

WHAT TO SEE

Little Bay Buffalo Company. Visitors cannot roam the range here, but the several dozen American bison ranging here are visible from an observation area and the parking lot. The store on the property sells bison-related gifts and top-quality bison meat. ✉ *50 Langley Rd.* ☎ *603/868–3300* ⊙ *Store Tues.–Sun. 10–5.*

SPORTS & THE OUTDOORS

You can hike several trails or picnic at 130-acre **Wagon Hill Farm** (✉ *U. S. 4 across from Emery Farm* ☎ *No phone*), overlooking the Oyster River. The old farm wagon on the top of a hill is one of the most-photographed sights in New England. Park next to the farmhouse and follow walking trails to the wagon and through the woods to the picnic area by the water. Sledding and cross-country skiing are winter activities.

SHOPPING

Emery Farm. In the same family for 11 generations, Emery Farm sells fruits and vegetables in summer (including pick-your-own raspberries, strawberries, and blueberries), pumpkins in fall, and Christmas trees in December. The farm shop carries breads, pies, and local crafts. Children can pet the resident goats and sheep and attend the storytelling events that are often held on Tuesday mornings in July and August. ✉ *U.S. 4, 1.5 mi east of Rte. 108* ☎ *603/742–8495* ⊙ *Late Apr.–Dec., daily 9–6.*

NIGHTLIFE & THE ARTS

NIGHTLIFE Students and local yupsters head to the **Stone Church** (✉ *5 Granite St., Newmarket* ☎ *603/659–6321*)—in an authentic 1835 former Methodist church—to listen to live rock, jazz, blues, and folk. The restaurant on the premises serves dinner Wednesday through Sunday.

THE ARTS The **Celebrity Series** (☎ *603/862–2290* ⊕ *www.unh.edu/celebrity*) at UNH brings music, theater, and dance to several venues. The **UNH Department of Theater and Dance** (✉ *Paul Creative Arts Center, 30 College Rd.* ☎ *603/862–2919*) produces a variety of shows. UNH's **Whittemore Center Arena** (✉ *128 Main St.* ☎ *603/862–4000* ⊕ *www. whittemorecenter.com*) hosts everything from Boston Pops concerts to home shows, plus college sports.

WHERE TO EAT & STAY

$$–$$$ ✕ **ffrost Sawyer Tavern.** That's not a typo, but an attempt to duplicate a ★ quirk in obsolete spelling (the way capital letters used to be designated) SEAFOOD/ of an old resident of this hilltop house. The eccentric stone basement AMERICAN tavern of this hilltop house has its original beams, from which hang collections of mugs, hats and—no way around it—bedpans. There's a terrific old bar. Choose from fine fare like grilled sea scallops or salmon and lobster seared in a tomato, lime, and coconut curry sauce; or lighter items like burgers, pizza, and fish-and-chips. ✉ *17 Newmarket Rd.* ☎ *603/868–7800* ▭ *AE, D, MC, V* ⊙ *No lunch.*

$$$ 🛏 **Three Chimneys Inn.** This stately yellow structure has graced a hill overlooking the Oyster River since 1649. Rooms in the house and the 1795 barn are named after plants from the gardens and filled with Georgian- and Federal-style antiques and reproductions, canopy or four-poster beds with Edwardian drapes, and Oriental rugs; half have fireplaces. There are two restaurants here: a formal dining room, and the ffrost Sawyer, quirky as the name implies. There's an afternoon wine and cheese social. **Pros:** intimate inn experience. **Cons:** have to

walk or drive into town. ✉17 Newmarket Rd. ☎603/868–7800 or 888/399–9777 ⊕www.threechimneysinn.com ⇗23 rooms ⚿In-room: Wi-Fi. In-hotel: 2 restaurants, room service, bar, no elevator, public Wi-Fi, some pets allowed, no-smoking rooms ▤AE, D, MC, V ❍❙BP.

LAKES REGION

Lake Winnipesaukee, an American Indian name for "smile of the great spirit," is the largest of the dozens of lakes scattered across the eastern half of central New Hampshire. With about 240 mi of shoreline full of inlets and coves, it's the largest in the state. Some claim Winnipesaukee has an island for each day of the year—the total, though impressive, falls well short: 274.

In contrast to Winnipesaukee, which bustles all summer long, is the more secluded Squam Lake. Its tranquillity is what no doubt attracted the producers of On Golden Pond; several scenes of the Oscar-winning film were shot here. Nearby Lake Wentworth is named for the state's first royal governor, who, in building his country manor here, established North America's first summer resort.

Well-preserved Colonial and 19th-century villages are among the region's many landmarks, and you'll find hiking trails, good antiques shops, and myriad water-oriented activities. This section begins at Wolfeboro, and more or less circles Lake Winnipesaukee clockwise, with several side trips.

WOLFEBORO

40 mi northeast of Concord, 49 mi northwest of Portsmouth.

Quietly upscale and decidedly preppy Wolfeboro has been a resort since Royal Governor John Wentworth built his summer home on the shores of Lake Wentworth in 1768. The town bills itself as the oldest summer resort in America. The town center, bursting with tony boutiques, fringes Lake Winnipesaukee and sees about a tenfold population increase each summer. In 2007 French President Nicolas Sarkozy summered here. Mitt Romney is another summer resident. The century-old, white clapboard buildings of the Brewster Academy prep school bracket the town's southern end. Wolfeboro marches to a steady, relaxed beat, comfortable for all ages.

WHAT TO SEE

New Hampshire Boat Museum. Two miles northeast of downtown, this museum celebrates the Lakes Region's boating legacy with displays of vintage Chris-Crafts, Jersey Speed Skiffs, three-point hydroplanes, and other fine watercraft, along with model boats, antique engines, racing photography and trophies, and old-time signs from marinas. ✉397 Center St. ☎603/569–4554 ⊕www.nhbm.org ▣$5 ⊙Memorial Day–Columbus Day, Mon.–Sat. 10–4, Sun. noon–4.

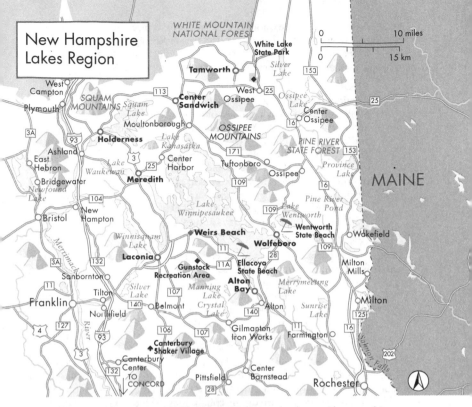

New Hampshire Lakes Region

Wright Museum. Uniforms, vehicles, and other artifacts at this museum illustrate the contributions of those on the home front to America's World War II effort. ✉ *77 Center St.* ☎ *603/569–1212* ⊕ *www.wright-museum.org* ✉ *$6* ⊙ *May–Oct., Mon.–Sat. 10–4, Sun. noon–4; Apr. and Nov., Sat. 10–4, Sun. noon–4.*

NEED A BREAK? Brewster Academy students and summer folk converge upon groovy little Lydia's (✉ *30 N. Main St.* ☎ *603/569–3991*) for espressos, hearty sandwiches, homemade soups, bagels, and desserts. Picking up pastries, cookies, freshly baked breads, and other sweets in the Yum Yum Shop (✉ *16 N. Main St.* ☎ *603/569–1919*) has been a tradition in these parts since 1948—the butter-crunch cookies are highly addictive.

SPORTS & THE OUTDOORS

BEACHES   **Wentworth State Beach** (✉ *Rte. 109* ☎ *603/569–3699* ✉ *$3*) has good swimming, fishing, picnicking areas, ball fields, and a bathhouse.

HIKING   A short (¼-mi) hike to the 100-foot post-and-beam **Abenaki Tower**, followed by a more rigorous climb to the top, rewards you with a vast view of Lake Winnipesaukee and the Ossipee mountain range. The trailhead is a few miles north of town on Route 109.

WATER
SPORTS
Scuba divers can explore a 130-foot-long cruise ship that sank in 30 feet of water off Glendale in 1895. **Dive Winnipesaukee Corp** (⊠4 N. Main St. ☎603/569–8080) runs charters out to wrecks and offers rentals, repairs, scuba sales, and lessons in waterskiing.

SHOPPING

American Home Gallery (⊠49 Center St., Wolfeboro Falls ☎603/569–8989) mixes an amazing array of antiques and housewares in with its architectural elements. You'll find an excellent regional-history section and plenty of children's titles at **Country Bookseller** (⊠23A N. Main St. ☎603/569–6030), Wolfeboro's fine general-interest bookstore. The artisans at **Hampshire Pewter Company** (⊠43 Mill St. ☎603/569–4944 or 800/639–7704 ⊕www.hampshirepewter.com) use 16th-century techniques to make pewter tableware and accessories. Come to shop or tour: free tours are given Memorial Day through Columbus Day at 9:30, 11, 1:30 and 3 most days and by appointment.

WHERE TO EAT

$-$$
ASIAN
✗**East of Suez.** Set in a countrified lodge on the south side of town, this warm and friendly restaurant serves creative Pan-Asian cuisine, with an emphasis on Philippine fare, such as *lumpia* (pork-and-shrimp spring rolls with a sweet-and-sour fruit sauce) and Philippine *pancit canton* (panfried egg noodles with sautéed shrimp and pork and Asian vegetables with a sweet oyster sauce). You can also sample Thai red curries, Japanese tempura, and Korean-style flank steak. ⊠775 S. Main St. ☎603/569–1648 ⊟AE, MC, V ☉Closed Oct.–mid-May.

$-$$
★
SEAFOOD
✗**Wolfetrap Grill and Raw Bar.** The seafood at this festive shanty on Lake Winnipesaukee comes right from the adjacent fish market. You'll find all your favorites here, including a renowned clam boil for one that includes steamers, corn on the cob, onions, baked potatoes, sweet potatoes, sausage, and a hot dog. The raw bar has oysters and clams on the half shell. ⊠19 Bay St. ☎603/569–1047 ⊟AE, D, MC, V ☉Closed Labor Day–Memorial Day.

WHERE TO STAY

$$
★
Topsides B & B. At this stylish retreat, refined rooms subtly convey the allure of a particular region, from coastal France to Martha's Vineyard to Virginia fox-hunting country. Lavish, custom bedding, Persian rugs, marble dressers, and fresh flowers lend an eclectic sophistication to this pale-gray clapboard inn that's steps from downtown shops and restaurants. High-speed wireless, homemade bath amenities, and highly personalized attention complete the experience. **Pros:** great location, clean simple rooms. **Cons:** just continental breakfast. ⊠209 S. Main St. ☎603/569–3834 ⊕www.topsidesbb.com ➠5 rooms ♿In-room: Wi-Fi. In-hotel: no elevator, public Internet, public Wi-Fi, no kids under 12, no-smoking rooms ⊟D, MC, V ◉CP.

$$$
★
Wolfeboro Inn. This inn with a great lakefront location opened in 1812 and has been a perennial favorite. In the second part of 2008 it is poised to take a radical step forward, to become, in fact, the freshest and most stylish hotel in the lake region. Call to find out if the rooms have been renovated yet; if so, and you like a contemporary luxurious boutique look, stay here—there will be nothing like it in the state out-

side of the stylish hotels the same owners have created from classic old properties in Exeter and Concord. **Pros:** lakefront setting, interesting pub, slated for massive renovation. **Cons:** pre-renovation property is tired. ⊠*90 N. Main St.* ☏*603/569–3016 or 800/451–2389* ⊕*www. wolfeboroinn.com* ↵*41 rooms, 3 suites, 1 apartment* ⚲*In-room: Wi-Fi. In-hotel: 2 restaurants, bar, public Internet, public Wi-Fi, no-smoking rooms* ⊟*AE, D, MC, V* ⦿*CP.*

ALTON BAY

3

10 mi southwest of Wolfeboro.

Lake Winnipesaukee's southern shore is alive with visitors from the moment the first flower blooms until the last maple sheds its leaves. Two mountain ridges hold 7 mi of the lake in Alton Bay, which is the name of both the inlet and the town at its tip. Cruise boats dock here, and small planes land here year-round, on both the water and the ice. There's a dance pavilion, along with miniature golf, a public beach, and a Victorian-style bandstand. Mt. Major, 5 mi north of Alton Bay on Route 11, has a 2.5-mi trail with views of Lake Winnipesaukee..

WHERE TO EAT

$$$$ ✕**Crystal Quail.** This 12-table restaurant, inside an 18th-century farm-house, is worth the drive for the sumptuous meals prepared by long-
★ time proprietors Harold and Cynthia Huckaby, who use free-range
AMERICAN meats and mostly organic produce and herbs in their cooking. The prix-fixe contemporary menu changes daily but might include saffron-garlic soup, a house pâté, quenelle-stuffed sole, or goose confit with apples and onions. ⊠*202 Pitman Rd., 12 mi south of Alton Bay, Center Barnstead* ☏*603/269–4151* ⊕*www.crystalquail.com* ⚏*Reservations essential* ⊟*No credit cards* ⛳*BYOB* ⦿*Closed Mon. and Tues. No lunch.*

WEIRS BEACH

☾ *17 mi northwest of Alton Bay.*

Weirs Beach is Lake Winnipesaukee's center for arcade activity. Anyone who loves souvenir shops, fireworks, waterslides, and hordes of children will feel right at home. Cruise boats also depart from here.

WHAT TO SEE

☾ **Funspot.** The mother ship of Lake Winnipesaukee's several giddy family-oriented amusement parks, Funspot claims to be the second-largest arcade in the country, but it's much more than just a video-game room. Here you can work your way through a miniature golf course, a golf driving range, an indoor golf simulator, 20 lanes of bowling, cash bingo, and more than 500 video games. Some outdoor attractions are closed in winter months. ⊠*Rte. 3, Weirs Beach* ☏*603/366–4377* ⊕*www. funspotnh.com* ⦿*Entry free; fee for each activity* ⦿*Mid-June–early Sept., daily 9 AM–midnight; early Sept.–mid-June, Sun.–Thurs. 10–10, Fri. and Sat. 10 AM–11 PM.*

○ **Surf Coaster.** The lake's ultimate water park, Surf Coaster has seven waterslides, a wave pool, and the Barefoot Action Lagoon, a large area for young children. Teams of six can also duke it out in a massive inflatable maze for a game of water tag. ⊠*1085 White Oaks Rd., Weirs Beach* ☎*603/366–5600* ⊕*www.surfcoasterusa.com* ⊠*$25* ⊙*Late June–early Sept., daily 10–6.*

○ **MS Mount Washington.** This 230-foot boat makes two-and-a-half-hour
Fodor'sChoice scenic cruises of Lake Winnipesaukee from Weirs Beach from mid-May
★ to late October, with stops in Wolfeboro, Alton Bay, Center Harbor, and Meredith (you can board at any of these stops). The cruise is a lake tradition. Evening cruises include live music and a buffet dinner. There are nightly music themes, check ahead for your favorites. The same company operates the MV *Sophie C.*, which has been the area's floating post office for more than a century. The boat departs from Weirs Beach with mail and passengers. Since the boat is delivering mail to homes along the shore, you can see areas of the lake not accessible by larger ships. Additionally, you can ride the MV *Doris E.* on one- and two-hour scenic cruises of Meredith Bay and the lake islands throughout summer. ☎*603/366–5531 or 888/843–6686* ⊕*www.cruisenh.com* ⊠*$25* ⊙*Day cruises, departures daily every few hours mid-June–Labor Day. Special cruises, departure times vary.*

★ **Winnipesaukee Scenic Railroad.** The period cars of this railroad carry you along the lakeshore on one- or two-hour rides; boarding is at Weirs Beach or Meredith. Special trips that include dinner are also available, as are foliage trains in fall and special Santa trains in December. ⊠*U. S. 3, Weirs Beach* ☎*603/279–5253 or 603/745–2135* ⊕*www.hoborr. com* ⊠*$9–$71* ⊙*July–mid-Sept., daily; Memorial Day–late June and mid-Sept.–mid-Oct., weekends only. Call for hours.*

SPORTS & THE OUTDOORS

BEACH & **Ellacoya State Beach** (⊠*Rte. 11* ☎*603/293–7821*) covers just 600
BOATING feet along the southwestern shore of Lake Winnipesaukee. In season, there's a bathhouse, picnic tables, and a fee ($3 from mid-May to Labor Day) for parking. **Thurston's Marina** (⊠*U.S. 3 at the bridge, Weirs Beach* ☎*603/366–4811*) rents watercraft such as pontoon boats and powerboats.

GOLF **Pheasant Ridge Golf Club** (⊠*140 Country Club Rd.* ☎*603/524–7808*) has an 18-hole layout with great mountain views. Green fees range from $31 to $40.

SKI AREAS **Gunstock USA.** High above Lake Winnipesaukee, this all-purpose area dates from the 1930s. It once had the country's longest rope tow lift— an advantage that helped local downhill skier and Olympic silver medalist Penny Pitou perfect her craft. Thrill Hill, a snow-tubing park, has 10 runs, multipassenger tubes, and lift service. Clever trail cutting along with grooming and surface sculpting three times daily has made this otherwise pedestrian mountain good for intermediates. That's how most of the 44 trails are rated, with a few more challenging runs as well as designated sections for slow skiers and learners. It's the state's largest night-skiing facility. Gunstock has 30 mi of trails for cross-country skiing and snowshoeing. In summer you'll find a swimming pool, a playground, hiking trails, mountain-bike rentals and trails, a skateboarding-blading park, guided horseback rides, pedal boats, and a campground. ⊠ *Rte. 11A* 🖃 *Box 1307, Laconia 03247* ☎ *603/293–4341 or 800/186 7862* ⊕ *www.gunstock.com.*

SHOPPING

Pepi Herrmann Crystal (⊠ *3 Waterford Pl.* ☎ *603/528–1020*) sells hand-cut crystal chandeliers and stemware. Take a tour and watch artists at work.

NIGHTLIFE & THE ARTS

The **New Hampshire Music Festival** (☎ *603/279–3300* ⊕ *www.nhmf.org*) presents award-winning orchestras from early July to mid-August; concerts occur at the Festival House on Symphony Lane in Center Harbor or at the Silver Cultural Arts Center on Main Street in Plymouth.

LACONIA

4 mi west of Gilford, 27 mi north of Concord.

The arrival in Laconia—then called Meredith Bridge—of the railroad in 1848 turned the once-sleepy hamlet into the Lakes Region's chief manufacturing hub. It acts today as the area's supply depot, a perfect role given its accessibility to both Winnisquam and Winnipesaukee lakes as well as Interstate 93. Come here when you need to find a chain superstore or fast-food restaurant.

WHAT TO SEE

Belknap Mill. The oldest unaltered, brick-built textile mill in the United States (1823), Belknap Mill contains a knitting museum devoted to the textile industry and a year-round cultural center that sponsors concerts, workshops, exhibits, and a lecture series. ⊠ *Mill Plaza, 25 Beacon St. E* ☎ *603/524–8813* ⊕ *www.belknapmill.org* 🎫 *Free* ⊙ *Weekdays 9–5.*

■ OFF THE
BEATEN
PATH

Canterbury Shaker Village. Shaker furniture and inventions are well regarded, and this National Historic Landmark helps illuminate the world of the people who created them. Established as a religious community in 1792, the village flourished in the 1800s and practiced equality of the sexes and races, common ownership, celibacy, and pacifism. The last member of the community passed away in 1992. Shakers invented such household items as the clothespin and the flat broom and were known for the simplicity and integrity of their designs. Engaging 90-minute tours pass through some of the 694-acre property's more than 25 restored buildings, many of them still with original Shaker furnishings, and crafts demonstrations take place daily. The Shaker Table restaurant ($$–$$$$) serves lunch daily and candlelight dinners Thursday–Sunday (reservations essential); the food blends contemporary and traditional Shaker recipes to delicious effect. A large shop sells fine Shaker reproductions. ⊠ *288 Shaker Rd., 15 mi south of Laconia via Rte. 106, Canterbury* ☎ *603/783–9511 or 866/783–9511* ⊕ *www.shakers.org* 🎫 *$15, good for 2 consecutive days* ⊙ *Mid-May–Oct., daily 10–5; Apr., Nov., and Dec., weekends 10–4.*

SPORTS & THE OUTDOORS

Bartlett Beach (✉ *Winnisquam Ave.*) has a playground and picnic area. **Opechee Park** (✉*N. Main St.*) has dressing rooms, a baseball field, tennis courts, and picnic areas.

SHOPPING

The more than 50 stores at the **Tanger Outlet Center** (✉ *120 Laconia Rd., I–93 Exit 20, Tilton* ☎*603/286–7880*) include Brooks Brothers, Eddie Bauer, Coach, and Mikasa.

WHERE TO STAY

$ 📺 **Ferry Point House.** Four miles southwest of Laconia, this home across the street from Lake Winnisquam gives you a quiet retreat with easy access to a private boat house, row boat, dock and a small beach. Built in the 1800s as a summer retreat for the Pillsbury family of baking fame, this red Victorian farmhouse has superb views of the lake. White wicker furniture and hanging baskets of flowers grace the 60-foot veranda, and the gazebo by the water's edge is a pleasant place to lounge and listen for loons. The pretty rooms have Victorian-style wallpaper. A parlor rooms has decantered sherry. **Pros:** affordable, lovely setting. **Cons:** have to cross street to lake, best for relaxed do-it-yourselfers. ✉*100 Lower Bay Rd., Sanbornton* ☎*603/524–0087* ⊕*www.ferrypointhouse.com* ⇆*9 rooms* ⚄*In-room: no a/c (some), no phone, no TV, Wi-Fi. In-hotel: water sports, no elevator, public Wi-Fi, no kids under 11, no-smoking rooms* ⊟*No credit cards* ⊘*Closed Dec. and Jan.* ⦿*BP.*

MEREDITH

11 mi north of Laconia.

Meredith, a onetime workaday mill town on U.S. 3 at Lake Winnipesaukee's western end, has watched its fortunes change for the better over the past decade or so. The opening of the Inns at Mills Falls has attracted hundreds of visitors, and crafts shops and art galleries have sprung up. You can pick up area information at a kiosk across from the town docks.

SPORTS & THE OUTDOORS

Red Hill, a hiking trail on Bean Road off Route 25, northeast of Center Harbor and about 7 mi northeast of Meredith, really does turn red in autumn. The reward at the end of the route is a view of Squam Lake and the mountains.

BOATING   Meredith is near the quaint village of Center Harbor, another boating hub that's in the middle of three bays at the northern end of Lake Winnipesaukee. **Meredith Marina and Boating Center** (✉*2 Bayshore Dr.* ☎*603/279–7921*) rents powerboats. **Wild Meadow Canoes & Kayaks** (✉*Rte. 25, between Center Harbor and Moultonboro* ☎*603/253–7536 or 800/427–7536*) has canoes and kayaks for rent.

SHOPPING

Annalee's Outlet Store (⊠*Annalee Pl., off Rte. 104* ☎*603/707–5388* ⊕*www.annalee.com* ☉*Daily 10–6*) sells, at a discount, the seasonal decorations and dolls of the Annalee company, famous for its felt dolls that Annalee Davis Thorndike began making here in 1933. The former museum is now closed. About 170 dealers operate out of the three-floor **Burlwood Antique Center** (⊠*U.S. 3* ☎*603/279–6387*), open May–October. **Keepsake Quilting & Country Pleasures** (⊠*Senter's Marketplace, Rte. 25B, Center Harbor, 5 mi northeast of Meredith* ☎*603/253–4026 or 800/965–9456*), reputedly America's largest quilt shop, contains 5,000 bolts of fabric, hundreds of quilting books, and countless supplies, as well as handmade quilts.

★ The **Meredith League of New Hampshire Craftsmen** (⊠*279 U.S. 3, ½ mi north of Rte. 104* ☎*603/279–7920*) sells works by area artisans. It's next to Church Landing. **Mill Falls Marketplace** (⊠*U.S. 3 at Rte. 25* ☎*603/279–7006*), part of the Inns at Mills Falls, contains shops with clothing, gifts, and books set around the old falls that run through it. The **Old Print Barn** (⊠*343 Winona Rd., New Hampton* ☎*603/279–6479*) carries rare prints—Currier & Ives, antique botanicals, and more—from around the world.

THE ARTS

The **Lakes Region Summer Theatre** (⊠*Interlakes Auditorium, Rte. 25* ☎*603/279–9933*) presents Broadway musicals during its 10-week season of summer stock.

WHERE TO EAT & STAY

$$–$$$
AMERICAN
✕**Lakehouse Grille.** With perhaps the best lake views of any restaurant in the region, this restaurant might be forgiven for ambitious dishes that fall short of being really good. Come here to be near the lake, especially in the convivial bar area, and you'll leave home quite happy. The setting is an upscale lodge, at Church Landing, within one of the Mill Falls hotels. The best dishes are old reliables like steak, ribs, and little pizzas. Breakfast is served daily. ⊠*Church Landing* ☎*603/279–5221* ⊟*AE, D, MC, V.*

$$–$$$
AMERICAN
✕**Mame's.** This 1820s tavern, once the home of the village doctor, now contains a warren of convivial dining rooms with exposed-brick walls, wooden beams, and wide-plank floors. Expect mostly American standbys of the fish, steak, veal, and chicken variety, including very good seafood Diane (shrimp, scallops, and salmon sautéed in butter and white wine); the mud pie is highly recommended. A tavern upstairs serves a cheaper menu. ⊠*8 Plymouth St.* ☎*603/279–4631* ⊟*AE, D, MC, V.*

$$
Fodor'sChoice
★
⌸**Inns and Spa at Mill Falls.** There are four separate hotels here—two new properties on the shore Lake Winnipesaukee, and two connected to a 19th-century mill (now a lively shopping area) and its roaring fall. Combined, the inns have all the amenities of a full resort as well as warmth and personality. The central-most Inn at Mills Falls, which adjoins an 18-shop market, has a pool and 54 spacious rooms. The lakefront Inn at Bay Point has 24 rooms—most with balconies, some with fireplaces. The 23 rooms at the lake-view Chase House at Mill Falls all have fireplaces; some have balconies. The star of the show is

camp-posh Church Landing, a dramatic lakefront lodge where most rooms have expansive decks with terrific water views. The Cascade Spa is one of the poshest in the state. A great heated pool crosses from indoors to outdoors. **Pros:** many lodging choices and prices, lakefront rooms available, fun environment. **Cons:** expensive; two buildings are not on lakefront. ✉ *312 Daniel Webster Hwy. (Rte 3), at Rte. 25* ☎ *603/279–7006 or 800/622–6455* 🌐 *www.millfalls.com* *148 rooms, 8 suites* *In-hotel: 5 restaurants, room service, bar, pools, gym, spa, water sports, laundry service, public Internet, public Wi-Fi, no-smoking rooms* *AE, D, DC, MC, V* *CP.*

HOLDERNESS

8 mi southeast of Plymouth, 8 mi northwest of Meredith.

Routes 25B and 25 lead to the small prim town of Holderness, between Squam and Little Squam lakes. *On Golden Pond,* starring Katharine Hepburn and Henry Fonda, was filmed on Squam, whose quiet beauty attracts nature lovers.

WHAT TO SEE

Fodor's Choice ★ **Squam Lakes Natural Science Center.** Trails on this 200-acre property include a ¾-mi path that passes black bears, bobcats, otters, and other native wildlife in trailside enclosures. Educational events such as the "Up Close to Animals" series in July and August also allow you to study a species in an intimate setting. The Gordon Children's Activity Center has interactive exhibits. A ride on a 28-foot pontoon boat is the best way to tour the lake: naturalists explain the science of the lake and describe the animals that make their home here. You'll learn a ton, too, about loon behavior and communication. ✉ *Rte. 113* ☎ *603/968–7194* 🌐 *www.nhnature.org* *Center $13. Boat tour $20. Combination ticket $30* *May–Oct., daily 9:30–4:30 (last entry at 3:30).*

WHERE TO EAT

$$$ AMERICAN **Manor on Golden Pond.** Leaded glass panes and wood paneling set the decidedly romantic and warm tone at this wonderful small dining room on a hill overlooking Squam Lake. The main dining room is in the manor's original billiard room and features the 1902 woodwork. An amuse-bouche of salmon tartare might start things off. A New Hampshire gumbo of duck breast and wild boar sausage in a spicy Cajun broth is unexpected and delicious, and quail and monkfish are very well prepared. A fabulous seven-course tasting menu is $75. ✉ *U. S. 3 and Shepard Hill Rd.* ☎ *603/968–3348* *Reservations required* *AE, D, MC, V.*

$–$$ AMERICAN **Walter's Basin.** A former bowling alley in the heart of Holderness makes an unlikely but charming setting for meals overlooking gentle Little Squam Lake—local boaters dock right beneath the dining room. Among the specialties on this seafood-intensive menu are crostini topped with lobster and fontina cheese, and almond-crusted rainbow trout with hazelnut beurre blanc. Burgers and sandwiches are served in the adjoining tavern. ✉ *15 Main St. (U.S. 3)* ☎ *603/968–4412* *AE, D, MC, V* *Closed Mon. and Tues.*

WHERE TO STAY

$$ **Glynn House Inn.** Jim and Gay Dunlop run this swank, three-story, 1890s Queen Anne–style Victorian with a turret and wraparound porch and, next door, a handsome 1920s carriage house. Expect the best in New England B&B comforts: plush beds, flat-screen TVs, free wine and cheese, and attentive service. Twelve of the 13 rooms have fireplaces; the bi-level Honeymoon Suite has a whirlpool tub and fireplace downstairs and a four-poster bed and skylights above. Breakfast usually includes freshly baked strudel. Squam Lake is minutes away. **Pros:** luxurious, well run B&B; clean, well-equipped; social atmosphere. **Cons:** not much to do in town of Ashland (though the charm in these parts is really the lake and outdoor activities). ⊠ *59 Highland St., Ashland 03217* ☎ *603/968–3775 or 800/637–9599* ⊕ *www.glynnhouse. com* ⇨ *5 rooms, 8 suites* ♿ *In-room: DVD, Wi-Fi. In-hotel: no-smoking rooms, public Internet, public Wi-Fi, some pets allowed, no kids under 12, no-smoking rooms* ▤ *MC, V* ⦿ *BP.*

$$ **Inn on Golden Pond.** Sweet-as-pie Bill and Bonnie Webb run this comfortable and informal B&B at a slight walk from the lake. Your hosts will provide walking trail maps to the private corners of the lake. In the living room you'll see maps pinned with the origin of guests, who come from all over (especially New York City and Boston). Rooms have hardwood floors, braided rugs, comfortable reading chairs, and country quilt bedspreads and curtains. The homemade jam at breakfast is made from rhubarb grown on the property. **Pros:** friendly innkeepers, very clean rooms and common spaces. **Cons:** 5-minute walk to access lake, not luxurious. ⊠ *Rte. 3* ☎ *603/968–7269* ⊕ *www.innongolden pond.com* ⇨ *6 rooms, 2 suites* ♿ *In-room: no phone, no TV, Wi-Fi. In-hotel: no elevator, public Internet, public Wi-Fi, no kids under 12, no-smoking rooms* ▤ *AE, D, MC, V* ⦿ *BP.*

$$$
Fodor's Choice
★
The Manor on Golden Pond. A name like that is a lot to live up to. Happily, the Manor is the most charming inn in the Lakes Region. Stroll down to the sandy private beach for a dip in the lake or to paddle their canoe for a bit—this is the only inn with private access to Squam Lake, though you'll need to walk a few minutes to get it. Back in the stately stucco-and-shingle inn, innkeeper and owners Brian and Mary Ellen Shields make sure you're comfortable. The house sits on a slight rise overlooking Squam Lake, on 15 acres of towering pines and hardwood trees. You can sit on the lawn in one of the Adirondack chairs, gazing out at the lake. Rooms in this house carry out a British country theme, most with wood-burning fireplaces and more than half with double whirlpool tubs. Canopy beds, vintage blanket chests, and tartan fabrics fill the sumptuous bedchambers. The restaurant is terrific, and the Three Cock Pub is endearing. There's a small spa, and afternoon tea is served in the library. **Pros:** wood fireplaces, private boathouse with free canoes and paddleboats, private lake access, great food, great hosts. **Cons:** expensive. ⊠ *U.S. 3 and Shepard Hill Rd. 03245* ☎ *603/968–3348 or 800/545–2141* ⊕ *www.manorongoldenpond.com* ⇨ *22 rooms, 2 suites, 1 cottage* ♿ *In-room: VCR, Wi-Fi. In-hotel: 2 restaurants, room service, bar, tennis court, pool, spa, water sports, no elevator, laundry service, public Internet, public Wi-Fi, no kids under 12, no-smoking rooms* ▤ *AE, D, MC, V* ⦿ *BP.*

CENTER SANDWICH

★ *12 mi northeast of Holderness.*

With Squam Lake to the west and the Sandwich Mountains to the north, Center Sandwich claims one of the prettiest settings of any Lakes Region community. So appealing are the town and its views that John Greenleaf Whittier used the Bearcamp River as the inspiration for his poem "Sunset on the Bearcamp." The town attracts artisans—crafts shops abound among its clutch of charming 18th- and 19th-century buildings.

WHAT TO SEE

Castle in the Clouds. This wonderful mountaintop estate was built in 1913–1914 without nails. The elaborate mansion has 16 rooms, eight bathrooms, and doors made of lead. Construction began in 1911 and continued for three years. Owner Thomas Gustave Plant spent $7 million, the bulk of his fortune, on this project and died penniless in 1946. A tour includes the mansion and the Castle Springs springwater facility on this 5,200-acre property overlooking Lake Winnepesaukee; there's also hiking and pony and horseback rides. ⊠ *Rte. 171, Moultonborough* ☎ *603/476–2352 or 800/729–2468* ⊕ *www.castleintheclouds. org* ⊑ *$10* ☉ *Weekends mid-May–early June; early June to mid-Oct., daily 10–4:30.*

SPORTS & THE OUTDOORS

The **Loon Center** at the **Frederick and Paula Anna Markus Wildlife Sanctuary** is the headquarters of the Loon Preservation Committee, an Audubon Society project. The loon, recognizable for its eerie calls and striking black-and-white coloring, resides on many New Hampshire lakes but is threatened by boat traffic, poor water quality, and habitat loss. Besides the changing exhibits about the birds, two trails wind through the 200-acre property: vantage points on the Loon Nest Trail overlook the spot resident loons sometimes occupy in late spring and summer. ⊠ *Lee's Mills Rd.* ☎ *603/476–5666* ⊕ *www.loon.org* ⊑ *Free* ☉ *Mon.–Sat. 9–5 early Oct.–June; daily 9–5 July–Columbus Day.*

SHOPPING

The **Old Country Store and Museum** (⊠ *Moultonborough Corner, 5 mi south of Center Sandwich* ☎ *603/476–5750*) has been selling maple products, cheeses aged on site, penny candy, and other items since 1781. Much of the equipment still used in the store is antique, and the museum (free) displays old farming and forging tools.

WHERE TO EAT

$–$$ ✕ **Corner House Inn.** This restaurant, in a converted barn adorned with
AMERICAN   local arts and crafts, serves classic American fare. Before you get to the white-chocolate cheesecake with key-lime filling, try the chef's lobster-and-mushroom bisque or tasty garlic-and-horseradish-crusted rack of lamb. There's storytelling Thursday evening. ⊠ *Rtes. 109 and 113* ☎ *603/284–6219* ⊟ *AE, MC, V* ☉ *No lunch Nov.–May.*

$$–$$$ ✕ **The Woodshed.** Farm implements and antiques hang on the walls of
AMERICAN   this enchanting, romantic 1860 barn. The fare is mostly traditional

New England—sea scallops baked in butter and lamb chops with mint sauce—but with some occasional surprises, such as Cajun-blackened pork tenderloin. Either way, the exceptionally fresh ingredients are sure to please. ✉ *128 Lee Rd., Moultonborough* ☎ *603/476–2311* ▭ *AE, D, DC, MC, V* ⊘ *Closed Mon. No lunch.*

TAMWORTH

13 mi east of Center Sandwich, 20 mi southwest of North Conway.

President Grover Cleveland summered in what remains a village of almost unreal quaintness—it's equally photogenic in verdant summer, during the fall foliage season, or under a blanket of winter snow. Cleveland's son, Francis, returned to stay and founded the acclaimed Barnstormers Theatre in 1931, one of America's first summer theaters, and one that continues to this day. Tamworth has a clutch of villages within its borders. At one of them—Chocorua—the view through the birches of Chocorua Lake has been so often photographed that you may experience déjà vu.

WHAT TO SEE

Remick Country Doctor Museum and Farm. For 99 years—from 1894 to 1993, Dr. Edwin Crafts Remick and his father provided medical services to the Tamworth area and operated a family farm. After he died, these two houses were turned into the Remick Country Doctor Museum and Farm. The exhibits focus on the life of a country doctor and on the activities of the still-working farm. You can tour the farm daily from July to October; during those months there's a daily historic activity, like candle making, at 12:30. The second floor of the house has been kept as it was when Remnick died about 15 years ago—and it's a great way to peer in to the life of a true Tamworth townsman. ✉ *58 Cleveland Hill Rd.* ☎ *603/323–7591 or 800/686–6117* ⊕ *www.remickmuseum.org* ▭ *$3* ⊘ *Nov.–June, weekdays 10–4; July–Oct., Mon.–Sat. 10–4.*

SPORTS & THE OUTDOORS

PARK **White Lake State Park.** The 72-acre stand of native pitch pine here is a National Natural Landmark. The park has hiking trails, a sandy beach, trout fishing, canoe rentals, two camping areas, a picnic area, and swimming. ✉ *Rte. 16, Tamworth* ☎ *603/323–7350.*

SHOPPING

The many rooms with themes—Christmas, bridal, and children's, among them—at the **Chocorua Dam Ice Cream & Gift Shop** (✉ *Rte. 16, Chocorua* ☎ *603/323–8745*) contain handcrafted items. When you've finished shopping, try the ice cream, coffee, or tea and scones.

NIGHTLIFE & THE ARTS

The **Arts Council of Tamworth** (☎ *603/323–8104* ⊕ *www.artstamworth. org*) produces concerts—soloists, string quartets, revues, children's programs—from September through June and an arts show in late July. **Barnstormers Summer Theatre** (✉ *Main St.* ☎ *603/323–8500* ⊕ *www.*

barnstormerstheatre.com) has performances in July and August. The box office opens in June.

WHERE TO EAT & STAY

¢–$

SEAFOOD

✕ **Jake's Seafood.** Oars and nautical trappings adorn the wood-paneled walls at this stop between West and Center Ossipee, about 8 mi southeast of Tamworth. The kitchen serves some of eastern New Hampshire's freshest and tastiest seafood, notably lobster pie, fried clams, and seafood casserole; other choices include steak, ribs, and chicken dishes. ⊠*2055 Rte. 16* ☎*603/539–2805* ▭*D, MC, V* ☉*Closed Mon.–Wed.*

¢–$

★

SOUTHERN

✕ **Yankee Smokehouse.** Need a rib fix? This down-home barbecue joint's logo depicting two happy pigs foreshadows the gleeful enthusiasm with which patrons dive into the hefty sandwiches of sliced pork and smoked chicken and immense platters of baby back ribs and smoked sliced beef. Ample sides of slaw, beans, fries, and garlic toast complement the hearty fare. Born-and-bred Southerners have been known to come away impressed. ⊠*Rtes. 16 and 25, about 5 mi southeast of Tamworth* ☎*603/539–7427* ▭*MC, V.*

$

★

▥ **Lazy Dog Inn.** If you travel with your dog, you've just found your new favorite hotel. What began as a stagecoach stop has been operating as an inn almost continuously since 1845. And when Laura and Steven Sousa took over earlier this decade, they converted the inn to a über-doggie friendly B&B. The barn became a "doggie lodge" with a number of runs, a canine lullaby CD plays, and the innkeepers care for the dogs during the day while guests explore the Lakes Region or the White Mountains. It's an exceptional niche, but it's not done at the expense of the rooms, which are the cleanest and best furnished within miles. The lodging rate includes dog care. **Pros:** mega pet friendly, super clean. **Cons:** some rooms share bath. ⊠*Rte. 16, Box 395, Chocorua 03817* ☎*603/323–8350 or 888/323–8350* ⊕*www.lazydoginn.com* ➟*6 rooms, 3 with bath* ♿*In-room: no phone, VCR, Wi-Fi. In-hotel: gym, no elevator, public Wi-Fi, some pets allowed, no kids under 14, no-smoking rooms* ▭*D, MC, V* ⦿*BP.*

THE WHITE MOUNTAINS

Sailors approaching East Coast harbors frequently mistake the pale peaks of the White Mountains—the highest range in the northeastern United States—for clouds. It was 1642 when explorer Darby Field could no longer contain his curiosity about one mountain in particular. He set off from his Exeter homestead and became the first man to climb what would eventually be called Mt. Washington. The 6,288-foot peak must have presented Field with formidable obstacles—its summit claims the highest wind velocity ever recorded and can see snow every month of the year.

Since Field's climb, curiosity about the mountains has not abated. Today an auto road and a cog railway lead to the top of Mt. Washington, and people come here by the tens of thousands to hike and climb, to photograph the vistas, and to ski. The peak is part of the Presidential

Range, whose other peaks are also named after early presidents, and part of the White Mountain National Forest, whose roughly 770,000 acres extend from northern New Hampshire into southwestern Maine. Among the forest's scenic notches (deep mountain passes) are Pinkham, Kinsman, Franconia, and Crawford.

This section begins in Waterville Valley, off Interstate 93, and continues to North Woodstock. It then follows portions of the White Mountains Trail, a 100-mi loop designated as a National Scenic & Cultural Byway.

WATERVILLE VALLEY

60 mi north of Concord.

The first visitors began arriving in Waterville Valley in 1835. A 10-mi-long cul-de-sac cut by one of New England's several Mad rivers and circled by mountains, the valley was first a summer resort and then more of a ski area. Although it's now a year-round getaway, it still has a small-town charm. There are inns, condos, restaurants, shops, conference facilities, a grocery store, and a post office.

SPORTS & THE OUTDOORS

The **White Mountain Athletic Club** (⊠ *Rte. 49* ☎ *603/236–8303*) has tennis, racquetball, and squash as well as a 25-meter indoor pool, a jogging track, exercise equipment, whirlpools, saunas, steam rooms, and a games room. The club is free to guests of many area lodgings.

SKI AREAS **Waterville Valley.** Former U.S. ski-team star Tom Corcoran designed this family oriented resort. The lodgings and various amenities are about 1 mi from the slopes, but a shuttle renders a car unnecessary. This ski area has hosted more World Cup races than any other in the East, so most advanced skiers will be challenged. Most of the 52 trails are intermediate: straight down the fall line, wide, and agreeably long. A 7-acre tree-skiing area adds variety. Snowmaking coverage of 100% ensures good skiing even when nature doesn't cooperate. The Waterville Valley cross-country network, with the ski center in the town square, has 65 mi of trails. About two-thirds of them are groomed; the rest are backcountry. ⊠ *1 Ski Area Rd.* ☎ *603/236–8311, 603/236–4144 snow conditions, 800/468–2553 lodging* ⊕ *www.waterville.com.*

WHERE TO STAY

$$–$$$ ⊞ **Black Bear Lodge.** This family-oriented property has one-bedroom suites that sleep up to six and have full kitchens. Each unit is individually owned and decorated. Children's movies are shown at night in season, and there's bus service to the slopes. Guests can use the White Mountain Athletic Club. There's a small heated pool and hot tub. **Pros:** affordable. **Cons:** basic in its decor and services. ⊠ *3 Village Rd* ☎ *603/236–4501 or 800/349–2327* ⊕ *www.black-bear-lodge.com* ⊷ *107 suites* ⊘ *In-room: no a/c (some), kitchen. In-hotel: pool, gym, public Internet, no-smoking rooms* ⊟ *AE, D, MC, V.*

$$$$ ⊞ **Golden Eagle Lodge.** Waterville's premier condominium property— with its steep roof punctuated by dozens of gabled dormers—recalls

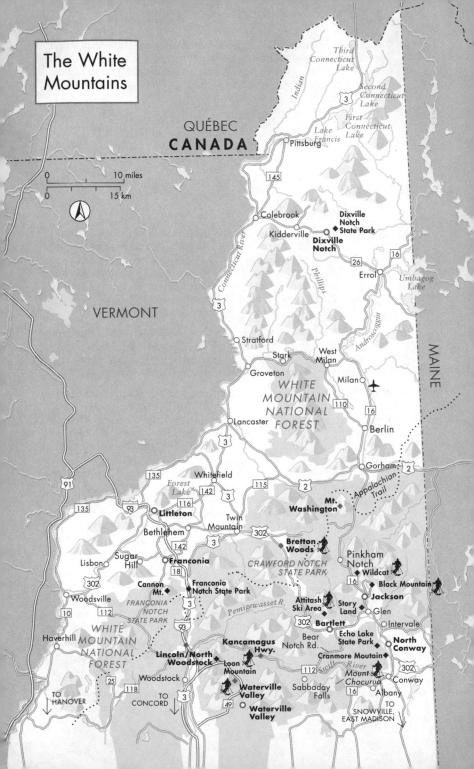

the grand hotels of an earlier era. Rooms, however, are contemporary with upscale light-wood furniture and well-equipped kitchens; many have views of the surrounding peaks. The full-service complex has a two-story lobby and a capable front-desk staff. Guests have access to the White Mountain Athletic Club. **Pros:** most reliable accommodation in town. **Cons:** somewhat bland architecture and decor. ⊠*6 Snow's Brook Rd., Box 495, 03215* ☎*603/236–4600 or 888/703–2453* ⊕*www.goldeneaglelodge.com* ⟿*139 condominiums* ⌂*In-room: kitchen, Wi-Fi. In-hotel: pool, public Internet, public Wi-Fi, laundry service, laundry facilities, no-smoking rooms* ▭*AE, D, DC, MC, V.*

$–$$ 🏨**Snowy Owl Inn.** You're treated to afternoon wine and cheese in the atrium lobby, which has a three-story fieldstone fireplace and many prints and watercolors of snowy owls. The fourth-floor bunk-bed lofts are ideal for families; first-floor rooms are suitable for couples seeking a quiet getaway. Four restaurants are within walking distance. Guests have access to the White Mountain Athletic Club. **Pros:** affordable. **Cons:** bland. ⊠*4 Village Rd., Box 407, 03215* ☎*603/236–8383 or 800/766–9969* ⊕*www.snowyowlinn.com* ⟿*85 rooms* ⌂*In-room: kitchen (some), VCR (some), Wi-Fi. In-hotel: pools, gym, public Internet, public Wi-Fi, no-smoking rooms* ▭*AE, D, DC, MC, V* 🍴*BP.*

LINCOLN/NORTH WOODSTOCK

14 mi northwest of Waterville Valley, 63 mi north of Concord.

These two neighboring towns at the southwestern end of the White Mountains National Forest and one end of the Kancamagus Highway (Route 112), are a lively resort area, especially for Bostonian families who can make an easy day trip straight up Interstate 93 to Exit 32. Festivals, such as the New Hampshire Scottish Highland Games in mid-September, keep Lincoln swarming with people year-round. The town itself is not much of an attraction. Tiny North Woodstock maintains more of a village feel.

WHAT TO SEE

☺ **Clarke's Trading Post.** It's undeniably hokey, but is a sure kids' favorite. It consists of a bear show, half-hour train rides over a 1904 covered bridge, a museum of Americana set inside an 1880s firehouse, a restored gas station filled with antique cars, and a replica of the Old Man of the Mountain that you can climb on. Tour guides tell tall tales and vendors sell popcorn, ice cream, pizza, and other snacks. There's also a mammoth gift shop, penny-candy store, and several other places to buy silly keepsakes. ⊠*U.S. 3, off I–93 (Exit 33), North Lincoln* ☎*603/745–8913* ⊕*www.clarkstradingpost.com* 🎟*$12* ☉*Memorial Day–Columbus Day daily 9–5 (and until 9 PM Sat. July 5–Aug. 16.*

FUN TOUR A ride on the Hobo Railroad yields scenic views of the Pemigewasset River and the White Mountain National Forest. The narrated excursions take 80 minutes. ⊠*Kancamagus Hwy. (Rte. 112), Lincoln* ☎*603/745–2135* ⊕*www. hoborr.com* 🎟*$10* ☉*Late June–early Sept., daily; May–late June and early Sept.–Oct., weekends; call for schedule.*

SPORTS & THE OUTDOORS

At **Whale's Tale Waterpark** (⊠*U.S. 3, I–93 Exit 33, North Lincoln* ☎*603/745–8810* ⊕*www.whalestalewaterpark.net* ⊠*$25* ⊙*Mid-June–Labor Day, daily 10–6*) you can float on an inner tube along a gentle river, careen down one of five water slides, take a trip in a multipassenger tube, or body-surf in the large wave pool. Whale Harbor and Orca Park Play Island contain water activities for small children and toddlers.

At **Lost River Gorge in Kinsman Notch** (⊠*Kancamagus Hwy. [Rte. 112], 6 mi west of North Woodstock* ☎*603/745–8720 or 800/346–3687* ⊕*www.findlostriver.com*) you can hike along the sheer granite river gorge and view such geological wonders as the Guillotine Rock and the Lemon Squeezer or pan for gemstones. A cafeteria, garden, and gift shop round out the amenities. It's open daily from mid-May to mid-October; admission is $10.

Pemi Valley Excursions (⊠*Main St., off I–93 (Exit 32), Lincoln* ☎*603/745–2744* ⊕*www.i93.com/pvsr*) offers a variety of recreational and scenic tours throughout the year. It's one of the best snowmobile outfitters in the region, offering one- to two-hour guided tours and half- and full-day snowmobile rentals. Spring through summer, you can ride horseback along wooded trails and along the Pemigewasset River, enjoy horse-drawn-carriage rides, and embark on moose-watching bus tours into the northernmost White Mountains.

SKI AREA   **Loon Mountain.** Wide, straight, and consistent intermediate trails prevail at Loon, a modern resort on the western edge of the Kancamagus Highway (Route 112) and the Pemigewasset River. Beginner trails and slopes are set apart. In winter 2007–08 Loon opened up the new South Peak, with new trails and an express quad. The most advanced among the 47 runs are grouped on the North Peak section farther from the main mountain. Snowboarders have a half-pipe and their own park; an alpine garden with bumps and jumps provides thrills for skiers. The vertical is 2,100 feet. In the base lodge and around the mountain are many food-service and lounge facilities. There's day and nighttime lift-served snow tubing on the lower slopes. The touring center at Loon Mountain has 22 mi of cross-country trails. There's also ice skating. ⊠*Kancamagus Hwy. (Rte. 112), Lincoln* ☎*603/745–8111, 603/745–8100 snow conditions, 800/227–4191 lodging* ⊕*www.loonmtn.com.*

NIGHTLIFE & THE ARTS

Skiers head to the **Black Diamond Lounge** (⊠*Kancamagus Hwy. [Rte. 112]* ☎*603/745–2244* ⊕*www.mtnclub.com*) in the Mountain Club at the Loon Mountain resort. The **Olde Timbermill** (⊠*Mill at Loon Mountain, Kancamagus Hwy. [Rte. 112]* ☎*603/745–3603*) has live dance music on weekends. The **North Country Center for the Arts** (⊠*Papermill Theatre, Kancamagus Hwy. [Rte. 112], Lincoln* ☎*603/745–6032, 603/745–2141 box office* ⊕*www.papermilltheatre.org*) presents theater for children and adults and art exhibitions in July and August. The draws at the **Thunderbird Lounge** (⊠*Indian Head Resort, 664 U.S. 3, North Lincoln* ☎*603/745–8000*) are nightly entertainment year-round and a large dance floor.

WHERE TO EAT & STAY

$ ✕**Woodstock Station.** If you like eateries loaded with character, don't
AMERICAN miss this restaurant, sited in the former Lincoln Railroad Station of the
late 1800s. Down the hall is a great brewery and pub that serves 13
handcrafted brews and is decorated with old maps and memorabilia.
You come here as much to mix with locals and feel part of the town as
to eat. The menu is what you might find at a Bennigan's: pizza, quesadilla, wings, chicken, and seafood. The lunch specials are a great value.
⊠*U.S. 3, North Woodstock* ☎*603/745–3951* ⊟*AE, D, MC, V.*

☺ $ ⬚**Indian Head Resort.** When you see the totem pole, you know you've
found this fun family resort. Views across the 180 acres of this motel's
property, near the Loon and Cannon Mountain ski areas, are of Indian
Head Rock Profile and the Franconia Mountains. Cross-country ski
trails and a mountain-bike trail from the resort connect to the Franconia Notch trail system. The Profile Room restaurant serves standard
American fare. **Pros:** best place for kids around. **Cons:** not directly
in town, farther from skiing. ⊠*U.S. 3, 5 mi north of North Woodstock* ⌂*R.R. 1, Box 99, North Lincoln 03251* ☎*603/745–8000 or
800/343–8000* ⊕*www.indianheadresort.com* ⇆*100 rooms, 40 cottages* ⬙*In-room: refrigerator, Wi-Fi. In-hotel: restaurant, room service,
bar, tennis court, pools, gym, no elevator, public Internet, public Wi-Fi,
no-smoking rooms* ⊟*AE, D, DC, MC, V.*

$$$ ⬚**Mountain Club on Loon.** If you want ski-in, ski-out on Loon Moun-
tain, this is your best—and only—option. A typical 1990s ski lodge
with a stone fireplace in the lobby, a heated outdoor pool with hot
tubs, and a small room with Ping-Pong and air hockey for kids, the
Club isn't thrilling, but it's clean and modern. There are suites that
sleep as many as eight, studios with Murphy beds, and many units
with kitchens. All rooms are within walking distance of the lifts, and
condominiums are on or near the slopes. Entertainers perform in the
lounge on most winter weekends. **Pros:** easy skiing, clean basic rooms,
easy access to national forest. **Cons:** unexciting decor. ⊠*Kancamagus
Hwy. (Rte. 112), Lincoln* ☎*603/745–2244 or 800/229–7829* ⊕*www.
mtnclub.com* ⇆*234 units* ⬙*In-room: kitchen (some). In-hotel: restau-
rant, bar, tennis courts, pool, gym, spa, laundry facilities, public Wi-Fi,
no-smoking rooms* ⊟*AE, D, MC, V.*

$ ⬚**Woodstock Inn.** The inexpensive inn and its restaurants and brew-
ery are the heart of cute little North Woodstock. Rooms in the main
inn—there are four other buildings associated with the inn as well—are
the quaintest, with sleigh beds, lace curtains, and warm wood accents
original to the late 1800s building. The Georgianna room has great
corner windows looking out over Main Street. The inn's building across
the street has a rustic theme. **Pros:** prime location in cute town location,
fun restaurants, inexpensive. **Cons:** rooms not luxurious. ⊠*U.S. 3, Box
118, North Woodstock* ☎*603/745–3951 or 800/321–3985* ⊕*www.
woodstockinnnh.com* ⇆*28 rooms, 5 suites, 2 with shared bath, 2
with hall bath* ⬙*In-room: DVD, Wi-Fi. In-hotel: 2 restaurants, bar,
no elevator, public Internet, public Wi-Fi, no-smoking rooms* ⊟*AE, D,
MC, V* ⍭*BP.*

3

FRANCONIA

16 mi northwest of Lincoln/North Woodstock.

Travelers have long passed through the White Mountains via Franconia Notch, and in the late 18th century a town evolved just to the north. It and the region's jagged rock formations and heavy coat of evergreens have stirred the imaginations of Washington Irving, Henry Wadsworth Longfellow, and Nathaniel Hawthorne, who penned a short story about the Old Man of the Mountain. There is almost no town proper to speak of here, just a handful of stores, touched though it is by Interstate 93 (aka the Franconia Notch Parkway).

Four miles west of Franconia, Sugar Hill is a town of about 500 people. It's famous for its spectacular sunsets and views of the Franconia Mountains, best seen from Sunset Hill, where formerly a row of grand hotels and mansions once stood.

WHAT TO SEE

Flume. This 800-foot-long chasm has narrow walls that give the gorge's running water an eerie echo. The route through it has been built up with a series of boardwalks and stairways. The visitor center has exhibits on the region's history. ⊠ *Franconia Notch Pkwy. Exit 34A* ☎ *603/745–8391* ⊕ *www.nhstateparks.com/franconia.html* ⊠ *$8* ☉ *Early May–late Oct., daily 9–5.*

Frost Place. His full-time home from 1915 to 1920 and also his summer home for 19 years, this is where Robert Frost soaked up the spirit of New England, which was the essence of his poetry. This place is imbued with the spirit of that work, down to the rusted mailbox in front that's painted R. FROST in simple lettering. Two rooms host occasional readings and contain memorabilia and signed editions of his books. Out back, you can follow short trails marked with lines from his poetry. A visit here will slow you down, and remind you of the intense beauty of the surrounding countryside. ⊠ *Ridge Rd. off Rte. 116* ☎ *603/823–5510* ⊕ *www.frostplace.org* ⊠ *$5* ☉ *Memorial Day–early Oct., Wed.–Mon. 1–5.*

Old Man of the Mountain. A famous New Hampshire's geological site is this naturally formed profile in the rock high above Franconia Notch, crumbled unexpectedly on May 3, 2003, from the strains of natural erosion. The iconic image had defined New Hampshire, and the Old Man's "death" stunned and saddened residents. You can still stop at the posted turnouts from Interstate 93 north- or southbound. In Franconia Notch State Park on the northbound side of the highway there is a pull-off and on the southbound side take Exit 34B and follow signs. Another option is to go along the shore of Profile Lake for the best views of the mountain face. There's a small, free Old Man of the Mountain Museum administered by Franconia Notch State Park at the southbound viewing area (by the Cannon Mountain tram parking area); it's open daily 9–5.

SPORTS & THE OUTDOORS

SKI AREAS **Cannon Mountain.** This was one of the nation's first ski areas, and the staff at this state-run facility in Franconia Notch State Park is attentive to skier services, family programs, snowmaking, and grooming. All this makes Cannon a very sound value. Cannon's 42 trails present challenges rarely found in New Hampshire—for instance the narrow, steep pitches off the peak of a 2,146-foot vertical rise. There are also two glade-skiing trails—Turnpike and Banshee—and a tubing park with lift service. Nordic skiing is on an 8-mi multiuse recreational path. In summer, for $10 round-trip, the Cannon Mountain Aerial Tramway can transport you up 2,022 feet. It's an eight-minute ride to the top, where marked trails lead to an observation platform. The tram runs daily from mid-May through late October.

The **New England Ski Museum** (☎603/823–7177 ⊕www.skimuseum. org) sits at the base of the tramway and traces the history of the sport with displays of early gear as well as photos, books, and videos. Admission is free, and the museum is open daily 10–5 from late December through March and from late May through mid-October. ⊠*Franconia Notch State Park, I–93 Exit 34B 03580* ☎*603/823–8800, 603/823–7771 snow conditions, 800/237–9007 lodging* ☉*Late May–mid-Oct. and late Dec.–Mar., daily 10–5.*

Franconia Village Cross-Country Ski Center. The cross-country ski center at the Franconia Inn has 39 mi of groomed trails and 24 mi of backcountry trails. One popular route leads to Bridal Veil Falls, a great spot for a picnic lunch. There are horse-drawn sleigh rides and ice-skating on a lighted rink. ⊠*1300 Easton Rd. 03580* ☎*603/823–5542 or 800/473–5299* ⊕*www.franconiainn.com.*

WHERE TO EAT

¢–$ ✗**Polly's Pancake Parlor.** Originally a carriage shed built in 1830, this
★ local institution was converted to a tearoom during the Depression,
AMERICAN when the Dexters began serving all-you-can-eat pancakes, waffles, and French toast for 50¢. The prices have gone up, but the descendants of the Dexters continue to serve pancakes and waffles made from grains ground on the property, their own country sausage, and pure maple syrup. The oatmeal-buttermilk pancakes with coconut, blueberries, or walnuts are other favorites. You can purchase home mixes and syrup at the adjoining store. ⊠*Rte. 117* ☎*603/823–5575* ▤*AE, D, MC, V* ☉*Closed mid-Oct.–mid-May. No dinner.*

$$–$$$ ✗**Sugar Hill Inn.** This 1789 farmhouse is the fine-dining option in these
AMERICAN neck of the woods. Chef Val Fortin serves such haute American fare as peppercorn-crusted sirloin steak with grilled mushrooms and truffle oil; the homemade desserts are always delicious. A four-course prix-fixe meal is $48. ⊠*116 Rte. 117* ☎*603/823–5621* ⚠*Reservations required* ▤*AE, MC, V* ☉*Closed Tues. and Wed. No lunch.*

WHERE TO STAY

$ 🏠**Franconia Inn.** At this 107-acre, family-friendly resort, you can play tennis on four clay courts, swim in the outdoor heated pool or hot tub, and hike. The cross-country ski barn doubles as a horseback-riding center in the warmer months. The white, three-story inn has unfussy country furnishings—you'll find canopy beds and country quilts in the rooms, most of which have period-style wallpapering or wood-paneling; many have working fireplaces. A sunny, plant-filled restaurant serves contemporary continental fare. **Pros:** good for kids, amazing views, outdoor heated pool. **Cons:** may be too remote for those who like town access. ⊠*1300 Easton Rd. 03580* ☎*603/823–5542 or 800/473–5299* ⊕*www.franconiainn.com* 🛏*34 rooms, 3 suites, 2 2-bedroom cottages* ♿*In-room: no phone, no TV, Wi-Fi. In-hotel: restaurant, bar, tennis courts, pool, bicycles, no elevator, public Wi-Fi, no-smoking rooms* ⊟*AE, MC, V* ☉*Closed May 1–15.*

$$–$$$ 🛏 **Sugar Hill Inn.** Hands down the nicest place in Franconia for a roman-
★   tic retreat is the Sugar Hill Inn. The lawn's old carriage and the wrap-around porch's wicker chairs put you in a nostalgic mood before you even enter this converted 1789 farmhouse. Antique-filled guest quarters are in the main house or one of three cottages. Many rooms and suites have hand-stenciled walls and views of the Franconia Mountains; some have fireplaces. Bette Davis visited friends in this house—the room with the best vistas is named after her. **Pros:** romantic, classic B&B; fine dinners. **Cons:** expensive. ⊠*116 Rte. 117 03586* ☎*603/823–5621 or 800/548–4748* ⊕*www.sugarhillinn.com* 🛏*13 rooms, 1 cottage* ♿*In-room: no phone, DVD (some), no TV (some), Wi-Fi. In-hotel: restaurant, room service, bar, pool, spa, no elevator, public Internet, public Wi-Fi, no-smoking rooms* ⊟*AE, MC, V* �’❘❙*BP, MAP.*

LITTLETON

9 mi northeast of Sugar Hill, 7 mi north of Franconia, 86 mi north of Concord.

One of northern New Hampshire's largest towns (this isn't saying much, mind you) is on a granite shelf along the Ammonoosuc River, whose swift current and drop of 235 feet enabled the community to flourish as a mill center in its early days. Later, the railroad came through, and Littleton grew into the region's commerce hub. In the minds of many, it's more a place to stock up on supplies than a bona fide destination, but few communities have worked harder at revitalization. Today, intriguing shops and eateries line the adorable main street, whose tidy 19th- and early-20th-century buildings suggest a set in a Jimmy Stewart movie.

WHAT TO SEE

Littleton Grist Mill. Stop by this restored 1798 mill just off Main Street of bustling Littleton. On the Ammonoosuc River, it contains a small shop selling stone-ground flour products, and a museum downstairs showcasing the original mill equipment. ⊠*18 Mill St.* ☎*603/444–7478 or 888/284–7478* ⊕*www.littletongristmill.com* ☉*July–Dec., 10–5; June–Apr., Wed.–Sat., 10–5.*

Thayers Inn. The heart of Main Street and Littleton is this hotel that functions as an informal museum, with old photos of town life in the lobby and halls. Reuqest a key to the cupola and climb up for the

360-degree views of town. Two rooms are open to the public: On the second floor is a room set up as it would have appeared in the 1840s. On the third floor is a diorama scene of a novel published by Eleanor Hodgman Porter, who was born in Littleton in 1868. She published her two Polyanna novels in 1913 and 1915. ✉ *111 Main St.* ☎ *603/444–6469* ⊕ *www.thayersinn.com.*

OFF THE BEATEN PATH

Whitefield. Like Dixville Notch and Bretton Woods, Whitefield, 11 mi northeast of Littleton, became a prominent summer resort in the late 19th century, when wealthy industrialists flocked to the small village in a rolling valley between two precipitous promontories to golf, ski, play polo, and hobnob with each other. The sprawling, yellow clapboard Mountain View hotel, which was established in 1865 and had grown to grand hotel status by the early 20th century, only to succumb to changing tourist habits and close by the 1980s, has been fully refurbished and is now open again as one of New England's grandest resort hotels. It's worth driving through the courtly Colonial center of town—Whitefield was settled in the early 1800s—and up Route 116 just beyond to see this magnificent structure atop a bluff overlooking the Presidentials.

Lancaster. About 8 mi north of Whitefield via U.S. 3, the affable seat of Coos County sits at the confluence of the Connecticut and Israel rivers, surrounded by low serrated peaks. Before becoming prosperous through commerce, Lancaster was an agricultural stronghold; at one time the only acceptable currency was the bushel of wheat. It's still an intimate mountain town. Like Littleton, though, it has restored much of its main street, which now has a dapper mix of Victorian homes, funky artisan and antiques shops, and prim churches and civic buildings.

SPORTS & THE OUTDOORS

The Society for the Protection of New Hampshire Forests owns two properties open to visitors in Bethlehem, 5 mi southeast of Littleton. **Bretzfelder Park** (✉ *Prospect St.* ☎ *603/444–6228*), a 77-acre nature and wildlife park, has a picnic shelter, hiking, and cross-country ski trails. The **Rocks Christmas Tree Farm** (✉ *4 Christmas La., Bethlehem* ☎ *603/444–6228*) is a working Christmas-tree farm with walking trails, historical buildings, and educational programs.

SHOPPING

ANTIQUES In a restored mill on the Ammonoosuc River, **ADMAC Salvage at the Tannery Marketplace** (✉ *111 Saranac St.* ☎ *603/444–1200*) contains an amazing array of architectural relics, antiques, collectibles, and estate leftovers. **Potato Barn Antiques Center** (✉ *U.S. 3, 6 mi north of Lancaster, Northumberland* ☎ *603/636–2611*) has several dealers under one roof—specialties include vintage farm tools, clothing, and costume jewelry.

BOOKS The **Village Book Store** (✉ *81 Main St.* ☎ *603/444–5263*) has comprehensive selections of both nonfiction and fiction titles.

BOUTIQUES & MORE Main Street and Union Street are filled with great little shops. **Pentimento** (✉ *34 Union St.* ☎ *603/444–7797*) is a small boutique filled floor to ceiling with eclectic gifts including candles, jewelry, and eyewear. **The League of New Hampshire Craftsman** (⊠ *81 Main St.* ☏ *603/444–1099*) has one of their seven great retail stores here.

NEED A BREAK?

Beside the Littleton Grist Mill, **Miller's Café & Bakery** (⊠ *16 Mill St.* ☏ *603/444– 2146* ⊕ *www.millerscafeandbakery.com* ☉ *Closed Sun. and Mon.*) serves coffees, microbrews and wines, baked goods, sandwiches, and salads.

WHERE TO EAT

$$–$$$
★
AMERICAN

✕ **Tim-bir Alley.** This is a rare find in New Hampshire: an independent restaurant in a contemporary setting that's been around a long time (since 1983) and yet still takes its food seriously. If you're in town, don't miss it. Tim Carr's menu changes weekly and uses regional American ingredients in creative ways. Main dishes might include rosemary-and-garlic lamb chops with spinach, feta, and pine nuts, or sunflower-encrusted salmon with a smoked-tomato puree. Save room for such desserts as white chocolate–coconut cheesecake. ⊠ *7 Main St.* ☏ *603/444–6142* ⊟ *No credit cards* ☉ *Closed Tues. and Wed. No lunch.*

WHERE TO STAY

$$
★

🏠 **Adair Country Inn.** An air of yesteryear refinement infuses Adair, a three-story Georgian-revival home that attorney Frank Hogan built as a wedding present for his daughter, Dorothy Adair, in 1927. Dorothy's hats adorn the place, as do books and old photos form the era. This is a luxurious, well-run country inn, with walking paths that wind through 200 acres of gardens designed by the Olmstead brothers. Rooms are furnished with period antiques and reproductions; many have fireplaces. Two more pluses: A generous afternoon tea is served in the elegant living room, and a great basement rec room has a 1929 billiards table and a 42-inch flat-screen with a big movie collection. **Pros:** clean, cozy rooms; refined book-filled spaces; good dinners. **Cons:** removed from town. ⊠ *80 Guider La., just off I–93 Exit 40* ☏ *603/444–2600 or 888/444–2600* ⊕ *www.adairinn.com* ⬧ *9 rooms, 1 cottage* ⚭ *Inroom: no phone, no TV, Wi-Fi. In-hotel: restaurant, tennis court, no elevator, public Wi-Fi, no kids under 12, no-smoking rooms* ⊟ *AE, D, MC, V* ◯| *BP.*

$$
☾
★

🏠 **Mountain View Grand Resort and Spa.** One of New England's most complete resorts, the Mountain View gives families and couples a seemingly endless array of things to do. For instance: horseback riding, a 9-hole golf course, four clay tennis courts, ice skating, tubing, snowmobiling, and cross-country skiing. Built in 1865 and for decades one of New England's grandest of the grande dames, the Mountain View reopened to great fanfare in summer 2002. Nearly all the rooms afford vast vistas of the mountains or golf course, and all are outfitted with plush Colonial-style mahogany furniture and floral-print bedspreads. The main restaurant, Juliet's, serves creative regional New England cuisine. The state-of-the-art Tower Spa provides myriad treatments. **Pros:** full-service resort in the grand tradition, full range of activities, free shuttle to Cannon. **Cons:** breakfast not included. ⊠ *120 Mountain View Rd., Whitefield* ☏ *603/837–2100 or 800/438–3017*

⊕*www.mountainviewgrand.com* ⟿*115 rooms, 30 suites* ♿*In-room: Wi-Fi. In-hotel: 4 restaurants, room service, bar, golf course, tennis courts, pools, gym, spa, bicycles, children's programs (ages 4–16), laundry service, concierge, public Internet, public Wi-Fi, no-smoking rooms* ⊟*AE, D, MC, V.*

¢ 🏨 **Thayers Inn.** This stately 1843 Greek-revival hotel is the essence of Littleton. It's not a luxury hotel. Thayers doesn't need to try to impress anyone. The well-kept rooms retain a quaintly old-fashioned look, with creaky floorboards, exposed pipes, vintage steam radiators, high ceilings, and comfy wing chairs. But of you're traveling on a budget, or just want an authentic northern town experience, history seems to radiate from this place. There's no elevator—good to know if you planned to book an upper-floor room. The Bailiwicks restaurant and bar downstairs is a typical delight: you'd never expect it as you head down the steps, but it's a charmer. **Pros:** one of the best values in New England. **Cons:** continental breakfast only. ⊠*111 Main St. 03561* ☎*603/444–6469 or 800/634–8179* ⊕*www.thayersinn.com* ⟿*22 rooms, 13 suites* ♿*In-room: VCR, Wi-Fi. In-hotel: restaurant, bar, no elevator, public Internet, public Wi-Fi, some pets allowed, no-smoking rooms* ⊟*AE, D, MC, V* ⫶◎⫶*CP.*

FodorsChoice ★

BRETTON WOODS

14 mi southeast of Bethlehem, 28 mi northeast of Lincoln and Woodstock.

In the early 1900s private railcars brought the elite from New York and Philadelphia to the Mount Washington Hotel, the jewel of the White Mountains. A visit to the hotel is not to be missed. The hotel was the site, in 1944, of a famous United Nations conference that created the International Monetary Fund and the International Bank for Reconstruction and Development and whose decisions governed international monetary and financial policy until the early 1970s. The area is also known for its cog railway and Bretton Woods ski resort.

WHAT TO SEE

⟲ In 1858 Sylvester Marsh petitioned the state legislature for permission
FodorsChoice to build a steam railway up Mt. Washington. A politico retorted that
★ he'd have better luck building a railroad to the moon. Just 11 years later, the **Mt. Washington Cog Railway** chugged its way along a 3-mi track up the west side of the mountain to the summit, and it is today one of the state's most beloved attractions—a thrill in either direction. In winter the train goes 4,100 feet up, an hour-long roundtrip ($31) with trains departing at 10 AM and 1 PM. The rest of the year the full trip ($59) is three hours, with 20 minutes at the summit; trains depart at 11 AM and 2 PM. ⊠*U.S. 302, 6 mi northeast of Bretton Woods* ☎*603/278–5404 or 800/922–8825* ⊕*www.thecog.com* ⟿*$59* ⊙*Two daily departures (hours vary).*

SPORTS & THE OUTDOORS

SKI AREA **Bretton Woods.** Skiing with your family? New Hampshire's largest ski
    ❄ area is considered one of the best family ski resorts in the country. It's
Fodor's Choice also probably the best place in New England to learn to ski. (If it's your
   ★ first time, get started at the free area reached by the Learning Center
Quad chairlift.) The views of Mt. Washington alone are worth the visit
to Bretton Woods; the scenery is especially beautiful from the **Top of
Quad restaurant**, which is open during ski season.

Trails will appeal mostly to novice and intermediate skiers, including
two magic carpets lifts for beginners. There are, however, some steeper
pitches near the top of the 1,500-foot vertical and glade skiing will satisfy experts. There's night skiing and snowboarding on weekends and
holidays. Four terrain parks, including an all-natural Wild West park,
will make snowboarders happy. Theres also a half-pipe.

The large, full-service cross-country ski center has 62 mi (100 km)
of groomed and double-track trails, many of them lift-serviced. The
Nordic ski center, which doubles as the golf clubhouse in summer, is
near the hotel.

Options for kids are plentiful. The Hobbit Ski and Snowboard School
for ages 4–12 have full- and half-day instruction. Hobbit Ski and
Snowplay program ages three to five is an introduction to skiing and
fun on the snow. There are also organized instructor activities in the
nursery. The complimentary Kinderwoods Winter Playground has a
sled carousel, igloos, and a zip line. Parents can buy an innovative
innovative interchangeable family ticket that allows parents to take
turns skiing while the other watches the kids—both passes come for
the price of one. ✉ *U.S. 302, 03575* ☎ *603/278–3320, 603/278–3333
weather conditions, 800/232–2972 information, 800/258–0330 lodging* ⊕ *www.brettonwoods.com.*

WHERE TO EAT

$$$ ✕ **The Bretton Arms Dining Room.** You're likely to have the best meal in the
AMERICAN area at the this intimate setting. Though the same executive chef over-
sees the Mount Washnigton Hotel dining room, the latter is immense,
and the Bretton Arms tiny; you seem to get more chef focus here. Three
small interconnected rooms, separated by fireplaces, are private and
romantic. Entrées include Maine lobster tossed with fresh pasta and
free-range Long Island duck breast. ✉ *U.S. 302* ☎ *603/278–1000*
🍽 *AE, D, MC, V* ⊗ *No lunch.*

$$$ ✕ **The Dining Room.** Wow. You'd be hard-pressed to find a larger or
 ★ grander dining room in New Hampshire (only the Balsams can com-
AMERICAN pare). The Mount Washington Hotel's huge octagonal dining room,
built in 1902 is adorned with Currier & Ives reproductions, Tiffany
glass, chandeliers galore, massive windows that open to the Presidential Range, and a nightly musical trio. Besides the Balsams, this is the
only restaurant in the state that requires a jacket—if you forgot yours,
fear not, they have about 30 you can borrow. Try seasonal dishes like
seared haddock and shrimp fricassee; lemon lobster ravioli with shrimp
and scallops; or roast pork with onions and mushrooms. ✉ *In Mount*

Washington Hotel, U.S. 302 ☎ *603/278–1000 Jacket required* ▤ *AE, D, MC, V.*

$-$$
AMERICAN
✕**Fabyan's Station.** In 1890, three score of tourist trains a day passed through this station, now a casual restaurant. If you're looking for an easygoing meal in the area, hop on over. Half the restaurant is a tavern with a long bar, and the other half serves sandwiches, fish, and steaks. There's a kids menu too. A model train circles above the dining room. ✉ *Rte. 302, 1 mi north of Bretton Woods ski area* ☎ *603/278–2222* ⚓ *Reservations not accepted* ▤ *AE, D, MC, V.*

3

WHERE TO STAY

¢
★
🏨**The Lodge.** A stay at this inexpensive roadside motel run by Bretton Woods gives you free access to all of the resort facilities at Mount Washington Hotel, including the pools, gym, and arcade. That makes it a great deal. You can also use the free shuttle to the hotel and the ski area. Even without all that rooms would be a great value: they're very clean and have private balconies that overlook the Presidential range. There's a pizzeria on site, a small arcade, a great indoor pool, and a cute hearthside common area. **Pros:** cheap, free access to Mount Washington amenities, free ski shuttle. Cons: across street from resort amenities, continental breakfast only. ✉ *U.S. 302, 03575* ☎ *603/278–1000 or 800/258–0330* ⊕ *www.mtwashington.com* 🛏 *50 rooms* ♿ *In-room: Wi-Fi. In-hotel: restaurant, golf courses, tennis courts, pool, bicycles, children's programs (ages 4–12), laundry facilities, laundry service, public Wi-Fi, no-smoking rooms* ▤ *AE, D, MC, V* ⑩ *CP.*

$$
☾
Fodor's Choice
★
🏨**The Mount Washington Hotel.** The two most memorable sights in the White Mountains would have to be (a) Mount Washington and (b) the Mount Washington Hotel. Its grand scale and exquisite setting foregrounded with the Presidentials is astonishing. This 1902 resort has a 900-foot-long veranda, stately public rooms, and, after a brilliant renovation, glimmers anew with an early-20th-century formality. It would take a full week to exhaust the recreational activities here: in winter there's tubing, ice skating, a great cross-country facility, a terrific downhill skiing complex, and sleigh rides; in summer, horseback riding, carriage rides, fly fishing, golf, mountain biking, etc. The adventure desk is a concierge area designed to keep you busy. The Cave provides nightly entertainment in a former 1930s speakeasy. Kids love to run around this huge hotel (so big it has its own post office), and there's an arcade, a sweet shop, playground, as well as kids club with themed day and evening programs. A 25,000-square-foot spa and a renovated 18-hole Donald Ross course (designed in 1915) are set to debut in fall 2008. Rooms aren't as lavish as the public spaces, but they have high ceilings and are comfortable. **Pros:** beautiful grand resort, loads of activities, free shuttle to skiing and activities. **Cons:** kids love to run around the hotel, big hotel, rooms not as luxurious as rest of property. ✉ *U.S. 302, 03575* ☎ *603/278–1000 or 800/258–0330* ⊕ *www.mtwashington.com* 🛏 *177 rooms, 23 suites* ♿ *In-room: Ethernet, Wi-Fi. In-hotel: 3 restaurants, room service, bars, golf courses, tennis courts, pool, gym, spa, bicycles, children's programs (ages 4–12), laundry service, concierge, public Internet, public Wi-Fi, no-smoking rooms* ▤ *AE, D, MC, V* ⑩ *EP, BP, MAP.*

$$ ⊞**The Notchland Inn.** To see this house is to believe in fairy tales. Built
Fodor'sChoice in 1862 by Sam Bemis, America's grandfather of landscape photog-
★ raphy, the house conveys mountain charm on a scale unmatched in
New England. It's simply a legenday setting, in Crawford Notch, in
the middle of the forest surrounded by the mountains: perhaps drop
any cute house here and you couldn't but fall in love. But to their
credit, innkeepers Les Schoof and Ed Butler have left wood-burning
fireplaces in every room (17 in total in the house) and do everything
else you'd hope for, like having a big library, leaving puzzles around,
serving five-course meals, and giving range of the place to Abby and
Crawford, the immense Bernese Mountain inn dogs. **Pros:** middle-of-
the-forest setting, marvelous house and common rooms, original fire-
places, good dinner. **Cons:** will be too isolated for some, rooms could
be better equipped (better bedding needed, for example). ⊠*Rte. 302,
Hart's Location* ☎*603/374–6131* ⊕*www.notchland.com* ☞*8 rooms,
5 suites, 3 cottages* ⚴*In-room: no phone, Wi-Fi. In-hotel: restaurant,
no elevator, public Wi-Fi, some pets allowed, no kids under 12, no-
smoking rooms* ▭*D, MC, V* ⑩*BP.*

**EN
ROUTE**

Scenic U.S. 302 winds through the steep, wooded mountains on either
side of spectacular Crawford Notch, southeast of Bretton Woods,
and passes through **Crawford Notch State Park** (⊠*U.S. 302, Harts Loca-
tion* ☎*603/374–2272*), where you can picnic and take a short hike
to Arethusa Falls or the Silver and Flume cascades. The visitor center
has a gift shop and a cafeteria; there's also a **campground.** ☎*603/271–
3628 reservations.*

BARTLETT

18 mi southeast of Bretton Woods.

With Bear Mountain to its south, Mt. Parker to its north, Mt. Cardi-
gan to its west, and the Saco River to its east, Bartlett, incorporated in
1790, has an unforgettable setting. Lovely Bear Notch Road (closed
in winter) has the only midpoint access to the Kancamagus Highway
(Route 112). There isn't much town here (dining options are just over
in Glen). It's best known for the Attitash ski area.

SPORTS & THE OUTDOORS

SKI AREA   **Attitash Ski Area.** Enhanced with massive snowmaking (98%), the trails
number 75 on two peaks—Attitash (with a vertical drop of 1,760 feet)
and Attitash Bear Peak (with a 1,450-foot vertical)—both with full-
service base lodges. The bulk of the skiing and boarding is geared to
intermediates and experts, with some steep pitches and glades. At 500
feet, the Ground Zero half pipe is New England's longest. The Attitash
Adventure Center has a rental shop, lessons desk, and children's pro-
grams. ⊠*U.S. 302* ☎*603/374–2368, 877/677–7609 snow conditions,
800/223–7669 lodging* ⊕*www.attitash.com.*

WHERE TO EAT

$$–$$$ ✕**Bernerhof Inn.** There are several options for dining at this inn. The
ECLECTIC dining room is the area's fine dining choice, preparing traditional Swiss
specialties such as fondue and Wiener schnitzel as well as contemporary dishes—Asian duck breast or venison filet, for instance. The Black
Bear pub pours microbrews and serves sandwiches and burgers, as well
as shepherds' pie and other dishes. The CyBear Lounge serves afternoon appetizers you can snack on while checking your e-mail. ⊠*U.S.
302, Glen* ☎*603/383–9132 or 800/548–8007* ⊕*www.bernerhofinn.
com* ⊟*AE, D, MC, V.*

$–$$ ✕**Margarita Grill.** Après-ski and hiking types congregate here—in
SOUTHWESTERN the dining room in cold weather and on the covered patio when it's
warm—for homemade salsas, wood-fired steaks, ribs, burgers, and a
smattering of Tex-Mex and Cajun specialties. Unwind at the tequila
bar after a day on the mountains. ⊠*U.S. 302, Glen* ☎*603/383–6556*
⊟*D, MC, V* ⊘*No lunch weekdays.*

$–$$ ✕**Red Parka Pub.** Practically an institution, this downtown Glen pub
AMERICAN has been here for more than two decades. The menu has everything
a family could want, from an all-you-can-eat salad bar to scallop pie.
The barbecued ribs are favorites, as are hand-carved steaks of every
type, from aged New York sirloin to prime rib. ⊠*U.S. 302, Glen*
☎*603/383–4344* ⚲*Reservations not accepted* ⊟*AE, D, MC, V.*

WHERE TO STAY

$$ 🏨**Attitash Mountain Village.** This place across the street form the entrance
to Attitash is deceptively large. You can't see the cluster of units form
the road because they're in the pine trees (there are also a few slope-
side condos). But they're there, along with hiking trails, a playground,
a clay tennis courts, two heated pools, an arcade, and free bike rent-
als. All in all it's a good deal for families on a budget and who want
to ski across the street. The look is a no-frills fun, family-style place.
There's a restaurant and a loose, sports-style pub. **Pros:** simple, no-frills
family place; playground. **Cons:** a bit run-down. ⊠*U.S. 302 03812*
☎*603/374–6501 or 800/862–1600* ⊕*www.attitashmtvillage.com*
⇝*350 units* ⚹*In-room: no a/c (some), kitchen, refrigerator (some),
DVD, Wi-Fi. In-hotel: restaurant, bar, tennis courts, pools, gym, bicy-
cles, laundry facilities, laundry service, public Internet, public Wi-Fi,
some pets allowed, no-smoking rooms* ⊟*AE, D, MC, V.*

$$ 🏨**Grand Summit Hotel & Conference Center.** The contemporary ski hotel
at the base of Attitash Bear Peak is the choice for skiers who want
ski-in, ski-out convenience. Attractive contemporary-style rooms have
kitchenettes, video game TVs, and stereos. Standard rooms have balconies. The main dining room serves passable American fare; dishes at
Crawford's Pub and Grill are lighter. **Pros:** ski-in ski-out, nice pool and
hot tubs, cheaper with ski package. **Cons:** gerneally bland accommodations. ⊠*U.S. 302 03812* ☎*603/374–1900 or 888/554–1900* ⊕*www.
attitash.com* ⇝*143 rooms* ⚹*In-room: kitchen (some), Wi-Fi. In-hotel:
2 restaurants, room service, bars, pool, gym, children's programs (ages
2–14), laundry facilities, laundry service, concierge, public Internet,
public Wi-Fi, no-smoking rooms* ⊟*AE, D, MC, V.*

3

JACKSON

★ *5 mi north of Glen.*

Just off Route 16 via a red covered bridge, Jackson has retained its storybook New England character. Art and antiques shopping, tennis, golf, fishing, and hiking to waterfalls are among the draws. When the snow falls, Jackson becomes the state's cross-country skiing capital. Four downhill ski areas are nearby.

WHAT TO SEE

☺ **Story Land.** That cluster of fluorescent buildings along Route 16 is a
Fodor'sChoice theme park with life-size storybook and nursery-rhyme characters. The
★ 20 rides and five shows include a flume ride, Victorian-theme river-raft ride, farm tractor–inspired kiddie ride, pumpkin coach, variety show (presented in a new theater, which opened in 2004), and swan boats. In early spring, only parts of the park are open and admission is reduced to $16. ⊠*Rte. 16* ☎*603/383–4186* ⊕*www.storylandnh.com* 🖃*$21* ☉*Mid-June–Labor Day, daily 9–6; Memorial Day–mid-June and Labor Day–Columbus Day, weekends 10–5.*

SPORTS & THE OUTDOORS

Nestlenook Farm (⊠*Dinsmore Rd.* ☎*603/383–9443*) maintains an outdoor ice-skating rink with rentals, music, and a bonfire. Going snowshoeing or taking a sleigh ride are other winter options; in summer you can fly-fish or ride in a horse-drawn carriage.

SKI AREAS **Black Mountain.** Friendly, informal, Black Mountain has a warming southern exposure. The Family Passport, which allows two adults and two juniors to ski at discounted rates, is a good value. Midweek rates here ($29) are usually the lowest in Mt. Washington Valley. The 40 trails and glades on the 1,100-vertical-foot mountain are evenly divided among beginner, intermediate, and expert. There's a nursery for kids six months and up. ⊠*Rte. 16B* ☎*603/383–4490, 800/475–4669 snow conditions* ⊕*www.blackmt.com.*

★ **Jackson Ski Touring Foundation.** One of the nation's top four cross-country skiing areas has 97 mi of trails. About 60 mi are track groomed, and 53 mi are skate groomed. There are roughly 39 mi of marked backcountry trails. You can arrange lessons and rentals at the lodge, in the center of Jackson Village. ⊠*153 Main St., Jackson* ☎*603/383–9355* ⊕*www.jacksonxc.org.*

WHERE TO EAT

$ ✗**Red Fox Bar & Grille.** Some say this big family restaurant overlooking
AMERICAN the Wentworth Golf Club gets its name from a wily fox with a penchant for stealing golf balls off the fairway. The wide-ranging menu has barbecued ribs, wood-fired pizzas, and blue-cheese-and-bacon burgers as well as more substantial dishes such as seared sea scallops with Grand Marnier sauce. The Sunday jazz breakfast buffet draws raves. ⊠*49 Rte. 16* ☎*603/383–4949* ⊟*AE, D, MC, V* ☉*No lunch weekdays.*

$$–$$$ ✗**Thompson House Eatery.** One of the most innovative restaurants in
★ generally staid northern New Hampshire, this romantic eatery inside a
AMERICAN rambling red farmhouse serves such world-beat fare as skewered apple-

wood-smoked shrimp over baby greens with fresh melon and balsamic vinegar. The entrée of grilled lamb chops with cucumber-tomato relish over Israeli couscous, Greek olives, and pancetta wins raves all around. ⊠ *193 Main St.* ☎*603/383–9341* ⊟*AE, D, MC, V* ⊘*Closed Apr.–early May. No lunch Mon.–Wed. late May–early Oct., no lunch Thurs. early Oct.–Mar.*

$$$
Fodor's Choice
★
AMERICAN

✗**Thorn Hill.** The dining room at the famous inn serves up one of New England's most memorable meals. In warm months dine on the decidedly romantic porch, which is lined with hanging candles and overlooks the Presidential mountain range. The wine list is the state's most lauded, with 1,900 labels. It's also fun: the three 2-ounce-glass tasting is affordable and the glasses come with identification tags near the stems. The curated "Top 50" list of changing reasonably priced bottles is a sure guide. Chef John Russ brings subtle and flavorful dishes. A roasted poussin, an organic free-range game hen with grilled bacon and jus, is served with a wonderful Jerusalem artichoke salad. ⊠*42 Thorn Hill Rd.* ☎*603/383–4242 or 800/289–8990* ⊴*Reservations essential* ⊟*AE, D, MC, V* ⊘*No lunch.*

WHERE TO STAY

$ 🏠**Christmas Farm Inn and Spa.** Despite its wintery name, this 1778 inn is an all-season retreat. Rooms in the main building and the saltbox next door have Laura Ashley and Ralph Lauren prints. Other rooms are set in a delightful old barn, in a sugarhouse, and in a few cottages set about the wooded grounds. In the main inn parlor, a Christmas tree is up all year, and there's a great fireplace. The inn's gardens are spectacular. The twelve suites in the contemporary carriage house have two-person whirlpool tubs and gas fireplaces. **Pros:** kids welcome, nice pools. **Cons:** saltbox rooms could use improvement. ⊠*Rte. 16B, Box CC 03846* ☎*603/383–4313 or 800/443–5837* ⊕*www.christmasfarminn. com* ⟿*22 rooms, 15 suites, 5 2-bedroom cottages* ⟳*In-room: Wi-Fi. In-hotel: restaurant, bar, pool, gym, spa, no elevator, public Wi-Fi, no-smoking rooms* ⊟*AE, MC, V* ⊺⊙⏽*BP.*

$ 🏠**Inn at Ellis River.** Most of the Victorian-style rooms in this unabashedly romantic 1893 inn on the Ellis River have fireplaces; some have balconies. Rooms are named after area waterfalls. A nice pub room has a pool table, darts, and games. Dinner is served with 48 hours advance reservation. **Pros:** pretty yard on river. **Cons:** slightly antiquated; needs some renovation work. ⊠*17 Harriman Rd., off Rte. 16, Box 656, 03846* ☎*603/383–9339 or 800/233–8309* ⊕*www.innatellis river.com* ⟿*17 rooms, 2 suites, 1 cottage* ⟳*In-room: DVD, VCR, Wi-Fi. In-hotel: bar, pool, no elevator, public Internet, public Wi-Fi, some pets allowed, no kids under 12, no-smoking rooms* ⊟*AE, D, MC, V* ⏽⊙⏽*BP.*

$
Fodor's Choice
★

🏠**Inn at Jackson.** This B&B is impeccably maintained, charmingly furnished, and bright: the pride of ownership shines through. The beautiful inn, a 1902 Victorian designed by Stanford White for the Baldwin family of piano fame, overlooks the village. The foyer's staircase is grand, but there's a remarkable relaxed and unpretentious ambience and a great value. The airy guest rooms have oversize windows; eight have fireplaces. The exceptional full breakfast may include anything from egg soufflé casserole to blueberry pancakes. **Pros:** super-clean rooms, great value, peaceful setting. **Cons:** third-floor rooms lack fireplaces. ⊠*Thorn Hill Rd., Box 822 03846* ☎*603/383–4321 or 800/289–8600* ⊕*www.innatjackson.com* ⟿*14 rooms* ⚲*In-room: DVD, Wi-Fi. In-hotel: no elevator, public Internet, public Wi-Fi, no kids under 7, no-smoking rooms* ⊟*AE, D, MC, V* �‖*BP.*

$ ❖ **Inn at Thorn Hill.** You won't find a more subtle sophistication any-

Fodor'sChoice where in New Hampshire than the total experience at Thorn Hill: the

★ dining (considered to be among the country's top hotel meals), service, and relaxed elegance here are unrivaled. Besides the setting and the great house (modeled after the Stanford White Victorian that burned down a decade ago), the brilliance stems from owner/innkeepers James and Ibby Cooper, wonderful hosts who run the place with aplomb. Much of the staff are young British interns, who add life and profes-sionalism to the inn and the dining. All of the rooms abound with cushy amenities: two-person Jacuzzis, fireplaces, and TVs with DVDs. The top units have steam showers, wet bars, and refrigerators. Cottages and rooms in the carriage house are less thrilling. A full spa provides a full range of beauty treatments and massages. Afternoon tea and a substantial full breakfast and dinner are included: it's a great value, too. **Pros:** great meals; great service; romantic setting. **Cons:** fee for wire-less Internet. ⊠*42 Thorn Hill Rd., Box A 03846* ☎*603/383–4242 or 800/289–8990* ⊕*www.innatthornhill.com* ⟿*15 rooms, 7 suites, 3 cottages* ⚲*In-room: refrigerator (some), DVD (some), no TV (some), Wi-Fi. In-hotel: restaurant, room service, bar, pool, gym, spa, laundry service, public Wi-Fi, no kids under 12, no-smoking rooms* ⊟*AE, D, MC, V* �‖*MAP.*

$$ ❖ **Wentworth.** This baronial 1869 Victorian was once one of New Eng-land's great hotels. Today the interior furnishings are unexciting, and the rooms in the main house are in poor shape. But wait: some of the rooms are fantastic. You can find them in the Arden cottage, one of a series of cottages on the national historic register beside the main house. Four rooms have wonderful hot tubs set in what look like giant whiskey barrels; these have wonderful views, and are worth a look. Arden rooms that don't have the hot tubs have big whirlpool baths. Weekends require a two-night stay and a dinner package. The 18-hole course at the Wentworth Golf Club is next door to the inn. **Pros:** professionally run, interesting architecture, restaurant with weekend entertainment. **Cons:** main inn rooms and bathrooms are older, unex-citing common areas. ⊠*1 Carter Notch Rd. 03846* ☎*603/383–9700 or 800/637–0013* ⊕*www.thewentworth.com* ⟿*44 rooms, 7 suites* ⚲*In-room: Wi-Fi. In-hotel: restaurant, room service, bar, tennis court, pool, public Internet, public Wi-Fi, no-smoking rooms* ⊟*AE, D, DC, MC, V* �‖*BP, MAP.*

MT. WASHINGTON

★ *20 mi northwest of Jackson.*

In summer you can drive to the top of Mt. Washington, the highest peak (6,288 feet) in the northeastern United States and the site of a weather station that recorded the world's highest winds, 231 mi per hour, in 1934. (⇨ Bretton Woods for information on the Mt. Washingtown Cog Railway.)

3

WHAT TO SEE

Mt. Washington Auto Road. Opened in 1861, this route begins at the Glen House, a gift shop and rest stop 15 mi north of Glen on Route 16, and winds its way up the east side of the mountain, ending at the top, an 8-mi and approximately half-hour drive later. At the summit is the Sherman Adams Summit Building, built in 1979 and containing a visitor center and a museum focusing on the mountain's geology and extreme weather conditions; you can stand in the glassed-in viewing area to hear the wind roar. The Mt. Washington Observatory is at the building's western end. There are rules limiting what cars may use the road. For instance, cars with automatic transmission must be able to shift down into first gear. It is also possible to reach the top along several rough hiking trails; those who hoof it can make the return trip via shuttle, tickets for which are sold at the Stage Office, at the summit at the end of the cog railway trestle. Remember that the temperature atop Mt. Washington will be much colder than down below—the average year-round is below freezing and the average wind velocity is 35 mph. ✉ *Rte. 16, Pinkham Notch* ☎ *603/466–3988* 🌐 *www.mountwashingtonautoroad.com* 🎟 *Car and driver $20, each additional adult passenger $7* ⏲ *Mid-June–early Sept., daily 7:30–6; May–mid-June and early Sept.–late Oct., daily 8–4, 8–5, or 8–5:30; call for specifics.*

SnowCoaches. In winter, when the road is closed to private vehicles, you can opt to reach the top of Mt. Washington via a guided tour in one of the four-wheel-drive vehicles that leave from Great Glen Trails Outdoor Center, just south of Gorham, on a first-come, first-served basis. Great Glen's nine-passenger vans are refitted with snowmobile-like treads and can travel to just above the tree line. You have the option of cross-country skiing, tubing, or snowshoeing down. ✉ *Rte. 16, Pinkham Notch* ☎ *603/466–2333* 🌐 *www.greatglentrails.com* 🎟 *$40 (includes all-day trail pass)* ⏲ *Dec.–Mar., snow necessary, most days, beginning at 9:15.*

SPORTS & THE OUTDOORS

Although not a town per se, scenic **Pinkham Notch** covers Mt. Washington's eastern side and includes several ravines, including Tuckerman Ravine, famous for spring skiing. The Appalachian Mountain Club maintains a large visitor center here on Route 16 that provides information to hikers and travelers and has guided hikes, outdoor skills workshops, a cafeteria, lodging, regional topography displays, and an outdoors shop.

HIKING The **Appalachian Mountain Club Pinkham Notch Visitor Center** (✉ *Rte. 16, Box 298, Gorham 03581* ☎ *603/466–2721, 603/466–2727 reservations* ⊕ *www.outdoors.org*) has lectures, workshops, slide shows, and outdoor skills instruction year-round. Accommodations include the adjacent Joe Dodge Lodge, the Highland Center at Crawford Notch with 100-plus beds and a 16-bed bunkhouse next to it, as well as the club's eight high-mountain huts spaced one day's hike from each other in the White Mountain National Forest portion of the Appalachian Trail. The huts provide meals and dorm-style lodging from June to late September or early October; the rest of the year they are self-service.

SKI AREAS **Great Glen Trails Outdoor Center.** Amenities at this fabulous new lodge at the base of Mt. Washington include a huge ski-gear and sports shop, food court, climbing wall, observation deck, and fieldstone fireplace. In winter it's renowned for its dramatic 24-mi cross-country trail system. Some trails have snowmaking, and there's access to more than 1,100 acres of backcountry. It's even possible to ski or snowshoe the lower half of the Mt. Washington Auto Road. Trees shelter most of the trails, so Mt. Washington's infamous weather isn't a concern. In summer it's the base from which hikers, mountain bikers, and trail runners can explore Mt. Washington. The center also has programs in canoeing, kayaking, and fly-fishing. ✉ *Rte. 16, Pinkham Notch* ☎ *603/466–2333* ⊕ *www.greatglentrails.com.*

Wildcat. Glade skiers favor Wildcat, with 28 acres of official tree skiing. The 47 runs include some stunning double-black-diamond trails. Skiers who can hold a wedge should check out the 2½-mi-long Polecat. Experts can zip down the Lynx. Views of Mt. Washington and Tuckerman Ravine are superb. The trails are classic New England—narrow and winding. Wildcat's expert runs deserve their designations and then some. Intermediates have mid-mountain–to-base trails, and beginners will find gentle terrain and a broad teaching slope. Snowboarders have several terrain parks and the run of the mountain. In summer you can ride to the top on the four-passenger gondola ($10) and hike the many well-kept trails. ✉ *Rte. 16, Pinkham Notch, Jackson* ☎ *603/466–3326, 888/754–9453 snow conditions, 800/255–6439 lodging* ⊕ *www.skiwildcat.com.*

WHERE TO STAY

¢ 🏨 **Joe Dodge Lodge at Pinkham Notch.** The Appalachian Mountain Club operates this rustic lodge at the base of Mt. Washington. Accommodations range from single-sex bunk rooms (rented by the bunk) for as many as five people, to private rooms—all have gleaming wood, cheerful quilts, and reading lights. The restaurant serves buffet breakfasts and lunches and family-style dinners. Packages include breakfast and dinner, plus skiing at Great Glen Trails and/or the Wildcat ski area. **Pros:** recreational access to mountain; AMC guides and educational oportunities. **Cons:** rustic conditions not right for those seeking luxury. ✉ *Rte. 16, Box 298, Gorham 03581* ☎ *603/466–2727* ⊕ *www.outdoors.org* ⇥ *102 beds without bath* ⚘ *In-room: no a/c, no phone, no TV. In-hotel: restaurant, no-smoking rooms* ⊟ *AE, MC, V* ❍ *MAP.*

DIXVILLE NOTCH

63 mi north of Mt. Washington, 66 mi northeast of Littleton, 149 mi north of Concord.

Just 12 mi from the Canadian border, this tiny community is known for two things. One is the Balsams, one of New Hampshire's oldest and most celebrated resorts. The other is the fact that Dixville Notch and another New Hampshire community, Hart's Location, are the first election districts in the nation to vote in presidential general elections. When the 30 or so Dixville Notch voters file into the little Balsams meeting room on the eve of election day and cast their ballots at the stroke of midnight, they invariably make national news.

One of the favorite pastimes in this area is spotting moose, those large, ungainly, yet elusive members of the deer family. Although you may catch sight of one or more yourself, **Northern Forest Moose Tours** (☎603/466–3103 or 800/992–7480) conducts bus tours of the region that have a 97% success rate for spotting moose.

OFF THE BEATEN PATH

Pittsburg. Well north of the White Mountains, in the Great North Woods, Pittsburg contains the four Connecticut Lakes and the springs that form the Connecticut River. The state's northern tip—a chunk of about 250 square mi—lies within the town's borders, the result of a dispute between the United States and Canada that began in 1832 and was resolved in 1842, when the international boundary was fixed.

Remote though it is, this frontier town teems with hunters, boaters, fishermen, hikers, and photographers from early summer through winter. Especially in the colder months, moose sightings are common. The town has more than a dozen lodges and several informal eateries. It's about a 90-minute drive from Littleton and 40-minute drive from Dixville Notch; add another 30 minutes to reach Fourth Connecticut Lake, nearly at the Canadian border. On your way, you pass the village of Stewartson, exactly midway between the Equator and the North Pole.

SPORTS & THE OUTDOORS

Dixville Notch State Park (✉ *Rte. 26* ☎603/538–6707), in the northernmost notch of the White Mountains, has picnic areas, a waterfall, two mountain brooks, and hiking trails.

SKI AREAS **Balsams.** Skiing was originally provided as an amenity for hotel guests at the Balsams, but the area has become popular with day-trippers as well. Slopes with such names as Sanguinary, Umbagog, and Magalloway may sound tough, but they're only moderately difficult, leaning toward intermediate. There are 16 trails and four glades for every skill level from the top of the 1,000-foot vertical. The Balsams has 59 mi of cross-country skiing, tracked and groomed for skating. Natural-history markers annotate some trails; you can also try telemark and backcountry skiing, and there are 21 mi of snowshoeing trails. ✉ *Rte. 26* ☎*603/255–3400, 603/255–3951 snow conditions, 800/255–0600, 800/255–0800 in New Hampshire* ⊕*www.thebalsams.com.*

WHERE TO EAT

Fodor'sChoice **Le Rendez Vous.** You might not expect to find an authentic French bak-
★ ery and pastry shop in the small workaday village of Colebrook, 10
FRENCH mi west of Dixville Notch, but Le Rendez Vous serves simply fabulous
tarts and treats—the owners came here directly from Paris. Drop in to
this quaint café furnished with several tables and armchairs for coffee,
hand-dipped Belgian chocolates, croissants, a tremendous variety of
fresh-baked breads, and all sorts of gourmet foods, from dried fruits
and nuts to lentils, olive oils, and balsamic vinegar. ✉ *146 Main St.,
Colebrook* ☎ *603/237–5150.*

WHERE TO STAY

$-$$ 🏨**The Balsams.** Nestled in the pine groves of the North Woods, this
★ lavish grande dame has been rolling out the red carpet since 1866. The
Balsams encompasses some 15,000 wooded acres—an area roughly
the size of the New York City borough of Manhattan. Even when the
resort is filled to capacity (figure about 400 guests and another 400
employees), it's still a remarkably solitary place. It draws families, golf
enthusiasts, skiers, and others for a varied slate of activities—from
dancing to cooking demonstrations. Rooms here are spacious, with
large cedar-lined closets and ample dressers. Floral-print wallpaper,
modern bathrooms, full-length mirrors, and reproduction antiques
impart a dignified old-world grace. Most rooms have views overlooking
the lake, gardens, and mountains; still, always inquire about the view
when booking, as a handful afford less-promising vistas (the parking
area, for example). In the dining room ($$$$; jacket and tie), you might
sample a chilled strawberry soup spiked with Grand Marnier, followed
by broiled swordfish with white beans and lemon coulis. Rates include
breakfast and dinner and unlimited use of the facilities. **Pros:** splendid
grand resort; activities galore. **Cons:** grand scale limits intimacy. ✉*Rte.
26 03576* ☎*603/255–3400, 800/255–0600, 800/255–0800 in NH*
🌐*www.thebalsams.com* ⇗*184 rooms, 20 suites* ⌂*In-room: no TV
(some). In-hotel: 3 restaurants, room service, bar, golf course, tennis
courts, pool, gym, bicycles, children's programs (ages 1–12), laundry
service, no-smoking rooms* ⊟*AE, D, MC, V* ⏍*FAP, MAP.*

$-$$ 🏨**The Glen.** This rustic lodge with stick furniture, fieldstone, and
cedar sits amid 180 pristine acres on First Connecticut Lake and is
surrounded by log cabins, seven of which are right on the water. The
cabins have efficiency kitchens and mini-refrigerators—not that you'll
need either, because rates include hearty meals, served family-style, in
the lodge restaurant. **Pros:** rustic, remote setting; charming lodge; loads
of character. **Cons:** remote; not luxurious. ✉*118 Glen Rd., 1 mi off
U.S. 3, Pittsburg* ☎*603/538–6500 or 800/445–4536* 🌐*www.theglen.
org* ⇗*6 rooms, 9 cabins* ⌂*In-room: no phone, kitchen, no TV. In-
hotel: restaurant, no-smoking rooms* ⊟*No credit cards* ☉*Closed mid-
Oct.–mid-May* ⏍*FAP.*

NORTH CONWAY

76 mi south of Dixville Notch, 7 mi south of Glen, 41 mi east of Lincoln/North Woodstock.

Before the arrival of the outlet stores, the town drew visitors for its inspiring scenery, ski resorts, and access to White Mountain National Forest. Today, however, the feeling of natural splendor is gone. Shopping is the big sport, and businesses line Route 16 for several miles. You'll get a close look at them because traffic slows to a crawl here. You can take scenic West Side Road from Conway to Intervale to circumvent the traffic and take in splendid views.

The **Conway Scenic Railroad** operates trips aboard vintage trains from historic North Conway Station. The Notch Train, through Crawford Notch to Crawford Depot (a 5-hour round trip) or Fabyan Station (5½ hours), offers wonderful scenic views from the domed observation coach. The Valley Train provides views of Mt. Washington countryside on a 55-minute round trip to Conway or a 1¾-hour trip to Bartlett—lunch and dinner are served on some departures. The 1874 station displays lanterns, old tickets and timetables, and other railroad artifacts. Reserve early during foliage season for the dining excursions. ⊠ *Rte. 16 (U.S. 302), 38 Norcross Circle* ☎ *603/356–5251 or 800/232–5251* ⊕ *www.conwayscenic.com* ☞ *$12–$60* ◷ *Mid-Apr.– mid Dec; call for times.*

WHAT TO SEE

Hartmann Model Railroad Museum. This building houses about 2,000 engines, more than 5,000 cars and coaches, and 14 operating layouts (from G to Z scales), in addition to a café, a crafts store, a hobby shop, and an outdoor miniature trains that you can sit on and ride. ⊠ *15 Town Hall Rd. at Rte. 16 (U.S. 302), Intervale* ☎ *603/356–9922* ⊕ *www.hartmannrr.com* ☞ *$6* ◷ *Daily 10–5.*

Weather Discovery Center. The hands-on exhibits at this meteorological educational facility teach how weather is monitored and how it affects us. The center is a collaboration between the National and Atmospheric Administration Forecast Systems lab and the Mt. Washington Observatory at the summit of Mt. Washington. ⊠ *Rte. 16 (U.S. 302), 1/5 mi south of rail tracks* ☎ *603/356–2137* ⊕ *www.mountwashington.org* ☞ *$5* ◷ *May–Oct., daily 10–5; Nov.–Apr., Sat.–Mon. 10–5 (also open daily during school vacation from mid-Feb. to early Mar.).*

SPORTS & THE OUTDOORS

Echo Lake State Park. You needn't be a rock climber to catch views from the 700-foot White Horse and Cathedral ledges in From the top you'll see the entire valley, in which Echo Lake shines like a diamond. An unmarked trailhead another .7 mi on West Side Road leads to Diana's Baths, a series of waterfalls. ⊠ *Off U.S 302* ☎ *603/271–3556* ☞ *$3* ◷ *Late May–mid-June, weekends dawn–dusk; mid-June–early Sept., daily dawn–dusk.*

CANOEING & River outfitter **Saco Bound Canoe & Kayak** (✉ *Rte. 16 [U.S. 302], Con-*
KAYAKING *way* 🕾*603/447–2177* ⊕*www.sacobound.com*) leads gentle canoeing
expeditions, guided kayak trips, and white-water rafting on seven rivers and provides lessons, equipment, and transportation.

FISHING **North Country Angler** (✉*2888 White Mountain Hwy.* 🕾*603/356–6000*
⊕*www.northcountryangler.com*) schedules intensive guided fly-fishing
weekends throughout the region. It's one of the best tackle shops in
the state.

SKI AREAS **Cranmore Mountain Resort.** This downhill ski area has been a favorite
of families since it began operating in 1938. Five glades have opened
more skiable terrain. The 39 trails are well laid out and fun to ski.
Most runs are naturally formed intermediates that weave in and out
of glades. Beginners have several slopes and routes from the summit;
experts must be content with a few short, steep pitches. In addition
to the trails, snowboarders have a terrain park and a half-pipe. Night
skiing is offered Thursday–Saturday and holidays. ✉ *1 Skimobile Rd.,*
North Conway 03860 🕾*603/356–5543, 603/356–8516 snow condi-*
tions, 800/786–6754 lodging ⊕*www.cranmore.com.*

King Pine Ski Area at Purity Spring Resort. Some 9 mi south of Conway,
this family-run ski area has been going strong since the late 19th century. Some ski-and-stay packages include free skiing for midweek
resort guests. Among the facilities and activities are an indoor pool
and fitness complex, and ice-skating. King Pine's 16 gentle trails are
ideal for beginner and intermediate skiers; experts won't be challenged
except for a brief pitch on the Pitch Pine trail. There's tubing on weekend afternoons and night skiing and tubing on Friday and Saturday.
There are 9 mi of cross-country skiing. An indoor fitness center is open
year-round. In summer this lively place is a big hit for waterskiing,
kayaking, loon-watching, tennis, hiking, and other activities; lodging
packages are available. ✉*Rte. 153, East Madison* 🕾*603/367–8896 or*
800/373–3754 ⊕*www.purityspring.com.*

Forty miles of groomed cross-country trails weave through North
Conway and the countryside along the **Mt. Washington Valley Ski Tour-**
ing Association Network (✉*Rte. 16, Intervale* 🕾*603/356–9920 or*
800/282–5220 ⊕*www.crosscountryskinh.com*).

SHOPPING

ANTIQUES **Richard Plusch Antiques** (✉*Rte. 16 [U.S. 302]* 🕾*603/356–3333*) deals
in period furniture and accessories, including glass, sterling silver, Oriental porcelains, rugs, and paintings.

CRAFTS **Handcrafters Barn** (✉*Main St.* 🕾*603/356–8996*) stocks the work of
350 area artists and artisans. The **League of New Hampshire Craftsmen**
(✉*2526 Main St.* 🕾*603/356–2441*) carries the creations of the state's
best artisans. **Zeb's General Store** (✉*2675 Main St.* 🕾*603/356–9294 or*
800/676–9294) looks just like an old-fashioned country store; it sells
food items, crafts, and other products made in New England.

CLOTHES More than 150 factory outlets—including L.L. Bean, Timberland,
Pfaltzgraff, London Fog, Polo, Nike, Anne Klein, and Woolrich—

line Route 16. A top pick for skiwear is **Joe Jones** (✉*2709 Main St.* ☎*603/356–9411*).

NIGHTLIFE & THE ARTS

Horsefeather's (✉*Main St.* ☎*603/356–6862*), a restaurant and bar, often has rock, blues, and folk music, especially on weekends. **Mt. Washington Valley Theater Company** (✉*Eastern Slope Inn Playhouse, Main St.* ☎*603/356–5776* ⊕*www.musical-theatre.org*) stages four productions from mid-June to late August.

WHERE TO EAT

$-$$ ✗**Delaney's Hole in the Wall.** This casual sports tavern has eclectic mem-
AMERICAN orabilia such as autographed baseballs and an early photo of skiing at Tuckerman Ravine hanging over the fireplace. Entrées range from fish-and-chips to fajitas to mussels and scallops sautéed with spiced sausage and Louisiana seasonings. There's live music most nights. ✉*Rte. 16, ¼ mi north of North Conway Village* ☎*603/356–7776* ▭*AE, D, MC, V.*

¢-$ ✗**Muddy Moose.** This family place is inviting and rustic thanks to its
AMERICAN fieldstone walls, exposed wood, and understated lighting. Dig into a Greek salad, grilled chicken Caesar wrap, char-grilled pork chops with a maple-cider glaze, or muddy moose pie, the signature ice cream, fudge and crumbled Oreo dessert. ✉*Rte. 16 just south of North Conway* ☎*603/356–7696* ▭*AE, D, MC, V* ♨*No reservations accepted.*

WHERE TO STAY

$ ▦**Buttonwood Inn.** A tranquil 17-acre oasis in this busy resort area, the Buttonwood is on Mt. Surprise, 2 mi northeast of North Conway Village. Staying here you can have a peaceful retreat and avoid the noise of downtown but still have access to area restaurants and shopping. Rooms in the 1820s farmhouse are furnished in Shaker style. Wide pine floors, quilts, and period stenciling add warmth. Two rooms have gas fireplaces. Downstairs is the Mt. Surprise room which has a self-serve bar, library, board games, and DVD library. **Pros:** good bedding and amenities, tranquil, clean. **Cons:** unexciting for those not wanting a remote getaway. ✉*Mt. Surprise Rd* ☎*603/356–2625 or 800/258–2625* ⊕*www.buttonwoodinn.com* ⇨*8 rooms, 2 suites* ♨*In-room: DVD (some), no TV. In-hotel: pool, no elevator, public Internet, public Wi-Fi, no-smoking rooms* ▭*AE, MC, V* ℺*BP.*

$ ▦**Darby Field Inn.** After a day of activity in the White Mountains, warm up by this inn's fieldstone fireplace or by the bar's woodstove. Most rooms in this unpretentious 1826 farmhouse have mountain views; several have fireplaces. There are 10 mi of cross-countrry and hiking trails, as well as carriage rides and sleigh rides. The inn's dining room prepares such haute regional American fare. **Pros:** clean, romantic, remote. **Cons:** best for couples. ✉*185 Chase Hill, Albany* ☎*603/447–2181 or 800/426–4147* ⊕*www.darbyfield.com* ⇨*9 rooms, 4 suites* ♨*In-room: no a/c (some), no phone, DVD (some), VCR (some), no TV (some), Wi-Fi. In-hotel: restaurant, bar, pool, no elevator, public Wi-Fi, no kids under 8, no-smoking rooms* ▭*AE, MC, V* ⊗*Closed Apr.* ℺*BP.*

$-$$ ⊞Inn at Crystal Lake. Just 5 mi south of Conway in the quaint village of Eaton Center, this gracious Greek-revival inn dates to 1884 and contains 11 finely appointed rooms with dramatic themes, each filled with a mix of curious and whimsical art and collectibles from the innkeepers' travels. The gardens surrounding the inn are spectacular. Breakfast is a tasty and filling country spread, including delicious baked goods; you can also enjoy afternoon snacks in the on-site Palmer Pub, which serves light dinner fare throughout the evening. **Pros:** Cute lodge, nice pub. **Cons:** no Wi-Fi. ⊠*Rte. 15, Eaton Center* ⌂*Box 12, 03832* ☎*603/447–2120 or 800/343–7336* ⊕*www.innatcrystallake. com* ➔*11 rooms* ⌂*In-room: VCR. In-hotel: bar, no-smoking rooms, no-smoking rooms* ▤*MC, V* ⧀*BP.*

$$-$$$ ⊞Snowvillage Inn. Journalist Frank Simonds built the gambrel-roofed
  ★   main house in 1916. To complement the tome-jammed bookshelves, guest rooms are named for famous authors; many have fireplaces. The nicest of the rooms, with 12 windows that look out over the Presidential Range, is a tribute to Robert Frost. Two additional buildings—the carriage house and the chimney house—also have libraries. The menu in the candlelit dining room ($$–$$$$; reservations essential) might include roasted rack of lamb with minted onion marmalade, pistachio-encrusted salmon, or a medley of young duckling prepared three ways. The inn is also home to the White Mountain Cooking School, and overnight packages with cooking classes are available. You can hike easily up to beautiful Foss Mountain, directly from the inn. **Pros:** adorable property; fine dining. **Cons:** on the pricier side. ⊠*Stewart Rd., 6 mi southeast of Conway, Snowville 03832* ☎*603/447–2818 or 800/447–4345* ⊕*www.snowvillageinn.com* ➔*18 rooms* ⌂*In-room: no TV. In-hotel: restaurant, no kids under 6, no-smoking rooms, no-smoking rooms* ▤*AE, D, MC, V* ⧀*BP, MAP.*

$$$ ⊞White Mountain Hotel and Resort. West of the traffic of North Conway, the scenery becomes splendid. Rooms in this hotel at the base of Whitehorse Ledge have mountain views. Proximity to the White Mountain National Forest and Echo Lake State Park makes you feel farther away from the outlet malls than you actually are. There's a 9-hole golf course and this is a great area for biking. Three meals a day are available at the at Ledges dining room; there's also a tavern. Kids 18 and under stay free. **Pros:** scenic setting that's close to shopping; lots of activities. **Cons:** two-night minimum summer weekends. ⊠*West Side Rd., 03860* ☎*800/533–6301* ☎*603/356–7100* ⊕*www.whitemountainhotel.com* ➔*80 rooms, 13 suites* ⌂*In-room: DVD, VCR, Wi-Fi. In-hotel: 2 restaurants, room service, bar, golf course, tennis court, pool, gym, public Internet, public Wi-Fi, no-smoking rooms* ▤*AE, D, MC, V* ⧀*BP, MAP.*

EN ROUTE   A great place to settle in to the White Mountains, take in one of the greatest panoramas of the muntains, and get visitor info is at the **Intervale Scenic Vista.** The stop, off Route 16 a few miles north of North Conway, is run by the DOT, has a helpful volunteer staff, and features a wonderful large topographical map and terrific bathrooms.

KANCAMAGUS HIGHWAY

★ *36 mi between Conway and Lincoln/North Woodstock.*

Interstate 93 is the fastest way to the White Mountains, but it's hardly the most appealing. The section of Route 112 known as the Kancamagus Highway passes through some of the state's most unspoiled mountain scenery—it was one of the first roads in the nation to be designated a National Scenic Byway. The Kanc, as it's called by locals, is punctuated by overlooks and picnic areas, erupts into fiery color each fall, when photo-snapping drivers can really slow things down. There are campgrounds off the highway. In bad weather, check with the White Mountains Visitors Bureau for road conditions.

SPORTS & THE OUTDOORS

A couple of short hiking trails off the Kancamagus Highway (Route 112) yield great rewards for relatively little effort. The **Lincoln Woods Trail** starts from the large parking lot of the Lincoln Woods Visitor Center, 4 mi east of Lincoln. You can purchase the recreation pass ($5 per vehicle, good for seven consecutive days) needed to park in any of the White Mountain National Forest lots or overlooks here; stopping briefly to take photos or to use the restrooms at the visitor center is permitted without a pass. The trail crosses a suspension bridge over the Pemigewasset River and follows an old railroad bed for 3 mi along the river. The parking and picnic area for **Sabbaday Falls**, about 15 mi west of Conway, is the trailhead for an easy ½-mi route to a multilevel cascade that plunges through two potholes and a flume.

DARTMOUTH–LAKE SUNAPEE

In the west-central part of the state, the towns around prestigious Dartmouth College and rippling Lake Sunapee vary from sleepy, old-fashioned outposts that haven't changed much in decades to bustling, sophisticated towns rife with cafés, art galleries, and boutiques. Among the latter, Hanover and New London are the area's main hubs, both of them becoming increasingly popular as vacation destinations and with telecommuters seeking a quieter, more economical home base. Although distinct from the Lakes Region, greater Lake Sunapee looks like a miniature Lake Winnipesaukee, albeit with far less commercial development. For a great drive, follow the Lake Sunapee Scenic & Cultural Byway, which runs for about 25 mi from Georges Mills (a bit northwest of New London) down into Warner, tracing much of the Lake Sunapee shoreline. When you've tired of climbing and swimming and visiting the past, look for small studios of area artists. This part of the state, along with the even quieter Monadnocks area to the south, has long been an informal artists' colony where people come to write, paint, and weave in solitude.

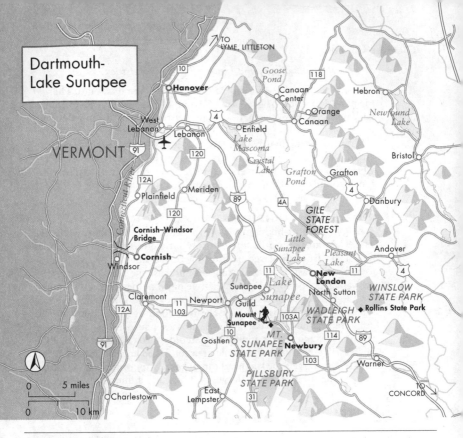

Dartmouth-
Lake Sunapee

NEW LONDON

16 mi northwest of Warner, 25 mi west of Tilton.

New London, the home of Colby-Sawyer College (1837), is a good base for exploring the Lake Sunapee region. A campus of stately Colonial-style buildings fronts the vibrant commercial district, where you'll find several cafés and boutiques.

SPORTS & THE OUTDOORS

A 3½-mi scenic auto road at **Rollins State Park** (⊠*Off Rte. 103, Main St., Warner* 🕾*603/456–3808* 🖅*$3*) snakes up the southern slope of Mt. Kearsarge, where you can hike a ½-mi trail to the summit. The road is closed mid-November through mid-June.

SHOPPING

Artisan's Workshop (⊠*Peter Christian's Tavern, 196 Main St.* 🕾*603/526–4227*) carries jewelry, glass, and other local handicrafts. Near New London in the tiny village of Elkins, **Mesa Home Factory Store** (⊠*Elkins Bus. Loop* 🕾*603/526–4497*) carries striking hand-painted dinnerware, handblown glassware, wrought-iron decorative arts, and other housewares at bargain prices.

THE ARTS

The **New London Barn Playhouse** (⊠*84 Main St.* ☎*603/526–6710 or 800/633–2276* ⊕*www.nlbarn.com*) presents Broadway-style and children's plays every summer in New Hampshire's oldest continuously operating theater.

WHERE TO EAT

$–$$ ✕**Four Corners Grille and Flying Goose Brew Pub.** South of downtown, this

AMERICAN inviting restaurant and adjoining pub is known for massive burgers, pit-barbecued meats, calamari in basil pesto, great ales, and exceptional views of Mt. Kearsarge. More substantial victuals include jambalaya with shrimp, scallops, mussels, and sausage, and char-grilled teriyaki steaks. There's live folk and light rock music many nights. ⊠*40 Andover Rd., Rtes. 11 and 114* ☎*603/526–6899* ▤*AE, D, MC, V.*

$ ✕**Jack's Coffee.** Nominally a coffeehouse, Jack's is actually much more,

CAFE presenting a nice range of bountiful salads (try the lemon Caesar) and designer sandwiches. It also has a great breakfast. The restaurant occupies a stately Greek-revival house in the heart of downtown, and a tree-shaded patio out front overlooks the pedestrian action. ⊠*207 Main St.* ☎*603/526–8003* ▤*D, MC, V* ☺*No dinner.*

WHERE TO STAY

$–$$ ▦**Inn at Pleasant Lake.** This 1790s inn lies just across Pleasant Lake

★ from majestic Mt. Kearsarge. Its spacious rooms have country antiques and modern bathrooms. The restaurant ($$$$; reservations essential) presents a nightly changing prix-fixe menu that draws raves for such entrées as roast tenderloin of Angus beef with a Calvados demi-glace and watercress pesto and such desserts as white-chocolate mousse with a trio of sauces. Afternoon tea and full breakfast are included. **Pros:** lakefront with a small beach; boating. **Cons:** away from town activities. ⊠*853 Pleasant St., 03257* ☎*603/526–6271 or 800/626–4907* ⊕*www.innatpleasantlake.com* ⇆*10 rooms* ⌂*In-room: no phone, no TV. In-hotel: restaurant, gym, beachfront, no-smoking rooms* ▤*MC, V* ⦿*BP.*

$–$$ ▦**Follansbee Inn.** Built in 1840, this quintessential country inn on the shore of Kezar Lake is a perfect fit in the 19th-century village of North Sutton, about 4 mi south of New London. The common rooms and bedrooms are loaded with collectibles—a traveling trunk here, a wooden school desk there. Each of the 18 rooms is filled with soft country quilts, and several of them overlook the water. In winter, you can ice-fish, borrow the inn's snowshoes, or ski across the lake; in summer you can swim or boat from the inn's pier. A 3-mi walking trail circles the lake. **Pros:** relaxed lakefront setting; clean rooms. **Cons:** young children aren't allowed. ⊠*Rte. 114, North Sutton* ☎*603/927–4221 or 800/626–4221* ⊕*www.follansbeeinn.com* ⇆*18 rooms* ⌂*In-room: no phone, no TV. In-hotel: water sports, bicycles, no kids under 10, no-smoking rooms* ▤*MC, V* ⦿*BP.*

$–$$ ▦**New London Inn.** The two porches of this rambling 1792 inn overlook Main Street. Clean rooms are brightly colored, with contemporary furnishings. Some have views of the Colby-Sawyer campus. The restaurant's ($$–$$$$) menu of innovative American cuisine has such starters as butternut squash with a sun-dried cranberry pesto and such entrées as grilled cilantro shrimp with a saffron risotto. **Pros:** Clean, contemporary, bright rooms; good service; day spa. **Cons:** Continental breakfast ends at 9 AM. ⊠*353 Main St., Box 8,* ☎*603/526–2791 or 800/526–2791* ⊕*www.newlondoninn.net* ↪*25 rooms* ⌂*In-room: no TV (some), Wi-Fi. In-hotel: restaurant, public Internet, public Wi-Fi, no-smoking rooms* ▭*AE, D, MC, V* ⏀*CP.*

EN ROUTE   About midway between New London and Newbury on the west side of the lake **Sunapee Harbor** is an old-fashioned, all-American summer resort community that feels a bit like a miniature version of Wolfeboro, with a large marina, a handful of restaurants and shops on the water, a tidy village green with a gazebo, and a small museum run by the historical society set in a Victorian stable. A plaque outside Wild Goose Country Store details some of Lake Sunapee's attributes—that it's one of the highest lakes in New Hampshire, at 1,091 feet above sea level, and that it's also one of the least polluted. An interpretive path runs along a short span of the Sugar River, the only outflow from Lake Sunapee, which winds for 18 mi to the Connecticut River.

NEWBURY

8 mi southwest of New London.

Newbury is on the edge of Mt. Sunapee State Park. The mountain, which rises to an elevation of nearly 3,000 feet, and the sparkling lake are the region's outdoor recreation centers. The popular League of New Hampshire Craftsmen's Fair, the nation's oldest crafts fair, is held at the base of Mt. Sunapee each August.

WHAT TO SEE

Fells. John M. Hay, who served as private secretary to Abraham Lincoln and secretary of state for Presidents McKinley and Roosevelt, built the Fells on Lake Sunapee as a summer home in 1890. House tours focus on his life in Newbury and Washington. Hay's son was responsible for the extensive gardens, a mix of formal and informal styles that include a 75-foot perennial border and a hillside planted with heather. More than 800 acres of the former estate are open for hiking and picnicking. ⊠*Rte. 103A* ☎*603/763–4789* ⊕*www.thefells.org* 🎟*$8* ☉*Labor Day–Columbus Day, daily 10–5; grounds daily dawn–dusk.*

SPORTS & THE OUTDOORS

BEACHES &   **Sunapee State Beach** has picnic areas, a beach, and a bathhouse. You
FISHING   can rent canoes here, too. ⊠*Rte. 103* ☎*603/763–5561* 🎟*$3* ☉*Daily dawn–dusk.* **Lake Sunapee** has brook and lake trout, salmon, smallmouth bass, and pickerel.

BOAT TOURS   Narrated cruises aboard the **MV Mt. Sunapee II** (⊠*Main St., Sunapee* ☎*603/938–6465* ⊕*www.sunapeecruises.com*) provide a closer look at Lake Sunapee's history and mountain scenery; they run from late May through mid-October, daily in summer and on weekends in spring and fall; the cost is $18. Dinner cruises are held on the **MV Kearsarge** (☎*603/938–6465* ⊕*www.mvkearsarge.com*); cruises leave from the dock at Sunapee Harbor, June through mid-October, Tuesday–Sunday evenings; the cost is $36, which includes a buffet dinner.

SKI AREA **Mount Sunapee.** Although the resort is state-owned, it's managed by Vermont's Okemo Mountain Resort (in Ludlow) known for being family friendly. The agreement has allowed the influx of capital necessary for operating extensive lifts, snowmaking (97% coverage), and trail grooming. This mountain is 1,510 vertical feet and has 60 trails, mostly intermediate. Experts can take to a dozen slopes, including three nice double-black diamonds. Boarders have a 420-foot-long half pipe and a terrain park with music. In summer, the Sunapee Express Quad zooms you to the summit. From here, it's just under a mile hike to Lake Solitude. Mountain bikers can use the lift to many trails, and an in-line skate park has beginner and advanced sections (plus equipment rentals). ⊠ *Rte. 103, 03772* ☎*603/763–2356, 603/763–4020 snow conditions, 877/687–8627 lodging* ⊕*www.mtsunapee.com.*

SHOPPING

Overlooking Lake Sunapee's southern tip, **Outspokin' Bicycle and Sport** (⊠*Rtes. 103 and 103A, at the harbor* ☎*603/763–9500*) has a tremendous selection of biking, hiking, skateboarding, waterskiing, skiing, and snowboarding clothing and equipment. Right on the harbor in Sunapee village, on the marina, **Wild Goose Country Store** (⊠*77 Main St.* ☎*603/763–5516*) carries quirky gifts, teddy bears, penny candy, pottery, and other engaging odds and ends.

WHERE TO EAT & STAY

$–$$ ✕**Anchorage at Sunapee Harbor.** Fans of this long gray restaurant with
AMERICAN a sprawling deck overlooking Sunapee Harbor's marina come as much for the great views as for the dependable—and occasionally creative—American chow. It's as likely a place for a burger or fried seafood platter as for homemade lobster spring rolls. There's also live entertainment some nights—in fact, this is where the founders of the rock band Aerosmith first met back in the early 1970s. ⊠*71 Main St., Sunapee Harbor* ☎*603/763–3334* ▭*D, MC, V* ☉*Closed mid-Oct.–late Apr. and Mon.*

$$$ ⬚**Sunapee Harbor Cottages.** A luxurious take on the classic cottage com-
★ pounds that dot the Sunapee and Lakes regions, this particular collection of six contemporary shingle bungalows tumbles down a gentle hillside just steps from Sunapee Harbor's marina and restaurants. Each light and airy unit sleeps from five to eight people, making this a good deal for larger groups and a bit of a splurge for couples—all have kitchens, gas fireplaces, porches, and a well-chosen mix of antiques and newer furnishings. Nice touches include grocery-delivery service, in-room massage, and even catered meals prepared by the nearby Millstone Restaurant. **Pros:** clean, contemporary, spacious units. **Cons:** units are close to each other. ⊠*4 Lake Ave., Sunapee Harbor* ☎*603/763–5052 or 866/763–5052* ⊕*www.sunapeeharborcottages. com* ⇌*6 cottages* ♿*In-room: kitchen, DVD, Wi-Fi, no elevator, no-smoking rooms* ▭*MC, V.*

Maple Sugaring

CLOSE UP

It's the quintessential condiment of New England breakfasts, the core ingredient of cutely shaped candies, and one of New Hampshire's legendary exports: maple syrup. In fact, the Granite State produces about 90,000 gallons of this sweet elixir every year. And throughout the state, particularly in the Monadnock and Sunapee regions, a number of private sugarhouses open their doors to the public—you can visit to watch maple-sugaring demonstrations, or just to buy fresh syrup. A few sugarhouses even hold parties and festivals.

Stop at a sugar shack to watch maple sap become maple syrup.

The season generally runs from about mid-February through mid-April, depending on weather conditions. Sap runs best when daytime temperatures rise above freezing. Once collected in buckets from the trees, sap is taken to the sugarhouses, where it's boiled down and ultimately reduced to pure maple syrup. You need to boil down about 40 gallons of raw sap to get just a gallon of refined syrup. It's a time-consuming and rather painstaking process, which in part accounts for the relative high cost of pure maple syrup versus the treacly imitation variety sold in many grocery stores.

Make a note on your calendar to attend the state's foremost sugaring event, New Hampshire Maple Weekend, held in mid- to late March, when some 50 sugarhouses open their doors to guests, host pancake breakfasts, and show off their often impressive sugaring operations. For a list of syrup producers throughout the state, contact **New Hampshire Maple Producers** (☎ *603/225–3757* ⊕ *www.nhmapleproducers.com*). The organization also produces a cookbook containing some 200 maple recipes; you can order this book from the Web site for $14, which includes shipping and handling.

—Andrew Collins

HANOVER

12 mi northwest of Enfield, 62 mi northwest of Concord.

Eleazer Wheelock founded Hanover's Dartmouth College in 1769 to educate the Abenaki "and other youth." When he arrived, the town consisted of about 20 families. The college and the town grew symbiotically, with Dartmouth becoming the northernmost Ivy League school. Hanover is still synonymous with Dartmouth, but it's also a respected medical and cultural center for the upper Connecticut River valley.

WHAT TO SEE

★ **Dartmouth College.** Robert Frost spent part of a brooding freshman semester at this Ivy League school before giving up college altogether. The buildings that cluster around the green include the **Baker Memorial Library,** which houses such literary treasures as 17th-century editions of Shakespeare's works. The library is also well known for the 3,000-square-foot murals by Mexican artist José Clemente Orozco that depict the story of civilization on the American continents. If the towering arcade at the entrance to the **Hopkins Center** (☎ *603/646–2422*) appears familiar, it's probably because it resembles the project that architect Wallace K. Harrison completed just after designing it: New York City's Metropolitan Opera House at Lincoln Center. The complex includes a 900-seat theater for film showings and concerts, a 400-seat theater for plays, and a black-box theater for new plays. The Dartmouth Symphony Orchestra performs here, as does the Big Apple Circus. In addition to African, Peruvian, Oceanic, Asian, European, and American art, the **Hood Museum of Art** (⊠ *Wheelock St.* ☎ *603/646–2808* ⊕ *www.dartmouth.edu/hood* ☜ *Free* ☉ *Tues. and Thurs.–Sat. 10–5, Wed. 10–9, Sun. noon–5*) owns the Picasso painting *Guitar on a Table,* silver by Paul Revere, and a set of Assyrian reliefs from the 9th century BC. The range of contemporary works, including pieces by John Sloan, William Glackens, Mark Rothko, Fernand Léger, and Joan Miró, is particularly notable. Rivaling the collection is the museum's architecture: a series of austere, copper-roofed, redbrick buildings arranged around a courtyard. Free campus tours are available on request. ⊠ *N. Main and Wentworth Sts.* ☎ *603/646–1110.*

NEED A BREAK?

Take a respite from museum-hopping with a cup of espresso, a ham-and-cheese scone, or a freshly baked brownie at the **Dirt Cowboy** (⊠ *7 S. Main St.* ☎ *603/643–1323*), a café across from the green and beside a used-book store. A local branch of a small Boston chain, **The Wrap** (⊠ *35 S. Main St.* ☎ *603/643–0202*), occupies a slick basement space with comfy sofas and has a small patio to the side. Drop by for healthful burritos, wraps, soups (try the carrot-ginger), and smoothies and energy drinks.

★ **Enfield Shaker Museum.** In 1782, two Shaker brothers from Mount Lebanon, New York, arrived on Lake Mascoma's northeastern side, about 12 mi southeast of Hanover. Eventually, they formed Enfield, the 9th of 18 Shaker communities in this country, and moved it to the lake's southern shore, where they erected more than 200 buildings. The Enfield Shaker Museum preserves the legacy of the Shakers, who numbered 330 members at the village's peak. By 1923, interest in the society had dwindled, and the last 10 members joined the Canterbury community, south of Laconia. A self-guided walking tour takes you through 13 of the remaining buildings, among them the Great Stone Dwelling (which served until recently as a hotel, the Shaker Inn) and an 1849 stone mill. Demonstrations of Shaker crafts techniques and numerous special events take place year-round. ⊠ *24 Caleb Dyer La., Enfield* ☎ *603/632–4346* ⊕ *www.shakermuseum.org* ☜ *$7* ☉ *Late May–late Oct., Mon.–Sat. 10–5, Sun. noon–5; late Oct.–late May, Sat. 10–4, Sun. noon–4.*

OFF THE BEATEN PATH

Upper Valley. From Hanover, you can make a 60-mi drive up Route 10 all the way to Littleton for a highly scenic tour of the upper Connecticut River valley. You'll have views of the river and Vermont's Green Mountains from many points. The road passes through groves of evergreens, over leafy ridges, and through delightful hamlets. Grab gourmet picnic provisions at the general store on Lyme's village common—probably the most pristine of any in the state—and stop at the bluff-top village green in historical Haverhill (28 mi north of Hanover) for a picnic amid the panorama of classic Georgian- and Federal-style mansions and faraway farmsteads. You can follow this scenic route all the way to the White Mountains region, or loop back south from Haverhill—along Route 25 to Route 118 to U.S. 4 west—to Enfield, a drive of about 45 mi (75 minutes).

SPORTS & THE OUTDOORS

Ledyard Canoe Club of Dartmouth (☎603/643–6709) provides canoe and kayak rentals and classes on the swift-flowing Connecticut River, which isn't suitable for beginners and is safest after mid-June.

SHOPPING

Shops, mostly of the independent variety but with a few upscale chains sprinkled in, line Hanover's main street. The commercial district blends almost imperceptibly with the Dartmouth campus. West Lebanon, south of Hanover on the Vermont border, has many more shops. Goldsmith Paul Gross of **Designer Gold** (⊠3 Lebanon St. ☎603/643–3864) designs settings for gemstones—all one-of-a-kind or limited-edition. **The League of New Hampshire Craftsman** (⊠83 Lebanon St. ☎603/643–5050) has a good craft and art shop. The **Powerhouse Mall** (⊠Rte. 12A, 1 mi north of I–89 Exit 20, West Lebanon ☎603/298–5236), a former power station, comprises three buildings of specialty stores, boutiques, and restaurants.

WHERE TO EAT

$$–$$$ **AMERICAN** ✕**Canoe Club.** This festive spot decked with canoes, paddles, classic Dartmouth paraphernalia presents live jazz and folk music many nights. The mood may be casual, but the kitchen presents rather fancy and imaginative food, including a memorable starter of shrimp, prosciutto, and almonds wrapped in bok choy with sweet-and-sour sauce. Among the main courses, roasted lamb sirloin with white beans, asparagus, and roasted garlic ragout stands out. There's also a lighter, late-night menu. ⊠27 S. Main St. ☎603/643–9660 ⊟AE, D, DC, MC, V.

$–$$ **ITALIAN** ✕**Lui Lui.** The creatively topped thin-crust pizzas and huge pasta portions are only part of the draw at this chatter-filled eatery. It also has a dramatic setting inside a former power station on the Mascoma River. Pizza picks include the Tuscan (mozzarella on the bottom, tomato, and roasted garlic) and the grilled chicken with barbecue sauce. Pasta fans should dive into a bowl of linguine with prosciutto, spinach, and mushrooms. The owners also run Molly's Restaurant and Jesse's Tavern, which are both nearby. ⊠Adjacent to Powerhouse Mall, off Rte. 12A, West Lebanon ☎603/298–7070 ⊟AE, MC, V.

¢
★
AMERICAN

✗**Lou's.** This is the only place in town where students and locals really mix. After all, it's hard to resist. A Hanover tradition since 1948, this diner-cum-café-cum-bakery serves possibly the best breakfast in the valley—a plate of *migas* (eggs, cheddar, salsa, and guacamole mixed with tortilla chips) can fill you up for the better part of the day; blueberry-cranberry buttermilk pancakes also satisfy. Or grab a seat at the old-fashioned soda fountain and order an ice-cream sundae. ⊠*30 S. Main St.* ☎*603/643–3321* ▭*AE, MC, V* ⊘*No dinner.*

$$–$$$
ECLECTIC

✗**Murphy's.** Students, visiting alums, and locals regularly descend upon this wildly popular pub, whose walls are lined with shelves of old books. The varied menu of consistently tasty chow lists both familiar and innovative fare: blackened-chicken wraps, char-grilled Black Angus steaks, Szechuan yellowfin tuna with red curry sauce and ginger cakes, lobster ravioli, and fajitas. Check out the extensive beer list. ⊠*11 S. Main St.* ☎*603/643–4075* ▭*AE, D, DC, MC, V.*

WHERE TO STAY

$$$$
★

🏨**Hanover Inn.** If you're in town for a Dartmouth event, there's no competition: you'll want to stay here on the town, and the college's, main square. You'll pay for the location, too. Owned by Dartmouth, this sprawling, Georgian-style brick structure rises four white-trimmed stories. The original building was converted to a tavern in 1780, and this expertly run inn, now greatly enlarged, has been operating ever since. Rooms have Colonial reproductions, Audubon prints, large sitting areas, and marble-accented bathrooms. The swank Zins Wine Bistro ($–$$) prepares lighter but highly innovative fare. **Pros:** center of campus and town location, well managed. **Cons:** breakfast not included, overpriced. ⊠*The Green, Main and Wheelock Sts., Box 151, 03755* ☎*603/643–4300 or 800/443–7024* ⊕*www.hanoverinn. com* ➷*92 rooms, 23 suites* ⊘*In-room: Wi-Fi. In-hotel: 2 restaurants, room service, bar, public Internet, public Wi-Fi, no-smoking rooms* ▭*AE, D, DC, MC, V.*

$$–$$$

🏨**Trumbull House.** The sunny guest rooms of this white Colonial-style house—on 16 acres in Hanover's outskirts—have king- or queen-size beds, window seats, writing desks, feather pillows, and other comfortable touches, as well as wireless Internet. There is also a romantic guesthouse, complete with a private deck, whirlpool tub, refrigerator, and wet bar. Breakfast, with a choice of entrées, is served in the formal dining room or in front of the living room fireplace. Rates include use of a nearby health club. **Pros:** quiet setting, lovely home, big breakfast. **Cons:** 5 mi east of town. ⊠*40 Etna Rd., 03755* ☎*603/643–2370 or 800/651–5141* ⊕*www.trumbullhouse.com* ➷*4 rooms, 1 suite, 1 cottage* ⊘*In-room: VCR, Wi-Fi. In-hotel: restaurant, no-smoking rooms* ▭*AE, D, DC, MC, V* ⊙*BP.*

CORNISH

22 mi south of Hanover.

Today Cornish is best known for its four covered bridges and for being the home of reclusive author J. D. Salinger, but at the turn of the 20th century the village was known primarily as the home of the country's then most popular novelist, Winston Churchill (no relation to the British prime minister). His novel *Richard Carvell* sold more than a million copies. Churchill was such a celebrity that he hosted Teddy Roosevelt during the president's 1902 visit. At that time Cornish was an enclave of artistic talent. Painter Maxfield Parrish lived and worked here, and sculptor Augustus Saint-Gaudens set up his studio and created the heroic bronzes for which he is known.

WHAT TO SEE
Cornish-Windsor Bridge. This 460-foot bridge, 1½ mi south of the Saint-Gaudens National Historic Site, connects New Hampshire to Vermont across the Connecticut River. It dates from 1866 and is the longest covered bridge in the United States. The notice on the bridge reads: WALK YOUR HORSES OR PAY TWO DOLLAR FINE.

Fodor'sChoice
★ **Saint-Gaudens National Historic Site.** Just south of Plainfield, where River Road rejoins Route 12A, a small lane leads to this historic site, where you can tour sculptor Augustus Saint-Gaudens's house, studio, gallery, and 150 acres of grounds and gardens. Scattered throughout are full-size casts of his works. The property has two hiking trails, the longer of which is the Blow-Me-Down Trail. Concerts are held every Sunday afternoon in July and August. ⊠ *Off Rte. 12A* ☎ *603/675–2175* ⊕ *www.sgnhs.org* 🎟 *$5* ⊙ *Buildings June–Oct., daily 9–4:30; grounds daily dawn–dusk.*

SPORTS & THE OUTDOORS
North Star Canoe Rentals (⊠ *Rte. 12A, Balloch's Crossing* ☎ *603/542–6929*) rents canoes for half- or full-day trips on the Connecticut River.

THE ARTS
The restored 19th-century **Claremont Opera House** (⊠ *Tremont Sq., Claremont* ☎ *603/542–4433* ⊕ *www.claremontoperahouse.com*) hosts plays and musicals throughout summer.

THE MONADNOCKS & MERRIMACK VALLEY

Southwestern and south-central New Hampshire mix village charm with city hustle across two distinct regions. The Merrimack River valley has the state's largest and fastest-growing cities: Nashua, Manchester, and Concord. To the west, in the state's sleepy southwestern corner, is the Monadnock region, one of New Hampshire's least-developed and most naturally stunning parts. Here you'll find plenty of hiking trails as well as peaceful hilltop hamlets that appear barely changed in the past two centuries. Mt. Monadnock, southern New Hampshire's largest peak, stands guard over the Monadnock region, which has more than 200 lakes and ponds. Rainbow trout, smallmouth and largemouth bass, and some northern pike swim in Chesterfield's Spofford Lake. Goose Pond in West Canaan, just north of Keene, holds smallmouth bass and white perch.

The towns are listed in counterclockwise order, beginning with Nashua and heading north to Manchester and Concord; then west to Henniker and Hillsborough and Charleston; south to Walpole; southwest to Keene and Jaffrey; and finally northeast to Peterborough.

NASHUA

98 mi south of Lincoln/North Woodstock, 48 mi northwest of Boston, 36 mi south of Concord, 50 mi southeast of Keene.

Once a prosperous manufacturing town that drew thousands of immigrant workers in the late 1800s and early 1900s, Nashua declined following World War II, as many factories shut down or moved to where labor was cheaper. Since the 1970s, however, the metro area has jumped in population, developing into a charming, old-fashioned community. Its low-key downtown has classic redbrick buildings along the Nashua River, a tributary of the Merrimack River. Though not visited by tourists as much as other communities in the region, Nashua (population 90,000) has some good restaurants and an engaging museum.

WHAT TO SEE

Florence Hyde Speare Memorial Museum. The city's impressive industrial history is retold at this museum that houses the Nashua Historical Society. In this two-story museum you'll find artifacts, early furnishings, photos, a vintage printing press, and a research library. Adjacent to the museum is the Federal-style **Abbot-Spalding House,** furnished with 18th- and 19th-century antiques, art, and household items. The house can be visited only on a guided tour that takes place one Saturday a month from April through November. ⊠ *5 Abbot St.* ☎ *603/883–0015* ⊕ *www.nashuahistoricalsociety.org* ☒ *Free* ☉ *Mar.–Thanksgiving, Tues.–Thurs. 10–4 (also one Sat. per month by appointment).*

WHERE TO EAT

$ **✕ Martha's Exchange.** A casual spot with copper brewing vats, original
AMERICAN   marble floors, and booth seating, Martha's appeals both to the after-work set and office workers on lunch breaks. Burgers and sandwiches, maple-stout-barbecued chicken and ribs, Mexican fare, seafood and steak grills, and salads—all in large portions—are your options here. There's also a sweets shop attached, and you can buy half-gallon jugs of house-brewed beers to go. ⊠ *185 Main St.* ☎ *603/883–8781* ☒ *AE, DC, MC, V.*

$$–$$$ **✕ Michael Timothy's Urban Bistro.** Part hip bistro, part jazzy wine bar
Fodor'sChoice   (with live music many nights), Michael Timothy's is so popular that
★   even foodies from Massachusetts drive here. The regularly chang-
BISTRO   ing menu might include stuffed pheasant with foie gras risotto and cranberry-clove jus, or wood-grilled venison loin with port reduction, herb spaetzle, creamed morel mushrooms, and stewed lentils. Wood-fired pizzas are also a specialty—try the one topped with sirloin tips, caramelized onions, mushrooms, salami, sautéed spinach, and three cheeses. Sunday brunch is a big hit here. ⊠ *212 Main St.* ☎ *603/595–9334* ☒ *AE, D, MC, V* ☉ *No lunch Sat.*

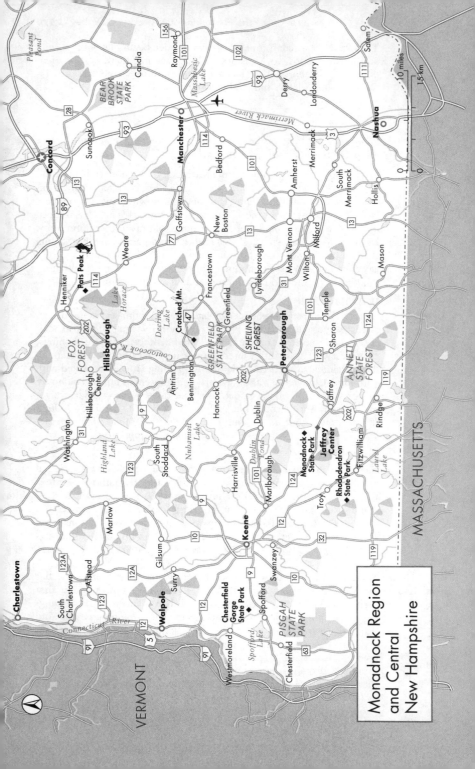

Monadnock Region
and Central
New Hampshire

$–$$
ITALIAN

×**Villa Banca.** On the ground floor of a dramatic, turreted office building, this airy spot with high ceilings and tall windows specializes in both traditional and contemporary Italian cooking. Get a little taste of everything by ordering a starter sampler platter consisting of seafood risotto cakes, lobster-stuffed artichokes, chicken sausage, fried spinach-and-artichoke ravioli, chicken in phyllo dough, and fried calamari. Then move on to the delicious pastas and grills, including gnocchi with wood-grilled turkey and prosciutto, and chicken-and-sausage lasagna. Note the exotic-martini menu—a big draw at happy hour. ⊠ *194 Main St.* ☎ *603/598–0500* ▭ *AE, D, DC, MC, V* ☉ *No lunch weekends.*

3

MANCHESTER

18 mi north of Nashua, 53 mi north of Boston.

Manchester, with 108,000-plus residents, is New Hampshire's largest city. The town grew up around the Amoskeag Falls on the Merrimack River, which fueled small textile mills through the 1700s. By 1828, Boston investors had bought the rights to the Merrimack's water power and built the Amoskeag Mills, which became a testament to New England's manufacturing capabilities. In 1906 the mills employed 17,000 people and weekly churned out more than 4 million yards of cloth. This vast enterprise served as Manchester's entire economic base; when it closed in 1936, the town was devastated.

Today Manchester is mainly a banking and business center. The old mill buildings have been converted into warehouses, classrooms, restaurants, museums, and office space. The city has the state's major airport, as well as the Verizon Wireless Arena, which hosts minor-league hockey matches, concerts, and conventions.

WHAT TO SEE

☉ Fodor's Choice ★

Amoskeag Mills. Miles of brick buildings comprise this mill. To get a sense of what they are and what they meant to Manchester, there are two key museums. The **SEE Science Center** (☎ *603/669–0400* ⊕ *www.see-sciencecenter.org* 🖃 *$5* ☉ *Weekdays 10–4, weekends 10–5*) is a hands-on science lab and children's museum with more than 70 exhibits. If you're in Manchester, child or adult, don't miss this. The world's largest permanent LEGO instillation of regular sized LEGOs is here, depicting the city's Amskeag Millyard and the ciy of Manchester as it was in 1915. This is a mind-blowing exhibit, making you awe at the craftsmanship of three million LEGOs across 2,000 square feet. Yes, you'll be awed. But more importantly, the exhibit directly conveys the massive size and importance of the mills, which ran a mile on each side of the Merrimack. It's an eye opener. Upstairs in the same building the **Millyard Museum** (☎ *603/625–2821* ⊕ *www.manchesterhistoric.org* 🖃 *$6* ☉ *Tues.–Sat. 10–4*) contains state-of-the-art exhibits depicting the region's history, from when Native Americans lived alongside and fished the Merrimack River to the heyday of Amoskeag Mills. The interactive Discovery Gallery is geared toward kids; there's also a lecture–concert hall and a large museum shop. ⊠ *Mill No. 3, 200 Bedford St. (entrance at 255 Commercial St.)* ☎ *603/625–2821.*

FodorsChoice **Currier Museum of Art.** New England's only Frank Lloyd Wright–designed
★ residence open to the public reopened in spring 2008 after a two-year,
$20 million renovation that doubled gallery space, and created new
shop, visitor entrance, café, and a winter garden with a Sol LeWitt
mural that faces the original 1929 Italianate entrance. There's a permanent collection of European and American paintings, sculpture, and
decorative arts from the 13th to the 20th century, including works by
Monet, Picasso, Hopper, Wyeth, and O'Keeffe. Also part of the museum
is the Frank Lloyd Wright–designed Zimmerman House, built in 1950.
Wright called this sparse, utterly functional living space "Usonian," an
invented term used to describe fifty such middle-income homes he built
with a vision of distinctly American architecture. ⊠*201 Myrtle Way*
☏*603/669–6144, 603/626–4158 Zimmerman House tours* ⊕*www.
currier.org* ⊠*$7, free Sat. 10–1; Zimmerman House $11 (reservations
essential)* ⊙*Sun., Mon., Wed., and Fri. 11–5; Thurs. 11–8; Sat. 10–5;
call for Zimmerman House tour hrs.*

NIGHTLIFE & THE ARTS

NIGHTLIFE **Club 313** (⊠*93 S. Maple St.* ☏*603/628–6813*) is New Hampshire's
most popular disco for lesbians and gays. It's open Wednesday–Sunday.
Revelers come from all over to drink at the **Yard** (⊠*1211 S. Mammoth
Rd.* ☏*603/623–3545*), which is also a steak and seafood restaurant.

THE ARTS The **Palace Theatre** (⊠*80 Hanover St.* ☏*603/668–5588 theater,
603/647–6476 philharmonic, 603/669–3559 symphony, 603/647–
6564 opera* ⊕*www.palacetheatre.org*) presents musicals and plays
throughout the year. It also hosts the state's philharmonic and symphony orchestras and the Opera League of New Hampshire.

WHERE TO EAT

$–$$ ✕**Cotton.** Mod lighting and furnishings and an arbored patio set a
★ swanky tone at this restaurant inside one of the old Amoskeag Mills
AMERICAN buildings. (You might recognize the neon sign that reads FOOD). The
kitchen churns out updated comfort food. Start with pan-seared crab
cakes or the lemongrass-chicken salad. Stellar entrée picks include possibly the best steaks in the state, including a huge 20-ounce porter-
house, as well as superb grilled pork "mignon" with sweet-potato hash
and a spicy honey-chipotle aioli. The same owners run the excellent
and similarly hip seafood restaurant, Starfish Grill, at 33 South Commercial Street. ⊠*75 Arms Park Dr.* ☏*603/622–5488* ▭*AE, D, DC,
MC, V* ⊙*No lunch weekends.*

$–$$ ✕**Fratello's.** Despite a seemingly endless supply of seating, the wait
ITALIAN for a table at this restaurant can be long on weekends. The huge bi-
level space inside a redbrick building at the north end of Amoskeag
Mills has high timber ceilings and exposed ducts. The kitchen prepares
Italian food from a lengthy menu. Try any of several mix-and-match
pastas and sauces, one of the wood-fired pizzas, or one of the many
seafood dishes, such as mussels Fratello, simmered with fresh garlic,
hot cherry peppers, extra virgin olive oil and white wine. ⊠*155 Dow
St.* ☏*603/624–2022* ⚒*Reservations not accepted* ▭*AE, D, MC, V.*

¢–$ ✗**Red Arrow Diner.** This tiny diner is ground zero for presidential hope-
Fodor'sChoice fuls in New Hampshire come primary season. The rest of the time,
★ a mix of hipsters and oldsters, including comedian and Manchester
AMERICAN native Adam Sandler, favor this neon-streaked, 24-hour greasy spoon,
which has been going strong since 1922. Filling fare—platters of
kielbasa, French toast, liver and onions, chicken Parmesan with spaghetti, and the diner's famous panfries—keeps patrons happy. ⊠61
Lowell St. ☎*603/626–1118* ▤*D, MC, V.*

$$–$$$ ✗**Richard's Bistro.** Whether you want to celebrate a special occasion or
BISTRO just crave first-rate regional American cuisine, head to this romantic
downtown bistro. The kitchen uses traditional New England ingredients in worldly preparations: try the char-broiled filet mignon with
Gorgonzola, baked-stuffed potato, and strawberries or the broiled haddock topped with shrimp and scallops on an herb-risotto cake with a
honey-peach sauce. ⊠*36 Lowell St.* ☎*603/644–1180* ▤*AE, D, MC,*
V ⊗*No lunch Sun.*

WHERE TO STAY

$$ ▦**Ash Street Inn.** Because it's in an attractive residential neighborhood
of striking Victorian homes, staying in this bright and clean, five-room
B&B will make you appreciate Manchester more. Every room in the
historic sage-green 1885 house, run by Darlene and Eric Johnston,
is painted a different warm color, and you can be safe knowing that
other details are equally well thought-out. There are good linens, and
there's decantered brandy in the sitting room, which has the house's
original stained glass. In the summer, a wraparound porch is a nice
place to sit on benches and enjoy a cooked-to-order breakfast, served
on a flexible schedule. **Pros:** spotless newly decorated rooms, residential
location appeal. **Cons:** not a full-service hotel. ⊠*118 Ash St., 03104*
☎*603/668–9908* ⊕*www.ashstreetinn.com* ⇆*5 rooms* ⌂*In-room:*
Wi-Fi. In-hotel: no elevator, public Wi-Fi, no kids under 12 ▤*AE,*
MC, V ⏻❘*BP.*

$$$–$$$$ ▦**Bedford Village Inn.** If you can trade direct downtown access for a
★ lovely manor outside of town, you'll be rewarded by the comforts of
this beautiful and well-run property. The hayloft and milking rooms
of this 1810 Federal farmstead, just a few miles southwest of Man-
chester, contain lavish suites with king-size four-poster beds, plus such
modern perks as two phones and high-speed wireless. The restaurant
($$–$$$$)—a warren of elegant dining rooms with fireplaces and wide-
pine floors—presents contemporary fare that might include a starter
of baked stuffed black mission figs with Gorgonzola, prosciutto, walnuts, and arugula, followed by pan-roasted sea bass with braised fennel
and carrots, saffron-whipped potatoes, and rock-shrimp vinaigrette.
There's also a casual tavern ($–$$$), where you might sample an herb-
grilled steak Cobb salad or tortellini filled with whipped mascarpone
cheese and pumpkin. **Pros:** relaxing property just outside Manchester,
exceptional grounds, great restaurant. **Cons:** outside of town. ⊠*2 Olde*
Bedford Way, Bedford ☎*603/472–2001 or 800/852–1166* ⊕*www.*
bedfordvillageinn.com ⇆*14 suites, 2 apartments* ⌂*In-room: DVD,*
Wi-Fi. In-hotel: restaurant, room service, bar, laundry service, public
Internet, public Wi-Fi, no-smoking rooms ▤*AE, D, DC, MC, V.*

$$ ⊡ **Radisson Manchester.** Of Manchester's many chain properties, the 12-story Radisson has the most central location—a short walk from Amoskeag Mills and great dining along Elm Street. Rooms are simple and clean, perfect for business travelers. Next door is the Center of New Hampshire conference center. Because of it's busy location, this is the only hotel in the state where you have to pay for parking. **Pros:** central downtown location. **Cons:** fee for parking, unexciting chain hotel. ⊠ *700 Elm St., 03101* ☎ *603/625–1000 or 800/333–3333* ⊕ *www.radisson.com/manchesternh* ⤣ *244 rooms, 6 suites* ⚭ *In-room: Wi-Fi. In-hotel: 2 restaurants, room service, bar, pool, gym, laundry service, public Internet, public Wi-Fi, parking (fee), some pets allowed, no-smoking rooms* ⊟ *AE, D, DC, MC, V.*

CONCORD

20 mi northwest of Manchester, 67 mi northwest of Boston, 46 mi northwest of Portsmouth.

New Hampshire's capital (population 42,000) is a quiet town that tends to the state's business but little else—the sidewalks roll up promptly at 6. The **Concord on Foot** walking trail winds through the historic district. Maps for the walk can be picked up at the **Chamber of Commerce** (⊠ *40 Commercial St.* ☎ *603/224–2508* ⊕ *www.concordnhchamber.com*) or stores along the trail.

WHAT TO SEE

☾ **Christa McAuliffe Planetarium.** Shows on the solar system, constellations, and space exploration that incorporate computer graphics, sound, and special effects are presented here in a 40-foot dome theater. Children love seeing the tornado tubes, magnetic marbles, and other hands-on exhibits. Outside, explore the scale-model planet walk and the human sundial. The planetarium was named for the Concord teacher who was selected among 11,000 applicants for NASA's Teacher in Space Project and was killed in the Space Shuttle *Challenger* explosion in 1986. ⊠ *New Hampshire Technical Institute campus, 2 Institute Dr.* ☎ *603/271–7831* ⊕ *www.starhop.com* ⊞ *Exhibit area free, shows $8* ⊗ *Tues.–Thurs. 9–5, Fri. 9–7, weekends 10–5; call for show times and reservations.*

Museum of New Hampshire History. Among the artifacts here is an original Concord Coach. During the 19th century, when more than 3,000 such conveyances were built in Concord, this was about as technologically perfect a vehicle as you could find—many say it's the coach that won the West. Other exhibits provide an overview of state history, from the Abenaki to the settlers of Portsmouth up to current residents. ⊠ *6 Eagle Sq.* ☎ *603/228–6688* ⊕ *www.nhhistory.org/museum.html* ⊞ *$5.50* ⊗ *Tues.–Sat. 9:30–5, Sun. noon–5 (also Mon. 9:30–5 in summer and Dec.).*

Pierce Manse. Franklin Pierce lived is this Greek-revival home before he moved to Washington to become the 14th U.S. president. He's buried nearby. ✉*14 Horseshoe Pond La.* ☎*603/225–4555* 💲*$5* ⊙*Mid-June–early Oct., Tues.–Sat. 11–3.*

State House. A self-guided tour of the neoclassical, gilt-domed state house, built in 1819, is a real treat. You get total access to the building, and can even take a photo with the governor. This is the oldest capitol building in the nation in which the legislature uses its original chambers. In January and June you can watch the assemblies in action once week: the 24 senators of the New Hampshire Senate (the fourth-smallest American lawmaking body) meet Thursdays. In a wild inversion, the state's representatives number 400—one representative per 3,000 residents, a world record. You can see them all when they meet one day a week in January and June (that day varies year to year). Grab a self-guided tour brochure at the visitor center, which has great dioramas and paraphenilia from decades of presidential primaries. Portaits of all New Hampshires governors line the halls. ✉*107 N. Main St.* ☎*603/271–2154* ⊕*www.ci.concord.nh.us/tourdest/statehs* 💲*Free* ⊙*Weekdays 8–4:30.*

SPORTS & THE OUTDOORS

Hannah's Paddles (✉*15 Hannah Dustin Dr.* ☎*603/753–6695*) rents canoes for use on the Merrimack River, which runs through Concord.

NIGHTLIFE & THE ARTS

The **Capitol Center for the Arts** (✉*44 S. Main St.* ☎*603/225–1111* ⊕*www.ccanh.com*) has been restored to reflect its Roaring '20s origins. It hosts touring Broadway shows, dance companies, and musical acts. The lounge at **Hermanos Cocina Mexicana** (✉*11 Hills Ave.* ☎*603/224–5669*) stages live jazz Sunday through Thursday nights.

SHOPPING

Capitol Craftsman Jewelers (✉*16 N. Main St.* ☎*603/224–6166*) sells fine jewelry and handicrafts. The **League of New Hampshire Craftsmen** (✉*36 N. Main St.* ☎*603/228–8171*) exhibits crafts in many media. **Mark Knipe Goldsmiths** (✉*2 Capitol Plaza, Main St.* ☎*603/224–2920*) sets antique stones in rings, earrings, and pendants.

WHERE TO EAT

¢–$
AMERICAN ✗**Barley House.** A lively, old-fashioned tavern practically across from the capitol building and usually buzzing with a mix of politicos, business folks, and tourists, the Barley House serves dependable American chow: chorizo-sausage pizzas, burgers smothered with peppercorn-whisky sauce and blue cheese, chicken potpies, Cuban sandwiches, beer-braised bratwurst, jambalaya, and Mediterranean chicken salad—it's an impressively comprehensive menu. The convivial bar turns out dozens of interesting beers, on tap and by the bottle, and there's also a decent wine list. It's open till 1 AM. ✉*132 N. Main St.* ☎*603/228–6363* ▭*AE, D, DC, MC, V* ⊙*Closed Sun.*

¢–$
★
PIZZA ✗**Foodee's.** A local chain with additional parlors in Keene, Dover, Tilton, Milford, and Wolfeboro, Foodee's serves creative pizzas with especially delicious crusts (sourdough, six-grain, deep-dish). The capital branch is in the heart of downtown and serves such pies as the Polish (with kielbasa, sauerkraut, and three cheeses) and the El Greco

(with sweet onions, sliced tomatoes, olive oil, and feta). You can also order pastas, salads, and calzones. The all-you-can-eat buffet, Tuesday through Friday for lunch and dinner, is a great bargain. ⊠2 S. Main St. ☎603/225–3834 ▤MC, V.

¢–$ ✕**Siam Orchid.** This dark, attractive Thai restaurant with a colorful
THAI   rickshaw gracing its dining room serves spicy and reasonably authentic Thai food. It draws a crowd from the capitol each day for lunch. Try the fiery broiled swordfish with shrimp curry sauce or the pine-nut chicken in an aromatic ginger sauce. There's a second location in Manchester. ⊠158 N. Main St. ☎603/228–3633 ▤AE, D, DC, MC, V ☙No lunch weekends.

WHERE TO STAY

$ ▦**The Centennial.** This is the most contemporary hotel in New Hampshire, and it's home to Granite, the state's most contemporary restaurant and bar, making it a draw for the state's politicians and those doing business here. The modernity is unexpected, since this imposing brick-and-stone building was constructed in 1892 for widows of Civil War veterans—but a head-to-toe renovation remade the interior. Boutique furniture and contemporary art sets the immediate tone in the lobby. Rooms have luxury linens, sleek carpet and furniture, and flat-screen TVs. Bathrooms have tumbled stone floors, granite countertops, and stand-alone showers. It's the state's first foray into a boutiquish, well-designed hotel, and it's a huge success. **Pros:** super contemporary and sleek hotel, very comfortable and clean rooms, great bar and restuarant. **Cons:** busy hotel. ⊠96 Pleasant St., 03301 ☎603/225–7102 or 800/360–4839 ⊕www.centennialhotel.com ➪27 rooms, 5 suites ⌂In-room: refrigerator, DVD, VCR, Wi-Fi. In-hotel: restaurant, room service, bar, gym, public Internet, public Wi-Fi, no-smoking rooms ▤AE, D, DC, MC, V.

HENNIKER

16 mi southwest of Concord.

Governor Wentworth, New Hampshire's first Royal Governor, named this town in honor of his friend John Henniker, a London merchant and member of the British Parliament (residents delight in their town's status as "the only Henniker in the world"). Once a mill town producing bicycle rims and other light-industrial items, Henniker reinvented itself after the factories were damaged, first by spring floods in 1936 and then by the hurricane and flood of 1938. New England College was established in the following decade, adding life to this town of about 4,000. One of the area's covered bridges is on the NEC campus.

SPORTS & THE OUTDOORS

SKI AREAS   **Pats Peak.** A quick trip up Interstate 93 from the Massachusetts border, Pats Peak is geared to families. Base facilities are rustic, and friendly personal attention is the rule. Despite Pats Peak's short 710-vertical-foot rise, the 21 trails and slopes have something for everyone, and the resort has some of the best snowmaking capacity in the state. New skiers and snowboarders can take advantage of a wide slope and several short trails; intermediates have wider trails from the top; and experts have a couple of real thrillers. Night skiing, snowboarding, and tubing take place in January and February. ⊠ *686 Flanders Rd., Rte. 114, 03242* ☎*603/428–3245 information, 888/728–7732 snow conditions* ⊕*www.patspeak.com.*

SHOPPING

The **Fiber Studio** (⊠*161 Foster Hill Rd.* ☎*603/428–7830*) sells beads, hand-spun natural-fiber yarns, spinning equipment, and looms.

NIGHTLIFE

There's often live folk music at **Upstairs at Daniel's** (⊠*30 Main St.* ☎*603/428–7621*), which occupies a rambling wood-frame building with great views of the Contoocook River. Daniel's, downstairs, is a good restaurant, serving American food in a casual environment.

WHERE TO EAT & STAY

$$$ ✕**Colby Hill Inn.** The fine dining in town takes place in the Colonial din-
CONTINENTAL ing room of this old inn, with a view out the floor-to-ceiling windows. The seasonally changing menu is excellent—fine choices include maca-damia-crusted seared sea scallops, and plank-roasted loin of venison with a spiced-rhubarb barbecue sauce and barley-risotto sauce. The good wine list emphasizes Californian bottles. Sunday brunch is served. ⊠*3 The Oaks* ☎*603/428–3281 603/428–3281* ▤*AE, D, DC, MC, V* ⊗*Closed Mon. and Tues. No lunch.*

$ ⊡**Colby Hill Inn.** Owner and innkeeper Mason Cobb, greets you with a
★ sincerity and kind inflection that you might expect from someone with the genuine name of Mason Cobb. This is a welcoming place—the old-style bar is in the lobby—and there are cookies and tea for guests all day by the parlor fireplace. You can stroll through the gardens and meadows, or play badminton out back. Rooms in the main house have comfortable four-poster and canopy beds with Colonial-style furnishings, and lace curtains. Bathrooms are on the small side, but are clean and new. The carriage house has four newly renovated suites, a step up in contemporary luxury from the main house; two have two-person whirlpool baths and backyard decks. **Pros:** comfortable, clean rooms, good dining. **Cons:** slightly out of the tourist loop; little by way of town life. ⊠*3 The Oaks, Box 779, 03242* ☎*603/428–3281 or 800/531–0330* ⊕*www.colbyhillinn.com* ⇲*14 rooms, 2 suites* ⟳*In-room: refrigerator (some), VCR (some), no TV (some), Wi-Fi. In-hotel: restaurant, bar, pool, no elevator, public Wi-Fi, no kids under 7, no-smoking rooms* ▤*AE, D, DC, MC, V* ⓘⓞⓘ*BP.*

HILLSBOROUGH

8 mi southwest of Henniker.

Hillsborough comprises four villages, the most prominent of which lies along the Contoocook River and grew up around a thriving woolen and hosiery industry in the mid-1800s. This section, which is really considered Hillsborough proper, is what you'll see as you roll through town on Route 9 (U.S. 202).

Turn north from downtown up School Street, and continue 3 mi past Fox State Forest to reach one of the state's best-preserved historic districts, Hillsborough Center, where 18th-century houses surround a green. Continue north 6 mi through the similarly quaint village of East Washington, and another 6 mi to reach the Colonial town center of Washington. One of the highest villages in New Hampshire, this picturesque arrangement of white clapboard buildings made the cover of *National Geographic* several years back. You can loop back to Hillsborough proper via Route 31 south.

The nation's 14th president, Franklin Pierce, was born in Hillsborough and lived here until he married. He is, alas, one of the least-appreciated presidents ever to serve.

WHAT TO SEE

Franklin Pierce Homestead. Operated by the Hillsborough Historical Society, the house is much as it was during Pierce's life. Guided tours are offered. ⊠ *Rte. 31 just north of Rte. 9* ☎ *603/478-3165* ⊕ *www. franklinpierce.ws/homestead* 🔳 *$3* ☉ *June and Sept., Sat. 10–4, Sun. 1–4; July and Aug., Mon.–Sat. 10–4, Sun. 1–4.*

SPORTS & THE OUTDOORS

Fox State Forest (⊠ *Center Rd.* ☎ *603/464-3453*) has 25 mi of hiking trails and an observation tower.

SHOPPING

At **Gibson Pewter** (⊠ *18 E. Washington Rd., Hillsborough Center* ☎ *603/464-3410* ⊕ *www.gibsonpewter.com*), Raymond Gibson and his son Jonathan create and sell museum-quality pewter pieces. It's open Monday–Saturday 10–4. Next door to the Franklin Pierce Homestead, **Richard Withington Antiques Auction** (⊠ *590 Center Rd., Hillsborough Center* ☎ *603/464-3232* ⊕ *www.withingtonauction.com*) hosts some of the best antiques auctions in New England and stocks an impressive selection of fine pieces for general sale.

CHARLESTOWN

40 mi northwest of Hillsborough, 20 mi south of Cornish.

Charlestown has the state's largest historic district. About 60 homes, handsome examples of Federal, Greek-revival, and Gothic-revival architecture, are clustered about the town center; 10 of them were built before 1800. Several merchants on the main street distribute brochures that describe an interesting walking tour of the district.

WHAT TO SEE

☉ **Fort at No. 4.** In 1747, this fort was an outpost on the periphery of Colonial civilization. That year fewer than 50 militiamen at the fort withstood an attack by 400 French soldiers, ensuring that northern New England remained under British rule. Today, costumed interpreters at this living-history museum cook dinner over an open hearth and demonstrate weaving, gardening, and candle making. Each year the museum holds reenactments of militia musters and battles of the French and Indian War. ✉*Rte. 11, ½ mi north of Charlestown* ☎*603/826–5700 or 888/367–8284* ⊕*www.fortat4.org* 🎟*$8* ⊙*Early June–Oct., Wed.–Sun. 10–4:30.*

SPORTS & THE OUTDOORS

On a bright, breezy day you might want to detour to the **Morningside Flight Park** (✉*357 Morningside La., off Rte. 12/11, 5 mi north of Charlestown* ☎*603/542–4416* ⊕*www.flymorningside.com*), considered to be among the best flying areas in the country. Watch the bright colors of gliders as they take off from the 450-foot peak, or take hanggliding lessons yourself.

WHERE TO STAY

$ 🏠**Dutch Treat.** The innkeepers live in the oldest section of this home, which dates from about 1755. Guest rooms, in the 1820 Federal-style part, are furnished with carefully chosen antiques. The Delfts Blue Room contains several pieces of the famed Dutch Delftware pottery, and in the Tulip Suite hangs a colorful history of the Netherlands' tulip-trade history. A bountiful breakfast is served in the formal dining room. **Pros:** middle of town. **Cons:** town it's located in is off-the-beaten track. ✉*355 Main St., Box 1000,* ☎*603/826–5565 or 877/344–0944* ⊕*www.thedutchtreat.com* ⮑*4 rooms, 1 suite* ⌕*In-room: no TV. In-hotel: no kids under 12, no elevator, no-smoking rooms* ▭*MC, V* ⏀*BP.*

WALPOLE

13 mi south of Charlestown.

Walpole possesses one of the state's most perfect town greens. This one, bordered by Elm and Washington streets, is surrounded by homes built about 1790, when the townsfolk constructed a canal around the Great Falls of the Connecticut River and brought commerce and wealth to the area. The town now has 3,200 inhabitants, more than a dozen of whom are millionaires.

OFF THE BEATEN PATH

Sugarhouses. Maple-sugar season occurs about the first week in March when days become warmer but nights are still frigid. A drive along maple-lined back roads reveals thousands of taps and buckets catching the labored flow of unrefined sap. Plumes of smoke rise from nearby sugarhouses, where sugaring off, the process of boiling down this precious liquid, takes place. Many sugarhouses are open to the public; after a tour and demonstration, you can sample the syrup. You can also buy them online. **Bascom Maple Farm** (✉*56 Sugarhouse Rd., Alstead* ☎*603/835–6361* ⊕*www.bascommaple.com*) has been family run since 1853 and produces more maple than anyone in New England. Visit the 2,200-acre farm and get maple pecan pie and maple milk shakes. **Stuart & John's Sugar House & Pancake Restaurant** (✉*Rtes. 12 and 63, Westmoreland* ☎*603/399–4486* ⊕*www.stuartandjohns sugarhouse.com*) conducts a tour and sells syrup and maple gifs in a roadside barn. It also serves a memorable pancake breakfast weekends mid-February–April and mid-September–November.

SHOPPING

★ At **Boggy Meadow Farm** (✉ *13 Boggy Meadow La.* ☎ *603/756–3300 or 877/541–3953*) you can watch the cheese process unfold, from the 200 cows being milked to the finer process of cheese-making. The farmstead raw-milk cheeses can be sampled and purchased in the store. It's worth it just to see the beautiful 400-acre farm. At **L.A. Burdick Chocolates** (✉ *45 Main Street* ☎ *603/756–2882*) you can choose from dozen of styles of chocolates and eat them in the café next door, or ship them anywhere.

WHERE TO EAT

$–$$

Fodor'sChoice

★

FRENCH

✕ **The Restaurant at L.A. Burdick Chocolate.** Famous candy maker Larry Burdick, who sells his artful hand-filled and hand-cut chocolates to top restaurants around the Northeast, is a Walpole resident. This restaurant has the easygoing sophistication of a Parisian café and may tempt you to linger over an incredibly rich hot chocolate. The Mediterranean-inspired menu utilizes fresh, often local ingredients and changes daily. Of course, dessert is a big treat here, featuring Burdick's tempting chocolates and pastries. For dinner, you might start with a selection of artisanal cheeses or the confit of duck with grilled plums and a red wine reduction, followed by striped bass with eggplant, tomatoes, and capers, or roasted chicken with garlic-mashed potato cake and fresh tarragon. ✉ *47 Main St.* ☎ *603/756–2882* ⊟ *AE, D, MC, V* ⊙ *No dinner Sun. and Mon.*

KEENE

17 mi southeast of Walpole; 20 mi northeast of Brattleboro, Vermont; 56 mi southwest of Manchester.

Keene is the largest city in the state's southwest corner. Its rapidly gentrifying main street, with several engaging boutiques and cafés, is America's widest (132 feet). Each year, on the Saturday before Halloween, locals use the street to hold a Pumpkin Festival, where they seek to retain their place in the record books for the most carved, lighted jack-o'-lanterns—more than 25,000 some years.

WHAT TO SEE

Keene State College. This hub of the local arts community is on the tree-lined main street and has a worthwhile art gallery and theater with select showings. The **Thorne-Sagendorph Art Gallery** (☎ *603/358–2720* ⊕ *www.keene.edu/tsag*) houses George Ridci's *Landscape* and presents traveling exhibitions. The **Putnam Theater** (☎ *603/358–2160*) shows foreign and art films.

OFF THE BEATEN PATH

Chesterfield's Route 63. If you're in the mood for a country drive or bike ride, head west from Keene along Route 9 to Route 63 (about 11 mi), and turn left toward the hilltop town of Chesterfield. This is an especially rewarding journey at sunset, as from many points along the road you can see west out over the Connecticut River valley and into Vermont. The village center consists of little more than a handful of dignified granite buildings and a small general store. You can loop back to Keene via Route 119 east in Hinsdale and then Route 10 north—the entire journey is about 40 mi.

NIGHTLIFE & THE ARTS

The **Colonial Theatre** (⊠95 Main St. ☎603/357–1233) opened in 1924 as a vaudeville stage. It now hosts music concerts, ballet, and has the town's largest movie screen. **Elm City Brewing Co.** (⊠222 West St. ☎603/355–3335), at the Colony Mill, serves light food and draws a mix of college students and young professionals. At Keene State College, the **Redfern Arts Center at Brickyard Pond** (⊠229 Main St. ☎603/358–2168) has year-round music, theater, and dance performances in two theaters and a recital hall.

SHOPPING

★ **Colony Mill Marketplace** (⊠222 West St. ☎603/357–1240), an old mill building, holds 30-plus stores and boutiques such as the Toadstool Bookshop, which carries many children's and regional travel and history books, and Ye Goodie Shoppe, whose specialty is handmade confections. Also popular is Antiques at Colony Mill, which sells the wares of more than 200 dealers. There's a food court, too.

Country Artisans (⊠53 Main St. ☎603/352–6980) showcases the stoneware, textiles, prints, and glassware of regional artists. **Hannah Grimes Marketplace** (⊠42 Main St. ☎603/352–686) overflows with mostly New Hampshire–made pottery, toys, kitchenware, soaps, greeting cards, and specialty foods.

The extraordinary collection of used books at the **Homestead Bookshop** (⊠Rtes. 101 and 124, Marlborough ☎603/876–4213) includes biographies, cookbooks, and town histories. It's 2 mi east of Keene on Rte 101. Just touring the six furniture- and collectibles-filled rooms is part of the fun at **Stone House Antiques** (⊠Rtes. 9 and 63, Chesterfield ☎603/363–4866), a stately, restored stagecoach tavern 6 mi SW of Keene.

WHERE TO EAT

$$ ✕**Luca's.** A deceptively simple storefront bistro overlooking Keene's
Fodor'sChoice graceful town square, Luca's dazzles with knowledgeable and help-
★ ful staff and some of the most deftly prepared cooking in this part
MEDITERRANEAN of the state. Pastas and grills reveal Italian, French, Greek, Spanish, and North African influences—consider salmon tagine in a sundried-tomato-and-whole-grain-mustard cream sauce, or shrimp and scallops El Greco, with plum tomatoes, feta, and baby spinach over linguine. Dine in the intimate art-filled dining room or at one of the sidewalk tables in summer. ⊠10 Central Sq. ☎603/358–3335 ▤AE, MC, V ⊗No lunch weekends Nov.–Mar.

WHERE TO STAY

¢ ▣**Carriage Barn.** Antiques and wide pine floors give this inn across from Keene State College charm. An expansive buffet is served each morning in the breakfast room, but many guests savor a second cup of coffee in the summerhouse. Pros: cheap. Cons: few amenities. ⊠358 Main St. ☎603/357–3812 ⊕www.carriagebarn.com ⇆4 rooms

⟨⟩*In-room: no phone, no TV. In-hotel: no-smoking rooms* ☰*AE, D, MC, V* ⑩*CP.*

$$–$$$ 🏠**Chesterfield Inn.** Surrounded by gardens, the Chesterfield sits above
★ Route 9, the main road between Keene and Brattleboro, Vermont. Fine
antiques and Colonial-style fabrics adorn the spacious guest quarters; 10
have fireplaces, and several have private decks or terraces that face the
stunning perennial gardens and verdant Vermont hills. In the restaurant
($$–$$$$) rosemary- and walnut-crusted rack of lamb and grilled blue-
corn-and-smoked-cheddar polenta with black bean ratatouille are among
the highlights. **Pros:** meticulously clean rooms, attractrive gardens, good
food. **Cons:** breakfast ends early. ⊠*Rte. 9* ✉*Box 155, Chesterfield
03443* ☎*603/256–3211 or 800/365–5515* ⊕*www.chesterfieldinn.com*
⟐*13 rooms, 2 suites* ⟨⟩*In-room: refrigerator, Wi-Fi. In-hotel: restau-
rant, no elevator, public Wi-Fi, some pets allowed, no-smoking rooms.*
☰*AE, D, MC, V* ⑩*BP.*

$ 🏠**E. F. Lane Hotel.** You can get a rare touch of urbanity in the sleepy
Monadnocks in this upscale redbrick hotel is in the middle of Main
Street. The hotel was retrofitted in 2000 from the former Goodnow
department store, a Keene landmark for over 100 years. That accounts
for some interesting room features, like a wall of exposed brick and
12-foot ceilings. Spacious rooms are furnished individually with repro-
duction Victorian antiques. "Chairman" suites have stairs that lead to
an upper level, and come with two bathrooms. Ask for your free movie
tickets and popcorn vouchers for the Colonial Theater across the street.
Pros: Spacious, interesting, comfortable rooms; center-of-town loca-
tion; free movie tickets. **Cons:** no restaurant or gym. ⊠*30 Main St.,
03431* ☎*603/357–7070 or 888/300–5056* ⊕*www.eflane.com* ⟐*32
rooms, 7 suites* ⟨⟩*In-room: refrigerator (some), Wi-Fi. In-hotel: bar,
public Internet, public Wi-Fi, some pets allowed, no-smoking rooms*
☰*AE, D, MC, V* ⑩*CP.*

$$ 🏠**Inn at East Hill Farm.** If you have kids, and they like animals, meet bliss:
☉ a family resort on a 170-acre 1830 farm overlooking Mt. Monadnock
with daylong kids' programs. Kids can start at 9 AM with cow milking.
Other activities include collecting chicken eggs, horseback- and pony
riding, arts and crafts, storytelling, hiking, sledding, hay rides in summer and horse-drawn sleigh rides in winter. You can feed sheep, don-
keys, cows, rabbits, horses, chickens, goats, ducks, and play with Chloe
the farm dog. Twice weekly in summer, trips are scheduled to a nearby
lake for boating, waterskiing, and fishing. Rates include most activities and three meals in a camplike dining hall. Rooms are comfortable,
not fancy. The inn is 10 mi southeast of Keene off Rte 124. **Pros:** rare
agri-tourism and family resort, activities galore, beautiful setting. **Cons:**
remote, rural location; noisy mess hall dining. ⊠*460 Monadnock St.,
Troy* ☎*603/242–6495 or 800/242–6495* ⊕*www.east-hill-farm.com*
⟐*70 rooms* ⟨⟩*In-room: no a/c (some), no phone, refrigerator, no TV
(some), Wi-Fi. In-hotel: restaurant, tennis court, pools, no elevator,
children's programs (ages 2–18), laundry facilities, public Wi-Fi, some
pets allowed, no-smoking rooms* ☰*D, MC, V* ⑩*FAP.*

JAFFREY CENTER

16 mi southeast of Keene.

Novelist Willa Cather came to Jaffrey Center in 1919 and stayed in the Shattuck Inn, which now stands empty on Old Meeting House Road. Not far from here, she pitched the tent in which she wrote several chapters of *My Ántonia*. She returned nearly every summer thereafter until her death and was buried in the Old Burying Ground.

WHAT TO SEE

Cathedral of the Pines. This outdoor memorial pays tribute to Americans who have sacrificed their lives in service to their country. There's an inspiring view of Mt. Monadnock and Mt. Kearsarge from the Altar of the Nation, which is composed of rock from every U.S. state and territory. All faiths are welcome to hold services here; organ music for meditation is played at midday from Tuesday through Thursday in July and August. The Memorial Bell Tower, with a carillon of bells from around the world, is built of native stone. Norman Rockwell designed the bronze tablets over the four arches. Flower gardens, an indoor chapel, and a museum of military memorabilia share the hilltop. It's 8 mi southeast of Jaffrey Center. ⊠*10 Hale Hill Rd., off Rte. 119, Rindge* ☎*603/899–3300 or 866/229–4520* ⊕*www.cathedralpines. com* 🖰*Donations accepted* ☉*May–Oct., daily 9–5.*

SPORTS & THE OUTDOORS

★ **Monadnock State Park.** The oft-quoted statistic about Mt. Monadnock is that it's America's most-climbed mountain—second in the world to Japan's Mt. Fuji. Whether this is true or not, locals agree that it's never lonely at the top. Some days more than 400 people crowd its bald peak. Monadnock rises to 3,165 feet, and on a clear day the hazy Boston skyline is visible from its summit. The park maintains picnic grounds and a small campground (RVs welcome, but no hookups) with 28 sites. Five trailheads branch into more than two dozen trails of varying difficulty that wend their way to the top. Allow between three and four hours for any round-trip hike. A visitor center has free trail maps as well as exhibits documenting the mountain's history. In winter, you can cross-country ski along roughly 12 mi of groomed trails on the lower elevations of the mountain. ⊠*Off Rte. 124, 2½ mi north of Jaffrey Center,* ☎*603/532–8862* 🖰*$3* ☉*Daily dawn–dusk* ⌖*No pets.*

Rhododendron State Park. More than 16 acres of wild rhododendrons bloom in mid-July at Fitzwilliam's park, which has the largest concentration of *Rhododendron maximum* north of the Allegheny Mountains. Bring a picnic lunch and sit in a nearby pine grove, or follow the marked footpaths through the flowers. On your way here, be sure to pass through Fitzwilliam's well-preserved historic district of Colonial and Federal-style houses, which have appeared on thousands of postcards. ⊠*Rte. 119 W, off Rte. 12, 10 mi southwest of Jaffrey Center, Fitzwilliam* ☎*603/239–8153* 🖰*$3 weekends and holidays, free at other times* ☉*Daily 8–sunset.*

SHOPPING

You'll find about 35 dealers at **Bloomin' Antiques** (⊠ *Rte. 12, 3 mi south of Rte. 119, Fitzwilliam* ☎ *603/585–6688*). Meanwhile, **Fitzwilliam Antiques Centre** (⊠ *Rtes. 12 and 119, Fitzwilliam* ☎ *603/585–9092*) sells the wares of some 40 dealers.

THE ARTS

Amos Fortune Forum, near the Old Burying Ground, brings nationally known speakers to the 1773 meetinghouse on summer evenings.

WHERE TO EAT

$-$$
AMERICAN

✕ **Lilly's on the Pond.** An appealing choice either for lunch or dinner, this rustic-timbered dining room overlooks a small mill pond in Rindge, about 8 mi south of Jaffrey Center. The extensive menu of mostly American fare includes chicken sautéed with lime and tequila, shrimp scampi, and burgers. ⊠ *U.S. 202, Rindge* ☎ *603/899–3322* ⊟ *D, MC, V* ⊙ *Closed Mon.*

WHERE TO STAY

$-$$

🏨 **Benjamin Prescott Inn.** Thanks to the working dairy farm surrounding this 1853 Colonial house—with its stenciling and wide pine floors—you feel as though you're miles out in the country rather than just minutes from Jaffrey Center. A full breakfast of Welsh miner's cakes and baked French toast with fruit and maple syrup prepares you for a day of antiquing or hiking. **Pros:** inexpensive. **Cons:** 2 mi east of town, outdated furnishings. ⊠ *433 Turnpike Rd. (Rt. 124E), 03452* ☎ *603/532–6637 or 888/950–6637* ⊕ *www.benjaminprescott inn.com* ⥩ *10 rooms, 3 suites* ⏶ *In-room: no phone, no TV, Wi-Fi. In-hotel: no kids under 10, public Wi-Fi, no-smoking rooms* ⊟ *AE, MC, V* ⊙ *BP.*

$

🏨 **Inn at Jaffrey Center.** Rooms in this beautiful home are painted in lively lavenders, yellows, or peaches, a cheery presence in the heart of pristine Jaffrey Center. Although full of period furnishings, they have a hip sensibility as well as high-thread-count bedding, fluffy towels, and fine toiletries. Rocking chairs set out on the front porch overlook the town and the golf course across the street. There's a good restaurant here with an impressive Sunday brunch. **Pros:** located in right in town, across from golf, good food. **Cons:** limited amentities. ⊠ *379 Main St., 03452* ☎ *603/532–7800 or 877/510–7019* ⊕ *www. theinnatjaffreycenter.com* ⥩ *9 rooms, 2 suites* ⏶ *In-room: no a/c, no phone, DVD (some), VCR (some), no TV (some), Wi-Fi. In-hotel: restaurant, bar, public Wi-Fi, no elevator, no-smoking rooms* ⊟ *AE, D, DC, MC, V* ⊙ *CP.*

$$-$$$

🏨 **Woodbound Inn.** A favorite with families and outdoors enthusiasts, this 1819 farmhouse became an inn in 1892. It occupies 200 acres on the shores of Contoocook Lake. Accommodations are functional but clean and cheerful; they range from quirky rooms in the main inn to modern hotel-style rooms in the Edgewood building to cabins by the water. There's a nine-hole, par-3 golf course, and of course lots of boating and fishing. **Pros:** relaxed, lakefront resort; new owners in 2008 bring focus on food. **Cons:** older, simple furnishings. ⊠ *247 Woodbound Rd., Rindge* ☎ *603/532–8341 or 800/688–7770*

⊕*www.woodboundinn.com* ⇆*44 rooms, 39 with bath; 11 cottages* ⌂*In-room: refrigerator (some), no TV (some). In-hotel: restaurant, bar, golf course, tennis court, no-smoking rooms* ⊟*AE, MC, V* ⏃⏃*BP, MAP.*

PETERBOROUGH

9 mi northeast of Jaffrey Center, 30 mi northwest of Nashua.

Do you remember Thorton Wilder's play *Our Town*? It's based on Peterborough. The nation's first free public library opened here in 1833. The town, which was the first in the region to be incorporated (1760), is still a commercial and cultural hub.

WHAT TO SEE

Mariposa Museum. You can play instruments from around the world, try on costumes from around the world, and indulge your cultural curiosity at this non-profit museum dedicated to hands-on exploration of international folklore and folk art. The three-floor museum is inside a historic redbrick Baptist church, across the Universalist church in the heart of town. The museum hosts a number of workshops and presentations on dance and arts and crafts. There's also a children's reading nook and a library. ✉*26 Main St.* ☎*603/924–4555* ⊕*www.mariposa museum.org* ▦*$5* ⏲*July and Aug., daily noon–4; Sept.–May, weekdays 3–5; live music performances year-round, Sun. at 3.*

SPORTS & THE OUTDOORS

PARKS **Miller State Park.** About 3 mi east of town, an auto road takes you almost 2,300 feet up Pack Monadnock Mountain. The road is closed mid-November through mid-April. ✉*Rte. 101* ☎*603/924–3672* ▦*$3.*

GOLF At the Donald Ross–designed **Crotched Mountain Golf Club** (✉*Off Rte. 47 near Bennington town line, Francestown* ☎*603/588–2923*), you'll find a hilly, rolling 18-hole layout with nice view of the Monadnocks. Greens fee are $30–$38.

SKI AREA **Crotched Mountain.** New Hampshire's southernmost skiing and snowboarding facility opened in 2004 with 17 trails, half of them intermediate, and the rest divided pretty evenly between beginner and expert. There's an 875-foot vertical drop. The slopes have ample snowmaking capacity, ensuring good skiing all winter long. Other facilities include a 40,000-square-foot lodge with a couple of restaurants, a ski school, and a snow camp for youngsters. ✉*615 Francestown Rd. (Rte. 47), Bennington* ☎*603/588–3668* ⊕*www.crotchedmountain.com.*

SHOPPING

The corporate headquarters and retail outlet of **Eastern Mountain Sports** (✉*1 Vose Farm Rd.* ☎*603/924–7231*) sells everything from tents to skis to hiking boots, offers hiking and camping classes, and conducts kayaking and canoeing demonstrations. **Harrisville Designs** (✉*Mill Alley, Harrisville* ☎*603/827–3333*) sells hand-spun and hand-dyed yarn as well as looms. The shop also conducts classes in knitting and weaving.

Sharon Arts Fine Crafts Store (⊠*Depot Sq.* ☎*603/924–2787*) exhibits locally made pottery, fabric, and woodwork and other crafts.

THE ARTS

From early July to late August, **Monadnock Music** (⊠*2A Concord St.* ☎*603/924–7610 or 800/868–9613* ⊕*www.monadnockmusic.org*) produces a series of solo recitals, chamber music concerts, and orchestra and opera performances by renowned musicians. Events take place throughout the area on Wednesday through Saturday evenings at 8 and on Sunday at 4; many are free. In winter, the **Peterborough Folk Music Society** (☎*603/827–2905* ⊕*http://pfmsconcerts.org*) presents folk music concerts. The **Peterborough Players** (⊠*Stearns Farm off Middle Hancock Rd.* ☎*603/924–7585* ⊕*www.peterboroughplayers.org*) have performed since 1933. Productions are staged in a converted barn.

WHERE TO EAT & STAY

$–$$
★
BISTRO
✕**Acqua Bistro.** Locals love to come to Peterborough's best restaurant for riverfront patio dining in warm weather. Start at the long bar for an aperitif before settling in for thin-crust pizza or an entrée of wild Arctic char with roasted vegetable-dill couscous and basil-walnut pesto. Save room for the bittersweet chocolate soufflé. ⊠*9 School St.* ☎*603/924–9905* ☰*MC, V* ☉*Closed Mon. No lunch.*

$
★
🏨**Hancock Inn.** This Federal-style 1789 inn is the real Colonial deal— the oldest in the state, and the pride of this idyllic town, 8 mi north of Peterborough. Common areas possess the warmth of a tavern, with fireplaces, big wing chairs, couches, dark-wood paneling. In fact, it happens to have a special tavern of its own, painted with Rufus Porter murals from 1825. Colonial rooms have antique four-poster beds over original wood floors. Because the inn is in the heart of Hancock, just over from the green, you're smack dab in the middle of a perfect hamlet. You don't need to go very far to eat—the restaurant here serves an excellent Shaker cranberry pot roast; and across the street is the town market and a very popular café—so you can put away your car keys and relax. **Pros:** quintessential Colonial inn in a perfect New England town, cozy rooms. **Cons:** remote location. ⊠*33 Main St., Hancock 03449* ☎*603/525–3318 or 800/525–1789* ⊕*www.hancockinn.com* ➟*15 rooms* ♿*In-room: DVD (some), Wi-Fi. In-hotel: restaurant, bar, no elevator, public Internet, public Wi-Fi, some pets allowed, no-smoking rooms* ☰*AE, D, DC, MC, V* ⍟*BP.*

¢–$
🏨**Inn at Crotched Mountain.** Three of the nine fireplaces in this 1822 inn are in Colonial-style guest rooms. The property, with stunning views of the Monadnocks, was once a stop on the Underground Railroad. At the inn's restaurant ($$), where Singapore native Rose Perry is at the helm, you can sample both American and Asian-inspired fare, such as cranberry-port pot roast and Indonesian charbroiled swordfish with a sauce of ginger, green pepper, onion, and lemon. Weekend rates include breakfast and dinner. **Pros:** spectacular country setting. **Cons:** might be too remote for some. ⊠*534 Mountain Rd., 12 mi northeast of Peterborough, Francestown* ☎*603/588–6840* ➟*13 rooms* ♿*In-hotel: restaurant, bar, tennis courts, pool, some pets allowed (fee), no-smoking rooms* ☰*No credit cards* ☉*Closed Apr. and Nov.* ⍟*BP, MAP.*

$ **Jack Daniels Motor Inn.** With so many dowdy motels in southwest-
★ ern New Hampshire, it's a pleasure to find one as bright and clean as
the Jack Daniels, just ½ mi north of downtown Peterborough. The
rooms are large and furnished with attractive cherrywood reproduction
antiques. Try to get one of two rooms looking out on the Contoocook
River; otherwise, second-floor rooms have chairs on the hallway overlooking the river. **Pros:** afforable and clean rooms, low-key atmosphere.
Cons: basic motel-style rooms, have to drive or walk into town. ☒ *80
Concord St. (U.S. 202), 03458* ☎ *603/924–7548* ⊕ *www.jackdan-
ielsmotorinn.com* ↩ *17 rooms* ⌂ *In-room: refrigerator (some), DVD
(some), VCR (some), Wi-Fi. In-hotel: no elevator, public Wi-Fi, some
pets allowed* ▭ *AE, D, DC, MC, V.*

NEW HAMPSHIRE ESSENTIALS

Research prices, get travel advice, and book your trip at fodors.com

TRANSPORATION

BY AIR

Manchester Airport (☒ *1 Airport Rd., Manchester* ☎ *603/624–6539* ⊕ *www.
flymanchester.com*), the state's largest airport, has rapidly become a cost-effective,
hassle-free alternative to Boston's airport. It has nonstop service to more than 20
cities. **Lebanon Municipal Airport** (☒ *5 Airpark Rd., West Lebanon* ☎ *603/298–
8878*), near Dartmouth College, is served by US Airways Express from New York.

BY BUS

C&J Trailways (☎ *603/430–1100 or 800/258–7111* ⊕ *www.cjtrailways.com*)
serves the seacoast area of New Hampshire from Boston, with stops in Portsmouth,
Durham and Dover. **Concord Coach Lines** (☎ *603/228–3300 or 800/639–3317,
603/448–2800 or 800/637–0123 Dartmouth Coach* ⊕ *www.concordcoachlines.
com*) links Boston's South Station and Logan International Airport with points all
along Interstate 93 as far north as Littleton and, around Lake Winnipesaukee and
the eastern White Mountains, along Route 16. Operated by Concord Coach Lines,
the Dartmouth Coach connects Boston's South Station and Logan International
Airport with Hanover, Lebanon, and New London. **Greyhound** (☎ *800/231–2222
or 214/849–8100* ⊕ *www.greyhound.com*) has service from Boston to Vermont
that stops in southern and western New Hampshire.

BY CAR

Interstate 93, running north from Massachusetts to Québec and passing through Manchester and Concord, is the principal south–north
route through central New Hampshire. To the west, Interstate 91 traces
the Vermont–New Hampshire border. To the east, Interstate 95, which
is a toll road, passes through southern New Hampshire's coastal area
on its way from Massachusetts to Maine. Interstate 89 travels from
Concord to Montpelier and Burlington, Vermont.

Speed limits on interstate and limited-access highways are generally 65
mph, except in heavily settled areas, where 55 mph is the norm. On state
and U.S. routes, speed limits vary considerably. On any given stretch,

SPORTS & OUTDOORS IN NEW HAMPSHIRE

BIKE TOURS

Bike the Whites (☎ *877/854–6535* ⊕ *www.bikethewhites.com*) organizes bike tours in New Hampshire and Vermont. **New England Hiking Holidays** (☎ *603/356–9696* or *800/869–0949* ⊕ *www.nehikingholidays.com*) arranges bicycling trips in the region.

BIRD-WATCHING

Audubon Society of New Hampshire (⊠ *3 Silk Farm Rd., Concord* ☎ *603/224–9909* ⊕ *www.nh audubon.org*) schedules monthly field trips throughout the state and a fall bird-watching tour to Star Isle and other parts of the Isles of Shoals.

CAMPING

New Hampshire Campground Owners Association (⌂ *Box 320, Twin Mountain, 03595* ☎ *603/846–5511* or *800/822–6764* ⊕ *www. ucampnh.com*) publishes a guide to private, state, and national-forest campgrounds. **White Mountain National Forest** (⊠ *U.S. Forest Service, 719 N. Main St., Laconia* ☎ *603/528–8721* or *877/444–6777* ⊕ *www.fs.fed.us/r9/forests/white_ mountain*) campground reservations has 20 campgrounds with more than 900 campsites spread across the region; only some take reservations. All sites have a 14-day limit.

FISHING

Many companies along the coast offer rentals and charters for deep-sea fishing and cruises. Inland, for trout and salmon fishing, try the Connecticut Lakes, though any clear White Mountain stream (there are 650 mi of them in the national forest alone) will do. Many streams are stocked. Conway Lake—the largest of the area's 45 lakes and ponds—is noted for smallmouth bass and, early and late in the season, good salmon fishing. For information about fishing and licenses, call the **New Hampshire Fish and Game Department** (☎ *603/271–3211* ⊕ *www.wildlife.state.nh.us*).

HIKING

Among the 86 major peaks in the White Mountains, hiking possibilities are endless. Innkeepers can usually point you toward the better nearby trails; some inns schedule guided day trips for guests. The **White Mountain National Forest** (⊠ *U.S. Forest Service, 719 Main St., Laconia* ☎ *603/528–8721* ⊕ *www.fs.fed. us/r9/forests/white_mountain*) office has information on hiking as well as on the parking passes ($5) that are required in the national forest. **New England Hiking Holidays** (☎ *603/356–9696* or *800/869–0949* ⊕ *www.nehikingholidays.com*) conducts hikes in the White Mountains with lodging in country inns for two to eight nights. Hikes, each with two guides, allow for different levels of ability and cover between 5 and 10 mi per day. The **New Hampshire Parks Department** (☎ *603/271–3556* ⊕ *www.nhparks.state.nh.us*) also general hiking information.

SKIING

Contacts Ski New Hampshire (⌂ *Box 10, North Woodstock, 03262* ☎ *603/745–9396* or *800/887–5464* ⊕ *www.skinh.com*).

the limit may be anywhere from 25 mph to 55 mph, so watch the signs carefully. Right turns are permitted on red lights unless indicated.

BY TRAIN

Amtrak (☎ 800/872-7245 ⊕ www.amtrak.com) runs its Downeaster service from Boston to Portland, Maine. It stops in Exeter, Durham, and Dover, New Hampshire.

CONTACTS & RESOURCES

VISITOR INFORMATION

State Contacts New Hampshire Fall Foliage hotline (☎ 800/258-3608). **New Hampshire Office of Travel and Tourism Development** (⊠ 172 Pembroke Rd., Concord ☎ 800/386-4664 free vacation guide ⊕ www.visitnh.gov).

Regional Contacts Lakes Region Association (⊠ Rte. 104 off I-93 Exit 23, New Hampton ☎ 800/605-2537 ⊕ www.lakesregion.org). **Lake Sunapee Region Chamber of Commerce** (⌖ Box 532, Sunapee 03782 ☎ 603/526-6575 or 877/526-6575 ⊕ www.sunapeevacations.com). **North Country Chamber of Commerce** (⌖ Box 1, Colebrook 03576 ☎ 603/237-8939 or 800/698-8939 ⊕ www.northcountrychamber.org). **White Mountains Visitors Bureau** (⊠ Kancamagus Hwy. (Rte. 112) at I-93 ⌖ Box 10, North Woodstock 03262 ☎ 603/745-8720 or 800/346-3687 ⊕ www.whitemtn.org).

Local Contacts Concord Chamber of Commerce (⊠ 40 Commercial St., Concord ☎ 603/224-2508 ⊕ www.concordnhchamber.com). **Exeter Area Chamber of Commerce** (⊠ 120 Water St., Exeter ☎ 603/772-2411 ⊕ www.exeterarea.org). **Greater Portsmouth Chamber of Commerce** (⊠ 500 Market St., Portsmouth ☎ 603/436-3988 ⊕ www.portcity.org). **Hanover Area Chamber of Commerce** (⊠ 216 Main St., Hanover ☎ 603/643-3115 ⊕ www.hanoverchamber.org). **Keene Chamber of Commerce** (⊠ 48 Central Sq., Keene ☎ 603/352-1303 ⊕ www.keenechamber.com). **Manchester Area Convention & Visitors Bureau** (⊠ 889 Elm St., Manchester ☎ 603/666-6600 ⊕ www.manchestercvb.com). **Monadnock Travel Council** (⌖ Box 358, Keene 03431 ☎ 800/432-7864 ⊕ www.monadnocktravel.com). **Seacoast New Hampshire Web site** (⊕ www.seacoastnh.com).

Maine, Vermont, & New Hampshire Essentials

PLANNING TOOLS, EXPERT INSIGHT, GREAT CONTACTS

There are planners and there are those who, excuse the pun, fly by the seat of their pants. We happily place ourselves among the planners. Our writers and editors try to anticipate all the issues you may face before and during any journey, and then they do their research. This section is the product of their efforts. Use it to get excited about your trip to Maine, Vermont, & New Hampshire, to inform your travel planning, or to guide you on the road should the seat of your pants start to feel threadbare.

GETTING STARTED

We're really proud of our Web site: Fodors.com is a great place to begin any journey. Scan Travel Wire for suggested itineraries, travel deals, new openings, and other up-to-the-minute info. Check out Booking to research prices and book flights, hotel rooms, rental cars, and vacation packages. Head to Talk for on-the-ground pointers from other travelers.

▌RESOURCES

ONLINE TRAVEL TOOLS

Check out the official home page of each Northern New England state for information on state government, as well as for links to state agencies with information on doing business, working, studying, living, and traveling in these areas. Gorp.com is a terrific general resource for just about every kind of recreational activity; just click on the state link under "Destinations," and you'll be flooded with links to myriad topics, from wildlife refuges to ski trips to backpacking advice. Citysearch.com offers a range of reviews and links to dining, culture, and services in major cities and destinations throughout Maine, New Hampshire, and Vermont.

ALL ABOUT NEW ENGLAND

New England's premier regional magazine also publishes an informative travel Web site at *www.yankeemagazine.com/travel*. Another great Web resource is *www.visitingnewengland.com*. and *www.visitnewengland.com* is a New England–wide information resource.

MAINE

MaineToday.com (⊕*www.travel.mainetoday.com*) provides travel information and is an excellent resource for arts, entertainment, and more. Maine's **Nordic Ski Club** (⊕*www.mainenordic.com*) provides cross-country info. The **Ski Maine Association** (⊕*www.skimaine.com*) has information about alpine snow sports.

NEW HAMPSHIRE

Look to **www.nh.com** for features on and anecdotes about New Hampshire, as well as advice on lodging, dining, recreation, and other aspects of New Hampshire. **Ski New Hampshire** (⊕*www.skinh.com*) has information on downhill and cross-country skiing.

VERMONT

The **Vermont Ski Areas Association** (⊕*www.skivermont.com*) covers the downhill scene. **Foliage reports** (⊕*www.foliage-vermont.com*) will keep you up to date; the site also posts information on driving tours, attractions, and hotels.

OTHER RESOURCES

BOOKS

Get a feel for classic Maine coast life by checking out *Ralph Stanley: Tales of a Maine Boatbuilder*. Written by Craig Milner and co-authored by Stanley, it includes a summary of boats built by the man many consider the finest wooden boat builder around. Photographer William Hubbell assembled 192 color images he made of these highly functional yet charming devices in *Good Fences: A Pictorial History of New England's Stone Wall*. In addition to photos, the book includes conversations with contemporary wall builders and a chronological history of styles. In *Wandering Home*, noted environmental author Bill McKibben walks for three weeks from his home in Vermont to his former home in the nearby Adirondack Mountains of New York via the Champlain Valley.

MOVIES

A winner in the 2005 Maine Documentary Film Competition, Red Door Media's *Closing the Circle* follows more than 100,000 of the tiny alewife—a type of herring—as they make their annual run up the Damariscotta River to Damariscotta Lake, their freshwater birthplace. In telling the tale, the filmakers discuss the impact of the fish on the culture and livelihood of the village alongside the lake. Henry Fonda gives one of his last great performances in 1981's *On Golden Pond*. Written by a screenwriter who spent summers lakeside in Belgrade, Maine, and filmed at Squam Lake in New Hampshire, the film gives a good if fictionalized feel for New England lake life.

VISITOR INFORMATION

Each Northern New England state provides helpful free information, including a map and listings of attractions, events, and lodging and dining establishments.

Contacts Maine Office of Tourism (✉59 State House Station, Augusta, ME ☎888/624–6345 ⊕www.visitmaine.com). **State of New Hampshire Division of Travel and Tourism Development** (✉Box 1856, Concord, NH 03302 ☎603/271–2665 or 800/386–4664 ⊕www.visitnh.gov). **Vermont Department of Tourism and Marketing** (✉National Life Bldg., 6th fl., Drawer 20, Montpelier, VT ☎802/828–3237 or 800/837–6668 brochures ⊕www.vermontvacation.com).

▌ THINGS TO CONSIDER

GEAR

The principal rule on weather in Northern New England is that there are no rules. A cold, foggy morning in spring can and often does become a bright, 60° afternoon. A summer breeze can suddenly turn chilly, and rain often appears with little warning. Thus, the best advice on how to dress is to layer your clothing so you can peel off or add garments as needed for comfort. Showers are frequent, so pack a raincoat and umbrella. Even in summer you should bring long pants, a sweater or two, and a waterproof windbreaker, because evenings are often chilly and sea spray can make things cool. Also in summer, bring a hat, sunscreen, and insect repellent.

Casual sportswear—walking shoes and jeans or khakis—will take you almost everywhere, but swimsuits and bare feet will not: shirts and shoes are required attire at even the most casual venues. Dress in restaurants is generally casual, except at some of the distinguished restaurants in Kennebunkport and Vermont. Upscale resorts will, at the very least, require men to wear collared shirts at dinner, and jeans are often frowned upon.

SHIPPING LUGGAGE AHEAD

Imagine globe-trotting with only a carry-on in tow. Shipping your luggage in advance via an air-freight service is a great way to cut down on backaches, hassles, and stress—especially if your packing list includes strollers, car seats, etc. There are some things to be aware of, though.

First, research carry-on restrictions; if you absolutely need something that's isn't practical to ship and isn't allowed in carry-ons, this strategy isn't for you. Second, plan to send your bags several days in advance to U.S. destinations and as much as two weeks in advance to some international destinations. Third, plan to spend some money: it will cost least $100 to send a small piece of luggage, a golf bag, or a pair of skis to a domestic destination, much more to places overseas.

Some people use Federal Express to ship their bags, but this can cost even more than air-freight services. All these services insure your bag (for most, the limit is $1,000, but you should verify that amount); you can, however, purchase additional insurance for about $1 per $100 of value.

Contacts Luggage Concierge (☎800/288–9818 ⊕www.luggageconcierge.com). **Luggage Express** (☎866/744–7224 ⊕www.usxpluggageexpress.com). **Luggage Free** (☎800/361–6871 ⊕www.luggagefree.com). **Sports Express** (☎800/357–4174 ⊕www.sportsexpress.com) specializes in shipping golf clubs and other sports equipment. **Virtual Bellhop** (☎877/235–5467 ⊕www.virtualbellhop.com).

PACKING 101

Why do some people travel with a convoy of huge suitcases yet never have a thing to wear? How do others pack a duffle with a week's worth of outfits *and* supplies for every contingency? We realize that packing is a matter of style, but there's a lot to be said for traveling light. These tips help fight the battle of the bulging bag.

Make a list. In a recent Fodor's survey, 29% of respondents said they make lists (and often pack) a week before a trip. You can use your list to pack and to repack at the end of your trip. It can also serve as record of the contents of your suitcase—in case it disappears in transit.

Think it through. What's the weather like? Is this a business trip? A cruise? Going abroad? In some places dress may be more or less conservative than you're used to. As you create your itinerary, note outfits next to each activity (don't forget accessories).

Edit your wardrobe. Plan to wear everything twice (better yet, thrice) and to do laundry along the way. Stick to one basic look—urban chic, sporty casual, etc. Build around one or two neutrals and an accent (e.g., black, white, and olive green). Women can freshen looks by changing scarves or jewelry. For a week's trip, you can look smashing with three bottoms, four or five tops, a sweater, and a jacket.

Be practical. Put comfortable shoes atop your list. Stack and roll clothes, so they'll wrinkle less. Unless you're on a guided tour or a cruise, select luggage you can readily carry. Porters are hard to find.

Check weight and size limitations. In the United States you may be charged extra for checked bags weighing more than 50 pounds. Abroad some airlines don't allow you to check bags over 60 to 70 pounds, or they charge outrageous fees for every excess pound—or bag. Carry-on size limitations can be stringent, too.

Check carry-on restrictions. Research restrictions with the TSA. Rules vary abroad, so check them with your airline if you're traveling overseas on a foreign carrier. Consider packing all but essentials (travel documents, prescription meds, wallet) in checked luggage. This leads to a "pack only what you can afford to lose" approach that might help you streamline.

Rethink valuables. On domestic flights, airlines are liable for only about $2,800 per person for bags. But items like computers, cameras, and jewelry aren't covered, and as gadgetry can go on and off the list of carry-on no-no's, you can't count on keeping things safe by keeping them close. Although comprehensive travel policies may cover luggage, the liability limit is often a pittance. It's a good idea to check your home-owner's policy, as it may cover you when you travel.

Lock it up. If you do pack valuables, use TSA-approved locks (about $10–$12) that can be unlocked by all U.S. security personnel.

Tag it. Always tag your luggage; use your business address if you don't want people to know your home address. Put the same information (and a copy of your itinerary with contact information) inside your luggage, too.

Report problems immediately. If your bags—or things in them—are damaged or go astray, file a written claim with your airline *before leaving the airport*. If the airline is at fault, it may give you money for essentials until your luggage arrives. Most lost bags are found within 48 hours, so alert the airline to your whereabouts for the next three days. If your bag was opened for security reasons in the States and something is missing, file a claim with the TSA.

BOOKING YOUR TRIP

▌ONLINE

Have you ever wondered what the differences are between online companies? An *online travel agent* is a Web site (like Expedia, Travelocity, and Orbitz) through which you make reservations instead of going directly to the airline, hotel, or car-rental company. A *discounter* is a firm that does a high volume of business with a hotel chain or airline and accordingly gets good prices. A *wholesaler* is one that makes cheap reservations in bulk and then re-sells them to people like you. An an *aggregator* is one that compares all the offerings so you don't have to.

As you may have discovered, to find a good deal online, you really have to shop around. A travel wholesaler such as Hotels.com or HotelClub.net can be a source of good rates, as can discounters such as Hotwire or Priceline, particularly if you can bid for your hotel room or airfare. Indeed, such sites sometimes have deals that are unavailable elsewhere. They do, however, tend to work only with hotel chains (which makes them rather useless for getting hotel reservations outside of major cities) or big airlines (so that often leaves out upstarts like JetBlue and some foreign carriers like Air India). Online travel agents, as well as airline travel packagers like American Airlines Vacations and Virgin Vacations, also may not work with all the world's hotels.

An aggregator site will search many sites and pull the best prices for airfares, hotels, and rental cars from them. Most aggregators compare the major travel-booking sites such as Expedia, Travelocity, and Orbitz; some also look at airline Web sites, though rarely the sites of smaller budget airlines. Some aggregators also compare other travel products, including complex packages—a good thing, as you can sometimes get the best overall deal by booking an air-and-hotel package.

With discounters and wholesalers you must generally prepay, and everything is nonrefundable. Before you fork over the dough, it's wise to check the terms and conditions, so you know what a given company will do for you if there's a problem and what you'll have to deal with on your own.

▪**TIP➔ To be absolutely sure everything was processed correctly, confirm reservations made through online travel agents, discounters, and wholesalers directly with your hotel before leaving home.**

▌WITH A TRAVEL AGENT

If you use an agent—brick-and-mortar or virtual—you'll pay a fee for the service. And know that the service you get from some online agents isn't comprehensive. For example Expedia and Travelocity don't search for prices on budget airlines like JetBlue, Southwest, or small foreign carriers. That said, some agents (online or not) *do* have access to fares that are difficult to find otherwise, and the savings can more than make up for any surcharge.

A knowledgeable brick-and-mortar travel agent can be a godsend if you're booking a cruise, a package trip that's not available to you directly, an air pass, or a complicated itinerary including several flights. What's more, travel agents that specialize in a destination may have exclusive access to certain deals and insider information on things such as charter flights. Agents who specialize in types of travelers or types of trips can also be invaluable.

▪**TIP➔ Remember that Expedia, Travelocity, and Orbitz are travel agents, not just booking engines. To resolve any problems with a reservation made through these companies, contact them first.**

Agent Resources American Society of Travel Agents (ASTA ☎703/739–2782 or 800/965–2782 ⊕www.travelsense.org).

Online Booking Resources

AGGREGATORS

Kayak	www.kayak.com	looks at cruises and vacation packages.
Mobissimo	www.mobissimo.com	examines airfare, hotels, cars, and tons of activities.
Qixo	www.qixo.com	compares cruises, vacation packages, and even travel insurance.
Sidestep	www.sidestep.com	compares vacation packages and lists travel deals and some activities.
Travelgrove	www.travelgrove.com	compares cruises and vacation packages and lets you search by themes.

BOOKING ENGINES

Cheap Tickets	www.cheaptickets.com	discounter.
Expedia	www.expedia.com	large online agency that charges a booking fee for airline tickets.
Hotwire	www.hotwire.com	discounter.
lastminute.com	www.lastminute.com	specializes in last-minute travel; the main site is for the U.K., but it has a link to a U.S. site.
Luxury Link	www.luxurylink.com	has auctions (surprisingly good deals) as well as offers on the high-end side of travel.
Onetravel.com	www.onetravel.com	discounter for hotels, car rentals, airfares, and packages.
Orbitz	www.orbitz.com	charges a booking fee for airline tickets, but gives a clear breakdown of fees and taxes before you book.
Priceline.com	www.priceline.com	discounter that also allows bidding.
Travel.com	www.travel.com	allows you to compare its rates with those of other booking engines.
Travelocity	www.travelocity.com	charges a booking fee for airline tickets, but promises good problem resolution.

ONLINE ACCOMMODATIONS

Hotelbook.com	www.hotelbook.com	focuses on independent hotels worldwide.
Hotel Club	www.hotelclub.net	good for major cities and some resort areas.
Hotels.com	www.hotels.com	big Expedia-owned wholesaler that offers rooms in hotels all over the world.
Quikbook	www.quikbook.com	offers "pay when you stay" reservations that allow you to settle your bill when you check out, not when you book; best for trips to U.S. and Canadian cities.

OTHER RESOURCES

Bidding For Travel	www.biddingfortravel.com	good place to figure out what you can get and for how much before you start bidding on, say, Priceline.

United States Tour Operators Association
(USTOA ☎212/599-6599 ⊕www.ustoa.com).

■ ACCOMMODATIONS

Northern New England can be a bit expensive when it comes to accommodations. Many areas are seasonal. Coastal sections tend to have the highest rates in summer, mountains regions can be pricey during the ski season, and virtually all of Northern New England can be expensive during the peak fall foliage times. In fact, it can be down-right tough to find weekend hotel rooms in summer and fall, so if you're planning to visit during that time, try to book your stay several weeks ahead.

Most hotels and other lodgings require you to give your credit-card details before they will confirm your reservation. If you don't feel comfortable e-mailing this information, ask if you can fax it (some places even prefer faxes). Whichever way you book, ask for confirmation in writing and have a copy of it handy when you check in.

Be sure you understand the hotel's cancellation policy. Some places allow you to cancel without any kind of penalty—even if you prepaid to secure a discounted rate—if you cancel at least 24 hours in advance. Others require you to cancel a week in advance or penalize you the cost of one night. Small inns and B&Bs are most likely to require you to cancel far in advance. Most hotels allow children under a certain age to stay in their parents' room at no extra charge, but others charge for them as extra adults; find out the cutoff age for discounts.

■TIP→ Assume that hotels operate on the European Plan (EP, no meals) unless we specify that they use the Breakfast Plan (BP, with full breakfast), Continental Plan (CP, Continental breakfast), Full American Plan (FAP, all meals), or are all-inclusive (AI, all meals and most activities).

APARTMENT & HOUSE RENTALS

You are most likely to find a house, apartment, or condo rental in areas in which ownership of second homes is common, such as beach resorts and near ski areas. A good strategy is to inquire about rentals in what would be the off-season for those resort areas—for instance, it's fairly easy to rent ski chalets in summer. Home-exchange directories sometimes list rentals as well as exchanges. Another good bet is to contact real estate agents in the area in which you are interested.

Contacts Forgetaway (☎no phone ⊕www. forgetaway.weather.com) **Home Away** (☎512/493-0382 ⊕www.homeaway.com) **Interhome** (☎954/791-8282 or 800/882-6864 ⊕www.interhome.us). **Vacation Home Rentals Worldwide** (☎201/767-9393 or 800/633-3284 ⊕www.vhrww.com). **Villas International** (☎415/499-9490 or 800/221-2260 ⊕www.villasintl.com).

BED & BREAKFASTS

Historic bed-and-breakfasts and inns proliferate throughout Northern New England. In many rural or less-touristy areas, B&Bs offer an affordable alternative to chain properties, but in tourism-dependent communities (i.e., most of the major towns in this region), you can expect to pay about the same or more for a historic inn as for a full-service hotel. Many of the region's finest restaurants are also found in country inns. Although many B&Bs and smaller establishments continue to offer a low-key, homey experience without TVs or numerous amenities, in recent years, especially in upscale resort areas, many such properties have begun to cater to business and luxury leisure travelers with high-speed Internet, voice mail, whirlpool tubs, and VCRs. Quite a few inns and B&Bs serve substantial full breakfasts—the kind that may keep your appetite in check for the better part of the day.

Reservation Services Bed & Breakfast.com (☎512/322-2710 or 800/462-2632 ⊕www. bedandbreakfast.com) also sends out an online newsletter. **Bed & Breakfast Inns Online** (☎615/868–1946 or 800/215–7365 ⊕www. bbonline.com). **BnB Finder.com** (☎212/432–7693 or 888/547–8226 ⊕www.bnbfinder.com).

CAMPING

The state offices of tourism *(⇨ Visitor Information)* supply information about privately operated campgrounds and campgrounds in parks run by state agencies and the federal government.

HOME EXCHANGES

With a direct home exchange you stay in someone else's home while they stay in yours. Some outfits also deal with vacation homes, so you're not actually staying in someone's full-time residence, just their vacant weekend place.

Exchange Clubs Home Exchange.com (☎800/877–8723 ⊕www.homeexchange. com); $59.95 for a 1-year online listing. **HomeLink International** (☎800/638–3841 ⊕www.homelink.org); $90 yearly for Web-only membership; $140 includes Web access and two catalogs. **Intervac U.S.** (☎800/756–4663 ⊕www.intervacus.com); $78.88 for Web-only membership; $126 includes Web access and a catalog.

HOSTELS

Hostels offer bare-bones lodging at low, low prices—often in shared dorm rooms with shared baths—to people of all ages, though the primary market is young travelers, especially students. Most hostels serve breakfast; dinner and/or shared cooking facilities may also be available. In some hostels you aren't allowed to be in your room during the day, and there may be a curfew at night. Nevertheless, hostels provide a sense of community, with public rooms where travelers often gather to share stories. Many hostels are affiliated with Hostelling International (HI), an umbrella group of hostel associations with some 4,000 member properties in more than 60 countries. Other hostels are completely independent and may be nothing more than a really cheap hotel.

10 WAYS TO SAVE

1. Join "frequent guest" programs. You may get preferential treatment in room choice and/or upgrades in your favorite chains.

2. Call direct. You can sometimes get a better price if you call a hotel's local toll-free number (if available) rather than a central reservations number.

3. Check online. Check hotel Web sites, as not all chains are represented on all travel sites.

4. Look for specials. Always inquire about packages and corporate rates.

5. Look for price guarantees. For overseas trips, look for guaranteed rates. With your rate locked in you won't pay more, even if the price goes up in the local currency.

6. Look for weekend deals at business hotels. High-end chains catering to business travelers are often busy only on weekdays; to fill rooms they often drop rates dramatically on weekends.

7. Ask about taxes. Verify whether local hotel taxes are included in quoted rates. In some places taxes can add 20% or more to your bill.

8. Read the fine print. Watch for add-ons, including resort fees, energy surcharges, and "convenience" fees for such things as unlimited local phone service you won't use or a free newspaper in a language you can't read.

9. Know when to go. If your destination's high season is December through April and you're trying to book, say, in late April, you might save money by changing your dates by a week or two. Ask when rates go down, though: if your dates straddle peak and non-peak seasons, a property may still charge peak-season rates for the entire stay.

10. Weigh your options (we can't say this enough). Weigh transportation times and costs against the savings of staying in a hotel that's cheaper because it's out of the way.

Membership in any HI association, open to travelers of all ages, allows you to stay in HI-affiliated hostels at member rates. One-year membership is about $28 for adults. Rates in dorm-style rooms run about $15–$25 per bed per night; private rooms are more, but are still generally well under $100 a night. Members have priority if the hostel is full; they're also eligible for discounts around the world, even on rail and bus travel in some countries.

New England communities with hostels include Bethel, Maine; White River Junction, Vermont; and Woodford, Vermont.

Information Hostelling International—USA (☎301/495–1240 ⊕www.hiusa.org).

HOTELS

All hotels listed have private bath unless otherwise noted.

Hotel and motel chains are amply represented in Maine, New Hampshire, and Vermont. Some of the large chains, such as Hilton, Holiday Inn, Hyatt, Marriott, and Ramada, operate all-suites, budget, business-oriented, or luxury resorts, often variations on the parent corporation's name (Courtyard by Marriott, for example). Though some chain hotels and motels may have a standardized look to them, this "cookie-cutter" approach also means that you can rely on the same level of comfort and efficiency at all properties in a chain, and at a chain's premier properties—its so-called flagship hotels—the decor and services may be outstanding.

Northern New England is liberally supplied with small, independent motels, which run the gamut from the tired to the tidy. Don't overlook these mom-and-pop operations; they frequently offer cheerful, convenient accommodations at lower rates than the chains.

Reservations are always a good idea, and they are particularly recommended in summer and in winter resort areas; in college towns in September and at

graduation time in spring; and at areas renowned for autumn foliage.

Most hotels and motels will hold your reservation until 6 PM; call ahead if you plan to arrive late. All will hold a late reservation for you if you guarantee your reservation with a credit-card number.

When you call to make a reservation, ask all the necessary questions up front. If you are arriving with a car, ask if there is a parking lot or covered garage and whether there is an extra fee for parking. If you like to eat your meals in, ask if the hotel has a restaurant or whether it has room service (most do, but not necessarily 24 hours a day—and be forewarned that it can be expensive). Most hotels and motels have in-room TVs, often with cable movies, but verify this if you like to watch TV. If you want an in-room crib for your child, there will probably be an additional charge.

Note that in Maine, hotels and inns (unless they have five or fewer rooms) are not allowed (again, by state law), to put age restrictions on children who can stay there with their parents.

Information New England Inns & Resorts Association (☎603/964–6689 ⊕www.new-englandinnsandresorts.com).

■ **TIP** ➔ **Ask the local tourist board about hotel packages that include tickets to major museum exhibits or other special events.**

■ AIRLINE TICKETS

Most domestic airline tickets are electronic; international tickets may be either electronic or paper. With an e-ticket the only thing you receive is an e-mailed receipt citing your itinerary and reservation and ticket numbers.

The greatest advantage of an e-ticket is that if you lose your receipt, you can simply print out another copy or ask the airline to do it for you at check-in. You usually pay a surcharge (up to $50) to get a paper ticket, if you can get one at all.

The sole advantage of a paper ticket is that it may be easier to endorse over to another airline if your flight is canceled and the airline with which you booked can't accommodate you on another flight.

■TIP→Discount air passes that let you travel economically in a country or region must often be purchased before you leave home. In some cases you can only get them through a travel agent.

The least expensive airfares to Northern New England are priced for round-trip travel. Airlines generally allow you to change your return date for a fee; most low-fare tickets, however, are nonrefundable. Airlines often post discounted "cyberfares" on their Web sites. The best bargains are on unsold seats on upcoming flights. If your plans are flexible, you can often save 60% to 70% by booking online. Discount travel Web sites such as Travelocity.com and Priceline.com also offer reduced fares.

FLIGHTS

Numerous airlines, large and small, fly to and from Boston, the main hub for New England air travel; additionally, discount carrier Southwest Airlines flies to Albany and Manchester. You can fly to Burlington from New York City on JetBlue.

Airline Contacts AirTran Airways

(☎800/247–8726 ⊕ www.airtran.com). **American Airlines** (☎800/433–7300 ⊕www.

10 WAYS TO SAVE

1. Nonrefundable is best. If saving money is more important than flexibility, then nonrefundable tickets work. That said, you'll pay dearly (often $100–$200) if you change your plans.

2. Comparison shop. Web sites and travel agents can have different arrangements with the airlines and offer different prices for exactly the same flights.

3. Beware the listed prices. Many airline Web sites—and most ads—show prices *without* taxes and surcharges. Don't buy until you know the full price.

4. Stay loyal. Stick with one or two frequent-flier programs. You'll rack up free trips faster and you'll accumulate more quickly the perks that make trips easier. On some airlines these include a special reservations number, early boarding, access to upgrades, and roomier economy seats.

5. Watch those ticketing fees. Surcharges are usually added when you buy your ticket anywhere but on an airline Web site. (That includes by phone—even if you call the airline directly—and paper tickets regardless of how you book).

6. Check often. Start looking for cheap fares from three months out to about one month.

7. Don't work alone. Some Web sites have tracking features that will e-mail you immediately when good deals are posted.

8. Jump on the good deals. Waiting even a few minutes might mean paying more.

9. Be flexible. Look for departures on Tuesday, Wednesday, and Saturday, typically the cheapest days to travel. And check on prices for departures at different times and to and from alternative airports.

10. Weigh your options. What you get can be as important as what you save. A cheaper flight might have a long layover or land at a secondary airport, where your ground transport costs are higher.

Car Rental Resources

LOCAL AGENCIES		
Car Rental Express		www.carrentalexpress.com.
MAJOR AGENCIES		
Alamo	800/462–5266	www.alamo.com.
Avis	800/331–1212	www.avis.com.
Budget	800/527–0700	www.budget.com.
Hertz	800/654–3131	www.hertz.com.
National Car Rental	800/227–7368	www.nationalcar.com.

aa.com). **Continental Airlines** (☎800/523–3273 for U.S. and Mexico reservations, 800/231–0856 for international reservations ⊕www.continental.com). **Delta Airlines** (☎800/221–1212 for U.S. reservations, 800/241–4141 for international reservations ⊕www.delta.com). **JetBlue** (☎800/538–2583 ⊕www.jetblue.com). **Northwest Airlines** (☎800/225–2525 ⊕www.nwa.com). **Southwest Airlines** (☎800/435–9792 ⊕www.southwest.com). **Spirit Airlines** (☎586/791–7300 or 800/772–7117 ⊕www.spiritair.com). **United Airlines** (☎800/864–8331 for U.S. reservations, 800/538–2929 for international reservations ⊕www.united.com). **USAirways** (☎800/428–4322 for U.S. and Canada reservations, 800/622–1015 for international reservations ⊕www.usairways.com).

For additional airline information, look under "By Air" in the Transportation section of this chapter.

▌ RENTAL CARS

When you reserve a car, ask about cancellation penalties, taxes, drop-off charges (if you're planning to pick up the car in one city and leave it in another), and surcharges (for being under or over a certain age, for additional drivers, or for driving across state or country borders or beyond a specific distance from your point of rental). All these things can add substantially to your costs. Request car seats and extras such as GPS when you book. As a rule, all vehicles feature auto-matic transmissions and air-conditioning and generally are low mileage.

Rates are sometimes—but not always—better if you book in advance or reserve through a rental agency's Web site. There are other reasons to book ahead, though: for popular destinations, during busy times of the year, or to ensure that you get certain types of cars (vans, SUVs, exotic sports cars).

▌TIP➔ **Make sure that a confirmed reservation guarantees you a car. Agencies sometimes overbook, particularly for busy weekends and holiday periods.**

A car is the most practical way to get around Maine, Vermont, and New Hampshire, so it's wise to rent one if you're not bringing your own. The major airports serving the region all have on-site car-rental agencies. If you're traveling to the area by bus or train, you might consider renting a car once you arrive. A few train or bus stations have one or two major car-rental agencies on site.

Rates at the area's major airport, Boston's Logan Airport, begin at around $50 a day and $250 a week for an economy car with air-conditioning, automatic transmission, and unlimited mileage. The same car might go for around $45 a day and $200 a week at a smaller airport such as Portland International Jetport. These rates do not include state tax on car rentals, which varies depending on the airport but generally runs 12% to 15%. Generally, it costs less to rent a car outside of an airport, but factor into the value whether it is easy or difficult to get there with all your luggage.

Most agencies won't rent to you if you're under the age of 21. When picking up a rental car, non-U.S. residents need a voucher for any prepaid reservations that were made in their home country, a passport, a driver's license, and a travel policy that covers each driver. Boston's Logan Airport is large, spread out, and usually congested, so if you will be returning a rental vehicle there, make sure to allow plenty of time to take care of it before heading for your flight.

CAR-RENTAL INSURANCE

Everyone who rents a car wonders whether the insurance that the rental companies offer is worth the expense. No one—including us—has a simple answer. It all depends on how much regular insurance you have, how comfortable you are with risk, and whether or not money is an issue.

If you own a car and carry comprehensive car insurance for both collision and liability, your personal auto insurance will probably cover a rental, but read your policy's fine print to be sure. If you don't have auto insurance, then you should probably buy the collision- or loss-damage waiver (CDW or LDW) from the rental company. This eliminates your liability for damage to the car.

Some credit cards offer CDW coverage, but it's usually supplemental to your own insurance and rarely covers SUVs, minivans, luxury models, and the like. If your coverage is secondary, you may still be liable for loss-of-use costs from the car-rental company (again, read the fine print). But no credit-card insurance is valid unless you use that card for *all* transactions, from reserving to paying the final bill.

■TIP➡ **Diners Club offers primary CDW coverage on all rentals reserved and paid**

10 WAYS TO SAVE 🚗

1. Beware of cheap rates. Those great rates aren't so great when you add in taxes, surcharges, and insurance. Such extras can double or triple the initial quote.

2. Rent weekly. Weekly rates are usually better than daily ones. Even if you only want to rent for five or six days, ask for the weekly rate; it may very well be cheaper than the daily rate for that period of time.

3. Don't forget the locals. Price local companies as well as the majors.

4. Airport rentals can cost more. Airports often add surcharges, which you can sometimes avoid by renting from an agency whose office is just off airport property.

5. Wholesalers can help. Investigate wholesalers, which don't own fleets but rent in bulk from firms that do, and which frequently offer better rates (note that you must usually pay for such rentals before leaving home).

6. Look for rate guarantees. With your rate locked in, you won't pay more, even if the price goes up in the local currency.

7. Fill up farther away. Avoid hefty refueling fees by filling the tank at a station well away from where you plan to turn in the car.

8. Pump it yourself. Don't pre-pay for rental car gas. The savings isn't that great, and unless you coast in on empty upon return, you wind up paying for gas you don't use.

9. Get all your discounts. Find out whether a credit card you carry or organization or frequent-renter program to which you belong has a discount program. And confirm that such discounts really are a deal. You can often do better with special weekend or weekly rates offered by a rental agency.

10. Check out packages. Adding a car rental onto your air/hotel vacation package may be cheaper than renting a car separately.

for with the card. This means that Diners Club's company—not your own car insurance—pays in case of an accident. It *doesn't* mean that your car-insurance company won't raise your rates once it discovers you had an accident.

You may also be offered supplemental liability coverage; the car-rental company is required to carry a minimal level of liability coverage insuring all renters, but it's rarely enough to cover claims in a really serious accident if you're at fault. Your own auto-insurance policy will protect you if you own a car; if you don't, you have to decide whether you are willing to take the risk.

U.S. rental companies sell CDWs and LDWs for about $15 to $25 a day; supplemental liability is usually more than $10 a day. The car-rental company may offer you all sorts of other policies, but they're rarely worth the cost. Personal accident insurance, which is basic hospitalization coverage, is an especially egregious rip-off if you already have health insurance.

■TIP➔ You can decline the insurance from the rental company and purchase it through a third-party provider such as Travel Guard (www.travelguard.com)—$9 per day for $35,000 of coverage. That's sometimes just under half the price of the CDW offered by some car-rental companies.

■ GUIDED TOURS

Guided tours are a good option when you don't want to do it all yourself. You travel along with a group (sometimes large, sometimes small), stay in prebooked hotels, eat with your fellow travelers (the cost of meals sometimes included in the price of your tour, sometimes not), and follow a schedule.

But not all guided tours are an if-it's-Tuesday-this-must-be-Portland experience. A knowledgeable guide can take you places that you might never discover on your own, and you may be pushed to

see more than you would have otherwise. Tours aren't for everyone, but they can be just the thing for trips to places where making travel arrangements is difficult or time-consuming (particularly when you don't speak the language).

Whenever you book a guided tour, find out what's included and what isn't. A "land-only" tour includes all your travel (by bus, in most cases) in the destination, but not necessarily your flights to and from or even within it. Also, in most cases prices in tour brochures don't include fees and taxes. And remember that you'll be expected to tip your guide (in cash) at the end of the tour.

Brennan Vacations and Insight Vacations both offer a selection of fall foliage tours. Contiki Holidays, specialists in vacations for 18- to 35-year-olds, has a few tours available that pass through parts of New England as well as the rest of the Northeast.

Recommended Companies Brennan Vacations (☎800/237–7249 ⊕www. brennanvacations.com). **Contiki Holidays** (☎866/266–8454 ⊕http://ca.contiki.com). **Insight Vacations** (☎800/582–8380 ⊕www. insightvacations.com).

SPECIAL-INTEREST TOURS

BICYCLING & HIKING

Contacts TrekAmerica ☎800/873–5872 ⊕www.trekamerica.com.

■TIP➔ Most airlines accommodate bikes as luggage, provided they're dismantled and boxed.

CULINARY

Contacts VacationsToGo.com ☎800/680–2858 ⊕www.tourvacationstogo.com/new_england_tours.cfm.

CULTURE

Contacts Country Squire Tours ☎800/966–9445 ⊕www.newenglandtours.com. **New England Vacation Tours** ☎800/742–7669 ⊕www.newenglandvacationtours.com. **VacationsToGo.com** ☎800/680–2858 ⊕www.

tourvacationstogo.com/new_england_tours.
cfm. **Wolfe Adventures & Tours** ☎888/449–6533 ⊕www.wolfetours.com.

SKIING

Contacts New England Vacation Tours
☎800/742–7669 ⊕www.newengland
vacationtours.com.

■ CRUISES

A handful of major cruise lines offer excursions that stop in a couple of spots along the Maine Coast. Most originate in New York City or New Jersey, and most stop in Portland or Bar Harbor—usually on the way to a destination in Canada, such as Nova Scotia or Montréal.

Cruise Lines Carnival Cruise Line (☎305/599–2600 or 800/227–6482 ⊕www.carnival.com). **Celebrity Cruises** (☎800/647–2251 ⊕www.celebrity.com). **Crystal Cruises** (☎310/785–9300 or 800/446–6620 ⊕www.crystalcruises.com). **Holland America Line** (☎206/281–3535 or 877/932–4259 ⊕www.hollandamerica.com). **Norwegian Cruise Line** (☎305/436–4000 or 800/327–7030 ⊕www.ncl.com). **Princess Cruises** (☎661/753–0000 or 800/774–6237 ⊕www.princess.com).

TRANSPORTATION

New England's largest city, Boston is the major transportation hub for reaching Maine, New Hampshire, and Vermont. Portland, Maine, is a secondary hub. How best to get around depends upon the extent of your itinerary—flying from one location to another once you reach the Maine, Vermont, and New Hampshire area can get expensive. Your best bet is to fly into Boston or Maine (or even Burlington, Vermont, or Manchester, New Hampshire), and then travel by car, planning your itinerary according to how much driving you're willing to do.

■ BY AIR

It's costly and generally impractical to fly within Northern New England, so most travelers visiting the region head for a major gateway, such as Boston, Manchester, or Portland, and then rent a car to explore the region. Maine, New Hampshire, and Vermont form a fairly compact region, with few important destinations more than six hours apart by car.

Boston's Logan Airport is one of the nation's most important domestic and international airports, with direct flights coming from all over North America and Europe as well as other continents. New England's other major airports receive few international flights (mostly from Canada) but do offer a wide range of direct domestic flights to East Coast and Midwest destinations, and to a lesser extent to the western United States. Some sample flying times to Boston are: from Chicago (2½ hours), London (6½ hours), and Los Angeles (6 hours). It's more difficult to find direct flights from major airports into Northern New England.

Always find out your carrier's check-in policy. Plan to arrive at the airport about 2 hours before your scheduled departure time for domestic flights and 2½ to 3 hours before international flights. You may need to arrive earlier if you're flying from one of the busier airports or during peak air-traffic times. Keep in mind you can probably arrive a bit later (60 to 90 minutes ahead of departure) for domestic flights from Manchester, Burlington, and Portland, which are smaller and more manageable than Logan.

All flights within the United States are strictly no-smoking. Canadian airlines don't allow smoking either. Some U.S. airports allow smoking in specially designated areas.

■TIP➔ If you travel frequently, look into the TSA's Registered Traveler program. The program, which is still being tested in several U.S. airports, is designed to cut down on gridlock at security checkpoints by allowing prescreened travelers to pass quickly through kiosks that scan an iris and/or a fingerprint. How sci-fi is that?

Air Travel Resources in New England New Hampshire Department of Justice (⊕http:// doj.nh.gov) is the place to file an airline complaint if you fly in or out of Manchester, NH. **Office of the Maine Attorney General** (⊕www.maine.gov/ag) is a good place to file any air-travel or airline related complaints. **Office of the Attorney General of Vermont** (⊕www.atg.state.vt.us) is the place to go for any air-travel or airline-related complaints.

AIRPORTS

The main gateway to Maine, Vermont, and New Hampshire is Boston's Logan International Airport (BOS), the region's largest. Manchester Boston Regional Airport (MHT) in New Hampshire is a rapidly growing, lower-cost alternative to Logan—it's about 50 mi north of Boston. Other regional airports are Portland International Jetport (PWM) and Bangor International Airport (BGR) in Maine; and Burlington International Airport (BTV) in Vermont. Albany International Airport (ALB) in Albany, New York, is also an option if your itinerary begins in Vermont.

Airport Information Albany International Airport (⊕www.albanyairport.com). **Bangor International Airport** (☎207/992–4600 ⊕www.flybangor.com). **Burlington International Airport** (☎802/863–1889 ⊕www.burlingtonintlairport.com). **Logan International Airport** (☎800/235–6426 ⊕www.massport.com/logan). **Manchester Boston Regional Airport** (☎603/624–6556 ⊕www.flymanchester.com). **Portland International Jetport** (☎207/874–8877 ⊕www.portlandjetport.org).

∎ BY BUS

Regional bus service is relatively plentiful throughout the most popular areas of Maine, Vermont, and New Hampshire. It can be a handy and somewhat affordable means of getting around, as buses travel many routes that trains do not; however, this style of travel prevents the sort of spontaneity and freedom to explore that you're afforded if traveling by car. Also, it's often a good idea to compare travel times and costs between bus and train routes to and within the region; in some cases, it's faster to take the train. Still, if it's a simple matter of getting from one city to another and you've got a bit of time on your hands, consider this option. Remember that buses sometimes make frequent stops, which may delay you but may also provide you the chance to see parts of the region you might not otherwise see.

Reservations are not required on buses serving the region, but they're a good idea for just about any bus trip.

Greyhound offers the **North America Discovery Pass,** which allows unlimited travel in the United States (excluding Alaska) within any 7-, 15-, 30-, or 60-day period ($283–$645, depending on length of the pass). You can also buy similar passes covering both the United States and Canada, and international travelers can purchase international versions of these same passes. Greyhound also has senior-citizen, military, children's, and student discounts applicable to individual fares and to the Discovery Pass.

Bus Information Greyhound Lines Inc. (☎800/231–2222 ⊕www.greyhound.com). **Peter Pan Bus Lines** (☎800/343–9999 ⊕www.peterpanbus.com).

∎ BY CAR

Northern New England is best explored by car. Public transportation options are limited in areas in the interior, however these areas are largely without heavy traffic and congestion, and parking is consistently easy to find. It is considerably more congested along the coast, and parking likewise can be hard to find or expensive. Morning and evening rush-hour traffic can also be a bit of a problem, especially along the coast. Note that I–95 is a toll highway throughout New England. If you rent a car at Logan International Airport, allow plenty of time to return it—as much as 60 minutes to be comfortable.

GASOLINE

Gas stations are easy to find along major highways and in most communities throughout the region. At this writing, the average price of a gallon of regular unleaded gas in Maine, Vermont, and New Hampshire is $4.12. However, prices vary from station to station within any city. The majority of stations are self-serve with pumps that accept credit cards, though you may find a holdout full-service station on occasion. Tipping is not expected at these.

PARKING

Parking in Northern New England is a familiar situation. In Boston and other large cities, finding a spot on the street can be time- and quarter-consuming. The best bet is to park in a garage, which can cost upward of $20 a day. In smaller cities, street parking is usually simpler, though parking garages are always convenient and less expensive than their big-city counterparts. Enforcement varies; in Portland, Maine, meter readers might sooner give a warning (a friendly reminder, really) than a ticket.

ROAD CONDITIONS

Major state and U.S. routes are generally well maintained, with snowplows at the ready during the winter to salt and plow road surfaces soon after the flakes begin to fall. Traffic is heaviest around Boston, especially during rush hour but pretty much any time of the day between sunrise and sunset. Secondary state routes and rural roads can be a mixed bag; generally, Route 1 is well maintained but with slower traffic that can get locally congested in even the smallest coastal towns.

Boston drivers are notorious for going all-for-broke, so only the adventurous should drive here. Once you're in Maine, New Hampshire, and Vermont it is far more relaxed. Rural drivers are known to stop to chat in the road.

RENTAL CARS

For rental car information, look under "Rental Cars" in the Booking Your Trip section of this chapter.

ROADSIDE EMERGENCIES

Throughout Northern New England, call 911 for any travel emergency, such as an accident or a serious health concern. For automotive breakdowns, 911 is not appropriate. Instead, find a local directory and dial a towing service. When out on the open highway, call the nonemergency central administration phone number of the State Police for assistance.

RULES OF THE ROAD

On city streets the speed limit is 30 mph unless otherwise posted; on rural roads, the speed limit ranges from 40 to 50 mph unless otherwise posted. Interstate speeds range from 50 to 65 mph, depending on how densely populated the area. Throughout the region, you're permitted to make a right turn on red except where posted.

State law requires that front-seat passengers wear seat belts at all times. Children under 16 must wear seat belts in both the front and back seats. Always strap children under age 5 into approved child-safety seats.

▌ BY TRAIN

Amtrak's *Downeaster* connects Boston with Portland, Maine, with stops in coastal New Hampshire. Other Amtrak services include the *Vermonter* between Washington, D.C., and St. Albans, Vermont; and the *Ethan Allen Express* between New York and Rutland, Vermont. These trains run on a daily basis. To avoid last-minute confusion, allow 15 to 30 minutes to make train connections.

Private rail lines have scenic train trips throughout Northern New England, particularly during fall foliage season. Several use vintage steam equipment; the most notable is the Cog Railway to Mt. Washington in New Hampshire.

Amtrak offers a **North America rail pass** that gives you unlimited travel within the United States and Canada within any 30-day period ($999 peak, $709 off-peak), and several kinds of **USA Rail passes** (for non-U.S. residents only) offering unlimited travel for 15 to 30 days. Amtrak also has senior-citizen, children's, disability, and student discounts, as well as occasional deals that allow a second or third accompanying passenger to travel for half price or even free. The **Amtrak Vacations** program customizes entire vacations, including hotels, car rentals, and tours.

Sample one-way fares and travel times (note that times vary greatly depending on the number of stops) on major routes from Philadelphia to Portland, 8–10 hours, $97–$194;

Amtrak (☎ 800/872-7245 ⊕ www.amtrak. com). **Mount Washington Cog Railway** (☎ 603/278-5404 or 800/922-8825 ⊕ www. thecog.com)

ON THE GROUND

■ CHILDREN IN NEW ENGLAND

Northern New England is an enjoyable part of the country for family road trips, and it's also relatively affordable, excepting some of the fancier resort towns. However, you'll have no problem finding comparatively inexpensive child-friendly hotels and family-style restaurants—as well as some top children's museums, beaches, parks, planetariums, and lighthouses. Just keep in mind that a number of fine, antiques-filled B&Bs and inns punctuate the landscape, and these places are not always suitable for kids—many flat-out refuse to accommodate children. Also, some of the quieter and more rural areas—although exuding history—lack child-oriented attractions.

Favorite destinations for family vacations in Northern New England include the White Mountains and coastal Maine, but in general, the entire region has plenty to offer families.

Be sure to plan ahead and **involve your youngsters** as you outline your trip. When packing, include things to keep them busy en route. On sightseeing days try to schedule activities of special interest to your children.

If you are renting a car, don't forget to arrange for a car seat when you reserve. For general advice about traveling with children, consult *Fodor's FYI: Travel with Your Baby* (available in bookstores everywhere).

FLYING

If your children are aged 2 or older, ask about children's airfares. As a general rule, infants under age 2 not occupying a seat fly at greatly reduced fares or even for free. But if you want to guarantee a seat for an infant, you have to pay full fare. Consider flying during off-peak days and times; most airlines will grant an infant a seat without a ticket if there are available seats.

When booking, confirm carry-on allowances if you're traveling with infants. In general, for babies charged 10% to 50% of the adult fare you are allowed one carry-on bag and a collapsible stroller; if the flight is full, the stroller may have to be checked or you may be limited to less.

Experts agree that it's a good idea to use safety seats aloft for children weighing less than 40 pounds. Airlines set their own policies: if you use a safety seat, U.S. carriers usually require that the child be ticketed, even if he or she is young enough to ride free, because the seats must be strapped into regular seats. And even if you pay the full adult fare for the seat, it may be worth it, especially on longer trips. Do **check your airline's policy about using safety seats during takeoff and landing.** Safety seats are not allowed everywhere in the plane, so get your seat assignments as early as possible.

When reserving, request children's meals or a freestanding bassinet (not available at all airlines) if you need them. But note that bulkhead seats, where you must sit to use the bassinet, may lack an overhead bin or storage space on the floor.

LODGING

Chain hotels and motels welcome children, and Maine, New Hampshire, and Vermont have many family-oriented resorts with lively children's programs. You'll also find farms that accept guests and can be lots of fun for children. Rental houses and apartments abound, particularly around ski areas; off-season, these can be economical as well as comfortable touring bases. Some country inns, especially those with a quiet, romantic atmosphere and those furnished with antiques, are less enthusiastic about little ones, so **be up front about your traveling companions** when you reserve. Many larger resorts and hotels will provide a babysitter at an additional cost. Others will provide a list of sitters in the area.

Most hotels in Northern New England allow children under a certain age to stay in their parents' room at no extra charge, but others charge for them as extra adults; be sure to find out the cutoff age for children's discounts.

Most lodgings that welcome infants and small children will provide a crib or cot, but **be sure to give advance notice** so that one will be available for you. Many family resorts make special accommodations for small children during meals. Be sure to ask in advance.

Most hotels in Northern New England allow children under a certain age to stay in their parents' room at no extra charge, but others charge for them as extra adults; be sure to find out the cutoff age for children's discounts. (Note that in Maine, by state law, hotels and inns [unless they have five or fewer rooms] cannot put age restrictions on children that can stay with adults.)

SIGHTS & ATTRACTIONS
Places that are especially appealing to children are indicated by a rubber-duckie icon (☺) in the margin.

TRANSPORTATION
Each Northern New England state has specific requirements regarding age and weight requirements for children in car seats. If you're renting a car, **be sure to ask about the state(s) you're planning to drive in.** If you will need a car seat, make sure the agency you select provides them and **reserve well in advance.**

▌ DISABILITIES & ACCESSIBILITY

Although rural and historic in many places, Northern New England has come a long way in making life easier for people with disabilities. The majority of businesses in the area are up to ADA standards (except some historic inns, B&Bs, and restaurants), and you'll find plenty of people who are more than happy to help you get around.

Even so, the definition of accessibility can differ from hotel to hotel. Some properties may be accessible by ADA standards for people with mobility problems but not for people with hearing or vision impairments, for example.

If you have mobility problems, ask for the lowest floor on which accessible services are offered. If you have a hearing impairment, check whether the hotel has devices to alert you visually to the ring of the telephone, a knock at the door, and a fire/emergency alarm. Some hotels provide these devices without charge. Discuss your needs with hotel personnel if this equipment isn't available, so a staff member can personally alert you in the event of an emergency.

If you're bringing a guide dog, get authorization ahead of time and write down the name of the person with whom you spoke.

RESERVATIONS
When discussing accessibility with an operator or reservations agent, ask hard questions. Are there any stairs, inside *or* out? Are there grab bars next to the toilet *and* in the shower/tub? How wide is the doorway to the room? To the bathroom? For the most extensive facilities meeting the latest legal specifications, opt for newer accommodations. If you reserve through a toll-free number, consider also calling the hotel's local number to confirm the information from the central reservations office. Get confirmation in writing when you can.

SIGHTS & ATTRACTIONS
In many coastal towns throughout the region, travelers with mobility impairments will have to cope with crowds as well as with narrow, uneven steps and sporadic curb cuts. L.L. Bean's outlet in

Freeport is fully accessible, and Acadia National Park has some 50 accessible miles of carriage roads that are closed to motor vehicles. In New Hampshire, many of Franconia Notch's natural attractions are accessible.

Local Resources The **Maine Office of Tourism**'s (⇨ *Visitor Information*) web site allows you to search according to facility accessibility on its Visitor Resources page. The **New Hampshire Division of Travel and Tourism Development** 's (⇨ *Visitor Information*) New Hampshire Guide Book includes accessibility ratings for lodgings and restaurants. The **Vermont Department of Tourism and Marketing** (⇨ *Visitor Information*) includes accessibility codes for attractions in the Vermont Traveler's Guidebook.

▌ COMMUNICATIONS

INTERNET

Most major chain hotels and many smaller motels throughout Northern New England now offer Wi-Fi or other Internet access at no cost to guests, both from individual rooms and in lobbies (which usually have a desktop computer available for guest use). Many coffee shops provide Wi-Fi free of charge, as well as most libraries—which also provide computers with free Internet access. If you have to bring your car in for service, there is a growing chance that the shop might have Wi-Fi, too.

Contacts Cybercafes (⊕ www.cybercafes. com) lists over 4,000 Internet cafés worldwide.

▌ EATING OUT

Although there are certain ingredients and preparations that are common to the region as a whole, Maine, New Hampshire, and Vermont's cuisine varies greatly from place to place. Especially in such urban areas as Portland, and in upscale resort areas such as coastal Maine and Stowe, Vermont, you can expect to find stellar restaurants, many of them with culinary luminaries at the helm and a reputation for creative, and occasionally daring, menus. Elsewhere, restaurant food tends more toward the simple, traditional, and conservative, though in some towns, especially in collegiate communities, there's a great variety of ethnic restaurants, such as Italian, French, Japanese, Indian, and Thai eateries. There are also quite a few diners, which typically present patrons with page after page of inexpensive, short-order cooking and often stay open until the wee hours; for a road-tripper, these down-home, locals' favorites make great alternatives to fast-food chains. The proximity to the ocean accounts for a number of restaurants, often tiny shacks, serving very fresh seafood, and the numerous boutique dairy, meat, and vegetable suppliers that have sprung up throughout Northern New England in the past couple of decades account for other choice ingredients. In fact, menus in the more upscale and tourism-driven communities often note from which Vermont dairy a particular goat cheese came.

For information on food-related health issues, see Health below.

MEALS & MEALTIMES

In general, the widest variety of mealtime options in Maine, New Hampshire, and Vermont is in larger cities and at resort areas, though you may be pleasantly surprised to hear about a creative café in a smaller town, especially along the Maine Coast.

For an early breakfast, pick places that cater to a working clientele. City, town, and roadside establishments specializing in breakfast for busy people often open their doors at 5 or 6 AM. At country inns and B&Bs, breakfast is seldom served before 8; if you need to get an earlier start, ask ahead of time if your host or hostess can accommodate you. Lunch in Northern New England generally runs from around 11 to 2:30; dinner is usually served from 6 to 9 (many restaurants have early-bird specials beginning at 5). Only in the larger cities will you find full dinners being offered much later than 9, although you can usually find a bar or bistro serving a limited menu late into the evening in all but the smallest towns. Many restaurants are closed Monday, and sometimes Sunday or Tuesday, although this is never true in resort areas in high season. However, resort-town eateries often shut down completely in the off-season.

Unless otherwise noted, the restaurants listed in this guide are open daily for lunch and dinner.

PAYING

Credit cards are accepted for meals throughout Northern New England in all but the most modest establishments. See price chart in each chapter for price categories for dining and lodging establishments.

For guidelines on tipping, see Tipping below.

RESERVATIONS & DRESS

Regardless of where you are, it's a good idea to make a reservation if you can. We only mention them specifically when reservations are essential (there's no other way you'll ever get a table) or when they are not accepted. For popular restaurants, book as far ahead as you can (often 30 days), and reconfirm as soon as you arrive. (Large parties should always call ahead to check the reservations policy.) We mention dress only when men are required to wear a jacket or a jacket and tie.

WINES, BEER & SPIRITS

Maine, New Hampshire, and Vermont are no stranger to microbrews. The granddaddy of Northern New England's independent beer makers is Boston's Samuel Adams, producing brews available throughout the region since 1985. Following the Sam Adams lead in offering hearty English-style ales and special seasonal brews are breweries such as Vermont's Long Trail, Maine's Shipyard, and New Hampshire's Old Nut Field.

Northern New England is beginning to earn some respect as a wine-producing region. Varieties capable of withstanding the region's harsh winters have been the basis of promising enterprises such as Vermont's Snow Farm Vineyard in the Lake Champlain Islands.

Although a patchwork of state and local regulations affect the hours and locations of places that sell alcoholic beverages, Northern New England licensing laws are fairly liberal. State-owned or -franchised stores sell hard liquor in Maine, New Hampshire, and Vermont; many travelers have found that New Hampshire offers the region's lowest prices. Look for state-run liquor "supermarkets" on interstate highways in the southern part of New Hampshire; these also have good wine selections.

∎ HEALTH

Lyme disease, so named for its having been first reported in the town of Lyme, Connecticut, is a potentially debilitating disease carried by deer ticks, which thrive in dry, brush-covered areas throughout Northern New England, but particularly on the coast. Always use insect repellent; outbreaks of Lyme disease all over the East Coast make it imperative that you protect yourself from ticks from early spring through summer. To prevent bites, wear light-color clothing and tuck pant legs into socks. Look for black ticks about the size of a pinhead around hairlines and the warmest parts of the body. If you have been bitten, consult a physician, especially if you see the telltale bull's-eye bite pattern. Influenza-like symptoms often accompany a Lyme infection. Early treatment is imperative.

Maine, New Hampshire, and Vermont's two greatest insect pests are black flies and mosquitoes. The former are a phenomenon of late spring and early summer and are generally a problem only in the densely wooded areas of the far north. Mosquitoes, however, can be a nuisance just about everywhere in summer—they're at their worst following snowy winters and wet springs. The best protection against both pests is repellent containing DEET; if you're camping in the woods during black fly season, you'll also want to use fine mesh screening in eating and sleeping areas, and even wear mesh headgear. A particular pest of coastal areas, especially salt marshes, is the greenhead fly. Their bite is nasty, and they are best repelled by a liberal application of Avon Skin So Soft.

Coastal waters attract seafood lovers who enjoy harvesting their own clams, mussels, and even lobsters; permits are required, and casual harvesting of lobsters is strictly forbidden. Amateur clammers should be aware that Northern New England shellfish beds are periodically visited by red tides, during which microorganisms can render shellfish poisonous. To keep abreast of the situation, inquire when you apply for a license (usually at town halls or police stations) and pay attention to red tide postings.

∎ HOURS OF OPERATION

Hours in Maine, New Hampshire, and Vermont differ little from those in other parts of the United States. Within the region, shops and other businesses tend to keep slightly later hours in larger cities and along the coast, which is generally more populated than interior communities.

Most major museums and attractions are open daily or six days a week (with Monday being the most likely day of closing). Hours are often shorter on Saturday and especially Sunday, and some prominent museums stay open late one or two nights a week, usually Tuesday, Thursday, or Friday. Northern New England also has quite a few smaller museums—historical societies, small art galleries, highly specialized collections—that open only a few days a week, and sometimes only by appointment in winter or slow periods.

Banks are usually open weekdays from 9 to 3 and some Saturday mornings. The post office is open from 8 to 5 weekdays and often on Saturday morning. Shops in urban and suburban areas, particularly in indoor and strip malls, typically open at 9 or 10 daily and stay open until anywhere from 6 PM to 10 PM on weekdays and Saturday, and until 5 or 6 on Sunday. Hours vary greatly. Bars and nightclubs have a last call of 1:40 AM and scoot people out by 2 AM.

On major highways and in densely populated areas you'll usually find at least one or two supermarkets, drugstores, and gas stations open 24 hours, and in a few big cities and also some college towns you'll find a smattering of all-night fast-food restaurants, diners, and coffeehouses.

∎ MONEY

It costs a bit more to travel in most of Northern New England than it does in the rest of the country, with the most costly areas being the resort areas along the Maine coast. There are also a fair number of somewhat posh inns and restaurants in parts of Vermont and New Hampshire. ATMs are plentiful, and larger denomination bills (as well as credit cards) are readily accepted in tourist destinations during the high season.

ITEM	AVERAGE COST
Cup of Coffee	$1.75
Glass of Wine	$6
Glass of Beer	$4
Sandwich	$6
Museum Admission	$12

Prices throughout this guide are given for adults. Substantially reduced fees are almost always available for children, students, and senior citizens.

CREDIT CARDS

Throughout this guide, the following abbreviations are used: **AE**, American Express; **D**, Discover; **DC**, Diners Club; **MC**, MasterCard; and **V**, Visa.

It's a good idea to inform your credit-card company before you travel, especially if you're going abroad and don't travel internationally very often. Otherwise, the credit-card company might put a hold on your card owing to unusual activity—not a good thing halfway through your trip. Record all your credit-card numbers—as well as the phone numbers to call if your cards are lost or stolen—in a safe place, so you're prepared should something go wrong. Both MasterCard and Visa have general numbers you can call (collect if you're abroad) if your card is lost, but you're better off calling the number of your issuing bank, since MasterCard and Visa usually just transfer you to your bank; your bank's number is usually printed on your card.

Major credit cards are readily accepted throughout Maine, New Hampshire, and Vermont, though in rural areas you may encounter difficulties or the acceptance of only MasterCard of Visa (also note that if you'll be making an excursion into Canada, many outlets there accept Visa but not MasterCard). Using a credit card on the road allows you to delay payment and gives you certain rights as a consumer.

Reporting Lost Cards American Express (☎800/528–4800 in the U.S. or 336/393–1111 collect from abroad ⊕www.american express.com). **Diners Club** (☎800/234–6377 in the U.S. or 303/799–1504 collect from abroad ⊕www.dinersclub.com). **Discover** (☎800/347–2683 in the U.S. or 801/902–3100 collect from abroad ⊕www.discovercard. com). **MasterCard** (☎800/627–8372 in the U.S. or 636/722–7111 collect from abroad

⊕www.mastercard.com). **Visa** (☎800/847–2911 in the U.S. or 410/581–9994 collect from abroad ⊕www.visa.com).

∎ SAFETY

Rural Northern New England is one of the country's safest regions, so much so that residents often leave their doors unlocked. In the cities, observe the usual precautions; it's worth noting, however, that crime rates have been dropping in metropolitan areas. You should avoid out-of-the-way or poorly lighted areas at night; clutch handbags close to your body and don't let them out of your sight; and be on your guard in subways, not only during the deserted wee hours but in crowded rush hours, when pickpockets are at work. Keep your valuables in hotel safes. Try to use ATMs in busy, well-lighted places such as bank lobbies.

If your vehicle breaks down in a rural area, pull as far off the road as possible, tie a handkerchief to your radio antenna (or use flares at night—check if your rental agency can provide them), and stay in your car with the doors locked until help arrives. Don't pick up hitchhikers. If you're planning to leave a car overnight to make use of off-road trails or camping facilities, make arrangements for a supervised parking area if at all possible. Cars left at trailhead parking lots are subject to theft and vandalism.

The universal telephone number for crime and other emergencies throughout Northern New England is 911.

∎TIP→ Distribute your cash, credit cards, I.D.s, and other valuables between a deep front pocket, an inside jacket or vest pocket, and a hidden money pouch. Don't reach for the money pouch once you're in public.

▌ TAXES

See Restaurant and Hotel charts at the beginning of each chapter for information about taxes on restaurant meals and accommodations. Sales taxes in Northern New England are as follows: Maine 5% and Vermont 6%. No sales tax is charged in New Hampshire. Some states and municipalities levy an additional tax (from 1% to 10%) on lodging or restaurant meals. Alcoholic beverages are sometimes taxed at a higher rate than that applied to meals.

▌ TIME

Northern New England operates on Eastern Standard Time and follows daylight saving time. When it is noon in Portland it is 9 AM in Los Angeles, 11 AM in Chicago, 5 PM in London, and 3 AM the following day in Sydney. When taking a ferry to Nova Scotia, note that the province operates on Atlantic Standard Time and therefore is an hour ahead.

▌ TIPPING

The customary tipping rate for taxi drivers in Maine, New Hampshire, and Vermont is 15%–20%, with a minimum of $2; bellhops are usually given $2 per bag in luxury hotels, $1 per bag elsewhere. Hotel maids should be tipped $2 per day of your stay. A doorman who hails or helps you into a cab can be tipped $1–$2. You should also tip your hotel concierge for services rendered; the size of the tip depends on the difficulty of your request, as well as the quality of the concierge's work. For an ordinary dinner reservation or tour arrangements, $3–$5 should do; if the concierge scores seats at a popular restaurant or show or performs unusual services (getting your laptop repaired, finding a good pet-sitter, etc.), $10 or more is appropriate.

Waiters should be tipped 15%–20%, though at higher-end restaurants, a solid 20% is more the norm. Many restaurants add a gratuity to the bill for parties of six or more. Ask what the percentage is if the menu or bill doesn't state it. Tip $1 per drink you order at the bar, though if at an upscale establishment, those $15 martinis might warrant a $2 tip.

TIPPING GUIDELINES FOR MAINE, NEW HAMPSHIRE, & VERMONT	
Bartender	$1 to $5 per round of drinks, depending on the number of drinks
Bellhop	$1 to $5 per bag, depending on the level of the hotel
Hotel Concierge	$5 or more, if he or she performs a service for you
Hotel Doorman	$1–$2 if he helps you get a cab
Hotel Maid	1$–$3 a day (either daily or at the end of your stay, in cash)
Hotel Room-Service Waiter	$1 to $2 per delivery, even if a service charge has been added
Porter at Airport or Train Station	$1 per bag
Restroom attendants	Restroom attendants in more expensive restaurants expect some small change or $1. Tip coat-check personnel at least $1–$2 per item checked unless there is a fee, then nothing.
Taxi Driver	15%–20%, but round up the fare to the next dollar amount
Tour Guide	10% of the cost of the tour
Valet Parking Attendant	$1–$2, but only when you get your car
Waiter	15%–20%, with 20% being the norm at high-end restaurants; nothing additional if a service charge is added to the bill.

INDEX

Photo Credits

NOTES

NOTES

NOTES

NOTES

ABOUT OUR WRITERS

Maine-based **Stephen and Neva Allen** have written extensively about travel for many newspapers and magazines as well as chapters for Fodor's. They moved to coastal Maine in 2000 and are devoted to the beautiful area they've come to call home.

Though based in Salt Lake City, Utah, **John Blodgett** still goes home to Maine—the place he spent much of his first 22 years. The lobster roll at Gilbert's Chowder House in Portland's Old Port alone is worth the airfare, but he also misses sitting next to the booming foghorn at Two Lights State Park and listening to the clang of buoys bobbing in Casco Bay.

A Maine Coast resident since the early 1990s, **Sherry Hanson** covers everything from the Civil War to how to kayak with a dog and brew beer at home. Her poetry has appeared in many journals as well as her own poetry book, a collection titled *A Cab to Stonehenge*, published in 2006.

A graduate of the University of Missouri School of Journalism, Maine-based writer **Mary Ruoff** has enjoyed writing articles about Maine travel, among other topics. She is married to a Mainer, Michael Hodsdon. Along with their son Dmitry ("Dima"), they spend as much time as they can at their family land "Way Down East," where Michael's grandfather was a fisherman.

Laura V. Scheel has spent a good portion of her years in Maine driving and exploring the state's numerous back roads and small towns. She has written frequently for Fodor's, contributing to titles such as *Fodor's Maine Coast* and *Fodor's The Thirteen Colonies*.

George Semler has been coming to Maine's Blue Hill Peninsula since the summer before he was born. A frequent writer for Fodor's (France, Spain, Cuba, Morocco, Andalusia, Barcelona-to-Bilbao, and Barcelona) as well as for *Saveur, Sky, Forbes,* and other publications, Semler writes about the outdoors, food, travel, and culture.

New York City–based **Michael de Zayas** has written about hotels on five continents, including covering them for Fodor's guides to Miami, Spain, the Caribbean, Chile, and New York City.